Alternatives to Animal Use in Research, Testing, and Education

OTA Reports are the principal documentation of formal assessment projects. These projects are approved in advance by the Technology Assessment Board. At the conclusion of a project, the Board has the opportunity to review the report, but its release does not necessarily imply endorsement of the results by the Board or its individual members.

CONGRESS OF THE UNITED STATES
Office of Technology Assessment
Washington, D. C. 20510

Recommended Citation:

U.S. Congress, Office of Technology Assessment, *Alternatives to Animal Use in Research, Testing, and Education* (Washington, DC: U.S. Government Printing Office, OTA-BA-273, February 1986).

Library of Congress Catalog Card Number 85-600621

For sale by the Superintendent of Documents
U.S. Government Printing Office, Washington, DC 20402

OTA Project Staff
Alternatives to Animal Use in Research, Testing, and Education

Roger C. Herdman, *Assistant Director, OTA Health and Life Sciences Division*

Gretchen S. Kolsrud, *Biological Applications Program Manager*

Gary B. Ellis, *Project Director* and *Analyst*
Judy K. Kosovich, *Principal Analyst*
Lisa J. Raines, *Legal Analyst*
Timothy J. Hart, *Project Director*[1]
Gregory A. Jaffe, *Research Assistant*[2]
Marcia D. Brody, *Research Assistant*[2]
James A. Thomas, *Research Assistant*[3]
Thomas M. Bugbee, *Research Assistant*[4]
Jeffrey S. Stryker, *Research Analyst*[5]

Support Staff

Sharon K. Smith, *Administrative Assistant*
Elma Rubright, *Administrative Assistant*[3]
Linda S. Rayford, *Secretary/Work Processing Specialist*
Barbara V. Ketchum, *Clerical Assistant*

Contractors

Linda Starke (Editor), Washington, DC

Battelle—Columbus Laboratories, Columbus, OH
Leonard M. Chanin, Washington, DC
Eileen M. Cline, Springfield, VA
Paul N. Craig, Shady Side, MD
Arthur H. Flemming, University of Chicago
Gordon G. Gallup, Jr., State University of New York at Albany
Gilbert S. Greenwald, University of Kansas Medical Center
Anne M. Guthrie, Arlington, VA
Health Designs, Inc., Rochester, NY
Henry R. Hertzfeld and Thomas D. Myers, Washington, DC
Meyer, Faller, and Weisman, P.C., Washington, DC
Roland M. Nardone and Lucille Ouellette, Catholic University, Washington, DC
Bennie I. Osburn, University of California, Davis
Stephen P. Push, Washington, DC

[1]Through December 1984.
[2]Through July 1985.
[3]Through August 1984.
[4]Through June 1984.
[5]Through January 1985.

CONTENTS

Chapter 1

Summary, Policy Issues, and Options for Congressional Action

CONTENTS

List of Tables

Figure

Chapter 1

Summary, Policy Issues, and Options for Congressional Action

- *A former high school teacher in New York organizes demonstrations and advertising campaigns opposing the use of rabbits and rodents in two product-safety tests. Industry responds by giving several million dollars in grants to university scientists searching for alternatives to animal testing.*
- *Researchers induce seizures in rats, draw their cerebrospinal fluid, and use it to quell seizures in other rats; the anticonvulsant substance produced during seizures could bear on the understanding and treatment of epilepsy.*
- *Industrial toxicologists in New Jersey adopt refined methods of testing potentially poisonous chemicals, reducing by 48 percent the number of animals used in acute toxicity studies and cutting the cost of compliance with government regulations.*
- *A Virginia woman donates $1,250,000 to the University of Pennsylvania to establish the Nation's first endowed professorship in humane ethics and animal welfare. One of the goals of the chair is to investigate alternatives to animal experiments for medical research.*
- *Members of the Animal Liberation Front break into a biomedical research laboratory in California and remove dogs being used in a cardiac pacemaker experiment.*
- *Veterinary students in Washington study principles of physiology without recourse to the traditional dog dissection. Instead, they use a computer simulation of canine physiology.*

These recent events illustrate the complex political, ethical, and economic issues raised by the use of animals in research, testing, and education. Concern about the continued use of animals has led to public calls for development of alternatives.

The popular debate over animal use has been taken up by proponents holding a wide spectrum of views, ranging from belief in abolition of animal use on moral and ethical grounds to belief in free rein on the use of animals in research, testing, and education. An increasing number of groups are taking a middle ground. In the mid-1980s, it is misleading—and often impossible—to characterize many vocal groups either as simply "pro-animal" or "pro-research."

In light of requests for "a scientific evaluation of alternative methods to animal research, experimentation, and testing" from the Chairman of the Senate Committee on Labor and Human Resources, Senator Orrin G. Hatch (R-UT), and from Senator Alan Cranston (D-CA), this assessment examines the reasons for seeking such alternatives and the prospects for developing them. It describes animal and nonanimal methods used by industry, academia, and government agencies; explains the roles and requirements of government regulation and self-regulation of animal use; and identifies policy issues and options that the debate over alternatives places before Congress.

The report covers three kinds of animal use: research in the biomedical and behavioral sciences; testing of products for toxicity; and education of students at all levels, including the advanced life sciences, and medical and veterinary training. The use of animals in these three situations—research, testing, and education—differs considerably, and each has different prospects for development of alternatives.

The assessment excludes examination of the use of animals in food and fiber production; their use in obtaining organs, antibodies, and other biological products; and their use for sport, entertainment, and companionship. Such purposes include numbers of animals generally estimated to be many multiples greater than the numbers used for purposes described in this report (see ch. 3). Issues of animal care, such as feeding and maintenance, are also beyond the scope of this assessment.

Replacement.

DEFINITION OF TERMS

Resusci-Dog, Canine Cardiopulmonary-Resuscitation Simulator

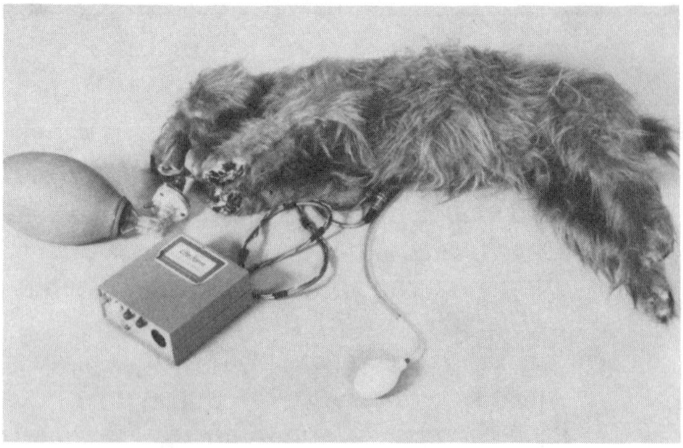

Photo credit: Charles R. Short, New York State College of Veterinary Medicine, Cornell University

Resusci-Dog, a plastic mannequin linked to a computer, can simulate an arterial pulse, and pressure can be applied to its rib cage for cardiac massage or cardiopulmonary resuscitation. Resusci-Dog has replaced about 100 dogs per year in the training of veterinary students at the New York State College of Veterinary Medicine.

In this report, animal is defined as any nonhuman member of the five classes of vertebrates: mammals, birds, reptiles, amphibians, and fish (see ch. 2). Within this group, two kinds of animals can be distinguished—warm-blooded animals (mammals and birds) and cold-blooded animals (reptiles, amphibians, and fish). Other creatures customarily included in the animal kingdom, such as invertebrates (e.g., worms, insects, and crustaceans), are excluded by this definition. The use of human subjects is not examined in this assessment.

The concept of alternatives to animal use has come to mean more than merely a one-to-one substitution of nonanimal methods for animal techniques. **For alternatives, OTA has chosen a definition characterized by the three Rs: replacement, reduction, and refinement.**

Scientists may **replace** methods that use animals with those that do not. For example, veterinary students may use a canine cardiopulmonary-resuscitation simulator, Resusci-Dog, instead of living dogs. Cell cultures may replace mice and rats that are fed new products to discover substances poisonous to humans. In addition, using the preceding definition of animal, an invertebrate (e.g., a horseshoe crab) could replace a vertebrate (e.g., a rabbit) in a testing protocol.

Reduction refers to the use of fewer animals. For instance, changing practices allow toxicologists to estimate the lethal dose of a chemical with as few as one-tenth the number of animals used in traditional tests. In biomedical research, long-lived animals, such as primates, may be shared, assuming sequential protocols are not deemed inhumane or scientifically conflicting. Designing experimental protocols with appropriate attention to statistical inference can lead to decreases (or to increases) in the numbers of animals used. Or several tissues may be simultaneously taken from a single animal as a result of coordination among investigators. Reduction can also refer to the minimization of any unintentionally duplicative experiments, perhaps through improvements in information resources.

Existing procedures may be **refined** so that animals are subjected to less pain and distress. Refinements include administration of anesthetics to animals undergoing otherwise painful procedures; administration of tranquilizers for distress; humane destruction prior to recovery from surgical anesthesia; and careful scrutiny of behavioral indices of pain or distress, followed by cessation of the procedure or the use of appropriate analgesics. Refinements also include the enhanced use of noninvasive imaging technologies that allow earlier detection of tumors, organ deterioration, or metabolic changes and the subsequent early euthanasia of test animals.

Pain is defined as discomfort resulting from injury or disease, while distress results from pain, anxiety, or fear. Pain may also be psychosomatic, resulting from emotional distress. Although these are subjective phenomena, pain and distress can sometimes be identified and quantified by observing an animal's behavior. Pain is relieved with analgesics or anesthetics; distress is eased with tranquilizers. Widely accepted ethical standards require that scientists subject animals to as little pain or distress as is necessary to accomplish the objectives of procedures. Professic quire scientists to provide relief to animals in p or distress, unless administering relief would interfere with the objective of the procedure (e.g., when the objective is a better understanding of the mechanisms of pain).

HOW MANY ANIMALS ARE USED?

Estimates of the animals used in the United States each year range from 10 million to upwards of 100 million. OTA scrutinized a variety of surveys (see ch. 3), including those of the National Research Council's Institute for Laboratory Animal Resources and the Animal and Plant Health Inspection Service (APHIS) of the U.S. Department of Agriculture (USDA). Indirect estimates of animal use were also based on data such as Federal funds spent on animal research and sales revenues of the Nation's largest commercial breeder of laboratory animals.

All these data are unreliable. No data source exists, for example, to enumerate how many institutions do not report animal use. In addition, nonreporting institutions may not be similar enough to reporting institutions to justify extrapolation. Thus every estimate of animal use stands as a rough approximation. With this caveat in mind, **the best data source available—the USDA/APHIS census—suggests that at least 17 million to 22 million animals were used in research and testing in the United States in 1983.** The majority of animals used—between 12 million and 15 million—were rats and mice. Current data permit no statement about any trends in animal use through recent years. Animal use in medical and veterinary education amounted to at least 53,000 animals in the school year 1983-84.

The Animal Welfare Act of 1966 (Public Law 89-544), as amended and presently enforced, requires research and testing facilities to report to USDA their annual use of dogs, cats, hamsters, rabbits, guinea pigs, and nonhuman primates (see ch. 13). (About two-thirds of the reporting institutions also volunteer the number of rats and mice used.) For fiscal year 1983, the USDA reporting forms indicate the facilities used nearly 1.8 million of these six kinds of animals (see table 1-1).

Table 1-1.—Animal Use Reported to the U.S. Department of Agriculture, 1983[a]

Animal	Number used in 1983
Dogs	182,425
Cats	55,346
Hamsters	454,479
Rabbits	509,052
Guinea pigs	521,237
Nonhuman primates	59,336
Total	1,781,875

[a]Totals do not include rats or mice, two species that together represent the majority of animals used.

SOURCE: Office of Technology Assessment.

USDA reports are of limited utility because:

- the Department counts only six kinds of animals that together account for an estimated 10 percent of the total animals used (reporting of rats, mice, birds, and fish is not required);
- the annual summary report does not tabulate reports received after December 31st of each year, resulting in a 10- to 20-percent underestimation of laboratory use of regulated species;
- ambiguities in the reporting form ask respondents to add figures in a way that can cause animals to be counted twice; and
- terms on the reporting form are undefined (e.g., the form has room for voluntary information about "wild animals," but does not specify what animals might be included).

In the absence of a comprehensive animal census, the USDA reports will continue to provide the best data. Imprecise as they are, these reports can identify major changes in the numbers of dogs, cats, hamsters, rabbits, guinea pigs, and nonhuman primates. (It is important to note that any change in the total number of animals used may reflect not only the adoption of alternative methods, but changes in research and testing budgets as well.)

laws

ETHICAL CONSIDERATIONS

At one end of a broad spectrum of ethical concerns about animal use is the belief that humans may use animals in any way they wish, without regard for the animals' suffering. At the other extreme is the notion—epitomized by the slogan "animals are people, too"—that each animal has the right not to be used for any purpose that does not benefit it. Each view is anchored in a school of philosophical thought, and people considering this issue can choose from a variety of arguable positions (see ch. 4).

Prominent within the Western philosophic and religious tradition is the view that humans have the right to use animals for the benefit of humankind. This view is predicated on the assumption that human beings have special intrinsic value and thus may use natural animate and inanimate objects, including animals, for purposes that will enhance the quality of human life. Yet this tradition suggests that because animals are intelligent and sentient beings, they should be treated in a humane manner. Current policies and trends within the scientific community have reinforced this conviction by advocating that pain and suffering be minimized when animals are used in research, testing, or education.

Advocates of what generally is called animal welfare frequently question the objectives of animal use, as well as the means. They point out that animals can experience pain, distress, and pleasure. Drawing on the utilitarian doctrine of providing the greatest good for the greatest number, some animal welfare advocates weigh animal interests against human interests. In this view, it might be permissible to use animals in research to find a cure for a fatal human disease, but it would be unjust to subject animals to pain to develop a product with purely cosmetic value.

Some animal rights advocates carry this concern a step further and do not balance human and animal rights. They generally invoke the principle of inalienable individual rights. They believe that animal use is unjustified unless it has the potential to benefit the particular animal being used. Animal rights advocates refer to the denial of animal rights as a form of "speciesism," a moral breach analogous to racism or sexism. Animals, by this reasoning, have a right not to be exploited by people.

People throughout the spectrum find common ground in the **principle of humane treatment**, but they fail to agree on how this principle should be applied. Society does not apply the principle of humane treatment equally to all animals. A cat may evoke more sympathy than a frog, for example, because the cat is a companion species and possesses apparently greater neurological sophistication than a frog, endowing it with both favored status and a familiarity that suggests to humans that they can interpret its behavior. Even within a species, all individuals are not treated consistently. Pet rabbits in the home and pest rabbits in the garden, like human friends and strangers, are treated differently.

The improvements in public health and safety made possible through the use of animals in research and testing are well known. But these questions remain: Do these advances justify animal use? How much of the improvements were actually dependent on the use of animals? Debate on these and other questions is bound to continue, but most parties agree that consideration of replacing, reducing, and refining the use of animals is desirable.

ALTERNATIVES IN RESEARCH

In research, scientists often explore uncharted territory in search of unpredictable events, a process that inherently involves uncertainty, missteps, and serendipity. Some biological research requires—and in the foreseeable future will continue to require—the use of live animals if the study of the complex interactions of the cells, tissues, and organs that make up an organism is to continue. Knowledge thus gained is applied to improving the health and well-being of humans and of animals themselves, and it may lead to the development of methods that would obviate the use of some animals.

Some nonanimal methods are becoming available in biomedical and behavioral research (see ch. 6). As more develop, animal use in research will likely become less common. It is important to note, however, that **even if animals cannot be replaced in certain experiments, researchers can attempt to reduce the number used and also to minimize pain and distress.**

Most alternatives to current animal use in research fall into one of four categories:

- **Continued, But Modified, Use of Animals.** This includes alleviation of pain and distress, substitution of cold-blooded for warm-blooded vertebrates, coordination among investigators, and use of experimental designs that provide reliable information with fewer animals than were used previously.
- **Living Systems.** These include micro-organisms, invertebrates, and the in vitro culture of organs, tissues, and cells.
- **Nonliving Systems.** These include epidemiologic databases and chemical and physical systems that mimic biological functions.
- **Computer Programs.** These simulate biological functions and interactions.

The many fields of research—ranging from anatomy to zoology—use animals differently, and each thus has different prospects for developing and implementing alternatives. To determine the prevalence of animal and nonanimal methods in varied disciplines of research, OTA surveyed 6,000 articles published between 1980 and 1983 in 12 biomedical research journals and 3 behavioral research journals (see ch. 5). Research disciplines were distinguished by their characteristic patterns of animal use, as measured by the percentages of published reports showing animal use, no animal use, and use of humans. Animal methods predominated in most of the journals surveyed, including the three behavioral research journals. The exceptions in the overall survey were cell biology, which used primarily nonanimal methods, and cardiology, which used primarily human subjects.

Pros

Using alternative methods in biomedical research holds several advantages from scientific, economic, and humane perspectives, including:

- reduction in the number of animals used;
- reduction in animal pain, distress, and experimental insult;
- reduction in investigator-induced, artifactual physiological phenomena;
- savings in time, with the benefit of obtaining results more quickly;
- the ability to perform replicative protocols on a routine basis;
- reduction in the cost of research;
- greater flexibility to alter conditions and variables of the experimental protocol;
- reduction of error stemming from interindividual variability; and
- the intrinsic potential of in vitro techniques to study cellular and molecular mechanisms.

Cons

Many of these alternative methods are accompanied by inherent disadvantages, including:

- reduced ability to study organismal growth processes;
- reduced ability to study cells, tissues, and organ systems acting in concert;
- reduced ability to study integrated biochemical and metabolic pathways;
- reduced ability to study behavior;
- reduced ability to study the recovery of damaged tissue;
- reduced ability to study interaction between the organism and its environment;
- reduced ability to study idiosyncratic or species-specific responses;
- reduced ability to distinguish between male- and female-specific phenomena; and
- a handicap to probing the unknown and phenomena not yet identified.

Behavior encompasses all the movements and sensations by which living things interact with both the living and nonliving components of their environment. Since one of the chief goals of behavioral research is an understanding of human behavior, there are obvious advantages to the use of human research subjects. There are also advantages to using animals, including the following:

- Laboratory research on animals offers a greater opportunity to control variables such as genetic background, prior experience, and environmental conditions, all of which affect behavior and can obscure the influence of the factor under study.

- The short lifespans of certain animals allow scientists to study behavior as it develops with age and across generations.
- Some animal behavior is less complex than human behavior, facilitating an understanding of basic elements and principles of behavior.
- The behavior of certain animals holds particular interest for humans. These animals include companion species, farm animals, and agricultural pests.

Although behavior is a biological phenomenon, behavioral research differs substantially from biomedical research in that researchers have fewer opportunities to study mechanisms isolated from living organisms. There is little prospect, for example, of using in vitro cultures to look at aggression, habitat and food selection, exploration patterns, or body maintenance activities—all topics studied by behavioral scientists. Yet in each of these disciplines, reduction or refinements of animal use may be possible. **It is the continued, but modified, use of animals that holds the most promise as an alternative in the field of behavioral research.**

ALTERNATIVES IN TESTING

Several million animals are used each year in testing substances for toxicity and establishing conditions for safe use. The resulting data—together with information about use and exposure, human epidemiologic data, and other information—are used in assessing and managing health risks.

As a reduction in the number of animals is a principal alternative, proper statistical design and analysis in testing protocols play an important role (see ch. 7). The total number of animals needed for statistically significant conclusions depends on the incidence of toxic effects without administration of the test substance, the degree of variation from animal to animal for the biological effect that is of interest, and the need to determine a quantitative relationship between the size of the dose and the magnitude of the response. Statistical analysis plays a similarly important role in research.

One of the oldest and, perhaps for that reason, least sophisticated tests is the **LD_{50}** ("lethal dose" for "50" percent of the test animals). In this short-term, or acute, test, a group of animals, usually rats or mice, are exposed to a single substance, and the measured end point is death (although other observations may be made). The LD_{50} is the dose at which half the test animals can be expected to die. A range of doses is administered to some 30 to 100 animals and the LD_{50} is calculated from the results. **Tests providing the same information have recently been developed using as few as 10 animals, i.e., a 3- to 10-fold reduction.**

The LD_{50} is used to screen substances for their relative toxicity and mode of toxic action. Scientists and animal welfare advocates have criticized it in recent years, in part because it cannot be extrapolated reliably to humans, and in part because the imposition of a highly toxic or lethal dose seems particularly inhumane.

Another often-criticized acute toxicity assay is the **Draize eye irritancy test.** This involves placing a test substance into one eye of four to six rabbits and evaluating its irritating effects. Results are used to develop precautionary information for situations in which exposure of the human eye to the substance is possible. Substances with certain properties—e.g., a caustic pH—could be assumed to be eye irritants and not tested. **Draize procedures may also be modified to reduce pain, and in vitro methods to test for irritancy are under development.** A promising new bioassay for tissue irritancy makes use of the chorioallantoic membrane of the chick embryo (see fig. 1-1).

Other common tests include those for long-term chronic effects, carcinogenicity, reproductive and developmental toxicity, skin irritancy, and neurotoxicity. In addition to such descriptive toxicology (i.e., tests that focus on the response of the organ-

Figure 1-1.—Chronological Sequence of Chick Embryo Chorioallantoic Membrane Assay

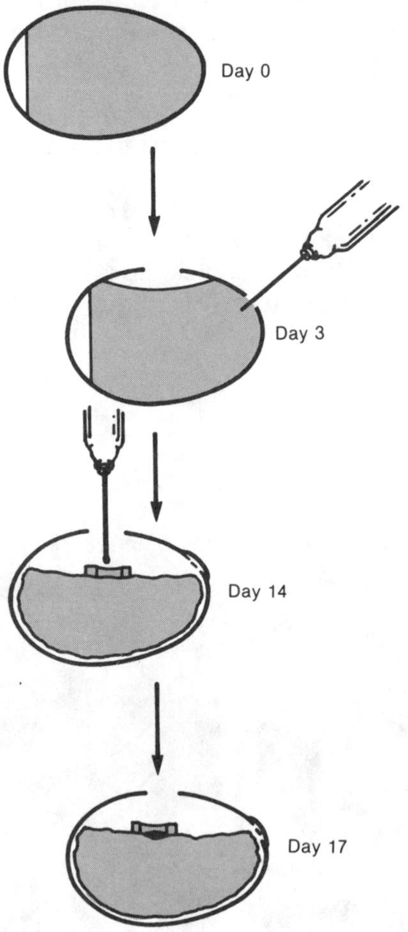

Day 0: Fertile eggs are incubated at 37°C. **Day 3:** The shell is penetrated in two places: A window is cut at the top, and 1.5 to 2 milliliters of albumin is removed with a needle and discarded. The chorioallantoic membrane forms on the floor of the air space, on top of the embryo. The window is taped. **Day 14:** A test sample is placed on the embryonic membrane and contained within a plastic ring. **Day 17:** The chorioallantoic membrane is evaluated for its response to the test substance, and the embryo is discarded.

SOURCE: J. Leighton, J. Nassauer, and R. Tchao, "The Chick Embryo in Toxicology: An Alternative to the Rabbit Eye," Food Chem. Toxicol. 23:293-298. Copyright 1985, Pergamon Press, Ltd.

Chick Embryo Chorioallantoic Membrane Assay

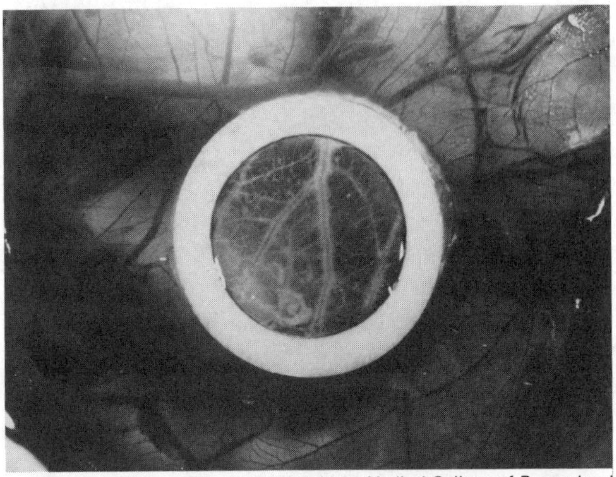

Photo credit: Joseph Leighton, Medical College of Pennsylvania

Typical reaction seen when certain concentrations of household products are placed on the 14-day-old chorioallantoic membrane and examined 3 days later on 17-day-old membranes. The thin white plastic ring has an internal diameter of 10 millimeters (0.4 inch). The area of injury occupies the entire plastic ring. Damaged blood vessels appear within the ring as an elaborate branching structure of pale, white, dead vessels of various sizes. The severity of the reaction is gauged by measuring the diameter of the injury, in this instance spanning the entire ring

ism as a whole), testing may also be done to determine the mechanisms by which a substance is metabolized or excreted, and the chemical reactions by which toxic effects are produced. Such studies of mechanistic toxicology aid in the selection and design of descriptive tests.

The Federal Government plays a major role in this area, both through laws that directly or indirectly require testing and through guidelines that influence testing procedures. The greatest amount of testing is done under laws administered by the Food and Drug Administration (FDA) requiring that products be safe and effective and that labeling claims be substantiated. The Environmental Protection Agency (EPA) requires testing to support pesticide registrations and in certain other cases. For substances other than pesticides, EPA relies largely on published literature and EPA-sponsored testing. Other agencies that use animal testing data include USDA, the Consumer Product Safety Commission, the Occupational Safety and Health Administration, the Department of Transportation, the Federal Trade Commission, and the Centers for Disease Control.

Although most laws do not explicitly require animal testing, requirements of safety implicitly require that the best available means for determining safety be used. Thus, alternatives are not likely to be used widely until they can be shown to be at least as valid and reliable as the tests being replaced. Meeting these criteria is probably not overly difficult with some alternatives that involve reduction or refinement, but it may be harder to replace whole-animal testing totally with in vitro methods.

Reductions in the number of animals used can be brought about by using no more animals than necessary to accomplish the purpose of the test, by combining tests in such a way that fewer animals are needed, and by retrieving information that allows any unintentional duplication of earlier work to be avoided (see chs. 8 and 10). Refinements include increased use of anesthetics and analgesics to ameliorate pain and tranquilizers to relieve distress. Replacements may involve human cell cultures obtained from cadavers or in surgery, animal cell cultures, invertebrates, or micro-organisms. For example, the use of an invertebrate in place of a vertebrate, as in the case of substituting horseshoe crabs for rabbits in testing drugs for their production of fever as a side effect, is increasingly accepted as a replacement.

The most promising in vitro methods are based on an understanding of whole-organ or organism responses that can be related to events at the cellular or subcellular level. Cells manifest a variety of reactions to toxins, including death, changes in permeability or metabolic activity, and damage to genetic material.

ALTERNATIVES IN EDUCATION

Finalist, 1985 Westinghouse Science Talent Search

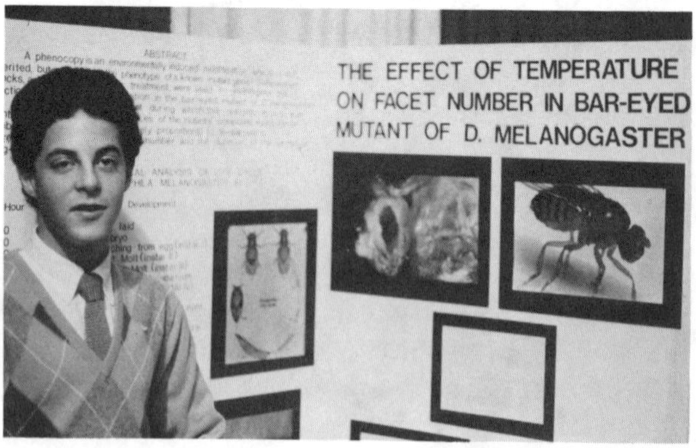

Photo credit: Gary B. Ellis

Louis C. Paul, age 18, Baldwin Senior High School, Baldwin, NY, with his research project, "Effect of Temperature on Facet Number in the Bar-Eyed Mutant of *Drosophila melanogaster.*"

Although far fewer animals are used in education than in either research or testing, animal use in the classroom plays an important role in shaping societal attitudes toward this subject. As educational goals vary from level to level, so does the use of animals and therefore the potential for alternatives (see ch. 9).

In elementary schools, live animals are generally present solely for observation and to acquaint students with the care and handling of different species. Although the guidelines set by many school boards and science teachers' associations limit the use of living vertebrates to procedures that neither cause pain or distress nor interfere with the animals' health, these guidelines are not observed in all secondary schools. Science fairs are an additional avenue for students to pursue original research. The Westinghouse Science Fair prohibits the invasive use of live vertebrates, whereas the International Science and Engineering Fair has no such prohibition.

In the college classroom and teaching laboratory, alternatives are being developed and implemented because they sometimes offer learning advantages, are cheaper than animal methods, and satisfy animal welfare concerns. As a student advances, animal use at the postsecondary level becomes increasingly tied to research and skill acquisition. As graduate education merges with laboratory research and training, animal use becomes largely a function of the questions under investigation. In disciplines such as surgical training in the health professions, some measure of animal use can be helpful but is not universally viewed as essential.

Many alternative methods in education are already accepted practice (see ch. 9). Replacements include computer simulations of physiological phenomena and pharmacologic reactions, cell culture studies, human and animal cadavers, and audiovisual materials. Clinical observation and instruction can also replace the use of animals in some laboratory exercises in medical and veterinary schools. Reduction techniques include the use of classroom demonstrations in place of individual students' animal surgery and multiple use of each animal, although subjecting an animal to multiple recovery procedures may be viewed as inhumane and counter to refined use. Refinements include the use of analgesics, euthanasia prior to recovery from surgery, observation of intact animals in the classroom or in their natural habitats, and the substitution of cold-blooded for warm-blooded vertebrates in laboratory exercises.

Humane education aspires to instill positive attitudes toward life and respect for living animals. Instruction in proper care and handling of various species may be complemented by exposure to the principles of animal use in research and testing and to alternative methods. This type of education promotes attitudes conducive to the development and adoption of alternatives.

COMPUTER SIMULATION AND INFORMATION RESOURCES

Recent advances in computer technology hold some potential for replacing and reducing the use of animals in research, testing, and education (see chs. 6, 8, 9, and 10). In most cases, however, research with animals will still be needed to provide basic data for writing computer software, as well as to prove the validity and reliability of computer alternatives.

In research, scientists are developing computer simulations of cells, tissues, fluids, organs, and organ systems. Use of such methods enables less use of some animals. Limitations on the utility of computer simulations are due to a lack of knowledge of all the parameters involved in the feedback mechanisms that constitute a living system, which means the information on which the computer must depend is incomplete.

In testing, computers allow toxicologists to develop mathematical models and algorithms that can predict the biological effects of new substances based on their chemical structure. If a new chemical has a structure similar to a known poison in certain key aspects, then the new substance also may be a poison. Such screening can thus preempt some animal use.

In education, computer programs simulate classroom experiments traditionally performed with animals. The most advanced systems are videodisks that combine visual, auditory, and interactive properties, much as a real classroom experiment would. Computer simulations can eliminate both the detailed work of conducting an experiment and the effects of extraneous variables, helping students concentrate on a lesson's main point.

Aside from their direct use in research, testing, and education, **computers also could reduce animal use by facilitating the flow of information about the results of research and testing.** Scientists routinely attempt to replicate results of experiments to ensure their accuracy and validity and the generality of the phenomenon. Unintentional duplication, however, can waste money and animal lives. To avoid such situations, the scientific community has established various modes of communication. Research and testing results are published in journals, summarized by abstracting services, discussed at conferences, and obtained through computer databases.

One way any existing unintentional duplication might be ended, and thus animal use reduced, is to establish or refine existing computer-based registries of research or testing data. The National Cancer Institute and the National Library of Medicine (NLM) developed a limited registry in the late 1970s, but it failed: The Laboratory Animal Data Bank (LADB) had few users, as it did not serve user needs.

Any new registry should contain descriptions of the methods of data collection and the laboratory results for both experimental and control groups of animals. Inclusion of negative results (which are seldom reported in journals) could also reduce animal use. Entries should undergo peer review before inclusion in the registry; that is, studies should be scrutinized to judge the validity and reliability of the data. A registry along these lines would probably be 3 to 15 times as complex and costly as the unsuccessful LADB.

As alternative methods are developed and implemented, a computerized registry of information about these novel techniques might serve to speed their adoption. In 1985, the NLM incorporated "animal testing alternatives" as a subject heading in its catalogs and databases, which help users throughout the world find biomedical books, articles, and audiovisual materials. In amending the Animal Welfare Act in 1985, Congress directed the National Agricultural Library to establish a service providing information on improved methods of animal experimentation, including methods that could reduce or replace animal use and minimize pain and distress to animals.

ECONOMIC CONSIDERATIONS

The total dollar cost of the acquisition and maintenance of laboratory animals is directly related to the length of time animals stay in the laboratory. With no accurate source of data on various species' length of stay, it is impossible to calculate the actual total dollar cost of animal use. Reducing the number of animals used can lower acquisition and maintenance costs. Yet, the overall savings will not be proportionate to the smaller number of animals used, as the overhead costs of breeding and laboratory animal facilities must still be met.

Animal use carries with it both great expense and major economic and health benefits (see chs. 5, 7, and 11). Nonetheless, it is difficult to express many of the costs and benefits monetarily. What price does society put on the pain and distress of an animal used in research, for example, or on the life of a person saved by a new medical treatment that was made possible by the use of animals?

In research, there is no way of knowing when a particular result would have been obtained if an experiment had not been done. Thus, it is impossible to predict many of the costs related to the use of alternatives in research. Attempts to do so are likely to result in economic predictions with little basis in fact.

The primary reason a company conducts animal tests is to meet its responsibilities to make safe products under safe conditions. For pharmaceuticals, the need extends to the assurance of product effectiveness. In testing, animal methods generally are more labor-intensive and time-consuming than nonanimal methods, due to the need, for example, to observe animals for toxic effects over lifetimes or generations. Testing can cause delays in marketing new products, including drugs and pesticides, and thus defer a company's revenue.

Rapid, inexpensive toxicity tests could yield major benefits to public health. There are more than 50,000 chemicals on the market, and 500 to 1,000 new ones are added each year. Not all must be tested, but toxicologists must expand their knowledge of toxic properties of commercial chemicals if human health is to be protected to the extent the public desires. Rapid and economical testing would facilitate the expansion of that knowledge.

Government regulatory practices can be read as promoting animal testing, although the laws and practices appear flexible enough to accept alternatives when such tests become scientifically acceptable. To date, regulatory practices have not, in fact, provided a basis for companies to expect that acceptance of alternative methods will be an expedient process. In addition to responding to regulatory requirements, companies conduct animal tests to protect themselves from product liability suits. Here, the necessary tests can exceed government requirements.

Because of the great expense and long time required for animal research and testing, priority in research results has considerable value to investigators and testing results bear considerable proprietary value for industry. Some data are made public by statute, and various arrangements can be made for sharing testing costs. Yet many data are held in confidence, for example, by the company that generated them.

FUNDING FOR THE DEVELOPMENT OF ALTERNATIVES

The Federal Government does not explicitly fund the development of alternatives to animal use per se. Because research on and development of alternatives is founded on a broad base of disciplines, it is difficult to ascertain the dimensions of the effective level of support. No category of research funds, for example, distributed by the National Institutes of Health (NIH) or the National Science Foundation is earmarked for the development of alternatives. Yet despite this lack of identifiable, targeted funding, Federal dollars do support areas of testing and research that generate alternatives.

In biomedical and behavioral research, it is not clear whether targeted funding efforts would produce alternatives faster than they are already being devised. **The research areas most likely to result in useful alternatives include computer simulation of living systems; cell, tissue, and organ culture technology; animal care and health; and mechanisms of pain and pain perception. Funding to improve animal facilities can result in healthier, less stressed animals and can free research from confounding variables bred by a less well defined or inferior environment.**

Some Federal agencies, notably the National Toxicology Program and FDA, conduct in-house research on alternatives to animal testing, as do some corporations. Industry has also committed funds to university researchers seeking alternatives. Revlon has given $1.25 million to the Rockefeller University to support research on alternatives to the Draize eye irritancy test. The Cosmetic, Toiletry, and Fragrance Association and Bristol Myers Company have given $2.1 million to the Center for Alternatives to Animal Testing at The Johns Hopkins University, which funds research into testing alternatives, especially in vitro methods.

Alternatives to animal use in education generally build on techniques developed in research and funded by research monies. Some Federal support for research in science education addresses the development of alternatives, particularly in the area of computer simulation. In 1985, the enactment of Public Law 99-129 authorized the Secretary of the Department of Health and Human Services to make grants to veterinary schools for the development of curriculum for training in the care of animals used in research, the treatment of animals while being used in research, and the development of alternatives to the use of animals in research.

Colleges and universities may offer courses related to humane principles or principles of experimentation. In addition, animal welfare groups are active sponsors in the areas of humane education and attitudes about animals.

A number of humane societies and animal welfare groups fund research on alternatives in research, testing, or education. Several private foundations, notably the Geraldine R. Dodge Foundation, designate support for research in animal welfare as among their funding missions.

REGULATION OF ANIMAL USE

Several Federal and State laws, regulations, guidelines, and institutional and professional societies' policies affect the use of animals in research and testing (see chs. 13, 14, and 15; app. B). Chief among these are the Animal Welfare Act, the Health Research Extension Act of 1985 (Public Law 99-158), rules on good laboratory practices established by FDA and EPA, the NIH *Guide for the Care and Use of Laboratory Animals* (revised in 1985), and the Public Health Service (PHS) *Policy on Humane Care and Use of Laboratory Animals by Awardee Institutions* (revised in 1985; see app. C).

Federal Regulation

Prompted by publicity about pet dogs used in research, Congress passed the Animal Welfare Act to halt the use of stolen pets in experimentation. Enacted in 1966 and amended in 1970, 1976, and

1985, the statute also contains provisions for the care and treatment of certain animals used in experiments. The act defines "animal" as:

> . . . any live or dead dog, cat, monkey (nonhuman primate animal), guinea pig, hamster, rabbit, or such other warm-blooded animal, as the Secretary [of the Department of Agriculture] may determine is being used, or is intended for use, for research, testing, experimentation or exhibition purposes . . .

USDA, empowered to identify other mammals and birds to be regulated, has done so only for marine mammals. In fact, in 1977, USDA promulgated a regulation excluding birds, rats, mice, and horses and other farm animals from coverage by the Animal Welfare Act. The use of rats and mice, the most common laboratory animals, is therefore not regulated.

The act does not cover facilities that use none of the regulated species. Facilities that use regulated species but that receive no Federal funds and maintain their own breeding colonies also fall outside the act's coverage.

The Animal Welfare Act regulates housing, feeding, and other aspects of animal care but bars USDA from regulating the design or performance of actual research or testing. A facility need only report annually that the provisions of the act are being followed and that professionally acceptable standards are being followed during actual experimentation. Facilities must also describe procedures likely to produce animal pain or distress and provide assurances that alternatives to those procedures were considered.

The Food Security Act of 1985 (Public Law 99-198) amended the Animal Welfare Act (amendments effective December 1986) to strengthen standards for laboratory animal care, increase enforcement of the Animal Welfare Act, provide for the dissemination of information to reduce unintended duplication of animal experiments, and mandate training for personnel who handle animals. For the first time, the Department of Health and Human Services is brought into the enforcement of the Animal Welfare Act, as the Secretary of Agriculture is directed to "consult with the Secretary of Health and Human Services prior to the issuance of regulations" under the act.

Each research facility covered by the Animal Welfare Act—including Federal facilities—is required to appoint an institutional animal committee that includes at least one doctor of veterinary medicine and one member not affiliated with the facility. The committee shall assess animal care, treatment, and practices in experimental research and shall inspect all animal study areas at least twice a year.

Many groups concerned about animal welfare want the act and its enforcement strengthened. They criticize USDA's exclusion of rats and mice, the level of funding for enforcement, and the choice of USDA's Animal and Plant Health Inspection Service as the enforcement agency. Inspectors, whose primary concern is preventing interstate transport of disease-carrying livestock and plants, spend about 6 percent of their time enforcing the research provisions of the Animal Welfare Act. Additional criticism is leveled at the act's failure to offer guidance in research practices during experimentation. A 1982 report by the Humane Society of the United States indicates that USDA regulations and guidelines failed to provide "information sufficient to demonstrate that researchers have used pain-relieving drugs 'appropriately' and in accordance with 'professionally acceptable standards'."

The Health Research Extension Act of 1985 mandates the establishment of animal care committees at all entities that conduct biomedical and behavioral research with PHS funds. It requires all applicants for NIH funding to submit assurances that they are in compliance with the law's provisions for the operation of animal care committees and that all personnel involved with animals have available to them training in the humane practice of animal maintenance and experimentation. The NIH Director is empowered to suspend or revoke funding if violations of the act are found and not corrected. In essence, **the act puts the force of Federal law behind certain elements of the PHS *Policy*.**

The act also directs the NIH Director to establish a plan for research into methods of biomedical research and experimentation that do not require the use of animals, that reduce the number of animals used, or that produce less pain and distress in experimental animals than methods currently in use.

FDA and EPA both established rules on good laboratory practices to ensure the quality of toxicity data submitted by industry in compliance with the agencies' regulations. Because proper animal care is essential to good animal tests, these rules indirectly benefit animals.

The NIH *Guide for the Care and Use of Laboratory Animals* prescribes detailed standards for animal care, maintenance, and housing. It applies to all research supported by NIH and is in fact used by most animal facilities throughout the public and private sector.

The Department of Defense (DOD) has been criticized for its use of animals in weapons research and in training for treatment of wounds. In 1973, Congress prohibited DOD from using dogs for research and development of chemical or biological weapons. In 1983, publicity caused an uproar about the use of dogs, pigs, and goats to train military surgeons in the treatment of gunshot wounds. The furor led to congressional action that prohibited DOD from using dogs and cats in such training during fiscal years 1984 and 1985.

State Regulation

Most State anticruelty statutes forbid both active cruelty and neglect (see ch. 14). Many of these laws incorporate vague terms, and alleged offenders offer a variety of defenses. Enforcement may be delegated to humane societies, whose members are not well trained to build criminal cases skillfully and are underfunded for the task.

Twenty States and the District of Columbia regulate the use of animals in research to some extent. As in the case of the Federal Animal Welfare Act, most State laws address such matters as procurement rather than the actual conduct of experiments.

All 50 States and the District of Columbia allow some form of pound animal use for research and training. In some States, laws permitting or requiring research and teaching facilities to purchase stray dogs and cats from pounds and shelters have been the targets of repeal efforts. To date, 9 States prohibit in-State procurement (although not importation from out-of-State) of pound animals for research and training. Of these, Massachusetts will in October 1986 prohibit the use of any animal obtained from a pound.

Institutional and Self-Regulation

Opponents of increased government regulation of research assert that investigators and their institutions are best suited to determine what constitutes appropriate care and use of animals. To regulate animal use at this level, the scientific community relies on a variety of policies and administrative structures (see ch. 15).

Taken together, the requirements for institutional animal committees contained in the Animal Welfare Act (as amended), the Health Research Extension Act of 1985, and the PHS *Policy* bring the overwhelming majority of experimental-animal users in the United States under the oversight of a structured, local review committee.

Institutions that receive funds from PHS for research on warm-blooded laboratory animals must have committees that oversee the housing and routine care of animals. NIH reports that about a quarter of these animal care and use committees currently review research proposals to determine whether experimental procedures satisfy concerns about animal welfare. Committees with such responsibility are not unique to research with animals: For 15 years, similar groups have been weighing ethical issues raised by the use of human research subjects, and these committees have served as models in the development of animal care and use committees.

Committees usually have included the institution's attending veterinarian, a representative of the institution's administration, and several users of research animals. Some committees also have nonscientist members, or lay members not affiliated with the institution. Nonscientist and lay seats have been filled by clergy, ethicists, lawyers, humane society officials, and animal rights advocates. **Animal care and use committees at PHS-supported facilities are today required to consist of not less than five members, and must include at least:**

- **one Doctor of Veterinary Medicine with training or experience in laboratory ani-**

mal science or medicine, who has responsibility for activities involving animals at the institution;

- **one practicing scientist experienced in research using animals;**
- **one member whose primary concerns are in a nonscientific area; and**
- **one individual who is not affiliated with the institution in any way.**

The minimum committee structure required by the PHS policy is thus more rigorous than that mandated by Federal law. The Animal Welfare Act and the Health Research Extension Act do not require, for example, that the committee veterinarian be trained in laboratory-animal medicine. The acts require a minimum committee of three individuals, whereas the PHS policy requires five.

Institutional regulation generally entails compliance with some type of minimum standards for an animal facility, usually those of the NIH *Guide for the Care and Use of Laboratory Animals*. Compliance can be checked in-house or through accreditation by the American Association for Accreditation of Laboratory Animal Care (AAALAC), a voluntary private organization. As of April 1985, a total of 483 institutions had received AAALAC accreditation, which requires site visits that include interviews, inspection of facilities, and review of policies and records. Accredited institutions include hospitals, universities, facilities of the Veterans' Administration (VA), and pharmaceutical manufacturers (see app. D).

A number of scientific and professional societies, universities, and corporations have promulgated statements of policy concerning their members' or employees' standards of conduct in animal use. These policies generally require:

- humane care and use of animals,
- minimization of the number of animals used,
- alleviation of pain and suffering, and
- supervision of animal use by qualified personnel.

Twelve of fifteen such policies reviewed by OTA encourage or require consideration of the use of alternatives. But only 3 of the 15 include enforcement provisions or mention sanctions against violators.

Regulation Within Federal Agencies

Six Federal departments and four independent agencies use laboratory animals intramurally and account for approximately one-tenth of the animal use in the United States. Beginning in December 1986, Federal facilities in those departments and agencies using animals will be required by the 1985 amendments to the Animal Welfare Act to install institutional animal committees. Each committee shall report to the head of the Federal agency conducting the experimentation.

Most Federal agencies that use animals in research or testing have formal policies and administrative structures to ensure that the animals receive humane treatment. At the request of the Executive Office of Science and Technology Policy, the Interagency Research Animal Committee developed a 450-word policy statement, *Principles for the Utilization and Care of Vertebrate Animals Used in Testing, Research, and Education,* to be followed by all Federal agencies supporting animal use (see ch. 13).

No one Federal agency policy on animal care and use has all the characteristics needed to address all issues adequately. Combining certain aspects from each would produce an effective uniform Federal policy. Almost all policies today require adherence to the NIH *Guide* and the Animal Welfare Act. Most agencies also require an attending veterinarian and an animal care and use committee at each facility. The committees generally review research protocols to ensure that animals are not used in excessive numbers, that adequate provisions are made for animal care and pain relief, and that alternatives are used whenever possible. Most committees and attending veterinarians have little enforcement power, and those who have such power rarely use it.

Some agencies' policies have features that would be considered advantageous by animal welfare advocates. NIH and the National Aeronautics and Space Administration have laypeople on their animal care and use committees. The VA requires all its animal facilities to acquire AAALAC accreditation. The Department of Defense has a separate policy and committee for nonhuman primates. The Air Force has solicited evaluation of its policies by a panel of independent experts and plans to implement the group's recommendations.

International Regulation

OTA surveyed laws controlling use of experimental animals in 10 foreign nations, including countries of Western Europe (see table 1-2) and Australia and Canada. Comparative analysis of regulation of animal use abroad can yield lessons from foreign regulatory experiences, models for regulation, and models for funding of alternatives.

A review of foreign laws, especially those revised or instituted in the last decade, indicates three trends of note in government control of animal research (see ch. 16):

- Attention is shifting away from intentionally or negligently "cruel" treatment and toward the avoidance of pain and suffering. This change in perspective raises the difficulty of defining prohibited conduct, and disagreement arises over the definition of animal pain and suffering. Newer statutes rely on authorized reviewers who check experimental plans in advance and apply their own sensibilities to satisfy themselves—and thereby the public interest—that pain and suffering are not being inflicted without justification.
- There is increasing emphasis on finding alternatives. The old method of justifying animal research by reference to its potential for providing new knowledge is being enhanced by the greater burden of demonstrating that no less painful method is available to achieve the same result. Increasingly, animals are being viewed as having an interest in not being hurt.
- Countries with comprehensive reporting systems (e.g., the United Kingdom) have found that fewer animals are now being used in experiments. The data are insufficient to determine the reasons for these reductions or what the effect may be on the production of new information.

These trends indicate a growing interest in Western Europe in replacing, reducing, or refining the use of animals through legislation.

It is not clear whether the tighter control found in some West European countries can be applied in the United States. Most West European nations are more homogeneous than is this country of federated States. In geographical dispersal and size, the research enterprises in those countries are small—there are fewer than 300 investigators using animals in Denmark, for example. The British system functions well, despite its complexity, because it has been refined over the course of a century. New scientists are weaned on it, and the inspector is a familiar sight in the laboratory. The British system's enforcement is based more on advice and negotiation than on confrontation.

POLICY ISSUES AND OPTIONS FOR CONGRESSIONAL ACTION

Seven policy issues related to alternatives to animal use in research, testing, and education were identified during the course of this assessment. The first concerns the implementation of alternatives and examines options that might encourage the research, testing, and education communities to adopt currently available methods of replacing, reducing, and refining their use of animals. The second issue explores options for promoting research and development leading to more and better alternatives. Both recognize that scientifically valid alternative methods can make positive contributions to research, testing, and education and might therefore be promoted.

The five additional policy issues examined are: disseminating information about animal experimentation, restricting animal use, counting animal use, establishing a Federal animal use policy, and changing the implementation of or amending the Animal Welfare Act. Although these policy issues do not explicitly address either the implementation or development of alternative methods, they are inextricably linked to the replacement, reduction, and refinement of animal use.

Associated with each policy issue are several options for congressional action, ranging in each case from taking no specific steps to making major

Table 1-2.—National Laws for the Protection of Animals in Selected European Countries

Provisions	Denmark	Federal Republic of Germany	Netherlands	Norway	Sweden	Switzerland	United Kingdom
Species protected	Vertebrates	All animals	Vertebrates, native species	Vertebrates, crustaceans	Vertebrates	Vertebrates	Vertebrates
Distinctions among species	Should use lowest rank; dogs, cats, monkeys purpose-bred	Better to use invertebrates or cold-blooded vertebrates	Vertebrates better protected	Monkeys, dogs, cats better protected	Should use lowest rank; all purpose-bred	Should use lowest rank	Primates, dogs, cats, equidae preferred; no stray dogs
Alternatives must be used if available	Yes	Yes	Vertebrates	Yes	Alternatives promoted	Yes	Alternatives encouraged
Anesthetics, analgesics, or approval required for painful experiments	Except for minor or transient pain	If pain, suffering, or injury likely	If injury or pain likely	If pain is possible (unless Board approves)	Surgery on mammals unless committee approves	Slight pain or anxiety; if too painful, must forgo	Statute does not specify, but certificate may require
Educational uses	Higher education, technique	High school and above	University and vocational	Professional training	Allowed, but restricted	Not allowed	Some demonstration; not for practicing
Ban on animal use for more than one painful experiment	All dogs, cats, monkeys; most experiments	No multiple surgeries on vertebrates	Rarely reused because of pain requirements	Only one experiment allowed per animal	Rarely reused because of pain requirements	Only reused if pain was slight	If anesthetized or because of pain requirements
License/permit for dealers, facilities, and investigators	All facilities, head investigators	Dealers, facilities, investigators	Dealers (dogs and cats), facilities	Investigators or facilities licensed	Breeders, facilities	Breeders, facilities	Facilities registered, investigators licensed
Review of experiments	Most experiments need approval by national Board	Not needed; proposed that facility's animal welfare officer review	Head of institute reviews	Investigator or facility (licensee) review	Notification/application; tiered system	2 State committees review	Home Office and Advisory Committee
Administration	Centralized, government/nongovernment board; licensee is responsible	States enforce and administer (proposed that facilities have animal welfare officer)	Central enforcement and reporting; administration by institute	Central coordination, some functions delegated to licensees	Central coordination with oversight by facility head and committee	Central coordination, administered by States	Centralized, shared by Head Office, Advisory Committee, Royal Society
Animal welfare representation	3 nominees to national Board	Being considered	Not required, but facility reports are public	Not required	On all committees; being reconsidered	Members of national commission	Advisory Committee
Reporting	Annual report	In-house recordkeeping	Annual report	Annual report	Government recordkeeping	In-house recordkeeping	Annual reports

SOURCE: Office of Technology Assessment.

changes. The order in which the options are presented should not imply their priority. Furthermore, the options are not, for the most part, mutually exclusive: Adopting one does not necessarily disqualify others in the same category or within any other category. A careful combination of options might produce the most desirable effects. In some cases, an option may suggest alterations in more than one aspect of alternatives to using animals. It is important to keep in mind that changes in one area have repercussions in others.

Some of the options involve direct legislative action. Others are oriented to the actions of the executive branch but involve congressional oversight or encouragement. Congress can promote alternatives in at least three ways. It can provide incentives through tax policies, grants, or educational assistance. It can mandate the adoption or development of alternatives by means of appropriations or legislation. And it can provide encouragement via oversight or resolutions. Table 1-3 summarizes the seven policy issues and associated options derived from this assessment.

ISSUE: Should steps be taken to encourage the use of available alternatives in research, testing, or education?

Alternatives to animals become accepted practice in the research, testing, and educational communities as methods are developed through research, validated by independent measurements, gradually accepted by the scientific community, and implemented as they come to be relied on or required. Several alternatives to the use of animals are in the validation or implementation phase today; for the most part, these methods are based on reductions and refinements. Approaches that replace the use of animals have generally not been completely validated and accepted. Instead, these represent possibilities for the longer term. (An exception may be educational simulations of living systems where an adequate range of physiological variables is known.) The processes of validation and gradual implementation are certain to continue, and they could be accelerated.

Analysis of alternatives in research (see ch. 6), testing (see ch. 8), and education (see ch. 9) demonstrates differing availability both among and within these three areas. In research, for example, animal methods can be complemented by computer models, and experiments may be designed to provide the desired information with fewer animals. Dissemination of information within the research community may reduce any instances of unintentional duplication, thereby lowering the number of animals used. In testing, the LD_{50} protocol has in many cases been modified to use fewer animals. And eye irritancy can be assumed—without testing—for substances exhibiting strong skin irritation or having a strongly acid or alkaline pH. In educational settings, exercises not involving animals may be substituted to teach the scientific method or to introduce biological concepts. In other instances, animals are destroyed humanely following a single surgery in a teaching session, rather than experiencing multiple recovery procedures. Four options address the implementation of alternatives such as these.

Option 1: Take no action.

As alternatives are developed and validated, they are likely to continue being implemented at an uneven pace, influenced by factors largely external to Congress. Science and technologies will continue to evolve, and as nonanimal methods emerge from research and validation, they may or may not be accepted and implemented by the scientific community.

This course does not necessarily pass judgment on the value of adopting alternatives per se. Nor does it mean that alternatives will not be implemented. It would merely indicate that Congress has decided against encouraging or forcing the implementation of alternatives beyond its direction in 1985 to NIH to establish a plan to develop and assess alternatives in biomedical research (Public Law 99-158). This option might illustrate the belief that external political, ethical, economic, and scientific factors are sufficient to govern the implementation of alternatives.

Further congressional action toward implementation might be judged unnecessary because various other sources are already acting to implement alternatives. For example, EPA has defined circumstances where the LD_{50} test can be replaced by a limit test (see ch. 8), and FDA has stated that it does not require data derived from the LD_{50} test; industry is watching to gauge the practical effects

Table 1-3.—Policy Issues Related to Alternatives to Animal Use and Options for Congressional Action

Policy issue: Using existing alternatives	Developing new alternatives	Disseminating information	Restricting animal use	Counting animals used	Establishing a Federal animal-use policy	Changing Animal Welfare Act
Options for congressional action						
Take no action Charge a Federal entity with coordinating the implementation of alternatives Encourage alternative methods in Federal testing requirements Ban procedures for which alternatives are available	Take no action Charge a Federal entity with coordinating the development of alternatives Fund development of alternatives	Take no action Mandate easy access to federally funded testing and research data Promote greater use of testing data submitted to Federal agencies Require literature searches Create new data-bases Translate foreign literature into English	Take no action Restrict use of certain kinds of animals Restrict use of certain protocols Restrict acquisition of animals from certain sources License animal users for certain protocols and/or kinds of animals Prohibit animal use	Take no action Eliminate APHIS[a] census Correct inadequacies in present APHIS[a] reporting system Expand APHIS[a] census to include rats and mice Establish independent census	Take no action Establish intramural Federal policy of minimum standards	Take no action Eliminate funding for enforcement Increase funding for enforcement Amend to expand coverage to include experimentation Amend to realign enforcement authority Amend to preempt State and local laws

[a]Animal and Plant Health Inspection Service.

SOURCE: Office of Technology Assessment.

of these statements. Also, members of the soap and detergent industry have implemented modifications of the LD_{50} test. Noteworthy, too, is the important role of institutional animal care and use committees in all phases of animal experimentation. In education, medical schools are conducting some laboratory exercises with computer simulations or video demonstrations in lieu of live animals. Medical students in some instances bypass experiments and training involving animals, proceeding from cadavers to people. Activities such as these are likely to continue without new congressional action.

Additional congressional steps may be deemed inappropriate because implementation of alternatives may be judged unimportant. Some people do not object to animal use, for example, in toxicological testing. They believe the status quo brings the comforts and health benefits of new products and technology and protects them from hazards.

Option 2: Require a new or existing Federal entity to coordinate the validation and implementation of alternatives.

This action is based on the assumption that validation and implementation of alternatives would occur more rapidly with enhanced Federal coordination. Along this line, an information service at the National Agricultural Library on improved methods of animal experimentation was mandated by Congress in 1985 (Public Law 99-198). A clearinghouse for resources required to implement alternatives would further hasten their adoption. This entity might, for example, be a central source for computer software or cell culture material.

Existing Federal entities that might be assigned such responsibilities include some component of the National Institutes of Health (e.g., the Division of Research Resources), the National Toxicology Program, or the National Center for Toxicological Research. Coordinating activities could include symposia, workshops, newsletters, scholarships, grants, and the issuance of model protocols or guidelines. The coordinating body could monitor both public and private initiatives. In 1985, Congress took a step toward coordination of the use of alternatives in biomedical research conducted by or through NIH. It directed NIH to disseminate information about alternatives found to be valid and reliable to those involved in animal experimentation (Public Law 99-158).

Educational programs play a central role in this type of effort. Training scientists in replacement methods and raising awareness about reductions and refinements is likely to increase the implementation of alternatives. This type of education is closely allied with the teaching of principles of humane care and use (see ch. 9).

Animal care and use committees at individual institutions might function as a relay between Federal coordination efforts and individual investigators (see ch. 15). The institutional animal care and use committee might be required to suggest alternative methods as part of its review of animal care and use. Linked in this way to a Federal implementation effort, these committees would both feed into and draw on the resources of the Federal entity.

A different type of coordination, particularly in research, would be the attachment of provisions to Federal grants regarding the implementation of alternatives. Research grant applications using alternative methods could be awarded higher priority scores in the grant evaluation process or be otherwise favored. This strategy would require sufficient flexibility to ensure that valuable, state-of-the-art scientific proposals that may not involve alternatives are not handicapped. Funding mechanisms could also be used to encourage coordination between laboratories. The responsibility for overseeing the implementation of alternatives via funding mechanisms could be borne by each source of Federal funding (see ch. 12).

Option 3: Encourage regulatory agencies to review existing testing guidelines and requirements and to substitute alternatives whenever scientifically feasible.

Through oversight or legislation, Congress could encourage or require Federal agencies to evaluate existing alternatives in testing, to participate in their validation, to adopt them where appropriate, and to report to Congress on their progress in implementing alternatives, as the NIH has been asked to do (Public Law 99-158). Such agency review would have to be a periodic or continuing effort, given rapid advances in the state of the art. Some review of testing guidelines now occurs in keeping requirements up to date, although the purpose of that review is to improve the science rather than to protect animals per se. Formal agency review of international testing guidelines, such as those of the Organization for Economic Cooperation and Development, could also be encouraged (see ch. 7 and app. E). The costs of agency review should be moderate, entailing input from agency experts, comment from outside experts, and publication. If Federal laboratories were involved in the validation of alternative testing methods, additional costs would be incurred. Such a policy could encourage industry to develop alternatives because the barriers to acceptance would be reduced.

Option 4: Ban procedures for which alternatives are available, or give a Federal agency authority to ban procedures as valid alternatives become available.

This option recognizes that prohibitions can be used to force technological change. Prohibiting procedures for which scientifically acceptable alternatives are already available would accelerate the implementation of such alternatives. Existing reductions and refinements in animal use include the greater use of analgesics in research, the use of fewer animals in the LD_{50} and Draize eye irritancy tests, and reliance on videotaped demonstrations and computer simulations in education.

A ban could not only force implementation of existing alternatives, but, over time, help focus the development of new techniques (as discussed in the next section) and allow considerable flexibility in achieving the desired end. A disadvantage of banning a specified procedure is that the replacement, or the process of developing one, may be even more politically unacceptable (e.g., the in vitro culture of human fetal nerve cells). A prohibition also takes no account of the question of judging the scientific acceptability of an alternative.

In pursuing this option or the preceding one, it is important to appreciate that the swiftest adoption of alternatives may come about if regulatory agencies avoid mandating specific testing requirements. Requiring specified tests might actually serve as a strong inhibitor to the implementation (and development) of alternative methods. Greater flexibility is achieved when testing requirements are defined in a manner that allows judgment and encourages use of alternate methods. Viewed from this perspective, the adoption of alternatives might be best stimulated by regulatory requirement for evaluation of a potential toxic response, such as mutagenicity, rather than requirement of a specified test for mutagenicity.

ISSUE: Should the more rapid development of new alternatives in research, testing, or education be stimulated?

Alternatives are currently being developed in many phases of animal use. It is worth noting that development of many of these techniques, especially their validation, cannot occur without animals being used (unless humans are used instead). In addition, many replacement systems will never be fully divorced from animal research and testing, and therefore they will serve to reduce but not eliminate animal use.

Certain research and testing methods now being developed, such as in vitro culture of animal components, bear great promise as alternatives. Similarly, the growing capabilities of computer modeling, for example biological simulation (see ch. 6) and pharmacology (see ch. 8), may reduce the number of animals needed. Development of an enhanced ability to detect and relieve pain can help refine animal use.

Research that spawns alternatives usually takes place across traditional disciplinary lines—principally within the life sciences—but also in applied mathematics, statistics, engineering, physics, and chemistry. The principal support for such research comes from Federal funds, predominantly NIH and the National Science Foundation. In general, there is little incentive for private investment in methodologies at a stage so remote from commercialization and, in the case of testing, so governed by regulation. Some private concerns, however, specifically fund research into alternative testing methods (see ch. 12).

Clearly, research and development require money. Determining the optimum level of funding, however, and the best way to distribute funds remains elusive. Nonetheless, the promotion of such research is likely to increase the number of alternatives available for implementation; in turn, increased implementation is likely to spur research in this area.

Option 1: Take no action.

If Congress takes no specific steps beyond its recent charge to NIH to establish a plan for the development of alternatives in biomedical research, the development of alternatives will continue to be a function of ethical, political, economic, and scientific factors.

That alternatives are being developed in the absence of direct legislation is best illustrated by research centers at Rockefeller University and The Johns Hopkins University funded by corporate and private donations (see ch. 12). In addition, corporations are undertaking work in-house or sponsoring it in universities, often in response to scientific, economic, animal welfare, and public relations considerations.

An uncertain pace of development marks the chief disadvantage of this option. Although alternatives may emerge, changing research priorities in both the public and private sectors will affect the rate of development. From another perspective, this is an advantage: It permits researchers to respond to changing needs and priorities with minimal Federal interference.

Option 2: Require a new or existing Federal entity to coordinate the development of alternatives.

Implementation of this option would have great symbolic value within the scientific and animal welfare communities and could lead to more rapid development of alternatives. A central clearinghouse for the development of alternatives could compile and maintain records of all federally funded research and development (R&D) on alternatives. Information on R&D in the private sector would be a valuable component of the coordination effort, though it may prove difficult to obtain.

Coordination could involve identifying research areas likely to lead to new alternatives and reviewing Federal support for those areas across agency lines. The latter responsibility might preclude housing this entity within an existing Federal agency involved in funding R&D on alternatives to avoid either a real or apparent conflict of interest.

As in the implementation of alternatives (see preceding issue), education plays a central role in the development of such approaches. Coordination of efforts aimed at informing investigators and students about animal research (see ch. 9) could be among the responsibilities of this Federal entity.

Option 3: Provide intramural and extramural Federal funding for the development of alternatives.

An effective mechanism for encouraging R&D on alternatives is funding. Small pilot programs might assess whether or not targeted development is effective.

Development of alternatives in testing within the Federal Government is a natural offshoot of and closely allied with toxicological research. The agencies most likely to produce alternatives in response to new Federal funding are the National Cancer Institute and NIH. Because testing is so closely tied to regulation, funding could also be directed to FDA, EPA, the Consumer Product Safety Commission, and the National Institute for Occupational Safety and Health. Regulatory agencies could be required to develop alternatives to specified tests or to spend funds generally toward their development.

To stimulate extramural R&D, granting agencies reviewing applications could be required to assign priority to those that contain research with promise for the development of new alternatives. Postdoctoral training programs could be established, along the lines of NIH's National Research Service Awards, to ensure a steady supply of young researchers schooled in traditional disciplines, ranging from molecular biology to animal behavior, with applications in the development of alternatives.

Financial incentives to private groups developing alternatives could take the form of tax incentives—perhaps tax credits in addition to those already in place for R&D. Such groups could also be eligible for a new program (analogous to the Small Business Innovation Research program) that would target the development of alternatives (see ch. 12).

ISSUE: Should improvements be made in information resources to reduce any unintentionally duplicative use of animals in research and testing?

Science is able to advance rapidly because information about what has been done is disseminated (see ch. 10). If attempts to find prior work are inadequate or prior work is not sufficiently accessible, unintentional duplication may occur. Such unnecessary repetition of experiments must be distinguished from replication of experiments to demonstrate the reproducibility of a method or to confirm the validity of results.

The amount of unintentional, largely duplicative research and testing that occurs today is unknown. Investigations into the amount and circumstances of unintentional duplication would be valuable in determining whether it results in substantial waste of animals or funds. Moreover, consultations with potential users of any new information resources would be essential in implementing certain options addressing this issue.

Although the storage and retrieval of data are costly, there are clear benefits to making information that reduces unintentional duplication readily available. Among these benefits are savings in the expense and time associated with animal research and testing. Other benefits are savings in animal lives and the additional work that might be done if resources are not wasted (see ch. 11).

Option 1: Take no action.

By making the National Agricultural Library the focus of a service to provide information on improved methods of animal experimentation (Public Law 99-198), Congress in 1985 indicated its intention to facilitate the dissemination of information about alternatives and to prevent unintended duplication of animal experimentation.

Even if no further improvements in information resources are made specifically for the sake of avoiding unintentionally duplicative animal use, general improvements in information resources will proceed as a matter of course. Many resources already exist. The National Library of Medicine, the National Toxicology Program, and other Federal entities maintain large databases that contain information or citations to published sources. Major commercial databases exist as well. National libraries and information centers provide the full text of articles and reports. The National Technical Information Service (NTIS) catalogs, stores, and distributes on request many unpublished Federal reports. Improvements in these resources can be expected, either to fill needs for which the benefits justify the costs or to achieve other information policy goals, such as openness in government or advancement of science.

Option 2: Require that results of all federally funded research and testing be conveniently accessible.

By means of oversight authority or legislation, all Federal entities could be required to provide convenient access to the results of all federally funded animal research and testing. Implementation could be largely through mechanisms already available—publishing in the scientific literature; circulating published reports or depositing them with NTIS, NLM, the National Agricultural Library, or other entity; or entering the results in a publicly available database. New databases might also be established. Requirements that results be made conveniently accessible could apply to Federal employees, contractors (through contract terms), and grantees (as a condition of awards). Contractors and grantees, however, may not be enthusiastic about assuming the burden of publicizing their results and responding to requests for information.

This option recognizes that much research and some testing using animals is federally funded, that dissemination of research and testing results could be more comprehensive, and that better dissemination might reduce any unintentional duplication. Because publication and information dissemination are normally much less costly than obtaining original data, the benefits of enhanced communication extend beyond saving animal lives.

It is important to note that most federally funded work, indeed the vast majority of significant work, is already accessible, although access comes with different levels of convenience. And the results of federally funded work (except some grants) are available under the Freedom of Information Act (FOIA). Requiring that all results be conveniently accessible may burden databases and libraries with inconclusive results or other information that will not be used.

Option 3: Promote greater use of animal testing data submitted by industry to Federal agencies, except where confidentiality protections apply.

Industry must submit data to regulatory agencies before it can market certain products or sometimes in response to reporting requirements. Statutory and regulatory provisions already exist that make some of this information publicly available, thus theoretically avoiding unintentional duplication. In addition, information that is voluntarily submitted and not claimed as confidential is available under FOIA.

Using oversight authority or legislation, greater use of nonconfidential information could be promoted, for example, by requiring that it be put into databases, compiled in reports, or summarized in newsletters. Industry could bear the cost of information dissemination, and any data submission to the Federal Government would have to be accompanied by evidence of intent to publish nonconfidential testing data. Industry may be unenthusiastic about such a procedure, because in some cases nonconfidential data provide direct clues to confidential data. Nevertheless, greater availability of nonconfidential data could aid in avoiding unintentionally duplicative testing.

The extent to which researchers who need such data already know how to obtain them is not known. The needs of those engaged in animal testing must be carefully gauged prior to consideration of this option. A further consideration is the willingness of those who generate the data to encourage others to benefit from their investment.

Option 4: Require comprehensive literature searches to ensure that federally funded research or testing involving animals is not duplicative.

A literature review is normally conducted by an investigator in the course of preparing a grant application, contract proposal, or data submission. In addition, the reviewers of such proposals are expected to be familiar with work that has already been done. Implementation of this option would require proof of a literature search through, for example, a companion document in any proposal to conduct federally funded research or testing. The funding entity would presumably have to judge the appropriateness of the literature search. Both the investigator's act of searching the literature and the funding agency's certification of the search may reduce any unintentional duplication. To make a mandatory literature search palatable to investigators, free access to some or all of the necessary information resources may have to be provided.

An alternative strategy is to require a literature search by the funding agency, or other entity, prior to the release of any funds. The disadvantages of requiring a comprehensive literature search before work could be funded include the delay that an additional step would cause, the cost of the search itself to the Federal Government, and possibly part of the cost of developing new information resources.

Option 5: Create new databases designed to reduce unintentional duplication of animal use in research and testing.

New computerized databases might play an important role in reducing any unintentionally duplicative animal use. There are at least three types that could contribute to this end:

- **Unpublished Results, Including Negative Results.** Such a database would disseminate results that are otherwise distributed narrowly or not at all. The major problem with unpublished information is that its quality is difficult to evaluate because it is rarely subjected to peer review. Another problem is that the most useful unpublished data are owned by industry and would not be disclosed because of their proprietary value (although provision could be made for voluntary submissions). A category of special interest, particularly from the standpoint of duplicative testing, is negative results (e.g., showing the absence of toxic effects). Few journals are willing to publish negative testing results. Dissemination of negative results could spare any unintentional duplication, direct investigators away from fruitless paths, or suggest improvements in methodologies.
- **Data From Untreated, or Control, Animals.** Data pertaining to the health or behavior of animals not given a test substance could be used in choosing the best species for experimentation (e.g., a species most likely to yield unambiguous results). This information might obviate the need to use more than one species or might allow smaller control groups in some experiments (see ch. 7). Compiling the database could be both difficult and costly because the necessary data are often not published (see ch. 10).
- **Experimental Protocols and Results.** This database could be as narrow as abbreviated listings of methods and results, perhaps arranged by species, or as comprehensive as the on-line full text of all published scientific literature. (The full text of a scientific report includes not only protocol and results, but also discussion and interpretation of the results, tables, figures, and bibliography. At present,

38-750 O - 86 - 2

the full text (minus figures and images) of a few dozen scientific journals is available on-line.) The greatest obstacle to the successful creation of a database of this size is catering to the diverse needs of animal users. In its fullest incarnation, this would cost hundreds of millions of dollars to start and maintain.

Most important, the extent to which any of these databases would be used is unknown. Within the Federal Government, the NLM has the greatest expertise in establishing and operating large databases, and implementation of any form of this option is likely to build on the experience and existing resources of that library.

Option 6: Facilitate the use of foreign data by providing translations of foreign journals.

An often-overlooked source of published data is foreign-language literature, although most important scientific work is routinely published in or translated into English. The advantages of providing translations of additional work are thought by many experts to be quite limited and economically unjustifiable. English translation costs for the four principal languages of science (French, German, Russian, and Japanese) range from $40 to $88 per thousand words. An estimated $4 billion to $5 billion would be required, for example, to translate the current foreign-language holdings of the NLM into English, with an ongoing yearly translation cost of $150 million (see ch. 10). Copyright protections might involve costly inconvenience as well. The impact of this option is uncertain, as English abstracts are today available for most foreign journals, and translations can be obtained on an ad hoc basis by those interested in a particular report.

ISSUE: Should animal use in research, testing, or education be restricted?

The use of animals for research, testing, and educational purposes is not closely restricted in the United States. Only four types of constraints can be identified. The Animal Welfare Act requires humane handling, care, and treatment of nonhuman primates, dogs, cats, rabbits, guinea pigs, and hamsters. However, any regulation of these animals within an actual experimental protocol is specifically excepted by the Animal Welfare Act (see ch. 13). Second, at the State and local levels, cruelty to animals is generally proscribed, although such statutes are generally not applied to animal use during experimentation (see ch. 14). Third, self-regulation takes place at individual institutions and facilities through the implementation of Federal policies. These call for assessment of animal care, treatment, and practices in experimentation by institutional animal care and use committees. Fourth, the Department of Defense was prohibited in fiscal years 1984 and 1985 from expending any funds for training surgical personnel by treating in dogs and cats wounds that had been produced by weapons (see app. B).

The few existing restrictions on animal use illustrate two phenomena. First, they show that primates and pets have a privileged position in public policy. The Animal Welfare Act names only six kinds of animals, omitting the rats and mice that together constitute approximately 75 percent of the animals used in research, testing, and education. It requires exercise for dogs and a physical environment adequate to promote the psychological well-being of primates. In the case of the DOD appropriation, dogs and cats were named, while goats and pigs (also used in surgical wound training) were not.

Second, the restrictions demarcate the long-standing frontier of legislative province over animal use—the laboratory door. The actual conduct of experiments stands largely outside of any specific mandatory provisions of law. (In contrast, British investigators are licensed to carry out specified procedures using specified animals and face inspection visits to the laboratory bench by government officials; see ch. 16.) Solely in the case of the prohibition of DOD expenditures is one use of two particular species addressed.

Considering the issue of restriction of animal use may require the resolution of four difficult questions:

- Are there **some kinds of animals** on which experimentation is inherently inappropriate?
- Are **some methods or procedures** beyond the realm of societal acceptability?
- Should **some sources of animals** be deemed off limits for animal use in research, testing, or education?
- Should **licensed investigators alone** be permitted to engage in animal experimentation?

The resolution of these questions turns on science, law, politics, and, to a large degree, ethics.

Six options for congressional action have been identified.

Option 1: Take no action.

In the absence of new restrictions, animal use in research, testing, and education will continue to be governed loosely at the Federal level. Like the American system of education, control of animal use can be largely a local issue, and institutional animal care and use committees stand as the arbiters of community standards. One drawback of a minimal Federal role is the possible development of conflicting or confusing State and local policies.

Maintenance of the status quo would reaffirm that Congress concurs that no methods or procedures are beyond the realm of societal acceptability (except the training of military personnel in surgical techniques on wounded dogs and cats in fiscal years 1984 and 1985). Maintenance of the status quo would leave unaffected the acquisition of animals for research, testing, and education: Sources of animals today include breeders, dealers, pounds, and in-house breeding. Some States will continue to bar the acquisition of pound animals for research (see ch. 14). Finally, in the absence of a licensing scheme, investigators and their areas of inquiry will remain wholly a function of available resources and individual interests.

Option 2: Restrict the use of certain kinds of animals.

Some people feel it is wrong to use particular animals in research, testing, or education. This belief may stem from respect for apparent intelligence, and animals most closely related to humans, such as nonhuman primates, may be considered off limits for investigation or manipulation. Similarly, attachment to companion animals such as dogs and cats or to pet species such as hamsters may lead to a desire for their legislated immunity from experimentation.

A restriction of this nature is likely to have several consequences. The restricted species would be protected while investigators faced, at a minimum, an inconvenience until new methods are developed. Development of new model systems would likely necessitate the generation of new fundamental data about the characteristics of the model system, while the existing base of data—which could be large—about the restricted animal is set aside because it is no longer useful. In some cases, new methods would lead to a substitution of a less favored species for the restricted one. Perhaps the most important consequence would be that where the restricted species (e.g., monkey or dog) is the most scientifically appropriate model for research or testing, a prohibition on the use of that species may affect the ability to extrapolate results to humans.

Given that few, if any, kinds of animals are exclusively used in testing, research, and education, a restriction of this nature would be difficult to impose. How, for example, might a restriction distinguish between primates under behavioral observation in a field colony and those observed by tourists at a safari-style game preserve? Restriction of the use of particular kinds of animals may be inconsistent with the popular treatment and use of those same animals (e.g., circus, zoological park, sport, hunt, or farm) throughout the United States. Combining this option with the next one—to restrict the use of a species in a certain protocol—would yield a more limited, more practicable form of restriction than a blanket prohibition on use of a species.

Option 3: Restrict the use of particular protocols.

Some people feel that it is inhumane to manipulate animals in certain ways, irrespective of the motivation for the procedure. Such concerns usually focus on procedures that cause the animal pain or are painful for humans to watch. The Draize eye irritancy test is such a procedure, as are inflictions of blunt head trauma in neurology research and of bullet wounds in surgical training.

In research, blanket prohibitions either of a particular animal's use (the preceding option) or of a specified procedure entail a risk of being overly inclusive. They could have unintended or unforeseen consequences, especially in the face of incomplete knowledge about how animals are used and in what protocols and what the results might portend. One risk of such a restriction would be the elimination of the use of animal models that may be the best available or the sole method of studying conditions present in humans but that do not lend themselves to systematic study in humans (see ch. 5).

In testing, procedures like the Draize test and the LD_{50} are used in part because investigators believe that Federal regulatory agencies, such as FDA and EPA, require the results of these tests in data submissions (see ch. 7). Exercise of oversight authority could induce Federal regulatory agencies to make explicit their disinterest in data derived from objectionable tests and to demonstrate their ready acceptance of data obtained through alternate means. Such oversight action, coupled with active research into alternative methods, would probably end most use of the targeted procedures.

It is likely that review of protocols by committee, particularly a committee with expertise in bioethics, laboratory animal science, and anesthesia, would effectively restrict procedures to those that are generally accepted as humane. In both research and testing, banning animal use for a specific purpose would reflect the judgment that knowledge gained via that procedure could never justify the cost in animal suffering or lives.

Option 4: Restrict the acquisition of animals from particular sources.

For several decades, States and municipalities have wrestled with the issue of the release of dogs and cats from pounds to research and educational institutions (see ch. 14). Some people feel that the release of pound animals for experimentation is wrong, because the animals are former pets or are too unhealthy to be proper subjects for study. In some jurisdictions, research and educational institutions are barred from acquiring pound animals, while other jurisdictions require that pound animals be released to researchers after a certain number of days in captivity.

As pound animals are usually sold at low cost (see ch. 11), banning their sale would lead to higher procurement costs as the pound animals were replaced with animals that are purposely bred for experimentation. (Some animals are already purpose-bred because certain pound animals are not suitable candidates for experimentation.) The purposeful breeding of such animals for experimentation in parallel with routine euthanasia of pound animals would probably work out to a net increase in dogs and cats being killed.

Option 5: License animal users (e.g., for specified uses or for particular kinds of animals).

Animal users could be granted licenses specifying the procedures they are authorized to perform or the animals with which they may work. Such a system is in place in the United Kingdom under the auspices of the Home Office (see ch. 16). Given that at least five to six times as many animals are used in the United States annually (17 million to 22 million) as in the United Kingdom (3 million to 4 million), achieving and maintaining licensure here would be a considerably larger and more costly enterprise than now exists in any country.

Implementation of this option would require a Federal licensing body with inspection and enforcement capability. If the British system is the model, licenses would be legally enforceable personal documents. A license to perform a particular experiment or a series of experiments or to work with a particular species would be nontransferable. Confidentiality would be guaranteed in order to protect, for example, an investigator's claim to priority in research results. Comprehensive annual reporting by licensees and auditing by an oversight body—both integral parts of the British system—would be necessary. It is noteworthy that in the United Kingdom this system allows every animal experiment to be logged (see ch. 16).

The British system works. It relies heavily on a tradition of cooperation between experimenter and Home Office inspector. The feasibility of such a system in the United States is difficult to predict because the dimensions of animal use are so poorly characterized. Hence, the number of licensees and the resources required for monitoring are unknown. Perhaps most important, the extent to which the parties involved would cooperate is uncertain.

Option 6: Prohibit the use of animals in research, testing, and education.

No other country and no jurisdiction in the United States has completely banned animal use in research, testing, or education. In Switzerland, a binding referendum of this nature was presented to the public for a vote in December 1985, but it was defeated (see ch. 16).

Action to ban animal use fully is the most extreme of the six options related to the issue of restriction. It would undeniably provide great impetus towards implementing alternatives. Indeed, the alternatives of **reduction** and **refinement** of animal use would be immediately and completely achieved. However, the development of many **replacements** to animal use depends itself on animals. A ban would, for example, eliminate the use of organ cultures, nonhuman tissue cultures, and cell cultures, except for those self-perpetuating ones already in existence. Replacements would have to be drawn from among human and veterinary patients, micro-organisms, plants, chemical and physical systems, and simulations of living systems. The development of new computer simulations would falter, with new data from animal systems being unavailable. The ability to verify new simulations or proposed replacements would also come to a halt.

Implementation of this option would effectively arrest most basic biomedical and behavioral research and toxicological testing in the United States. Education would be affected, too, although perhaps not as severely as research and testing. In the advanced life sciences and in medical and veterinary training, students might be handicapped, although not to as great a degree as once thought. Some medical schools today, for example, use no animals in physiology curricula (see ch. 9).

The economic and public health consequences of a ban on animal use are so unpredictable and speculative that this course of action must be considered dangerous. Caution would demand, for example, that any new products or processes have substantial advantages over available ones to merit the risk of using them without animal testing.

ISSUE: Should more accurate data be obtained on the kinds and numbers of animals used in research, testing, and education?

Accurate data on the kinds and numbers of animals used in research, testing, and education in the United States do not exist (see chs. 3 and 9). The best numbers now available on the use of certain species (nonhuman primates, dogs, cats, rabbits, guinea pigs, and hamsters) are produced by the Animal and Plant Health Inspection Service of the USDA. The APHIS *Animal Welfare Enforcement Report* submitted to Congress each year is best viewed as a rough estimate of animal use. It records approximately 10 percent of all animals used annually; omitted are rats, mice, birds, fish, reptiles, and amphibians.

Estimates of animals used yearly in the United States range to 100 million and more. Although the development and implementation of alternatives do not require an accurate count, public policy formation would be helped by better data. Regulating animal use, for example, or funding the development or validation of alternatives to a particular procedure, may depend on how many animals are used and what fraction of the total this represents. Trends in animal use have similar applications. In the United Kingdom, the exact animal use records kept since 1876 have influenced policymakers (see ch. 16).

Some animal welfare advocates suggest that the moral and ethical issues surrounding animal use are independent of the precise number of animals used. Others question whether the value of the data obtained is worth the cost of obtaining accurate numbers. A rough estimate based on minimal data may be all that is necessary to put the relevant issues into context. Selecting among the following options will depend, therefore, on judgment of how important it is to know the number and kinds of animals used, who uses them, and what trends exist.

Option 1: Take no action.

The primary advantage of this option is that no additional funding would be required, since nothing within the system would change. Continued funding of current APHIS activities would keep yielding rough estimates of the use of six kinds of animals that account for about 10 percent of total animal use.

The major disadvantage of maintaining the status quo is that an inaccurate and ambiguous reporting system would be perpetuated, yielding marginally useful analysis of animal use in the United States. The APHIS counting system is ineffective because of problems with ambiguous reporting forms and a failure to audit the forms that are returned.

Funding for the APHIS survey has been derived from the approximately $5 million allocated annually in recent years to APHIS to enforce the Animal Welfare Act. Depending on the uses to which data on animal use are put, maintaining the status quo may be adequate, an unnecessary expense, or not nearly enough.

Option 2: Eliminate the APHIS reporting system.

If the value of the information obtained by the APHIS system is not justified by the money allocated for its collection, the APHIS reporting system could be terminated. In adopting this option, Congress would signal a willingness to rely on estimates produced by nongovernment organizations and individuals without the benefit of reports or inspections.

Option 3: Correct inadequacies in the present APHIS system of reporting use of animals mandated by the Animal Welfare Act.

To gain a more accurate picture of the use of nonhuman primates, dogs, cats, rabbits, guinea pigs, and hamsters in the United States, oversight authority could be used to require that APHIS alter its present practices in one or more of the following ways:

- correct its reporting form to eliminate ambiguities;
- change the reporting deadline or publication schedule for the annual *Animal Welfare Enforcement Report,* so that fewer institutional reports are excluded;
- audit or spot-check the "Annual Report of Research Facility" forms and facilities;
- strictly enforce the regulation requiring that all institutions within the United States using mandated species register with APHIS and complete the "Annual Report of Research Facility" forms as required by law; or
- allocate more of APHIS' resources for enforcement of the Animal Welfare Act to reporting.

These changes would require little additional government funding or expenditure by regulated entities, although it could affect how they allocate their resources. Adoption of this option would bring APHIS closer to delivering the information it is obliged to deliver under the Animal Welfare Act.

Option 4: Alter the APHIS system to count additional kinds of animals (e.g., rats and mice).

Rats and mice account for approximately 75 percent of the animals used in research, testing, and education in the United States. They go uncounted because a USDA regulation under the Animal Welfare Act excludes them from its definition of animals. There is, however, some voluntary reporting of the use of these species on the APHIS "Annual Report of Research Facility" forms.

Data on rats and mice (or other currently unregulated animals) could be obtained in either of two ways. Congressional oversight of the Secretary of Agriculture could lead to a requirement that the use of rats and mice be reported. This would require additional funding for APHIS, because the number of facilities under the act's regulations would increase. On the other hand, the counting mechanism is already in place, and only minor changes would be needed.

Expanding the APHIS animal counting requirement to include rats and mice would raise costs for some members of the research and testing communities. Accurate counting of these species, including categorization of experiments for pain and pain relief, is a labor-intensive activity and hence costly. Such costs will be of exceptional concern to institutions using large numbers of rats and mice, and these users can be expected to question whether accounting needs for policy evaluation require the extra expense.

A broadening of the APHIS census to include rats and mice would still leave some uncounted. The Animal Welfare Act's definition of research facility covers any institution that uses primates, dogs, cats, rabbits, guinea pigs, hamsters, or other warm-blooded animals, as the Secretary of Agriculture may determine are used in experimentation, and that either purchases or transports animals in commerce or receives Federal funds for experiments. Thus, a facility that breeds all its animals in-house—most likely rats or mice—falls outside the scope of the Animal Welfare Act and accompanying USDA regulations. The number of facilities breeding and using rats and/or mice exclusively is unknown. Some toxicological testing laboratories are likely to fall into this group.

Option 5: Establish an independent census of animal use, either on a one-time or periodic basis.

Fundamental changes could be made in the ways animals are counted. An animal census could be periodic—e.g., occurring every 2, 5, or 10 years. An organization other than APHIS, such as the private Institute for Laboratory Animal Resources (ILAR) of the National Research Council, could do the counting. In 1986, ILAR will undertake another in its series of surveys of laboratory-animal facilities and resources in the United States. (The last survey was conducted in 1978.) ILAR will survey the use of two classes of vertebrates—mammals and birds—at approximately 3,000 facilities.

Another approach to gathering information on the kinds and numbers of animals used would be to conduct a comprehensive, one-time study of research, testing, and education. Such a study could survey all species acquired or bred for research, testing, and education; count the number of animals actually used in experimentation; record the length of stay in animals in the facility; and categorize the purposes of the experimental-animal use. Such a comprehensive survey would not merit repetition every year—the purposes of animal use in research, for instance, do not change that quickly.

A different way to count animals used would be to obtain figures from breeders on the number of animals bred for experimentation. This would not take into account the percentage of animals bred that are never used in experimentation, or animals bred within a laboratory, but it would yield a valuable index of animal use. Yet another source of information would be to count the number of facilities or individuals using animals for specified activities.

It is noteworthy that the revised PHS *Policy on Humane Care and Use of Laboratory Animals by Awardee Institutions* (effective Dec. 31, 1985) requires listing the average daily inventory, by species (with none excepted), of each animal facility, as part of each institution's annual report to the NIH Office for Protection from Research Risks. Thus, PHS-supported facilities are now required to report more complete census data to NIH than facilities covered by the Animal Welfare Act report to APHIS. Consequently, a portion of animal use in research (e.g., NIH-supported animal research) and testing (e.g., FDA-supported animal testing) is about to become more closely censused.

The choice among census types under this option will depend on the ways in which the information is to be used, the resources available for obtaining it, and the utility of the new census required by PHS.

ISSUE: Should Federal departments and agencies be subject to minimum standards for animal use?

The Federal Government has six cabinet departments and four independent agencies involved in intramural animal research or testing (see ch. 13 and app. B). These departments and agencies account for at least 1.6 million animals for intramural research (see ch. 3). Federal agencies have generally followed the existing PHS policy and as of December 1986 will be required to operate institutional animal committees (Public Law 99-198). Many departments and agencies also follow the NIH *Guide for the Care and Use of Laboratory Animals*. Yet there is no stated, detailed policy of minimum standards for animal use within the Federal Government. Therefore, this issue has just two options: either maintaining the present system or establishing a minimum policy for intramural animal use. Financial considerations are not a major factor because funds will be needed either to continue the present system of variable policies or to implement and enforce a minimum, government-wide policy.

Option 1: Take no action.

The advantages of the present system are its flexibility and minimal bureaucratic structure. The policies mentioned previously, along with the Interagency Research Animal Committee's *Principles for the Utilization and Care of Vertebrate Animals Used in Testing, Research, and Training,* allow each agency or department to have policies and mechanisms unique to its situation. The disadvantages are the potential for conflicting policies and the lack of a neutral enforcement authority.

Option 2: Establish minimum standards for all intramural animal use in Federal departments and agencies.

This option would require that a policy be developed and perhaps that an organizational entity be established to oversee its implementation and enforcement. This could be accomplished by an interagency committee or by a designated agency.

Setting minimum standards would still give each agency and department the flexibility to tailor specific policies to unique situations, yet it would establish a Federal model for standards of animal care in experimentation and ensure humane procedures in Federal facilities.

A Federal intramural policy might incorporate policies and procedures that address facility accreditation and institutional review of research proposals. A composite, minimum Federal policy could reflect the most progressive parts of various current agency standards.

It is noteworthy that this type of action has been taken to protect human research subjects. A *Model Federal Policy for the Protection of Human Research Subjects* involved in research conducted, supported, or regulated by Federal departments or agencies is now in draft form. The policy will be implemented through routine policy and procedural channels of the departments and agencies. The advantage of minimum standards is that all concerned parties know the policy and can immediately and permanently put in place the appropriate organizational structure and facilities to guarantee adherence.

ISSUE: Should the Animal Welfare Act of 1966 be further amended, or its enforcement enhanced?

One criticism of the Animal Welfare Act is the lack of coverage of practices other than anesthesia and analgesia during actual experimentation. Although the most recent amendments to the act, in 1985, direct institutional animal committees to assess practices in experimentation and require that professionally acceptable standards are followed during experimentation, the act at the same time forbids any regulation related to the design or performance of experiments. Additional complaints concern the adequacy of resources for its enforcement, the enforcement structure, the choice of APHIS as the primary enforcement agency, and the cumbersome recordkeeping.

In considering whether the act should be strengthened, some related issues must be kept in mind. First, a change in authority may require funding for implementation and enforcement. Second, any change must take into account the present resources of those affected and their ability to achieve compliance without compromising other objectives. Thus, an important consideration is whether or not regulated institutions have sufficient institutional and independent veterinary resources to effect meaningful compliance with a strengthened law and still meet their testing or research objectives. Finally, strengthening the Animal Welfare Act in the face of differences within the scientific and animal welfare communities will carry considerable symbolic value.

Option 1: Take no action.

By maintaining the status quo, Congress would give a strong signal to all concerned parties that it is satisfied with the present regulatory structure for animal use in the United States and that no change is deemed necessary. More specifically, selection of this option would imply that current enforcement efforts are sufficient and that it is not necessary to regulate rats and mice used in experimentation.

Option 2: Eliminate funding for enforcement of the Animal Welfare Act.

Elimination of funding for enforcement of the Animal Welfare Act by APHIS would save the Federal Government approximately $5 million annually. Without these funds, there would be no inspections of facilities (including exhibitors, dealers, and research institutions) using nonhuman primates, dogs, cats, rabbits, guinea pigs, or hamsters and no annual census of these six kinds of animals. Action taken by APHIS against violators would cease. Therefore, the objective of the Animal Welfare Act—to safeguard the humane care and treatment of certain animals—would no longer be met.

Option 3: Increase funding for enforcement of the Animal Welfare Act.

Increased funding for the enforcement of the Animal Welfare Act would bolster enforcement of the present law. Additional funds could be used to:

- increase the training of inspectors;
- increase the number of enforcement agents in the field, so as to raise the number of inspections;
- oversee consistent interpretation of existing regulation by inspection and enforcement agents in the field; and/or

- replace voluntary assurances and simple certifications of compliance with more rigorous procedures.

Additional funding could help stimulate the present passive regulatory situation to become a more active, aggressive regulatory environment. Such a transition would rest on APHIS' level of enthusiasm for enforcing the Animal Welfare Act.

Option 4: Expand the jurisdiction of enforcing agencies to include standards of care, treatment, and use during the actual conduct of experimentation.

The Animal Welfare Act exempts the treatment of animals while they are actually involved in experimentation, except for a requirement for appropriate anesthesia or analgesia and the use of professionally acceptable standards in the care, treatment, and use of animals. The original law exempted actual experimentation because Congress did not want to interfere with the conduct of the scientific process (see ch. 13). Animal care and treatment are essentially regulated only before and after a scientific procedure. Implementation of this option would broach the design and execution of experimental protocols and would require statutory change. Such action would increase the responsibility of APHIS and its enforcement would require additional funding. A deterrent to implementation of this option is APHIS' lack of expertise in reviewing experimental protocols.

Option 5: Realign existing and any new responsibilities for enforcement among Federal departments and agencies.

APHIS spends little of its resources, either monetary or personnel, enforcing the Animal Welfare Act (see ch. 13). It was selected by Congress in 1966 to enforce the act because it had some expertise in animal issues but did not have the conflict of interest that an entity such as NIH or DHHS might have.

Enforcement power could be changed by transferring enforcement authority for violations of the Animal Welfare Act from USDA (APHIS) to DHHS. This would set up a potential conflict of interest: A single department would both sponsor animal experimentation and have oversight authority. In addition, many of the regulations in the Animal Welfare Act affect areas in which DHHS has no expertise (e.g., animal use by exhibitors).

In amending the Animal Welfare Act in 1985, Congress mandated that the Secretary of Agriculture consult with the Secretary of Health and Human Services prior to issuing regulations under authority of the act. The implementation of this provision may lead to DHHS having increased influence on the enforcement of the act.

Option 6: Amend the Animal Welfare Act to preempt State and local laws concerning animal use in areas not already covered by the Animal Welfare Act.

Although the *Edward Taub* case in Maryland (see ch. 14) did not decide the preemption question, it did bring up the issue of whether the Animal Welfare Act could preempt a State statute. Congress may wish to examine its authority to preempt State anticruelty statutes and may then wish to specify for the judiciary whether it intended its law to supersede any State or local laws on this issue. In doing so, Congress could remove uncertainty in the law by making clear whether it intends the Animal Welfare Act to be a comprehensive, exclusive system of control over the use of animals in experimental facilities and activities in interstate and foreign commerce. Without such clarification, the possibility exists for local criminal prosecution, seizure of animals, injunctions to close facilities, and cessation of animal investigations.

Current State and local efforts to assure humane treatment have been criticized for several reasons. Compliance schemes are overly complex, training and resources are inadequate, and existing laws are not specific enough in their standards for care, treatment, and use. If Federal preemption is not exercised, then State and local laws will be considered concurrent and complementary to existing Federal laws.

It is important to note that Federal preemption means that the administrative system for monitoring, including on-site inspection, should be made adequate to ensure continued compliance with national standards for humane treatment. Otherwise, State-level organizations with a sincere and reasonable concern about the care of animals will be justified in demanding local enforcement and surveillance of research, testing, and education involving animals.

Finally, it should be recognized that if Federal preemption is deemed necessary, the constitutional question of whether the Federal Government has the authority to assert itself into areas traditionally regulated by the States (e.g., pound animal use) may well land in the courts.

Chapter 2

Introduction

Donahue: *What doesn't feel pain? When do you stop feeling pain? Does a frog feel pain?*
McArdle: *Yes.*
Donahue: *Frogs feel pain? . . . now what about laboratory high school? You remember, you had to dissect the frog? . . . Should we eliminate that? How about fishing? . . . how about baiting a hook with a worm? Is that fair? In other words, where do we stop?*
McArdle: *You bring up fishing and I think that's a good point. I used to wonder whether or not the nonvertebrate animals would feel pain. A few years ago they found endorphins, which are substances that handle chronic pain, in earth worms. So, earth worms may in fact be subject to chronic pain when you're putting them on that hook.*

Phil Donahue with John E. McArdle, Humane Society of the United States
Donahue (transcript #02065)
February 1985

Although the highest standard of protection must be applied to all animals, we acknowledge that it is right to pay special attention to the companions of man [non-human primates, cats, dogs, and equidae] for whom there is the greatest public concern.

Scientific Procedures on Living Animals, Command 9521
British Home Office
May 1985

CONTENTS

Table

Chapter 2
Introduction

This report assesses the state of the art and the potential for alternatives to using animals in three contexts: biomedical and behavioral research, testing of products for toxicity, and education. Distinguishing among these three areas is important because both the patterns of animal use and the potential for alternatives vary among them. Research develops new knowledge and new technologies; although prediction of results is one goal, unpredictable results may prove even more significant. Testing relies on standardized procedures that have been demonstrated to predict certain health effects in humans or animals. It entails the measurement of biological phenomena, such as the presence or absence of cancer or of skin irritation, or the concentration of certain substances in tissue or in bodily fluids. Education involves teaching students in the life sciences, health professionals and preprofessionals, and research scientists, as well as the cultivation of humane attitudes toward animals at all levels. Alternatives in each of these three areas consist of procedures that replace animals with nonanimal methods, that reduce the number of animals used, or that refine existing protocols to make them more humane.

In addition to evaluating alternatives in three areas, the assessment also examines ethical concerns regarding the use of animals, economic considerations of their use and the alternatives, funding for the development of alternatives, and current regulation of animal use. Most important, this report delineates seven major public policy issues (and associated options for congressional action) in relation to alternatives (see ch. 1).

With a focus on the prospects for alternatives to animal use in research, testing, and education, this assessment necessarily excludes certain related topics and treats others only in brief. The role of animals in food and fiber production falls outside the scope of this study, as does the role of animals in the commercial production of antibodies and other biological materials. In addition, OTA has not evaluated the use of animals for companionship, sport, or entertainment. Although laboratory animals are an integral part of this assessment, OTA did not examine contemporary standards of their care (e.g., cage size, sanitation, ventilation, feeding, and watering). Lastly, the use of human subjects is not considered in this assessment.

WHAT IS AN ANIMAL?

In any biological definition of the word "animal," all vertebrate and invertebrate organisms are included and plants and unicellular organisms are excluded. For the purposes of this report, however, **an "animal" is defined as any member of the five classes of vertebrates (nonhuman mammals, birds, reptiles, amphibians, and fish).** These five classes of vertebrates can be further divided into two major groups, cold-blooded vertebrates (reptiles, amphibians, and fish) and warm-blooded vertebrates (mammals and birds). Invertebrates, therefore, are not discussed as animals.

Political and scientific discussions often incorporate other subdivisions for the term "animal." Although not strictly part of the definition in this report, the terms "lower" and "higher" are used in many discussions of alternatives that refine existing animal procedures or that replace certain animal species with other ones. In these contexts, the substitution of "lower" animals for "higher" animals usually refers to using cold-blooded vertebrates instead of warm-blooded vertebrates. In addition, within the class of mammals, "lower" is generally used to designate, for example, rodents, while "higher" refers to primates, companion animal species (e.g., dogs, cats, or rabbits), and domestic farm animals (e.g., horses, cattle, or pigs).

Table 2-1 is a classification of the principal living organisms that are used in research, testing, and education. It indicates the laboratory species falling within this assessment's definition of an animal and the species that can be classified as "alternatives."

Table 2-1.—Some Types of Living Organisms Used in Research, Testing, and Education

Alternatives:

I. Prokaryotes (any living organism without a nuclear membrane)
- A. Bacteria
  - 1. *Escherichia coli*
  - 2. *Salmonella*
  - 3. *Streptococcus*
  - 4. *Bacillus*
- B. Fungi—e.g., yeast

II. Eukaryotes (any living organism with a nuclear membrane)
- A. Plants
- B. Invertebrates
  - 1. Protozoa
    - a. *Paramecium*
    - b. *Amoeba*
  - 2. Porifera—e.g., sponges
  - 3. Coelenterates—e.g., *Hydra* and Jellyfish
  - 4. Flatworms—e.g., *Planaria*
  - 5. Segmented worms
    - a. Earthworms
    - b. Leeches
    - c. Annelids
  - 6. Nematodes—e.g., *Caenorhabditis elegans*
  - 7. Molluscs
    - a. Gastropods—e.g., snails and *Aplysia*
    - b. Pelecypods—e.g., mussels
    - c. Cephalopods—e.g., squids and octopuses
  - 8. Arthropods
    - a. *Limulus* (horseshoe crabs)
    - b. Arachnids
      - (1) Spiders
      - (2) Ticks
      - (3) Mites
      - (4) Scorpions
    - c. Crustaceans
      - (1) *Daphnia*
      - (2) Brine shrimp
      - (3) Crayfish
    - d. Insects
      - (1) Crickets
      - (2) Cockroaches
      - (3) *Drosophila* (fruit flies)
      - (4) Lice
      - (5) Beetles
      - (6) Moths
      - (7) Butterflies
  - 9. Echinoderms
    - a. Sea urchins
    - b. Sand dollars
    - c. Sea cucumbers

Animals:
- C. Vertebrates
  - 1. Cold-blooded vertebrates
    - a. Fish
      - (1) Jawless fish—e.g., lampreys
      - (2) Cartilaginous fish—e.g., sharks
      - (3) Bony fish
    - b. Amphibians
      - (1) Frogs—e.g., *Rana*
      - (2) Toads—e.g., *Xenopus*
      - (3) Salamanders
    - c. Reptiles
      - (1) Turtles
      - (2) Crocodiles
      - (3) Alligators
      - (4) Snakes
      - (5) Lizards
  - 2. Warm-blooded vertebrates
    - a. Birds
      - (1) Quail
      - (2) Chickens
      - (3) Pigeons
      - (4) Doves
      - (5) Ducks
    - b. Mammals
      - (1) Bats
      - (2) Rodents
        - (a) Mice
        - (b) Rats
        - (c) Gerbils
        - (d) Guinea pigs
        - (e) Hamsters
        - (f) Squirrels
      - (3) Marine mammals
        - (a) Dolphins
        - (b) Whales
        - (c) Seals
        - (d) Sea lions
      - (4) Rabbits
      - (5) Armadillos
      - (6) Carnivores
        - (a) Dogs
        - (b) Cats
        - (c) Ferrets
      - (7) Ungulates
        - (a) Cattle
        - (b) Sheep
        - (c) Horses
        - (d) Pigs
        - (e) Miniature pigs
        - (f) Goats
        - (g) Donkeys
        - (h) Burros
      - (8) Primates
        - (a) Baboons
        - (b) Capuchins
        - (c) Chimpanzees
        - (d) Macaques, Cynomolgous
        - (e) Macaques, Pig-tailed
        - (f) Macaques, Rhesus
        - (g) Marmosets
        - (h) Squirrel monkeys

SOURCE: Office of Technology Assessment.

WHAT IS AN ALTERNATIVE?

Defining the word "alternative" is in a sense always doomed to failure: Regardless of how accommodating or strict the definition, many will fault it. The term evolved in the political arena, coined by animal welfare activists and for the most part nonscientists, and yet it has direct implications for scientists using laboratory animals. Its meaning varies greatly, depending on who uses it and the context in which it is used.

The definition of "alternatives" employed by OTA obviously affects this entire assessment: It defines the scope of the study. Too narrow a definition would dispose of the need for this report, while too broad a definition would render it unmanageable. Defining alternatives as the nonuse of animals, as some would have it, would restrict the bounds of the study to the consideration of invertebrate organisms, chemicals, plants, and computers. On the other hand, stretching the definition to include humans, for example, would create a whole new series of issues that would be virtually impossible to address within one assessment. With these concerns in mind, **OTA chose to define "alternatives" as encompassing any subjects, protocols, or technologies that "*replace* the use of laboratory animals altogether, *reduce* the number of animals required, or *refine* existing procedures or techniques so as to minimize the level of stress endured by the animal"** (4; adapted from 5).

Some examples of alternatives under this definition include computer simulations to demonstrate principles of physiology to medical students, the use of the approximate lethal dose methodology in acute toxicity studies, and the increased use of anesthetics with pain research subjects. The "reduction" part of the definition indicates that the increased use of cultured cells, tissues, and organs instead of whole animals is also an alternative. A very broad interpretation of alternatives might also include the substitution of cold-blooded for warm-blooded vertebrates.

BIOLOGICAL MODELS

When animals—or alternatives—are used in research, testing, and education, it is because they possess a simpler or more accessible structure or mechanism in comparison with the object of primary interest (which is often the human) or are themselves the object of primary interest, or because certain procedures cannot be carried out on humans. Viewed from this perspective, both animals and alternatives stand as models. In the broadest sense, a biological model is a surrogate, or substitute, for any process or organism of ultimate interest to the investigator. It is a representation of or analog to some living structure, organism, or process.

In addition to analogy, biology has another analytical tool at its disposal—homology, which is correspondence in structure and function derived from a common evolutionary origin (i.e., a common gene sequence). The most closely related species are generally presumed to offer the best homologs. Relationships between species are not always known in detail, however, and unresolved questions about evolutionary events and pathways are numerous. Care must therefore be used in evaluating the degree of homology and the extent to which it relates to analogy (3).

Some biological mechanisms, such as the coding of genetic information and the pathways of metabolism, arose early in evolution. These mechanisms have been highly conserved and are widely shared by organisms, including humans, at the cellular and molecular levels. Thus, good models for these fundamental molecular mechanisms in humans can be found in a wide array of organisms, some of which, such as bacteria, have structures and functions far less complex than those of mammals (3).

Several characteristics are important in choosing a model for research, testing, or educational purposes. The most important is the model's discrimination—the extent to which it reproduces the particular property in which the investigator is interested. With greater discrimination, the predictability between the model and the property under study increases.

After the discrimination or predictability of a model, certain other criteria stand out as being necessary for a good biological model (1,2). A model should:

- accurately reproduce the disease or lesion under study;
- be available to multiple investigators;
- be exportable from one laboratory to another;
- be large enough to yield multiple samples;
- fit into available facilities of most laboratories;
- be capable of being handled by most investigators;
- survive long enough to be usable;
- exhibit the phenomenon under study with relative frequency;
- be of defined genetic homogeneity or heterogeneity;
- possess unique anatomical, physiological, or behavioral attributes;
- be accompanied by readily available background data; and
- be amenable to investigation with available, sophisticated techniques.

Depending on the type and needs of the investigation, certain of these criteria might be more important than others. Overall, a model with more of these characteristics will have higher discrimination and stronger predictive ability.

In research, testing, and education, a small number of species have achieved prominence as experimental tools because they have been extensively studied from a number of perspectives and thus provide well-understood paradigms that have been described in detail in terms of genetics, biochemistry, physiology, and other aspects. These organisms include the laboratory rat, laboratory mouse, fruit fly, and bacterium *Escherichia coli*. Yet taxonomic breadth is also required in research and testing, since it is often impossible to predict what species will lend themselves particularly well to the study of specific problems. In biological modeling, concentration on selected species and taxonomic diversity are not mutually exclusive; both play a role in the establishment of a maximally useful matrix of biological knowledge (3).

CHAPTER 2 REFERENCES

1. Leader R.A., and Padgett, G.A., "The Genesis and Validation of Animal Models," *Am. J. Pathol.* 101:s11-s16, 1980.
2. National Research Council, *Mammalian Models for Research on Aging* (Washington, DC: National Academy Press, 1981).
3. National Research Council, *Models for Biomedical Research: A New Perspective* (Washington, DC: National Academy Press, 1985).
4. Rowan, A.N., *Of Mice, Models, & Men: A Critical Evaluation of Animal Research* (Albany, NY: State University of New York Press, 1984).
5. Russell, W.M.S., and Burch, R.L., *Principles of Humane Experimental Technique* (Springfield, IL: Charles C. Thomas, 1959).

Chapter 3

Patterns of Animal Use

Twenty million rats, rabbits, cats, dogs, mice, and monkeys are killed each year in the name of science. And the number has quadrupled in recent years . . . 150 living creatures are sacrificed every minute.

Paul Harvey
Radio broadcast of April 30, 1985

Each minute around the clock, 150 creatures are sacrificed . . . a total of 70 million a year. Included are 25,000 primates . . . and nearly 500,000 dogs and cats.

Parade, January 13, 1985

Each year in the United States, almost 100 million animals are used in scientific research. Nearly a million are dogs and cats.

Ed Bradley
CBS News, *60 MINUTES*
October 14, 1984

OTA ignores the fact that more than one-half of all research goes unreported because unfunded. Secondly, funded researchers consistently understate the number of animals used for several reasons I won't enumerate. My personal guess is that 120-150 million animals is the right ballpark figure.

Sidney Gendin
Eastern Michigan University
The Research News 36(3-4):17, 1985

CONTENTS

List of Tables

List of Figures

Chapter 3

Patterns of Animal Use

Humans "use" animals in several different ways. In addition to animal use in research, testing, and education, animals are involved in food and fiber production, the production of biological products, sports, and entertainment. Animals can also be kept as pets for the purpose of companionship. It has been roughly estimated that 2 billion to 4 billion animals are used in food and fiber production every year and that Americans have approximately 75 million dogs and cats as household pets. The uses not considered in this assessment therefore account for many times more animals than the estimated 17 million to 22 million animals used annually in research, testing, and education.

There are no easily obtainable data in the United States allowing an accurate estimate of animal use for research, testing, and education that satisfies all interested parties; estimates range over a full order of magnitude, from approximately 10 million to 100 million animals. These estimates have all been prepared by different people or institutions with different data sources under different standards (e.g., different time periods or definitions). Comparison of the various estimates is difficult and, in many cases, impossible.

The issue of numbers is important to any discussion of animal use in research, testing, and education. Most basically, a number is needed from which to consider arguments to decrease or eliminate animal use. In addition, comparing absolute numbers in different years would provide some idea of whether laboratory-animal use is increasing or decreasing in the United States; these numbers are powerful and important to many people. A high overall total, or high numbers of certain species (such as nonhuman primates or companion species), supports the claims of interest groups hoping to restrict or ban such experimentation. On the other hand, a low number indicates the issue is not as important as some claim. In addition, a decreasing trend in animal use supports the position that the present system will lower animal use on its own.

For this assessment, some idea was needed of the scope of animal use in terms of both the numbers of particular species used and the different major users. In addition, an analysis of different data sources helps put the various estimates of animal use into some comparative perspective. It provides the context in which to discuss alternatives and how much effect they might have. Although it is true that the development of alternatives and alternative methods does not require a perfectly accurate estimate of usage, the planning of public policy certainly should be based on firm data.

By looking critically at the different data sources and coming up with possible estimates of laboratory-animal use in the United States, this assessment attempts to base discussions on a realistic, factually backed range of figures. Without such an analysis, any discussion or decisions on policy issues and possible solutions lack an important perspective.

THE FEDERAL GOVERNMENT'S USE OF ANIMALS

To document the scope and extent of animal use for research by Federal departments and agencies, information was obtained from the Animal and Plant Health Inspection Service (APHIS) annual reports for Federal research facilities for 1983, the *Animal Welfare Enforcement Reports* for fiscal years 1978 through 1983 (both obtained from the U.S. Department of Agriculture (USDA)), and personal communications or written material about animal use in each department or agency. Together, the information illustrates:

- the extent of animal use in different departments,
- the amount and type of animals being used in the Federal Government,
- the experimental conditions under which most animal experiments are carried out,

- the general purpose for which animal research and testing is carried out in different departments and agencies, and
- how much research and testing for the Federal Government is conducted intramurally (i.e., within Federal facilities).

Federal Departments and Agencies Using Animals in Research

Six departments and four independent Federal agencies conduct intramural research or testing involving animals. Uses of animals range from combat-casualty-care investigations in the Department of the Army, to acute toxicity studies by the Consumer Product Safety Commission of potentially hazardous substances, to National Aeronautics and Space Administration research on protecting the health of American astronauts. (For additional information on the use of animals within the Federal Government, see chs. 7 and 13 and app. B.)

Department of Agriculture

USDA performs biomedical research using animals under the authority of the Animal Welfare Act in order to improve animal breeds, food, and fibers. Most of the research is conducted intramurally by the Agricultural Research Service, although some extramural research (i.e., research supported by USDA, but conducted in non-USDA facilities) is contracted out by the Cooperative State Research Service. Some of this USDA animal research involves farm animals, however, which are largely excluded from Government regulatory policies and are exempt from the Animal Welfare Act and APHIS regulations (44).

Department of Commerce

The Department of Commerce conducts a small amount of intramural research with animals and lets some extramural contracts that involve animal studies. There are no specific Commerce guidelines or policies governing the humane treatment and appropriate veterinary care for laboratory animals (33).

Department of Defense

The divisions within the Department of Defense (DOD) that conduct experimental research on animals are the Air Force, the Army, the Navy, the Uniformed Services University of the Health Sciences, the Defense Nuclear Agency, and the Armed Forces Institute of Pathology; the first three of these account for most of the research. Together, all the divisions have approximately 40 research facilities that conduct animal experimentation.

The Aerospace Medical Division (AMD) of the Air Force accounts for about 95 percent of that service's use of animals. Of this, 84 percent is due to intramural research (9). AMD research and development projects fall within the following areas:

- humans in space,
- chemical defense and threat countermeasures,
- safety and environment,
- logistics and technical training,
- air combat training,
- human components of weapons systems, and
- personnel and force management.

The safety and environment program uses the most animals, while those on human components of weapons systems and chemical defense also have some animal use (50).

The Army does medical research to protect the soldier by the authority in the mission of the U.S. Army Medical Research and Development Command. Medical research and development (R&D) are carried out in five areas: infectious diseases (tropical disease and biological warfare defense), combat casualty care, combat systems, dental research (facial injuries), and chemical defense. About one-third of the research is done in-house and two-thirds is contracted out (38).

The Navy in fiscal year 1985 allocated $58 million for the life sciences or biomedical research. Of this, $37 million (64 percent) is for extramural research while the remainder is for intramural use. The two main branches of the service doing research involving animals are the Naval Medical Research and Development Command and the Office of Naval Research (ONR). The Naval Medical Research and Development Command does research in:

- submarine and diving medicine,
- electromagnetic radiation,
- aviation medicine/human performance,
- fleet health care systems,
- infectious diseases, and
- oral and dental health.

ONR conducts research using animals in four major areas: molecular biology, neurophysiology/physiology, cellular biosystems, and psychological sciences (45).

Department of Energy

The Department of Energy has no intramural research facilities and so contracts out all its research (47). The primary research objective within its Office of Health and Environmental Research is to study the health and environmental effects of energy technologies and programs. To do this, in the past, the Department's contractor used dogs. Recently, though, there has been a gradual shift from whole animals to cellular and molecular research and a much greater emphasis on rodents as opposed to companion species or primates (12).

Department of Health and Human Services

Intramural animal research or testing is carried out by four components of the Department of Health and Human Services' Public Health Service: the National Institutes of Health (NIH), the Food and Drug Administration (FDA), the National Institute on Drug Abuse (NIDA) (a part of the Alcohol, Drug Abuse, and Mental Health Administration), and the National Institute for Occupational Safety and Health (NIOSH) (a part of the Centers for Disease Control).

NIH is the largest research institution in the Federal Government and uses more animals than any other department or agency. The mission of NIH is to uncover new knowledge that will lead to better health (51). It does this by both intramural and extramural research. Approximately 88 percent of the NIH budget is spent on extramural programs while 10 percent goes to intramural research and 2 percent is used for NIH administration. Some 44 percent of the research awards go to research involving animals (28).

Research in the FDA is mission-oriented, with the principal objective being to provide data to support regulatory decisions. Research is conducted to determine the safety of human and animal foods; detect contaminants in human and animal foods; determine the safety and efficacy of human and animal drugs, biological products, and medical devices; reduce unnecessary exposure to artificial radiation; and increase fundamental understanding of the toxicological effects of chemicals. Ninety percent of the dollar budget for FDA research is allocated to intramural research studies while the other 10 percent goes to extramural research (5).

Department of the Interior

The Department of the Interior does more than 95 percent of its research in-house (31). Most animal research is performed by the U.S. Fish and Wildlife Service to support its mission "to provide the Federal leadership to conserve, protect, and enhance fish and wildlife and their habitats for the continuing benefit of people." This involves maintenance of relevant research and education programs in cooperation with other State and private organizations to enhance fish and wildlife resource management (53).

Department of Transportation

The Department of Transportation conducts animal research under the authority of the Hazardous Transportation Act of 1974 to determine the level at which substances become Class B poisons (see ch. 7). Most of the research involving animals is conducted extramurally (42). The Department also performs animal research under the authority of the National Traffic and Motor Vehicle Safety Act of 1966 (10).

Consumer Product Safety Commission

The Consumer Product Safety Commission (CPSC) both relies on data provided by manufacturers and conducts its own testing to determine the toxic potential of consumer products. Animals are used by CPSC's Directorate for Health Sciences in determinations of substances' acute oral toxicity, their potential for skin and eye irritation, and their combustion toxicity (16).

Environmental Protection Agency

The Environmental Protection Agency (EPA) performs research involving animals under the statutory and regulatory authority of the Toxic Substances Control Act and the Federal Insecticide, Fungicide, and Rodenticide Act. The general purpose of this research fits into one of three categories: methods development to assess potential hazards to the environment, dose-response data for risk assessment, or low-dose to high-dose data for risk assessment. EPA has two major research facilities, one in Cincinnati, OH, and the other in Research Triangle Park, NC. In addition to the intramural research done in these facilities, EPA does contract extramural research. The amount done outside the agency varies from year to year and depends on the program, but it usually does not exceed 40 percent of total research (48).

National Aeronautics and Space Administration

The National Aeronautics and Space Administration (NASA) has three facilities that maintain or conduct research with animals, although approximately 65 percent of NASA's Life Sciences research is conducted extramurally. About 12 percent of the life sciences budget was used to fund animal research in fiscal year 1984 (37).

The general purpose of NASA's research is to acquire knowledge that can be used to protect and ensure the health of American astronauts, both during their missions in space and after their return to Earth.

National Science Foundation

The National Science Foundation awards grants for scientific research involving animals but performs no intramural research.

Veterans' Administration

The Veterans' Administration (VA) has 174 facilities, 91 of which have the ability and authorization to do animal research. The VA's mandate to do research that may involve animals comes from part of the agency's defined mission to understand health maladies better, with a special emphasis on those that affect veterans. The VA uses animals in its research and development divisions and its education programs, which are located in many of its local facilities. All research funded by the VA is done intramurally, and some of the research done by the VA is funded by other agencies, such as NIH (29).

Research and development within the VA has three elements: the Medical Research Program, Rehabilitative R&D, and Health Services R&D. The Medical Research Program includes research basic to disease and deformities, while Rehabilitative R&D includes studies on artificial appliances or substances for use in restoring structure or function of parts of the human body. Finally, Health Services R&D includes research toward improvement, replacement, or discontinuance of health care delivery systems (32). Thus, the VA's mandate for research and development is extremely broad and holds the potential to use animals in many programs.

Patterns of Federal Animal Use

APHIS is the agency within the U.S. Department of Agriculture responsible for administering and enforcing the Animal Welfare Act of 1966 (Public Law 89-544) and its amendments (see ch. 13). The act defines research facility as any individual, institution, organization, or postsecondary school that uses or intends to use live animals in research, tests, or experiments *and* that purchases or transports live animals in commerce *or* that receives Federal funds for research, tests, or experiments. It defines "animal" to include "any live or dead dog, cat, monkey (nonhuman primate mammal), guinea pig, hamster, rabbit, or such other warm-blooded animal, as the Secretary [of the Department of Agriculture] may determine is being used, or is intended for use, for research, testing, experimentation, or exhibition purposes, or as a pet." The act excludes horses not used for research purposes and other

Primate Involved in Behavioral Research

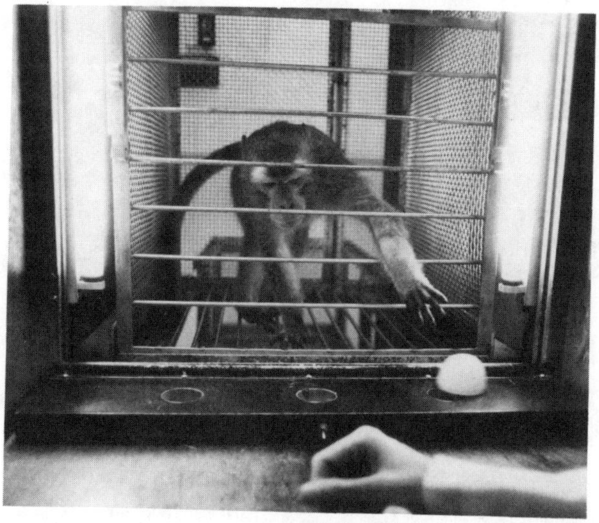

Photo credit: David Hathcox ©, 1985

farm animals intended for use as food or fiber. Under this definition, dead frogs used in biology classes or animals killed prior to usage are not included. Rats, mice, and birds were specifically excluded from the act's coverage by regulations promulgated in 1977 by the Secretary of Agriculture (9 C.F.R. 1.1(n); 42 FR 31022); reporting the use of these animals is voluntary.

The regulations that APHIS enforces require that each research facility fill out an Annual Report of Research Facility (see fig. 3-1) by December 1 on the preceding Federal fiscal year (October 1 - September 30). Elementary and secondary schools are exempt, as are facilities using only exempt species (rats, mice, or birds). In addition, any facility that does its own in-house breeding and does not receive Federal funds does not have to file a report. Although Federal research facilities are not required to register with APHIS, many of them do fill out the annual reporting forms. Each year, APHIS reports to Congress on the data collected from these forms in its *Animal Welfare Enforcement Report.*

Since 1982, two lines on the Annual Report of Research Facility have listed rats and mice under column A, "Animals Covered by the Act" (which is therefore no longer an accurate heading). Although not legally required, many respondents who used mandated species filled in the number of rats and mice anyway, either not realizing that reporting on these species is voluntary or electing to report their use. Thus, for many institutions a usage figure for rats and mice is given. In other cases, though, facilities reporting on mandated species omitted data on rats and mice.

Table 3-1 details the total reported animal use by research facilities within the Federal Government broken down by departments, major divisions, and agencies for fiscal year 1983. The Annual Report of Research Facility requires not only that total animals used be reported, but that the animals used be categorized as being used in research, experiments, or tests: 1) involving no pain or distress; 2) where appropriate anesthetic, analgesic, or tranquilizer drugs were administered to avoid pain or distress; or 3) involving pain or distress without administration of appropriate anesthetic, analgesic, or tranquilizer drugs (see fig. 3-1).

Several qualifications are necessary on the numbers reported in table 3-1, which are based on the annual reports obtained from APHIS:

- The 131 research reports include only intramural Federal research done at Federal facilities.
- The 131 facilities are not all the Federal facilities that might have used animals in 1983; at least 25 facilities did not file a report for that year.
- The numbers obtained were tabulated from each report. The reports were checked and corrected for improper coding of information and inaccurate addition. In many cases, these changes reflected substantial differences in the number of animals used for specific institutions.
- The numbers for mice and rats are included from any institution that reported them voluntarily. Several facilities, however, specifically mentioned that they were not required to submit these data and did not do so.

In addition to these general limitations on overall numbers, some specific qualifications for individual departments and agencies are also warranted:

- For FDA, table 3-1 does not include its primary research facility, the National Center for Toxicological Research (NCTR), since no report

Figure 3-1.—USDA/APHIS "Annual Report of Research Facility"

This report is required by law (7 USC 2143). Failure to report according to the regulations can result in an order to cease and desist and to be subject to penalties as provided for in Section 2150.

UNITED STATES DEPARTMENT OF AGRICULTURE
ANIMAL AND PLANT HEALTH INSPECTION SERVICE
VETERINARY SERVICES

1. DATE OF REPORT

FORM APPROVED
OMB NO. 0579-0036

2. HEADQUARTERS RESEARCH FACILITY *(Name & Address, as registered with USDA, include Zip Code)*

ANNUAL REPORT OF RESEARCH FACILITY
(Required For Each Reporting Facility Where Animals Are Held And An Attending Veterinarian Has Responsibility)

INSTRUCTIONS

Reporting Facility - complete items 1 through 24 and submit to your Headquarters Facility. Attach additional sheets if necessary.

Headquarters Facility - complete items 25 through 27 and submit on or before December 1 of each year for the preceding Federal fiscal year (October 1, to September 30) to the Veterinarian in Charge for the State where the research facility headquarters is registered.

3. REGISTRATION NO.

4. REPORTING FACILITY *(Name and Address, include Zip Code)*

REPORT OF ANIMALS USED IN ACTUAL RESEARCH, TESTING, OR EXPERIMENTATION - Section 2.28 of Animal Welfare Regulations requires appropriate use of anesthetics, analgesics, and tranquilizing drugs during research, testing, or experimentation. Experiments involving pain or distress without use of these drugs must be reported and a brief statement explaining the research.

A. Animals Covered By Act	B. New Animals Added this Year	C. Number of animals used in research, experiments, or tests involving no pain or distress.	D. Number of animals used in research, experiments, or tests where appropriate anesthetic, analgesic, or tranquilizer drugs were administered to avoid pain or distress.	E. Number of animals used in research, experiments, or tests involving pain or distress without administration of appropriate anesthetic, analgesic, or tranquilizer drugs. *(Attach brief explanation)*	F. TOTAL NO. Of Animals *(Cols. ~~B~~ + C + D + E)*
5. Dogs					
6. Cats					
7. Guinea Pigs					
8. Hamsters					
9. Rabbits					
10. Primates					
11. Rats					
12. Mice					
13. Wild Animals *(specify)*					
14.					
15.					

CERTIFICATION BY ATTENDING VETERINARIAN FOR REPORTING FACILITY OR INSTITUTIONAL COMMITTEE

I (We) hereby certify that the type and amount of analgesic, anesthetic, and tranquilizing drugs used on animals during actual research, testing or experimentation including post-operative and post-procedural care was deemed appropriate to relieve pain and distress for the subject animal.

16. SIGNATURE OF ATTENDING VETERINARIAN	17. TITLE	18. DATE SIGNED
19. SIGNATURE OF COMMITTEE MEMBER	20. TITLE	21. DATE SIGNED
22. SIGNATURE OF COMMITTEE MEMBER	23. TITLE	24. DATE SIGNED

CERTIFICATION BY HEADQUARTERS RESEARCH FACILITY OFFICIAL

I certify that the above is true, correct, and complete and that professionally acceptable standards governing the care, treatment, and use of animals including appropriate use of anesthetic, analgesic, and tranquilizing drugs, during actual research, testing, or experimentation including post-operative and post-procedural care are being followed by the above research facilities or sites (7 U.S.C. Section 2143).

25. SIGNATURE OF RESPONSIBLE OFFICIAL	26. TITLE	27. DATE SIGNED

VS FORM 18-23 *Previous edition obsolete*
(AUG 81)

SOURCE: Animal and Plant Health Inspection Service, U.S. Department of Agriculture.

was filed for 1983. This probably excludes a substantial number of animals since the fiscal year 1984 annual report for NCTR reported the use of 8 dogs, 334 rabbits, 29 primates, 14,621 rats, and 11,744 mice.

- The VA has 81 facilities accredited by the American Association for Accreditation of Laboratory Animal Care (AAALAC) yet only 63 reports were filed for 1983. Therefore, there is a strong possibility that the numbers for the VA are underreported.

Bearing in mind all the limitations and qualifications of the data used to generate table 3-1, **OTA estimates that a minimum of 1.6 million animals are used annually by the Federal Government in intramural research. The Department of Defense, the Department of Health and Human Services, and the Veterans' Administration together account for 96 percent of reported Federal animal use. DHHS alone reported 49 percent of the total.**

Among the six kind of animals whose inclusion in annual reporting forms is mandated by the Animal Welfare Act, guinea pigs are used most often—twice as frequently as hamsters or rabbits (the second and third most used species). Overall, about the same number of dogs and primates are used, while far fewer cats are involved in Government experiments. Finally, table 3-1 suggests that certain agencies do research on specific species. For example, the VA uses a disproportionately large number of dogs and the Department of the Interior is the major user of wild animals.

Reports of Federal facilities indicate that most animal use falls into the experimental situation categorized as involving no pain or distress. Sixty-three percent of the animals used were in this category while 32 percent were given drugs to avoid pain or distress and only 5 percent experienced pain or distress without receiving anesthetics, analgesics, or tranquilizers. The largest user of drugs in experiments was the VA (62 percent of the animals in this category), whereas the largest user of animals experiencing pain or distress was the Department of Defense (84 percent of the animals in this category). The latter figure may be inflated, however, by the fact that DOD has reported mice and rats voluntarily under these categories in many cases and has listed in this column all animals dying in infectious and neoplastic disease studies, which many Federal agencies may not do (43).

Table 3-2 shows the trends in animal use for Federal agencies as a group from 1978 to 1983, according to the *Animal Welfare Enforcement Reports* submitted by APHIS to Congress (49). As with the numbers from the 1983 Annual Reports of Research Facilities, these data do not tell the whole story. Most important, these data do not include rats and mice, which together make up a majority of the animals used. Second, only reports that have been received by December 31 each year (the reports are due December 1) are included (26). It has been estimated that between 10 percent and 20 percent of the total reporting institutions fail to report by December 31 and are therefore not included in the *Animal Welfare Enforcement Reports* (17). (Thus, the 1983 data are lower in table 3-2 than in 3-1, which included all available annual reports.)

The data are difficult to interpret due to the different numbers of research facilities included each year. Therefore, no conclusions can be drawn about whether the trend in animal use is increasing or decreasing. This is also the case for trends in the use of individual species. The 1983 data do indicate, however, that no more than 8 percent of animals used in Federal programs reported here have experienced pain or distress in an experiment since 1978. The percentage of animals experiencing no pain or distress has remained between 50 and 60 percent, while drugs have been used to alleviate pain or distress for 30 to 40 percent of the animals.

ANIMAL USE IN THE UNITED STATES

OTA surveyed the available data concerning the numbers of laboratory animals used for research, testing, and education. These were summarized, corrected for methodological deficiencies, and evaluated for their statistical reliability. As a final step, estimates were made of current levels of an-

Table 3-1.—Research-Animal Use in the Federal Government, by Major Department and Division for Fiscal Year 1983

			Department of Defense					Department of Health and Human Services	
Animals used	USDA	Commerce	Misc.	Air Force	Army	Navy	Total	FDA	NIDA
Facilities reporting	11	1	3	6	20	10	**39**	1	1
Dogs	25	0	994	635	827	344	**2,800**	113	51
% row	<1	0	11	7	9	4	**31**	1	<1
Cats	39	0	491	61	214	36	**802**	0	84
% row	1	0	18	2	8	1	**29**	0	3
Guinea pigs	6,105	0	1,601	586	26,695	609	**29,491**	0	98
% row	9	0	2	1	41	1	**46**	0	<1
Hamsters	7,487	0	627	1,352	4,822	417	**7,218**	0	0
% row	21	0	2	4	14	1	**21**	0	0
Rabbits	1,047	0	1,863	703	3,731	264	**6,561**	0	0
% row	4	0	6	2	13	1	**23**	0	0
Primates	0	0	418	527	676	219	**1,840**	0	0
% row	0	0	6	7	9	3	**25**	0	0
Rats	7,862	0	25,259	10,570	55,057	4,243	**95,129**	0	312
% row	2	0	6	2	13	1	**22**	0	<1
Mice	30,625	0	72,085	6,140	143,503	42,094	**263,822**	0	600
% row	3	0	7	1	14	4	**26**	0	<1
Wild animals	24	43	1,377	34	2,762	479	**4,652**	0	0
% row	<1	<1	10	<1	19	3	**32**	0	0
Total	**53,214**	**43**	**104,715**	**20,608**	**238,287**	**48,705**	**412,315**	**113**	**1145**
% row	**3**	**<1**	**6**	**1**	**15**	**3**	**25**	**<1**	**<1**

KEY: USDA-United States Department of Agriculture; FDA-Food and Drug Administration; NIDA-National Institute on Drug Abuse; NIH-National Institutes of Health; CDC-Centers for Disease Control; NIOSH-National Institute for Occupational Safety and Health; DOT-Department of Transportation; EPA-Environmental Protection Agency; NASA-National Aeronautics and Space Administration; VA-Veterans' Administration; CPSC-Consumer Product Safety Commission.

Percentages may not add up to 100 due to rounding.

SOURCE: Office of Technology Assessment, from 1983 APHIS Annual Reports of Research Facilities (Form 18-23); CPSC data from K.C. Gupta, Deputy Director, Division of Health Sciences Laboratory, Directorate for Health Sciences, U.S. Consumer Product Safety Commission, Washington, DC, personal communication, Sept. 24, 1985.

nual animal use in the United States. The purpose of this exercise was to examine numbers on animal use and compare the reliability of estimates from different data sources.

The figures published in this assessment on the number of animals used are not absolute. They are only as accurate as the data from which they were obtained. All publicly available information on past and current animal use was collected from a variety of sources, often through personal contacts. Data from the two most reliable sources, the Institute of Laboratory Animal Resources (ILAR) of the National Research Council and the USDA's Animal and Plant Health Inspection Service, were corrected to take into account the actual years of reporting and the omission of certain data that were not received before a deadline.

Laboratory-animal use was then estimated and projected using statistical techniques where appropriate. For this purpose, the corrected ILAR and APHIS data were used, as well as more indirect means based on National Institutes of Health funding, National Cancer Institute (NCI) usage, and NIH total usage as a function of NIH intramural use. Although the number of animals bred should lead to good estimates of animals used in the laboratory, the larger laboratory-animal breeders would not confirm or deny sales figures that had appeared in the news media and literature. Therefore, estimates based on such reports are of uncertain reliability.

Limitations of Animal-Use Study

Two types of limits on this study exist: intrinsic and extrinsic. The major intrinsic limitations were funding constraints and a limited time span during which the study could be performed. This prohibited the collection of raw data and required that OTA rely on existing data sources. The extrinsic

Table 3-1.—Research-Animal Use in the Federal Government, by Major Department and Division for Fiscal Year 1983 (Continued)

Animals used	Department of Health and Human Services									
	NIH	CDC/NIOSH	Total	Interior	DOT	EPA	NASA	VA	CPSC	Total
Facilities reporting	3	2	**7**	2	1	4	2	63	1	**131**
Dogs	756	0	**920**	0	30	2	14	5,187	0	**8,978**
% row	8	0	**10**	0	<1	<1	<1	58	0	**100**
Cats	503	0	**587**	0	0	0	40	1,304	0	**2,772**
% row	18	0	**21**	0	0	0	1	47	0	**100**
Guinea pigs	23,973	0	**24,071**	0	0	978	58	3,747	0	**64,450**
% row	37	0	**37**	0	0	2	<1	6	0	**100**
Hamsters	14,003	10	**14,013**	0	0	1,723	0	4,732	0	**35,173**
% row	40	0	**40**	0	0	5	0	14	0	**100**
Rabbits	8,783	30	**8,813**	0	0	842	74	11,508	600	**29,445**
% row	30	<1	**30**	0	0	3	<1	39	2	**100**
Primates	4,452	287	**4,739**	0	0	33	184	461	0	**7,257**
% row	61	4	**65**	0	0	<1	3	6	0	**100**
Rats	196,458	3,750	**200,520**	900	150	0	3,936	122,872	2,080	**433,449**
% row	45	<1	**46**	<1	0	0	1	28	<1	**100**
Mice	533,094	1,120	**534,814**	923	4,552	0	622	188,560	0	**1,023,918**
% row	52	<1	**52**	<1	<1	0	<1	18	0	**100**
Wild animals	2,787	0	**2,787**	4,228	0	0	232	2,393	0	**14,359**
% row	19	0	**19**	29	0	0	2	17	0	**100**
Total	**784,809**	**5,197**	**791,264**	**6,051**	**4,732**	**3,578**	**5,160**	**340,764**	**2,680**	**1,619,801**
% row	**48**	**<1**	**49**	**<1**	**<1**	**<1**	**<1**	**21**	**<1**	**100**

KEY: USDA-United States Department of Agriculture; FDA-Food and Drug Administration; NIDA-National Institute on Drug Abuse; NIH-National Institutes of Health; CDC-Centers for Disease Control; NIOSH-National Institute for Occupational Safety and Health; DOT-Department of Transportation; EPA-Environmental Protection Agency; NASA-National Aeronautics and Space Administration; VA-Veterans' Administration; CPSC-Consumer Product Safety Commission.

Percentages may not add up to 100 due to rounding.

SOURCE: Office of Technology Assessment, from 1983 APHIS Annual Reports of Research Facilities (Form 18–23); CPSC data from K.C. Gupta, Deputy Director, Division of Health Sciences Laboratory, Directorate for Health Sciences, U.S. Consumer Product Safety Commission, Washington, DC, personal communication, Sept. 24, 1985.

Table 3-2.—Total Numbers of Animals Used in Federal Government Facilities as Reported to Congress in APHIS Animal Welfare Enforcement Reports, 1978-83

	Fiscal year					
	1978	1979	1980	1981	1982	1983
Federal facilities included in reports	188	150	118	131	131	88
Dogs	20,128	15,605	13,153	13,930	6,369	6,668
Cats	5,354	4,709	3,368	3,183	1,940	1,825
Primates	7,286	5,031	3,459	3,081	6,907	1,837
Guinea pigs	65,009	40,425	25,402	33,495	45,972	36,033
Hamsters	45,291	25,213	17,830	32,367	35,220	18,992
Rabbits	43,867	32,205	21,631	21,962	16,209	16,355
Wild animals	5,537	4,137	3,209	2,007	7,618	8,037
Total animals[a]	192,472	127,325	88,052	110,025	120,235	89,747

[a]Totals do not include rats or mice, two species that together account for the majority of animals used.

SOURCE: Office Technology Assessment, from APHIS Animal Welfare Enforcement Reports, 1978–1983.

limitations include various information deficiencies, such as:

- inadequacies of information on most of the survey and data collection methodologies,
- difficulties with definitions,
- problems with categorizing animals under areas of use,
- reporting requirements of different data sources, and
- an inability to verify completeness of data sources.

For example, there is often a discrepancy in the definition of the term "use." In some cases, the term reflects the number of animals acquired; in other cases, it corresponds only to those used in laboratory experiments. This distinction is frequently obscured in the data sources, and only after careful reading of the documents (and, sometimes, personal inquiry) was the definition used in each case clarified. This leads to large differences in numbers, since not all animals acquired are used in experiments. It also makes any comparative analysis between surveys very unsound.

In addition to this problem of the difference between production and use, the extrinsic problem of the number of animals not used in a procedure because they do not fit the proper criteria comes into any extrapolation of animal use from laboratory-animal market share data. A substantial proportion of the animals bred for research die or must be discarded because they do not meet protocol specifications (age, sex, weight, general health). The number has been estimated as between a few percent of those acquired to almost 50 percent. In general, the unused proportion of a species is inversely related to the cost of the animals. In other words, the more expensive the animal, the less likely it will be unused, once bred or purchased. Thus, nonhuman primates are much less likely to go unused than are mice or rats; in some cases 50 percent of a rodent species may go unused. Using only one sex of a rodent species in a given experiment, for example, would account for 50 percent of the animals going unused. This information must be borne in mind when comparing "production" with "use" and when estimating animal use.

Overall, these limitations reflect on the accuracy of the data and any projections based on them. The limitations are such that the only reasonably credible source for current use and projections is APHIS, particularly its institutional data sheets (the Annual Report of Research Facility discussed earlier). Only the detailed APHIS institutional data sheets for fiscal years 1982 and 1983 were used in this assessment, though those for earlier years were also available (although they would not have had any data on mice or rats, which were not even listed on the form until 1982). Consequently, the APHIS data are less reliable for the years before 1982 inasmuch as these are based on reports to Congress that did not contain late-reporting institutions. (The *Animal Welfare Enforcement Reports* to Congress underestimate use of the mandated species by 10 to 20 percent due to the cutoff date and do not treat data from Federal institutions consistently (17).) For some species, such as fish and birds, only rough estimates of use could be obtained, due to the diffuse nature of use and the fact that they are not included in the APHIS data.

Critical Evaluation of Animal-Use Estimates

In evaluating the reliability of various data sources, the following parameters were considered:

- ability to trace the methodology used in producing the numbers, including the survey technique;
- ability to extrapolate to nonreporting institutions, which implies that there is a clear statement as to which institutions did or did not report data;
- method of data collection, whether some formal manner or through a few interviews, resulting in broad estimates; and
- ability to determine the fraction of animals reported as being actually used in lab experimentation, as contrasted to, for example, animal husbandry.

These parameters were chosen because meeting these criteria permits extrapolation of the limited data to the entire population of institutions.

In general, if the numbers cannot be justified through some rational process (such as the above), too much significance should not be attached to them.

These four criteria were used to assign a confidence rating to each data source. The confidence categories are: "excellent," "good," "fair," "poor," and "indeterminate." (These ratings refer only to the published numbers, not to their usefulness as a predictive tool.) Such a confidence rating is necessarily subjective; the categories are comparative and should not be viewed as absolute.

Upon reviewing all the data sources available for predicting the laboratory-animal use in the United States, it is clear that no source accurately portrays the number of animals being used. Each has methodological problems that prevented it from accurately counting all users of animals. What follows is an analysis of the available data sources and how they rank in comparison with the other surveys in terms of confidence and reliability.

USDA Animal and Plant Health Inspection Service (APHIS)

The 1982 and 1983 data were analyzed on a case-by-case basis. Copies of the original report forms were obtained from USDA; they were sorted by institution type, checked, coded, and entered into a computer database. Comparing the 1982 and 1983 APHIS data (see table 3-5, in the "Summary and Analysis of Estimates" section) with the USDA *Animal Welfare Enforcement Report* for 1980 (the APHIS 1980 data in table 3-5) reveals a large discrepancy. The USDA reports invariably contain lower numbers for all species, as the data sheets received after the December 31 cutoff date are not included in reports in either the current or the next fiscal year. It is estimated that between 10 and 20 percent of the reports are not used to compile the report to Congress in a given year (17). This limitation does not apply to the results contained in the present compilation for 1982 and 1983, since all data for a given year were used no matter when received. The assumption is made that copies of virtually all of the data sheets received by USDA in the 1982 and 1983 are used in this study. No verification was made of which institutions did not report.

The number of institutions reporting to APHIS has hovered around 1,000 since 1972. The numbers for 1982 and 1983 (shown in table 3-6, in the "Summary and Analysis of Estimates" section) were tabulated from the actual summary data sheets provided to APHIS by the institutions and include all possible reports. Even these figures—1,127 for 1982 and 1,146 for 1983—are probably low, as not all institutions submit reports. (The total number of institutions registered by APHIS was 1,113 in 1982 and 1,166 in 1983; this excludes Federal agencies, which are not required to register.) Some of the institutions may not report because they have not used any animals that year, or because they have only used exempt species.

For the six required species listed on the form (dogs, cats, guinea pigs, hamsters, rabbits, and primates), the numbers reported provide a very close approximation of the animals actually used. Thus these data were assigned a confidence rating of "excellent." (For a summary of all the data sources discussed in this section and their confidence ratings, see table 3-3.) For exempt species (primarily rats and mice), it is possible to estimate the number of unreported rats and mice by extrapolating from the numbers reported (see the section on "Estimate Using Corrected APHIS Data"). Some commentators (1,3,27) claim, however, that a certain number of exempt animals go unreported—and would be missed in an extrapolation—because they are purchased directly by the user and not reported to the central facility. This contention could not be confirmed. Therefore, the voluntarily reported data on rats and mice on the 1982 and 1983 APHIS annual reports received a confidence rating of "good."

ILAR Surveys

The Institute for Laboratory Animal Resources, a component of the National Research Council, periodically surveys users of laboratory animals (18,19,20,21,22,23), although it is generally more concerned with facilities and personnel than with quantity of animals used. The ILAR data represent the number of animals "acquired by own

Table 3-3.—Reliability of Various Data Sources

Source	Years covered	Confidence rating	Strength(s)	Limitation(s)
USDA/APHIS:				
Mandated species	1982-83	Excellent	Required by law. Data available by institution, thus extrapolation to nonreporters is possible	
Mandated species	1972-81	Fair	Required by law. Data by institution available, but not used	10 to 20 percent of institutions not included in reports to Congress. Totals not consistent (some years include Federal agencies, others do not)
Exempt species	1982-83	Good	Data by institution available. Rats and mice were on the form so anyone who reported probably provided an accurate number. Many did not realize that these were voluntary since they were listed on form. Extrapolation possible	Not required by law
ILAR Surveys of Laboratory Animal Use	1965-71	Poor	Of some use in establishing trends for that period	Old data. Cannot extrapolate to missing data
1968 Survey	1967	Fair	Statistically sound survey. Possibility of extrapolating to other institutions	Limited to 683 Federal-grant-eligible institutions
1980 Survey	1978	Fair	Thorough and statistically solid. Extrapolation to non-reporting institutions possible	Primary attention given to nonprofit Federal-grant-eligible institutions. Not required by law to be filled out
W.B. Saunders & Co.	1965	Indeterminate		Company defunct, survey methodology unclear; no evaluation possible
Foster D. Snell	1975	Indeterminate		Data appear to be based on interviews with two breeders Methodology unclear. Personnel no longer available

SOURCE: Office of Technology Assessment.

breeding and from commercial sources," not necessarily the number actually used in experimentation.

The ILAR and APHIS surveys are so different in their organization and methodology that it is not meaningful to compare the two sources, even in years for which data from both are available. It is also difficult to point out significant changes within this data source because the ILAR methodology varied over time and could not be verified adequately, so changes in numbers are difficult to substantiate.

ILAR *Surveys of Laboratory Animal Use* (20) consist of tables summarizing the results of questionnaires on the number of animals used for research. As ILAR personnel cannot discern who was surveyed and who responded, extrapolation for missing data is impossible. The surveys could, however, be of some use in assessing trends between 1965 and 1971. A "poor" confidence rating was given.

The *1968 Survey of Laboratory Animal Facilities and Resources* (21) appears to have been a very thorough and statistically sound survey including all known users of laboratory animals. The results shown, however, are only for the 683 organizations eligible for Federal grants that responded because of the interest of the survey sponsor (NIH). It is possible, however, to normalize for missing data based on the reported biomedical research expenditures for these 683 organizations of $920

Table 3-3.—Reliability of Various Data Sources (Continued)

Source	Years covered	Confidence rating	Strength(s)	Limitation(s)
Alex Brown & Sons	1981	Poor	At the time, it was thought to represent best estimate for lab animals in U.S. market	Data based on a few interviews, and mostly broad estimates
Andrew N. Rowan	1985	Poor	Data distinguishes between production, acquisition, and actual use	Broad analysis with many assumptions. Based mainly on one breeding facility
Amphibians:				
Emmons	1969	Indeterminate		Global estimates
Culley	1981	Indeterminate		Many assumptions
Nace	1974-81	Fair	Fair detail for basis of estimates	Difficult to know actual numbers due to large number of users
Various, on fish usage	1983	Fair	Data consistent	Global estimates only
Various, on bird usage	1983	Poor	Good detail by institutions	Uncertainty about nonreporting institutions, and fraction of fowl used by lab experimentation
Data on animal trends:				
Wadsworth Center, NY	1980-83	Poor	Good detail of different species used	Difficult to predict any trends
Johns Hopkins, MD	1975-85	Poor		Limited data that are impossible to analyze

SOURCE: Office of Technology Assessment.

million in fiscal year 1967. (The results for all respondents, while not mentioned in the report, were compiled and reported for comparison purposes in the ILAR 1980 survey.) The confidence rating was "fair."

The ILAR *National Survey of Laboratory Animal Facilities and Resources* (22) also appears to be a thorough and statistically solid report, although the data (for fiscal year 1978) are now 8 years old. Since it also was funded by NIH, primary attention was given to nonprofit biomedical research institutions eligible for Federal grants. In addition, data were received from Federal organizations, commercial research labs, and the pharmaceutical industry. Seventy-two percent of the 2,637 questionnaires were returned; 47 percent of those were acceptable, thus providing 1,252 respondents (including 992 nonprofit Federal-grant-eligibles, 137 commercial laboratories, 25 components of the DOD, 21 units of NIH, and 77 components of other Federal agencies). Although the individual identities of the respondents are unknown, the biomedical research expenditures of the nonprofit organizations are known. Since their data are reported separately from all respondents, an extrapolation to the unknown cases can be attempted based on the known national (meaning "all use in the United States") biomedical research expenditures. This source was assigned a confidence rating of "fair."

W.B. Saunders & Company

W.B. Saunders & Company (41) surveyed the laboratory animal market in 1965 and projected figures for 1970. The survey and its estimates are widely quoted as one of the first estimates of animal use. The survey methodology is unclear and the company no longer exists, so these data fall under the "indeterminate" category.

Foster D. Snell, Inc., for Manufacturing Chemists Association

A study performed by Foster D. Snell, Inc., for the Manufacturing Chemists Association (25) estimated that 35 million mice and 40 million rats were produced domestically in the United States in 1975, and that 20,000 monkeys were imported from India. The report's authors could not be located and the methodology is unclear, thus making it impossible to validate. It appears that the data are based on interviews with personnel at two animal breeding facilities (Charles River Breeding Labs, Inc., and White Eagle Farms) and perhaps a few other people in industry, academia, and government. As it is difficult to give any credibility to such data, the source was assigned a confidence rating of "indeterminate."

Alex Brown & Sons

An Alex Brown & Sons (2) report on Charles River Breeding Labs, Inc., stated that the company produces 22 million animals annually worldwide, specializing in mice, rats, guinea pigs, hamsters, and primates. It did not give any breakdown by species, nor do any other analyses of Charles River. The number was primarily a guess based on a few interviews and so its value must be questioned. The confidence rating of this source was "poor."

Andrew N. Rowan

In a 1984 book, *Of Mice, Models, & Men: A Critical Evaluation of Animal Research,* Andrew N. Rowan estimated that approximately 71 million laboratory animals are used each year, including 45 million mice and 15 million rats (39). These figures were obtained by looking at all the available data sources for animal use in the United States, especially information on Charles River breeding production. In 1985, Rowan revised these estimates to distinguish between production, acquisition, and actual use. The new estimates on animals used suggest that between 25 and 35 million animals are used per year (40). As these are based on a very broad analysis with many assumptions, they have been given a confidence rating of "poor."

Surveys and Estimates on Amphibians, Fish, and Birds

There is little good survey information on laboratory use of amphibians, fish, or birds. Use of these animals is not required to be reported on the USDA/APHIS annual reports. Therefore, the only sources of estimates are personal communications with experts in these fields.

The most recent assessments of amphibian use were the ILAR surveys of 1965-71, which indicated the use of 3.37 million amphibians in 1971. As mentioned earlier, however, it is not known how to normalize for institutions that did not report, so the usefulness of these data are questionable and the confidence rating is "indeterminate."

Several individuals who use or produce amphibians were surveyed, yielding a wide range of estimates. A former general manager of a major supplier of amphibians estimated that approximately 9 million frogs were shipped by suppliers in 1969 for educational and teaching purposes (13). This is a global estimate and so its confidence rating was considered "indeterminate." An amphibian researcher at Louisiana State University did a survey of the use of bullfrogs that estimated that 150,000 bullfrogs and 200,000 tadpoles could have been used in 1981 (a decrease since 1971, he found). He then assumed that bullfrogs represent roughly 10 percent of amphibian use and estimated that about 1 million frogs and 2 million tadpoles were used in the United States for teaching and research in 1981 (8). The assumptions in this method are very general and so the value of this estimate is questionable; an "indeterminate" rating was assigned. Finally, George Nace (34,35) estimated that about 9 million frogs were shipped by suppliers in 1971, but that this dropped to roughly 4.5 million in 1981 and stabilized at that level in 1984, with 90 percent of the usage educational and 10 percent research. There is fairly good detail for the basis of the estimates, but it is difficult to confirm the totals due to the large number of users. This source was given a confidence rating of "fair."

Reliable data on fish used in laboratories were particularly difficult to obtain. Estimates were received from commercial and institutional (including Government) users in the field. For fish over half an inch long, the yearly use appears to range between 500,000 and 1 million. For smaller fish, the best estimate is that 2 million to 3 million are used yearly. Most are used for toxicological studies. Although the numbers are fairly consistent from source to source, they are only global estimates and so were given a confidence rating of "fair." These numbers apply only to laboratory use. They do not include fish that are used in the wild in propagation, contamination, feeding, and other ecological studies.

For birds, many of those completing the APHIS data sheets voluntarily reported bird use under the "wild animal" category. According to these data, at least 33,910 birds were used in fiscal year 1982 and 29,781 in fiscal year 1983. Of these, the University of Maryland used 17,915 birds in 1982, and 12,305 in 1983 (46). Since this one institution used such a large fraction of the reported total, inquiries about other large possible users indicated that many of the poultry research institutions (mostly land-grant universities in the East and South) did not report birds on their APHIS forms. The largest of these, in terms of poultry research, is North Carolina State University, from whom it was learned that approximately 41,000 birds were used for poultry science and 1,100 in veterinary schools (7). Checking the APHIS data sheets for other land-grant institutions showed that most had reported bird usage. In addition, discussions with researchers at several institutions established that only 80 to 85 percent of the poultry science usage is in laboratories with the remainder mostly in feeding, management, and breeding studies. Therefore, although there is good detail for many institutions on bird use, there is uncertainty in the APHIS data about nonreporting institutions and about the proportion of fowl used in actual experimentation.

Several individuals have estimated bird use in the United States. James Will of the Animal Resource Center at the University of Wisconsin in Madison, WI, estimated that 25,000 to 100,000 avian individuals are used for laboratory experimentation (54). Andrew N. Rowan of Tufts University School of Veterinary Medicine in Boston, MA, estimated that at least 500,000 birds are used in biomedical research (40). Both of these figures are based on very weak data and so are assigned a confidence rating of "poor." Thus, using these estimates and the APHIS bird data, an annual use of between 100,000 and 500,000 birds is as accurate an estimate as can be made.

Data on Trends in Animal Use

Several limited data sources exist that suggest trends in animal use in the past several years. At Wadsworth Center for Laboratories and Research, New York State Department of Health (Albany, NY), the use of mandated species decreased 40 percent from 2,925 in 1980 to 1,754 in 1983. The use of rats and mice also decreased substantially (22 percent), from 72,796 in 1980 to 56,681 in 1983, at a time when total research dollars available continued to increase (11). At The John Hopkins School of Hygiene and Public Health in Baltimore, MD, the daily census of animals decreased from over 8,000 in 1975 to approximately 2,000 in 1985 while animal care personnel dropped from 10 to 4 and research expenditures more than doubled (14). These data sources are limited in scope, use different counting mechanisms, and can be considered anecdotal in nature. They were assigned a confidence rating of "poor."

Calculating Rat and Mouse Usage

Using these same data sources, estimates for annual laboratory use of rats and mice in the United States were calculated. The criteria and scales described earlier were also applied to assign confidence ratings to the estimates. To gauge annual laboratory-animal use, minimum average costs of $4 per rat and $2 per mouse (6,15,24,30,36,55) were assumed to represent conservative prices for a typical research subject. This permitted extrapolations based on price to represent an expected maximum of animals that could be purchased.

Three different methods were used to estimate the use of rats and mice in the United States. The first involved using indirect means for the calculations, while a second method used 1978 ILAR data. The third, and most reliable, method relied on corrected USDA/APHIS data and involved calculations using regression equations.

Indirect Estimates

Possible methods for estimating rat and mouse usage under this category involve extrapolations from data based on NIH funding, NCI usage, NIH total use as a function of intramural use, and animal breeder information. For example, an estimate based on NIH funding involves the following steps and assumptions:

- NIH funds 37 percent of all national biomedical research expenditures (52).
- In 1983, NIH awarded $582,571,000 in direct costs to 5,011 extramural projects utilizing rats and other species (4). If it is assumed that all

38-750 O - 86 - 3

expenditures went to projects that used only rats, an upper limit can be extrapolated for rats purchasable using NIH funds.

- Twelve percent of direct costs of NIH-sponsored research funds go toward the purchase of supplies, glassware, chemicals, research animals, and items listed as expendable (55).
- If it is assumed that half of the supply funds went toward the purchase of animals, then $34,954,260 would be available for the purchase of rats.
- At $4 a rat, 8.7 million rats could be purchased.
- In 1983, NIH awarded $531,519,000 in direct costs to 4,080 projects using mice. At an average cost of $2 per mouse, 16 million mice could be purchased with NIH funds.
- Assuming that NIH supports 37 percent of animal use in the country, then the potential number of these two species purchasable in the United States is estimated at 23.6 million rats and 43.1 million mice.This indirect method (whether it uses NIH data or NCI data or animal breeder information) involves many assumptions, limited data sources, and cannot be considered very reliable. It was assigned a "poor" confidence rating.

Estimate Using Corrected ILAR Data, 1978

The results of the 1978 *National Survey* (22) permit approximation of animal use for all users with techniques that fill in the missing data of nonrespondents based on a method such as the following:

- The NIH-grant-eligible nonprofit biomedical research organizations responding to the survey reported biomedical research expenditures of $2.2 billion for 1978.
- Total national biomedical research expenditures are estimated at $6.27 billion for 1978 (52).
- If it is assumed that animal use (in numbers) is proportional to the dollar amount spent on research utilizing them and that the usage rate of animals by all institutions is proportional to that of nonprofit institutions, national usage equals (nonprofit ILAR 1980) $\times$ 6.27 $\div$ 2.2. This yields an estimate of 16 million mice and 5.6 million rats used in 1978. Such methods do involve some assumptions not easily justifiable and so the confidence rating is somewhat lower than for the ILAR data on which they are based. In addition, they are based on information already 8 years old.

Estimate Using Corrected APHIS Data

About two-thirds of the institutions completing APHIS annual reports for 1982 and 1983 volunteered information on the number of rats and mice used. Regression equations based on those institutions reporting the specific species on the Annual Report of Research Facility forms were used to estimate the numbers of rats and mice for those institutions not reporting these species (17). The estimates obtained using these regression equations and then simply applying the mean value for reporting institutions to the nonreporters are shown in table 3-4 (which summarizes all the estimates discussed). These regression equations yield estimates of 8.5 million mice and between 3.4 million and 3.7 million rats used annually in 1982 and 1983; applying the mean value for reporting institutions to those that did not report yields higher estimates. Given the fairly detailed database to which the regression equations were applied, these estimates received a confidence rating of "good." The estimates generated from these corrected APHIS data are likely the most accurate that can be obtained with data currently available.

Summary and Analysis of Estimates

Table 3-5 summarizes the various estimates on animal use discussed in this chapter. Several factors reduce the usefulness of these data, however: APHIS's definition of animal (which excludes rats, mice, and birds) and the exemption from regulation of research facilities that do in-house breeding and receive no Federal funds. These limitations may cause the numbers generated from the APHIS data to be underestimations of the total animal use in the United States for research, testing, and education. For example, the Directory of Toxicology Testing Laboratories published by the Chemical Specialties Manufacturers Association, Inc., lists 110 facilities in the United States. In checking these against the list of APHIS registered research facil-

Table 3-4—Estimates of Rat and Mouse Usage in Laboratories, 1978, 1982, 1983

	Mice (millions)			Rats (millions)			
Basis of estimation	1978	1982	1983	1978	1982	1983	Confidence rating
Indirect means—NIH funding	—	—	43.1	—	—	23.6	Poor
Corrected ILAR data:							
Nonprofit funding share.	16.0	—	—	5.6	—	—	Fair
Corrected APHIS data:							
Regression	—	8.5	8.5	—	3.4	3.7	Good
Average	—	10.2	11.2	—	4.1	4.6	Good

SOURCE: Office of Technology Assessment.

ities, 40 percent were not registered and so would not file a report. Any animals used in those facilities would not be reported in the APHIS data. The 1978 ILAR *National Survey of Laboratory Animal Facilities and Resources* stated that 35 percent of mice and 19 percent of rats acquired for research were bred in-house by the researchers (22), so these too might not appear on the the APHIS data sheets. Thus, all these limitations mean the APHIS data may be underestimations of total animal use, but it is impossible to estimate if the difference is significant. Ideally, the results based on APHIS data could be compared with estimates based on animal breeder numbers. However, since information on distribution of costs per animal is proprietary, such an analysis is impossible. Therefore, although the data contained in the APHIS reports are the most reliable, they do not include all possible users of laboratory animals.

Inspection of some 150 institutional Annual Report of Research Facility forms raises several other doubts as to the accuracy of the data collected by APHIS. In general, the form seems to lack any instruction to the individual institutions on how it should be filled out. As a result, there is no consistency in the ways in which forms are completed. The reliability of the data on the forms today is in question. Figures 3-2, 3-3, and 3-4, which exemplify the reporting problems, are actual forms returned to APHIS for 1983, although the institution names have been deleted. For example:

- Some forms have an error that can lead to miscalculations of the number of animals used: Column F asks for the addition of columns B+C+D+E. The actual number desired is C+D+E. **Thus, some reports have doubled the number of animals used** (since B=C+D+E) (see fig. 3-2). These types of miscalculations, along with normal mathematical errors, were corrected in the OTA estimate of animal use in the Federal Government. Thus, the numbers for Federal agencies in these two sections are different for the same APHIS institutional reports. (For Federal agencies, this difference is fairly small.)
- In many cases, respondents did not seem to understand how to classify the animals used in the different experimental categories. **If the APHIS form is read literally, any animal given drugs to avoid pain or distress is also an animal that experiences no pain or distress and could be counted in both categories** (see fig. 3-3).
- **The answers to the category "wild animals" differed greatly.** Some forms listed legitimate wild animals, such as seals, while others included as wild such animals as gerbils, cattle, sheep, and pigs (see fig. 3-4). In fact, the "wild animals" line was often filled in with farm animals, which are exempt from being reported.
- **The forms are now improperly labeled in that rats and mice are included under column A, "Animals Covered by the Act," yet they are specifically exempted by USDA regulation from coverage by the Animal Welfare Act.** Many institutions that filled out APHIS forms may have been unaware that reporting rats and mice was voluntary.

These examples serve to characterize the present system as lacking clarity and uniformity in definition and accurate reporting. Redesign and enhanced explanation of the APHIS form would lead to collection of more accurate data on animal use.

Table 3-5.—Various Estimates of the Number of Animals Used in the United States

Group	Species	W. B. Saunders (estimate) 1965	W. B. Saunders (projection) 1970	ILAR 1967	ILAR 1970	ILAR 1978	APHIS 1980[a]	APHIS 1982[b]	APHIS 1983[b]	Health Designs (estimate) 1983
Number of reporting institutions		—	—	1,371	1,523	1,252	975	1,127	1,146	—
Rodents	**Total**	**58,440,000**	**94,480,000**	**30,363,000**	**37,247,377**	**18,648,171**	**828,216**	**10,530,685**	**12,158,377**	**13,175,716**
	Mice	36,840,000	59,560,000	22,772,300	25,687,067	13,413,813	—	6,889,744	7,913,137	8,500,000
	Rats	15,660,000	25,320,000	6,131,000	9,870,628	4,358,766	—	2,725,814	3,269,434	3,700,000
	Hamsters	3,300,000	5,340,000	785,900	870,056	368,934	405,826	417,267	454,479	454,479
	Guinea pigs	2,520,000	4,070,000	613,300	737,899	426,665	422,390	497,860	521,237	521,237
	Other rodents	120,000	190,000	60,500	81,727	79,993	—	—	—	—
Rabbits	**Total**	**1,560,000**	**2,520,000**	**504,500**	**494,591**	**439,986**	**471,297**	**547,312**	**509,052**	**509,052**
Carnivores	**Total**	—	—	**370,400**	**247,310**	**242,961**	**257,265**	**254,828**	**237,771**	**237,771**
	Cats	—	—	99,300	56,646	54,908	68,482	59,961	55,346	55,346
	Dogs	—	—	262,000	182,728	183,063	188,783	194,867	182,425	182,425
	Other carnivores	—	—	9,100	7,936	4,990	—	—	—	—
Ungulates	**Total**	—	—	**106,200**	**95,636**	**144,595**	—	—	—	—
Nonhuman primates	**Total**	—	—	**57,700**	**54,437**	**30,323**	**56,024**	**54,565**	**59,333**	**59,336**
Birds	**Total**	—	—	**2,070,500**	**887,263**	**450,352**	—	—	—	**100,000**[c]
Amphibians	**Total**	—	—	—	**2,039,490**	—	—	—	—	**500,000**[c]
	Frogs and toads	—	—	—	2,022,755	—	—	—	—	—
Other	**Total**	—	—	—	**601,663**[d]	—	**49,102**[e]	—	—	**4,000,000**[c,f]
ALL ANIMALS	**TOTAL**	**60,000,000**	**97,000,000**	**33,472,300**	**41,667,767**	**19,956,388**	**1,661,904**	**11,387,390**	**12,964,536**	**18,581,875**

[a]Data obtained from *Animal Welfare Enforcement Report* to Congress for 1980. They do not include any numbers for rats and mice.
[b]Data compiled by Health Designs, Inc. (Rochester, NY) with all available Annual Reports of Research Facilities. The data for rats and mice are from voluntary reporting of the use of these species.
[c]Estimates stated are highest value of a rough range.
[d]Marine mammals, fish, and reptiles.
[e]Wild animals.
[f]Fish.

SOURCE: Office of Technology Assessment.

Figure 3-2.—Example A of APHIS "Annual Report of Research Facility"

This report is required by law (7 USC 2143). Failu ɔ report according to the regulations can result in an order to cease and desist and to be subj ɔ penalties as provided for in Section 2150.

UNITED STATES DEPARTMENT OF AGRICULTURE
ANIMAL AND PLANT HEALTH INSPECTION SERVICE
VETERINARY SERVICES

1. DATE OF REPORT
March 7, 1984

FORM APPROVED
OMB NO. 0579-0036

2. HEADQUARTERS RESEARCH FACILITY *(Name & Address, as registered with USDA, include Zip Code)*

ANNUAL REPORT OF RESEARCH FACILITY

(Required For Each Reporting Facility Where Animals Are Held And An Attending Veterinarian Has Responsibility)

INSTRUCTIONS

Reporting Facility - complete items 1 through 24 and submit to your Headquarters Facility. Attach additional sheets if necessary.

Headquarters Facility - complete items 25 through 27 and submit on or before December 1 of each year for the preceding Federal fiscal year (October 1, to September 30) to the Veterinarian in Charge for the State where the research facility headquarters is registered.

3. REGISTRATION NO.

4. REPORTING FACILITY *(Name and Address, include Zip Code)*

REPORT OF ANIMALS USED IN ACTUAL RESEARCH, TESTING, OR EXPERIMENTATION - Section 2.28 of Animal Welfare Regulations requires appropriate use of anesthetics, analgesics, and tranquilizing drugs during research, testing, or experimentation. Experiments involving pain or distress without use of these drugs must be reported and a brief statement explaining the research.

A. Animals Covered By Act	B. New Animals Added this Year	C. Number of animals used in research, experiments, or tests involving no pain or distress.	D. Number of animals used in research, experiments, or tests where appropriate anesthetic, analgesic, or tranquilizer drugs were administered to avoid pain or distress.	E. Number of animals used in research, experiments, or tests involving pain or distress without administration of appropriate anesthetic, analgesic, or tranquilizer drugs. *(Attach brief explanation)*	F. TOTAL NO. Of Animals *(Cols. B + C + D + E)*
5. Dogs	610	0	610	0	1220
6. Cats	0	0	0	0	0
7. Guinea Pigs	0	0			0
8. Hamsters	0	0			0
9. Rabbits	24	24	0	0	48
10. Primates	0	0	0	0	0
11. Rats	4500	0	4500	0	9000
12. Mice	2000	1200	800	0	4000
~~Wild Animals~~ *(specify)* 13. Gerbils	50	0	0	0	50
14. Sheep	8	1	7		16
15. Cattle	10	0	10	0	20

CERTIFICATION BY ATTENDING VETERINARIAN FOR REPORTING FACILITY OR INSTITUTIONAL COMMITTEE

I (We) hereby certify that the type and amount of analgesic, anesthetic, and tranquilizing drugs used on animals during actual research, testing or experimentation including post-operative and post-procedural care was deemed appropriate to relieve pain and distress for the subject animal.

16. SIGNATURE OF ATTENDING VETERINARIAN	17. TITLE	18. DATE SIGNED 3/5/84
19. SIGNATURE OF COMMITTEE MEMBER	20. TITLE	21. DATE SIGNED 3/6/84
22. SIGNATURE OF COMMITTEE MEMBER	23. TITLE	24. DATE SIGNED 3/6/84

CERTIFICATION BY HEADQUARTERS RESEARCH FACILITY OFFICIAL

I certify that the above is true, correct, and complete and that professionally acceptable standards governing the care, treatment, and use of animals including appropriate use of anesthetic, analgesic, and tranquilizing drugs, during actual research, testing, or experimentation including post-operative and post-procedural care are being followed by the above research facilities or sites (7 U.S.C. Section 2143).

25. SIGNATURE OF RESPONSIBLE OFFICIAL	26. TITLE	27. DATE SIGNED

VS FORM 18-23 (AUG 81) *Previous edition obsolete*

SOURCE: Animal and Plant Health Inspection Service, U.S. Department of Agriculture.

Figure 3-3.—Example B of APHIS "Annual Report of Research Facility"

This report is required by law (7 USC 2143). Failure to report according to the regulations can result in an order to cease and desist and to be subject to penalties as provided for in Section 2150.

UNITED STATES DEPARTMENT OF AGRICULTURE
ANIMAL AND PLANT HEALTH INSPECTION SERVICE
VETERINARY SERVICES

1. DATE OF REPORT 10/17/83

FORM APPROVED
OMB NO. 0579-0036

2. HEADQUARTERS RESEARCH FACILITY *(Name & Address, as registered with USDA, include Zip Code)*

ANNUAL REPORT OF RESEARCH FACILITY

(Required For Each Reporting Facility Where Animals Are Held And An Attending Veterinarian Has Responsibility)

3. REGISTRATION NO.

4. REPORTING FACILITY *(Name and Address, include Zip Code)*

INSTRUCTIONS

Reporting Facility - complete items 1 through 24 and submit to your Headquarters Facility. Attach additional sheets if necessary.

Headquarters Facility - complete items 25 through 27 and submit on or before December 1 of each year for the preceding Federal fiscal year (October 1, to September 30) to the Veterinarian in Charge for the State where the research facility headquarters is registered.

REPORT OF ANIMALS USED IN ACTUAL RESEARCH, TESTING, OR EXPERIMENTATION - Section 2.28 of Animal Welfare Regulations requires appropriate use of anesthetics, analgesics, and tranquilizing drugs during research, testing, or experimentation. Experiments involving pain or distress without use of these drugs must be reported and a brief statement explaining the research.

A. Animals Covered By Act	B. New Animals Added this Year	C. Number of animals used in research, experiments, or tests involving no pain or distress.	D. Number of animals used in research, experiments, or tests where appropriate anesthetic, analgesic, or tranquilizer drugs were administered to avoid pain or distress.	E. Number of animals used in research, experiments, or tests involving pain or distress without administration of appropriate anesthetic, analgesic, or tranquilizer drugs. *(Attach brief explanation)*	F. TOTAL NO. Of Animals *(Cols. + C + D + E)*
5. Dogs			14		14
6. Cats		6	6		12
7. Guinea Pigs		18	18		36
8. Hamsters					
9. Rabbits		130	130		260
10. Primates					
11. Rats		20	20		40
12. Mice		250	250		500
13. Wild Animals *(specify)*					
14.					
15.					

CERTIFICATION BY ATTENDING VETERINARIAN FOR REPORTING FACILITY OR INSTITUTIONAL COMMITTEE

I (We) hereby certify that the type and amount of analgesic, anesthetic, and tranquilizing drugs used on animals during actual research, testing or experimentation including post-operative and post-procedural care was deemed appropriate to relieve pain and distress for the subject animal.

16. SIGNATURE OF ATTENDING VETERINARIAN	17. TITLE	18. DATE SIGNED 10/24/83
19. SIGNATURE OF COMMITTEE MEMBER	20. TITLE	21. DATE SIGNED
22. SIGNATURE OF COMMITTEE MEMBER	23. TITLE	24. DATE SIGNED

CERTIFICATION BY HEADQUARTERS RESEARCH FACILITY OFFICIAL

I certify that the above is true, correct, and complete and that professionally acceptable standards governing the care, treatment, and use of animals including appropriate use of anesthetic, analgesic, and tranquilizing drugs, during actual research, testing, or experimentation including post-operative and post-procedural care are being followed by the above research facilities or sites (7 U.S.C. Section 2143).

25. SIGNATURE OF RESPONSIBLE OFFICIAL	26. TITLE	27. DATE SIGNED 10-31-83

VS FORM 18-23 (AUG 81) *Previous edition obsolete*

SOURCE: Animal and Plant Health Inspection Service, U.S. Department of Agriculture.

Figure 3-4.—Example C of APHIS "Annual Report of Research Facility"

RECEIVED ... law (7 USC 2143). Failure to report according to the regulations can result in an order to cease and desist and to be subject to penalties as provided for in Section 2150.

DEC 2 1983

USDA, APHIS, VS

UNITED STATES DEPARTMENT OF AGRICULTURE
ANIMAL AND PLANT HEALTH INSPECTION SERVICE
VETERINARY SERVICES

ANNUAL REPORT OF RESEARCH FACILITY

(Required For Each Reporting Facility Where Animals Are Held And An Attending Veterinarian Has Responsibility)

1. DATE OF REPORT
30 NOV 83

FORM APPROVED
OMB NO. 0579-0036

2. HEADQUARTERS RESEARCH FACILITY *(Name & Address, as registered with USDA, include Zip Code)*

INSTRUCTIONS

Reporting Facility - complete items 1 through 24 and submit to your Headquarters Facility. Attach additional sheets if necessary.

Headquarters Facility - complete items 25 through 27 and submit on or before December 1 of each year for the preceding Federal fiscal year (October 1, to September 30) to the Veterinarian in Charge for the State where the research facility headquarters is registered.

3. REGISTRATION NO.

4. REPORTING FACILITY *(Name and Address, include Zip Code)*

REPORT OF ANIMALS USED IN ACTUAL RESEARCH, TESTING, OR EXPERIMENTATION - Section 2.28 of Animal Welfare Regulations requires appropriate use of anesthetics, analgesics, and tranquilizing drugs during research, testing, or experimentation. Experiments involving pain or distress without use of these drugs must be reported and a brief statement explaining the research.

A. Animals Covered By Act	B. New Animals Added this Year	C. Number of animals used in research, experiments, or tests involving no pain or distress.	D. Number of animals used in research, experiments, or tests where appropriate anesthetic, analgesic, or tranquilizer drugs were administered to avoid pain or distress.	E. Number of animals used in research, experiments, or tests involving pain or distress without administration of appropriate anesthetic, analgesic, or tranquilizer drugs. *(Attach brief explanation)*	F. TOTAL NO. Of Animals *(Cols. B + C + D + E)*
5. Dogs	44	12	189	0	201
6. Cats	0	0	0	0	0
7. Guinea Pigs	383	137	186	0	323
8. Hamsters	207	0	207	0	207
9. Rabbits	638	40	598	0	638
10. Primates	0	12	119	0	131
11. Rats	4357	1940	1444	0	3384
12. Mice	1373	363	739	0	1102
13. Wild Animals *(specify)* TURTLES	293	0	293	0	293
14. DOMESTIC PIGS	609	0	609	0	609
15. GERBILS	100	0	100	0	100

CERTIFICATION BY ATTENDING VETERINARIAN FOR REPORTING FACILITY OR INSTITUTIONAL COMMITTEE

I (We) hereby certify that the type and amount of analgesic, anesthetic, and tranquilizing drugs used on animals during actual research, testing or experimentation including post-operative and post-procedural care was deemed appropriate to relieve pain and distress for the subject animal.

16. SIGNATURE OF ATTENDING VETERINARIAN	17. TITLE	18. DATE SIGNED 30 NOV 83
19. SIGNATURE OF COMMITTEE MEMBER	20. TITLE	21. DATE SIGNED 30 NOV 83
22. SIGNATURE OF COMMITTEE MEMBER	23. TITLE	24. DATE SIGNED

CERTIFICATION BY HEADQUARTERS RESEARCH FACILITY OFFICIAL

I certify that the above is true, correct, and complete and that professionally acceptable standards governing the care, treatment, and use of animals including appropriate use of anesthetic, analgesic, and tranquilizing drugs, during actual research, testing, or experimentation including post-operative and post-procedural care are being followed by the above research facilities or sites (7 U.S.C. Section 2143).

25. SIGNATURE OF RESPONSIBLE OFFICIAL	26. TITLE	27. DATE SIGNED 30 NOV 83

VS FORM 18-23 (AUG 81) *Previous edition obsolete*

SOURCE: Animal and Plant Health Inspection Service, U.S. Department of Agriculture.

Even with these limitations and qualifications, the numbers generated by the APHIS data provide a range that can be used in discussions of animal use. The totals include: 1.8 million mandated species, 100,000 to 500,000 birds, 100,000 to 500,000 amphibians, 2.5 million to 4.0 million fish, and 12.2 million to 15.25 million mice and rats. Therefore, **it appears that between 17 million and 22 million animals are used in United States laboratories annually.**

The largest group is represented by mice and rats. For reporting institutions, mice represent 60.8 percent of all animals used, and rats 25.1 percent. In addition, for the mandated species, certain institutions use specific species disproportionately to their percentage of overall total use (see table 3-6). Fifty percent or more of all cats and dogs are used by universities and medical schools. Guinea pigs are used mostly by the pharmaceutical industry, whereas hamsters are used more often in biomedical research, and to a lesser extent in universities, medical schools, and the pharmaceutical firms. Sixty-two percent of rabbits are used in universities, medical schools, and the pharmaceutical industry, as are 75.6 percent of the primates.

For rats and mice, the trends indicated in table 3-6 are clouded by the fact that there was more reporting of rat and mouse usage in 1983 than in

Table 3-6.—USDA/APHIS Data, Changes 1982-83 (reporting institutions only)

	Institution type									
	Universities & medical schools	Hospitals nonuniversity	Bio-medical research	Toxicology testing labs	Chemical companies	Pharmaceutical, device & diagnosis	State & local government	Food, feed & miscellaneous	Federal agencies	Total
Year										
Rats:										
1982	1,079,208	86,472	343,915	97,237	176,874	558,630	11,299	12,700	359,479	2,725,814
1983	1,234,864	106,430	406,936	144,162	114,215	778,425	30,378	14,355	439,729	3,269,494
% change	14	23	18	48	−35	39	168	13	22	19
Mice:										
1982	1,678,300	203,768	1,579,664	431,464	161,659	1,669,629	200,150	6,247	958,863	6,889,744
1983	1,951,466	222,080	1,512,424	495,067	158,752	2,021,157	477,250	3,632	1,071,339	7,913,167
% change	16	8	−4	14	−1	21	138	−41	11	14
Dogs:										
1982	98,983	13,622	22,291	3,457	2,194	37,604	322	3,698	12,696	194,867
1983	90,001	12,605	21,483	5,003	1,591	38,311	436	3,400	9,595	182,425
% change	−9	−7	−3	44	−27	1	35	−8	−24	−6
Cats:										
1982	34,555	2,716	7,697	137	115	9,073	87	2,040	3,541	59.961
1983	32,535	2,265	6,768	172	44	8,624	72	2,092	2,774	55,346
% change	−5	−16	−12	25	−61	−4	−17	2	−21	−7
Guinea pigs:										
1982	82,198	6,104	25,225	35,145	18,182	272,405	9,044	1,504	48,053	497,860
1983	64,554	7,195	30,696	28,753	14,722	297,849	10,090	930	66,448	521,237
% change	−21	17	21	−18	−19	9	11	−38	38	4
Hamsters:										
1982	151,365	5,501	65,146	12,954	3,160	131,227	8,401	23	39,490	417,267
1983	115,483	5,472	169,272	11,922	612	112,618	3,193	22	35,885	454,479
% change	−23	−0.5	159	−7	−80	−14	−61	−4	−9	9
Rabbits:										
1982	173,716	15,171	63,863	60,785	20,970	177,289	2,102	1,862	31,554	547,312
1983	158,058	15,042	64,626	55,785	22,034	159,276	1,948	2,504	29,779	509,052
% change	−9	−0.8	1	−8	5	−10	−7	34	−5	−6
Primates:										
1982	23,353	557	13,543	2,577	144	7,709	329	66	6,287	54,565
1983	22,201	1,059	13,272	5,809	25	9,376	243	82	7,269	59,336
% change	−4	90	−2	125	−82	21	−26	24	15	8
Institutions reporting:										
1982	410	129	167	79	27	145	19	26	125	1,127
1983	402	140	159	86	31	155	18	32	123	1,146
% change	−2	8	−4	8	14	6	−5	23	−2	2

SOURCE: Office of Technology Assessment.

1982. So, although it appears from table 3-6 that the usage increased, this was in fact not so (as can be seen from table 3-4). Data for all institutions from the regression equations show no change in mice and a small increase in the use of rats. However, since the same pattern of increase by institutional group reporting can be seen from table 3-6, there has likely been no increase or decrease in use of these two species between 1982 and 1983.

In table 3-6, the number of reporting institutions includes those that reported any number for any species, whether these included rats or mice or not. Few significant changes occurred as a function of institution type for the 2 years surveyed. **No trend in animal use can be identified between 1982 and 1983, and the available data provide no justification for predicting either increases or decreases in future years.** It would have been possible to examine the 1981 APHIS data sheets and determine whether, on the basis of 3 years' data, a trend for the mandated species existed, but the 1981 data sheets would not indicate trends for rats and mice. The other methods of estimating laboratory-animal use do not match the reliability of the APHIS data, and thus do not lend much credence to the numbers reported in the past.

Future Animal Censuses

The major limitation with this estimate of annual laboratory-animal usage was the need to depend on available data sources, with all the limitations just described. Although the APHIS data sheets were of considerable value, they still do not substitute for an appropriately designed stratified random sampling of all possible users. Only then would all possible institutions be represented. The APHIS scheme depends on institutions to request certification. Some may be operating and not reporting to APHIS. Still, with considerable further effort, a post-hoc stratification could be done based on the APHIS data.

Estimates could be improved by two major approaches. The first, and least expensive, would involve the use of all annual APHIS reporting forms—following an imperative redesign of the form—as well as thoroughly determining which registered institutions in each year did and did not report. Then appropriate statistical estimation techniques could be used on an institution-type and year-specific basis to correct for missing data. The second, and more ambitious, approach would be to conduct a stratified random sample study of all possible users. The stratification would be by type of institution, size of institution, and species of animals. From such a sample, appropriate statistical techniques could be used to project to the entire population of user institutions.

In 1985, the National Research Council's Institute of Laboratory Animal Resources announced plans for another in its series of surveys of experimental animal usage. The 1986 census will include mammals and birds, but omit fish, amphibians, and reptiles.

SUMMARY AND CONCLUSIONS

A rough analysis of the number of laboratory animals used is important to provide some context in which to discuss alternatives to using animals, evaluate progress toward the goal of using fewer animals, and judge the effect that alternatives might have. OTA therefore evaluated existing data on the number of laboratory animals used each year in the United States.

The data sources considered included various reports and surveys published by the National Research Council's Institute of Laboratory Animal Resources, various market surveys, and the annual reports submitted to USDA's Animal and Plant Health Inspection Service. For the latter source, the individual annual reports furnished by each registered facility for 1982 and 1983 were evaluated. Generally, it was found that great disparities existed among the different sources. No single data source presents an accurate count of the number of laboratory animals used in the United States since not one includes all potential users. In addition, it is impossible to compare data among sources due to the inadequacy of information on survey and data collection methodologies, definitions, areas of use, reporting requirements, and the inability to justify completeness of the data.

In a comparative analysis of data sources, it was found that the most useful data were the APHIS data sheets completed by every institution that uses laboratory species regulated under the Animal Welfare Act. APHIS requires that registered institutions report all use of dogs, cats, guinea pigs, hamsters, rabbits, and nonhuman primates. Even with this requirement, though, it seems that APHIS does not receive animal-use information from all possible users. The data from these forms were found to be more accurate than the *Animal Welfare Enforcement Report,* a summary submitted annually by APHIS to Congress. This report usually neglects 10 to 20 percent of the annual reports (those submitted late, usually after December 31) and so underestimates the actual number of dogs, cats, guinea pigs, hamsters, rabbits, and nonhuman primates used.

For fiscal years 1982 and 1983, the numbers of these kinds of animals used, according to the APHIS data sheets, are shown in table 3-7. For other laboratory species—mice, rats, birds, amphibians, and fish—the ability to obtain accurate estimates of the number used is impaired by a lack of reliable data sources. The best estimates are that 100,000 to 500,000 birds, 100,000 to 500,000 amphibians, 2.5 million to 4.0 million fish, and 12.2 million to 15.25 million rats and mice were used. (Animal use in medical and veterinary education is estimated to be at least 53,000 animals per year and is discussed in ch. 9.) Total animal use in the United States, therefore, is estimated as between 17 million and 22 million a year.

The great discrepancies in data sources meant no trends could be observed over time and among different types of institution. Even within the APHIS data for six kinds of animals, no clear trends were found. Indeed, the most important finding was that no accurate source exists on the numbers of animals used annually in the United States. A stratified random sample of all possible user institutions done with a correct statistical analysis would probably be the best way to estimate laboratory-animal use in the United States.

Table 3-7.—Animal Use Reported to the U.S. Department of Agriculture, 1982 and 1983[a]

Animal	Number used in 1982	Number used in 1983
Dogs	194,867	182,425
Cats	59,961	55,346
Hamsters	417,267	454,479
Rabbits	547,312	509,052
Guinea pigs	497,860	521,237
Nonhuman primates	54,565	59,336
Total	**1,771,832**	**1,781,875**

[a]Totals **do not include rats or mice,** two species that together represent the majority of animals used.

SOURCE: Office of Technology Assessment.

In the Federal Government, six departments and four agencies use animals for intramural research and testing. These investigative efforts range from uncovering new knowledge that will lead to better health (within the National Institutes of Health), to evaluating hazardous substances in consumer products (within the Consumer Product Safety Commission's Directorate for Health Sciences), to protecting the health of American astronauts (within the National Aeronautic and Space Administration's Life Sciences Division).

OTA used the APHIS Annual Report of Research Facility forms to track animal use within the Federal Government itself by department (and by division within departments) and by species. In this way, it was possible to identify what portion of the estimated 17 million to 22 million animals used yearly were used within Federal facilities. In 1983, the Federal Government used at least 1.6 million animals, largely rats and mice. Ninety-six percent of the 1.6 million animals were used by DOD, DHHS, and the VA. Of the total, about 9 percent were dogs, cats, hamsters, rabbits, guinea pigs, and nonhuman primates.

The APHIS forms require that all experiments be categorized as: 1) involving no pain or distress; 2) involving appropriate anesthetic, analgesic, or tranquilizer drugs to avoid pain or distress; or 3) involving pain or distress without administration of appropriate anesthetic, analgesic, or tranquilizer drugs. Sixty-three percent of the animals used within Federal departments and agencies were in the experimental situation categorized as involving no pain or distress while 32 percent were given drugs and only 5 percent experienced pain or distress.

The APHIS reporting system lacks clear definitions and uniform reporting. If accurate data are to be obtained, the forms must be revised and better explanations of how to complete them must be provided.

CHAPTER 3 REFERENCES

1. Abood, L.G., Professor, Center for Brain Research, University of Rochester, Rochester, NY, personal communication, 1984.
2. Alex Brown & Sons, Inc., *Charles River Breeding Laboratories, Inc., Market Survey* (Baltimore, MD: 1981).
3. Bier, R., Bio-Research Laboratories, Ltd., Sennerville, Quebec, Canada, personal communication, 1984.
4. Bohrer, D., Division of Research Grants, National Institutes of Health, Bethesda, MD, personal communication, 1984.
5. Borsetti, A., Staff Scientist, Office of Science Coordination, Food and Drug Administration, U.S. Department of Health and Human Services, Rockville, MD, personal communication, 1984.
6. Charles River Breeding Laboratories, Inc., price list, Wilmington, MA, 1983.
7. Cook, R., North Carolina State University, Raleigh, NC, personal communication, 1984.
8. Culley, D., Louisiana State University, Baton Rouge, LA, personal communication, 1984.
9. David, T., Staff Veterinarian, Aerospace Medical Division, Air Force, U.S. Department of Defense, Brooks Air Force Base, TX, personal communication, Jan. 18, 1985.
10. Digges, K., Deputy Associate Administrator for Research Development, National Highway Traffic Safety Administration, U.S. Department of Transportation, Washington, DC, personal communication, March 1985.
11. Dodds, W.J., Division of Laboratories and Research, New York State Department of Health, Albany, NY, personal communication, April 1985.
12. Edington, C., Associate Director, Office of Health and Environmental Research, Office of Energy Research, U.S. Department of Energy, Washington, DC, personal communication, Nov. 16, 1984.
13. Emmons, M.B., "Secondary and Elementary School Use of Live and Preserved Animals," *Animals in Education*, H. McGriffin and N. Brownley (eds.) (Washington, DC: Institute for Study of Animal Problems, 1980).
14. Goldberg, A.M., Director, The Johns Hopkins Center for Alternatives to Animal Testing, Baltimore, MD, personal communication, April 1985.
15. Guilloud, N., Ortho Pharmaceutical Corporation, Raritan, NJ, personal communication, 1984.
16. Gupta, K.C., Deputy Director, Division of Health Sciences Laboratory, Directorate for Health Sciences, U.S. Consumer Product Safety Commission, Washington, DC, personal communication, Sept. 24, 1985.
17. Health Designs Inc., "Survey and Estimates of Laboratory Animal Use in the United States," contract report prepared for the Office of Technology Assessment, U.S. Congress, July 1984.
18. Institute of Laboratory Animal Resources, *Animal Facilities in Medical Research (Final Report),* A Report of the Committee on the Animal Facilities Survey (2 parts) (Washington, DC: National Academy of Sciences, 1964).
19. Institute of Laboratory Animal Resources, *Animal Facilities in Medical Research: A Preliminary Study* (Washington, DC: National Academy of Sciences, 1962).
20. Institute of Laboratory Animal Resources, *Annual Surveys of Animals Used for Research Purposes* (Washington, DC: National Academy of Sciences, 1965-71).
21. Institute of Laboratory Animal Resources, "Laboratory Animal Facilities and Resources Supporting Biomedical Research, 1967-68," *Lab Anim. Care* 20: 795-869, 1970.
22. Institute of Laboratory Animal Resources, *National Survey of Laboratory Animal Facilities and Resources* (Washington, DC: National Academy of Sciences, 1980).
23. Institute of Laboratory Animal Resources, *Non-Human Primates: Usage and Availability for Biomedical Programs* (Washington, DC: National Academy of Sciences, 1975).
24. Kellogg, C., Department of Psychology, University of Rochester, Rochester, NY, personal communication, 1984.
25. Manufacturing Chemists Association, *Study of Potential Economic Impacts of the Proposed Toxic Substances Control Act as Illustrated by Senate Bill S776* (Florham Park, NJ: Foster F. Snell, Inc., 1975).
26. Matchett, A., Animal Care Staff, U.S. Department of Agriculture, Washington, DC, personal communication, 1984.
27. McArdle, J.E., Director, Laboratory Animal Welfare, Humane Society of the United States, Washington, DC, personal communication, 1984.
28. McCarthy, C., Director, Office for Protection from Research Risks, National Institutes of Health, Public Health Service, U.S. Department of Health and Human Services, Bethesda, MD, personal communication, October 1984.
29. Middleton, C., Chief Veterinary Medical Officer, Veterans' Administration, Washington, DC, personal communication, Oct. 3, 1984.
30. Miller, T., McNeil Laboratories, Ft. Washington, PA, personal communication, 1984.
31. Moorehouse, K., Division of Wildlife Service, Fish

and Wildlife Service, U.S. Department of the Interior, Washington, DC, personal communication, October 1984.
32. Moreland, A., "Animal Research Protocol Review Within the Veterans' Administration" (draft), Gainesville, FL, 1984.
33. Mosed, R., Executive Director for Oceanic and Atmospheric Administration, National Oceanic and Atmospheric Administration, U.S. Department of Commerce, Rockville, MD, personal communication, September 1984.
34. Nace, G.W., Professor of Zoology, University of Michigan, Ann Arbor, MI, personal communication, 1984.
35. Nace, G.W., Response to a questionnaire on the use of frogs in the United States, questionnaire prepared by Rolf Martin, Department of Chemistry, Brooklyn College of the City University of New York, Brooklyn, NY, 1984.
36. New A., Director, Laboratory Animal Science, National Cancer Institute, Public Health Service, U.S. Department of Health and Human Services, Bethesda, MD, personal communication, 1984.
37. Nicogossian, A., Director, Life Sciences Division, National Aeronautics and Space Administration, Washington, DC, personal communication, 1984.
38. Roberts, C., Director, Division of Veterinary Medicine, U.S. Department of Defense, Washington, DC, personal communication, September 1984.
39. Rowan, A.N., *Of Mice, Models, & Men: A Critical Evaluation of Animal Research* (Albany, NY: State University of New York Press, 1984).
40. Rowan, A.N., Assistant Dean for New Programs, Tufts University School of Veterinary Medicine, Boston, MA, personal communication, 1985.
41. W.B. Saunders and Company, "Market Survey," *Inform. Lab. Anim. Res.* 9(3):10, 1965.
42. Schultz, C., Chief, Sciences Branch, Technology Division, Office of Hazardous Materials Regulation, Materials Transportation Bureau, Research and Special Programs Administration, U.S. Department of Transportation, Washington, DC, personal communication, September 1984.
43. Simmonds, R., Director of Instructional and Research Support, Uniformed Service University of the Health Sciences, Bethesda, MD, personal communication, April 1985.
44. Stewart, W., Senior Veterinarian, Animal and Plant Health Inspection Service, U.S. Department of Agriculture, Hyattsville, MD, personal communication, November 1984.
45. Taylor, J., Staff Veterinary Officer, Naval Command, U.S. Department of Defense, Washington, DC, personal communication, November 1984.
46. Thomas, O., Professor of Poultry Science, University of Maryland, College Park, MD, personal communication, 1984.
47. Thomas, R., U.S. Department of Energy, Washington, DC, personal communication, October 1984.
48. Ulvedal, F., Acting Director, Water and Toxic Substances Health Effects Research Division, U.S. Environmental Protection Agency, Washington, DC, personal communication, September 1984.
49. U.S. Department of Agriculture, Animal and Plant Health Inspection Service, *Animal Welfare Enforcement: Report of the Secretary of Agriculture to the President of the Senate and the Speaker of the House of Representatives* (annual) (Washington, DC: 1972 through 1983).
50. U.S. Department of Defense, Air Force Division, *Aerospace Medical Division Animal Use Review Panel Meetings* (Washington, DC: May 1984).
51. U.S. Department of Health and Human Services, Public Health Service, National Institutes of Health, *1983 NIH Almanac* (Bethesda, MD: 1983).
52. U.S. Department of Health and Human Services, Public Health Service, National Institutes of Health, *NIH Data Book* (Bethesda, MD: 1983).
53. U.S. Department of the Interior, U.S. Fish and Wildlife Service, *Service Managment Plan* (draft) (Washington, DC: October 1984).
54. Will, J.A., Director, Research Animal Resources Center, University of Wisconsin, Madison, WI, personal communication, 1984.
55. Willett, J.D., Project Officer, Biological Models and Materials Resource Section, Animal Resource Program, Division of Research Resources, National Institutes of Health, Public Health Service, U.S. Department of Health and Human Services, Bethesda, MD, personal communication, 1983.

Chapter 4

Ethical Considerations

To use either human or non-human animals for purposes that are not in their own interests is both ethically unjustifiable and, in the long run, counter-productive.

Alex Pacheco
People for the Ethical Treatment of Animals
March 15, 1985

Fortunately, there are many who, while deeply and appropriately concerned for the compassionate treatment of animals, recognize that human welfare is and should be our primary concern.

Frederick A. King
Yerkes Regional Primate Research Center
Psychology Today, September 1984

One cannot intelligently assess vivisection in isolation from animal exploitation in other areas of human life: for food, furs, leather, in so-called sports, in movies, in the wild. Vivisection, properly seen, is simply one variation on the cultural theme of animal sacrifice.

Michael A. Giannelli
The Fund for Animals, Inc.
March 10, 1985

The use of any particular animal—say, a sheep—in medical research is more important than its use as lamb chops.

Carl Cohen
The University of Michigan
The Research News 35(10-12):9, 1984

CONTENTS

Chapter 4

Ethical Considerations

The range of opinion on the rights and wrongs of using animals to satisfy human needs is as broad as the political spectrum itself. At one extreme, animals are thought to be entitled to at least a portion of the respect, individual freedom, and dignity that are considered to be basic human rights. Some say that animals should be recognized as belonging to a community that includes humans. At the other extreme, humans are thought to have broad and absolute authority over the lives and interests of animals. From this perspective, expediency alone, not morality, dictates what we may do with animals.

To illustrate the distance between these extremes, a recent legal brief for animal rights can be contrasted with a televised interview with three scientists who perform animal experimentation. According to the brief (43):

> If being alive is the basis for being a moral object, and if all other interests and needs are predicated upon life, then the most basic, morally relevant aspect of a creature is its life. We may correlatively suggest that any animal, therefore, has a *right to life.*

The scientists, in a televised exchange with Harvard philosopher Robert Nozick, were asked whether the fact that an experiment will kill hundreds of animals is ever regarded by scientists as a reason for not performing it. One answered: "Not that I know of." When Nozick asked whether the animals count at all, one scientist replied, "Why should they?" while another added that he did not think that experimenting on animals raised a moral issue at all (45).

People at both extremes would probably agree that, given a choice between experiments equivalent in cost and scientific value, one that does not require the destruction of animals would be preferable to one that does. This consensus, however, would probably evaporate if animal experimentation produced greater scientific validity or the technique that used animals had significant cost advantages.

In morals, as in politics, most people tend to shun extremes. However, a middle view is at once the most defensible and the most difficult to defend. Pitted against extreme or esoteric positions, the numbers on its side create a presumption in its favor. Yet a presumption given only by the weight of opinion will not amount to a moral justification. A belief is not shown to be true simply by counting the votes of those who accept it. Some *basis* for an opinion, independent of it being accepted, must be found.

Adoption of a middle view is hazardous in two respects. First, it runs the risk of inconsistency. Propositions located at polar extremes will usually contradict one another, and a position that seeks to incorporate both may find itself embracing a contradiction. In the case of toxicity testing, for example, it may not seem possible to respect the interests of experimental animals and yet use them as tools for enhancing human health and safety.

The second risk is that consistency will be secured at a price too high, by way of a theoretically unattractive ad hoc device. In principle, two contradictory propositions can be reconciled simply by making one an exception to the other. It could, for example, be stipulated that the general rule against harming animals does not hold when they are used to test for toxicity. But it is one thing to say this and another to give a reason for it. Complex rules, introduced for no reason other than to remove a particular inconsistency, muddy a point of view without shedding any light on the hard moral cases it must address. More important, they are arbitrary.

THE RELIGIOUS AND PHILOSOPHICAL TRADITIONS

Interest in the moral status of animals is by no means modern. The ancient religions had much to say about the place that animals were to occupy in the cosmic scheme of things. Oriental creeds were, as a rule, reluctant to draw a sharp distinction between humans and other species. All animal lives were judged worthy of protection and some were thought to be sacred. The doctrine of transmigration left still more room for caution—any animal body might house a soul entitled to special care. The various forms of the doctrine of transmigration share the thesis that a single, continuous, immaterial individual may pass from one body to another, which may be of the same or a different species. If the latter, its conduct in the earlier incarnation may determine the kind of body it inhabits next. For such reasons, the prescribed dietary regimen in the Orient was frequently vegetarian. Modern influences have relaxed, but not wholly removed, the grip of these beliefs.

In the West, a different tradition took root, one that seems to have assigned value to animals only as they serve human purposes. Judeo-Christian doctrine appears to have condoned an indifferent, if not openly exploitative, attitude toward nonhuman animals (38,45). (For an opposing view, see refs. 6 and 49.) The Genesis account suggests that humans are the last and most perfected of God's creatures. Humans alone, of all living things, bear the likeness of God, and receive the divine commission to exercise "dominion over the fish of the sea, and over the birds of the air, and over the cattle, and over all the earth, and over every creeping thing that creeps upon the earth" (Genesis 1:26-28; all Biblical references and quotations are to the Revised Standard Version). After the flood, God rewarded Noah and his sons with this blessing: "Every moving thing that lives shall be food for you; and as I gave you the green plants, I give you everything" (Genesis 9:3). A brief Talmudic story indicates that Judaic practice was to the same effect: "A calf was being taken to the slaughterer, when it broke away, hid his head under the Rabbi's skirts, and lowed in terror. 'Go,' said he, 'for this wast thou created' " (12).

These passages do not warrant the inference that humans are permitted to treat animals in any way they please. Even when suffering is inflicted as a means to some human end, humans are subject to the condition of *using* the animal. Wanton cruelty would not be allowed. Nor is it clear just what human dominion includes, until the terms of a model ruler-subject relation are spelled out. Humans must presumably rule well, and the good ruler does not take authorized but unjustified actions. Much depends, too, on whether human sovereignty over nature is to be thought absolute or limited by a divine will that may have set some value on animals in addition to their utility for humans.

In a number of passages, the scriptures seem to place a rein on the use of animals. Genesis confirms that God had already judged the world as good—that is, possessed of some value—before humans were created (Genesis 1:3,10,13,18,21). And on several occasions in the later books of the Old Testament, humans are expressly directed to show kindness to the animals under their control. Thus, "you shall not muzzle an ox when it treads out the grain" (Deuteronomy 25:4). And, "a righteous man has regard for the life of his beast, but the mercy of the wicked is cruel" (Proverbs 12:10).

The most persuasive evidence for restraint may lie in the role-model of the good shepherd, often cited in both testaments. At one point, by report of the prophet Ezekiel, God becomes annoyed (Ezekiel 34:2,4):

> Ho, shepherds of Israel who have been feeding yourselves! Should not shepherds feed the sheep? . . . The weak you have not strengthened, the sick you have not healed, the crippled you have not bound up, the strayed you have not brought back, the lost you have not sought, and with force and harshness you have ruled them.

God's own rule is often compared with the concern that shepherds should have for their flocks (Ezekiel 34:11-13; John 10:11; Luke 15:4-7). Designed to show that God stands to humans as they stand to animals—a kind provider even if there are no duties to provide for them—that simile would fail if the shepherds could wholly disregard the welfare of their animals.

Aside from this figurative guide, the New Testament is spare in its references to handling animals. Saint Paul's discussion of the proscription against muzzling the ox suggests a human benefit: "Is it for oxen that God is concerned? Does he not speak entirely for our sake? It was written for our sake, because the plowman should plow in hope and the thresher thresh in hope of a share in the crop" (I Corinthians 9:9-10). Thus, the thresher was to let the ox feed from the corn being worked, not so much for the good of the ox, but because a well-fed animal would yield a larger return.

This passage suggests a shift in sentiment from the Old to the New Testament. For Christians, the paramount practical concern is the condition and future of the immortal soul possessed by human beings. Animals are not believed to have immortal souls, nor be repositories for human souls. In the Christian world view, then, animals are left without the one thing that has special value in itself—a soul. An animal's welfare is a good thing only as it is good for the human being.

The letter containing Paul's reading of the Old Testament rule was written only a generation after Christ's death, when Christianity was still a new faith. The distinction between humans and other animals hardened as the creed acquired the trappings of theory, but in such a way as to raise new questions about its real source. The legacy of Greek philosophy exercised such a pervasive influence over Christian theology in its formative years that the distinction could be traced to Athens as easily as to Jerusalem.

It might be said that in theology all roads lead back to Augustine or Aquinas. On the subject of animals, the Augustinian position finds expression in his critique of a competing doctrine, which, on the premise that animals also had souls, would not allow killing them. Augustine cited the conduct of Christ as a lesson to the contrary (7):

> Christ himself shows that to refrain from the killing of animals and the destroying of plants is the height of superstition, for judging that there are no common rights between us and the beasts and trees, he sent the devils into a herd of swine and with a curse withered the tree on which he found no fruit.

If Christ could use animals for his own purposes, then so apparently could we. Augustine's view, however, was tempered in two respects. First, he denied that animals were mere instruments of humans. As creatures made by God, they also possessed a good of their own (7,8). Second, animals' utility was the use to which human intelligence might put them, not the convenience or inconvenience that they might present. Augustine did not hold that humans were to treat animals according to their own pleasure or displeasure (8).

Aquinas' view of animals was more sophisticated and less sympathetic. Every natural being that underwent development had an end or perfected state that God had created it to achieve. God made humans, however, as free and rational agents, with control over their actions. People's lives took their objectives from their designs. Being neither free nor rational, an animal was merely a means to an end existing outside it (in the form of some purpose that a rational individual might have for it). Thus, the nonhuman animal was ordered, by nature and providence, to the use of humans (1).

From Aquinas' perspective, the Old Testament concern for animals had been appropriately characterized by Saint Paul. People should avoid mistreating animals not because this would be best for the animals, but because cruelty could be harmful to humans. Strictly understood, disinterested charity towards animals was impossible, since there was no common fellowship between humans and them (2).

In its essentials, this view prevails within the Catholic Church today. Its implications for research in the life sciences have not gone unnoticed. Writing at the turn of this century, Father Joseph Rickaby, the English Catholic moral theorist, denied that the suffering of animals was an obstacle to biological inquiry (42):

> Brutes are as things in our regard: so far as they are useful to us, they exist for us, not for themselves; and we do right in using them unsparingly for our need and convenience, though not for our wantonness. If then any special case of pain to a brute creature be a fact of considerable value for observation in biological science or the medical art, no reasoned considerations of morality

> can stand in the way of man making the experiment, yet so that even in the quest of science he be *mindful* of mercy.

Protestantism retains the thesis that humans enjoy a rightful hegemony over other animals, but suggests a shift towards a "stewardship" interpretation of that role. John Calvin, the 16th-century Reformation theologian, maintained that when God placed animals "in subjection unto us, He did it with the condition that we should treat them gently" (13). They were brute beasts, to be sure, but for Calvin as for Augustine they were also creatures of God. Calvin went a step further, however, in making this fact about animals a limitation on humans' use of them. Here humans would seem to be less the sovereigns of nature than deputies appointed to manage God's earthly estate. Every creature would still be subject to God's ownership and control. A person was still worth more than any number of sparrows, yet "no one of them will fall to the ground without your Father's will" (Matthew 10:29). Thus, Karl Barth, a leading modern Protestant theologian, urged that people possess the right to use and sometimes to kill animals, but only because God has so authorized it in order that humans might live (9).

There have been a few distinguished Judeo-Christian defenders of a position much closer to the Oriental view. Saint Francis and Albert Schweitzer both pressed for a principle of reverence toward every living thing. But their ideal has been received as just that: a norm perhaps for saints, and something all should desire, but not binding on imperfect individuals in less-than-ideal circumstances. In the absence of mainstream philosophical support, the intellectual authority of the reverence-for-all-life rule is thought to be outweighed by the personal prestige of its practitioners (21).

Until 1600, the philosophical mainstream was Aristotelian. Using a much broader conception of the soul than the current one, Aristotle distinguished living from nonliving beings by the presence or absence of some form of a soul, or life-giving power. Its function might be nutrition, sensation, desire, locomotion, or thought. The first of these, but not the rest, was found in plants. All animals had sensation and desire as well, and most also had locomotion. Humans alone had the power of thought (4). This advantage made humans naturally suited to rule over other living beings and made animals natural slaves. Aristotle reached this conclusion by generalizing from phenomena already at work within humans: Those with greater rationality exhibited an internal mastery of reason over desire and an external mastery over those who, because they lacked the mental equipment to tend to more than their bodily needs, required direction from others (5). This resulted in leadership by those most competent to rule.

Natural fitness implied that nature worked toward certain ends that together formed a master plan. The significance of the 17th-century scientific revolution lay not so much in its overthrow of church authority in the empirical realm as in its discovery of a method and a subject matter (i.e., mechanics treated as a branch of physics) that dispensed with the hypothesis that nature had purposes. Nature became simply the sum of matter in motion, mathematically describable without reference to goals that phenomena might serve.

The philosophical foundations for the new world view were supplied by Rene Descartes, who recognized only two kinds of existence, material and mental. Bodies were extended in space and time and divisible into parts, with properties of size, shape, and weight. Minds contained beliefs, emotions, and intentions, but no physical properties. The human was a composite being—the only one—with both a body and a mind (18).

Animals did not fit comfortably into the Cartesian scheme. They obviously had bodies, but did they not also have sensations and desires? Descartes answered that in a sense they did, but that their behavior could be duplicated by a machine, while human behavior could not. In their use of language and thought, humans revealed a capacity to respond to stimuli in a variety of ways, whereas animals would respond in only one, "according to the arrangements of their organs" (19).

For all their differences, the Aristotelian and Cartesian theories joined hands in making the activities that required reasoning the distinctive mark of humanity. Both defined the human being as a rational animal. That thesis was not questioned until the following century, when British empiricists criticized it as inflated claims for the power of reason. The Scottish skeptic David Hume concurred with Descartes that the human mind was capable of creatively entertaining a variety of possible conclusions from a given body of experience. But this, Hume argued (29), was nothing more than a habit of inference formed from repeated observations, something that dogs could do as well (30):

> 'Tis necessary in the first place, that there be some impression immediately present to their memory or senses, in order to be the foundation of their judgment. From the tone of voice the dog infers his master's anger, and foresees his own punishment. From a certain sensation affecting his smell, he judges his game not to be far distant from him.
>
> Secondly, the inference he draws from the present impression is built on experience, and on his observation of the conjunction of objects in past instances. As you vary the experience, he varies his reasoning. Make a beating follow upon one sign or motion for some time, and afterwards upon another; and he will successively draw different conclusions according to this most recent experience.

The issue dividing Descartes and Hume survives, still unsettled, in current controversies over artificial intelligence and animal cognition. Recent decades have witnessed an explosion of empirical investigations into the behavior of nonhuman animals (26,35,50). Among these, various efforts to teach higher primates how to use a nonverbal language have captured the public's imagination. Inferences drawn from such studies, however, encounter two obstacles. First, to argue that chimps consciously use gestures in the same way that human deaf-mutes do is to assume a certain theory about the relation between bodily behavior and mental operations. No consensus on mind-body relations exists today. The same difficulty, it is worth noting, affects various efforts to use similarities in brain structure and function as evidence for similarities in thought.

Even if such matters could be resolved, a greater conceptual hurdle would remain: What is the connection between language and thought? Language requires combining terms into well-formed sentences using rules of grammar and meaning. Linguistic mastery includes the capacity to create novel sentences in situations not precisely like those already encountered and the resources to express thoughts in different modalities (as descriptions, questions, commands, and so on) (48). It also seems to require recognition that something said is true, false, or uncertain (17,24).

Although no one knows whether other primates will ever approach human beings in linguistic performance, it would be a mistake to focus on that issue. Evidence is mounting that animals can recognize visual patterns, remember where their food is located, learn how to perform nonmechanical tasks, and foresee where a moving prey will eventually be positioned, even if they cannot master a language (26,50). In this sense, animals exhibit intelligence as defined by ability to adapt to environmental conditions. From a Darwinian (evolutionary) perspective, humans do not hold a privileged status over animals. Humans are not more highly evolved than other animals; all have evolved to fill their respective niches.

Neither linguistic nor nonlinguistic findings hold all the answers. The moral issue is not simply whether animals have some and lack other abilities that human beings possess, but whether the differences between them make for differences in how humans and animals should be treated. Sometimes the differences matter, common sense might say, and sometimes they do not.

THE ETHICAL QUESTIONS

How, if at all, should animals be used in research, testing, and education? Before this can be answered, a preliminary question must be asked (14,15,44,47): What moral standing does an animal have? Is it the kind of being to which humans could possibly have moral duties and obligations? Taking one side or another on the question need not include any particular moral judgment. Whatever its resolution, the separable moral issue remains: What constraints, if any, regulate humans' use of animals? These constraints might be weaker if animals lack moral standing, but not necessarily absent altogether.

Moral Standing

Modern moral theory operates under a "law conception" of ethics (3). It judges particular human actions as right (lawful) or wrong (unlawful) as they comply with or violate some universal principle of conduct. In this, it departs from the classical theory of the virtues, which makes individual character the unit of evaluation and does not attempt to reduce ethics to a system of rules. Under the law conception, moral standing also goes to persons, but it is not conferred by an individual, institution, or community. From this point of view, an individual counts as a person because of some inherent characteristic. This is the chief reason why it is within the moral domain to speak of the natural duties and the natural rights of a person. A legal system can, of course, recognize natural duties and rights.

For obvious reasons, no one has ever argued that animals can have moral duties (40). That would require that they freely choose to act among alternatives they judge to be right or wrong—a skill as demanding as full-blown linguistic competence would be. Nevertheless, it is possible to take the view that animals have moral standing but do not have rights.

There are two broad theoretical approaches to the subject of rights. The first, sometimes called the *will theory*, would discourage efforts to attribute rights to animals. In its classical form, as given by Emmanuel Kant, it would define a right as a capacity to obligate others to a duty. Possession of a right carries with it an authorization to use coercion to enforce the correlative duty (31). This, in turn, implies that the right-holder's capacity is a power of discretion, either to enforce or waive the right. A right is therefore something that a right-holder may choose to exercise or not. The choice itself will be an act of will.

H.L.A. Hart, a leading contemporary defender of the will theory, treats a right as a choice that gives the right-holder authority to control the actions of someone else. The possessor of a moral right has a moral justification for limiting the freedom of another, not because the action the right-holder is entitled to require has some moral quality, but simply because in the circumstances a certain distribution of human freedom will be maintained if the right-holder has the choice to determine how that other shall act (28).

The will theory helps to avoid confusion between claims of right, and other, separable requirements to promote or secure some valued state of affairs (e.g., to assist someone in need). Since animals could not be said to have waived or exercised the rights they had, all references to animal rights could simply be translated into talk of human duties.

Those who would assign rights to animals have embraced the alternative *interest theory* of what it means to have a right. A right, in their view, is a claim to the performance of a duty by someone else, but the right-holder need not be in a position or possess the competence to make this claim by an act of will. It is enough that the right-holder has interests that can be represented (by others) in a normative forum (20). These interests will include things that are intrinsically good and things in which the right-holder "takes an interest," selfish or not (40). To have a right, then, will be simply to have interests that can be affected by someone else.

The interest theory surfaces in Peter Singer's *Animal Liberation,* among the first contemporary theoretical statements of the case for animals. In that work, Singer uses the term "right" to describe any claim that individuals may make to have their interests equally considered with those of others. It implies, therefore, nothing more than a capacity for suffering, which both humans and animals possess (45).

The modest measure of animal awareness that such a test demands has been one source of its appeal. It has not, however, been free of controversy. Some have objected that animals cannot have interests because interests require beliefs and animals cannot have beliefs in the strict sense (24, 36). This criticism suggests that pain-avoidance is not an "interest" because it is not a "belief," a distinction that seems more semantical than useful. Nevertheless, a more serious charge remains. As stated, the interest theory shows only that having interests is a necessary condition for having rights, not that it is sufficient. Singer himself has since abandoned the attempt to show sufficiency and, accordingly, recanted his earlier references to the language of rights (46):

> I could easily have dispensed with it altogether. I think that the only right I ever attribute to animals is the "right" to equal consideration of interests, and anything that is expressed by talking of such a right could equally be expressed by the assertion that animals' interests ought to be given equal consideration with the interests of humans.

Singer effectively acknowledges Hart's charge that the notion of a right has lost its distinctive function in this context because it no longer refers to the discretionary control that one individual has over the conduct of another.

There is one very general consideration that appears to weigh against the will theory, if not entirely in favor of the interest theory. It underlies a form of argument so ubiquitous in the animal-rights literature that it deserves a name. The *consistency argument* is exemplified in the following passage from an essay on vegetarianism by Tom Regan. Rejecting rationality, freedom of choice, and self-consciousness as conditions for having a right to life, Regan adds (41):

> It is reasonably clear that not all human beings satisfy them. The severely mentally feeble, for example, fail to satisfy them. Accordingly, *if* we want to insist that they have a right to life, then we cannot also maintain that they have it because they satisfy one or another of these conditions. Thus, *if* we want to insist that they have an equal right to life, despite their failure to satisfy these conditions, we cannot consistently maintain that animals, because they fail to satisfy these conditions, therefore lack this right.
>
> Another possible ground is that of sentience, by which I understand the capacity to experience pleasure and pain. But this view, too, must encounter a familiar difficulty—namely, that it could not justify restricting the right *only* to human beings.

In short, given that some human beings (infants, mental defectives, and senile adults) lack such capacity as well, Regan points to the inconsistency of holding both that this capacity is a condition of having a right *and* that *all* humans and *only* humans have moral rights. Any less burdensome test, however, will presumably admit animals as possible right-holders (33,45). (For an opposing perspective, see refs. 22 and 24.)

This reasoning appears to overlook a significant difference between an incompetent human being and an animal. In most cases, human beings have the capacity for rationality, freedom of choice, and self-consciousness, whereas in all cases animals do not. If most humans have these characteristics, it might be appropriate (or at least convenient) to treat humans as a homogenous group, even though some members lack these characteristics. If all animals lack certain characteristics, it may be similarly appropriate to treat them as a group, regardless of whether some humans also lack these characteristics.

Furthermore, if rights do not imply *present* possession of the qualifying condition (as suggested by the way that people treat those who are mentally incapacitated only for a time), then babies who have yet to mature and people who have become incapacitated after a period of competence will still have rights. The animal, as far as can be ascertained, has never met and will never meet this qualification. The rare human being whose deficiency is complete over a lifespan is nevertheless differently situated from the animal. The condition is a *dis*ability—the loss of some skill the person would normally be expected to have. The animal's condition is not disabling, even though it lacks the same skill. The very fact that the human has been deprived of an ability implies that the person has been harmed; a human's failure to acquire an ability means that person is in need of help. The condition of the animal does not call for either inference. This difference, to be sure, makes no mention of rights. Yet it creates a special duty to meet the human need that would not extend to animals. Because the animal without a will has not lost what it was biologically programmed to possess, it "needs" a will only as a human might "need" to fly. In neither case does the condition give rise to a moral demand for assistance.

Ironically, the consistency argument contains a basic inconsistency. On the one hand, the argument asserts that humans are not superior to animals; animals should therefore be treated like humans. On the other hand, the very nature of the moral argument is promotion of morally superior behavior: Humans should refuse to exploit other species, even though the other species exploit each other.

The consistency argument nevertheless succeeds to the extent that it shows that the *general* reason for moral concern in the cases discussed cannot be limited to humans. Other things being equal, the fact that a condition is harmful or threatens harm to an individual—human or animal—creates a moral reason to intervene. That reason need not take the form of a duty owed to the victim, with a correlative right that this would entail. It need not always be a duty of any sort. The highest approval is often reserved for the good deed that, like the good samaritan's, goes beyond what duty strictly requires.

There is a spectrum of possible positions, beginning at one end with a strict prohibition against the cruel infliction of suffering, moving to a still powerful requirement to lend help when the individual alone is in a position to provide it for someone in great need, and then to the milder requirements of charity and generosity when the individual can provide them without great personal sacrifice (even if others can do the same), and finally, at the other extreme, to the highly praised but not binding act of genuine self-sacrifice that distinguishes the moral saint. The moral vernacular covers this spectrum with a single term. The act in question is called the "humane" thing to do, and sometimes failure to perform it is labeled inhumane.

The term itself refers to the actor, not the recipient. Humane treatment, following the Oxford English Dictionary, is "characterized by such behavior or disposition toward others as befits a man." This meaning, which dates back to the 18th century, applies to conduct marked by empathy with and consideration for the needs and distresses of others, which can include both human beings and animals.

This does not mean that animals will generally command the same degree of affection and attention as humans. The attitude of empathy, which is the psychological spring for humane treatment, consists in "feeling like" the object of sympathy, and the basis for this response must be a certain understanding of what it is like to be in the other's position. Other human beings are much more accessible in this respect, not only because they are structurally and functionally like each other, but because they can communicate their feelings in ways that animals can scarcely approach. In such areas as the capacity for experiencing pain, however, the differences across species are by no means so great as to make empathetic identification impossible. Here the mark of the humane individual will be the extent to which sympathy jumps the barrier between species (11).

There are differences among animals, too, in the capacities they have, the things they do, and the relations they have with humans, all of which affect the moral weight that humane considerations will have. A gorilla will gather more sympathy than a trout, not so much because it is more intelligent as because it exhibits a range of needs and emotional responses to those needs that is missing altogether in the trout, in which evidence of pain can barely be detected. Predatory animals and wild rodents rarely elicit affection because their characteristic activities do not mark them as helpless and in need. Even within one species, the regard an animal may receive will rise with the social ties and responsibilities that human beings have developed with it. As a possible recipient of humane treatment, the garden-pest rabbit will stand to the pet rabbit much as the stranger does to an acquaintance.

Each of the morally significant differences among animal recipients of humane treatment builds on an analogy to the human case. Thus, whatever the merits of the consistency argument on the score of rights, it applies here because the humane treatment principle crosses the species border. Mary Midgeley has put the point eloquently in another context (33):

> [Animals] can be in terrible need, and they can be brought into that need by human action. When they are, it is not obvious why the absence of close kinship, acquaintance or the admiration which is due to human rationality should entirely cancel the claim. Nor do we behave as if they obviously did so. Someone who sees an injured dog lying writhing in the road after being hit by a car may well think, not just that he will do something about it, but that he ought to. If he has hit it himself, the grounds for this will seem stronger. It is not obvious that his reasons for thinking like this are of a different kind from those that would arise if (like the Samaritan) he saw an injured hu-

man being. And he too may feel about equally justified in both cases in being late for his uncle's party.

Humane treatment is the most commonly cited standard in Federal legislation concerning animals. Its wide range of application due to its lack of precision, however, leads to a temptation to dismiss it as a pious but essentially vacuous sentiment. A theory of moral constraints is needed to determine whether this or some other standard is sufficiently precise to serve as a guide for legislation regulating the use of animals.

Moral Constraints

A rule that allows an individual to do whatever that person wished would not be a moral rule. Morality by its very nature operates as a check on the tendency to go wherever desire leads. The constraints it imposes can be applied prospectively, contemporaneously, or retrospectively. Prospective analysis looks ahead to the possible consequences, while retrospective analysis may restrict the results it is permissible to promote (37). Before the action is taken, it can be said that the action that morally ought to be performed is the one with the best consequences. An individual succeeds in this objective to the extent that an action produces as much benefit and as little harm as possible. During the course of the action, conditions concerning the intention of the individual and the consent of the recipient may have to be met before a moral license to pursue the best consequences is granted. The fact that a lie will produce more benefit than the truth will not necessarily make it the right thing to do.

Moral theories divide according to the weight they give to one or the other kind of constraint. In its purest form, the prospective approach holds that an action or policy is right if it has better consequences, for everyone affected by it, than any available alternative. The language here is carefully drawn. "Better" does not mean "morally better." A good consequence is simply an outcome that someone finds desirable. If an action gives pleasure to someone, the enjoyment is a good thing; if it causes pain, the person's suffering would be a bad thing. It is not necessary to ask whether the pleasure or pain is morally fitting.

Intuition will ideally play no part in determining an outcome. One consequence will count as better than another if, after assigning positive numerical values to its good elements and negative values to its bad ones, the sum of positive values exceeds that of negative values (10).

Better for whom? The utilitarian principle, still the most influential formulation of the forward-looking approach, holds that actions and policies are to be evaluated by their effects, for good or ill, on everyone, not just the individual alone or some select group of individuals. Between an individual's own good and the good of others, "utilitarianism requires him to be as strictly impartial as a disinterested and benevolent spectator" (10,34). The interests of each affected individual are to count equally. Any two experiences that are alike except that they occur in different individuals are to be given the same value. Among utilitarians, enjoyment is a good and suffering an evil, and so every animal with the capacity for such experiences will also count as one individual. Sentience suffices for possessing this value, even if it does not confer rights. "The question," as Bentham once put it, "is not, Can they reason? nor Can they talk?, but Can they suffer?"(10).

Because it extends the scope of moral concern to animals without committing itself to a vulnerable theory of animal rights, utilitarianism has become the theory of choice among those who would press for more constraints on humans' treatment of animals. Singer derives the credo that all animals are equal from the utilitarian conception of equality (45). If the principle of utility requires that suffering be minimized, and if some kinds of suffering are found in animals as well as humans, then to count human suffering while ignoring animal suffering would violate the canon of equality. It would make a simple difference of location—in one species rather than another—the basis for a distinction in value. Like racism, such "speciesism" enshrines an arbitrary preference for interests simply because of their location in some set of individuals (45). (For arguments that speciesism is not immoral, see refs. 16,23,51,52.)

As a general moral principle, utilitarianism is subject to several objections, the most serious being that its standard of equality is much too weak to satisfy the demands of justice (25,37,39). Since it only requires that individuals with interests be given the same consideration, but in its summation of interests allows the claims of any one individual to be overridden by the sheer weight of numbers on the other side, it seems to sanction a tyranny of the majority that permits violations of individual rights. This may not, however, undermine the utilitarian case for animals if animals have doubtful standing as right-holders.

Some commentators have suggested that there may be an acceptable double standard in morals, consisting of a nonutilitarian principle for agents with standing as persons and a utilitarian rule for handling individuals with interests but not rights (21,37). The use of different rules for different kinds of individuals is already well established. Rules that would be objectionably paternalistic if applied to adults are admissible if restricted to children. The dangers are that inconsistent standards might hold for the same individual or that differences between the two classes of individuals might be arbitrary.

The suggestion that the adult-child and human-animal distinctions are comparably rational and justifiable (21) is superficial for two reasons. First, it does not seem to be arbitrary to distinguish between the adult and the child, because human society understands that children may be intellectually and experientially unable to make wise choices. Thus, society can choose for children that which society believes is in their best interests. The problem with the human-animal distinction is that an animal may in fact be able to make and communicate a decision that expresses the animal's self-interest: It wants no part of any scientific procedure that results in pain or distress. Even if the animal could not make or communicate a decision, it may be arbitrary to distinguish between such animals and humans who are similar in their inability to make such decisions (the profoundly mentally handicapped), allowing society to use the former but not the latter as research subjects.

The second difference between the adult-child and human-animal distinctions relates to the *purpose* for distinguishing between two groups. The first distinction is permissible because it allows society to *protect* the interests of the child, while the purpose of the human-animal distinction is to allow society to *ignore*, or at least *diminish*, the interests of the animal.

The device of a double standard is often used to explain the sharp differences in the constraints governing the treatment of animals and humans as experimental subjects. For animals the standard is humane treatment, which forbids unnecessary suffering but otherwise allows experiments that harm and even kill the animal. That same rule, proposed for human subjects, is generally considered unethical. There are many experiments in which perfectly reliable results can only be obtained by doing to a human what is now done to an animal. Nevertheless, without the subject's informed consent—indeed, sometimes even with it—such experiments are absolutely impermissible, no matter how beneficial the consequence might be. They would violate the rights of the human subject.

The proscription against unnecessary suffering is best understood as a corollary of the principle of utility. Since suffering is a bad consequence, there is an initial utilitarian onus against behavior that would produce it. Such treatment calls for justification. To meet this burden, a bare appeal to some offsetting good consequence will not be sufficient. The principle of utility, as formulated, is comparative. It requires that an action or policy have better consequences than any available alternative. Among the alternatives will be uses that do not involve animal suffering. If one of them has consequences at least as good as or better than the one proposed, the suffering will be unnecessary. Other things being equal, then, it should prove harder to establish necessity than the contrary, since the former must rule out all the alternatives while the latter need find only one.

Necessity is a relation between a means (an action or policy) and an end (its objective). *Restricted necessity* takes the end as given—that is, not subject to evaluation—and asks only whether the course of action suggested is an indispensable means to that end. For example, in an LD_{50} test for toxicity that uses 40 rats as subjects (see chs. 7 and 8), if no alternative procedure using fewer or no rats could get the same results with the same reliability, that test would be necessary in the restricted sense. In *unrestricted* necessity, the end is open to assessment on utilitarian grounds:

- How likely is the objective to be met, in comparison with other possible goals? If the LD_{50} test yields unreliable results, its necessity in the unrestricted sense would be open to challenge.
- Assuming that the objective will be met, how beneficial will it be? Suppose, for instance, that an LD_{50} test were to be run on a new cosmetic not significantly different from those already on the market. The test may be considered unnecessary because the objective is unnecessary.

Unrestricted necessity is more difficult to prove, because it always includes restricted necessity and more. Thus, a stringent standard of necessity, one that lets fewer procedures through, would require that a procedure be necessary in the unrestricted sense. In addition, since necessity is more difficult to establish than the possibility of substitution, the burden of proving both the existence of necessity and the absence of alternatives could be placed on those who would use the procedure. A more lenient test could invert these priorities by presuming that the procedure is necessary and that alternatives are lacking unless shown otherwise. This approach would not expect the user to show beforehand that no other alternative was available; it is generally followed when a research proposal is reviewed by a scientist's peers or an institutional animal care and use committee (27).

Nonutilitarian positions on the use of animals have one feature in common: Although virtually none ignores consequences, they unite in denying that a course of action can be justified wholly by appeal to the value of its consequences (39). This leaves room for substantial variation, with the differences traceable to the considerations they would add in order to complete a moral assessment.

Ironically, both extremes in the animal treatment debate are nonutilitarian. The hard line supporting unlimited exploitation of animals builds from the premise that animals lack moral standing. Without rights, they cannot be recipients of a duty owed to them. On some theories of value, moreover, enjoyment does not count as a good thing in itself, nor is suffering per se an evil. Kant, for example, thought that the only unconditional good was a will whose choices are undetermined by desire for enjoyment or fear of punishment (31). Not having a will, animals could not have this value. Morally, they were indistinguishable from inanimate tools—mere means to be used for the purposes of beings who do have a will. Like Aquinas, however, Kant did acknowledge an *indirect duty* of kindness, given that "tender feelings toward dumb animals develop humane feelings toward mankind" (32).

The indirect duty theory stumbles in the attempt to explain why there should be any empirical connection at all between people's feelings for animals and their feelings for other humans. Some similarity must be seen in the objects of the two sentiments if one is to influence the other; yet the theory says that there is no such likeness in reality. Thus either a person's motive is proof by itself that humans have a direct moral interest in animals, in which case the theory is mistaken; or the theory is correct and the individual has misunderstood it, in which case the person will be free, once educated in the theory, to abuse animals without fear that this will tempt abuse of human beings. Kant cannot have it both ways: He cannot require individuals to act on a belief that his own theory alleges to be false (33).

The Kantian position could be turned on its head if animals had moral standing after all. In *The Case for Animal Rights,* Regan gives the most cogent defense to date for that view. He concedes that animals are not moral agents: Since they are unable to choose freely among impartially determined moral alternatives, they cannot have any moral duties. At least some animals, however, have beliefs, desires, memory, a sense of the future, preferences, an identity over time, and an individual welfare of their own (41). In these respects, they are indistinguishable from human infants and mental defectives, who also fail to qualify as moral agents. Nevertheless, these animals possess an inherent value, independent of the value that their experiences may have, that gives them standing as "moral patients" — that is, as individuals on the receiving end of the right and wrong actions of moral agents. They have this value equally, and equally with moral agents (40). Inherent value in turn gives them a claim, or right, to certain treatment.

Regan's major thesis is that, as moral patients, animals enjoy a presumptive right not to be harmed. He considers this principle a radical alternative to utilitarianism. But once the reference to rights is filtered out, the utilitarian might find Regan's theory quite congenial. Both Regan and utilitarians would hold that harm to animals is a bad consequence and so it would be wrong, in the absence of an overriding consideration, to harm them. The conflict between the two theories, therefore, lies in the kind of justification that each theory would permit to overturn this presumption.

Regan offers two guiding principles (40). By the first, when the choice is between harm to a few and harm to many and when each affected individual would be harmed in a comparable way, then the rights of the few ought to be overridden. As Regan acknowledges, the utilitarian commitment to minimize suffering would have the same result. By the second principle, when the choice is between harm to a few and harm to many, if a member of the affected few would be worse off than any member of the affected many, the rights of the many ought to be overridden. This "worse-off" rule parts company with utilitarianism in setting aggregate consequences aside and protecting minority interests.

In view of this possibility, it is surprising to find that Regan calls for a blanket prohibition against the use of animals in research and toxicity testing. That conclusion would follow only if his two rules for defeating the right not to be harmed could never be successfully invoked in these areas. Regan is apparently drawn to this result by a constraint he attaches to the rules: They hold only for harms suffered by innocent victims. Animals are always innocent, in the sense that Regan gives to that term (41). But human patients will be, too, and at least sometimes human agents will also be. Regan would have to show that these occasions can never arise in research, testing, or education, or that, if they do, the human agent/patient never faces the greater harm. His analysis does not show this.

This difficulty aside, Regan's theory can be read as holding, first, that the necessity standard cannot be applied until the innocence of all parties has been established and, second, that when it does apply, the worse-off rule should replace the utility principle in cases where they diverge.

It is unclear whether the worse-off rule is preferable to the utilitarian principle for the purposes of animal use. But the notion of innocence, with its judicial implications, appears to have no place in the issue of experimental-subject rights for three reasons. First, the notion that animals are always innocent because they cannot be otherwise is problematic. Innocence makes sense only when guilt does, because innocence means that one has done no wrong *though doing wrong was an option*. If animals are not rational decisionmakers, if they cannot choose between right and wrong, then the concept of innocence has little meaning. Second, most human subjects are probably innocent in the sense that Regan uses the term, so that the concept does little to advance the theory that experimenting on humans is preferable to experimenting on animals. Finally, even a guilty person may have certain rights. While a person guilty of a crime against society may be imprisoned or otherwise punished, society holds that the guilty have a right to avoid cruel and inhumane punishments. Bioethics similarly rejects the involuntary use of guilty prisoners in medical experiments.

SUMMARY AND CONCLUSIONS

The present debate over animal use in research, testing, and education is marked by a cacophony of voices. A critical survey of the religious and philosophical backgrounds to the debate yields some hope that, if the competing voices were muted by reflection, they would begin to coalesce as variations around a single theme. That theme would be the standard of humane treatment, extended to animals as well as to humans.

Much has been made of the historical contrast between Western and Oriental religious views on animals. The biblical and theological texts in the Judeo-Christian tradition do not give us a principle of unconditional respect for animals. Humans alone are accorded inherent value as being created in the image of God, and this gives them a license to use animals for their own purposes. Not, however, to abuse them. Cruelty and callous indifference to the needs of animals find no scriptural support, and virtually all religious thinkers condemn them. If God is a good shepherd, treating humans kindly without being bound to, humans can be as much to the animals in their care. The Christian position thus amounts to a synthesis of two elements in tension. On the one hand, animals are inferior in worth to humans, as the body of a person is inferior to the soul. On the other hand, they are not so inferior that their own welfare cannot stand in the way of unbridled use of them.

Modern religious and philosophical patterns of thought are branches of the same ancestral trunk. It should not be surprising, then, that the philosophical tradition exhibits the same tension on the subject of animals. Humans have standing as persons—that is, as individuals who can assume duties and enjoy rights. To join them, animals must at least be capable of possessing rights. But they cannot assume duties and do not have the power of discretion that gives rights a distinctive role in morals. Consistency suggests rights should be ascribed to animals once rights are given to infants and mentally handicapped humans who also lack discretion. Yet it would be inconsistent to assert that humans are not superior to animals while suggesting that humans should refuse to exploit other species, even though other species exploit each other.

Even if animals are not moral persons, however, it does not follow that they are mere things, morally indistinguishable from machines. They are sufficiently like humans in one morally relevant respect—their capacity for suffering in basic forms—to generate a moral claim on humans. It would be inconsistent to hold that, other things being equal, human suffering ought to be relieved, but animal suffering ought not.

Because it extends the scope of moral concern to animals without committing itself to a vulnerable theory of animal rights, utilitarianism has become the theory of choice among those who would press for more constraints on humans' treatment of animals. If the principle of utility requires that suffering be minimized, and if some kinds of suffering are found in animals as well as humans, then to count human suffering while ignoring animal suffering would violate the canon of equality. It would make a simple difference of location—in one species rather than another—the basis for a distinction in value. Like racism, such "speciesism" enshrines an arbitrary preference for interests simply because of their location in some set of individuals.

The rule that suffering ought to be relieved, in humans or animals, is the principle of humane treatment. It covers a large and heterogeneous range of situations; the most germane, for the debate over animal use, are those in which someone inflicts suffering on someone else. The humane treatment principle establishes a presumption against doing this, but that presumption can be overcome—always in the case of animals, and sometimes even in the case of a human—by showing that the harm done is necessary. Necessity here is not bare utility, but necessity overall. The harm must not only be a means to a good end, it must be the only means. A broader definition of necessity might also require that the harm be a means to an end whose value is considered in light of the degree of harm necessary to achieve that end. In addition, necessity always implies a comparison with available alternatives.

Animal use in research, testing, and education creates a conflict of interests between the liberty that humans have to use animals for human ends (knowledge, health, safety) and the need that animals have to be free of suffering. There is no reason why either one of these broad interests should always prevail over the other. The fulcrum on which they are balanced is the necessity standard itself. That is, when the suffering inflicted on animals is not necessary to satisfy a desirable human objective, the animal interest will prevail. And when the suffering is unavoidable, the human interest will be controlling. Animals are morally entitled to be treated humanely; whether they are entitled to more than that is unclear.

Reprinted with permission from CHEMTECH 15(1):63. Copyright 1985, American Chemical Society.

CHAPTER 4 REFERENCES

1. Aquinas, T., *Summa Contra Gentiles,* tr. English Dominican Fathers (New York: Benzinger Brothers, 1928).
2. Aquinas, T., *Summa Theological,* tr. English Dominican Fathers (New York: Benzinger Brothers, 1918).
3. Ancombe, G.E.M., "Modern Moral Philosophy," *Philosophy* 33:1-19, 1958.
4. Aristotle, *De Animal,* tr. K. Foster and S. Humphries (New Haven, CT: Yale University Press, 1954).
5. Aristotle, *Politics,* tr. E. Barker (Oxford, England: The Clarendon Press, 1952).
6. Attfield, R., *The Ethics of Environmental Concern* (New York: Columbia University Press, 1983).
7. Augustine, *The Catholic and Manichean Ways of Life,* tr. D.A. Gallagher and I.J. Gallagher (Boston, MA: The Catholic University Press, 1966).
8. Augustine, *The City of God,* tr. H. Bettenson (New York: Penguin, 1972).
9. Barth, K., *Church Dogmatics,* tr. G.T. Thompson (New York: Charles Scribner's Sons, 1955).
10. Bentham, J., *Introduction to the Principles of Morals and Legislation* (New York: Columbia University Press, 1945).
11. Boyce, J.R., and Lutes, C., "Animal Rights: How Much Pain is a Cure Worth?" *Christianity Today* 29(Sept. 6):35-38, 1985.
12. Brody, B., "Morality and Religion Reconsidered," *Readings in the Philosophy of Religion,* B. Brody (ed.) (Englewood Cliffs, NJ: Prentice-Hall, 1974).
13. Calvin, J., *Sermons of M. John Calvin Upon . . . Deuteronomie,* tr. A. Golding (1583).
14. Caplan, A.L., "Beastly Conduct: Ethical Issues in Animal Experimentation," *Ann. N.Y. Acad. Sci.* 406:159-169, 1983.
15. Caplan, A.L., "Animal Husbandry and Moral Duty," presentation at Second CFN Symposium, *The Ethics of Animal Experimentation,* Stockholm, Sweden, Aug. 12-14, 1985.
16. Cigman, R., "Death, Misfortune, and Species Inequality," *Phil. Public Affairs* 10:47-64, 1981.
17. Davidson, D., "Thought and Talk," *Mind and Language,* S. Gutterplan (ed.) (New York: Oxford University Press, 1975).
18. Descartes, R., "Principles of Philosophy," *Descartes: Philosophical Writings,* E. Anscombe and P.T. Geach (eds.) (London: Nelson, 1969).
19. Descartes, R., "Discourse of Method," *Descartes: Philosophical Writings,* E.Anscombe and P.T. Geach (eds.) (London: Nelson, 1969).
20. Feinberg, J., "The Rights of Animals and Unborn Generations," *Rights, Justice, and the Bounds of Liberty,* J. Feinberg (ed.) (Princeton, NJ: Princeton University Press, 1980).
21. Flemming, A.H., "Ethical Considerations," contract

report prepared for the Office of Technology Assessment, U.S. Congress, 1984.

22. Fox, M.A., *The Case for Animal Experimentation: An Evolutionary and Ethical Perspective* (Berkeley, CA: University of California Press, 1985).
23. Francis, L.P., and Norman, R., "Some Animals Are More Equal Than Others," *Philosophy* 53:507-527, 1978.
24. Frey, R.G., *Interests and Rights: The Case Against Animals* (Oxford, England: Clarendon Press, 1980).
25. Gewirth, A., *Reason and Morality* (Chicago: University of Chicago Press, 1978).
26. Griffin, D.R., *Animal Thinking* (Cambridge, MA: Harvard University Press, 1984).
27. Halvorsyn, H.O., "Ethics of Animal Research: Philosophy and Practice," *Am. Soc. Microbiol. News* 51(8):375-377, 1985.
28. Hart, H.L.A., "Are There Any Natural Rights?" *Rights,* D. Lyons (ed.) (Belmont, CA: Wadsworth, 1980).
29. Hume, D., *An Enquiry Concerning Human Understanding* (Indianapolis, IN: Hackett Publishing Company, 1977).
30. Hume, D., *A Treatise of Human Nature,* L.A. Selby-Bigge (ed.) (Oxford, England: Clarendon Press, 1967).
31. Kant, E., *Foundations of Metaphysics of Morals,* tr. L.W. Beck (Indianapolis, IN: Bobbs-Merrill, 1969).
32. Kant, E., *Lectures on Ethics,* tr. L. Infield (New York: Harper and Row, 1941).
33. Midgeley, M., *Animals and Why They Matter* (Athens, GA: University of Georgia Press, 1983).
34. Mill, J.S., *Utilitarianism, Liberty, Representative Government* (New York: Dutton, 1910).
35. Miller, N.E., "The Value of Behavioral Research in Animals," *Am. Psychologist* 40(4):423-440, 1985.
36. McCloskey, H.J., "Rights," *Phil. Quart.* 15:113-127, 1965.
37. Nozick, R., *Anarchy, State, and Utopia* (New York: Basic Books, 1974).
38. Passmore, J., *Man's Responsibility for Nature* (New York: Charles Scribner's Sons, 1974).
39. Rawls, J., *A Theory of Justice* (Cambridge, MA: Harvard University Press, 1971).
40. Regan, T., *The Case for Animal Rights* (Berkeley, CA: University of California Press, 1983).
41. Regan, T., "The Moral Basis of Vegetarianism," *All That Dwell Within,* T. Regan (ed.) (Berkeley, CA: University of California Press, 1982).
42. Rickaby, J., *Moral Philosophy* (London: Longmans, 1905).
43. Rollin, B.E., *Animal Rights and Human Morality* (Buffalo, NY: Prometheus Books, 1981).
44. Rowan, A.N., *Of Mice, Models & Men: A Critical Evaluation of Animal Research* (Albany, NY: State University of New York Press, 1984).
45. Singer, P., *Animal Liberation* (New York: Avon Books, 1975).
46. Singer, P., "The Parable of the Fox and the Unliberated Animals," *Ethics* 88:122, 1978.
47. Tannenbaum, J., and Rowan, A.N., "Rethinking the Morality of Animal Research," *Hastings Center Report* 15(5):32-43, 1985.
48. Terrace, H.S., *Nim: A Chimpanzee Who Learned Sign Language* (New York: Random House, 1979).
49. Thomas, K., *Man and the Natural World* (New York: Pantheon Books, 1983).
50. Walker, S., *Animal Thought* (London: Routledge & Kegan Paul, 1983).
51. Watson, R.A., "Self-Consciousness and the Rights of Nonhuman Animals and Nature," *Environ. Ethics* 1:99-129, 1979.
52. Williams, M., "Rights, Interest, and Moral Equality," *Environ. Ethics* 2:149-161, 1980.

Chapter 5

The Use of Animals in Research

I know that half of what I teach as fact," said a wise medical pedagogue, "will be proved false in 10 years. The hard part is that I don't know which half." His statistics may not be exact, but the notion is right enough. No one knows which half, and it is impossible to know except in retrospect.

That is what research is—the reason for the prefix. The half that is wrong is at least as important as the half that is right, because the new questions come in ferreting out the errors—and new answers too.

Kenneth L. Brigham
Vanderbilt University School of Medicine
N. Engl. J. Med. 312:794, 1985

CONTENTS

List of Tables

Figure

Chapter 5
The Use of Animals in Research

Research, as the word denotes, is an ongoing search—a search for new information and for novel ways to apply existing information. Research assumes a multitude of directions in a wide variety of disciplines. It is not surprising, then, that the use of animals in research—and the potential for alternatives to using them—mirrors the multifaceted nature of research itself.

Viewed broadly, almost any research investigation involving members of the animal kingdom, including humans, and sometimes even members of the plant kingdom, can be categorized as biomedical research. In this sense, biomedical research covers a long list of disciplines: anatomy, anesthesiology, behavioral biology, biochemistry, biomedical engineering, biophysics, cardiology, cell biology, dentistry, developmental biology, endocrinology, entomology, epidemiology, genetics, gerontology, histology, immunology, metabolism, microbiology, molecular biology, neurology, nutrition, oncology, parasitology, pathology, pharmacology, physiology, psychology, radiology, reproductive biology, surgery, teratology, toxicology, veterinary science, virology, and zoology.

When considering animal use—and alternatives to animal use—in research, it is useful to isolate behavioral research from the broader category of biomedical research. Behavioral research is a part of biomedical research, yet is distinguished from the larger topic by the nature of the experiments, the identity of the researchers, and the kinds of alternatives available (see ch. 6).

This chapter defines and describes animal use in biomedical and behavioral research. Also included are the results of a brief survey done by OTA of the use of animal and nonanimal methods in published research reports in selected disciplines of biomedical and behavioral research.

THE ROLE OF ANIMALS IN BIOMEDICAL RESEARCH

To discuss alternatives to using animals in biomedical research, it is important to review the context in which animals are presently included. A comprehensive review of this subject (see ref. 41) is beyond the scope of the present assessment. However, animals' broad role in contemporary biomedical research can be at least partly delineated by considering:

- the manifold contributions to biomedical research of a single group of animals—nonhuman primates;
- the role of experimental animals in the development of a single medical procedure, namely coronary artery bypass surgery; and
- the reasons multiple species are used in biomedical research.

These perspectives illustrate two fundamental principles of animal use in biomedical research. First, a single species or group of animals often serves a multitude of purposes in widely varying research enterprises. Second, a single advance in applied research often represents results generated from many species.

Nonhuman Primates in Biomedical Research

Primates—humans, monkeys, and apes—share a common genetic basis and anatomical, physiological, biochemical, and behavioral traits that provide unique research opportunities. As a consequence, humans and other primates are susceptible to many of the same diseases and have many of the same disease-fighting capabilities. Reviewing the use of nonhuman primates is also appropriate because they are relatively expensive research animals (e.g., a rhesus monkey costs from $600 to $2,000) and the object of much public interest. Two recent reports describe the role of primates in biomedical research (29,45). Those

38-750 O - 86 - 4

reports are summarized in table 5-1; highlights of the studies follow.

Polio

The development of the polio vaccine exemplifies the key role of primates in the research laboratory. Many thorough studies of polio in humans had been made by the early 1900s, but the cause of the disease was still unknown. A breakthrough occurred in 1908, when scientists experimentally transmitted the poliovirus to monkeys for the first time. Studies in rhesus and cynomolgus monkeys and in chimpanzees followed isolation of the virus, but a vaccine remained elusive. After nearly a half-century, researchers were able

Table 5-1.—Some Uses of Nonhuman Primates in Research on Human Health and Disease

Human health concern	Primate experimental model
Acquired immune deficiency syndrome (AIDS)	Chimpanzee, African green monkey
Atherosclerosis	Cynomolgus monkey
Balding	Stumptail monkey
Cancer from solid tumors	Chimpanzee
Cholesterol gallstones	Squirrel monkey
Circadian rhythms	Squirrel monkey
Cornea transplant	Rhesus monkey, African green monkey, Stumptail monkey, Patas monkey, Cynomolgus monkey
Dental implants	Pig-tailed monkey
Diabetes	Celebes black macaque
Dietary fats and heart disease	Cynomolgus monkey
Embryo transfer	Rhesus monkey, Cynomolgus monkey
Eye damage from ultraviolet radiation	Rhesus monkey
Eye disorders in children	Rhesus monkey
Fetal alcohol syndrome	Pig-tailed monkey
Fetal surgery	Rhesus monkey
Genital herpes	African green monkey
Gilbert's syndrome	Bolivian squirrel monkey
Glaucoma	Rhesus monkey
Hearing impairment	Rhesus monkey
Hepatitis B	Rhesus monkey, Chimpanzee, African green monkey
Herpes-virus-induced cancer	Owl monkey, Marmoset
High blood pressure	Cynomolgus monkey
Hyaline membrane disease in newborns	Rhesus monkey, Pig-tailed monkey
In vitro fertilization	Rhesus monkey, Chimpanzee, Baboon, Cynomolgus monkey
Infertility	Rhesus monkey
Inflammatory bowel disease	Marmoset
Laser surgery on damaged nerves	Baboon
Leprosy	Sooty mangabey
Liver disorders	Rhesus monkey
Malaria	Chimpanzee, Owl monkey, Rhesus monkey
Male and female behavior patterns	Rhesus monkey
Male birth control	Rhesus monkey, Cynomolgus monkey
Menopausal problems	Rhesus monkey, Stumptail monkey
Mother-infant behavior	Rhesus monkey
Motion sickness	Squirrel monkey
Nonhormonal fertility regulation	Bonnet monkey, Chimpanzee
Obesity	Baboon
Parkinson's disease	Rhesus monkey
Polio	Rhesus monkey, Cynomolgus monkey, Chimpanzee
Premature labor	Rhesus monkey, Baboon
Rh factor disease	Rhesus monkey
Slow viruses	Owl monkey, Squirrel monkey, Stumptail monkey
Systemic lupus erythematosus	Cynomolgus monkey

SOURCES: Adapted from "Toward Better Health: The Role of Primates in Medical Research," *Primate News* 21(1):1-24, 1984; and F. A. King and C. J. Yarbrough, "Medical and Behavioral Benefits From Primate Research," *Physiologist* 28:75-87, 1985.

to grow the poliovirus in human tissue culture (15), and an effective vaccine became available to the public in 1955. When the vaccine was developed, monkey kidney tissue was essential for production of pure virus in great quantities, and live monkeys were essential for safety and effectiveness testing. Today, noninfectious polio vaccine can be produced in continuously propagating cells without the need for monkeys, although monkeys are required to test for safety. The impact of the polio vaccine has been dramatic: In 1952, at the height of one epidemic, 58,000 cases of polio occurred in the United States; in 1984, just 4 cases were reported (39).

Hepatitis B

Hepatitis B is the most dangerous form of hepatitis, a debilitating liver disease characterized by fever, weakness, loss of appetite, headache, and muscle pain. There are nearly 1 million hepatitis B virus carriers in the United States today, and the infection is estimated to cost $1 million per day in this country. Worldwide, there are some 200 million carriers, primarily in Asia and Africa. Up to 1 percent of those infected with hepatitis B die of the disease, and 5 to 10 percent become chronic carriers of the virus who can remain infectious indefinitely (21). Since there is no known treatment for hepatitis B infection, prevention is essential.

Research with rhesus monkeys and chimpanzees led to the development just a few years ago of a vaccine, derived from human plasma, against hepatitis B infection. In 1981, the Food and Drug Administration (FDA) licensed this vaccine for human use. In 1984, recombinant DNA technology was used to prepare a hepatitis B vaccine from yeast cells (the first vaccine for human use so produced). Prior to its trial in 37 human volunteers, this yeast recombinant hepatitis B vaccine was administered to African green monkeys in order to gauge its effectiveness (52). These new vaccines are expected to have a worldwide impact on the disease, and they may also reduce the incidence of hepatocellular carcinoma, a form of liver cancer associated with chronic hepatitis B infection (40).

Herpes

Estimates of the number of persons afflicted with recurrent genital herpes virus infections range from 5 million to 20 million worldwide (61). A new antiviral drug, acyclovir, was recently licensed for use against human genital herpes infections and appears to yield antiviral and clinical benefits when taken orally (48). Acyclovir was extensively tested in African green monkeys. The opportunity to run such tests arose because of a natural outbreak of a virus closely related to that causing both chickenpox and shingles (i.e., herpes zoster) in humans. The infected monkey colony at the Delta Regional Primate Research Center in Louisiana enabled scientists to study the herpes disease process and test antiviral drugs. In 1984, researchers reported an in vitro model system for studying the herpes simplex virus, using human fetal nerve cells as the host. This in vitro model is expected to enable analysis of the state of the herpes virus as it establishes and remains latent in human nerve cells (62).

High Blood Pressure

High blood pressure, when untreated, increases the risk of stroke, heart disease, and kidney failure. In most cases, the cause or causes of high blood pressure remain unknown, and the condition is a public health problem of immense proportions. Data from the early 1980s indicate that fully one-third of Americans use medication to control blood pressure. From 1971 to 1981, visits to physicians for diagnosis and therapy of high blood pressure increased by 55 percent, while visits for all other causes decreased by approximately 5 percent (32).

Monkeys are used to examine mechanisms of high blood pressure because the natural hormone molecules controlling blood pressure (e.g., the kidney hormone renin) are identical in humans and other primates. In contrast, the renin molecules of humans and nonprimate species are dissimilar. In addition to using monkeys to study the effects of diet and drugs on high blood pressure, researchers are examining the genetic transmission of high blood pressure. One breeding colony of cynomolgus monkeys exhibiting high blood pressure has been monitored for 5 years; this permits the study of high blood pressure in parents, offspring, and future generations to analyze the tendency to inherit the condition.

Parkinson's Disease

Parkinson's disease is a neurological disorder of older adults characterized by palsy and rigid muscles. Progress in understanding the cause and development of the disease and in refining methods of long-term drug therapy has been hampered by lack of an adequate animal model. Attempts to induce the disease in rats, guinea pigs, and cats either have failed to produce all the symptoms or have yielded symptoms that do not last long and so cannot be effectively researched.

In 1983, the first animal model of Parkinson's disease was developed. Scientists at the National Institute of Mental Health (NIMH) induced a form of parkinsonism in eight rhesus monkeys by giving them a drug, 1-methyl-4-phenyl-1,2,3,6-tetrahydropyridine (MPTP), that selectively destroys specific cells in the substantia nigra, a region of the brain destroyed in humans by Parkinson's disease. The monkeys exhibited all the major clinical features of Parkinson's disease in humans. They also responded dramatically to L-dopa, the standard medication for people with this disease (8). NIMH researchers have speculated that the availability of this new animal model may lead to understanding the reason Parkinson's disease occurs in older adults, the course of the disease, and drug therapy and its side effects (30).

In 1984, squirrel monkeys were used to shed further light on the mechanism of MPTP-induced parkinsonism. Pargyline, a drug currently prescribed for high blood pressure in humans (Eutonyl, Abbott Laboratories, North Chicago, IL), was used to prevent the neurotoxic effects of MPTP (31). These results in squirrel monkeys suggested that MPTP itself may not be the actual neurotoxic agent. Instead, attention is now focused on an MPTP metabolite and on the mechanism of MPTP metabolism in the brain (33).

Baldness

Like many men, stumptail monkeys become bald as they age. This trait has made the stumptail monkey the animal of choice in baldness research. Although it is not life-threatening, baldness is a matter of concern for many people: Hair-combing patterns suggest that many men desire to have hair where there is none, and advertisements for hair restoration abound in the popular media. The public spends large sums on hair-restoration nostrums, and in 1985 the FDA proposed banning the sale of all nonprescription drug products sold to prevent or reverse baldness, having concluded there is no scientific evidence that such lotions and creams are effective (50 FR 2191).

A drug originally developed to manage high blood pressure, minoxidil, has the unexpected side effect of causing thick hair growth from follicles that normally produce only fine, downy hair. To test the potential of minoxidil for hair growth, researchers applied it externally to the bald front scalp of stumptail monkeys. The results with monkeys showed promise, and clinical trials are now in progress with bald men across the United States. Monkey studies are continuing to assess the effects and safety of minoxidil as a means of counteracting hair loss.

Menopausal Hot Flashes

Of the 30 million postmenopausal women in the United States, as many as 75 percent have experienced or will experience hot flashes brought on by increased blood flow to the skin. Hot flashes produce a feeling of warmth for several minutes, and they are often followed by sweating. These physical symptoms may be accompanied by nervousness, irritability, and depression. At present, physicians can treat the symptoms of menopause, but the causes of the symptoms remain unknown. Research into the mechanisms of menopause and the development of therapy for menopausal problems has been hampered by the difficulty of studying this condition in animals. This difficulty stems from three facts: Only primates, and no other nonhuman species, have menstrual cycles; monkeys do not exhibit symptoms of menopause until at least age 25; and monkeys brought into the laboratory from the wild are rarely of menopausal age.

Throughout the last decade, researchers have studied the menstrual cycle and its cessation in

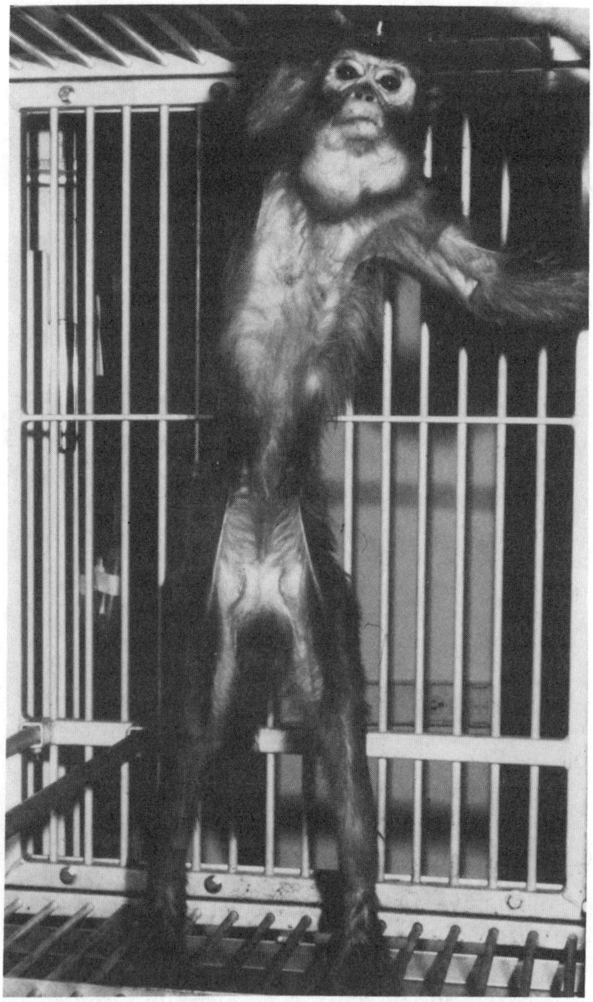

Left: Bent, flexed posture and absence of movement exhibited by a rhesus monkey treated with the drug MPTP to induce Parkinson's disease. Other symptoms in both monkeys and humans include tremor, eyelid closure, difficulty swallowing (drooling), and difficulty with vocalization and speech.

Right: Reversal of abnormal posture and return of normal movement following treatment with L-dopa. The *right* photograph was taken 2 hours after the *left* one.

Photo credit: R. Stanley Burns, National Institute of Mental Health

First animal model of Parkinson's disease, developed in 1983

a limited number of rhesus monkeys reaching 25 to 30 years of age (11). In 1984, hot flashes were described in another primate, the stumptail monkey (25). The aim of developing an animal model for hot flashes is to determine the role of the brain and of hormones in the control of this problem. Once the underlying mechanisms that produce hot flashes are better understood, more effective treatments may be developed for women who suffer from menopausal problems.

Experimental Animals' Contribution to Coronary Artery Bypass Graft Surgery

A second way to describe the role of animals in biomedical research is to review the ways in which a single advance in applied biomedical research came about. As an illustration of this process, the development of the coronary artery bypass graft operation, recently recounted (9,46), is summarized here.

Coronary or arteriosclerotic heart disease, often caused by a narrowing or blocking of the arteries supplying blood to the heart, is the number one cause of death in the United States. In 1982, it was responsible for approximately 500,000 deaths (59). Coronary artery bypass graft surgery was introduced in the early 1970s. In this procedure, which has become the primary surgical approach to treatment of coronary artery disease, a grafted vessel is attached to the coronary artery to circumvent the constricted portion. The graft improves the blood and oxygen supply to the heart muscle. The growth of the procedure has been quite rapid: Approximately 70,000 operations were performed in 1977; 160,000 in 1981 (7); and 191,000 in 1983 (38).

Coronary artery bypass graft surgery is now the most commonly performed major operation in the United States (7). It is accepted as far more effective than medication in relieving the severe chest pain, or angina pectoris, associated with coronary heart disease (47). The long-term benefit of this procedure, in terms of mortality, varies among patient groups (60).

The experimental steps leading to the successful coronary artery bypass graft operation are depicted in figure 5-1, in which the cardiac surgeon stands at the summit of Mt. Coronary Artery Bypass. In the early stages of research—that is, in the foothills of the mountain—there was a great deal of variability in the kinds of animals required. Studies in frogs, reptiles, horses, cats, dogs, sheep, and deer contributed to scientists' understanding of the fundamental principles of circulation, blood pressure, and temperature regulation. As problems became more specialized, the choices of animal species became more restricted. Dogs, chimpanzees, and, ultimately, humans contributed to the later stages of research leading to the coronary artery bypass. Virtually every step up Mt. Coronary Artery Bypass required initial stages of study on living animal models of various species.

Today, in retrospect, the experimental steps leading to this surgical procedure appear as a simple and logical progression. In this sense, figure 5-1 is deceptive. It is important to note that the first step was not predictive of the second step, the second not predictive of the third, and so on. The advance from each step involved uncertainty, missteps, and serendipity. All are inherent in the process of basic biomedical research. Moreover, only a poor understanding exists of the path leading from basic to applied biomedical research. Although Mt. Coronary Artery Bypass stands as a bona fide illustration of the integration of data drawn from several species, it was formed without a blueprint.

Use of Multiple Species in Biomedical Research

The contributions of animals are an important part of the history of human health, disease, and medicine. It is noteworthy that animals have not only contributed to human welfare, but deterred from it as well. The benefits and detriments derived from animals involve numerous species.

The number of animal diseases labeled zoonoses—diseases transmissible from animals to humans—now stands at about 200. These exact a heavy toll of human morbidity and mortality on a worldwide scale. Research to combat zoonoses logically focuses on the species that are the principal sources of the diseases. And the more species that are infected by a particular agent, the greater are the biological resources available for research to overcome it. Numerous animal vectors of an infectious agent provide increased opportunities for the study of variation among species in the incubation of, transmission of, and susceptibility to the infectious agent. Most of the threats to humans from animals—including rabies, tuberculosis, brucellosis, toxoplasmosis, anthrax, and dengue fever—infect a sufficient va-

Figure 5-1.—Steps in Biomedical Research That Preceded Successful Coronary Artery Bypass Graft Surgery

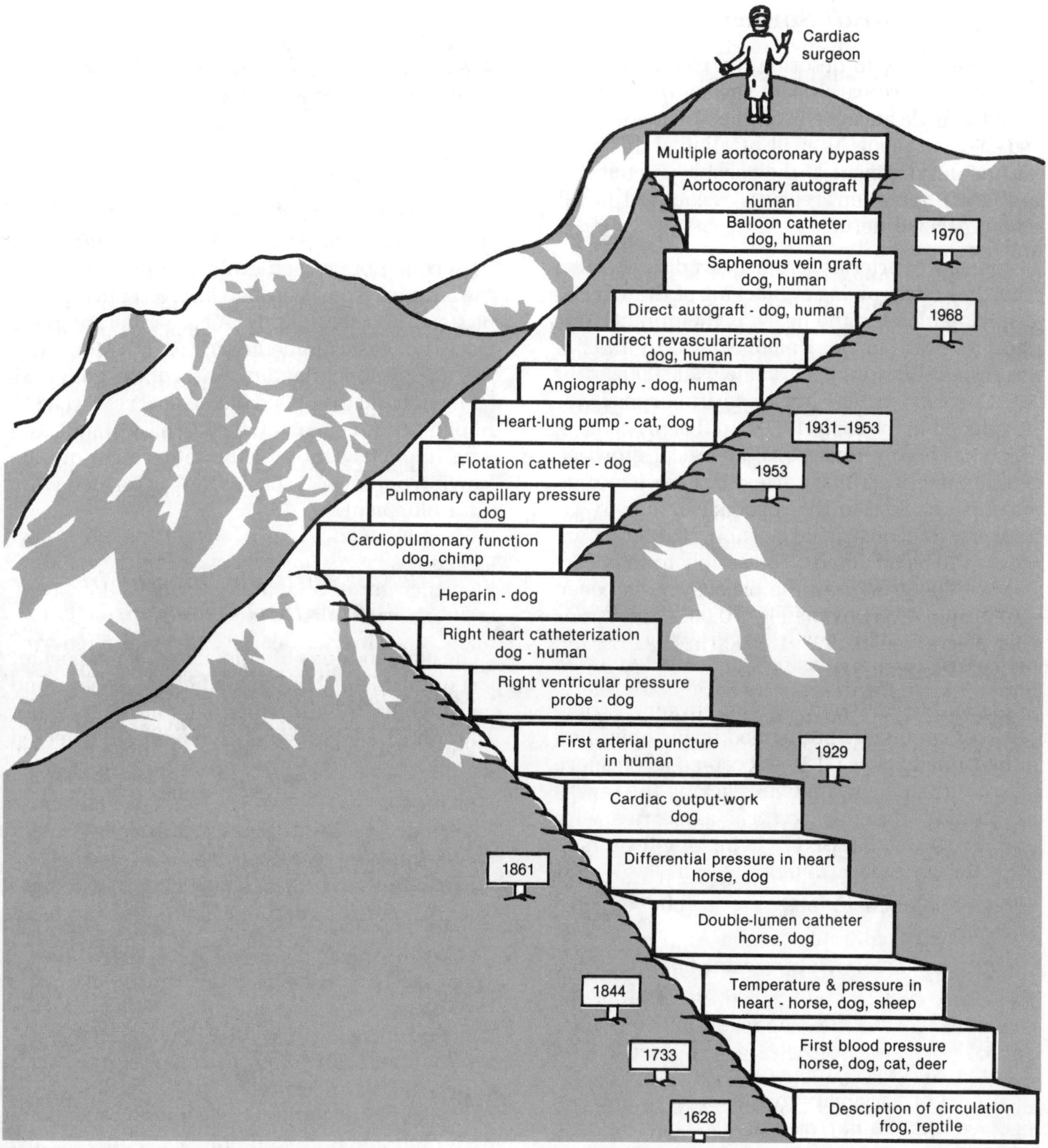

SOURCE: Redrawn from W. C. Randall, "Crises in Physiological Research," *Physiologist* 26:351-356, 1983, after J. H. Comroe, Jr., and R. D. Dripps, "Ben Franklin and Open Heart Surgery," *Circ. Res.* 35:661-669, 1974.

riety of species that effective research on their control has been possible (19). Perhaps ironically, the same diverse mix of species that transmits disease to humans forms the substrate for research to ameliorate human disease.

Infection of multiple animal species has led to virtual control in industrial countries of the plagues just mentioned. Yet a paucity of animal vectors or models hampers control of certain other human infectious diseases. Leprosy, herpes, and gonorrhea (which are not zoonoses) have yet to be brought under control, owing partly to the lack of effective animal models. Recent discoveries of leprosy and herpes infections in primates, the culture of the leprosy bacillus in armadillos, and adaptation of the gonorrheal organisms to some species of laboratory animals offer promise that effective animal models will soon become available for research (19). Yet research on other conditions of still-unknown etiology, such as Alzheimer's disease, remains impeded by the inability to identify an appropriate animal model.

Additional impetus for employing a variety of species in the course of research comes from a consideration of the immune response, which recognizes material that is foreign to the body. The immune system thus serves as an animal's defense against infections due to viruses, fungi, or bacteria. When foreign proteins, or antigens, are introduced into an animal, the immune system responds by manufacturing a protein of its own, an antibody, to counter the invader. This is the principle on which the development of vaccines is based: An antigen is injected, and it stimulates production of an antibody that combats the foreign antigen.

The strength of an immune response varies from species to species, and even within a species, according to the genetic constitution of the animal used. Researchers often cannot gain a full understanding of how to develop useful vaccines unless they test several species to examine subtle differences in immune responses. In this way, species differences in response to foreign antigens are found and can be exploited in the production of effective vaccines for humans and animals. It is this use of the immune system that has controlled most of the major infectious viral diseases, including smallpox, which was controlled through the use of the cowpox, or vaccinia, virus.

No one animal species is the complete research model for the human. In general, nonhuman primate species have the greatest anatomical, physiological, and metabolic similarities to humans. Yet, as table 5-2 indicates, much important biological information can be provided by using dissimilar organisms. (This table oversimplifies the use of various animals in studying human health and disease because it does not rate the closeness of the similarity of the conditions between humans and animals (19).)

It is important to establish any new biological principle or a new phase of understanding a disease condition in as many species as possible in order to improve safely the extrapolation from one animal to another and to humans (19). Research results derived from multiple systems in varied species, such as those listed in table 5-2, complement each other to approximate human anatomy, physiology, and metabolism.

Some biomedical research, collectively known as veterinary research, seeks to understand the life processes of animals and applies this knowledge to serve animals themselves, as well as humans. Veterinary research addresses the normal structure and function of animals and the causes, diagnosis, prevention, and treatment of disease in experimental animals and clinical (i.e., patient) animals. Research on food- and fiber-producing domestic animals supports the utilization of plant and animal resources for human sustenance. Veterinary research plays a prominent role in controlling diseases of importance in food-producing animals and, hence, of importance to humans.

Veterinary research supports, and is closely allied with, veterinary medicine. Practitioners of veterinary medicine maintain and improve the health and well-being of animals. The profession concentrates on the health of animals important for food and fiber and on companion animals. Other species receiving veterinary attention include laboratory animals, fish and aquatic animals, and zoo and wild animals. Thus, the majority of veterinary medicine addresses 30 to 40 different species of economic, ecologic, and environmental importance. These include:

- domestic animals (e.g., cats, cattle, chickens, dogs, donkeys, goats, horses, sheep, and turkeys);

Table 5-2.—Some Anatomical, Physiological, and Metabolic Similarities and Differences Between Humans and Various Laboratory Animals

	Conditions, systems, or structures	
Animal	Similarities to humans	Differences from humans
Cat	Splenic vasculature Sphenoid sinus in skull Liver Middle ear and ear drum Epidermis	Spleen Reaction to foreign protein Laryngeal structures Sweat glands Mediastinum (interior chest tissue) Development of embryonic gonads Sleep Heat regulation
Cattle	Ascending colon Electrolyte excretion	Digestion Plasma gamma globulins in newborn Sleep Heat regulation Vomiting Sweat glands
Chicken	Palate	Retinal vessels Lymphoid tissue in liver Pituitary gland Respiratory system Oviduct Reproductive system Acetate metabolism
Chinchilla	Inner ear structures	
Dog	Pituitary gland vasculature Renal arteries Splenic vasculature Sphenoid sinus in skull Superficial kidney vasculature Liver Epidermis Adrenal gland innervation	Intestinal circulation Anal sacs Sweat glands Pancreatic ducts Heat regulation Sleep Laryngeal nerves Mediastinum
Goat	Embryonic blood circulation	Stomach and digestion Heat regulation Sweat glands Vomiting Sleep Plasma gamma globulins in newborn
Guinea pig	Spleen Immune system	Sweat glands
Horse	Pulmonary vasculature Bile duct Pancreatic duct Lung	Carotid body Spleen Cecum and colon Gall bladder Plasma gamma globulins in newborn
Mouse	Senile hepatic changes	Spleen
Pig	Maturation of red blood cells Cardiovascular tree Teeth Adrenal gland Skin Penile urethra Retinal vessels	Spleen Liver Plasma gamma globulins in newborn Sweat glands

Table 5-2.—Some Anatomical, Physiological, and Metabolic Similarities and Differences Between Humans and Various Laboratory Animals (Continued)

	Conditions, systems, or structures	
Animal	Similarities to humans	Differences from humans
Nonhuman primates	Brain vasculature Intestinal circulation Placenta Pancreatic duct Adrenal gland Innervation Nucleic acid metabolism Teeth and mandible Brain Larynx Kidney Reproductive performance Menstrual cycle Spermatozoa	Inguinal canal
Rabbit	Splenic vasculature Spleen Immunity Innervation Middle ear and ear drum	Liver Sweat glands Lung elasticity
Rat	Spleen Senile splenic changes Senile pancreatic changes	Cardiac circulation Abdominal circulation No gall bladder
Sheep	Splenic vasculature Sweat glands	Stomach and digestion Heat regulation Breeding Vomiting Sleep Plasma gamma globulins in newborn

SOURCES: Adapted from B.M. Mitruka, H.M. Rawnsley, and D.V. Vadehra, *Animals for Research, Models for the Study of Human Disease* (New York: John Wiley & Sons, 1976); and W.I. Gay and J.D. Willett, "The Spectrum of Biological Systems and the Selection of Models," in *National Symposium on Imperatives in Research Animal Use: Scientific Needs and Animal Welfare*, NIH Pub. No. 85-2746 (Bethesda, MD: National Institutes of Health, 1985).

- laboratory animals (e.g., mice, rats, guinea pigs, rabbits, hamsters, and ferrets);
- nonhuman primates (e.g., baboons, new-world monkeys, and old-world monkeys);
- exotic birds (e.g., parakeets, parrots, cockatiels, and cockatoos);
- birds of prey (e.g., falcons, hawks, and eagles);
- freshwater and marine fish;
- marine mammals (e.g., porpoises and whales);
- large terrestrial mammals (e.g., deer, antelope, elk, lion, tigers, elephants, and llamas); and
- assorted reptiles and amphibians.

Choice of Species

The variety of animal species used in research spans the animal kingdom, and some species are used more often than others (see ch. 3). Various reasons exist for using particular species in research:

- Some species are more available than others. For example, certain primate species are in chronic short supply. Conversely, in the case of rats and mice, large numbers of commercial breeding businesses can supply particular strains, ages, and sex on the purchaser's demand.
- Existing databases and literature have been built on a particular species. Additional work, in order to contribute to the field in a direct way, needs to be based on the same species.
- For most research purposes, nonendangered, commercially available animals are preferred over endangered ones.
- Some species exhibit the physiology or behavior of interest in a more vivid and robust form than do other species. For example, the desert-adapted kangaroo rat is the species of

choice for studies of the kidney's role in water conservation.
- Certain aspects of physiology or behavior are exhibited by only a limited number of species. For example, studies of echolocation are best done with bats, which emit sounds in radar-type fashion.
- The costs of acquisition vary widely among species. For example, a mouse costs approximately $2, a hamster approximately $5, and a guinea pig approximately $19. (The actual cost for a particular species varies with the sex, strain, weight, age, quantity ordered, method of shipping, and distance shipped.)
- Maintenance costs vary widely among species. Depending on the laboratory lifetime of the animal, maintenance expenses can quickly exceed acquisition costs. For example, maintaining a mouse in a research laboratory costs approximately 5 cents per day, a hamster approximately 11 cents per day, and a guinea pig approximately 40 cents per day. (The actual per diem cost varies among different animal facilities, depending, for example, on accounting practices and local labor costs.)
- Results obtained from different species vary in their ability to be generalized, both among animals and between animals and humans. Generalizations are more readily made among species that are more closely related than among species that are less closely related.

Attempts to identify alternatives to using animals in research are likely to be influenced by these considerations.

THE ROLE OF ANIMALS IN BEHAVIORAL RESEARCH

Like all of biomedical research, behavioral research relies on animals to identify models for and aid in the understanding of human phenomena. Behavioral research has the further goal of understanding the behavior of animal species of economic or intrinsic interest to people.

Behavior encompasses all the movements and sensations by which organisms interact with both the living and nonliving components of their environment (2). The environment includes not only objects and events external to the organism, but internal events as well (e.g., visceral cues, motivations, and emotions). Behavior is not an object or a thing. It is a process that continues in most organisms until they die. Even sleep is a form of behavior. Unlike coloration or size, behavior is a dynamic property that functions primarily to enable an organism to adapt to changing environmental conditions.

What is Behavioral Research?

Classes of Behavioral Research

There are several classes of behavioral research, each with a distinct focus:

- **Abnormal Behavior.** In the broadest sense, abnormal behavior is any that deviates from normal patterns. Instances among animals include seemingly suicidal, self-induced beachings by whales, phobic and neurotic problems in pets, and various laboratory-induced animal models of human psychopathology (e.g., depression, drug addiction, or obesity).
- **Aggression.** Aggression can be defined as an organism's threatening to inflict, attempting to inflict, or actually doing physical harm to another organism.
- **Animal Movements.** Animal movements represent major changes in location over time and space, such as patterns of migration, herding, homing, navigation, orientation, and dispersal.
- **Body Maintenance.** Behaviors that function to provide body maintenance and homeostasis include hunger, thirst, respiration, thermoregulation, excretion, grooming, preening, and parasite removal.
- **Cognition.** Although this label has been used indiscriminately to encompass practically all aspects of learned behavior (36), the term is more strictly applied to instances of apparent mentalistic activity in animals (e.g., consciousness, thinking, imagery, self-awareness, intention, or attribution).
- **Communication.** Communication consists of an exchange of information between two

or more organisms that results in a change in behavior. Instances of this range from those that are stereotyped and instinctive, such as the dance "language" of honey bees, to those that might appear to have a symbolic basis, as in the case of the recent attempts to teach chimpanzees various forms of sign language. Depending on species, communication can involve visual, auditory, olfactory, or tactile cues.

- **Exploration and Activity.** In addition to instances of curiosity and exploratory behavior, patterns of activity included in this discipline are circadian rhythms, sleep, hibernation, roost-time restlessness, and different patterns of locomotion (e.g., swimming, swinging, or flying).
- **Habitat and Food Selection.** Habitat and food selection refer to the areas where animals live under natural conditions (e.g., freshwater streams, forests, or deserts) and the ways they exploit resources. Areas of inquiry by behavioral researchers include competition between species and optimal foraging strategies.
- **Learning, Memory, and Problem Solving.** These behaviors are represented by the acquisition and retention of new information that allows organisms to anticipate recurring environmental events, as well as changes in behavior that maximize or minimize certain outcomes. Included in this discipline is the cultural transmission of information from one generation to the next and imitation.
- **Motivation and Emotion.** The study of motivation looks at mechanisms and manipulations that activate and sustain behavior. Emotion typically includes reactions that accompany different motivational states and is often associated, for example, with fear, anxiety, apprehension, pleasure, and rage.
- **Predator-Prey Relations.** As a consequence of selective pressure associated with predation, many prey species have developed an extensive and elaborate array of predator defenses couched in terms of sensory and/or behavioral adaptations, such as burrowing or voluntary immobility. Likewise, predators use a variety of behavioral strategies in prey identification and capture.
- **Reproduction and Parental Care.** Patterns of courtship, mate selection, copulatory behavior, nest building, nurturing, and care of offspring all fall within this discipline.
- **Sensation and Perception.** Sensation and perception refers to the ways in which organisms detect and interpret their environment. Topics included in this discipline include studies of sensory mechanisms, the development of search images, and highly specialized sensory mechanisms, such as echolocation.
- **Social Behavior.** Social behavior is defined by a situation in which the behavior of one organism serves as a stimulus for the behavior of another, and vice versa. Instances of social behavior range from simple forms of aggregation to complex exchanges among individuals (e.g., dominance, cooperation, and reciprocal altruism).
- **Spacing Mechanisms.** Spacing mechanisms are intimately tied to social behavior, and range from such topics as individual distance to the maintenance of territories.

Behavioral v. Biomedical Research

Distinctions between behavioral and biomedical research, although they are commonly made (and are followed in this assessment), frequently break down. Behavior, in the final analysis, is a biological phenomenon. Behavior presupposes a living organism, and the way that organism behaves is influenced in complex ways by its genetic makeup, hormonal status, physiology, and neurochemistry. Intervening between the input of environmental events and the output of behavioral events are complex neuroanatomical networks involving receptors, electrochemical reactions, nerve impulses, and effector organs. Behavior does not occur in a vacuum. The biology of the organism provides the foundation that makes behavioral events possible.

It is increasingly apparent that many aspects of behavioral research must be viewed in conjunction with biomedical research. Strong components of both behavioral and biomedical research are evident, for example, in the study of obesity, hypertension, drug addiction, headaches, aggression, alcoholism, sexual dysfunction, brain damage, epilepsy, schizophrenia, depression, learning disorders, smoking, anorexia nervosa, stomach ulcers, mental retardation, and a variety of other psychological disorders.

Why Are Animals Used in Behavioral Research?

Control

The use of animals under laboratory conditions enables the manipulation and control of a variety of factors that in different settings would confuse, contaminate, and confound any attempt to interpret a behavioral outcome. Animal models also allow the control of genetic background, prior experience, temperature, humidity, diet, and previous social encounters. When these variables are uncontrolled, observed behavioral responses can be virtually impossible to interpret.

Objectivity

Two prerequisites to any research are objectivity and impartiality. When humans study humans, as can be the case in behavioral research, unique problems may arise. Not only can it be difficult for the investigator to remain objective in interpreting behavioral phenomena, but a variety of other complications can arise from the social relationship among those conducting the research and those participating as subjects (50). The use of nonhuman species partially ameliorates this problem.

Developmental Effects

Among many species behavior changes as a function of age. The problem this poses for human research is one of time. Human development continues for many decades. To chart behavioral changes within the same persons would take many years, involving exhaustive followup studies and the ever-present danger of losing research subjects, for example, because of death or relocation. The alternative to such longitudinal work is to conduct cross-sectional studies, where simultaneous samples are drawn from different age groups. A problem in this case is that sociological and cultural changes over time (e.g., 50 years ago, an eighth-grade education was the norm) confound apparent differences between people of different ages. Because a range of lifespans is available among laboratory species, the use of animal models can minimize or circumvent altogether some problems associated with the study of behavior over time.

Genetic Effects

There is growing evidence of a variety of genetic effects on behavior (23). With animal models, selective breeding studies can establish, pinpoint, and quantify genetic effects on behavior. The opportunity for human research in this area, apart from studies of identical twins, is limited.

Methodology

The fact that animals cannot talk seems at first to constitute a serious disadvantage to conducting behavioral research with animals. Yet, the stark limits of trans-species communication help to keep human investigators unbiased in their work. The use of animal models forces the behavioral scientist to develop objective, operational definitions and research techniques that may later be applied to humans.

Lower Complexity

Behavior, notably human behavior, can be extremely complex. The use of animals that appear to be structurally and functionally less complex presents a way to identify some of the basic elements and principles of behavior that might otherwise remain inextricably embedded in a mosaic of other factors.

Species-Specific Behaviors

Certain behavioral phenomena fall outside the realm of human sensory or motor abilities. For example, flight, echolocation, infrared detection, and homing require the use of nonhuman species as subjects for research purposes.

Heuristic Value

Research on the behavior of animals has been an important source of hypotheses about human behavior and an impetus to research on humans (35). Much of what is now known about the principles of learning, for example, was initially derived from research on animals. Likewise, a variety of therapeutic techniques (e.g., desensitization) were derived from work with animals. Human studies were done to verify what was learned from animal research and to gauge the limits of extrapolation from animals to humans.

Practical Application to Animal Species

In addition to providing models of a variety of biomedical and psychological problems in humans, research on animal behavior is in many instances focused on benefits to the animals themselves. For example, an understanding of behavior has proved crucial for designing optimal captive environments for the protection and breeding of endangered species (55). Increased attention has also been paid to the behavior of farm animals. The study of mother-infant attachments, social behavior in groups, stress resulting from overcrowding and confinement, and habitat preferences has led to important insights into farm-animal welfare and husbandry (13,27,54).

It is also noteworthy in this context that knowledge gained about behavioral problems in humans through animal research is now being applied to animals. Effective treatments have been developed for aggressive problems in cats (5) and fears and phobias in dogs (24,58).

A knowledge of animal behavior has helped identify and solve ecologic problems. The discovery and subsequent synthesis of insect sex attractants, or pheromones, has important implications for the control of agricultural pests. Rather than having to use toxic pesticides applied over vast areas, there is already some application and much future potential in baiting traps with specific pheromones, which precludes environmental contamination.

One unique application of laboratory findings to the solution of ecologic problems involved studies of taste-aversion conditioning in rats (18). Researchers paired unpleasant, chemical- or radiation-induced illness with different flavors. After just one or two trials, rats developed highly durable aversions to the flavors paired with unpleasant stimuli. Outside the laboratory, by pairing lithium-chloride-induced illness with the flesh of various prey species, it is now possible to control coyote attacks on sheep and turkeys (14). Indeed, one or two trials is sufficient to eliminate attacks on specific domestic farm animals but leave the coyote free to feed on alternative prey (22).

This procedure has recently been extended to reducing crop damage by crows and even appears to have promise for dealing with cancer patients undergoing radiation therapy (1). (A frequent complication of radiation therapy has been unpleasant gastrointestinal illness that the patient generalizes to all food; the patient may be unable to eat. Using the principles of conditioned taste aversion developed in rats, it is now possible to circumvent the problem by restricting patients to one particular kind of food during radiation treatment, so that the aversion that develops is specific to that food alone.)

Individual Animals in the Service of Humans

Behavioral research occasionally centers on a trait of a particular species that may be especially well suited to assist humans. For example, using animals to help handicapped persons has required a knowledge of animal behavior. Seeing-eye guide dogs, usually German shepherds or golden retrievers, assist the blind (20), and trained capuchin monkeys perform as aides for quadriplegics (63). Pet dogs and cats have been shown to have therapeutic value for psychiatric patients (10), the handicapped (12), and the elderly (49), and they may even hold promise for alleviating depression resulting from loss of a child (57).

Methods of Behavioral Research

The methods of behavioral research are as varied as the disciplines, but most fall into one of three general categories: field studies and naturalistic observation; developmental studies; and laboratory studies.

Field studies represent an attempt to examine the behavior in question as it occurs under natural circumstances. Such studies do not typically involve attempts to manipulate or control the conditions of observation. Watching animals in natural conditions has frequently been suggested as an alternative to using them in laboratory research (6,44). The following benefits and limitations of naturalistic observation have been recognized:

- Naturalistic observation is frequently a starting point. Observation of animals in the field provides a base of descriptive information and serves as a source of hypotheses to be subsequently tested under laboratory conditions.
- Naturalistic observation can be used to compare behavior observed in the field with that occurring in the laboratory to assess the extent to which an artificial environment may alter behavior, and whether the results can be generalized.
- Field studies can increase the efficiency with which animals are used by providing important information on natural species variables and biological constraints on behavior.
- The principal drawback to naturalistic observation is the absence of control. Under natural conditions, events frequently change in both important and spurious ways, often making it impossible to establish cause-and-effect relations (37).

Behavioral research often requires study of one animal or a group through time, as development proceeds. Among many species the emergence of different patterns of behavior is a reflection of both maturational and experiential factors. Developmental variables have been identified as being important in the expression of such diverse behaviors as aggression, communication, activity, learning, and social behavior.

Laboratory studies undertake to manipulate and control the condition of observation so as to specify more precisely the variables and conditions that influence the behavior in question. Most laboratory studies of behavior can be subdivided into those that attempt to identify the environmental determinants of behavior and those concerned with the organic basis for behavior. Within the latter category are a number of approaches involving attempts to identify the neuroanatomical, neurochemical, endocrinological, and genetic underpinnings for behavior.

Use of Multiple Species in Behavioral Research

Many behavioral phenomena appear common to different species. Patterns of migration, for example, are common to such diverse groups as insects, fish, birds, and even some species of mammals. Much the same appears true for learning, motivation, and bodily maintenance. Yet, generalizations about categories of behavior (e.g., parental care or hoarding) in unrelated species may be misleading, because the species evolved independently (34). Moreover, comparing the performance of different species on a simple task may have no bearing on larger issues such as intelligence (26). What used to be seen as general principles and "laws" of learning, for example, now turn out to be specific to certain species under certain situations (3,4,53).

There are some behaviors that are of limited scope across species but of profound importance in terms of their bearing on the question of human behavior. For example, the capacity to recognize one's own reflection in a mirror has only been found in humans, chimpanzees, and orangutans, and much the same may apply to instances of intentional deception, gratitude, grudging, sympathy, empathy, attribution, reconciliation, and sorrow (17).

PAIN AND DISTRESS IN RESEARCH ANIMALS

There are two general kinds of animal experimentation in which pain may occur. First, there are studies that investigate the nature of pain itself and the anatomical, behavioral, chemical, pharmacological, and physiological mechanisms responsible for it. In such studies, the infliction of pain and the monitoring of the responses to pain are usually integral parts of the experimental procedure. The goal is the prevention, treatment, and amelioration of human and animal pain. The second, and much larger, class of animal experimentation in which pain may occur consists of those studies in which pain is but a byproduct of the procedures used (28).

When indices of pain are observed or anticipated in living research animals as byproducts of an experimental protocol, the investigator is both informally and formally obliged to supply pain relief. (For a further discussion of the investigator's responsibilities in this area, see chs. 4, 13, 14, 15, and 16.)

Pain relief for a laboratory animal is usually accomplished by one of three means. An **analgesic** is an agent that relieves pain without causing loss of consciousness. The most frequent use of analgesic drugs in laboratory animals is likely to be in the postoperative period. An **anesthetic** is an agent that causes loss of the sensation of pain, usually without loss of consciousness. An anesthetic may be classified as topical, local, or general, according to the breadth of its effect. Topical anesthetics find only limited use in animal research, usually as components of ointments applied to minor injuries, whereas local anesthetics are used for many minor surgical procedures. The use of local anesthetics requires postsurgical care, because anesthetized surfaces are particularly liable to accidental and self-inflicted damage (43). General anesthetic, either injected or inhaled, is widely used in research. A **tranquilizer** is an agent that quiets, calms, and reduces anxiety and tension with some alteration of the level of consciousness and without effecting analgesia. Tranquilizers are particularly useful in reducing distress and resistance to confinement.

The perception of pain is largely subjective. It is best described as an awareness of discomfort resulting from injury, disease, or emotional distress and evidenced by biological or behavioral changes. A frequent companion to pain is distress—the undesirable stress resulting from pain, anxiety, or fear (51). Distress can also occur in the absence of pain. An animal struggling in a restraint device may be free from any pain, but it may be in distress.

Despite the difficulty associated with objectively defining pain, it can usually be recognized. The most obvious sign is an animal's behavior (16,42, 56). Signs of pain include the following:

- **Impaired activity.** Animals may be relatively inactive or may remain completely immobile within their pen or cage. If they do move, it is often with an abnormal gait, such as limping or not using a leg.
- **Change in personality.** Pain may result in guarding behavior (attempting to protect or move away). Animals may also be uncharacteristically aggressive.
- **Restlessness.** Animals may move about continually or may rise up and lie down repeatedly.
- **Decreased intake.** Food and water consumption are usually severely retarded, often to the extent that moderate or severe dehydration can occur.
- **Abnormal vocalization.** Dogs may whine or whimper, rats and hamsters may squeak at a high pitch, and primates may scream or grunt.
- **Abnormal posture.** Dogs, cats, and rodents may tense the muscles of the back and abdomen to effect a "tucked-up" appearance.
- **Self-mutilation.** Dogs and rodents may gnaw at the site of a lesion on their own flesh or, for example, remove their own tumor.

In identifying pain, all these criteria must be considered in conjunction with the nature of the experimental procedure and the previous normal behavioral characteristics of the animal. Also, it should be noted that no one criterion is a wholly reliable indicator of pain.

An experimental procedure probably involves pain if it includes, for example, induction of any pathological state, administration of toxic substances, long-term physical restraint, aversive training, or major operative procedures such as surgery and induction of physical trauma. Various procedures employed in the research laboratory can be compared, ranking each for the estimated degree of pain for the animal subject (see table 5-3). Educated estimates of pain perception in animals can be made by understanding animal behavior; by drawing analogies based on compar-

Table 5-3.—Classification of Research Experiments and Procedures According to the Degree of Pain or Distress for the Animal

Level of pain/distress	Examples of types of experiments	Examples of procedures
Absent or negligible	• Noninvasive behavioral testing • Studies of migration or homing • Dietary preference studies	• Banding for identification or tracking • Field observation • Fecal examination • Conditioned learning with food reward
Low	• Determination of pain threshold • Manipulation of blood chemistry • Experiments carried out on anesthetized animals that do not wake up again	• Flinch or jump response • Injections • Tube feeding • Tattooing • Administration of anesthetic • Surgery under deep anesthesia and subsequent sacrifice —Removal of organs for histological or biochemical investigation —Culture of surviving organs • Blood sampling
Moderate	• Behavioral study of flight or avoidance reactions • Operations carried out under anesthesia or analgesia, with the animal waking up or experiencing the cessation of the action of the painkiller (postoperative pain)	• Stimulation of unanesthetized animal • Biopsies • Implantation of chronic catheters • Castration • Mild electric shock • Implantation of electrodes • Central nervous system lesions • Exposure of internal organs • Food or water restriction for more than 24 hours
High	• Chronic stress studies • Drug withdrawal studies • Studies of certain infectious agents • Experiments on mechanisms of pain in conscious animals • Experiments on mechanisms of healing • Studies of radiation toxicity	• Prolonged physical restraint • Chronic sleep deprivation • Intense electric shock • Production of pain clearly beyond threshold tolerance • Induction of burns or wounds • Surgery on conscious animal

SOURCE: Office of Technology Assessment.

ative anatomy, physiology, and pathology; and by basing inferences on subjective responses to pain experiences by humans. Careful attempts to estimate and categorize the degree of pain experienced by laboratory animals—ranging from absent or negligible to high—can provide a basis for efforts to minimize the pain or distress caused by research procedures.

ANIMAL AND NONANIMAL PROTOCOLS IN BIOMEDICAL AND BEHAVIORAL RESEARCH REPORTS

One way to measure the balance of animal and nonanimal methods in research is to survey the end-product of experimentation—the published literature. OTA examined approximately 6,000 research reports published from 1980 through 1983 in an effort to document the prevalence of animal and nonanimal protocols in contemporary research.

Fifteen leading scientific journals were selected to represent disciplines within biomedical and behavioral research. These journals were chosen because of their primary emphasis on research done in the United States by American scientists and because of the respect accorded them by scientists in each discipline. The editors of all 15 subject manuscripts to independent peer review prior to publication.

For each year from 1980 through 1983, OTA examined the first 100 research papers published in each journal; in a few cases, fewer than 100 papers were published in a given year. Short communications and review articles were not included. In each report, OTA checked whether animals were used. Thus, the materials and methods employed in each article were categorized as either use of animals, no use of animals, or use of humans. "Animal" is defined as described earlier (see ch. 2), any nonhuman vertebrate. "Use" of animals is defined conservatively as **any** use of an animal in an experiment. Table 5-4 lists some examples of the ways specific protocols were categorized by OTA.

Survey Findings

The results of this survey indicate that the research journals—and perhaps the disciplines they represent—fall into two categories:

Table 5-4.—Classification of Published Research Protocols in OTA Survey of 15 Journals

Examples of protocols classified as use of animals:
Whole animals used as experimental subjects
Animals used to obtain cell, tissue, or organ of interest
Animals used in the establishment of new cell, tissue, or organ cultures
Extraction of protein or other biological molecule from animals
Production of antibodies by whole animals or animal components
Use of egg, sperm, or embryo from animal source
Use of animal epidemiologic data
Examples of protocols classified as no use of animals:
Use of invertebrate organisms
Use of computer systems
Use of previously established cell lines
Acquisition of biological molecules from a commercial manufacturer
Use of physical or chemical systems
Examples of protocols classified as use of humans:
Use of living human subjects
Use of cadavers
Use of human placenta
Use of human blood cells or components
Use of human epidemiologic data

SOURCE: Office of Technology Assessment.

- journals representing disciplines that have already largely incorporated nonanimal methods into the research process; and
- journals representing disciplines that either have not incorporated, or may not have available, nonanimal methods.

For most of the 15 journals (see table 5-5), published protocols fall predominantly into just one of the three categories of methods; in many cases, over 80 percent of the protocols are in one category. Only *Cell*, representing cell biology, had a majority of articles using nonanimal methods. The *American Journal of Cardiology* contained a majority of articles using humans or human materials as research subjects. All the remaining journals except *Developmental Biology* and the *Journal of Biological Chemistry* included a majority of articles using animals. *Developmental Biology* and the *Journal of Biological Chemistry* contained approximately equal percentages of articles employing animal and nonanimal methods.

The 12 biomedical research journals included in this survey cover a diverse array of disciplines under this one rubric. The differing patterns of animal, nonanimal, and human use make generalizations misleading at best and perhaps impossible. In the same way that biomedical research itself is not monolithic, the patterns of animal use among disciplines of biomedical research are not uniform. Perhaps not surprisingly, veterinary research, insofar as it is represented by two journals, relies primarily on animals, a minimal percentage of nonanimal methods, and no protocols with humans.

The three behavioral research journals included in this survey registered a predominance of animal methods—more than 90 percent of the protocols in each case. The research reported in these journals involved minimal use of humans or nonanimal methods. Other behavioral research journals, for example those reporting on clinical psychology, largely publish reports of research with human subjects.

Survey Limitations

This attempt to gauge the implementation of nonanimal methods in selected areas of biomedical and behavioral research had certain limita-

Table 5-5.—Percentage of Papers (Average, 1980-83) Using Animal, Nonanimal, and Human Subjects in 15 Biomedical and Behavioral Research Journals Surveyed by OTA

	Percentage of papers using:		
Journal	Animals	Nonanimals	Humans
Biomedical research:			
American Journal of Veterinary Research	96	4[a]	0
Journal of Animal Science	96	4[b]	0
Endocrinology	91	8	1
American Journal of Physiology	90	6	4
Anatomical Record	88	3	9
Proceedings of the Society of Experimental Biology and Medicine	83	10	7
Journal of Immunology	71	10	19
Journal of the National Cancer Institute	60	9	31
Developmental Biology	54	46	0
Journal of Biological Chemistry	39	52	9
Cell	31	67	2
American Journal of Cardiology	12	0	88
Behavioral research:			
Behavioral and Neural Biology	96	4	0
Journal of Comparative and Physiological Psychology	96	3	1
Physiology and Behavior	93	1	6

[a]Primarily virus research.
[b]Primarily computer modeling or grain fermentation applicable to ruminant nutrition.

SOURCE: Office of Technology Assessment.

tions. The conservative scoring procedure tended to underestimate the use of alternatives to animals as defined in this assessment (see ch. 2). For instance, if an experimental protocol used both animal and nonanimal methods, it was categorized under use of animals. If a study involved both nonanimal methods and humans, it was counted as use of humans. Further, if a study involved both animal methods and humans, it was counted as use of animals. The approach used to categorize protocols took into consideration only the replacement, not the reduction or refinement, of animal methods. Whether a protocol involved 1 or 100 animals, it still fell under the category of "use of animals," and all reports bore equal weight in determining percentage of protocols using humans or animal or nonanimal methods. In addition, there was no attempt to quantify the pain or stress of an animal in an experiment or to distinguish between different vertebrate species. Any alternative protocol, therefore, that tended to reduce or refine an existing animal procedure was still categorized as "use of animals."

An example of the problem of overestimation of animal use by a survey such as this exists in immunology. Today, antibodies, needed in most immunology research, can be obtained by injecting rabbits with foreign proteins, or antigens, and extracting the antibodies that the rabbit produced or by using mouse spleens and the monoclonal antibody technique to produce antibodies to an antigen. Each process requires animals. Once the monoclonal cells are in culture, however, there is a virtually unlimited supply of the needed antibody, and there is essentially no further need for animals. Thus the monoclonal technique can decrease animal use, as was the case in many of the most recent articles surveyed in the *Journal of Immunology*. These articles, though, were still coded under the "use of animals" category because the primary methods and materials involved animals. But the total number of animals in a given experiment decreased, for they were used in just one aspect of the experiment instead of two. The monoclonal antibody technique is being used as an alternative to the repeated use of rabbits, yet its impact is underestimated in a survey such as this. The OTA scoring of protocols published in the *Journal of Immunology* did not reflect certain reductions that are currently being implemented.

Along with underestimating the implementation of nonanimal methods, the boundaries within which the OTA survey was carried out also tended to overestimate the use of animals as experimental subjects. This was due principally to two factors included in the scoring procedure under animal use—epidemiologic studies and the study of biological molecules obtained from animals.

Epidemiologic data are the primary sources in some articles in the *American Journal of Cardiology,* the *Journal of the National Cancer Institute,* and in many veterinary studies. These protocols were included under "use of animals," yet they did not manipulate animals in any way as experimental subjects.

Obtaining many biological molecules that are studied experimentally requires that they be extracted from animals who produce them. Subsequent experiments on these molecules themselves (reported, for example, in the *Journal of Biological Chemistry*) do not involve animals at all. In such cases, animals may be used in preparation for an experiment but are not actually involved in the experiment being performed. Therefore, protocols that involved animals as donors of biological molecules (e.g., bodily fluids) for an experiment prior to its initiation were also included under use of animals, and this tended to overestimate the use of animals as research subjects.

It is important to distinguish between the number of published articles involving animal methods and the actual number of animals used in research. The OTA survey provides no information on the latter. Some protocols may involve only a few animals, while others may employ tens or hundreds. Moreover, depending on the species and type of research, some subjects might be used in multiple experiments. In primate research, for example, it is not uncommon for animals to be used in a succession of either related or unrelated studies over a period of years; this would not be the case for rodents.

SUMMARY AND CONCLUSIONS

Biomedical and behavioral research center on the understanding of human health and disease and rely on animals to achieve this goal. They use animal subjects to understand not only human phenomena, but animal phenomena as well. The broad spectrum of enterprises involved in these fields of research includes disciplines ranging from anatomy to zoology. Although the varied disciplines that make up biomedical and behavioral research have distinct foci, they often overlap.

Animals are used throughout these disciplines to address an array of questions. Nonhuman primates, for example, have contributed to an understanding of polio, hepatitis B, high blood pressure, Parkinson's disease, baldness, menopausal hot flashes, and other human conditions. Beyond the nonhuman primates, diverse species are used in biomedical research because of their anatomical, physiological, and metabolic similarities to or differences from humans. Principles and techniques developed in varied animal species (e.g., dog, horse, and sheep) may combine to support a single application to humans, as in the case of coronary artery bypass graft surgery. In behavioral research, different animal species may also be used to learn about characteristics unique to the species under study, usually one of economic importance or intrinsic interest to humans.

Animals may suffer pain or distress in the course of research on the mechanism of pain, or, more generally, as a byproduct of experimental procedures. In such cases, the investigator is obliged to supply pain relief to the animal or to justify withholding pain-relieving drugs as necessary to the experiment. Institutional animal care and use committees play an important role in overseeing this process (see ch. 15). Pain relief is usually effected by the administration of analgesic, anesthetic, or tranquilizing agents. Indices of pain can usually be recognized in experimental animals, and experimental procedures can be ranked according to estimates of the degree of pain produced. Such a ranking provides a basis for efforts to minimize the pain caused by research procedures.

An OTA survey of published research reports in 15 scientific journals documented the prevalence of animal v. nonanimal protocols in contemporary research. Each research journal, and perhaps the discipline it represents, can be identified by a characteristic balance of protocols using animals, nonanimals, and humans. The data permit research journals to be classified as representing disciplines that either rely on nonanimal methods or that do not incorporate such methods (or do not have them available). In the same way that research itself is not monolithic, patterns of animal use and the use of nonanimal methods among research disciplines are not uniform.

CHAPTER 5 REFERENCES

1. Adams, P.M., "Animal Research and Animal Welfare: An Overview of the Issues," paper presented at the 92d Annual Meeting of the American Psychological Association, Toronto, Aug. 26, 1984.
2. Alexander, R.D., "The Search for a General Theory of Behavior," *Behav. Sci.* 20:77-100, 1975.
3. Bitterman, M.E., "Phyletic Differences in Learning," *Am. Psychol.* 20:396-410, 1965.
4. Bitterman, M.E., "The Comparative Analysis of Learning," *Science* 188:699-709, 1975.
5. Borschelt, P.L., and Voith, V.L., "Diagnosis and Treatment of Aggression Problems in Cats," *Vet. Clin. North Am. (Small Anim. Prac.)* 12:665-671, 1982.
6. Bowd, A.D., "Ethical Reservations About Psychological Research With Animals," *Psychol. Rec.* 30:201-210, 1980.
7. Braunwald, E., "Effects of Coronary-Artery Bypass Grafting on Survival," *N. Engl. J. Med.* 309:1181-1184, 1983.
8. Burns, R.S., Chiueh, C.C., Markey, S.P., et al., "A Primate Model of Parkinsonism: Selective Destruction of Dopaminergic Neurons in the Pars Compacta of the Substantia Nigra by *N*-methyl-4-phenyl-1,2,3,6-tetrahydropyridine," *Proc. Natl. Acad. Sci. USA* 80:4546-4550, 1983.
9. Comroe, J.H., Jr., and Dripps, R.D., "Ben Franklin and Open Heart Surgery," *Circ. Res.* 35:661-669, 1974.
10. Corson, S.A., Corson, E.O.L., Gwynne, P., et al., "Pet Dogs as Nonverbal Communication Links in Hospital Psychiatry," *Comprehen. Psychiat.* 18:61-72, 1977.
11. Cowen, R., "Rhesus Monkeys Provide Model for Symptoms of Menopause," *Res. Resources Reporter* 8(11):1-3, 1983.
12. Curtis, P., "Animals Are Good for the Handicapped, Perhaps All of Us," *Smithsonian* 12(1):48-57, 1981.
13. Curtis, S.E., and McGlone, J.J. "Status of Farm Animal Behavioral Research in North America," *J. Anim. Sci.* 54:450-455, 1982.
14. Ellins, S.R., and Catalano, S.M., "Field Application of the Conditioned Taste Aversion Paradigm to the Control of Coyote Predation on Sheep and Turkeys," *Behav. Neural Biol.* 29:532-536, 1980.
15. Enders, J.F., Weller, T.H., and Robbins, F.C., "Cultivation of the Lansing Strain of Poliomyelitis Virus in Cultures of Various Human Embryonic Tissue," *Science* 109:85-87, 1949.
16. Flecknell, P.A., "The Relief of Pain in Laboratory Animals," *Lab. Anim.* 18:147-160, 1984.
17. Gallup, G.G., Jr., "Toward a Comparative Psychology of Mind," *Animal Cognition and Behavior,* R.L. Mellgren (ed.) (New York: North-Holland, 1983).
18. Garcia, J., and Koelling, R.A., "The Relation of Cue to Consequence in Avoidance Learning," *Psychonom. Sci.* 4:123-124, 1966.
19. Gay, W.I., and Willett, J.D., "The Spectrum of Biological Systems and the Selection of Models," *National Symposium on Imperatives in Research Animal Use: Scientific Needs and Animal Welfare,* NIH Pub. No. 85-2746 (Bethesda, MD: National Institutes of Health, 1985).
20. Goddard, M.E, and Beilharz, R.G., "Genetic and Environmental Factors Affecting the Suitability of Dogs as Guide Dogs for the Blind," *Theor. Appl. Gen.* 62:97-102, 1982.
21. Goldsmith, M.F., "Crossing 'Threshold' of Hepatitis B Control Awaits Greater Vaccine Use," *JAMA* 251:2765-2772, 1984.
22. Gustavson, C.R., Garcia, J., Hankins, W.G., et al., "Coyote Predation Control Through Aversive Conditioning," *Science* 184:581-583, 1974.
23. Hirsch, J. (ed.), *Behavioral Genetic Analysis* (New York: McGraw-Hill, 1967).
24. Hothersall, D., and Tuber, D.S., "Fears in Companion Dogs: Characteristics and Treatment," *Psychopathology in Animals,* J.D. Keehn (ed.) (New York: Academic Press, 1979).
25. Jelinek, J., Kappen, A., Schonbaum, E., et al., "A Primate Model of Human Postmenopausal Hot Flushes," *J. Clin. Endocrinol. Metab.* 59:1224-1228, 1984.
26. Kalat, J.W., "Evolutionary Thinking in the History of the Comparative Psychology of Learning," *Neurosci. Biobehav. Rev.* 7:309-314, 1983.
27. Kilgour, R., "The Contributions of Psychology to a Knowledge of Farm Animal Behavior," *Appl. Anim. Ethol.* 2:197-205, 1976.
28. King, F.A., "The Concept of Pain and Its Reduction in Animal Research," paper presented at the 92d Annual Meeting of the American Psychological Association, Toronto, Aug. 25, 1984.
29. King, F.A., and Yarbrough, C.J., "Medical and Behavioral Benefits From Primate Research," *Physiologists* 28:75-87, 1985.
30. Kolata, G., "Monkey Model of Parkinson's Disease," *Science* 220:705, 1983.
31. Langston, J.W., Irwin, I., and Langston, E.B., "Pargyline Prevents MPTP-Induced Parkinsonism in Primates," *Science* 225:1480-1482, 1984.
32. Lenfant, C., and Roccella, E.J., "Trends in Hypertension Control in the United States," *Chest* 86:459-462, 1984.
33. Lewin, R.L., "Brain Enzyme is the Target of Drug Toxin," *Science* 225:1460-1462, 1984.
34. Lockard, R.B., "The Albino Rat: A Defensible Choice or a Bad Habit?" *Am. Psychol.* 23:734-742, 1968.

35. Maser, J.D., and Seligman, M.E.P. (eds.), *Psychopathology: Experimental Models* (San Francisco: W.H. Freeman, 1977).
36. Mellgren, R.L. (ed.), *Animal Cognition and Behavior* (New York: North-Holland, 1983).
37. Miller, D.B., "Roles of Naturalistic Observation in Comparative Psychology," *Am. Psychol.* 32:211-219, 1977.
38. Mock, M.B., Reeder, G.S., Schaff, H.V., et al., "Percutaneous Transluminal Coronary Angioplasty Versus Coronary Artery Bypass," *N. Engl. J. Med.* 312:916-918, 1985.
39. *Morbidity and Mortality Weekly Report,* "Summary —Cases of Specified Notifiable Diseases, United States," 33(51/52):726, 1985.
40. Moriarty, A.M., Alexander, H., Lerner, R.A., et al., "Antibodies to Peptides Detect New Hepatitis B Antigen: Serological Correlation With Hepatocellular Carcinoma," *Science* 227:429-433, 1985.
41. National Research Council, *Models for Biomedical Research: A New Perspective* (Washington, DC: National Academy Press, 1985).
42. Orlans, F.B., "Classification of Animal Pain: Review of Protocols for Animal Welfare Concerns," paper presented at Animals and the Scientists: Institutional Responsibilities, The Johns Hopkins University, Baltimore, MD, May 21-22, 1984.
43. Paton, W., *Man and Mouse: Animals in Medical Research* (New York: Oxford University Press, 1984).
44. Pratt, D., *Alternatives to Pain in Experiments on Animals* (New York: Argus Archives, 1980).
45. *Primate News,* "Toward Better Health: The Role of Primates in Medical Research," 21(1):1-24, January 1984.
46. Randall, W.C., "Crises in Physiological Research," *Physiologist* 26:351-356, 1983.
47. Rapaport, E., "An Overview of Issues," Part II of *Circulation* 66(5):III-3-III-5, 1982.
48. Reichman, R.C., Badger, G.J., Mertz, G.J., et al., "Treatment of Recurrent Genital Herpes Simplex Infections With Oral Acyclovir," *JAMA* 251:2103-2107, 1984.
49. Robb, S.S., and Stegman, C.E., "Companion Animals and Elderly People: A Challenge for Evaluators of Social Support," *Gerontologist* 23:277-282, 1983.
50. Rosenthal, R., "Biasing Effects of Experimenters," *Etcetera* 34:253-264, 1977.
51. Rowan, A.N., *Of Mice, Models, & Men: A Critical Evaluation of Animal Research* (Albany, NY: State University of New York Press, 1984).
52. Scolnick, E.M., McLean, A.A., West, D.J., et al., "Clinical Evaluation in Healthy Adults of a Hepatitis B Vaccine Made by Recombinant DNA," *JAMA* 251: 2812-2815, 1984.
53. Seligman, M.E.P., "On the Generality of the Laws of Learning," *Psychol. Rev.* 77:406-418, 1970.
54. Simonsen, H.B., "Role of Applied Ethology in International Work on Farm Animal Welfare," *Vet. Rec.* 111:341-342, 1982.
55. Snowdon, C.T., "Ethology, Comparative Psychology, and Animal Behavior," *Ann. Rev. Psychol.* 34:63-94, 1983.
56. Soma, L.R., "Analgesic Management of the Experimental Animal," *National Symposium on Imperatives in Research Animal Use: Scientific Needs and Animal Welfare,* NIH Pub. No. 85-2746 (Bethesda, MD: National Institutes of Health, 1985).
57. Suarez, S.D., and Gallup, G.G., Jr., "Depression as a Response to Reproductive Failure," *J. Soc. Biol. Struct.,* in press.
58. Tuber, D.S., Hothersall, D., and Peters, M.F., "Treatment of Fears and Phobias in Dogs," *Vet. Clin. North Am. (Small Anim. Prac.)* 12:607-624, 1982.
59. U.S. Department of Health and Human Services, Public Health Service, National Center for Health Statistics, *Health, United States, 1983,* DHHS Pub. No. (PHS) 84-1232 (Washington, DC: U.S. Government Printing Office, December 1983).
60. U.S. Veterans' Administration Coronary Artery Bypass Surgery Cooperative Study Group, "Eleven-Year Survival in the Veterans Administration Randomized Trial of Coronary Bypass Surgery for Stable Angina," *N. Engl. J. Med.* 311:1333-1339, 1984.
61. Whittington, W., and Cates, W.J., Jr., "Acyclovir Therapy for Genital Herpes: Enthusiasm and Caution in Equal Doses," *JAMA* 251:2116-2117, 1984.
62. Wigdahl, B., Smith, C.A., Traglia, H.M., et al., "Herpes Simplex Virus Latency in Isolated Human Neurons," *Proc. Natl. Acad. Sci. USA* 81:6217-6221, 1984.
63. Willard, M.J., Dana, K., Stark, L., et al., "Training a Capuchin (*Cebus apella*) to Perform as an Aid for a Quadriplegic," *Primates* 23:520-532, 1982.

Chapter 6

Alternatives to Animal Use in Research

Unless we get a handle on what is happening in the mammalian *brain, there's no way of knowing whether any of these [invertebrate] models is right or not.*

Richard F. Thompson
Stanford University
Science 85 6(4):33, 1985

Investigators often ask statisticians how many observations they should make (fortunately, usually before the study begins). To be answerable, this question needs fuller formulation. There is a resemblance to the question, How much money should I take when I go on vacation? Fuller information is needed there too. How long a vacation? Where? With whom?

Three questions need to be answered before the sample size is determined. How variable are the data that will be collected? How precise an answer is needed? How much confidence should there be in the answer obtained? These questions can be well worth probing even if the question of sample size will foreseeably be answered by the size of the budget or the time available for the study. Sometimes a planned study is dropped because sample-size analysis shows that it has almost no chance of providing a useful answer under the constraints of time or budget that apply.

Lincoln E. Moses
Stanford University
N. Engl. J. Med. 312:890-897, 1985

CONTENTS

List of Tables

List of Figures

Alternatives to Animal Use in Research

Alternatives to animal use in biomedical and behavioral research fall into four broad categories:

- **continued, but modified, animal use,** including a reduction in the number of animals used, improved experimental design and statistical analyses of results, substitution of cold-blooded for warm-blooded vertebrates, substitution of laboratory mammals for domestic or companion mammals, and reduction of pain or experimental insult;
- **use of living systems,** including in vitro cultures (of cells, tissues, and organs; see table 6-1), embryos, invertebrates, micro-organisms, and plants;
- **use of nonliving systems,** such as chemical or physical systems; and
- **computer simulation.**

In this chapter, various disciplines within biomedical and behavioral research are surveyed in order to focus attention on the most promising areas for development of alternatives to animal methods. Areas not amenable to the implementation of such alternatives are also identified.

As noted in chapter 5, distinctions within and among the varied disciplines of biomedical and behavioral research are artificial in one sense: Boundaries among disciplines are often blurred, and broad areas of overlap exist. Yet the examination of discrete areas of research highlights the great variability among disciplines in the potential for using alternatives to animals.

Using alternative methods in research holds several advantages from scientific, economic, and humane perspectives, including:

- reduction in the number of animals used;
- reduction in animal pain, suffering, and experimental insult;
- reduction in investigator-induced, artifactual physiological phenomena;
- savings in time, with the benefit of obtaining results more quickly;
- the ability to perform replicative protocols on a routine basis;
- reduction in the cost of research;
- a greater flexibility to alter conditions and variables of the experimental protocol;
- reduction of error stemming from inter-individual variability; and
- the intrinsic potential of in vitro techniques to study cellular and molecular mechanisms.

At the same time, these methods are fraught with inherent disadvantages, including:

- reduced ability to study organismal growth processes;
- reduced ability to study cells, tissues, and organ systems acting in concert;
- reduced ability to study integrated biochemical and metabolic pathways;

Table 6-1.—Research Methods Involving Living Components

Isolated perfused organs using:	Isolated tissue or tissue sample using:	Isolated single cell using:	Subcellular constituents using:
liver	striated muscle	fat cells	nuclei
muscle	iris	liver cells	mitochondria
heart	trachea	neurons	microsomes
lung	bronchi	glial cells	lysosomes
adrenal gland	lung	striated muscle cells	synaptosomes
pituitary gland	uterus	smooth muscle cells	cell membranes
intestine	intestine	red blood cells	muscle actin/myosin
testis	seminal vesicle	leukocytes	
skin	vas deferens	platelets	
spleen	bladder	mast cells	
kidney	spleen		
	salivary gland		
	fat pads		
	liver slice		

SOURCE: Adapted from W. Paton, *Man and Mouse: Animals in Medical Research* (New York: Oxford University Press, 1984).

- reduced ability to study behavior;
- reduced ability to study the recovery of damaged tissue;
- reduced ability to study interaction between the organism and its environment;
- reduced ability to study idiosyncratic or species-specific responses;
- reduced ability to distinguish between male- and female-specific phenomena; and
- a handicap to probing the unknown and phenomena not yet identified.

This general listing of advantages and disadvantages provides a framework for examining the use of alternatives in specific disciplines of biomedical and behavioral research. Many of these pros and cons are cited in this chapter's detailed description of alternatives.

CONTINUED, BUT MODIFIED, USE OF ANIMALS IN BIOMEDICAL RESEARCH

Animal use in biomedical research can be modified in a number of ways, including strengthening experimental design to use fewer animals, reducing the degree of experimental insult, and substituting one organism for another. In the case of substitution, cold-blooded vertebrates may supplant warm-blooded ones.

Reduction in the Number of Animals Used

Up to half the animals used in research protocols may be untreated, or control, animals. The importance of using parallel, internally controlled designs for experimentation may be one of the first lessons learned by science students whose results are rejected for not providing comparable data from treatment groups of animals matched for size, age, sex, and dosage. Studies with investigator-initiated, internal controls support substantially stronger inferences than those without them.

Common and Historical Controls

Fewer animals may be used in an experiment by sharing a control group with other investigators or by not using a concurrent control group. In both cases, all the physical and genetic characteristics of the treatment group(s) must be matched to those of the control group, and the conditions under which the data are collected must be as precisely duplicated as possible. There are difficulties unique to each method. Investigators may encounter constraints on their particular study when sharing controls. For example, sharing may be impossible if one group needs to extend its studies beyond the time agreed for termination and autopsy of the shared animals, or if the actions of one group adversely affect the other, as might happen by the inadvertent spreading of a parasite or pathogen. In the case of historical controls, the difficulty rests in exactly duplicating earlier conditions. Use of such controls must be carefully documented and justified (82).

Animal Sharing

Another way to use fewer animals is to share individual experimental animals or their tissues between research groups. Although this method may encounter the same types of difficulties described for the sharing of controls, it appears to be gaining in popularity among compatible groups. At the University of Virginia, investigators in endocrinology (Department of Internal Medicine) and in the molecular genetics of heme synthesis (Department of Biology) use the pituitaries and livers of the same rats even though the two departments are on opposite sides of the campus (54).

Research animals may also be shared among different sites. This is especially practicable in the case of long-lived primates. As long as sequential protocols are not deemed inhumane or scientifically conflicting, primates may be shipped from one research site to another. The Primate Research Institute (PRI) of New Mexico State University, for example, will loan chimpanzees and rhesus and cynomolgus monkeys to qualified U.S. scientists. PRI currently has 240 chimpanzees on campus, with another 150 animals on loan.

Using animals maximally in a confined area is a mandatory part of experimental design in the research program of the National Aeronautics and Space Administration (NASA). Protocols typically call for investigators to combine projects and make efficient use of one small group of animals (125).

Improved Experimental or Statistical Design

"Every time a particle of statistical method is properly used, fewer animals are employed than would otherwise have been necessary," wrote Russell and Burch some 27 years ago (174). Since then, progress has been made both in the number of statistical tools available and in the training of investigators in the use of these tools. Yet training still lags behind the availability of tools. Insufficient information for critical evaluation and inappropriate statistical analyses appear frequently in the literature, particularly with investigators using the t-test in cases for which analysis of variance is the appropriate measure (82).

An analysis of variance simultaneously tests two or more parameters of treatment groups for indication of significant difference. When the test statistic falls in the rejection region, the researcher can be reasonably sure that a real difference exists between treatments. The t-test estimates the difference between the mean values of one parameter of two treatments. It is a powerful measure of significance when the number of comparisons is small, but it is subject to an increasingly large potential for error as the number of parameters grows. Using multiple t-tests increases the risk of finding a significant difference between treatments where there is none. Such observations are not esoteric, since poor summarization and statistical usage may reflect poor experimental design, calling into question the results of an investigation and leading to otherwise unnecessary repetition. At least one group, the Harvard Study Group on Statistics in the Biomedical Sciences, is pursuing ways to improve statistical practice and reporting (64).

Serial sacrifice, crossover, and group sequential testing are three experimental designs that can reduce animal use in laboratory research (82). In serial sacrifice, animals with induced effects are randomly selected for sacrifice and examination for the occurrence and progress of effects over time. Such studies, as in radiation oncology (22), have the dual advantage of cutting short the time some animals must spend in an affected state and providing information about changes within the animal other than those observed when it is allowed to die without further interference. The primary disadvantage is that survival information is compromised; therefore, the resulting data cannot be compared with other studies in which survival serves as an end point.

A crossover design may be appropriate for studies in which short-term effects are expected. Each animal serves as its own control by first receiving either a drug or a placebo, and then receiving the reverse. Such a design can be highly useful in laboratory and clinical testing, but crossovers must be used judiciously. Should there be any unexpected long-term effects, the entire test is invalidated and would need to be repeated as two separate tests.

In the group sequential design, treatment groups are compared with each other in stages. For example, if two groups are given the same dosage of two different drugs, experimentation at higher dosages is undertaken only if there is no statistically significant difference between the responses of the two groups. The sooner a difference between groups is observed, the fewer the number of trials run. Both crossover and group sequential designs have potential applications in anesthesiology, endocrinology, nutrition, pharmacology, radiology, teratology, and toxicology.

A commonly mentioned method of reducing the number of animals used is smaller treatment groups. Yet within the biomedical research community a frequently heard complaint is that too few animals to yield useful estimates are likely to be included in each treatment group, particularly in fields such as radiology (95). Problems of this nature generally grow out of the extreme economic pressures being applied to investigators to control animal costs. Well-established techniques such as saturation analyses, particularly radioimmunoassays, have radically reduced the number of animals used for any one procedure, but they may have resulted in little or no reduction in overall use, since they have made previously difficult analyses more accessible to many more investigators.

Substituting One Species for Another

In some instances, laboratory mammals (e.g., rodents) or nonmammalian vertebrates can be used in place of companion mammals (e.g., dogs), domestic species (e.g., sheep), or primates (e.g., monkeys). As more information on the physiology, biochemistry, and endocrinology of laboratory mammals and nonmammalian species accumulates and is demonstrated to be like or unlike that of humans, greater use can be made of laboratory species, which in turn can generate more information and reduce future needs for research. Comparative neuroscience is perhaps the most rapidly expanding field and is related to physiology, biochemistry, pharmacology, developmental biology, and zoology (33). Some brain components have been found to be remarkably similar between vertebrate species (69).

Economics plays a large part in the selection of how many and what kind of animals will be used in some research (see ch. 11). An investigator following up on previous work will generally begin with the species already in use, changing only if money becomes scarcer or if a better model is clearly demonstrated. Investigators starting anew are likely to seek the advice of a facility veterinarian or of colleagues as to which species best fits their needs and to begin with the smallest acceptable animal. Still other researchers deliberately begin work with a novel animal model in order to create a new research niche.

One of the principal reasons for the increased use of rodents in all areas of biomedical research has been the availability of genetically homogeneous or pathogen-free strains. For some studies, however, a further degree of genetic definition is needed. These studies require that the research animal carry some specific genetic traits that are suited to the objectives of the research. Because of their high reproductive potential, rodents are ideal for this type of "custom designing" and extensive use is being made of these animals in a variety of disciplines (109). Oncology and immunology are two of the more familiar areas of use (92). Pharmacological research using an ethanol-preferring strain of rats has prepared the way for exploration of the genetics of alcoholism (212). Further, the male Lewis rat, an animal that rapidly acquires testicular lesions and antibodies to sperm after vasectomy, is a candidate for study of the reversal of vasectomy. This research could answer questions of human concern in anatomy, physiology, immunology, endocrinology, and reconstructive surgery (100).

Chickens and their embryos play an important role in developmental biology, endocrinology, histology, and zoology. Other current uses are in molecular biology, in which embryonic chicken brain tissue is being cultured to study the neural-cell adhesion molecule (193), and biochemistry, in which the embryonic chicken liver is being used to study the acquisition of hormone responsiveness during embryogenesis (62). In cardiology, turkeys with inherited Turkey Round Heart disease serve as models of cardiomyopathy (107), and turkey erythrocytes are fused with amphibian erythrocytes to study receptors that mediate physiological functions in heart, smooth muscle, and other tissues (199).

Frogs have long been used in anatomy, biochemistry, developmental biology, physiology, and zoology. They continue to be widely used in those disciplines and, additionally, are currently being used by NASA in radiology studies (125). In dental research, frogs are used to assess digital transplants to augment tooth and jaw regeneration (101). The newt *Triturus*—able to regenerate its limbs, eye lens, tail, and spinal cord—is used in developmental biology to explore mechanisms of organ regeneration (90). Turtles are used in physiology to study, for example, retinal mechanisms subserving color vision. The cone cells of the turtle retina are especially conducive to such research (161).

Fish are used in research to a lesser degree than other vertebrates, considering that there are over 30,000 species and their care is relatively uncomplicated. It has been suggested that fish would make excellent subjects for nutritional research, since many are known to show specific vitamin deficiency symptoms (210). Physiologists have used goldfish to study the implications of myelin-sheath resistances in demyelinating diseases (73). Rainbow trout embryos are being used in oncology research (93). Further, there has been recent interest in a specialized feature of some piscine species: the electric organ. This tissue is exceptionally rich in a single class of cholinergic synapses. Biochemists, geneticists, and molecular biologists working with this material have determined that the structure of the acetylcholine receptor protein is remarkably like a human's (39).

Reduction of Pain or Experimental Insult

Until recently, the probability of a research animal receiving the correct amount or type of anesthetic depended largely on the inclination of individual investigators. They could accept information about anesthesia available from previous research or attempt to improve on it. In some cases where little information was available, guesswork was required. Now, the enhanced presence of facility veterinarians and animal care and use committees with oversight authority (see ch. 15) has resulted in experimental animals being recognized as veterinary patients entitled to protection from as much pain and distress as possible, while maintaining the integrity of research.

Analgesics, anesthetics, and tranquilizers are the principle tools for the reduction of experimental pain and distress (see ch. 5). Terminal anesthesia and death has become the method of choice following major organ surgery on animals, even though it might be argued that observation of the healing process logically constitutes a part of surgical research (224). Where postsurgical study is considered necessary, as in cardiology, intensive postoperative control of pain can be used in lieu of maintaining the animal under general anesthesia until death (24).

Advances in Instrumentation

New types of instruments are critical to a reduction in experimental insult, as they can lead directly to the more refined or reduced use of live animals or living material. In the past decade, practically every piece of instrumentation in biomedical laboratories has been adapted to handle "micro" samples or has been replaced by new microtechnology. Some examples of microinstrumentation include:

- In reproductive physiology, a 1.0 microliter sample of rat epididymal fluid collected by micropuncture can be used to examine sperm motility, determine total protein, and determine androgen-binding protein activity (207).
- In biochemistry and molecular genetics, electrophysiological techniques are being used to explore the possibility of recording the opening and closing of single membrane channels, tiny pores controlling cellular function (105).
- To study leukemias, blood diseases, and inborn errors in metabolism, a method for measuring the enzyme kinetics within a single white blood cell has been developed (134).
- A device is available that will dispense a 1.0 microliter sample as 1,000 aliquots (1 nanoliter each) for use in biochemical enzyme research or for clinical samples such as cerebrospinal fluid from infants (97).

The use of small samples for analysis by mass spectrometry (146) and by gas or liquid chromatography (86,208) exemplifies minimally invasive technology. Each year, an entire issue of *Science* magazine is devoted to trends in analytical instrumentation (2,3). Continued developments in analytical instrumentation, including noninvasive imaging techniques such as magnetic resonance imaging (MRI), will likely reduce the experimental insults faces by research animals.

In vivo measurements using fiber optics now provide miniaturized spectrophotometric analysis from within the ducts and blood vessels, determine blood velocity, measure temperature changes, monitor intracranial and intracardiac pressure, measure fluorescent marker molecules in tumors, measure pH, and even determine glucose concentration (166). Fiber optics offer great promise: They can be inserted into vessels and ducts via small catheters with little discomfort and into the abdominal cavity using local anesthetics (a laparoscopy), and they can be used repeatedly within the same animal to obtain measurements without permanent damage. Chronic intravascular catheters are used in a similar way to obtain repeated blood samples for hormone measurement from freely moving, undisturbed animals (see fig. 6-1) (189).

Other minimally invasive techniques in animal research include immunoscintigraphy, amniocentesis, and use of the laser. In immunoscintigraphy,

Figure 6-1.—Apparatus for Remote Blood-Sampling via Chronic, Intravascular Catheter From Unrestrained Ferret

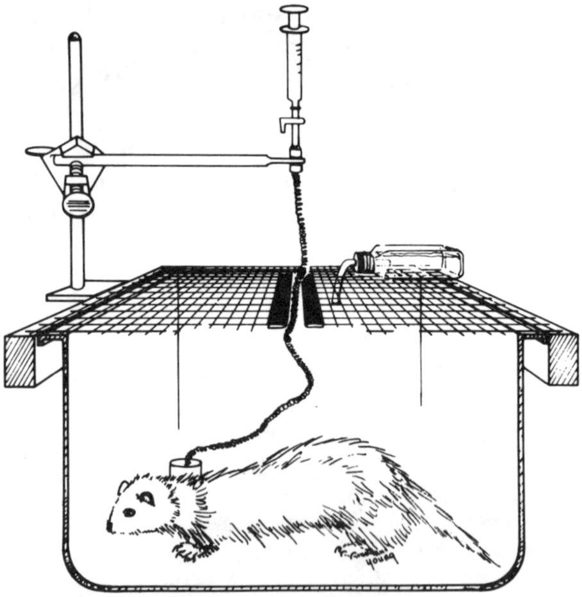

SOURCE: C.L. Sisk, Michigan State University.

the production of target-specific monoclonal antibodies has improved the ability of external radioimaging techniques to locate tumors and to identify certain noncancerous diseases; radiolabeled antibodies attach to the target tissue and are then visualized (59). Amniocentesis is used for the early detection of genetic diseases, teratological events, and fetal distress, particularly in domestic species (67). A new application of the laser in oncology involves its ability to initiate a lethal photochemical reaction in cancerous tissue during photoradiation therapy (41).

Some apparently new noninvasive techniques are actually adapted, miniaturized, or computerized versions of older methods. One such example is a small, inflatable tail cuff used to measure blood pressure in a rat's tail during hypertension studies (225). In another example, urine is used in some specialized methods: In physiological research, electrical impedance measures canine urinary output (1).

Tandem mass spectrometry is being used for breath analysis to screen for diabetes, cirrhosis, renal disease, and ovulation. Many diseases remain to be examined, but there is potential for use of this technique in toxicology, nutrition, metabolic diseases, endocrinology, anesthesia, physiology, and pathology (133).

A technique developed for the determination of the quality of agricultural crops (162) and the percent of fat in beef (135) uses amplified, digitized, computer-corrected diffuse reflectance spectrophotometry in the near-infrared region. It involves simply placing an appropriate sensor on the surface of the skin and it can be adapted for oncological, physiological, and nutritional research (102).

Other increasingly popular noninvasive techniques include ultrasonography—which is used in cardiology to locate vessels (145), to determine blood-flow velocity (176), and to detect early atherosclerosis (108)—and magnetic resonance imaging, used to examine the energetics of skeletal muscle in gerontological research (201), to diagnose metabolic disorders (32), and to provide details of molecular structure and dynamics in liquids and solids (130).

USE OF LIVING SYSTEMS IN BIOMEDICAL RESEARCH

In Vitro Research

In vitro biomedical research entails the maintenance of organs, tissues (or fragments of organs and tissues), and cells outside of the body. Depending on the conditions of harvesting and preparing the living material for in vitro maintenance, the cells may be grown as a population of independent cells (cell culture) or with the normal tissue or organ architecture preserved. In the former, the cells may be encouraged to proliferate, resulting in numerous descendant cell populations suitable for studies on growth, nutrition, cell division, and gene expression and regulation.

Table 6-2, which summarizes the characteristics of in vitro systems, makes it clear that as organization is disrupted or lost, the in vitro system has less and less of the kind of intercellular and intracellular interactions that characterize organs,

Table 6-2.—Properties of In Vitro Culture Systems

Preparation and consequences	Level of tissue organization	Reproducibility	Expression similar to in vivo	Genetic alteration by mutation and/or selection	Environmental control
Intact system (no consequence)	++++	++++	++++	+	+
Organ culture (remove influences of whole organism)	++++	++++	+ to +++	+	++
Tissue culture (remove influences of whole organisms)	+++	+++	+ to +++	+	+++
Primary cell cultures (disrupt intercellular relationships)	0	++	+ to +++	+	++++
Cell lines (intercellular relationships are reduced; cell proliferation is enhanced, at times with little control)	0	++++	+ to +++	+ to ++++	++++

KEY: ++++ = High degree; +++ = Moderate degree; ++ = Modest degree; + = Some degree; 0 = None.

SOURCE: Adapted from R.M. Nardone and L.A. Ouellette, "Scope of 'Alternatives': Overview of the State of the Art," contract report prepared for the Office of Technology Assessment, U.S. Congress, July 1984.

tissues, and cells in the body. Nevertheless, improved accessibility of added chemicals and the opportunity to achieve genetic homogeneity by cloning and genetic manipulation by selection and fusion are important trade-offs. Indeed, at times cell-to-cell interaction may interfere with an experimental objective (156).

The explosive growth of in vitro research during the 1960s and 1970s is illustrated by the fact that the *Index of Tissue Culture* had 84 pages of entries in 1965, 207 pages in 1970, 566 pages in 1975, and 636 pages in 1980, when the publication was discontinued because computerized information retrieval was warranted. There is virtually no field of biomedical research that has not been affected by in vitro technology. In vitro models for the study of cell senescence, atherosclerosis, development, growth, and immune reactions are illustrative of the diversity of applications in biomedical research (156).

The specific conditions that best support the maintenance, growth, or differentiation of each type of culture must be determined before any useful information can be garnered. Some of the general requirements of culture systems are combinations of the proper gas atmosphere, humidity, temperature, pH, and nutrients. Other culture systems may also have specific light, motion, pressure, and physical or chemical support requirements. Under the proper conditions, many can be subcultured for months or frozen in liquid nitrogen for years without loss of their unique, differentiated properties.

The ability to maintain many continuous cell lines has opened the floodgates of experimentation and made the new technologies accessible to all the disciplines of biomedical research. Other advantages include ease of transport from one laboratory or country to another, the ability to culture both normal and abnormal tissue for comparison and research, the use of human cells to eliminate species variation, and the ability to expose cultures directly to exogenous molecules at specific concentrations for precise time periods. Disadvantages include the changes in structure or function observed in some cultures, and the fact that isolated systems give isolated results that may bear little relation to results obtained from the integrated systems of whole animals.

Organ Culture

At some point in the history of research, investigators have attempted with varying success to isolate and maintain every major and minor mammalian organ, for a variety of purposes. In recent years, improved techniques, such as the availability of artificial blood media, have increased the probability of successful organ culture. Blood, or artificial blood media, can be pumped through the organ to sustain it ("perfusion") (see fig. 6-2). Current applications of organ perfusion include the study of protein synthesis in lactating guinea pig mammary tissue (136) and the use of human placentas in toxicology studies, with additional potential for use in oncology and gerontology research (99).

Figure 6-2—Schematic of Experimental Organ Perfusion

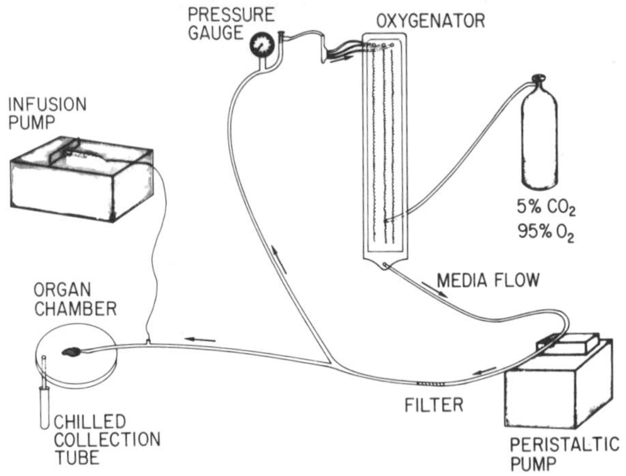

SOURCE: C. Chubb, The University of Texas Health Science Center at Dallas.

Organ Perfusion: Mouse Testis With Pipette Introduced Into Artery

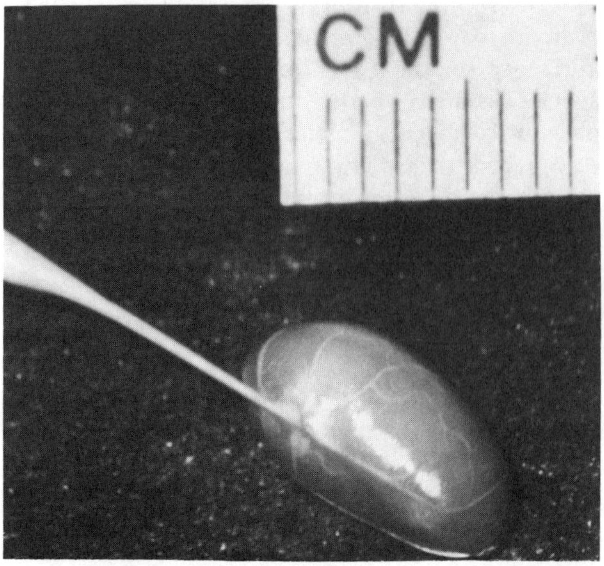

Photo credit: C. Chubb, The University of Texas Health Science Center at Dallas

Whole organs are not generally amenable to long-term in vitro culture or growth. The size and complexity of whole organs make it impossible for them to receive sufficient nourishment for normal function without external support. Nevertheless, whole organs are fundamental to many types of anatomy, histology, and pathology because of their suitability for the examination of relationships between cells and tissues, and they can be sustained in culture for hours or days.

Cryostat sections (thin slices of frozen tissue cut with a microtome) through organs are maintained in vitro for oncology studies into organ-specific adhesion of metastatic tumor cells. This method closely reflects the in vivo event and therefore could eventually reduce the use of whole animals in a very active research area (159).

Whole mammalian embryos, in addition to their obligatory use in the investigation of basic developmental biology, have been cultured in vitro for other purposes. Protocols have included examinations of the effects of hormones and teratogens (42).

Tissue Culture

Many normal and pathological tissues from humans and a variety of animal species can be successfully maintained and studied in culture. Indeed, the progress that has been achieved since 1907, when R.G. Harrison first maintained frog neural tissue outside of the body for weeks, has changed the field of tissue culture from an art into a science. Keeping cultures of anything other than bacteria or viruses alive for more than a few hours was problematic until the 1950s, when investigators began to gain a better understanding of the requirements of cells and the addition of antibiotics to culture systems. The viability of cultures was extended substantially by controlling bacterial contamination.

In tissue culture, isolated pieces of a living organism are maintained with their various cell types arranged as they were in the original organism and with their differentiated functions intact. Such cultures are both "better" and "worse" than cultures of a single cell type. They are better in that the effects of manipulation can be observed in a more natural environment and different cell types can interact as they would in vivo. They are worse in that they are much more difficult to maintain. Although tissue-culture experiments require the sacrifice of an animal, they can be viewed as alternatives to animal use since numerous sections of adjoining tissue can be removed and compared. In this way, two or more treatments are administered to tissues, rather than to a number of individual animals.

Tissue culture is being successfully employed in many disciplines of biomedical research. In neurology, the use of embryonic rat mesencephalon tissues to examine the destruction of dopamine neurons has replaced the use of primates (154). Prior to this development, the monkey had served as the best model for the study of degenerative effects observed in humans. Adult rats, cats, and guinea pigs have been shown to be resistant to the destruction of dopamine neurons. Metabolic studies of an experimental antiarthritis agent have made use of the inside of hamster and rat intestinal walls (202). Physiological experiments examined the dynamics of secretion with mouse epididymis (70).

Cell Culture

Although cell culture is not a new technique, developments and applications during the past decade have come so rapidly as to create whole new research institutions and industries. Cell culture today touches every discipline of biomedical research, as well as clinical practice. The following illustrates the pervasiveness of this approach in biomedical research:

- Eggs and sperm from many species have been used by endocrinologists, physiologists, and biochemists to study the mechanisms involved in fertilization and early development (58,157).
- A hamster ovary cell line and its mutants are being used to explore the biochemistry of a membrane-associated protein essential to all animal cell function (175).
- In oncology, human interferon derived from bacterial recombinant DNA induces a transformation of human white blood cells similar to that observed during infection, cancer, and rheumatoid arthritis. This change in white blood cells provides clues to the pathology of cancer (216).
- Steroid metabolism is being studied using cultured rat epididymal cells (29).
- A monkey kidney cell line was employed to demonstrate the metabolic effects of several general anesthetics (26).
- Geneticists are developing an in vitro method of studying heme gene expression (54).
- Surgical research into the use of cultured human epithelium for permanent coverage of large burn wounds has moved from the laboratory into clinical trials (76).

In immunology, studies on antibody synthesis and response have been bolstered by the Nobel-prize-winning elucidation of monoclonal antibodies. In its initial steps, this technique consumes large numbers of animals, as the varying immune responses of many mice are probed. Then, cloned cells from the spleen of one mouse can be exploited to produce valuable, highly specific antibodies. Antibodies so produced can obviate the need for many rabbits, sheep, and even humans in the large-scale production of antibodies. Perhaps of even greater importance for research is the high quality of the antibody produced by monoclonal cells. A comprehensive listing of current research being conducted with monoclonal antibodies from cloned cells is beyond the scope of this assessment. Some of the diagnostic potentials of monoclonal antibodies being explored in biomedical research are:

- the characterization of malignant and benign tumors;
- the identification of autoimmune antibodies in rheumatoid arthritis, systemic lupus erythematosus, myasthenia gravis, and other autoimmune diseases;
- the identification and quantification of serum proteins, hormones, and their cell-surface receptors;
- the monitoring of therapeutic drugs and identification of novel therapeutic drugs;
- the rapid diagnosis of bacterial, viral, fungal, and parasitic diseases;
- the monitoring and identification of lymphoid and hematopoietic cells in disease states; and
- pregnancy testing.

Biologists have developed techniques for the controlled disruption of cells that can leave many organelles intact or allow the harvesting of selected intracellular membranes. These fractions have proved to be invaluable in the search for information at the molecular level. For example, microsomal membrane fractions from rat and human liver have been used in comparative anesthesia research (27). In endocrinology, human placental and ovarian microsomes were used to demonstrate inhibition of steroid hormone synthesis by plant chemicals (112). In dentistry, proteins purified from unerupted fetal buds were shown to be in-

38-750 0 - 86 - 5

hibitory toward seeded enamel growth in culture (56). In virology, infected cell nuclei isolated from a hamster cell line were used to study influenza virion RNA replication (16). In metabolic studies, the inhibition of chick-embryo-derived collagen fibril formation by glucose suggests a direct relationship between excess glucose and poor wound healing observed in people with diabetes mellitus (126). One of the most unique uses of subcellular fractions involves the bringing together of mixed species systems in biochemical studies of protein transport across intercellular membranes. For example, researchers studying intracellular protein translocation used dog pancreatic microsomes, bovine pituitary and rabbit reticulocyte messenger RNA, bacterial nuclease, and a wheat germ cell-free system to elucidate the structure of the signal recognition particle (213).

Human Tissues and Cells

Cultured human fetal lung cells have been found to be excellent hosts to support the developmental cycle of a protozoan parasite that causes severe, persistent, life-threatening diarrhea in immunodeficient patients. There has been no effective therapy for this illness, so the in vitro system offers an opportunity to study the parasite's behavior, development, and metabolism and provides a potential method for screening therapeutic agents (50).

Virologists and oncologists have been very quick to take advantage of new human in vitro culture systems. For example, an embryonal carcinoma cell line from the stem cells of a teratocarcinoma is being used to study cytomegalovirus replication (83). Lysis of herpes simplex virus (HSV) type 2 is being investigated using human monocytes (117), and HSV latency is studied by using isolated neurons obtained from human fetuses (220).

The use of postmortem material from humans has significance in many areas of biomedical research, but particularly in neurology. Investigators studying the unconventional slow-virus diseases use brain tissue from humans with Creutzfeldt-Jakob disease and from animals with scrapie (144). Postmortem material from schizophrenics has provided evidence for two distinct categories of that disease (181), and temporal lobe structures from Alzheimer patients have revealed specific pathological cellular patterns in the brain hippocampal formation (104).

Examples of the use of human tissue for investigations aimed at human treatment can today be drawn from every discipline of biomedical research. Advances in in-vitro culture methods are likely to increase this use further. Postmortem tissue use is likely to continue.

Invertebrates

Invertebrates represent over 90 percent of nonplant species on the earth. Although their body structure is much less similar to humans than is vertebrate body structure, invertebrate anatomy, physiology, and biochemistry offer avenues for new approaches that have been only partially explored.

Caenorhabditis elegans, a 1 millimeter roundworm, is of intense interest to developmental biologists. As they have traced this nematode's complete cell lineage, it offers an unprecedented opportunity for the study of individual living cells (38).

Other terrestrial invertebrates are used in many disciplines of biomedical research. For example, flies, bees, earthworms, and leeches are involved in various aspects of anatomy, physiology, and biochemistry (5,33). Ants and bees are used in vision research (4). Fruit flies are well known for their participation in genetic studies. Age-related metabolic changes in other insects are being investigated for possible use in aging research (184).

Marine invertebrates represent an important, largely untapped research resource. One commentator (190) has suggested that the lack of opportunity by medical scientists to learn marine biology and the failure of marine biologists to learn pathology have combined to leave marine species overlooked. A notable exception to the underuse of marine invertebrates is neurobiology. The coelenterates, including hydra, corals, anemones, and jellyfish, have helped scientists understand primitive nervous system biochemistry. Lobsters and squid have contributed to knowledge of brain anatomy and physiology, and the grazing snail and crayfish have broadened understanding of cell biology (33).

Four advantages of using invertebrates in biomedical research are:

- different phylogenetic levels of structural and functional specialization can be exploited (e.g., different types of circulatory systems, novel chemical compounds);
- invertebrates reproduce rapidly and produce numerous offspring; experiments can be executed in days and weeks instead of months and years;
- storage, upkeep, and maintenance are inexpensive; and
- invertebrates are not prone to spreading disease throughout a colony;

The overwhelming disadvantage is the considerable phylogenetic distance between invertebrates and humans.

Micro-organisms

From its origins within the medical disciplines of bacteriology, pathology, and virology, the study and use of micro-organisms has branched out to influence practically every area of biomedical research, as these examples indicate:

- *Salmonella typhimurium*—bacteria used in mechanistic studies in genetics (124) as well as the Ames mutagenicity/carcinogenicity test (see ch. 8);
- *Escherichia coli*—bacteria used by developmental biologists to derive theories of gene control (90) and by molecular biologists in recombinant DNA research (75);
- *Streptococcus mutans*—bacteria used in dental research on the metabolic activity of plaque (91);
- *Bacillus subtilis* (bacteria) spores, *Artemina salina* (brine shrimp) eggs, and *Sordaria fimilcula* (fungi) ascospores—all incorporated into NASA's biostack (monolayers of biological test organisms sandwiched between thin foils of different types of nuclear track detectors) radiology experiments inside Spacelab I (31);
- *Tetrahymena pyriformis*—a ciliate protozoan being used to study the effects of anesthetics on metabolism (44); and
- a host of microscopic protozoans, metazoans, and rotifers used to investigate the physiology and biochemistry of photoreception and vision (4).

The advantages of using micro-organisms in biomedical research are fourfold: They reproduce rapidly at body temperature; rapid division (every 20 to 30 minutes) makes them useful for short-term studies; multigenerational studies can be performed in a short period of time; and they are inexpensive in terms of storage, upkeep, and maintenance. The major disadvantage stems from the fact that these are unicellular organisms: As a consequence, the interaction of cells cannot be studied (156).

Plants

One advantage of using organisms from the plant kingdom is that they lack anything resembling a nervous system. Presumably, plants do not feel pain; they appear to be good potential alternatives to animals. Plants, like micro-organisms, are relatively easy and inexpensive to propagate (156).

Although there is some interest in the potential use of plant cells in toxicology and oncology research (191), the use of whole cells from plants is obstructed by their very rigid cell-wall structure compared with the relatively fluid animal cell membrane. This prevents their use in many disciplines where intimate cell surface contact or transmembrane communication is essential.

Once removed from the cell, comparable organelles from plants and animals (including micro-organisms) are essentially indistinguishable in both appearance and function. For example, in studies having potentially broad applications in endocrinology and immunology, yeasts have been found to contain active steroid hormone systems (118). Yeast is used in cell biology in studies of the import of proteins into mitochondria, organelles that are essentially the same whatever their source (129). An extensive literature in cell biology, genetics, molecular biology, and virology supports the use of subcellular fractions from plants and animals, separately or together, for research into basic molecular mechanisms (213).

USE OF NONLIVING SYSTEMS IN BIOMEDICAL RESEARCH

Chemical and Physical Systems

Long before the advent of modern technology, researchers were constructing chemical models of certain phenomena that occur in living systems. There is a long and rich history in biochemistry, for example, of the application of nonliving systems to experimentation (128,147).

Enzyme biochemistry continues to be a principal area of application of nonliving methodology in biomedical research. Enzyme mechanisms may be studied in a totally chemical system. Magnetic resonance imaging is used to obtain from enzymes in solution detailed structural data and information about the mechanism of enzyme action. By combining MRI with cryoenzymology—the use of enzyme solutions held at subzero temperatures—enzymatic reactions can be slowed enough to study intermediate products that would ordinarily exist for too short a time to be detected. Investigations that had been restricted to in vivo manipulations can now be expanded into a far wider range in vitro (131).

In dental research, a chemical system mimics the mechanics of the formation of dental caries. A two-chambered diffusion cell pairs an excess amount of specific protein crystals with a chemical solution of artificial "plaque-saliva." Dissolution of the crystals can be studied under varying chemical conditions relevant to a better understanding of the caries process (40).

In the field of membrane biophysics, the advent of synthetic membranes has proved a boon to research and stands as one of the premier examples of nonliving alternatives to animal use. Liposomes are synthetic vesicles made of protein and fatty molecules. Their structure can be dictated by the investigator, who can combine proteins and lipids of different types and in different ratios to yield an artificial membrane. As with true biological membranes, the barriers formed by liposomes are selectively permeable. These artificial membranes are particularly useful in basic studies of the transport of molecules across membranes and of membrane damage (12).

Except for the use of mannequins to simulate accident victims in the transportation industry and in trauma centers, the principal use of physical and mechanical systems today is in education (see ch. 9) rather than in biomedical research. However, it is not inconceivable that future combinations of mechanical and electronic technology could provide biomedical researchers with artificial research subjects capable of independent, unanticipated responses.

Epidemiology: Using Existing Databases

The use of existing databases to gain new information and insights in biomedical research may be a major underused resource, if the paucity of published results is any criteria. One study that relied on such information concentrated on the relationship between 17 nutrients and the potential for development of hypertension cardiovascular disease in more than 10,000 people from the database of the National Center for Health Statistics' Health and Nutrition Examination Survey (HANES I) (137). The results proved to be highly controversial, with some of the criticism aimed at the use of the database (119).

Too little information is currently available to evaluate fully the potential dimensions of the salutary use of epidemiologic databases in basic biomedical research. The possibility exists that their enhanced use may constitute an important nonanimal method.

COMPUTER SIMULATION IN BIOMEDICAL RESEARCH

Modern approaches to biomedical research describe the functions of living systems at all organizational levels by the language of science—mathematics. Knowledge is acquired by investigating relationships among cells, tissues, fluids, organs, and organ systems. By the processes of trial and error and of hypothesis and testing, relationships begin to be understood and can be described by mathematical expressions. These can range from simple, linear functions to various types of curved functions to multidimensional surface functions and may involve kinetic data expressed by differential equations. Variables in these equations include physical terms, such as time, temperature, weight, energy, force, volume, and motion. Complex mathematical relationships may be developed to express these cause-and-effect relationships more clearly. In some instances, a relatively simple relationship may be shown to exist, but this is unusual, since living systems are highly interactive and multidimensional in nature (48).

A relationship that can be reasonably expressed in a mathematical equation may be considered to be a candidate biological model. The limits within which the expression will hold determine the utility and validity of the model. If it is possible to change one or more parameters in the equation, and thereby obtain the same response or responses as found in live animal research, the model may be used to "simulate" a biological preparation. Simulation implies that an investigator can manipulate the parameters at will and observe the resultant effects on the model. Used in this way, computer simulation is a useful tool for research and especially for suggesting new mechanisms or hypotheses for further study (48).

At the subcellular level, information is usually gained by electron microscopic examination or by analytical methods for the sequencing of amino acids and nucleic acids. Such information tends to be of a descriptive or topological nature rather than numerical. Recent strides in genetic engineering based on increased knowledge of DNA, RNA, and protein amino acid sequencing have required computers to store and match nucleic acid and amino acid sequences numbering in the millions (163). These capabilities are not equivalent to simulation, but they share with simulation a reliance on computers for storage and processing.

At the level of one or a few cells, models are being sought for computer simulation of sliding filament systems—believed to be the basic movement of muscle fibers, cilia, and flagella (28). Modeling of the function of individual cone cells in the eye is under study at the National Institutes of Health (NIH) (167).

Most efforts toward computer simulation of biological systems are directed at higher levels of organization, such as organs and organ systems. This bias is a consequence of the need to understand numerous feedback systems within living systems. Feedback systems are the basis for an organism's ability to maintain a homeostatic, or steady, state. Feedback mechanisms involve several organs as well as communication via the bloodstream and nervous system. For a simulation to succeed, the system must be considered as a whole. In modeling the cardiovascular system, for example, a simulation must take into account the heart, brain, lungs, and kidneys.

In the 1980s, computer modeling of organ systems is progressing on many fronts. The brief sampling of simulations listed in table 6-3 illustrates the variety of organ systems under study.

One development in this field deserving particular attention was the establishment by NIH's Division of Research Resources in 1984 of the National Biomedical Simulation Resource, a computer facility at Duke University that may be used onsite or over a telephone data network. Any project in which the results are free to be published in open scientific journals and where no profit is involved can apply to use the facility. Training sessions introduce biological scientists to the concepts of modeling, and special aid is provided in the development of simulation software (120). Projects under

Table 6-3.—Some Examples of Computer Simulation of Phenomena in Biomedical Research

Kidney function:
- Transport of electrolytes, nonelectrolytes, and water into and out of the kidney (142)

Cardiac function:
- Enzyme metabolism in cardiac muscle (214)
- Cardiac pressure-flow-volume relationships (152)
- Malfunctions of instrumented cardiovascular control systems (9)

Lung function:
- Respiratory mechanics (150)

Sensory physiology:
- Peripheral auditory system, and single auditory nerve fiber transmission of vibrations (180)

Neurophysiology:
- Impulse propagation along myelinated axons (73)

Developmental biology:
- Shape changes in embryonic cells that develop into mature organs (98)

SOURCE: Office of Technology Assessment.

way in 1985 involved research in cardiology, physiology, endocrinology, toxicology, and neurology. Specific simulations included:

- regulation of sodium, potassium, and calcium in heart muscle;
- electrolyte diffusion in heart muscle;
- propagation of activity in heart muscle;
- heart volume potentials;
- mathematical modeling of blood coagulation;
- regional dose responses in the human and animal lung;
- ciliary motility;
- cochlear function in the inner ear; and
- a molecular model of ion transport in nerves and muscles.

Limitations on the utility of computer simulations stem from the lack of knowledge of all possible parameters that may play a role, however slight, in the melange of feedback mechanisms that constitute living systems. Basic biomedical research at all levels, some of it involving live animals, will continue to provide the new knowledge required to improve existing simulations and develop models where no satisfactory one exists. The development of increasingly powerful computer programs depends on the use of animals in biomedical research.

CONTINUED, BUT MODIFIED, USE OF ANIMALS IN BEHAVIORAL RESEARCH

As in biomedical research, the continued, but modified, use of animals in behavioral research encompasses reducing the number of animals used through changes in experimental design and statistical analyses, substituting cold- for warm-blooded vertebrates, and lessening the degree of pain or experimental insult in general, and in pain research in particular. Compared with biomedical research, behavioral research offers markedly fewer opportunities to substitute cold-for warm-blooded vertebrates and to use in vitro cultures, and it holds little chance of using nonliving systems.

Reduction in the Number of Animals Used

Improved Experimental Design and Statistical Analyses

Individual animals vary in their behavior both between subjects and, in the case of one subject, over time. The goal of a behavioral experiment is to identify patterns that remain when these two sources of variability have been eliminated or taken into account. An investigator attempts to conclude that observed effects are due to the conditions being manipulated in the experiment and not to extraneous factors. This decision usually rests on the outcome of statistical tests. Ensuring the validity of such tests or improving their design can mean that fewer experiments are needed. Enhanced statistical rigor, however, may lead to increases or decreases in the number of animals required in a particular protocol.

Statistical Power.—A statistical test's sensitivity in detecting experimental effects is termed its "power." The most widely recognized method of increasing power and, hence, the sensitivity of an experiment is to use a large sample of subjects. Typically, the more variable the results, the more power is needed to detect an effect and, therefore, the greater the need for large samples. Although the magnitude of variability cannot be determined prior to an experiment, the amount of variability likely to be encountered can be estimated by conducting small, pilot studies or by examining previous research in the same or related areas. Given an estimate of variability, statistical tables can be used to determine the sample size needed to attain certain levels of power (221).

In certain instances, the methods of increasing power may reduce, not increase, the number of animals needed:

- Choosing a lower level of statistical significance (i.e., the likelihood that the results were due to chance) increases power and reduces the number of subjects needed. However, this also increases the chances of concluding that the experimental procedure produced an effect when in fact the effect was due to chance alone. By convention, researchers generally accept the probability of a chance effect of 5 percent or less as a statistically significant result.

- Greater precision in the conduct of an experiment may reduce variability and increase power. For example, highly precise behavioral measurements coupled with the elimination or control of extraneous variables would reduce the need for large numbers of subjects (198).
- The use of different statistical analyses can increase the sensitivity and power of a protocol (e.g., analysis of the data by parametric rather than nonparametric statistical tests) (198).
- Alterations in experimental designs can increase power. Factorial designs (where two or more treatments are manipulated concurrently), for example, are more powerful and can be used instead of testing the effects of different treatments in separate experiments. Not only does the use of factorial designs increase power, it requires fewer untreated, control subjects than multiple concurrent studies do. It is important to note, however, that in areas that have not been heavily researched there are inherent dangers to the use of factorial designs. For example, there may be no observed effect of treatments given in combination, as one treatment cancels the effect of another. Without sufficient background information on the effects of the treatments administered individually, this finding would be erroneously interpreted.
- Power is increased as the magnitude of the treatment effect is increased. Treatment effects can be maximized by choosing widely spaced levels of the treatment variables or by including conditions that are thought to maximize the appearance of the phenomenon under study (113).

Within-Subjects Design.—Many experiments on animal behavior are conducted using a between-subjects design. That is, different groups of animals are given different treatments, and the performances of the different groups are compared. However, individuals also vary in their behavior. Depending on the degree of variability, large numbers of subjects may be needed in each group to obtain statistically significant results. Under certain conditions, however, a within-subjects (or repeated measures) design can be used that requires only one group of animals instead of many. Under these conditions all members of the group serve in all treatment conditions. The advantage of this technique is that it minimizes variability by taking into account individual differences. The major drawback, however, is the possibility of contaminating the data and nullifying the results: Treatments already received by a subject may influence, and thereby confound, performance under subsequent treatments. Carry-over effects can be partially offset by counter-balancing, wherein the experimenter ensures an equal occurrence of each experimental treatment at each stage of the experiment; this balances any effect of prior testing equally over all treatment conditions (113). Although within-subjects designs are effective in reducing both variability and the number of subjects needed, the inherent danger of carry-over effects in many instances may invalidate the use of such designs.

Random Block Design.—Randomized block design consists of assigning subjects to groups based on evidence of their being similar to one another in one or more characteristics known to be related to the behavior under investigation. Two or more such blocks are formed and then each block is assigned randomly to the treatment conditions. This design reduces variability by restricting the degree of individual differences within blocks, and thereby increases power (113). Although randomized block designs are effective in lowering the number of animals needed in an experiment, they are not applicable to all areas of behavioral research. The technique requires substantial prior knowledge of the behavior being investigated and is therefore limited to intensively researched areas.

Analysis of Covariance.—An analysis of covariance uses the same information as randomized block designs except that an estimate of variability is not needed beforehand. The covariance procedure is applied to data after they are collected to adjust for chance differences among groups. The analysis increases power, and fewer animals may be needed to obtain statistically significant results (113).

Single-Subject Design.—In some instances inferences can be made about populations from very small samples. This is common in psychophysical experiments in which there is a substantial prior body of evidence indicating that the behaviors under investigation do not vary appreciably within the population at large (e.g., visual sensitivity to light). Although such experiments can be conducted using just one subject, two or three are typically used to guard against the possibility of misleading results from an atypical subject (198).

In other than psychophysical experiments, the general procedure in single-subject research consists of choosing a baseline (which involves measuring the frequency of occurrence of the behavior of interest), changing one treatment variable at a time, temporarily withdrawing the experimental treatment to assess its causal effects, and repeatedly measuring the baseline behavior before and after each treatment. (More sophisticated experimental designs available for single-subject research are reviewed in ref. 96.) Single-subject designs are increasingly used in animal operant conditioning and human clinical research (187). Statistical analyses of these are reported infrequently due to the lack of many statistical techniques for handling such data, although using time-series analyses to test for changes over time is one acceptable method available (111).

A limitation to studying a single subject is the uncertainty of the generality of the findings, a problem commonly dealt with by replicating the experiment with different subjects (96). Thus the reduction in animals used may be illusory.

Inbred Strains.—One way of reducing variability (and hence increasing power) is to use highly homogeneous populations of subjects. Inbred strains of animals, produced as a result of 20 or more generations of brother-sister matings, represent one approach, though it is usually much more expensive than using randomly bred animals. In most inbred strains all subjects are highly identical genetically and genetically stable; they change only as a result of the slow accumulation of mutations. In contrast, outbred stocks of animals are genetically variable. They contain an unknown and uncontrollable degree of genetic variation that may obscure or mask experimental treatment effects. Inbred strains not only increase statistical power, they also reduce variability between experiments conducted in different laboratories or in the same laboratory at different times (68).

It can be argued that experiments should rely on animals drawn from heterogeneous, outbred populations in order to get a broad genetic basis for results that can be extrapolated, for example, to heterogeneous human populations. Yet the differences between different inbred strains are usually greater than the differences between individuals of an outbred stock. Greater generality, then, may be obtained by conducting experiments with two or more inbred strains (68).

Sharing Animals.—A team approach to research questions across biomedical and behavioral research disciplines could reduce the number of animals needed for behavioral research (173). For example, researchers studying a behavioral phenomenon by noninvasive means could, at the experiment's conclusion, give their animals to biologists investigating the anatomy or physiology of that species. Likewise, scientists from different disciplines could collaborate on research proposals: A psychologist may be interested in studying predator-prey relations, while a biologist wants to study endocrinological changes in response to stress; effective collaboration could yield two different data sets from the same animals.

Substitution of Cold-Blooded for Warm-Blooded Vertebrates

The modified use of animals in biomedical research includes the replacement of mammals and birds with fish, amphibians, and reptiles. In behavioral research, however, the often vast differences between species are likely to make such substitutions difficult. At the moment, researchers know more about why warm-blooded vertebrates **cannot** be replaced with cold-blooded ones, as this description of seven behavioral research disciplines illustrates.

Aggression

Aggressive interactions between members of the same species have been studied in a variety of fish and reptile species under both laboratory and field conditions. Considerable work has been done on intermale rivalry among stickleback (183) and cichlid fish (11). Aggressive interactions among cold-blooded vertebrates are frequently stereotyped and species-specific. Among stickleback fish, for example, full-fledged attacks can be elicited by a model that is the same color but a different shape (30). In contrast, aggression in primates can embody a variety of highly sophisticated introspective social strategies such as deception, grudging, delayed retaliation, and reconciliation (77). Thus extrapolation among all vertebrates of the results of research into aggression is difficult.

Animal Movements

Migration and homing abilities have been intensively studied in several species of fish, particularly eels and Pacific salmon. Among American and European eels, for example, the eggs hatch in the Sargasso Sea, near Bermuda. The juvenile fish make a year-long migration toward the coasts of North America and Europe. On reaching sexual maturity in 7 to 15 years, the adult eels migrate back to the Sargasso Sea to breed (217), a movement primarily dependent on the use of chemical cues in the water (60). In contrast, birds use solar, stellar, and magnetic cues to navigate, and whales use the topography of the ocean floor and coastline to remain on course for migratory purposes. Such dramatic differences in the way different species respond to and perceive the environment limit the use of cold-blooded vertebrates in modeling animal movements of warm-blooded ones.

Communication

Visual cues, such as changes in coloration, posture, or body appearance, have been shown to be important determinants of social interaction among fish (30), which, unlike most mammals, generally have color vision. Fish also exhibit dramatic changes in appearance, such as flaring of the gill apertures, which are relatively rare among mammals. Auditory communication is marked by species differences, too. Communication among amphibians and reptiles, primarily to attract a mate, consists of simple one- or two-note utterances. Vocalization in birds and mammals consists of a wide range and variety of sounds. Moreover, unlike cold-blooded species, many birds have to learn species-specific songs. Many rodents communicate by ultrasonic vocalizations (123) that have no apparent counterpart among cold-blooded species.

Learning, Memory, and Problem Solving

Learning has been studied in a variety of diverse species (179,183), and many differences are manifested. Comparing learning in goldfish and turtles with that in rats yields both similar and distinguishing features. For example, rats show a decrement in performance when an accustomed reward is changed, while goldfish and turtles do not (23). The existence of so-called biological boundaries of learning (182), apparently shaped by unique ecological pressures, precludes most substitutions of one species for another in learning paradigms.

Predator-Prey Relations

Prey-catching behavior and predator avoidance have been studied in fish, frogs, and turtles (60, 103,203). The similarity across species in behaviors used by prey to avoid being caught suggests that when a general question about reactions to predation (rather than the behavior of a given species) is of interest, cold-blooded vertebrates can substitute for warm-blooded ones (103). But there is growing evidence of neurochemical differences underlying predator avoidance behaviors even among birds and mammals (78).

Predators exhibit marked differences across species. Frogs, for example, sit passively and wait for an insect to come within striking distance, while some carnivores have developed sophisticated hunting strategies that often embody elements of cooperation and may even culminate in sharing foods (30).

Reproduction and Parental Care

With some notable exceptions (e.g., the African Mouthbreeder fish), parental care of offspring is absent in most cold-blooded vertebrates, since the eggs are typically abandoned shortly after fertilization. In contrast, all birds are subject to some type of parental care, and mammalian parent-offspring relations become even more complicated. Species differences in external versus internal fertilization, seasonal breeding, courtship, pair-bonding, and nest-building preclude substitutions of one species for another in this research.

Sensation and Perception

The sensory and perceptual differences among species are vast. For example, many snakes' primary mode of prey identification is chemical cues transferred from the tongue to a structure at the roof of the mouth, called Jacobsen's organ. Ingestively naive baby snakes appear to have an innate preference for prey extracts that represent species-typical foods across a variety of different snakes. Each species shows unique attack profiles that appear to be independent of maternal diet and not subject to modification by experience (e.g., baby snakes of a minnow-eating species that are force-fed liver still show attack responses to minnow extracts but not to liver) (34,35).

In contrast, baby rats seem predisposed to eat the same diet as their mother, and the flavor of the maternal milk serves as a medium for the transmission of cues that rat pups use to make their initial food choices. Manipulating maternal diet during lactation has produced corresponding changes in subsequent pup food preferences. Moreover, rat pups poisoned in association with a mother's milk later avoid the types of food she had been eating (74).

Reduction of Pain or Experimental Insult

As noted earlier, a general anesthetic is preferable to a local one for surgical manipulations because it suppresses both pain and fear (114). Pain-relieving drugs should be administered to animals after surgery whenever this would not interfere with the behavior under study, and animals should be carefully monitored so that any complications that develop may be treated (197).

Transection of the spine or brain stem is recommended for surgical experiments when possible, because it renders the animal incapable of feeling pain (114). This technique has limited applicability in behavioral research, however, as postsurgical behavioral assessment requires a relatively intact animal. Similarly, the nonrecovery experiments on completely anesthetized animals that were described earlier, in the biomedical research section, are rarely used in behavioral research, since most behaviors of interest do not occur when the animal is unconscious and behavioral testing is typically conducted postsurgically. Multiple surgeries on the same animal are to be avoided whenever possible, because painful consequences may be cumulative (197).

The analysis of pain in behavioral research is complicated by recent theoretical and empirical developments suggesting that fear and pain activate quite different kinds of behavior (25). Rather than being on a continuum, as might seem to be the case intuitively, data suggest that fear and pain are associated with fundamentally different motivational systems. Fear activates species-specific defensive behaviors, such as freezing, flight, or fighting, that serve to minimize encounters with pain-producing stimuli (e.g., predators). Pain, on the other hand, appears conducive to the kinds of behaviors that provide for healing and recuperation (e.g., rest, grooming, licking the affected area, and sleep). A growing body of evidence shows that fear takes priority over pain, and that fear can actually inhibit pain under some circumstances (possibly through the release of endogenous opiates). For example, soldiers who are wounded in battle frequently continue fighting and feel no pain from their injuries until after they are removed from the front lines (211). Likewise, a deer wounded by hunters may flee the scene with defensive behavior indistinguishable from that of uninjured animals. But once the deer is out of danger, pain-related recuperative behaviors predominate (25).

Brain Manipulation

In studies of the physiological bases of behavior, the recording of brain-wave patterns may be substituted for electrical stimulation whenever possible, and brain areas may be stimulated instead of lesioning or ablating sections of the brain (121). These techniques, however, are not completely interchangeable. Recording neuronal firing as an animal behaves allows correlational inferences to be made, but not causal ones. If the experimental goal is to determine a particular brain area that is responsible for a certain behavior, that area must be manipulated directly. Electrical stimulation of brain areas is useful in establishing causal relationships, and the most definitive and reliable results are obtained when stimulation is used in conjunction with lesioning or ablation (20).

Drug Administration

In research on the behavioral effects of experimental or currently available drugs, animals are injected either intraperitoneally (within the body cavity), intravenously, intramuscularly, or intracranially (within the skull, via an implanted cannula). Depending on whether the drug must be given repeatedly, the injection procedure can be stressful and may cause discomfort. Within the last decade alternative administration methods have been developed that may replace the need for multiple injections in some chronic drug treatment studies. Capsules of porous rubber (Silastic®, produced by Dow-Corning) implanted beneath the skin release a drug slowly into the animal's body, and stress produced by repeated injections is avoided. The method produces minimal discomfort and is well tolerated by animals (63). Small, implantable minipumps are also available to deliver drugs for days or weeks.

The use of aerosols has also been suggested (174); although this would seem to hold promise for alleviating the stress of injections, it has drawbacks. For example, animals may differ greatly in their inhalation rates, and dispersal of the drug into the air prevents adequate control of drug dosage.

Food Deprivation

It is important to distinguish between the different methods of depriving animals of food and the reasons for using any method. In most cases, animals are deprived of food to motivate them to perform various tasks or behaviors for food reward. The nature of the subject's performance of such tasks—and not the food deprivation—is the object of study.

Food deprivation is typically applied one of two ways: Animals are deprived of food for a standard period of time (e.g., 24 hours) prior to testing or they are maintained at some percentage of their normal body weight (e.g., 80 percent) (43). Each procedure has advantages and disadvantages. Food deprivation for specified intervals of time is easy to implement, but it fails to take into account species differences in metabolic rates. For example, 24 hours of food deprivation for a mammal is less severe than it would be for a bird, while for a snake it would be inconsequential. Maintaining animals at a percentage of normal body weight avoids this problem, but it requires daily handling and the delay of the trial for long periods of time to stabilize body weights.

When food deprivation is applied according to a standard time period in behavioral protocols, the most common interval is 24 hours (43). It is noteworthy that the feeding of domestic pets once a day parallels this laboratory protocol. When maintaining animals at some percentage of their normal body weight, behavioral protocols usually involve up to 20 percent weight loss (43). Experimental animals' reduced food intake is associated in some instances with enhanced longevity (172).

Several suggestions have been made to reduce, ameliorate, or eliminate food deprivation in behavioral research:

- Water deprivation, sometimes used concurrently with food deprivation, should be used to motivate behavior only if thirst or drinking is the object of study. Water deprivation affects an animal's physical condition more severely than food deprivation does, because death by dehydration occurs much more rapidly than death by starvation (121).
- The normal eating pattern of a species should be taken into account when deciding on the duration of food deprivation. For example, sparrows eat only during the light hours of the day; hamsters feed largely at night.
- In some cases, food deprivation might be avoided by using a highly preferred food as a reward (121).
- Food deprivation may also be avoided by taking the experiment into the animal's living quarters, so that it is required to perform for

food as and when it wants to eat. In this way, any deprivation would be self-imposed as under natural conditions (121,151). This technique has been used successfully in work on sensory-motor functioning in monkeys (168).

Pain Research and the Use of Electric Shock

The experience of pain is a highly adaptive capacity. It prevents organisms from engaging in behaviors that would otherwise prove maladaptive. For example, humans who are congenitally insensitive to pain become terribly scarred and mutilated, often develop a sense of being invincible, and have short life expectancies (141,143,196). Perhaps because pain plays such an essential role in regulating the behavior of organisms, pain thresholds are surprisingly consistent across a great diversity of species (115). The discovery of endogenous opiates in earthworms (5) and recent findings with spiders (61) suggest that invertebrates may also feel pain.

Pain can be induced through mechanical, thermal, electrical, or chemical stimuli (127). Of the various stimuli used for research purposes, electric shock at the levels normally used in experimentation is the only one that does not damage tissue. Most studies of pain in animals use what are called flinch-and-jump thresholds—an index of the minimal amount of electric shock or heat needed to produce a reaction. Electric shock is used as a stimulus for research into the mechanism of pain for several reasons:

- Electric shock is easily quantifiable. The parameters of shock can be manipulated and specified with a high degree of precision over a wide range.
- Electric shock can be administered so as to have a discrete or gradual onset and offset.
- Electric shock of the type most often used (i.e., a brief current of 0.001 amperes, the equivalent of a tingling sensation in the finger) does not yield physical damage, bleeding, or tissue destruction.

However, electric shock is a highly atypical stimulus (79). No contemporary terrestrial species appears to have evolved under conditions of electric shock. The question of whether data obtained this way are widely generalizable in mechanisms of pain remains unanswered.

A survey of the 608 articles appearing from 1979 through 1983 in the American Psychological Association journals that typically publish animal research (e.g., *Journal of Comparative and Physiological Psychology* and its successors *Behavioral Neuroscience* and *Journal of Comparative Psychology*) identified 10 percent of the studies as using electric shock. Four percent of the studies administered inescapable shocks stronger than 0.001 amperes. Most of the experiments with electric shock involved rodents; those with monkeys, dogs, and cats accounted for 0.5 percent of the total 608 articles (43).

Recommendations that have been made to reduce pain or discomfort in animal experiments involving aversive stimulation include:

- The lowest possible level of electric shock should be used that will at the same time maintain the behavior under study (52). However, this may reduce the statistical power and require a large sample size.
- Animals should be given predictable rather than unpredictable shock and an opportunity to control its termination (52). Rats, for example, will choose to receive more shocks at greater intensity in order to receive a warning cue prior to each shock delivery (10).
- If aversive stimulation must be used, alternatives to electric shock such as loud noise or bright lights should be considered (121).
- In developing models of chronic pain, the model should closely simulate a particular chronic pain syndrome in humans (e.g., arthritis or cancer). Otherwise, there is no justification for the procedure (114).
- Animals should have an opportunity to control the intensity of the stimulus in chronic pain studies. While the objection to this might be that, given this option, the animal would "turn off" the pain stimulus, this might be circumvented by giving a preferred food reward for keeping the stimulus "on" at a given level, as in experiments with electric shock titration techniques (114).
- A reward, such as a preferred food, should be used for the correct responses instead of a punisher, such as electric shock, for incorrect response (121).

USE OF LIVING SYSTEMS IN BEHAVIORAL RESEARCH

In behavioral research, using living components derived from whole animals or living nonanimal systems as alternatives to animals could conceivably involve embryos; cell, tissue, and organ cultures; invertebrates; and plants. The greatest potential in this area, however, appears to rest with the use of invertebrates.

Several factors limit the use of embryos (used here to refer to the conceptus, embryo, and fetus prior to birth) as an alternative or complement to young or adult animals:

- Some studies involving embryos may be conducted when the subject is very close to birth or hatching. The advanced developmental status of the organism at this point raises the same kinds of ethical considerations that would apply to the use of postnatal animals (see ch. 4).
- In behavioral studies involving mammalian embryos, the mother is necessarily involved in most experimental manipulations performed on the embryo. As a consequence, embryological manipulations on mammals cannot logically avoid the use of adult mammals.
- Behavioral studies using embryos may involve testing for effects later in adult life (e.g., behavioral teratological studies). In these instances, embryos are not being used as alternatives, since the procedures also require postnatal assessment.
- Only a limited number of behaviors can be studied in embryos, partly because of practical problems associated with access to the embryo.
- Embryos live in a dramatically different environment than fully developed adult animals. This difference constrains the generalizability of behavioral data obtained from them.

Cell, tissue, and organ cultures do not figure prominently in the equation of alternatives to animal use in behavioral research. In isolation and in culture, cells, tissues, and organs exhibit few activities that fall among the disciplines of behavioral research.

A rare example of the use of cell culture in behavioral research comes from studies of the biochemical basis of depression and manic mood changes. Skin fibroblast cells obtained from humans and maintained in culture for several months were assessed for their ability to bind a variety of pharmacologic agents. The cultured cells of patients and relatives of patients with manic-depressive illness exhibited markedly different biochemical properties than the cultured cells of persons without a history of manic depression (155). One commentator characterized this as "a step forward, applying to psychiatry the techniques of tissue sampling and cell culture that have been of great value in characterizing molecular abnormalities in numerous medical diseases" (192). Continued development of this line of research could reduce the use of animals in such investigations.

Invertebrates

Few behavioral studies use invertebrates as subjects (139). As a consequence, relatively little is known about invertebrate behavior. In behavioral research, invertebrates offer a fertile testing ground for any theory that claims to be broadly based across the phyla of the animal kingdom (138). Certain groups of invertebrates are promising subjects for behavioral research.

The brains of octopuses and squid approach those of vertebrates in relative size and complexity (178). Visual discrimination learning has been studied extensively in the octopus. Octopuses can discriminate between pairs of geometric shapes that differ with respect to vertical, horizontal, and oblique orientations. The octopus and squid show learning performance on a par with mammals on such tasks as detour problems, reversal learning, delayed response, and delayed reinforcement (178,218).

Among all the invertebrates, the only species with a neuroanatomy and learning ability comparable to vertebrates are the octopus and squid. Practical problems in obtaining, transporting, and housing these marine species have always precluded their widespread use as alternatives in behavioral research (178). However, recent advances in the laboratory culture of octopuses make them promising research candidates, although providing live food (e.g., shrimp) on a consistent basis remains a major logistical obstacle. The development of a dead or artificial food ration is currently a high priority in octopus culture (88). The same highly developed nervous system that makes the octopus and squid desirable replacements for vertebrates may cause some ethical objections to use of these invertebrates. In addition, their adaptation to a completely aquatic existence would also make tenuous any extrapolations to the behavior of terrestrial mammals.

Starfish and sea urchins exhibit habituation—the waning of a response to stimuli, as a result of repeated elicitation of that response—and they can learn escape behaviors in response to a cue paired with aversive stimulation (46).

Earthworms exhibit habituation (45), can learn to associate light with a food reward (66), and can learn to travel a maze to receive darkness and moisture as reinforcing stimuli (85). Flatworms are also of considerable interest, since they represent a bilateral body form, as do mammals. Flatworms exhibit a concentration of nervous tissue and sensory organs in the anterior, or head, portion of their bodies, and they have refined internal organ systems (47). Flatworms exhibit habituation, can be conditioned to avoid a light after it has been paired with shock, and can learn to approach an area for food reward. There are also claims that such learned events are remembered after these worms undergo regeneration, and that learning can be transferred from one animal to another by cannibalism (reviewed in ref. 47).

Insects are valuable behavioral models in communication, navigation, learning and memory, and behavioral genetics.

Octopus (*Octopus bimaculoides*) Cultured From the Egg in the Laboratory

Photo credit: Lab. Anim. Sci. 35(1):34. Copyright 1985, American Association for Laboratory Animal Science

- **Communication.** Honeybees recruit others to a new food source through a dance performed at the hive that conveys distance and directional information (209). Many species of insects (e.g., moths and ants) communicate chemically by pheromones, which serve sex attractant, repellant, and/or trail-marking functions (reviewed in ref. 30). Other species, such as the cricket, communicate by songs produced by rubbing body parts together (19).
- **Navigation.** Honeybees have demonstrated extraordinary abilities to locate and return to a food source "mapped out" for them by other bees. They can also return to an artificial feeding source designed for experimental purposes to test their navigation abilities (37, 209,215).
- **Learning and Memory.** Habituation has been demonstrated in a variety of insect species (46). Honeybees also appear capable of more advanced forms of learning, such as learning to associate a specific color with a food reward, and they can remember this association after a 2-week interval (219). Cockroaches can learn to leave their preferred dark retreats and stay in the light to avoid being shocked; ants have been trained to travel a maze to receive food rewards (85).
- **Behavioral Genetics.** Because of the relative ease with which their chromosomes and individual genes can be identified, fruit flies have been used extensively to elucidate the genetic basis for a variety of behaviors (132).

Habituation has been demonstrated in a variety of spiders (45), and spiders are capable of learning and remembering the location of prey in their webs (85). They can also be trained to associate food dipped in quinine or sugar with different tones (46).

Even though protozoa possess both plant- and animal-like characteristics and lack nervous tissue, some forms of learning have been demonstrated in these single-celled organisms. Habituation has been demonstrated in paramecia (45). Although the results generated much controversy (reviewed in ref. 45), one investigator claimed to have trained paramecia to enter a specific area of their water container in order to receive food reinforcement (81). It has also been reported that paramecia show spontaneous alternation in a T-maze, a phenomenon also observed in rodents (139).

A recent study of learning ability in paramecia has demonstrated classical conditioning of an escape movement (94). This study also found that paramecia develop memory for the training event, since significantly fewer trials were needed 24 hours later to relearn the response. Data such as these challenge the widely held assumption that learning is a property of synaptic interactions between nerve cells—absent in protozoa—and not of individual cells themselves.

Plants

From a behavioral perspective, plants differ from animals in two principal ways. First, plants lack the means of achieving rapid intra- and inter-organismal communication and coordination due to the absence of a nervous system. However, plants do regulate intra-organismal activities occurring at different sites through the use of hormones. Plants and animals thus share the basic principles of endocrine function. Second, plants differ from animals in that they are stationary. They must wait for energy to come to them, while most animals move about to obtain different sources of energy.

Despite these differences, plants do show rudimentary forms of behavior (188). Plants can grow and move in response to light, and some plants have achieved the capacity for relatively rapid movement to exploit certain animals as prey (e.g., the venus fly trap). The mimosa plant, which can fold its leaves when touched, has been a subject of particular interest. Certain of its cells appear to generate primitive action potentials—electrical activity that may be analogous to neuronal functioning in animals (186). There have also been reports that the folding response of the mimosa plant shows habituation (6) and even some of the rudiments of classical conditioning (8). Although some claim evidence of feelings, emotions, and even thinking in plants based on polygraph recordings (206), others contend these are artifactual (80).

A number of plants defend themselves from predators via thorns, stickers, or toxic chemicals that produce sickness, irritation, or even death if touched or consumed. It has been demonstrated that some plants, under attack by insects and micro-organisms, develop highly sophisticated defenses involving the emission of antibiotic-like substances and chemicals that inhibit insect digestive enzymes. Indeed, some plants can apparently communicate chemically with as-yet-unaffected neighboring plants to induce leaf-chemistry changes in advance of infestation (reviewed in ref. 164).

These impressive features of the botanical world notwithstanding, it is unlikely that plants will make an important contribution to behavioral research. The lack of a central nervous system, and in particular a brain, renders the plant an inappropriate model for use among the disciplines of behavioral research.

USE OF NONLIVING SYSTEMS IN BEHAVIORAL RESEARCH

Inanimate chemical or physical systems are unlikely to prove useful in behavioral research, for reasons intrinsic to the nature of behavior. A dynamic, emergent process, behavior functions to allow organisms to adapt to moment-to-moment changes in the environment. In a sense, all behavior ultimately functions to aid and abet survival and reproduction (51). Adaptation, survival, and reproduction are not properties of nonliving systems. And behavior involves information processing and a continuous series of choices among an array of alternatives (140). Although chemical or physical systems may change in response to certain environmental stimuli, the nature of such changes does not involve decisionmaking or information-processing.

Behavior is a byproduct of interactions between sensory, neural, hormonal, genetic, and experiential factors. As such, it is influenced by the situation at hand, the developmental history of the organism, and prior experience with similar and related situations. It appears inappropriate to imbue inanimate chemical or physical systems with the capacity for experience. Devoid of such a capacity for experience, nonliving systems are unlikely alternatives to using animals in behavioral research.

Examples of the application of chemical or physical systems to behavioral research are sparse. One involves the use of chemical reagents to mimic the properties of rhythmic behavioral phenomena in animals. Certain chemical reagents exhibit changes in state that oscillate periodically in a fashion similar to some biologically based rhythms. However, the chemical reactions themselves remain poorly understood (222).

COMPUTER SIMULATION IN BEHAVIORAL RESEARCH

A computer simulation is an operating model that depicts not only the state of a behavioral system at a particular point in time but also changes that occur in that system over time. Because dynamic processes are of quintessential importance in behavioral research, computer simulation stands as a potentially useful tool for the behavioral scientist.

In order to simulate a living system, a computer programmer must have information about that system. The more information at hand, the better the simulation (53). In the strictest sense, a completely accurate simulation presupposes that everything that there is to know about the system in question is known. To construct a computer simulation that would fully replace the use of a live organism in behavioral research would require knowing everything about the behavior in question, which in turn would preclude the need for a computer simulation for research purposes.

Yet, if computer simulation cannot fully replace living organisms, it can and does contribute to behavioral research. Although the fundamental behavioral qualities of adaptation, survival, and reproduction do not pertain to computer programs, computer software does, for example, embody information processing and decisionmaking. Examples of recent attempts toward computer simulation in behavioral research are listed in table 6-4.

Computer simulations are used in behavioral research in a number of ways. Statistical simulations, in particular, are increasingly frequent. For example, one computer program simulates random-choice behavior in mazes (194), and two programs simulate random movements of animals under various conditions (17,49). The output generated by these kinds of simulations is compared with animal-generated data to see if factors other than pure chance are influencing the animals' behavior.

Statistical simulations are also used to test hypotheses that may not be subject to empirical confirmation. One investigator used a computer simulation to test the proposition that "if enough monkeys were allowed to pound away at typewriters for enough time, all the great works of literature would result" (21). The larger objective

Table 6-4.—Some Examples of Computer Simulation of Behavioral Phenomena

Spacing mechanisms and animal movements:
- Space use and movement patterns (17,49)
- Movements of juvenile Atlantic herring (110)
- Animal spacing (153)
- Mosquito flight patterns (165)
- Foraging of the honeyeater bird (169)
- Random choice in radial arm mazes (194)

Learning, memory, and problem solving:
- Classical conditioning (15,18)
- Learning in neural systems (177)
- Habituation (195)
- Behavior in a psychoecological space (84)
- Mechanisms for reducing inhibition (223)

Sensation and perception:
- Visual pattern analysis (13)
- Landmark learning by bees (37)
- Chemical recruitment in ants (106)

Communication:
- Bird song (55,185)
- Animal vocalizations (57)

Sensation and perception:
- Neuron models (122)
- Neural basis for pain and touch (148)

Body maintenance:
- Food intake (14)
- Control of drinking behavior (204)

Reproduction and parental care:
- Sexual behavior of the male rat (72,205)
- Infanticide in langurs (89)
- Evolution of reproductive synchrony (116)
- Mating behavior of *Spodoptera littoralis* (200)

SOURCE: Office of Technology Assessment.

in this study was to determine if the extreme cases of human genius could be accounted for through chance processes.

The simulation was based on an initial assumption that monkeys typing at random— or a computer simulation using random numbers—would generate huge volumes of nonsense. Statistical properties of the English language (e.g., the relative frequencies of individual characters or sequences of characters) were added to the simulation. As higher-order properties of English (i.e., the relative frequencies of three- and four-letter sequences) were incorporated into the algorithm, the rate of generation of intelligible words, phrases, and sentences increased. These results led to a hypothesis that genius could be simulated by a process of random choice with a weighting procedure, subject to a prior preparatory process in which an individual absorbs the necessary operational patterns that characterize the discipline. In studies such as this, it is not merely the output generated by the computer model that is of interest, but the simulation process as well.

Computer simulations have considerable heuristic value (65): They may yield insight about the system or phenomenon being modeled (71) and, as a consequence, stimulate additional research. The value of computer simulation as a heuristic device has been summarized as follows (158):

> Simulation gives a means of exploring the plausibility of models in which theoretical sophistication exceeds the state of the art in empirical testing. Simulations provide tools for empirically analyzing theories in order to better understand their implications and predictions. Simulations are a means of exploring interactions between components of complex models. They pose a practical challenge to operationalize theoretical constructs, which can lead to incidental discoveries about related processes. Finally, they engender a concern with issues of process control that contributes to the development of general principles with broad applications.

Computer simulation holds promise for understanding complex cognitive processes. For example, the computer is often considered analogous, at least in some ways, to the human brain (7)— both process large amounts of information, and their respective outcomes are a consequence of multiple, relatively simple operations. On the other hand, there are major differences:

- computers have larger and many fewer components than the brain;
- computer operations occur with much greater speed than neural operations;
- computers operate through sequential processing; and
- computers attend to all input, while the brain is selectively attentive.

Such differences do not, however, preclude the use of computers as functional models (170). Moreover, one advantage of computers is that they demand rigorous and exact description. And an investigator need not invoke a variety of hypothetical or mentalistic variables (e.g., hope, fear, desire, and intention) to describe their functioning (171).

It is important to note that any predictions generated by a computer simulation must be tested and verified using the system the computer was designed to replace (149). In this sense, the use of animals in behavioral research is likely to continue in lockstep with the development of computer simulation software.

One commentator summarized the use of computers as an alternative to animals in behavioral research in this way (114):

> At the present time and for the foreseeable future it seems clear that the computer will not be a feasible substitute for experiments on animals. The fundamental reason is that a computer cannot acquire data other than those that are generated by carefully designed experimental studies in animals. What the computer does provide is a superb technique for processing vast amounts of data with great speed and accuracy and for presenting them in almost any manner the investigator desires. To suggest that enough data are already available from previous work, so that from them programs can be generated and subjected to a variety of permutations that would lead to new insights, overlooks an important fact. In any animal experiment there are numerous variables over which we have little control, and there are virtually always as many more about which we as yet know nothing but which may have very significant influences on the phenomenon under investigation. In real life, which after all is what matters in biologic research, these variables may be crucial and may give important clues to entirely unsuspected phenomena that are sometimes far more important than the original subject of the study. In a word, computers do not generate new concepts or acquire new data. They process data and permit the investigator to view it in more manageable or novel ways, and this may facilitate new hypotheses or insights.

In summary, computer simulation can serve to facilitate behavioral research. The need for certain protocols may be precluded, or protocols may be refocused by computer simulation before they commence. Modeling techniques using computer simulation lead to the refinement of experimental protocols to be conducted on animals (36). Yet as the preceding quote implies, in facilitating behavioral research computer simulation may actually increase, rather than decrease, the use of animals because data can be analyzed more quickly and in much greater detail, leading to proportionately more hypotheses to investigate (87,160).

SUMMARY AND CONCLUSIONS

Animal use in research can be modified in a number of ways, including strengthening experimental design to minimize the number of animals used, reducing the degree of experimental insult, and substituting one species for another. The outright replacement of animals with nonanimal methods in research is not at hand, and, because of the nature of biomedical and behavioral research, in many instances it is not likely to become feasible.

Advances in instrumentation are critical to the more refined or reduced use of live animals or living material. In the past decade, practically every piece of instrumentation in biomedical laboratories has been adapted to handle "micro" samples or has been replaced by new microtechnology. The use of small samples for analysis by mass spectrometry and by gas or liquid chromatography leads to less invasive technology. Fiber optics, for example, can be used to perform analyses inside ducts and blood vessels with little discomfort and no permanent damage to the animal. Continued developments in analytical instrumentation, including noninvasive imaging techniques such as magnetic resonance imaging, will likely ameliorate the degree of experimental insult faced by research animals.

In vitro technology has affected virtually every field of biomedical research. This technology entails the maintenance of organs, tissues, and cells outside of the body and may affect research animal use in two important ways. First, when organs, tissues, or cells are removed from animals and cultured, experiments may be conducted with fewer animals than would be necessary in whole-animal experiments and, of course, without pain. Cells from one animal, for example, may be divided among a dozen experimental cultures and a dozen control cultures, replacing 24 animals that might be used in a comparable whole-animal experiment.

Second, when cells proliferate in culture, commercially available cell lines can completely eliminate animal use in some experiments. Such cell cultures are derived directly from preexisting cell cultures—not animals. Researchers have used, for example, a monkey kidney cell line to study the metabolic effects of general anesthetics.

In vitro experiments are not equivalent to whole-animal experiments. In in-vitro systems, as organization is disrupted or lost, the in vitro system has less and less of the kind of interactions that characterize cells in the body. This can be an advantage and a disadvantage. Interactions may cause extraneous phenomena that obscure the process under study. Conversely, the absence of interactions may produce results that are at variance with what actually occurs in the live animal. Conclusions drawn from in vitro studies must eventually be validated by comparison with results of whole-animal experiments.

In some areas of biomedical research, invertebrates and micro-organisms can be used, and even plant parts can yield information about animal systems. Structures within plant and animal cells, when removed from the cells, are essentially indistinguishable in both appearance and function. Cell biologists, for example, use yeast cells as a source of mitochondria—the energy-generating structures present in all plant and animal cells.

Hard and fast distinctions between biomedical and behavioral research are difficult to sustain. Nevertheless, it is apparent that there is even less potential for replacement of animals in behavioral than in biomedical research. In vitro techniques and nonliving systems are not viable alternatives to the use of animals in behavioral research.

Invertebrates are used extensively in behavioral research. Octopuses and squid are studied because of their highly developed brains. In addition, the discovery of learning and memory in single-cell organisms has challenged the widely held assumption that these phenomena are properties of the interactions of nerve cells rather than of individual cells, and has opened new avenues of research with nonanimal methods.

Computer simulation is a valuable tool in biomedical and behavioral research, but it does not stand as a replacement for animal use. The development of new and more sophisticated computer simulations in biomedical and behavioral research is predicated on data derived from animals. Increased use of computer simulation may have the paradoxical effect of leading to an increase in the number of animals used in experimentation, as more hypotheses and experimental questions are generated more rapidly.

CHAPTER 6 REFERENCES

1. Abbey, J., Close, L., and Jacobs, M., "Pilot Study: Use of Electrical Impedance to Measure Urinary Volume in Canines," *Communic. Nurs. Res.* 11:22, 1977.
2. Abelson, P.H., "Analytical Instruments," *Science* 226:249, 1984.
3. Abelson, P.H., "Instrumentation," *Science* 230:245, 1985.
4. Ali, M.A. (ed.), *Photoreception and Vision in Invertebrates* (New York: Plenum Press, 1984).
5. Alumets, J., Hakanson, R., Sundler, F., et al., "Neuronal Localisation of Immunoreactive Enkepha-

lin and B-endorphin in the Earthworm," *Nature* 279:805-806, 1979.
6. Applewhite, P.B., "Behavioral Plasticity in the Sensitive Plant, *Mimosa*," *Behav. Biol.* 7:47-53, 1972.
7. Apter, M.J., *The Computer Simulation of Behaviour* (London: Hutchinson, 1970).
8. Armus, H.L., "Conditioning of the Sensitive Plant, *Mimosa pudica*," *Comparative Psychology: Research in Animal Behavior*, M.R. Denny and S.C. Ratner (eds.) (Homewood, IL: Dorsey Press, 1970).
9. Attinger, E.O., Chairman, Department of Biomedical Engineering, University of Virginia Medical Center, Charlottesville, VA, personal communication, Aug. 14, 1984.
10. Badia, P., Culbertson, S., and Harsh, J., "Choice of Longer or Stronger Signaled Shock Over Shorter or Weaker Unsignaled Shock," *J. Exper. Anal. Behav.* 19:25-33, 1973.
11. Baerends, G.P., and Baerends-Van Roon, J.M., "An Introduction to the Ethology of Cichlid Fishes," *Behaviour* [Suppl.] 1:1-243, 1950.
12. Bangham, A.D., Hill, M.W., and Miller, N.G., "Preparation and Use of Liposomes as Models of Biological Membranes," *Methods in Membrane Biology, Vol. 1*, E.D. Korn (ed.) (New York: Plenum Press, 1974).
13. Barlow, H.B., Narasimham, R., and Rosenfeld, A., "Visual Pattern Analysis in Machines and Animals," *Science* 177:567-575, 1972.
14. Barnwell, G.M., and Stafford, F.S., "Mathematical Model for Decision Making Neural Circuits Controlling Food Intake," *Bull. Psychonom. Soc.* 5:473-476, 1975.
15. Barto, A.G., and Sutton, R.S., "Simulation of Anticipatory Responses in Classical Conditioning by a Neuron-like Adaptive Element," *Behav. Brain Res.* 4:221-235, 1982.
16. Beaton, A.R., and Krug, R.M., "Synthesis of the Templates for Influenza Virion RNA Replication In Vitro," *Biochemistry* 81:4682-4686, 1984.
17. Bekoff, M., and Wieland, C., "SPACE-OUT: Graphics Programs to Study and to Simulate Space Use and Movement Patterns," *Behav. Res. Meth. Instru.* 14:34-36, 1982.
18. Benedict, J.O., "CLASCONISM: A Computer Program to Simulate Experiments in Classical Conditioning," *Behav. Res. Meth. Instru.* 11:603-604, 1979.
19. Bennet-Clark, H.C., "A New French Mole Cricket, Differing in Song and Morphology From *Gryllotalpa gryllotalpa L.* (Orthoptera: Gryllotalpidae)," *Proc. Royal Entomolog. Soc. London (B)* 39:125-132, 1970.
20. Bennett, T.L., *Introduction to Physiological Psychology* (Monterey, CA: Brooks, Cole, 1982).
21. Bennett, W.R., "How Artificial Is Intelligence?" *Am. Sci.* 65:694-702, 1977.
22. Berlin, B., Brodsky, J., and Clifford, P., "Testing Disease Dependence in Survival Experiments With Serial Sacrifice," *J. Am. Stat. Assoc.* 74:5-14, 1979.
23. Bitterman, M.E., "The Comparative Analysis of Learning," *Science* 188:699-709, 1975.
24. Bloom, S., "Alternative Method for Heart Attack Studies Reduces Animal Pain," *Sci. Center Newsletter* 6(2):4, 1984.
25. Bolles, R.C., and Fanselow, M.S., "A Perceptual-Defensive-Recuperative Model of Fear and Pain," *Behav. Brain Sci.* 3:291-323, 1980.
26. Brabec, M.J., Bedows, E., Davidson, B.A., et al., "Effect of General Anesthetics and Pressure on Aerobic Metabolism of Monkey Kidney Cells," *Anesthesiology* 61:43-47, 1984.
27. Bradshaw, J.J., and Ivanetich, K.M., "Isoflurane: A Comparison of Its Metabolism by Human and Rat Hepatic Cytochrome P-450," *Anesth. Analg.* 63:805-813, 1984.
28. Brokaw, C.J., "Models for Oscillation and Bend Propagation by Flagella," *Symp. Soc. Exp. Biol.* 35:313-338, 1982.
29. Brown, D.V., and Amann, R.P., "Inhibition of Testosterone Metabolism in Cultured Rat Epididymal Principal Cells by Dihydrotestosterone and Progesterone," *Biol. Reprod.* 30:67-73, 1984.
30. Brown, J.L., *The Evolution of Behavior* (New York: W.W. Norton & Co., 1975).
31. Bucker, H., Horneck, G., Facius, R., et al., "Radiobiological Advanced Biostack Experiment," *Science* 225:222-224, 1984.
32. Budinger, T.F., and Lauterbur, P.C., "Nuclear Magnetic Resonance Technology for Medical Studies," *Science* 226:288-297, 1984.
33. Bullock, T.H., "Comparative Neuroscience Holds Promise for Quiet Revolutions," *Science* 225:473-478, 1984.
34. Burghardt, G.M., "Chemical-Cue Preferences of Inexperienced Snakes: Comparative Aspects," *Science* 157:718-721, 1967.
35. Burghardt, G.M., "Intraspecific Geographical Variation in Chemical Food Cue Preferences of Newborn Garter Snakes (*Thamnophis sirtalis*)," *Behaviour* 36:246-257, 1970.
36. Carson, E.R., "The Role of Mathematical Models in Biochemical Research," *Animals in Scientific Research: An Effective Substitute for Man?* (London: Macmillan, 1983).
37. Cartwright, B.A., and Collett, T.S., "Landmark

Learning in Bees," *J. Comp. Physiol.* 151:521-543, 1983.
38. Chalfie, M., "Neuronal Development in *Caenorhabditis elegans," Trends in Neuroscience,* June 1984.
39. Changeux, J., Devillers-Thiery, A., and Chemouilli, P., "Acetylcholine Receptor: An Allosteric Protein," *Science* 225:1335-1345, 1984.
40. Chow, L.C., and Brown, W.E., "A Physiocochemical Bench-Scale Caries Model," *J. Dent. Res.* 63:868-873, 1984.
41. Christensen, C.P., "New Laser Source Technology," *Science* 224:117-123, 1984.
42. Cline, E.M., Randall, P.A., and Oliphant, E.E., "Hormone Mediated Oviductal Influence on Mouse Embryo Development," *Fert. Steril.* 28:766-771, 1977.
43. Coile, D.C., and Miller, N.E., "How Radical Animal Activists Try to Mislead Humane People," *Am. Psychol.* 39:700-701, 1984.
44. Conklin, K.A., and Lau, S., "Halothane Effects on AT Content and Uridine Uptake and Phosphorylation in *Tetrahymena pyriformis," Anesthesiology* 61:78-82, 1984.
45. Corning, W.C., Dyal, J.A., and Willows, A.O.D. (eds.), *Invertebrate Learning, Vol. 1: Protozoans Through Annelids* (New York: Plenum Press, 1973).
46. Corning, W.C., Dyal, J.A., and Willows, A.O.D. (eds.), *Invertebrate Learning, Vol. 2 Arthropods and Gastropod Mollusks* (New York: Plenum Press, 1973).
47. Corning, W.C., and Kelly, S., "Platyhelminthes: The Turbellarians," *Invertebrate Learning Vol. 1: Protozoans Through Annelids,* W.C. Corning, J.A. Dyal, and A.O.D. Willows (eds.) (New York: Plenum Press, 1973).
48. Craig, P.N., "Overview of Computer Use in Research, Testing, and Education," contract report prepared for the Office of Technology Assessment, U.S. Congress, August 1984.
49. Cubiciotti, D., "DOPPELGANGER: A FORTRAN Program for Simulating Time-Sampled Spatial Locations of 'Phantom' Animals Performing Discrete Pseudorandom Walks," *Behav. Res. Meth. Instru.* 14:485-486, 1982.
50. Current, W.L., and Haynes, T.B., "Complete Development of *Cryptosporidium* in Cell Culture," *Science* 224:603-605, 1984.
51. Daly, M., and Wilson, M., *Sex, Evolution, and Behavior* (Boston, MA: Willard Grant Press, 1983).
52. Davis, H., "Ethical Considerations in the Aversive Control of Behavior," *Soc. Sci. Med.* 15F:61-67, 1981.
53. Dennett, D.C., "Commentary/Pylyshyn: Computational Models and Empirical Constraints," *Behav. Brain Sci.* 1:103-104, 1978.
54. Dierks, P.M., Associate Professor, Department of Biology, University of Virginia, Charlottesville, VA, personal communication, Aug. 21, 1984.
55. Dobson, C.W., and Lemon, R.E., "Markov Sequences in Songs of American Thrushes," *Behaviour* 68:86-105, 1979.
56. Doi, Y., Eanes, E.D., Shimokawa, H., et al., "Inhibition of Seeded Growth of Enamel Apatite Crystals by Amelogenin and Enamelin Proteins In Vitro," *J. Dent. Res.* 63:98-105, 1984.
57. Dooling, R.J., Clark, C., Miller, R., et al., "Program Package for the Analysis and Synthesis of Animal Vocalizations," *Behav. Res. Meth. Instru.* 14:487, 1982.
58. Dukelow, W.R., Chan, P.J., Hutz, R.J., et al., "Preimplantation Development of the Primate Embryo after In Vitro Fertilization," *J. Exp. Zool.* 228:215-221, 1983.
59. East, I.J., Keenan, A.M., Larson, S.M., et al., "Scintigraphy of Normal Mouse Ovaries With Monoclonal Antibodies to ZP-2, the Major Zona Pellucida Protein," *Science* 225:938-941, 1984.
60. Eibl-Eibesfeldt, I., *Ethology: The Biology of Behavior* (New York: Holt, Rinehart & Winston, 1975).
61. Eisner, T., and Camazine, S., "Spider Leg Autotomy Induced By Prey Venom Injection: An Adaptive Response to 'Pain'?" *Proc. Natl. Acad. Sci. USA* 80:3382-3385, 1983.
62. Elbrecht, A., Lazier, C.B., Protter, A.A., et al., "Independent Development Programs for Two Estrogen-Regulated Genes," *Science* 225:639-641, 1984.
63. Ellison, G., Nielsen, E.B., and Lyon, M., "Animal Models of Psychosis: Hallucinatory Behaviors in Monkeys During the Late Stage of Continuous Amphetamine Intoxication," *J. Psychiat. Res.* 16:13-22, 1981.
64. Emerson, J.D., and Colditz, G.A., "Use of Statistical Analysis in The New England Journal of Medicine," *N. Engl. J. Med.* 309:709-713, 1983.
65. Estes, W.K., "Some Targets for Mathematical Psychology," *J. Math. Psychol.* 12:263-282, 1975.
66. Evans, S.M., *Studies in Invertebrate Behavior* (London: Heinemann, 1968).
67. Ewald, B.H., and Gregg, D.A., "Animal Research for Animals," *Ann. N.Y. Acad. Sci.* 406:48-58, 1983.
68. Festing, M.F.W., *Inbred Strains in Biomedical Research* (New York: Oxford University Press, 1979).
69. Field, D.J., Collins, R.A., and Lee, J.C., "Heterogeneity of Vertebrate Brain Tubulins," *Biochemistry* 81:4041-4045, 1984.
70. Flickinger, C.J., "Radioautographic Analysis of the Secretory Pathway for Glycoproteins in Principal Cells of the Mouse Epididymis Exposed to Tritiated Fucose," *Biol. Reprod.* 32:377-390, 1985.

71. Freeman, L., "Two Problems in Computer Simulation in the Social and Behavioral Sciences," *Soc. Sci. Info.* 10:103-109, 1971.
72. Freeman, S., and McFarland, D., "Towards a Model for the Copulatory Behavior of the Male Rat: II. RATSEX—An Exercise in Simulation," *Motivational Control Systems Analysis,* D.J. McFarland (ed.) (London: Academic Press, 1974).
73. Funch, P.G., and Faber, D.S., "Measurement of Myelin Sheath Resistances: Implications for Axonal Conduction and Pathophysiology," *Science* 225: 538-540, 1984.
74. Galef, B.G., Jr., and Sherry, D.F., "Mother's Milk: A Medium for Transmission of Cues Reflecting the Flavor of Mother's Diet," *J. Comp. Physiol. Psychol.* 83:374-378, 1973.
75. Gall, J., "Recombinant DNA Research," *Laboratory Animal Use in Basic Biomedical Research* (draft) (Bethesda, MD: American Society for Cell Biology, 1984).
76. Gallico, G.G., III, O'Connor, N.E., Compton, C.C., et al., "Permanent Coverage of Large Burn Wounds With Autologous Cultured Human Epithelium," *N. Engl. J. Med.* 311:448-451, 1984.
77. Gallup, G.G., Jr., "Toward a Comparative Psychology of Mind," *Animal Cognition and Behavior,* R.L. Mellgren (ed.) (New York: North Holland, 1983).
78. Gallup, G.G., Jr., Boren, J.L., Suarez, S.D., et al., "The Psychopharmacology of Tonic Immobility in Chickens," *The Brain and Behavior of the Fowl,* T. Ookawa (ed.) (Tokyo: Japan Scientific Societies Press, 1983).
79. Gallup, G.G., Jr., and Suarez, S.D., "On the Use of Animals in Psychological Research," *Psychol. Rec.* 30:211-218, 1980.
80. Galston, A.W., and Slayman, C.L., "The Not-So-Secret Life of Plants," *Am. Sci.* 67:337-344, 1979.
81. Gelber, B., "Investigations of the Behavior of *Paramecium aurelia:* I. Modification of Behavior After Training With Food Reinforcement," *J. Comp. Physiol. Psychol.* 45:58-65, 1952.
82. Geller, N.L., "Statistical Strategies for Animal Conservation," *Ann. N.Y. Acad. Sci.* 406:20-31, 1983.
83. Gonczol, E., Andrews, P.W., and Plotkin, S.A., "Cytomegovirus Replicates in Differentiated But Not in Undifferentiated Human Embryonal Carcinoma Cells," *Science* 224:159-161, 1984.
84. Goude, G., "A Theory of Behavior in a Two-Balanced Psychoecological Space," *Scand. J. Psychol.* 22:225-242, 1981.
85. Grier, J.W., *Biology of Animal Behavior* (St. Louis, MO: Times Mirror/Mosby, 1984).
86. Gross, M.L., and Rempel, D.L.,"Fourier Transform Mass Spectrometry," *Science* 226:261-267, 1984.
87. Guyton, A.C., "Physiological System Modeling as an Alternative Model Procedure," in U.S. Department of Health and Human Services, Public Health Service, National Institutes of Health, *Trends in Bioassay Methodology: In Vivo, In Vitro and Mathematical Approaches,* NIH Pub. No. 82-2382 (Washington, DC, 1981).
88. Hanlon, R.T., and Forsythe, J.W., "Advances in the Laboratory Culture of Octopuses for Biomedical Research," *Lab. Anim. Sci.* 35(1):33-40, 1985.
89. Hausfater, G., Aref, S., and Cairns, S.J., "Infanticide as an Alternative Male Reproductive Strategy in Langurs: A Mathematical Model," *J. Theor. Biol.* 94:391-412, 1982.
90. Hay, E.A., "Development of Systems Which Do Not Focus on Whole Animals," *Laboratory Animal Use in Basic Biomedical Research* (draft) (Bethesda, MD: American Society for Cell Biology, 1984).
91. Hayes, M.L., "The Effects of Fatty Acids and Their Monoesters on the Metabolic Activity of Dental Plaque," *J. Dent. Res.* 63: 2-5, 1984.
92. Held, J.R., Doherty, J., and King, N.B., "Societal Benefits Derived From Animal Research," *J. Am. Vet. Med. Assoc.* 185: 268-269, 1984.
93. Hendricks, J.D., Meyers, T.R., Casteel, J.L., et al., "Rainbow Trout Embryos: Advantages and Limitations for Carcinogenesis Research," in U.S. Department of Health and Human Services, Public Health Service, National Cancer Institute, *Use of Small Fish Species in Carcinogenicity Testing,* Monograph 65, NIH Pub. No. (PHS) 84-2652 (Bethesda, MD, May 1984).
94. Hennessey, T.M., Rucker, W.B., and McDiarmid, C.G., "Classical Conditioning in Paramecia," *Anim. Learn. Behav.* 7:417-423, 1979.
95. Herbert, D.E., Associate Professor, Department of Radiology, University of South Alabama, Mobile, AL, personal communication, July 24, 1984.
96. Hersen, M., and Barlow, D.H. (eds.), *Single Case Experimental Designs* (New York: Pergamon Press, 1976).
97. Hieftje, G.M., "New Techniques and Tools in Clinical Chemistry," *Clin. Chem.* 29: 1659-1644, 1983.
98. Hilfer, S.R., and Hilfer, E.S., "Computer Simulation of Organogenesis: An Approach to the Analysis of Shape Changes in Epithelial Organs," *Dev. Biol.* 97:444-453, 1983.
99. Hodgkinson, L., "Tree of Life," *Progress Without Pain* (Lord Dowding Fund, National Anti-Vivisection Society, Ltd., London) 21:20-25, 1984.
100. Howards, S.S., Professor, Departments of Urology and Physiology, University of Virginia, Charlottesville, VA, personal communication, Oct. 10, 1984.
101. Howes, R.I., and Eakers, E.C., "Augmentation of

Tooth and Jaw Regeneration in the Frog With a Digital Transplant," *J. Dent. Res.* 63:670-674, 1984.
102. Hruschka, W.R., Instrumentation Research Laboratory, BARC, Agricultural Research Service, U.S. Department of Agriculture, Beltsville, MD, personal communication, July 26, 1984.
103. Huntingford, F.A., "Some Ethical Issues Raised By Studies of Predation and Aggression," *Anim. Behav.* 32:210-215, 1984.
104. Hyman, B.T., Van Hoesen, G.W., Damasio, A.R., et al., "Alzheimer's Disease: Cell-Specific Pathology Isolates the Hippocampal Formation," *Science* 225:1168-1170, 1984.
105. Iverson, L.L., "Molecular Neurobiology," *Science* 225:1468, 1984.
106. Jaffe, K., "Theoretical Analysis of the Communication System for Chemical Mass Recruitment in Ants," *J. Theor. Biol.* 84:589-610, 1980.
107. Jankus, E.F., Staley, N.A., and Noren, G.R., "Turkey Round Heart Disease: A Model Cardiomyopathy," *Research Animals in Medicine,* Lowell T. Harmison (ed.) (Washington, DC: U.S. Department of Health and Human Services, Public Health Service, National Institutes of Health, 1984).
108. Johnston, K.W., Hager, M., and Cobbold, R.S.C., "Detection of Early Atherosclerosis Using the Systolic Pressure Slope," *Non-Invasive Clinical Measurement,* D.E.M. Taylor and J. Whamond (eds.) (Baltimore, MD: University Park Press, 1977).
109. Jonas, A.M., "The Mouse in Biomedical Research," *Physiologist* 27:330-346, 1984.
110. Jovellanos, C.L., and Gaskin, D.E., "Predicting the Movements of Juvenile Atlantic Herring *Clupea harengus* in the Southwest Bay of Fundy Using Computer Simulation Techniques," *Can. J. Fish Aquat. Sci.* 40:139-146, 1983.
111. Kazdin, A.E., "Statistical Analyses for Single-Case Experimental Designs," *Single Case Experimental Designs,* M. Hersen and D.H. Barlow (eds.) (New York: Pergamon Press, 1976).
112. Kellis, J.T., Jr., and Vickery, L.E., "Inhibition of Human Estrogen Synthetase (Aromatase) by Flavones," *Science* 225:1032-1034, 1984.
113. Keppel, G., *Design and Analysis: A Researcher's Handbook* (Englewood Cliffs, NJ: Prentice-Hall, 1973).
114. Kerr, F.W.L., "The Investigator's Responsibilities in Research Using Animals," *Scientific Perspectives on Animal Welfare,* W.J. Dodds and F.B. Orlans (eds.) (New York: Academic Press, 1982).
115. Kitchell, R.L., and Erickson, H.H. (eds.), *Animal Pain: Perception and Alleviation* (Bethesda, MD: American Physiological Society, 1983).
116. Knowlton, N., "Reproductive Synchrony, Parental Investment, and the Evolutionary Dynamics of Sexual Selection," *Anim. Behav.* 27:1022-1033, 1979.
117. Koff, W.C., Fidler, I.J., Showalter, S.D., et al., "Human Monocytes Activated by Immunomodulators in Liposomes Lyse Herpesvirus-Infected But Not Normal Cells," *Science* 224:1007-1009, 1984.
118. Kolata, G., "Steroid Hormone Systems Found in Yeast," *Science* 225:913-914, 1984.
119. Kolata, G., "A New Kind of Epidemiology," *Science* 224:481, 1984.
120. Kootsey, J.M., Director, National Biomedical Simulation Resource, Duke University Medical Center, Durham, NC, personal communication, Oct. 11, 1984.
121. Lea, S.E.G., "Alternatives to the Use of Painful Stimuli in Physiological Psychology and the Study of Animal Behaviour," *ATLA Abstr.* 7:20-21, 1979.
122. Lee, M.H., and Marudarajan, A.R., "A Computer Package for the Evaluation of Neuron Models Involving Large Uniform Networks," *Int. J. Man-Machine Stud.* 17:189-210, 1982.
123. Leshner, A.I., *An Introduction to Behavioral Endocrinology* (New York: Oxford University Press, 1978).
124. Levin, D.E., Marnett, L.J., and Ames, B.N., "Spontaneous and Mutagen-Induced Deletions: Mechanistic Studies in *Salmonella* Tester Strain TA102," *Genetics* 81:4457-4461, 1984.
125. Lewis, C.S., "NASA's Use of Animals in Research," prepared for the Life Sciences Division, National Aeronautics and Space Administration, Washington, DC, Sept. 28, 1983.
126. Lien, Y., Stern, R., Fu, J.C.C., et al., "Inhibition of Collagen Fibril Formation In Vitro and Subsequent Cross-Linking by Glucose," *Science* 225:1489-1491, 1984.
127. Lineberry, C.G., "Laboratory Animals in Pain Research," *Methods of Animal Experimentation,* W.I. Gay (ed.) (New York: Academic Press, 1981).
128. Lineweaver, H., and Burk, D., "Determination of Enzyme Dissociation Constants," *J. Am. Chem. Soc.* 56:658-666, 1934.
129. Maccecchini, M., Rudin, Y., Blobel, G., et al., "Import of Proteins Into Mitochondria: Precursor Forms of the Extramitochondrially Made F1-ATPase Subunits in Yeast," *Proc. Natl. Acad. Sci. USA* 76:343-347, 1979.
130. Maciel, G.E., "High-Resolution Nuclear Magnetic Resonance of Solids," *Science* 226:282-287, 1984.
131. Mackenzie, N.E., Malthouse, J.P.G., and Scott, A.I., "Studying Enzyme Mechanism by Carbon-13 Nuclear Magnetic Resonance," *Science* 225:883-889, 1984.

132. Manning, A., "The Effects of Artificial Selection for Mating Speeds in *Drosophilia melanogaster*," *Anim. Behav.* 9:82-92, 1961.
133. Manolis, A., "The Diagnostic Potential of Breath Analysis," *Clin. Chem.* 29:5-15, 1983.
134. Markovic, N.S., Markovic, O.T., and Young, D.S., "Simplified Methods for Measuring Enzyme Kinetics in a Single Cell," *Clin. Chem.* 29:1578-1581, 1983.
135. Massie, D.R., "Fat Measurement of Ground Beef With a Gallium Arsenide Infrared Emitter," *Quality Detection in Foods* (St. Joseph, MI: American Society of Agricultural Engineers, 1976).
136. Mather, I.H., Jarasch, E., Bruder, G., et al., "Protein Synthesis in Lactating Guinea-pig Mammary Tissue Perfused In Vitro," *Exp. Cell Res.* 151:208-223, 1984.
137. McCarron, D.A., Morris, C.D., Henry, H.J., et al., "Blood Pressure and Nutrient Intake in the United States," *Science* 226:386-388, 1984.
138. McConnell, J.V., "Comparative Physiology: Learning in Invertebrates," *Ann. Rev. Physiol.* 28:107-136, 1966.
139. McConnell, J.V., and Jacobson, A.L., "Learning in Invertebrates," *Comparative Psychology: A Modern Survey,* D.A. Dewsbury and D.A. Rethlingshafer (eds.) (New York: McGraw-Hill, 1973).
140. McFarland, D.J., "Decision Making in Animals," *Nature* 269:15-21, 1977.
141. McMurray, G.A., "Congenital Insensitivity to Pain and Its Implications for Motivation Theory," *Can. J. Psychol.* 9:650-667, 1955.
142. Mejia, R., "Computer Simulation of Renal Function-Project 1Z01HL03202-11," in U.S. Department of Health and Human Services, Public Health Service, National Heart, Lung, and Blood Institute , *CRISP Report, 1982* (Bethesda, MD, 1982).
143. Melzack, R., *The Puzzle of Pain* (New York: Penguin, 1973).
144. Merz, P.A., Rohwer, R.G., Kascsak, R., et al., "Infection-Specific Particle From the Unconventional Slow Virus Diseases," *Science* 225:437-440, 1984.
145. Metz, S., Horrow, J.C., and Balcar, I., "A Controlled Comparison of Techniques for Locating the Internal Jugular Vein Using Ultrasonography," *Anesth. Analg.* 63:673-679, 1984.
146. Meuzelaar, H.L.C., Windig, W., Harper, A.M., et. al., "Pyrolysis Mass Spectrometry of Complex Organic Materials," *Science* 226:268-274, 1984.
147. Michaelis, L., and Menten, M.L., "Kinetics of Invertase Action," *Biochemistry* 49:333-369, 1913.
148. Minamitani, H., and Hagita, N., "A Neutral Network Model of Pain Mechanisms: Computer Simulation of the Central Neural Activities Essential for the Pain and Touch Sensations," *IEEE Transactions on Systems, Man, and Cybernetics* 11:481-493, 1981.
149. Mirham, G.A., "Simulation Methodology," *Theory and Decision* 7:67-94, 1976.
150. Moffatt, D.S., Guyton, A.C., and Adair, T.H., "Functional Diagrams of Flow and Volume for the Dog's Lung," *J. Appl. Physiol.* 52:1035-1042, 1982.
151. Moran, G., "Severe Food Deprivation: Some Thoughts Regarding Its Exclusive Use," *Psychol. Bull.* 82:543-557, 1975.
152. Moses, R.D., "Computer Simulation of the Cardiovascular System-Project 1Z01HL02719-01," in U.S. Department of Health and Human Services, Public Health Service, National Heart, Lung, and Blood Institute, *CRISP Report, 1982* (Bethesda, MD, 1982).
153. Murai, M., Thompson, W.A., and Wellington, W.G., "Simple Computer Model of Animal Spacing," *Res. Pop. Ecol.* 20:165-178, 1979.
154. Mytilineou, C., and Cohen, G., "1-Methyl-4-Phenyl-1,2,3,6-Tetrahydropyridine Destroys Dopamine Neurons in Explants of Rat Embryo Mesencephalon," *Science* 225:529-531, 1984.
155. Nadi, N.S., Nurnberger, J.I., and Gershon, E.S., "Muscarinic Cholinergic Receptors on Skin Fibroblasts in Familial Affective Disorder," *N. Engl. J. Med.* 311:225-230, 1984.
156. Nardone, R.M., and Ouellette, L.A., "Scope of 'Alternatives': Overview of the State of the Art," contract report prepared for the Office of Technology Assessment, U.S. Congress, July 1984.
157. Naz, R.K., Alexander, N.J., Isahakia, M., et al., "Monoclonal Antibody to a Human Germ Cell Membrane Glycoprotein That Inhibits Fertilization," *Science* 224:342-344, 1984.
158. Neches, R., "Simulation Systems for Cognitive Psychology," *Behav. Res. Meth. Instru.* 14:77-91, 1982.
159. Netland, P.A., and Zetter, B.R. "Organ-Specific Adhesion of Metastatic Tumor Cells in Vitro," *Science* 224:1113-1115, 1984.
160. Newton, C.M., "Biostatistical and Biomathematical Methods in Efficient Animal Experimentation," in National Research Council/National Academy of Sciences, *The Future of Animals, Cells, Models, and Systems in Research, Development, Education, and Testing* (Washington, DC: National Academy of Sciences, 1975).
161. Normann, R.A., Perlman, I., Kolb, H., et al., "Direct Excitatory Interactions Between Cones of Different Spectral Types in the Turtle Retina," *Science* 224:625-627, 1984.
162. Norris, K.H., "Near Infrared Reflectance Spectroscop—The Present and Future," *Cereals '78: Better Nutrition for the World's Millions,* Proceedings of the Sixth International Cereal and Bread Congress, May 1978.

163. Orcutt, B.C., George, D.G., and Dayhoff, M.O., "Protein and Nucleic Acid Sequence Data Base Systems," *Ann. Rev. Biophys. Bioengin.* 12:419-441, 1983.
164. Patrusky, B., "Plants in Their Own Behalf," *Mosaic* 14(2):32-39, 1983.
165. Peterson, E.L., "The Temporal Pattern of Mosquito Flight Activity," *Behaviour* 72:1-25, 1980.
166. Peterson, J.I., and Vurek, G.G., "Fiber-Optic Sensors for Biomedical Applications," *Science* 224:123-127, 1984.
167. Pottala, E.W., Colburn, T.R., Covacci, R., et al., "Hardware Cone Cell Model: Operational Characteristics," *Med. Biol. Engin. Comput.* 20:437, 1982.
168. Preilowski, B., Reger, M., and Engele, H., "Combining Scientific Experimentation With Species Adequate Housing in Laboratory Studies of Non-Human Primates," *Am. J. Primatol.* 5:374, 1984.
169. Pyke, G.H., "Honeyeater Foraging: A Test of Optimal Foraging Theory," *Anim. Behav.* 29:878-888, 1981.
170. Pylyshyn, Z.W., "Computational Models and Empirical Restraints," *Behav. Brain Sci.* 1:93-99, 1978.
171. Reed, S.C., "Problems in Assessing Intelligence in Artifacts," *IEEE Transactions on Systems, Man, and Cybernetics* 4:97-100, 1974.
172. Ross, M.H., "Nutrition and Longevity in Experimental Animals," *Nutrition and Aging,* M. Wineck (ed.) (New York: John Wiley & Sons, 1976).
173. Rowsell, H.C., "The Ethics of Biomedical Experimentation," in National Research Council/National Academy of Sciences, *The Future of Animals, Cells, Models, and Systems in Research, Development, Education, and Testing* (Washington, DC: National Academy of Sciences, 1975).
174. Russell, W.M.S., and Burch, R.L., *Principles of Humane Experimental Technique* (Springfield, IL: Charles C. Thomas, 1959).
175. Sahagian, G.G., and Neufeld, E.F., "Biosynthesis and Turnover of the Mannose 6-Phosphate Receptor in Cultured Chinese Hamster Ovary Cells," *J. Biol. Chem.* 258:7121-7128, 1983.
176. Sainz, A., Roberts, V.C., Pinardi, G., et al., "Blood Flow Velocity and Acceleration Measurement by Doppler-shift Ultrasound," *Non-Invasive Clinical Measurement,* D.E.M. Taylor and J. Whamond (eds.) (Baltimore, MD: University Park Press, 1977).
177. Salu, Y., "Computer Simulations of Learning in Neural Systems," *Comput. Biomed. Res.* 16:176-189, 1983.
178. Sanders, G.D., "The Cephalopods," *Invertebrate Learning, Vol. 3: Cephalopods and Echinoderms,* W.C. Corning, J.A. Dyal, and A.O.D. Willows (eds.) (New York: Plenum Press, 1975).
179. Schwartz, J.M., and Cogan, D.C., "Position Discrimination in the Salamander, *Ambystoma tigrinum,*" *Devel. Psychobiol.* 10:355-358, 1977.
180. Schwid, H.A., and Geisler, C.D., "Multiple Reservoir Model of Neurotransmitter Release by a Cochlear Inner Hair Cell," *J. Acoust. Soc. Am.* 72:1435-1440, 1982.
181. Seeman, P., Ulpian, C., Bergeron, C., et al., "Bimodal Distribution of Dopamine Receptor Densities in Brains of Schizophrenics," *Science* 225:728-731, 1984.
182. Seligman, M.E.P., "On the Generality of the Laws of Learning," *Psychol. Rev.* 77:406-418, 1970.
183. Sevenster, P., "Motivation and Learning in Sticklebacks *(Gasterosteus aculeatus L.),*" *The Central Nervous System and Fish Behavior,* D. Ingle (ed.) (Chicago: University of Chicago Press, 1968).
184. Sharma, S.P., Jit, I., and Rai, N., "Age-Related Changes in Nucleic Acids and Protein in *Callosobruchus maculatus* Fabr. (Coleoptera)," *Gerontology* 30:26-29, 1984.
185. Shiovitz, K.A., and Lemon, R.E., "Species Identification of Song by Indigo Buntings as Determined by Responses to Computer Generated Sounds," *Behaviour* 74:167-199, 1980.
186. Sibaoka, T., "Action Potentials in Plant Organs," *Nerv. Horm. Mech. Integr.* 20:40-73, 1966.
187. Sidman, M., *Tactics of Scientific Research* (New York: Basic Books, 1960).
188. Simon, A., "A Theoretical Approach to the Classical Conditioning of Botanical Subjects," *J. Biol. Psychol.* 20:35-43, 1978.
189. Sisk, C.L., and Desjardins, C., "Changes in LH Pulse Amplitude and Frequency as a Function of Time After Castration of Male Ferrets," *Soc. Neurosci. Abstr.* 9:708, 1983.
190. Smith, A.C., "Marine Animals in Medical Research," *JAMA* 242:2847, 1979.
191. Smyth, D.H., *Alternatives to Animal Experiments* (London: Scholar Press Ltd, 1978).
192. Snyder, S.H., "Cholinergic Mechanisms in Affective Disorders," *N. Engl. J. Med.* 311:254-255, 1984.
193. Sorkin, B.C., Hoffman, S., Edelman, G.M., et al., "Sulfation and Phosphorylation of the Neural Cell Adhesion Molecule, N-CAM," *Science* 225:1476-1478, 1984.
194. Spetch, M.L., and Wilkie, D.M., "A Program That Simulates Random Choice in Radial Arm Mazes and Similar Choice Situations," *Behav. Res. Meth. Instru.* 12:377-378, 1980.
195. Stanley, S.M., *Macroevolution: Patterns and Process* (San Francisco: W.H. Freeman, 1979).
196. Sternback, R.A., *Pain: A Psychophysiological Analysis* (New York: Academic Press, 1968).

197. Stevens, C.G., "Human Perspectives," in National Research Council/National Academy of Sciences, *The Future of Animals, Cells, Models, and Systems in Research, Development, Education, and Testing* (Washington, DC: National Academy of Sciences, 1975).
198. Still, A.W., "On the Number of Subjects Used in Animal Behaviour Experiments," *Anim. Behav.* 30:873-880, 1982.
199. Strulovici, B., Carione, R.A., Kilpatric, B.F., et al., "Direct Demonstration of Impaired Functionality of a Purified Desensitized B-Adrenergic Receptor in a Reconstituted System," *Science* 225:837-840, 1984.
200. Symmons, P.M., and Rosenberg, L.J., "A Model Simulating Mating Behavior of *Spodoptera littoralis*," *J. Appl. Ecol.* 15:423-438, 1978.
201. Taylor, D.J., Crowe, M., Bore, P.J., et al., "Examination of the Energetics of Aging Skeletal Muscle Using Nuclear Magnetic Resonance," *Gerontology* 30:2-7, 1984.
202. Tepperman, K., Finer, R., Donovan, S., et al., "Intestinal Uptake and Metabolism of Auranofin, A New Oral Gold-Based Antiarthritis Drug," *Science* 225:430-432, 1984.
203. Tinbergen, N., *The Study of Instinct* (New York: Oxford University Press, 1951).
204. Toates, F., "Computer Simulation and the Homeostatic Control of Behavior" *Motivational Control Systems Analysis,* D.J. McFarland (ed.) (London: Academic Press, 1974).
205. Toates, F., and O'Rourke, C., "Computer Simulation of Male Rat Sexual Behavior," *Med. Biol. Engin. Comput.* 16:98-104, 1978.
206. Tompkins, P., and Bird, C., *The Secret Life of Plants* (New York: Harper & Row, 1973).
207. Turner, T.T., Plesums, J.L., and Cabot, C.L., "Luminal Fluid Proteins of the Male Reproductive Tract," *Biol. Reprod.* 21:883-890, 1979.
208. Vestal, M.L., "High-Performance Liquid Chromatography-Mass Spectrometry," *Science* 226:275-281, 1984.
209. Von Frisch, K., *The Dance Language and Orientation of Bees* (Cambridge, MA: Harvard University Press, 1967).
210. Waddell, C.A., and Desai, I.D., "The Use of Laboratory Animals in Nutrition Research," *World Rev. Nutr. Diet.* 36:206-222, 1981.
211. Wall, P.D., "On the Relation of Injury to Pain," *Pain* 6:253-264, 1979.
212. Waller, M.B., Bride, W.J., Gatto, G.J., et al., "Intragastric Self-Infusion of Ethanol by Ethanol-Preferring and Nonpreferring Lines of Rats," *Science* 225:78-80, 1984.
213. Walter, P., and Blobel, G., "Signal Recognition Particle Contains a 7S RNA Essential for Protein Translocation Across the Endoplasmic Reticulum," *Nature* 299:691-698, 1982.
214. Waser, M.R., Garfinkel, L., Kohn, M.C., et al,. "Computer Modeling of Muscle Phosphofructokinase Kinetics," *J. Theor. Biol.* 103:295-312, 1983.
215. Wehner, R., "Spatial Vision in Arthropods," *Handbook of Sensory Physiology Vol. VII/6C,* H. Autrum (ed.) (New York: Springer, 1981).
216. Weinberg, J.B., Hobbs, M.M., and Misukonis, M.A., "Recombinant Human Interferon Induces Human Monocyte Polykaryon Formation," *Proc. Natl. Acad. Sci USA* 81:4554-4557, 1984.
217. Weisz, P.B., *The Science of Biology* (New York: McGraw-Hill, 4th ed., 1971).
218. Wells, M.J., *Octopus: Physiology and Behaviour of an Advanced Invertebrate* (London: Chapman & Hall, 1978).
219. Wells, P.H., "Honeybees," *Invertebrate Learning, Vol. 2: Arthropods and Gastropod Mollusks,* W.C. Corning, J.A. Dyal, and A.O.D. Willows (eds.) (New York: Plenum Press, 1973).
220. Wigdahl, B., Smith, C.A., Traglia, H.M., et al., "Herpes Simplex Virus Latency in Isolated Human Neurons," *Proc. Natl. Acad. Sci. USA* 81:6217-6221, 1984.
221. Winer, B.J., *Statistical Principles in Experimental Design* (New York: McGraw-Hill, 1971).
222. Winfree, A.T., "Rotating Chemical Reactions," *Sci. Am.* 230:82-95, 1974.
223. Woodward, W.T., and Bitterman, M.E., "Asymptotic Reversal Learning in Pigeons: Mechanisms for Reducing Inhibition," *J. Exp. Psychol.* (Animal Behavior Processes) 2:57-66, 1976.
224. Wright, E.M., Jr., Vice-Chairman, Department of Comparative Medicine, University of Virginia, Charlottesville, VA, personal communication, Aug. 16, 1984.
225. Zanberg, P., "Animal Models in Experimental Hypertension: Relevance to Drug Testing and Discovery," *Handbook of Hypertension, Vol. 3: Pharmacology of Antihypertensive Drugs,* P.A. van Zweiten (ed.) (Amsterdam: Elsevier Science Publishers B.W., 1984).

Chapter 7

The Use of Animals in Testing

Distress caused by the Draize eye test is sometimes so acute that rabbits do *scream out in pain.*

Close-Up Report
Humane Society of the United States
1985

Laws should neither push the science where it is not yet ready to go nor hold the science to procedures that have been modified or replaced.

Geraldine V. Cox
Chemical Manufacturers Association
March 20, 1985

CONTENTS

Table

Chapter 7

The Use of Animals in Testing

Testing for the safety or efficacy of a substance or product accounts for a major use of animals as defined in this assessment, most of which are rats and mice (see ch. 3). Of these, probably the largest portion are used in developing drugs. A significant portion are also used to test other substances—pesticides, industrial chemicals, and consumer products—to assess possible toxicity and to establish conditions under which they can be used safely.

Research and testing have been differentiated for purposes of this assessment, but the boundary between them is not sharp. From the standpoint of developing alternatives, a key difference is that a particular test may be performed for hundreds, perhaps thousands of substances and use hundreds or thousands of animals, whereas a given research method will be used on far fewer. As a corollary there are far more research procedures than testing procedures from which to choose. Furthermore, individual researchers are much more likely to develop their own methods than are those conducting testing. These differences make the task of developing alternatives more manageable for testing than for research.

Testing for efficacy has some attributes of research and some of toxicity testing. A particular protocol may be used on a small number of substances and is likely to be tailored either to the application or to the family of substances being tested. Experimenters testing for efficacy need to have a better understanding of the mechanisms by which a particular effect occurs than those testing for toxicity, primarily because efficacy testing is closely related to the physiological mechanisms that the new drug may affect, whereas toxic effects may be quite independent. Finally, an important distinction of efficacy testing is that the animals used would ordinarily be diseased.

Other kinds of tests include those for safety other than for toxicity, as in testing of diagnostic techniques or quality control tests in the manufacture of medical devices. These have end points even more specific than those for toxicity, and are thus good candidates for the development of alternatives (see ch. 8).

Toxicity testing is the focus of this and the following chapter for three reasons. First, this is an area of animal use in testing in which the government has great influence on nongovernmental activities. Second, these tests are used in a more routine fashion than are tests for efficacy or general safety and therefore have a greater tendency to lag in the application of state-of-the-art technology. Third, toxicity tests include methods that have attracted the largest political attack.

All substances can be toxic at some exposure level, even water. Conversely, even substances known to be highly toxic may be harmless at low doses or under certain circumstances. Determining the hazard to humans requires information about the potential hazard and the expected level of exposure, resulting in an estimate of the probability that a substance will produce harm under certain conditions (8). This assessment of risk is a scientific endeavor, whereas the management of risk is a sociopolitical one (31,36).

Although toxicity data on humans are invaluable in conducting risk assessments, they are usually unavailable. Some information comes from epidemiologic studies or episodes of accidental human exposure. Most often, however, testing on animals is used. An appropriate weight is given to the following factors on a case-by-case basis, considering the seriousness of the hazard and the kind of assumptions needed to estimate risks to humans:

- the relationship between dose and response;
- the effects at the molecular, cellular, organ, organ system, and whole-organism levels;
- conflicting results between studies and possible explanations for the conflicts;
- the effects of structurally similar substances on humans or animals;
- any known metabolic differences between humans and the test species that could affect the toxic response; and
- statistical uncertainties and difficulties in extrapolating to a low dose (55).

TESTING METHODS

Toxicology as a science began in the 16th century and has advanced with the growth of the chemical, pesticide, drug, and cosmetic industries. The concept of protecting the public from harmful effects of chemicals dates back to laws of ancient civilizations that made it illegal to adulterate the food supply (25). The importance of toxicology to public health has received considerable attention in the United States since the 1930s. Public awareness of the value of toxicological testing has also been furthered by disasters such as Minamata disease (methyl mercury poisoning in Japan), the thalidomide tragedy, and, more recently, the development of cancer in those exposed to diethylstilbestrol (DES) in utero.

Designing a Test

There are two approaches to toxicology—mechanistic and descriptive—and these affect the design of experiments and the choice of biological end points to be measured. Mechanistic toxicology focuses on the chemical processes by which a toxic effect occurs and relies heavily on the techniques of physiology, biochemistry, and analytical chemistry to monitor these processes. A simple example of this approach would be a series of experiments showing that a certain substance is metabolized in the liver, that one of the byproducts of metabolism happens to be a potent liver carcinogen, and that liver cancer typically follows administration of that substance. Mechanistic tests are custom-designed and are closely related to research. They can contribute greatly to the design and interpretation of descriptive tests. Mechanistic toxicology plays a major role in the development of methodologies that could replace whole-animal testing.

Descriptive toxicology deals with phenomena above the molecular level and may rely heavily on the techniques of pathology, statistics, physiology, and pharmacology, e.g., the evaluation of changes in the appearance of an organ or its constituent cells, the presence of tumors, or signs of irritation. This approach does not necessarily require an understanding of the mechanisms by which toxic effects occur, although if mechanistic information were available, it would be used. In terms of the test substance and species in the preceding hypothetical case, descriptive toxicology would show that a certain substance causes liver cancer in a particular species within a certain time. It might also show the approximate relationship between the substance dose and the incidence of the liver cancer. Regulatory schemes requiring testing most often rely on descriptive toxicology.

Mechanistic toxicology provides an approach to extrapolation from one species to another based on known similarities and differences in physiology. The closer the test animal is biologically to humans or the greater the number of species in which the effect is detected, the more likely it will occur in humans as well. The reliability of extrapolations from descriptive experiments is greatly enhanced when mechanistic information is also used. Similarly, the use of mechanistic information in the design of descriptive tests contributes greatly to the reasonableness of any later extrapolation to humans if human toxicity data are lacking.

Most state-of-the-art toxicological tests require whole animals. Although in vitro alternatives are being developed (see ch. 8), different end points would be measured. For example, whole animals will probably continue to be needed to look for effects in previously unknown target organs, to evaluate effects that represent an interaction of multiple organ systems, to monitor metabolism and pharmacokinetics, or to evaluate healing or diminished responsiveness to the toxic substance. Thus, whole-animal use is unlikely to stop entirely in the foreseeable future.

Choice of Species and Strain

In 1904, the Food and Drug Administration (FDA) was still using human employees to test food preservatives (e.g., boric acid, salicylic acid, their derivatives, and formaldehyde) for toxicity (25). Use of animals remained limited until a few decades ago, when breeding technology provided large numbers of animals with carefully controlled genetic characteristics, thus allowing toxic effects to be more easily detected than had previously been the case. Animal use has grown with increasing demands by the public for safe and effective products.

The most appropriate animals are ideally those that, for the substance being tested, predict the human response most accurately. There is no other animal wholly identical to humans in terms of toxic effects. The choice of animal is influenced by known similarity to humans for the organ system or mechanism of interest, as well as convenience of breeding or purchasing, familiarity with the species, existing data, lifespan, ease of handling under experimental conditions, cost of obtaining and maintaining, litter size, and gestation period. Rodents have been used extensively, as have rabbits, primates, and dogs.

Rodents have been used in almost all carcinogenicity testing despite the fact that such tests are the most difficult to extrapolate to humans. Mice and rats have been used because their lifespan is short, they are small and easily handled, and they have a number of metabolic pathways and pathological responses similar to those of humans. Some specially developed strains are sufficiently susceptible to cancer that test groups can be small. These factors contribute greatly to the economic feasibility of conducting carcinogenicity testing with rodents. Extensive experience in using them, and in using particular strains, is often an important reason for continuing their use (55). A large amount of data are already available on spontaneous tumors at specific organ sites (1).

Although rodents are routinely used for many kinds of tests, other animals may be used for specific reasons. For example, the rabbit is used for eye irritation tests because it has large, easily manipulated eyes and because its eyes have many characteristics found in human eyes (19). Hens have been shown to be a good model for delayed neurotoxic effects of organophosphorous compounds (12).

Dose Levels and Route and Duration of Exposure

The way in which exposure to a substance occurs can affect the kind and severity of toxic effects. For example, if a chemical does not present a hazard when applied to skin because it is not absorbed, it may nonetheless be very toxic if taken orally. When the route of exposure does not affect the portion of the dose taken up or its distribution in the body, testing might be done in the manner most easily controlled. For other than the most preliminary tests to characterize toxicity, most would administer the substance by the same route as would occur in the course of accidental exposure or use by humans. Sometimes the palatability, solubility, stability, or volatility of a substance will determine which routes are feasible.

Certain tests, such as the acute toxicity for a single exposure, are used as inexpensive screening tools for estimating the relative hazard presented by a substance. As discussed later in this chapter, the acute toxicity test known as the LD_{50} is used in classification schemes for the transportation or disposal of chemicals. Acute toxicity testing might also be used to determine the risks of one-time exposure, as might occur in an accident. Ordinarily, the duration of exposure in an animal study is greater (at least in proportion to the lifespan) than the exposure period for which data will be used in extrapolating the risks to humans.

The dose levels administered depend on a variety of factors. On the one hand, it is not possible to detect long-term effects if the dose is so large that many animals die before the end of the test. On the other hand, administered doses representative of human exposure levels may not produce detectable effects with what may be considered a reasonable number of test animals. Generally, three dose levels are used; they are chosen so as to span the range of responses from a "no-observed-effect level" to fully observable toxic effects.

For carcinogenicity and other long-term testing, the highest dose should be one that will produce measurable toxicity without significantly altering lifespan. Other levels may depend on whether the carcinogenicity is being looked for in combination with chronic toxicity (55). The lowest dose could be one for which there are no observed effects or it might be related to the level of estimated human exposure (38).

Another approach is to choose doses that will yield levels in the blood similar to those expected for humans. Although this is perhaps a more realistic test, effects may be more difficult to detect. In addition, the criterion of similarity may require more than one administration per day because metabolic rates and excretion rates tend to be faster in small animals than in humans (24).

Statistical Considerations

To obtain valid results, an experiment must be designed so that what is measured provides useful and sufficiently accurate information. Statistical methods allow a scientist to estimate the minimum number of test animals from which conclusions can be drawn to estimate the reliability of any conclusions. Statistical analysis can help reduce the number of animals needed for a particular test procedure.

To allow for the unexpected (including death, illness, or error), the number of animals used always exceeds the minimum number needed to detect expected effects reliably. Determining that minimum number of animals is more difficult for longer tests, both because the passage of time makes the probability of something going wrong during the experiment increase, and because certain problems are more likely to occur as the animals age.

Another factor affecting the number of animals needed is the variability in the sensitivity of individual animals to the substance involved. Thus, as few as 6 animals might be used for an eye irritation test or 10 per dose level for an acute toxicity test. In carcinogenicity or teratogenicity testing, many of the animals may be unaffected by the test substance, and 100 animals may be needed for each dose level.

Most species experience some cancer and other diseases during their life. Any measurement of incidence as it relates to the dose given must be taken against this background incidence, which is gauged in an (untreated) control group. Control groups may also be important if a test substance is being carried in a particular vehicle needed to administer the test substance, such as in solution with another chemical, that is not itself being tested (vehicle control group). The sensitivity of the test animals to a substance known to be toxic may also be measured for comparison (a positive control group). Because there are so many variables that can influence a test, toxicologists consider it vital that the control and test groups be drawn from the same pool of animals and be tested concurrently.

Any experiment suffers from experimental error, of which there are three sources: the natural variation due to differences among test animals, the variation in experimental conditions, and error arising in measurement. Determining the amount of error is crucial to drawing reliable conclusions from experimental results, but it is also important to keep the error as low as possible by controlling conditions carefully. Differences among test animals are controlled by using genetically similar and sufficiently large groups for each condition. Even minor environmental factors can influence toxic response (15,23). Sources of measurement error depend on the measurement technique and the equipment.

Use of Standardized Test Methods and Guidelines

Testing methodologies are standardized to control experimental variables, thus allowing results to be easily compared. Methodologies may become standardized through round-robin testing in many labs, through publication and imitation, and through development by recognized organizations or agencies. Methodologies or guidelines are published by the Food and Drug Administration, the Environmental Protection Agency (EPA), the Organization for Economic Cooperation and Development (OECD), the National Cancer Institute, the American Society for Testing and Materials, the American National Standards Institute, the British Standards Institute, the International Agency for Research on Cancer, and others (see app. A for information on FDA, EPA, and OECD guidelines).

The most important reason to strive for compatibility among guidelines is to avoid the need to repeat identical tests to satisfy particular requirements of various governments and agencies. Compatibility can also avoid nontariff trade barriers. Any government that would like to change its testing requirements to further the cause of animal welfare needs to consider the effects of its policies on testing in other countries.

Pharmacokinetics

Pharmacokinetic studies provide information about the mechanisms of absorption, about a substance's distribution among the various body compartments, and about metabolism and elimination. They facilitate the interpretation of results from other tests and their extrapolation to humans because the distribution and elimination of a foreign substance will often explain its toxicity or lack thereof.

Absorption of a substance into the body can occur by a variety of routes. If exposure is by inhalation, absorption can occur in the lungs, in the pathways leading to the lungs, and sometimes in the gastrointestinal tract. If exposure is by mouth, absorption would occur as the substance passes through the gastrointestinal tract. What is not absorbed is excreted in the feces. With dermal exposure, the substance must be absorbed through the skin. If exposure is via injection into a body cavity, the substance cannot be removed without the involvement of other parts of the body.

Once a substance is absorbed, it may be excreted unchanged. Excretion could be through the skin, in the urine, feces, semen, or breast milk, or, if it is volatile, in exhaled air. It might also be stored in tissues, organs, or body fluids, perhaps for the life of the organism. A substance might also be chemically modified until it can be excreted or until the body is unable to metabolize it any further. This metabolism normally takes place in the liver, the site where detoxification of substances takes place. A test substance or its metabolic products can react with the chemicals that make up the body, perhaps resulting in toxic effects.

Pharmacokinetic studies are usually conducted through the sampling of body fluids, both those that are excreted (urine, saliva) and those that are not (blood, cerebrospinal fluid). Tissue samples are often taken, although normally not until the end of a study (4).

Acute Toxicity Tests

Acute toxicity testing is used to detect the toxic effects of single or multiple exposures occurring within 24 hours. These are frequently the first tests performed in determining the toxic characteristics of a substance and may serve as a basis for classification or labeling or for concerns about accidental exposure. The results are used to establish toxicity relative to other substances, to determine specific toxic effects, and to provide information on the mode of toxic action and the relationship between dose and adverse effects. Results may also help in designing long-term tests.

One of the most common acute toxicity tests is the LD_{50} (from Lethal Dose for 50 percent), developed in 1927 for comparing batches of dangerous drugs (52). The LD_{50} is calculated to be the dose, within statistically established confidence intervals, at which half the test animals can be expected to die upon exposure to a test substance. A substance is administered once by the oral, dermal, or parenteral (injection into a vein or the body cavity) route or it is inhaled. The animals, usually rodents, are observed for 14 days and then sacrificed so that their organs and tissues can be evaluated for gross changes. Other measurements and observations can be added to increase the amount of information this test provides.

A related procedure is the limit test. A high dose is given, often 5 g/kg body weight (54); if no animals die, the test ends. This is based on the assumption that if an organism is not killed by an extremely large dose, it does not matter what dose it takes to actually cause death. Other tests using fewer animals have been devised and are receiving growing acceptance (see ch. 8).

Acute toxicity testing has its limitations, particularly because the end point is death. Death can come about in many ways and the mechanism is not conveyed in the numerical value of an LD_{50}. In addition, the results may vary greatly both among and within species, with the animals' sex, age, and diet, and with other test conditions. Acute toxicity testing, although not necessarily the classic LD_{50} procedures, will continue to be of interest because there are many substances for which the toxic effects of acute exposure are quite different from those produced by chronic exposure (8). It may also continue to be used in selecting doses for long-term studies. Nonetheless, circumstances may be identified in which acute toxicity testing is not needed because other tests more relevant to the use should be performed. The Toxicity Committee of the Fund for the Replacement of Ani-

38-750 O - 86 - 6

mals in Medical Experiments recommended that study of the consequences of not acquiring knowledge of acute toxicity of products be undertaken and that in the case of products such as drugs, LD_{50} tests should be replaced by acute toxicity tests that emphasize the nature of the effects observed (18).

Skin and Eye Irritation/Corrosion Tests

Irritation is the production of reversible tissue damage such as swelling, while corrosion is the production of irreversible tissue damage. Skin and eye irritation tests normally involve acute exposure. Repeated exposure can be used to test for allergic reactions, which involve the organism's immune system, and cumulative effects. Skin irritation studies are used to initially characterize a substance's toxicity and to develop precautionary information for situations in which human skin or eye exposure is possible.

Although it is not yet possible to reliably predict the degree of irritation or corrosion a substance will cause, a considerable body of knowledge exists. The factors that determine damaging effects to eyes or skin are:

- intimacy and duration of contact,
- physical properties that determine the amount of penetration, and
- the reactivity of the substance with tissues (10).

Intimacy is affected by both the ability of the substance to spread over the surface (such as soaps or detergents) and its concentration. Penetration of the skin or other membranes is greatest in substances with small molecular size and with abilities to mix with both water and oil. A substance that can react with proteins and enzymes in tissues is especially damaging if it can penetrate to the delicate structures of the eye (50).

Skin irritation tests are usually conducted on rabbits, guinea pigs, rats, and mice, although other mammals may also be used. The test substance is applied to a small area of skin from which the fur has been clipped or shaved and may be held in place with a dressing. Using untreated skin of the same animal for comparison, the degree of redness or blistering is scored at intervals (e.g., 38,54).

There are many similarities between the skin cells of humans and other mammals, but there are important differences as well. For example, there are structural differences that affect permeability (32). Animal models have been shown to be particularly poor in the evaluation of mild irritants (27). The extrapolation of animal models is further complicated by large differences in the race, age, and skin condition of humans (21,26,58).

The method most commonly used to evaluate eye irritation is the Draize test, which has remained largely unaltered since it was introduced more than 40 years ago (9). A single dose of a substance is applied to one eye of at least three adult rabbits. The other eye remains untreated. The degree of irritation or corrosion to the cornea, iris, and conjunctiva is scored by comparison with standard pictures over a period of 3 days. The rabbits may be observed for 3 weeks to determine whether the effects are reversible.

A substance shown to be highly corrosive to skin will be highly irritating to the eye and thus might not be tested. Similarly, a substance with a pH of 2 or less (strongly acid) or 11.5 or more (strongly alkaline) is assumed to be highly irritating or corrosive to skin or eye and need not be tested (38,54). The cornea tolerates substances with a pH ranging from 3 to 11 variably, with the severity of a reaction depending in large part on a substance's ability to affect protein structure or function (17,35).

Repeated-Dose Toxicity Tests

Humans are often exposed repeatedly to a substance and this does not necessarily cause the same effects as an acute, one-time exposure. Chronic toxicity effects differ from acute toxicity ones when the test substance or its metabolites accumulate in the organism to a toxic level or when it causes irreversible toxic effects that accumulate with each administration (8). Rats are most frequently used, and testing in a second, nonrodent species, usually a dog, is also common.

Repeated or prolonged exposure to the test substance is used in chronic, subchronic, and short-term toxicity tests. The term chronic generally refers to tests with exposure for at least 1 year or most of the lifetime of the test species. Subchronic usually refers to tests of intermediate duration—3 to 6 months. Short-term repeated-dose toxicity tests last from 2 to 4 weeks.

Some have suggested that there is little to be gained by exposures of more than 6 months duration for chronic toxicity testing (18,34). One commentator has argued that studies of 3 to 6 months are easier to interpret because the complicating effects of aging are avoided (44,45). Another finds longer tests necessary for detecting effects that occur only late in life or for which cumulative toxicity is an important consequence (42).

Throughout repeated-dose testing, animals would be observed for general appearance, respiratory problems, central and peripheral nervous system function, coordination, and behavioral changes. During and following the course of exposure, observations are made of hematology (hematocrit, white cell count, platelet count, clotting factors), ophthalmology, electrolyte balance, carbohydrate metabolism, liver and kidney function (as determined from concentrations of certain substances in the blood), body weight, and the appearance of lesions. After the animals have been sacrificed, observations are made of body surfaces, orifices, cavities, and organs. Microscopic examinations are made of selected tissues and organs, of gross lesions, and of organs that changed in size. One technique used in repeated-dose toxicity testing to determine whether the toxic effects are reversible is to give a satellite group the highest dose of the test substance and then give the animals time to recover before sacrificing them.

Carcinogenicity

Cancer is a major human health concern, striking one out of four and killing one out of five Americans (53). Consequently, carcinogenicity is an important animal test. Detecting human carcinogens presents special problems because a latency period of 20 years or more can occur. Animal testing, particularly in rodents, is useful because the latency period for tumor formation is much shorter (1 to 2 years for rodents), thus allowing potential human carcinogens to be detected during testing and before use, at which point they could become major public health problems. It is also much easier to control the animal environment than the human environment, and therefore to investigate causal relationships.

Although many human carcinogens were discovered without animal testing, several have been identified by first using such tests, e.g., DES, vinyl chloride, and bis(chloro-methyl) ether (55). Animal use has its limitations; many substances cause cancer only in certain species. The known human carcinogens benzene and arsenic have never proved to be animal carcinogens. Hundreds of substances have been identified as carcinogens in tests with one or more animal species but not in humans, in part because of insufficient human epidemiologic data and in part because some of them undoubtedly do not cause cancer in humans (41). Nonetheless, the use of animals in testing for carcinogenicity is widely endorsed (55).

Carcinogenicity testing is more costly and requires far more animals than other tests. Chronic toxicity testing may use about 160 rats and 32 dogs, whereas carcinogenicity testing would use about 400 rats and 400 mice. (In order to economize, carcinogenicity testing and chronic toxicity testing are often combined.) Cancer is easy to detect if tumors are visible, but it can only be detected in its early stages by microscopic examination of multiple samples of 30 or more tissues and organs that may appear normal. Typically, 500,000 data points must be analyzed (41).

These large numbers of animals and multiple data points are needed for statistical reasons. Cancer has a high background incidence and large variations from animal to animal, making it difficult to establish that cancer was caused by the test substance. The higher the incidence of spontaneous cancers, the more difficult it is to establish a link between cancer and the test substance. For example, if the background rate of cancer is 10 percent and the common criterion for statistical significance of 0.05 is used, the number of animals required to detect carcinogenicity in 90 percent of the tests is as shown in table 7-1. As can be seen, if a test substance causes cancer in 80 percent of the animals, 48 animals are needed to demonstrate carcinogenicity. If the incidence is only 15 percent, over 3,000 animals are needed. It has been suggested that the background incidence could be re-

Table 7-1.—Number of Animals Needed to Detect Carcinogenicity in 90 Percent of All Tests for a Statistical Significance of 0.05

Rate of incidence caused by test substance (percent)	Number of animals (3 dose levels plus control group)
80	48
60	84
40	184
20	1,020
15	3,304

SOURCE: Adapted from I.F.H. Purchase, "Carcinogenicity," *Animals and Alternatives in Toxicity Testing,* M. Balls, R.J. Riddell, and A.N. Worden (eds.) (New York: Academic Press, 1983).

duced, and the sensitivity of the method thereby improved, if animals were not kept under conditions that aggravate cancer (excessively nutritious diet, little exercise, and isolation) (42).

Developmental and Reproductive Toxicity

The effects of chemicals on human reproduction are difficult to assess because of the complexity of the reproductive process and the many kinds of insults that can be inflicted before reproductive maturity as well as during fetal development (8). Reproductive functions that can be harmed by foreign substances include the storage and maturation of the germ cells, fertility (including factors that affect sperm maturation and implantation of the fertilized egg), and the development of the fetus. Possible toxic effects to the fetus include birth defects (teratogenicity), low birth weight, abnormal gestation time, and prenatal or postnatal death (7).

There are a variety of experimental protocols by which these effects can be determined in animals. Some involve more than one generation; others involve evaluation of a fetus before birth. Exposure to a substance can start before the female ovulates or as late as some specific stage of fetal development. Exposure can be chronic or acute. The great variety of procedures available can lead to a certain amount of overlapping testing (2).

Rats and rabbits are the most commonly used species. Mice and hamsters and other mammals are used as well. Three dose levels are normally used, the highest of which causes minimal toxicity in the adult female. Groups of about 20 pregnant females are typically used. In the OECD Testing Guidelines, if no teratogenic effects are observed at a dose of 1,000 mg/kg body weight, other dose levels are not necessary (38).

Neurotoxicity

Neurotoxicity (damage to the nervous system) is observed in acute and chronic testing, but the range of neurotoxic effects is so great and the signs so varied that special tests for damage to the nervous system are sometimes warranted. Neurotoxic effects that tend to be associated with acute exposure are functional, sometimes reversible changes in the nervous system that might not involve structural damage or degeneration. Most chronic neurotoxic effects do involve structural changes or degeneration and are not readily reversible (6). The type of neurotoxic effect tends to depend on the size of the dose and the duration of exposure (46).

There are many types of nerve cells, each performing special functions. Damage can occur to the functioning of the cell itself, to its connections to other nerve cells or to muscle cells, or to the supporting cells. Neurotoxicity can be manifested in the following ways: motor disorders such as weakness, lack of coordination, paralysis, tremor, convulsions, or slurred speech; sensory disorders such as numbness, pain, or auditory, olfactory, or visual deficits; disturbances of autonomic function such as sweating, incontinence, vomiting, impotence, or tear formation; increased state of excitability such as hyperactivity, irritability, or euphoria; impairment of short- or long-term memory, disorientation, or confusion; sleep disorders; psychiatric disturbances; impaired temperature regulation; or alterations in appetite, or weight gain or loss (6).

More than any other kind of toxicity test, neurotoxicity does not lend itself to standard procedures or in vitro tests because the range of effects is so broad. There are considerable differences among species, and little standardization of tests across species has occurred. Neurotoxicity tests would typically follow acute or chronic toxicity ones in which neurotoxic effects had been observed or were suspected (6).

Mutagenicity

A mutation is a permanent change in a gene that is passed along to any descendants of the cell. Thus, mutations in germ cells will be passed along to offspring. If recessive, the mutation will not be observed in the offspring but will become part of the gene pool from which future generations will draw. If the mutation is dominant, it may be lethal to the developing fetus or it might affect the offspring in a variety of ways, including impairing its fertility. If the damage is to a somatic cell, the mutation could lead to cancer or, in a developing fetus, birth defects.

There are several nonanimal and in vitro tests based on mammalian or human cells that would be considered alternative mutagenicity tests (see ch. 8). There are several whole-animal tests as well. One is the dominant lethal assay, in which a male is exposed to the test substance and then mated with an untreated female. Part way through the pregnancy, the female is killed and the number and condition of the fetuses observed. Another is the heritable translocation assay, in which the male progeny of treated males are mated with untreated females and the effect on fetuses determined. The mutations transmissible to the next generation are of special interest because of their implications for the human gene pool (5).

The in vivo sister chromatid exchange and mouse micronucleus tests rely on microscopic examination of the chromosomes themselves after the test substance has been administered to the whole animal. In vitro versions of these techniques also exist (see ch. 8). Changes can be observed using a microscope. Host-mediated assays are a hybrid of nonanimal and whole-animal techniques in which the test substance and a micro-organism are administered to an animal and the effects on the microorganism determined (5).

Current Trends

Many factors are likely to influence testing practices in the near future. Public pressure to use alternatives to whole animals, increasing costs of using animals, and improvements in toxicological methods are likely to reduce the use of some tests, such as the LD_{50} and the Draize eye irritation tests. This pressure is also likely to result in changes in some existing tests in order to reduce animal suffering.

These developments could bring about a review of current legal requirements for testing, perhaps reducing the amount of testing per chemical and the number of animals per test. Such a review, as well as advances in the state of the art, might better tailor testing to the substance being examined and to the circumstances of human exposure. On the other hand, the number of substances being tested could increase with greater regulatory or product liability requirements, with greater funding available for testing, or with less expensive tests available.

Interpretation and extrapolation of test results to humans can be expected to improve as the mechanisms of toxic responses are better understood. Increasing use of pharmacokinetics and mechanistic studies is likely to result in improved designs and better selection of tests.

THE ROLE OF GOVERNMENT IN TESTING

The Federal Government and each of the States are involved in testing in a variety of ways. Perhaps the most important are various explicit and implicit requirements for testing under existing statutes. Another area is the funding of research and development leading to new methods (see ch. 12). Yet another is the funding of toxicological testing, conducted primarily by the National Toxicology Program (NTP), supported largely by the National Institute of Environmental Health Sciences. This program, chartered in 1978, is a cooperative effort among agencies within the Department of Health and Human Services (see chs. 11 and 12).

Four principal Federal agencies have a significant role in animal testing for regulatory purposes: FDA, EPA, the Consumer Product Safety Commission (CPSC), and the Occupational Safety and Health Administration (OSHA). Other agencies whose regulatory activities affect animal use include the

Centers for Disease Control (CDC), the Department of Transportation (DOT), the Federal Trade Commission (FTC), and the U.S. Department of Agriculture (USDA). Animal testing is also funded by the Department of Defense.

Testing is covered by several types of statutes and regulations. Most common are laws that require a product to be safe and effective. Given the state of currently accepted technology and practice, such a statute implicitly (although not explicitly) calls for animal testing. Such tests are routinely expected as an indication of meeting the standard of product safety and effectiveness. A second stimulus for animal testing involves premarket approval. Under this authority, testing with animals is explicitly required by regulations of the agency involved. Or, animal testing may be explicitly required by statute, as in the case of the Federal Hazardous Substances Act administered by CPSC. As a practical matter, it makes little difference whether the tests involving animals occur under implicit or explicit statutory or regulatory authority: The procedures used are quite similar.

The specific tests performed and the methodologies used may be dictated by informal or formal requirements of the agency. These may take the form of promulgated regulations, published guidelines, unpublished guidelines, or customary practices. Some guidelines and the use of specific tests are accepted internationally (see app. A.)

With these general principles in mind, this discussion summarizes current Federal regulatory requirements relating to testing with animals (see also app. B). This review is not intended to evaluate the justification of such testing, only to describe its scope and magnitude. It is meant to provide sufficient background to permit an evaluation of the reasons testing is conducted and of the regulatory needs that any alternatives to such testing must satisfy.

Food and Drug Administration

FDA is responsible for administering several statutes that regulate animal and human food, animal and human drugs, medical devices, cosmetics, color additives, and radiological products. This regulation takes place primarily under the 1938 Federal Food, Drug, and Cosmetic Act as amended (21 U.S.C. 301 et seq.) and the Public Health Service Act of 1944 (42 U.S.C. 200 et seq.).

FDA evaluates each product on a case-by-case basis. The exact testing regime is determined by considering the type of product, the method of exposure, the amount and duration of intended use, and the potential hazards associated with the specific product. In support of its regulatory responsibilities and to assure quality testing, FDA has issued standards for good laboratory practice (see ch. 13) and has developed guidelines and testing protocols. Although some special guidelines or testing protocols are established for specific products, most tests are the same as or similar to the toxicological tests used by other agencies. Appendix A lists the types of tests used.

The National Center for Toxicological Research (NCTR) in Jefferson, AR, and the National Toxicology Program are the research and testing arms of FDA. Although NCTR and NTP have no direct regulatory responsibilities, they provide information needed to evaluate the safety of chemicals. Research that involves the use of animals or alternative methods includes studies of effects of low-dose, long-term exposure to chemicals; development of new methodology to investigate toxic effects; study of biological mechanisms of toxicity; and investigation of methods for estimating human health risks using experimental laboratory data.

The misbranding or adulteration of virtually any product regulated by FDA is prohibited. In addition, testing is required both to substantiate labeling claims and to demonstrate safety. These requirements should be assumed to apply to the substances and products discussed in this section unless otherwise stated.

Food for Humans

Under the law, a food additive is defined as a food substance that is not "generally recognized as safe" (as defined in the Federal Food, Drug, and Cosmetic Act) and that has not previously been approved as safe by FDA or USDA between 1938 and 1958. No such additive may be used until it has been subjected to extensive toxicity testing, a food additive petition has been submitted to FDA, and FDA has approved the additive as safe and promulgated a food additive regulation governing its use.

The safety of an additive is established by evaluating data from combinations of tests. The amount of testing that must be performed is determined by the amount of information already available and the degree of toxicological concern. Guidelines have been developed (*Toxicological Principles for the Safety Assessment of Direct Food Additives and Color Additives Used in Food* (56), known as the Red Book) that contain detailed procedures adequate to meet minimum requirements. However, manufacturers are permitted to modify the testing as they deem necessary as long as the data are equal to or better than what would be derived by using the guidelines.

Food safety has been important to FDA since the early 1900s. However, the use of animals to test food additives was not begun until the passage of the 1954 Pesticide Chemical Amendments and the 1958 Food Additive Amendments. The most famous amendment, sponsored by Delaney, required that any additive that induces cancer in animals or in humans be banned.

Drugs for Humans

FDA regulates all human drugs, including biological ones. The 1938 amendments of the Federal Food, Drug, and Cosmetic Act require drug manufacturers to submit evidence to FDA that a new drug is safe prior to commercialization. Safety evaluations are primarily based on preclinical animal testing and subsequent clinical testing in humans. In 1962, amendments to the act required that the effectiveness of a new drug also be demonstrated, and this is accomplished through clinical testing.

The requirements to use animals to test new human drugs depend on the proposed scope of clinical investigation and on the drug's anticipated use. Determining the best procedures for testing is complex because of the variation that exists in the use and activity of drugs. Testing must be tailored to each drug and specific requirements are determined by considering the route of administration, the target population, the length of treatment, and the relationship of the drug to others already in use. In addition to the formal procedures required under the Good Laboratory Practices regulations (see ch. 13), guidelines are available to aid manufacturers in designing test protocols. Manufacturers commonly discuss their programs with FDA before and during testing, as well as afterward.

Guidelines are available for tests required for drugs intended for oral, parenteral, dermal, inhalation, ophthalmic, vaginal, and rectal uses, and those used in combination. Duration of proposed human administration is a major factor for determining the particular animal test species, the number of animals, and the duration of the test.

Biological products—any virus, therapeutic serum, toxin, antitoxin, vaccine, blood, blood component or derivative, or allergenic product used to prevent, treat, or cure human diseases or injuries—are regulated under the Public Health Service Act and the Federal Food, Drug, and Cosmetic Act. As with drugs, before a new vaccine or allergenic can be marketed, the manufacturer must provide test data to show that the product is safe and effective. FDA's Center for Drugs and Biologics licenses the product and the manufacturing facility. For some products, tests are performed on each batch to assure that standards of potency and safety are met prior to release. For most of these, requirements are specified in the Code of Federal Regulations.

Food and Drugs for Animals

Food for pets, food-producing animals, and any other animal is subject to the same basic regulatory requirements as food for humans, with the addition of testing in the target species.

The Federal regulation of animal drugs, medicated feeds, and feed additives began under the 1938 act. The 1968 Animal Drug Amendments consolidated animal food and drug laws, keeping the 1962 standard for safety and effectiveness. The basic intent of these statutes and their resultant regulations is to avoid using substances that may leave harmful residues in animal products intended for human consumption, and to avoid harm to food-producing and other animals.

FDA regulates all animal drugs except those derived from living matter (biologics), which are regulated by USDA. Animal drugs may not be misbranded or adulterated. Testing is done to substantiate labeling claims and to prove safety. A "new animal drug" is defined as one not "generally recognized as safe" and effective. It must be tested to demonstrate both safety and effectiveness before marketing is permitted.

Medical Devices

Extensive regulatory provisions relating to the safety and effectiveness of medical devices for humans were enacted in 1976 (21 U.S.C. 321). For devices available before then, FDA may at any time require that proof of safety and effectiveness be submitted. For post-1976 medical devices that are substantially equivalent to those for humans before 1976, the same rule applies. But for those not substantially equivalent, testing must be undertaken to prove both safety and effectiveness, a premarket approval application must be submitted to FDA, and FDA must approve the device as safe and effective before it may be marketed. Because of the diversity of medical devices, the testing required is tailored specifically to the product involved and there are relatively few guidelines.

As the materials involved and methods of application are often unique, determining the safety of medical devices from the standpoint of toxicity presents special problems. Consequently, recommendations for specific tests are based on an evaluation of the following factors:

- the population for which the device is intended, with special reference to the target group's age and sex, and the benefit to be derived;
- the intended use of the device and its potential to contact the body or, for leachable or absorbable materials, to be distributed in the body;
- the location of the device in the immediate vicinity of various organs that might be adversely affected by its presence;
- the size of the device and the amount of leachate potentially available to the body; and
- chemical or toxicological information suggesting the potential for adverse toxic effects, such as when a leachable substance belongs to a chemical family that contains compounds with known potential for these effects.

Requirements for testing ophthalmic devices and products, color additives used in devices, and female contraceptive devices are more standardized. For color additives used in devices, the same types of tests are recommended as for color additives used in foods. For female contraceptive devices, the requirements are the same as those used for contraceptive drugs.

Medical devices for animals may not be misbranded or adulterated either. Testing can involve animals and is undertaken to substantiate labeling claims and safety. The law does not require premarket approval of such devices, however.

Cosmetics

Although the law prohibits misbranding or adulteration of cosmetics, FDA has no statutory authority to require testing of cosmetics for safety (other than their color additives) before they are marketed. However, animal testing is commonly undertaken to substantiate labeling claims and, by regulation, FDA has stated that any cosmetic with an ingredient that has not been substantiated for safety or that itself has not been substantiated for safety in its final product form must bear a prominent label declaration that the safety of the product has not been determined.

Color Additives

The law requires that any color additive used in food or drugs for animals or humans, in medical devices for humans, or in a cosmetic must be proved safe; must be the subject of a color additive petition filed with FDA; and must be determined by FDA to be safe before it is used (21 U.S.C. 321 et seq.). Color additives in use at the time of the enactment of this provision in 1960 have been placed on a provisional list and are subject to the same requirements for testing and approval as post-1960 color additives.

Radiological Products

The law authorizes FDA to regulate the emission of radiation from electronic products through the establishment of performance standards and a program of research and other activities to minimize human exposure. Testing on electronic product radiation is undertaken both in relation to proposed and promulgated performance standards and to determine other aspects of potential hazard for humans from such emissions.

Environmental Protection Agency

In fulfilling its statutory responsibilities, EPA uses toxicity data derived from animal testing in a variety of ways. EPA has the authority to require such data be submitted under laws it administers, but data are obtained through other means as well. They are submitted voluntarily by those who conduct or sponsor testing and are obtained from the open literature, from other government agencies, through contracts and grants, and from EPA laboratories.

This section describes the regulatory programs for which animal testing data are needed and the authorities under which existing data or testing can be required. (EPA's testing guidelines are described in app. A.)

Pesticides

The Federal Insecticide, Fungicide, and Rodenticide Act (FIFRA) (Public Law 92-516, 7 U.S.C. 136 et seq.) is designed to protect human health and the environment from adverse effects of pesticides while allowing the benefits of their use. This is done by granting or denying registrations; approving labeling; setting maximum residue levels on or in raw agricultural commodities; and establishing procedures for safe application, storage, and disposal. In registering the approximately 50,000 formulations of "pesticide products," EPA uses comprehensive registration standards that include animal testing data, as well as physical properties, analytical methods, and descriptions of manufacturing and use conditions.

EPA also relies on animal toxicity data when it issues emergency exemptions, experimental-use permits, and temporary tolerances for experimental purposes in response to unexpected and temporary food or health emergencies. Emergency exemptions may be granted to State or Federal agencies for uses not included in the registration. Experimental-use permits allow large-scale testing of new pesticides or new uses of a registered pesticide.

The Agency's Data Requirements for Pesticide Registration specify the kinds of material that must be submitted to EPA to support registration of each pesticide under Section 3 of FIFRA. EPA uses the information to determine the identity and composition of pesticides and to evaluate their potential adverse effects and environmental fate. Tests are either "required" or "conditionally required" depending on such factors as the results of preliminary tests, whether the pesticide use is for a food crop, whether the use is experimental, where and how the pesticide is to be applied, and the fate of the pesticide residue. Certain tests are required for new products, and guidelines for conducting these tests have also been developed (40 CFR 158, 49 FR 42856). Many are conditionally required through "tiered testing," whereby the results of the first tier of tests determine the need for additional ones. Three tiers have been described.

There is some flexibility in the application of these testing requirements, but EPA is to be consulted if test protocols other than those described are to be used. Additional flexibility in the testing requirements is available through EPA's procedures for waivers and for minor uses (40 CFR 158).

Virtually all data are submitted in the context of obtaining, maintaining, or renewing a registration. Another requirement is that the registrant must submit any health or safety information that would be of interest to EPA regarding a registered pesticide. This includes the submission of ongoing or completed studies for pesticides subject to registration standards, cancellation, or review; incidents involving adverse effects to human or nontarget organisms resulting from exposure; or incidents regarding lack of efficacy that could indirectly pose a hazard to human life.

Industrial Chemicals

The Toxic Substances Control Act (TSCA) (15 U.S.C. 2601) authorizes EPA to regulate chemical substances that present an "unreasonable risk" of injury to health or the environment and to require the reporting or development of data necessary for EPA to assess risks posed by a given substance. Toxicological testing data derived from animals form the basis for risk assessment and subsequent regulatory actions taken by EPA in implementing TSCA.

If a chemical substance presents an unreasonable risk, EPA can regulate its manufacturing, processing, distribution in commerce, use, or disposal.

Such regulatory actions would be based on toxicity data and exposure data, as well as on data regarding the beneficial uses of the substance. Regulation can be in the form of prohibiting or limiting certain actions, requiring warnings or instructions for use, or requiring the submission or retention of certain records.

If EPA has reason to believe that a substance presents an unreasonable risk but the agency lacks sufficient information to make such a finding, it can require reporting of existing toxicity or exposure data. EPA can also require that a substance be tested in animals for specific toxic effects.

Under TSCA, EPA has authority to require testing of industrial chemicals if testing is needed to perform a risk assessment. To aid in identifying relevant chemical substances, TSCA authorized an interagency testing committee to make suggestions. EPA must consider these suggestions and either initiate rulemaking or publish reasons for not doing so.

TSCA requires that 90 days before the manufacture or import of a "new" chemical (a chemical not on the TSCA Inventory of Chemical Substances) can begin, a Premanufacture Notification must be submitted to EPA. The submitters must provide all information in their possession or control related to health or environmental effects or to exposure. EPA can also require hazard or exposure information for substances already in commerce.

Air

The Clean Air Act (42 U.S.C. 7401 et seq.) requires the Federal and State Governments to take certain actions to improve or maintain the quality of ambient air. Animal testing data support various activities under the act. EPA designates certain substances as "criteria pollutants" and establishes national standards for ambient air based on toxicity and other concerns. Under Section 112, EPA also designates certain very toxic pollutants as "hazardous" and establishes standards for their emission or other control.

For registrations of any fuel or fuel additive, the EPA Administrator may require the manufacturer to conduct tests to determine whether there are potential short- or long-term health effects. Tests may be for acute effects, chronic effects, immunotoxicity, carcinogenicity, teratogenicity, or mutagenicity.

Radiation

EPA's authority over radiation was delegated in the President's Reorganization Plan of 1970 (35 FR 15623), under which EPA makes recommendations to other Federal agencies (the Nuclear Regulatory Commission, the Department of Energy, and OSHA) regarding acceptable levels of emissions for the byproducts of producing fuel-grade uranium and from other low-level wastes. Most of the data used to develop regulatory standards were gathered from humans inadvertently exposed to radiation, but data from animals are used for genetic and other effects, dose-response relationships, and metabolism.

Water

The Clean Water Act (33 U.S.C. 466) requires Federal and State efforts to restore and maintain the integrity of U.S. waters. Data needed to fulfill these requirements are obtained primarily from testing fish and other aquatic organisms.

The 1977 amendments to the act listed toxic substances that are commonly referred to as the 126 priority pollutants, primarily because of their toxic effects on humans and animals. These are controlled through nationally uniform limitations on the effluents containing them. Water Quality Criteria have also been promulgated for permissible ambient concentrations of these substances and are used to establish State water quality standards. Other toxic chemicals will also be regulated under the Clean Water Act.

The Clean Water Act calls for National Water Quality Criteria to be derived. The complete data set is developed by conducting a series of acute and long-term bioassays using organisms from at least eight different families. Acute tests are required on a salmonid, another family belonging to the class Osteichthyes (bony fish), and another representative of the phylum Chordata. The long-term tests required are chronic tests with one species of fish and a bioconcentration test with one aquatic species.

In 1982, EPA published a Water Quality Standards Handbook that provides guidance for developing site-specific water quality criteria that reflect local environmental conditions based on toxicity testing in fish.

The Safe Drinking Water Act (42 U.S.C. 300) is designed to protect public drinking water supplies through minimum national standards that are implemented by the States. Under this act, EPA also regulates the underground injection of fluids and other imminent or substantial hazards to drinking water. In addition, health advisories are prepared on specific problems.

Primary drinking water regulations are developed for certain contaminants that may have adverse effects on human health. Maximum contaminant levels are established or health advisories published using mammalian testing data.

EPA's authority over groundwater is based on a number of the laws that the agency administers. The management of groundwater is a joint Federal and State responsibility, but EPA provides technical assistance to State agencies and prepares advisories dealing with common problems that endanger groundwater. To some extent, these support activities rely on toxicity data.

Because groundwater is the source of drinking water for about half the U.S. population, the identification and characterization of groundwater problems is an important part of the drinking water program. Over 700 synthetic organic chemicals have been identified in various drinking water supplies. Some epidemiologic evidence is available, and more is being collected to help characterize the toxicity of these contaminants, but animal testing data are mainly used.

Solid Waste

The Resource Conservation and Recovery Act (RCRA) (Public Law 94-580, 48 U.S.C. 6901) protects public health and the environment by controlling the disposal of solid waste and by regulating the management and handling of hazardous waste materials. EPA is authorized to develop regulations governing the generation, transportation, treatment, storage, and disposal of hazardous wastes. These regulations, in addition to State laws on waste, are enforced by the States.

Animal testing is used to identify hazardous wastes. Toxicity is one of the criteria. RCRA regulations list chemicals that have been determined to be hazardous and processes that are presumed to generate hazardous waste. Analytical procedures for determining the contents of waste are also described, as are criteria for determining whether the contents are toxic or otherwise hazardous. When information does not exist for certain wastes, EPA must develop it. RCRA does not require those who generate hazardous waste to test the toxicity of the waste.

Because RCRA deals with solid waste, the predominant health problems arise from the leaching of waste from disposal sites. EPA is in the process of selecting and validating tests for characterizing waste. These will look for acute and chronic effects on aquatic animals, primarily fathead minnows. Partial or full life-cycle bioassays and fish bioaccumulation tests will also be required. The potential hazards to humans are characterized with several mutagenicity tests.

Data from tests with humans and animals are used under RCRA to develop "acceptable daily intake" levels that are regulated under the act. Because of the nature of exposure to these wastes, data from short-term and dermal tests are not used.

Superfund

The Comprehensive Environmental Response, Compensation, and Liability Act (CERCLA) (42 U.S.C. 9601), known as Superfund, authorizes the Federal Government to clean up or otherwise respond to the release of hazardous substances or other pollutants that may endanger public welfare. The most significant activity under CERCLA, from the standpoint of animal testing, is the designation of hazardous substances. Substances designated as hazardous under certain sections of other laws (TSCA, the Clean Air Act, the Clean Water Act, and RCRA) are also considered hazardous under CERCLA, and the EPA Administrator is to designate specific amounts of hazardous substances to be "reportable quantities," based in part on toxicity data.

One activity under CERCLA that diminishes the need for animal testing (because it assembles data on humans) is the compilation of a Toxic Substances and Disease Registry under the Department of Health and Human Services. This registry will track persons exposed to hazardous substances, along with the medical testing and evaluation that follows the exposure.

Consumer Product Safety Commission

The CPSC administers the Consumer Product Safety Act (15 U.S.C. 401 et seq.), the Federal Hazardous Substances Act (15 U.S.C. 1261 et seq.), the Poison Prevention Packaging Act (15 U.S.C. 1471 et seq.), and the Flammable Fabrics Act (15 U.S.C. 1191 et seq.).

The Consumer Product Safety Act empowers CPSC to prevent unreasonable risks of injury from consumer products. Included are both the risk of acute and chronic toxicity and the risk of physical injury. Under this statute, industry regularly conducts animal toxicity testing to determine the safety of consumer products.

The Federal Hazardous Substances Act provides for the regulation of hazardous substances used in or around the household. These are defined as any substance or mixture that is toxic, corrosive, flammable, or combustible, that is an irritant or a strong sensitizer, or that generates pressure through decomposition, heat, or other means, if such substance may cause substantial personal injury or illness during customary or reasonably foreseeable handling or use. Unlike its usual method of letting a regulatory agency or the manufacturer determine what kind of testing is needed to determine safety, in this act Congress defines a "highly toxic" substance in terms of the results of the LD_{50} test and requires certain labeling when the LD_{50} is less than 50 mg/kg body weight, 2 mg/l of air inhaled for an hour or less, or 200 mg/kg of dermal exposure for 24 hours or less. Although the act does not literally require that these tests be done, a manufacturer cannot know whether they are in compliance with the act unless they perform the tests. CPSC has issued regulations regarding testing requirements needed to determine whether a substance is a skin or an eye irritant (16 CFR 1500).

The Flammable Fabrics Act authorized regulation of wearing apparel and fabrics that are flammable. Industry regularly conducts animal testing to determine the toxicity of substances applied to fabric in order to reduce or eliminate flammability.

Department of Labor

The Occupational Safety and Health Act of 1970 (29 U.S.C. 651 et seq.) requires the National Institute for Occupational Safety and Health (NIOSH) to conduct health hazard evaluations of the workplace (see section on Centers for Disease Control).

A goal of the act is that no employee suffer diminished health as a result of conditions in the workplace. To this end, employers have a duty to communicate safety information about substances present in the workplace through labels, material safety data sheets, and training. Most safety testing is done with animals.

Under the Federal Mine Safety and Health Act of 1977 (30 U.S.C. 801 et seq.), employers must determine whether substances found or used in mines are potentially toxic at the concentrations at which they occur.

Department of Transportation

The Hazardous Materials Transportation Act (49 U.S.C. 1801 et seq.) requires that any materials shipped in interstate commerce be properly labeled and contained in a manner reflecting the degree of hazard present. DOT requires that acute toxicity studies be carried out on substances not already classified or for which toxic effects to humans or test animals are not already known. A substance would be treated as a class B poison (and thus as presenting a health hazard during transportation) if its administration to 10 or more rats at a single dose of a specified amount (orally, dermally, or by inhalation) killed at least half the animals within 48 hours. Analogous authority exists for the U.S. Coast Guard under the Dangerous Cargo Act (46 U.S.C. 179) and the Ports and Waterways Safety Act (33 U.S.C. 1221 et seq.).

Department of Agriculture

USDA administers the Virus-Serum-Toxin Act of 1913 (21 U.S.C. 151 et seq.), under which it licenses animal biologics. The regulatory requirements are similar to those administered by FDA for other animal drugs. Animal testing is undertaken to substantiate labeling claims for animal drugs and to prove their safety. The testing required by USDA for proof of safety and effectiveness of these animal biological drugs is extensive.

Under a series of statutes, USDA exercises close inspection authority over the processing of meat, poultry, and eggs for human consumption. These statutes prohibit any misbranding or adulteration. Testing is required to substantiate labeling claims. Although most safety issues are handled by FDA, testing may also on occasion be required by USDA to demonstrate safety under particular conditions.

USDA administers a number of statutes designed to control and eradicate disease in plants and animals. This authority extends from research through to control of interstate and foreign transportation. Substantial testing is undertaken by USDA in pursuing these statutory mandates.

Centers for Disease Control

The Public Health Service Act (42 U.S.C. 201 et seq.) authorizes CDC to take appropriate action to prevent the spread of communicable disease. Pursuant to this authority, CDC regulates any agent that could cause such illnesses. CDC uses animal data to determine the agents that should be regulated.

Under the authority of the Occupational Safety and Health Act of 1970, the National Institute for Occupational Safety and Health, a component of CDC, develops and periodically revises recommendations for limits of exposure to potentially hazardous substances or conditions in the workplace. When morbidity cannot be explained on the basis of current toxicological knowledge, NIOSH must design toxicological investigations to discover the cause. Such occupational hazard assessments are based on data on humans and animals collected by NIOSH.

Federal Trade Commission

The Federal Trade Commission Act (15 U.S.C. 41 et seq.) prohibits any advertisement that is misleading in a material respect. FTC has adopted the position that an advertiser must have adequate substantiation for any claims relating to safety or effectiveness. Thus, manufacturers and distributors regularly test their products, using data on humans and animals to substantiate their claims.

STATE USES OF ANIMAL TESTING DATA

States engage in a variety of regulatory activities that rely directly or indirectly on animal testing data. One of the most important longstanding uses is the registration of pesticides. Air, water, and waste have also been the subject of State legislation in recent years. State laws often use animal testing data for the identification and classification of substances for control. Several States have also enacted right-to-know laws that may give people greater access to testing data, although such legislation does not necessarily affect the amount of testing done.

Pesticide Registrations

All States are required to register pesticides under Section 24 of FIFRA. Most States have 5,000 to 10,000 pesticides registered and grant 5 to 10 emergency exemptions per year. As part of the registration process, States receive animal testing data for evaluation. Much of the time, the information is required only in summary form, unless the State specifically requests the raw data. The data are usually obtained directly from the registrant to avoid possible delays or confidentiality problems. Although States generally rely on EPA's assessment of data for registration purposes, they regularly review it for emergency exemptions and special local needs (22).

California and Florida have the largest pesticide programs. These States also have the authority to require additional testing (e.g., field testing locally). In addition, California also recently passed a law giving its Director of Food and Agriculture the authority to require data for which EPA has granted a waiver or exemption (e.g., experimental-use permits). California law also requires that data gaps for 200 pesticides be filled and that the first report of an injury to a worker exposed to a pesticide be reported to the Health Department (California Food and Agriculture Code, Div. 7, ch. 2).

Identification and Classification of Toxic Substances

Identification and classification of substances is an important function in most environmental laws. Such activities take place under each Federal environmental statute. Coordination among offices in EPA or with other agencies is common. State agencies also coordinate these activities with their Federal counterparts.

Sometimes, Federal law or regulations are simply adopted by a State and recodified. For example, certain provisions of the New York and Florida regulations governing hazardous wastes incorporate, by reference, EPA regulations appearing at 40 CFR 261 and its Appendices (New York Compilation of Rules and Regulations, Title 6, ch. 366). These regulations list hazardous waste and their constituents, provide analytical procedures to determine the composition of a waste so that it can be classified, and provide for variances from these regulations that may be granted by EPA's Administrator. Much more common are statutes that incorporate Federal laws and regulations and that add other requirements or combine Federal requirements in new ways.

The Wisconsin Pollution Discharge Elimination Law (Wisconsin Statutes Annotated, ch. 147) adopts EPA effluent limitations, effluent standards, and prohibitions. In addition to substances already regulated by EPA, Wisconsin effluent limitations apply to all toxic pollutants "referred to in table 1 of committee print number 95-30 of the Committee on Public Works and Transportation of the U.S. House of Representatives." Additional pollutants are to be identified under Section 147.07 of the Wisconsin law.

The Colorado Hazardous Waste Management Regulations (Code of Colorado Regulations, Title 5, ch. 1007) adopt EPA toxicity provisions of 40 CFR 261 but include "any other substance which has been found to be fatal to humans at low doses, or in the absence of human data, has an oral LD_{50} in the rat of 50 mg/kg or less, an inhalation LC_{50} (lethal concentration) in the rat of 2 mg/l or less, or a dermal LD_{50} in the rabbit of 200 mg/kg or less."

The Texas Water Quality Acts (Texas Water Code, Title 2, chs. 5, 26, 30, 313) use several Federal laws to classify a substance as hazardous: CERCLA; the Water Pollution Control Act; the Solid Waste Disposal Act; the Clean Air Act; and TSCA. If it is hazardous under any one of these laws, it is hazardous for purposes of Texas law.

Under Oregon Hazardous Waste Management Regulations (Oregon Administrative Rules, ch. 340, div. 62, 63), a substance is considered toxic if it is a pesticide or pesticide manufacturing residue and has one of the following properties:

- oral toxicity in a 14-day test with an LD_{50} less than 500 mg/kg,
- inhalation toxicity over 1 hour with an LC_{50} less than 2 mg/l gas or 200 mg/m^3 dust or mist,
- dermal toxicity over 14 days with an LD_{50} less than 200 mg/kg, or
- aquatic toxicity over 96 hours at an LC_{50} less than 250 mg/l.

It would also be considered toxic if it contains a carcinogen identified by OSHA at 29 CFR 1910.93(c).

Washington Dangerous Waste Regulations (Washington Administrative Code, Title 173, ch. 303) require the polluter to use EPA toxicity information, EPA's Spill Table, NIOSH's Registry of Toxic Effects of Chemicals (see ch. 10), and any other reasonably available sources to determine if a pollutant is toxic. Carcinogens are identified by an International Agency for Research on Cancer finding that a substance is a positive or suspected human or animal carcinogen. Additional criteria are provided in the Toxic Category Table, which contains five categories of hazards based on an LC_{50} test for fish, an oral LD_{50} for rats, an inhalation LC_{50} for rats, and a dermal LD_{50} for rabbits.

Some State laws do not explicitly provide for harmonization with Federal requirements regarding the identification and classification of toxic substances. Under the California Air Pollution Laws (California Air Pollution Control Laws, 1979 Edition), the California Air Resources Board and the State Department of Health Service are to prepare recommendations for substances to be regulated and to consider all relevant data. State officials may request information on any substance under evaluation, although they do not have the authority to require testing. However, any person who wishes the board to review one of its determinations must specify additional evidence that is to be considered. Similarly, the California Hazardous Waste Control Act (California Health and Safety Code, Div. 20, chs. 6.5, 1039; California Administrative Code, Title 22, div. 4, ch. 30) directs the California Department of Health Services to prepare lists of hazardous waste and extremely hazardous waste and to develop regulations for their management.

PRODUCT LIABILITY CONSIDERATIONS

Toxicological testing and research play an important role in the law of product liability. Manufacturers are responsible for knowing what dangers their products may present and must pay for any damages these products cause. Animals are used to discover possible dangers, and courts may award damages to a party whose injuries could have been prevented with additional testing or research (see ch. 11).

This discussion of product liability law focuses primarily on drugs because animal use plays such an important role in determining safety. Drugs are also an interesting case study because they are reviewed for safety and effectiveness by the Food and Drug Administration before they are marketed, and yet satisfying FDA's testing requirements does not necessarily fulfill the manufacturer's duty to test.

The Manufacturer's Duty to Produce a Safe Product

In general, a manufacturer has a duty to produce a safe product with appropriate warnings and instructions. This is based on an individual's responsibility to exercise care to avoid unreasonable risks of harm to others. The duty extends to all persons who might foreseeably be injured by the product manufactured. Under the Uniform Commercial Code—a law governing commercial transactions involving goods, which varies only slightly from State to State—failure to produce a safe product results in liability for the manufacturer for the damages thereby caused.

Generally, an injured plaintiff must prove that the drug in question was unreasonably dangerous, that the defect existed at the time the drug left the manufacturer's control, that the consumer was injured or suffered damages from the use of the drug, and that the defect in the drug was the proximate cause of the injury (13,37).

Product liability law in most jurisdictions follows the "strict liability" standard—that is, no matter how careful a manufacturer is, it is liable for injuries caused by its products. Some jurisdictions only hold the manufacturer to a high standard of care, and many that do have strict liability standards also have exceptions.

One exception is for drugs that are necessary but that cannot be made safe. Some have a high risk of harmful side effects but treat conditions that are even more harmful if left untreated, such as rabies (57). (Conversely, when the advantages a product offers are small, such as where vaccines were combined instead of using multiple injections, the manufacturer is more likely to be held liable (51).) Another exception is for products for which no developed skill or foresight could have avoided the harm (14). Even though a toxic effect might not have been tested for using existing methods with animals, a manufacturer must not ignore injuries its product may cause after marketing (13). Similarly, if a new test becomes available, the manufacturer may be required to use it (14,29,47).

Methods of Testing Required

A manufacturer must normally use the safest and most effective testing method available. Thus, when monkeys provided the only reliable means for testing polio vaccine, they had to be used to test individual batches of drugs, despite the difficulty and expense of obtaining them (20). Although no cases could be found pertaining to drugs, this standard might not apply when testing is impractical in relation to the risk of harm (30,48).

Testing must reflect conditions of actual use as closely as possible. Thus, where the drug DES was to be used on pregnant women, the manufacturer should have tested pregnant animals and was held liable for cancer in offspring (3). Several smokers have tried to recover from cigarette manufacturers. They have been denied recovery to date because when they started smoking, the risk of cancer had not been demonstrated (28,40,43).

A judge or jury would normally decide whether testing was adequate, but if there was a failure to comply with regulatory requirements, this would normally prove insufficient testing (16,33,39). However, compliance with such requirements would not prove that testing was adequate (14).

In addition to examining what tests were done, the judge or jury might look at the adequacy of the test protocols themselves. For example, the injured plaintiff might argue that the number of test animals was not large enough to determine if a risk was presented (11) or that the conditions under which the drug was tested did not represent actual use conditions (49,51).

SUMMARY AND CONCLUSIONS

The most widespread kind of testing with animals is conducted for the elucidation of toxicity from drugs, chemicals, and so forth. Toxicology has advanced with the growth of the synthetic chemical industries and the use of chemicals in consumer products. Toxicological testing is used in the assessment of hazards and the management of health risks to humans. The use of animals for such testing did not become common until a few decades ago; it now accounts for several million animals per year.

Many toxicological tests are standardized to aid in the comparison of results and because they have been shown to be acceptable tools for measuring certain phenomena. Most of the standard tests are descriptive in that they indicate an end result but do not necessarily elucidate the processes leading to it. Knowledge of the mechanisms by which a toxic effect occurs allows much greater reliability in extrapolation to humans.

The design of a test involves many trade-offs. The choice of species is affected by its physiological similarity to humans, its cost and availability, and the amount of data for other substances available for comparison. The route of exposure, duration of exposure, and size of doses are affected by the possible nature and extent of exposure in humans, by the dose needed to produce a measurable toxic effect, and by convenience. Expected variability in the toxic response governs the numbers of animals used.

Commonly used tests include the following:

- **acute toxicity**—a single dose at high enough concentrations to produce toxic effects or death, often used to screen substances for relative toxicity;
- **eye and skin irritation**—usually a single exposure, generally used to develop warnings for handling and predict accidental exposure toxicity;
- **repeated-dose chronic toxicity**—repeated exposure for periods ranging from 2 weeks to more than a year, used to determine the possible effects of long-term human exposure;
- **carcinogenicity**—repeated exposure for most of lifespan, used to detect possible human carcinogens;
- **developmental and reproductive toxicity**—

a variety of exposures to determine the possible production of infertility, miscarriages, and birth defects;

- **neurotoxicity**—a variety of doses and routes to determine toxic effects to nerves, with toxic end points such as behavioral changes, lack of coordination, or learning disabilities; and
- **mutagenicity**—a variety of methods for determining if genetic material of germ or somatic cells has been changed.

To aid in the design of tests and in the extrapolation of results to humans, studies are sometimes done to determine the mechanisms by which toxicity occurs or to characterize the processes by which the test substance enters, is handled, and leaves the body.

The Federal Government has considerable impact on testing practices through a variety of laws and regulations. Sometimes testing is required for premarket approval; more often, it is implied by requirements for safe and effective products. In only a handful of instances, such as the Federal Hazardous Substances Act administered by the Consumer Product Safety Commission and the Hazardous Materials Transportation Act administered by the Department of Transportation, do Federal statutes explicitly require animal testing.

The four agencies with the largest roles are the Food and Drug Administration, the Environmental Protection Agency, the Consumer Product Safety Commission, and the Occupational Safety and Health Administration. FDA uses animal testing data in the approval of food additives, drugs, biologics, medical devices, and color additives for humans and animals. EPA and State Governments use such test results in the registration of pesticides and the regulation of industrial chemicals, as well as in the protection of water and air and in the regulation of waste disposal. CPSC relies on animal data in identifying and regulating risks to consumers, while OSHA indirectly uses them in requiring employers to maintain a safe workplace.

Testing also plays an important role in the liability of a manufacturer for unsafe products. In most States, a manufacturer is responsible for any injuries arising from use of its products, regardless of how much testing was done. Exceptions may be made where suitable tests do not exist or the product is known to present risks but those risks are preferable to the harm that would occur without the product, as in the case of rabies vaccine.

Despite the problems of extrapolating to humans and other shortcomings of animal testing techniques, the use of animals in testing is an integral part of the Nation's attempt to protect human health. Ideally, as the practice of toxicology advances, there will be less emphasis on numerical values in certain tests and more consideration of the mechanisms by which toxic effects occur.

CHAPTER 7 REFERENCES

1. Altman, P.L. (ed.), *Pathology of Laboratory Mice and Rats* (New York: Pergamon Press, 1985).
2. Berry, C.L., "Reproductive Toxicity," *Animals and Alternatives in Toxicity Testing*, M. Balls, R.J. Riddell, and A.N. Worden (eds.) (New York: Academic Press, 1983).
3. *Bichler* v. *Eli Lilly and Company*, 436 N.Y.S.2d 625 (1981).
4. Bridges, J.W., Chasseaud, L.F., Cohen, G.M., et al., "Application of Pharmacokinetics," *Animals and Alternatives in Toxicity Testing*, M.Balls, R.J. Riddell, and A.N. Worden (eds.) (New York: Academic Press, 1983).
5. Brusick, D., *Principles of Genetic Toxicology* (New York: Plenum Press, 1980).
6. Dewar, A.J., "Neurotoxicity," *Animals and Alternatives in Toxicity Testing*, M. Balls, R.J. Riddell, and A.N. Worden (eds.) (New York: Academic Press, 1983).
7. Diszfalusy, E. (ed.), *Regulation of Human Fertility-Proceedings, Symposium on Advances in Fertility Regulation* (Geneva: World Health Organization, 1977).
8. Doull, J., Klassen, C.D., and Amdur, M.O. (eds.), *Casarett and Doull's Toxicology: The Basic Science of Poisons* (New York: Macmillan Publishing Co., 2d ed., 1980).
9. Draize, J.H., Woodward, G., and Calvery, H.O., "Method for the Study of Irritation and Toxicity of Substances Applied Topically to the Skin and Mu-

cous Membranes," *J. Pharm. Exper.* 82:377-389, 1944.

10. Duke-Elder, S., *Textbook of Ophthalmology Therapeutics* (St. Louis, MO: C.V. Mosby, 1954).
11. *Edison Pharmaceutical* v. *FDA*, 600 F.2d 831 (D.C. Cir. 1979).
12. Eto, M., *Organophosophorous Pesticides: Organic and Biological Chemistry* (Cleveland, OH: Chemical Rubber Co., 1974).
13. *Ferebee* v. *Chevron Chemical Co.*, 736 F.2d 1529, 1536 (D.C. Cir. 1984).
14. *Ferrigno* v. *Eli Lilly and Company*, 175 N.J. Super 420, 420 A.2d 1305 (1980).
15. Fortmeyer, H.P., "The Influence of Exogenous Factors Such as Maintenance and Nutrition on the Course and Results of Animal Experiments," *Animals in Toxicological Research*, I. Bartosek, A. Guaitani, and R. Pacei (eds.) (New York: Raven Press, 1982).
16. *Frankel* v. *Styer*, 386 F.2d 151 (3rd Cir. 1967).
17. Freidenwald, J.S., Hughes, W.F., and Hermann, H., "Acid Burns of the Eye," *Arch. Ophthalmol.* 35:98-108, 1946.
18. Fund for the Replacement of Animals in Medical Experiments, "Report of the FRAME Toxicity Committee," *Animals and Alternatives in Toxicity Testing*, M. Balls, R.J. Riddell, and A.N. Worden (eds.) (New York: Academic Press, 1983).
19. Goldberg, A.M., Director, The Johns Hopkins Center for Alternatives to Animal Testing, Baltimore, MD, personal communication, April 1985.
20. *Griffin* v. *U.S.*, 351 F.Supp. 10 (E.D.Pa. 1972).
21. Grove, G.L., Duncan, S., and Kingman, A.M., "Effect of Aging on the Blistering of Human Skin With Ammonium Hydroxide," *Br. J. Dermatol.* 107:393-400, 1982.
22. Hart, A., National Agricultural Chemicals Association, Washington, DC, personal communication, September 1984.
23. Heine, W., "Importance of Quality Standard and Quality Control in Small Laboratory Animals for Toxicological Research," *Animals in Toxicological Research*, I. Bartosek, A. Guaitani, and R. Pacei (eds.) (New York: Raven Press, 1982).
24. Heywood, R., "Long-Term Toxicity," *Animals and Alternatives in Toxicity Testing*, M. Balls, R.J. Riddell, and A.N. Worden (eds.) (New York: Academic Press, 1983).
25. Hutt, P.B., and Hutt, P.B., II, "A History of Government Regulation of Adulteration and Misbranding of Food," *Food Drug Cosmetic Law J.* 39:2-73, 1984.
26. Kingston, T., and Marks, R., "Irritant Reactions to Dithranol in Normal Subjects and Psoriatic Patients," *Br. J. Dermatol.* 108:307-313, 1983.
27. Kligman, A.M., "Assessment of Mild Irritants," *Principles of Cosmetics for the Dermatologist*, P. Frost and S.N. Horwitz (eds.) (St. Louis, MO: C.V. Mosby, 1982).
28. *Lartique* v. *R.J. Reynolds Tobacco Company*, 317 F.2d 19 (1963).
29. *Leibowitz* v. *Ortho Pharmaceutical Co.*, 224 Pa.Super. 418, 307 A.2d 449 (1973).
30. *Livesley* v. *Continental Motors Corporation*, 331 Mich. 434, 49 N.W.2d 365 (1951).
31. Lowrance, W.W., *Of Acceptable Risk—Science and Determination of Safety* (Los Altos, CA: William Kaufmann, Inc., 1976).
32. Marks, R., "Testing for Cutaneous Toxicity," *Animals and Alternatives in Toxicity Testing*, M. Balls, R.J. Riddell, and A.N. Worden (eds.) (New York: Academic Press, 1983).
33. *McComish* v. *DeSoi*, 42 N.J. 274, 200 A.2d 116 (1964).
34. McNamara, B.P., "Concepts in Health Evaluation of Commercial and Industrial Chemicals," *New Concepts in Safety Evaluation*, M.A. Mehlman, R.E. Shapiro, and H. Blumenthal (eds.) (New York: John Wiley & Sons, 1976).
35. Morton-Grant, W., and Kern, H.L., "Cations and the Cornea," *Am. J. Ophthalmol.* 42:167-181, 1956.
36. National Academy of Sciences, *Toxicity Testing Strategies to Determine Needs and Priorities* (Washington, DC: National Academy Press, 1984).
37. *Nicklaus* v. *Hughes Tool Company*, 417 F.2d 983 (8th Cir. 1969).
38. Organization for Economic Cooperation and Development, *Guidelines for Testing of Chemicals*, and addenda (Paris: 1981).
39. *Orthopedic Equipment Company* v. *Eutsler*, 276 F.2d 455 (4th Cir. 1960).
40. *Pritchard* v. *Liggett and Meyers Tobacco Company*, 295 F.2d 292 (3rd Cir. 1961).
41. Purchase, I.F.H., "Carcinogenicity," *Animals and Alternatives in Toxicity Testing*, M. Balls, R.J. Riddell, and A.N. Worden (eds.) (New York: Academic Press, 1983).
42. Roe, F.J.C., "Carcinogenicity Testing," *Animals and Alternatives in Toxicity Testing*, M. Balls, R.J. Riddell, and A.N. Worden (eds.) (New York: Academic Press, 1983).
43. *Ross* v. *Phillip Morris and Company*, 328 F.2d 3 (8th Cir. 1964).
44. Salsburg, D.S., "The Effects of Lifetime Feeding Studies on Patterns of Senile Lesions in Mice and Rats," *Drugs Chem. Tox.* 3:1-33, 1980.
45. Salsburg, D.S., "Statistics and Toxicology: An Overview," *Scientific Considerations in Monitoring and Evaluating Toxicological Research*, E.J. Gralla (ed.) (Washington, DC: Hemisphere, 1981).

46. Schaumburg, H.H., and Spencer, P., "Central and Peripheral Nervous System Degeneration Produced by Pure n-Hexane: An Experimental Study," *Brain* 99:183-192, 1976.
47. *Schenebeck* v. *Sterling Drug, Inc.*, 423 F.2d 919 (8th Cir. 1970).
48. *Sieracki* v. *Seas Shipping Company*, 57 F.Supp. 724 (E.D.Pa. 1944).
49. *Stromsodt* v. *Parke-Davis and Company*, 257 F.Supp. 991 (D.N.D. 1966), affirmed, 411 F.2d 1390 (8th Cir. 1969).
50. Swanston, D.W., "Eye Irritancy Testing," *Animals and Alternatives in Toxicity Testing*, M. Balls, R.J. Riddell, and A.N. Worden (eds.) (New York: Academic Press, 1983).
51. *Tinnerholm* v. *Parke-Davis and Company*, 411 F.2d 48 (2nd Cir. 1969).
52. Trevan, J.W., "The Error of Determination of Toxicity," *Proc. R. Soc. Lond. (Biol.)* 101:483 (1927).
53. U.S. Congress, Office of Technology Assessment, *Assessment of Technologies for Determining Cancer Risks From the Environment*, OTA-H-138 (Washington, DC: U.S. Government Printing Office, June 1981).
54. U.S. Environmental Protection Agency, "Acute Exposure: Oral Toxicity," *Office of Toxic Substances Health and Environmental Effects Test Guidelines* (Washington, DC: updated October 1984).
55. U.S. Executive Office of the President, Office of Science and Technology Policy, "Chemical Carcinogens: A Review of the Science and Its Associated Principles," Mar. 14, 1985.
56. U.S. Food and Drug Administration, *Toxicological Principles for the Safety Assessment of Direct Food Additives and Color Additives Used in Food* (Washington, DC: Bureau of Foods, 1982.)
57. *U.S.* v. *An Article of Drug—Bacto Unidisk*, 394 U.S. 784, 792 (1968).
58. Weigland, D.A., Haygood, C., and Gaylor, J.R., "Cell Layer and Density of Negro and Caucasian Stratum Corneum," *J. Invest. Dermatol.* 62:563-568, 1974.

Chapter 8

Alternatives to Animal Use in Testing

Queen: I will try the forces
Of these compounds on such creatures as
We count not worth the hanging, but none human . . .
Cornelius: Your Highness
Shall from this practice but make hard your heart.

Shakespeare, *Cymbeline*
Act I, Scene VI

The experimental means to be used for safety evaluations is left open to suggestion. As unorthodox as this might sound, leaving such means open for consideration is the best solution. Safety evaluations should not be based on standard, specified series of tests. They are best approached by first raising all pertinent safety questions and then searching for the experimental means to provide the best answers. Under such circumstances, even the standard LD test might on occasion be the best experimental means to resolve outstanding safety questions.

Constantine Zervos
Food and Drug Administration
Safety Evaluation and Regulation of Chemicals 2,
D. Homburger (ed.) (Basel: Karger, 1985)

CONTENTS

Table

Figure

Chapter 8

Alternatives to Animal Use in Testing

Alternatives to using animals in testing serve the same purposes that using whole animals does—protecting and improving human health and comfort. The technologies on which alternatives are based result primarily from biomedical and biochemical research. Several of them are reviewed in this chapter, though they are discussed in greater detail in chapter 6. Some alternatives that might eventually replace the tests covered in chapter 7 are also described here.

Notable progress in the move to alternatives has been achieved in certain areas (78). For example, biochemical tests to diagnose pregnancy have replaced those using rabbits, and the *Limulus* amebocyte lysate test, which relies on the coagulation of a small amount of blood from a horseshoe crab, has replaced rabbits in testing for the presence of bacterial endotoxins that would cause fever (25,117). Many companies have modified the widely used LD_{50} test to use fewer animals (22) and have otherwise refined the methods used to test for toxicity (100). Mammalian cell culture assays are used extensively in industrial laboratories for safety testing of medical devices (52,53) and pharmaceutical substances (1,84) and as immune response assays (97,98).

The development of alternatives to animals in testing has accelerated in recent years with the establishment of programs having development and implementation of alternatives as their goal (see ch. 12). However, the barriers to adoption of these tests are more than the technical barrier of developing and validating a new technology. Testing is an integral part of many regulatory schemes and product liability law, and validation ultimately rests on acceptance by the scientific, regulatory, and legal communities.

Public concern over animal use in testing appears to be increasing in tandem with public concern for product and drug safety. Ironically, the public's increasing concern for safety could lead to more testing. Yet it also provides an incentive to develop new techniques, particularly those that promise to be cheaper and faster than current whole-animal methods. A further irony is that developing alternatives, as well as validating them, sometimes requires animal use.

CONTINUED, BUT MODIFIED, USE OF ANIMALS IN TESTING

It has been suggested that many more animals are used for testing than are needed (90) and that changes in experimental design or improved methods of data analysis could substantially reduce the number of animals used. Each experiment has unique requirements (see ch. 7), and the ways in which the number of animals might be reduced will vary accordingly.

Many of the methods discussed in chapter 6 for the modified use of animals in research are also applicable to testing, such as gathering more data from each animal or improving the analysis of results by using random block design or covariance analysis. In random block design, animals with a particular characteristic, such as litter mates or animals of a certain size, are randomly assigned to different groups to balance whatever effect these variables might have. If the groups being distributed are sufficiently large, the results can also be analyzed to determine the effect of the masking variable (47). Covariance can be used to analyze results when some of the experimental variables are uncontrolled but known, thus estimating their effect on the results.

As in research, the number of animals needed as controls can be reduced by using the same group as a control for several simultaneous experiments. A laboratory's ability to do this will be limited by its size and the amount of lead time available to allow testing to be coordinated. Another difficulty is that environmental conditions must be exactly the same and the tests must start and finish at exactly the same times. The reduction in animal use that simultaneous experiments brings about is modest because the control group should be larger if it is being used in several simultaneous experiments (34).

The use of historical data for control groups is constrained by the difficulty of exactly duplicating the conditions of a study. However, the size of the groups and other controlled variables can be better planned if historical data are used to discover the background incidence of specific tumors or other diseases before testing begins. This use of historic controls has been recognized by the National Cancer Institute, the World Health Organization, the Canadian Government, and the now-defunct Interagency Regulatory Liaison Group (104). The Federation of American Societies for Experimental Biology has developed a data book containing such information based on the Laboratory Animal Data Bank (see ch. 10) (2).

Avoiding Duplicative Testing

Animal use in testing can and has been reduced by industry and others through improved communication and cooperation in the planning and execution of testing, thereby avoiding unintentional duplication. Trade groups such as the Chemical Manufacturers Association, the Pharmaceutical Manufacturers Association, and the Soap and Detergent Association play important roles in this coordination.

The sharing of data after testing has occurred is often done for pesticides (see chs. 10 and 11). And in 1978, the Food and Drug Administration implemented a policy of permitting approval of new drug applications solely on the basis of published scientific papers (113). The possibility of an unintentional repetition of an experiment is also avoided through the work of organizations such as the Chemical Industry Institute of Toxicology (CIIT) (Research Triangle Park, NC). Using contributions from member companies, CIIT conducts toxicological tests and distributes the results widely.

Governments contribute greatly to information sharing, which allows duplicative testing to be avoided, by providing both access to test results and information about their own planned and ongoing tests. The International Agency for Research on Cancer makes it easy for duplicative carcinogenicity testing to be avoided by informing testing facilities and governments about planned and ongoing testing. Federal and international databases and publications also contain information about planned tests and those under way (see ch. 10).

Reducing Pain and Distress

As with research, testing can be modified to reduce animal pain or distress in two ways: by providing relief with drugs or by changing the procedures so that less pain or distress is produced (see ch. 6). A third alternative might be to use a less sensitive species, but there is no method by which relative distress among species can be discerned. Relief from pain and distress is accomplished through analgesics, anesthetics, tranquilizers, or sedatives and modification of the test itself.

Few pain-relieving drugs have been developed and marketed for animals. Little information is available on recommended doses (122) or on the likely effect on test results. Thus, before pain relief could be incorporated into a test, it would be necessary to determine the needed dose and the effect on the toxic response, thus using additional animals as well as subjecting them to pain.

Several small changes that do not interfere with the experimental design can be made by an investigator. Small needles can be substituted for large. Animals can be comforted by petting. Social animals can be caged in groups, although there are often reasons that multiple housing cannot be used. Smaller doses can be used and tests can be ended at the earliest feasible time. Sometimes, smaller doses will actually result in increased sensitivity of the test (38). Making such changes sometimes depends on the attitude and expertise of individual researchers rather than the contents of testing guidelines, which may not be sufficiently detailed.

USE OF LIVING SYSTEMS IN TESTING

As detailed in chapter 6, two kinds of living systems can reduce whole-animal use—in vitro systems based on animal or human components (cell, tissue, and organ cultures) and systems based on organisms not considered animals for purposes of this report (micro-organisms and invertebrates). (Some people consider both of these in vitro systems.)

In Vitro Systems

Cells, tissues, and organs can be kept alive outside a living organism and used for testing. Although animals are still required as a source for these in vitro systems, the animal would experience distress for a much shorter time, and perhaps less distress overall, than occurs with whole-animal testing because it would be killed before any experimental manipulations were carried out. Occasionally, different cells, tissues, or organs from the same animals can be used for different investigations. In addition, many fewer animals would be required for a given test, in part because variability in the toxic response is smaller than it is with whole-animal tests and in part because one animal can be used for multiple data points, further reducing variability. The fact that human tissues sometimes can be used confers an additional advantage because the need for extrapolation from animal data is obviated.

These isolated components also have disadvantages. They are usually unable to produce the complete physiologic responses of a whole organism. The components often become undifferentiated and lose their ability to perform their special functions when isolated from the organism, particularly when the sample is broken up into its constituent cells, and even more so when the cells replicate. Another disadvantage is that the effect of the route of exposure, a variable that can have profound effects on test results, is often impossible to determine.

There are many measures of damage to differentiated or undifferentiated cells—the rate of reproduction, the rate of synthesis of certain substances,

Microscopic View of Cell Culture From Rabbit Corneal Epithelium

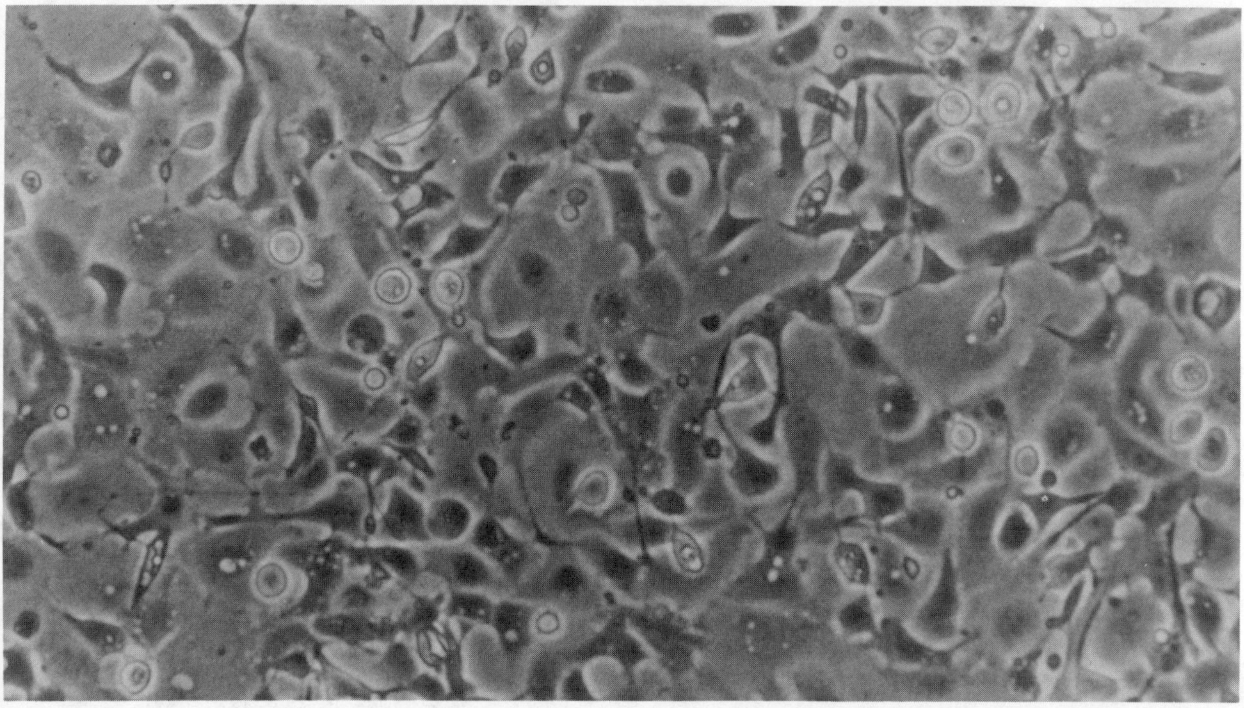

Photo credit: Kwan Y. Chan, University of Washington

changes in membrane permeability, and damage to some part of the cell structure. Those functions having to do with viability and growth are most frequently measured because they require an integration of many physiologic events within the cell, are sensitive, and lend themselves to automation (73).

Quantifiable tests are preferred over subjective ones, and a wide variety of quantitative approaches are available to measure irritation, including the release of prostaglandins (35); the production of enzymes (46), proteins (57), antigens, antibodies, or hormones (73); and the migration of certain white blood cells (macrophages) to the area of irritation (12,101). Irritation can also be measured by the extent to which cells exfoliate from the surface of the tissue. The extent of damage can be determined by counting cells and by examining the nuclei (102). Another indicator of irritation, the integrity of cell membranes, can be monitored through the uptake of nutrients through the cell wall. Where the nutrient uptake is active (that is, when the cell is required to expend energy for transport), uptake can also be used to indicate changes in metabolism (86,102).

Liver cells have been the subject of considerable research, in part because they play such an important role in an organism's removal of toxic substances and in part because they retain most of their special functions when cultured. The response of liver cells to toxic substances may be measured in many ways: the use of sugar as an indication of metabolic activity; the production of proteins or other substances that have been correlated with toxicity; uptake of amino acids as an indication of protein synthesis; changes in appearance that parallel those observed in livers of whole animals (106); and morphological changes and reductions in viability (75). Other promising techniques in this rapidly expanding field include culturing:

- beating heart cells to detect the effect of certain vapors on irregularities in heartbeat (68);
- rabbit kidney tubules to detect substances that can cause acute renal failure, and rat vaginal tissue to test vaginal irritancy of contraceptives (27);
- various kinds of cells to test for biocompatibility of implants (15,52,53); and
- nerve cells to test for the synthesis of neuro-

Dispensing Apparatus for Delivery of Culture Medium to Cells Within a Plastic Culture Plate

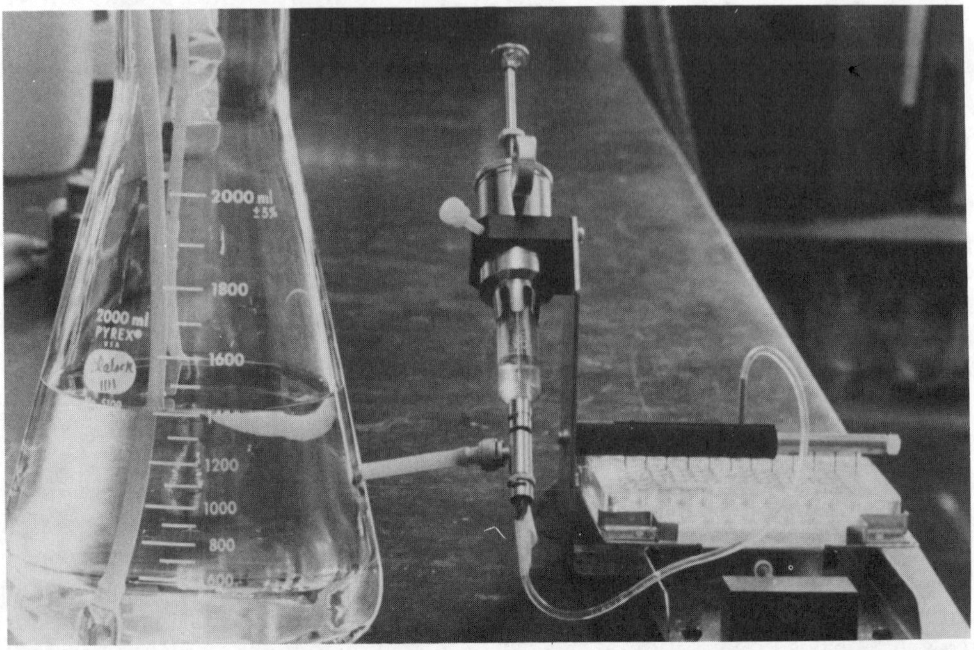

Photo credit: The Johns Hopkins University

transmitter chemicals, the formation of synapses, and the conduction of impulses (7).

Although tissue and organ cultures may approximate more closely the physiology of the human or whole-animal model, they are more difficult to manipulate than cell cultures (see ch. 6). Sophisticated equipment must be used to monitor and control the environment and to perfuse the sample with nutrients. Where the sample is more than a few cell layers thick, uniform delivery of the test substance, nutrients, and oxygen is difficult, as is the removal of waste products. Cell differentiation can usually be maintained in tissue and organ cultures, albeit with some difficulty (50).

Human placentas have proved quite useful in testing the ability of a drug to cross the placenta from mother to fetus. There are certain logistical problems with this method, however. The placenta must be transferred to the perfusion apparatus within 5 minutes after it is eliminated from the uterus, and it is only useful for about 3 hours afterward (77).

Nonanimal Organisms

There are a variety of nonanimal organisms that can replace some animals in testing, ranging from plants to single-celled organisms to invertebrates. All of these can respond to certain noxious stimuli, and some may experience pain. However, many commentators believe that they do not experience pain or suffering in the same way that animals do, particularly in those cases where there is no brain or neural tissue (90). The use of such organisms, which has never been controlled under any Federal or State law, is regarded as a replacement for animals in this report.

Micro-organisms

In recent years, increased emphasis has been placed on the use of bacteria and fungi to measure certain genotoxic effects. A major advantage of these organisms is that they can be cultivated much more easily and quickly than most animal or human cells. Their genetic makeup is simple compared with that of animals and humans and the fact that a great deal is known about it facilitates their use, particularly in toxicological research leading to new methods (74). A change in genetic material is relatively easy to detect and characterize. Fungal systems have been shown to be especially useful in mutagenicity testing and seem to be more sensitive than bacteria (126), perhaps at the expense of falsely indicating a hazard. Other species that have proved useful include slime molds, algae, and protozoa (74).

Protozoa, although rather primitive overall, frequently have specialized functions that mimic those of humans. For example, the cilia of protozoa respond to smoke or phenols as do the cilia in the human bronchial tube (5). Various protozoans have been used in toxicity testing of cigarette smoke. Protozoans are currently being evaluated for use in screening tests for carcinogenesis, mutagenesis, and reproductive toxicity (93).

Invertebrates

Invertebrates have made major contributions in biomedical research because certain aspects of their physiology are sufficiently similar to that of mammals (74). Although models for toxicity testing require greater similarity to animals or more thorough characterization of differences than models for research, invertebrates offer exciting possibilities.

Of the invertebrates, insects offer the greatest selection of models, there being over 2 million species from which to choose (74). Among them, the fruit fly, *Drosophila melanogaster,* is the best understood. Procedures have been developed for detecting mutagenicity (18), as well as teratogenicity (11) and reproductive toxicity (93).

The sea urchin has long been a favored test organism for basic reproductive research (74). Consequently, the mechanisms and procedures of testing this invertebrate can easily be developed and performed. The sea urchin model for fertilization and development can be used in screening for reproductive toxicity, teratogenicity, and mutagenicity. Nematodes, annelids, and mollusks are also used for alternative mutagenesis testing regimes and, additionally, mollusks are used in the area of reproductive toxicology. Sponges, mollusks, crustaceans, and echinoderms are being used in metabolism studies, as understanding metabolite formation in nonmammalian species can lend insight to interspecies variation (93).

USE OF NONLIVING SYSTEMS IN TESTING

Animal use can sometimes be avoided altogether with nonliving biochemical or physicochemical systems, although most such systems currently require animal-derived components. Computer simulation can also be used when there are sufficient data available for substances related to the one of interest and when the mechanisms of toxicity are at least partially understood.

Chemical Systems

Whole animals have been replaced with analytical chemistry for tests involving detection of a substance or measurement of potency or concentration, such as for vaccines, anticancer drugs, and vitamins (10). However, toxicity testing in nonliving systems is quite limited at this time.

Recently developed methods of detection or measurement are based on the selective binding that occurs between a particular substance and the antibodies to it. In an assay for botulism toxin (which traditionally required up to 200 mice), antibodies obtained from rabbits are modified so that the binding of the toxin can be detected easily. The rabbits are initially injected with a small, harmless dose of the botulism toxin. Small amounts of blood are then removed from the rabbits at regular intervals. In 4 weeks, a rabbit can produce enough antibody, with little discomfort, to perform tests that would otherwise require thousands of mice (32).

Chemical systems that test for toxicity are based on determining whether a substance undergoes a specific reaction. For example, it is well known that carbon monoxide binds to hemoglobin in the blood, thus greatly reducing the blood's ability to carry oxygen. The extent to which a substance would displace oxygen in hemoglobin can be a measure of its ability to produce asphyxiation. Substances can also be tested in isolation for their effects on enzymes crucial to certain bodily functions.

An important limit of chemical systems is that they do not indicate the extent to which an organism can recover from or prevent these reactions. For example, a substance that binds strongly to hemoglobin may not be a problem because it is not absorbed. A substance will not have a significant effect on an enzyme of interest if it is excreted before it has an effect.

Physicochemical systems have some ability to determine whether a substance will be absorbed and what will happen to it. The tendency of a substance to accumulate in a biological system can be roughly estimated by the relative proportions that dissolve in equal volumes of water and the organic solvent octanol (34,55). Artificial skin made with filter paper and fats is being tried as a means of mimicking absorption of cosmetics and drugs (45). Reactivity and other toxicity-related properties can be deduced from chemical structure alone (109).

Mathematical and Computer Models

Advances in computer technology during the past 20 years have contributed to the development of sophisticated mathematical models of quantitative structure activity relationships (QSAR). These models are used to predict biological responses on the basis of physical and chemical properties, structure, and available toxicological data. The limitations of such models are due in part to a lack of understanding of the mechanisms by which toxic effects occur.

In applying QSAR, the biological effects of chemicals are expressed in quantitative terms. These effects can be correlated with physicochemical properties, composition, and/or structure. Frequently used properties include an affinity for fats versus water (octanol/water partition coefficient), the presence of certain reactive groups, the size and shape of molecules, and the way reactive fragments are linked together.

The simplest extrapolation is for a series of closely related chemicals. The several characteristics they have in common need not be incorporated into the model as variables. This type of analysis has been performed for several hundred families of chemicals and has established that relationships within a series are fairly predictable (64).

Another approach, more broadly applicable, is to examine the contributions of various portions of a molecule. In more elaborate computer programs, it is possible to identify likely reactions and cascading physiological events in various species, techniques first developed for pharmacology (54). A similar approach is the use of multitiered classification schemes that use large databases to draw semiempirical conclusions (36).

Epidemiologic Data on Humans

Perhaps the most useful alternative to animal testing is epidemiologic studies on humans. Such studies were used to detect carcinogenicity in humans as early as the 18th century (49,85,87). The most well known study detected scrotal cancer in chimney sweeps (85). A more recent example in which epidemiologic evidence was used to detect a human carcinogen was the finding that vinyl chloride causes a rare liver cancer in humans (26). A major disadvantage of epidemiologic studies is that considerable human exposure can take place before a toxic effect is detectable, particularly in the case of diseases that take many years to develop. Another disadvantage is that they can be quite expensive to conduct. Privacy must also be considered (112), preventing many data that would be useful from being collected or analyzed.

Epidemiologic studies may be divided into three general types: experimental, descriptive, and observational. Experimental epidemiology is the human equivalent of animal testing—providing or withholding a substance to determine its toxic or beneficial effects. Such studies are greatly limited by ethical and legal considerations, as well as the difficulties involved in securing the cooperation of a large number of people.

Descriptive epidemiology analyzes data on the distribution and extent of health problems or other conditions in various populations, trying to find correlations among characteristics such as diet, air quality, and occupation. Such comparisons are frequently done between countries or smaller geographic regions, as is the case for cancer statistics collected and analyzed by the National Cancer Institute (9).

Observational epidemiology uses data derived from individuals or small groups. Data would be evaluated statistically to determine the strength of the association between the variable of interest and the disease. In cohort studies, a well-characterized and homogenous group is studied over time. In case-control studies, a control group is selected retrospectively based on variables thought to be relevant to the effect. Both methods rely on an accurate prediction of the variables that are important and are subject to various selection biases (62,112).

THE LD_{50} TEST

The LD_{50} test is one of the most widely used toxicity tests, and the development of alternatives to it is regarded by many as a high priority. As described in chapter 7, this acute toxicity test measures the amount of a substance needed to kill half the population of the test species. The LD_{50} is used as a rough indicator of the acute toxicity of a chemical.

The LD_{50} is useful for testing biological therapeutics, although there remain few such substances for which the LD_{50} is the only available means of standardization (13,90). Other applications, perhaps not so well justified (90), are determining doses for other toxicological tests and setting regulatory priorities.

There has been political pressure to abolish the LD_{50} and it has been criticized by many toxicologists on scientific grounds. It has poor reproducibility and the results are difficult to extrapolate to humans because there are so many mechanisms by which death could occur (70,90,125).

Despite the many criticisms of the LD_{50}, most toxicologists agree that acute toxicity information has valid uses, and that measurements of lethality also are important. Nevertheless, the precision with which the LD_{50} is measured is often unjustified for several reasons. First, most applications of the information do not require precision. Second, even if the information were precise for a given species, the LD_{50} varies so much from species to species that extrapolation to humans is only rough. Third, the LD_{50} of a given substance varies significantly from laboratory to laboratory, and even in the same laboratory.

Various regulatory classification schemes make distinctions between levels of toxicity ("highly toxic" versus "toxic," versus "moderately toxic," versus "nontoxic"). The LD_{50} for two neighboring levels typically differs by a factor of 4 to 10. Yet, the reproducibility of test results does not justify even these distinctions. A recent study, though not necessarily typical, indicates the magnitude of the problem. A series of LD_{50} tests were performed in 60 European laboratories for five substances on one species. The LD_{50} for one substance ranged from 46 mg/kg body weight to 522 mg/kg, possibly ranging over three toxicity levels in some classification schemes. Although the variations were not this large for the four other chemicals tested, the smallest variation was 350 to 1,280 mg/kg. Each test was done with 50 or more animals so that the results would be precise (61).

Using Fewer Animals

The standard LD_{50} requires at least three groups of 10 animals or more each. An alternative procedure for determining the Approximate Lethal Dose (ALD) was developed as early as the 1940s (29), in which individual animals are administered doses that increase by 50 percent over the previous dose. Depending on the initial dose level, the total number of animals needed is usually 4 to 10. Because the test substance might not be cleared between doses or because there may be cumulative effects, the ALD can be lower than the LD_{50}, perhaps by 70 percent, though more typically by less than 20 percent (29).

Many other acute toxicity tests that require fewer animals than the LD_{50} have been developed (14, 17,33,61,69,71,94,105,107). Most require that the doses increase sequentially, thereby allowing the experiment to stop when a certain limit is reached. Thus, fewer animals die in the conduct of a test, but its duration could increase from 2 weeks to a month or more. Although many investigators are moving to less precise LD_{50} tests, no generally accepted alternative seems to have emerged.

The Limit Test and Other Refinements

If a substance is not lethal at high doses, its precise LD_{50} is not very important. In the limit test (80), a small number of animals is given a single oral dose, e.g., 5 g/kg body weight. If no animals die and no major ill effects occur, no further testing is needed. However, this limit is so high that this approach may have little practical value in reducing animal use (24).

Rather than determining the dose that is lethal, studies can also be done to detect toxic effects at doses that are not lethal. As with the LD_{50}, increasing doses can be administered to a small number of animals, perhaps stopping when some limit is reached. This approach can be further refined so that animals that are in distress could be sacrificed without affecting the outcome of the test (14).

In Vitro and Nonanimal Methods

Cell toxicity—changes in cell function or death of cells—can sometimes be used to detect acute toxicity. However, cell toxicity cannot be expected to function as a replacement for the LD_{50} because lethality can occur by so many mechanisms that are supercellular. Cell toxicity is particularly useful in comparing members of chemical families, such as alcohols and alkaloids (79).

At present, mathematical modeling has limitations, although it may have some utility in range-finding and in screening substances for testing (109). Modeling of acute toxicity fails to meet one of the criteria suggested by a working party on quantitative structure activity relationships, namely that the mechanism by which the response occurs should involve a common rate-determining step (88). Nonetheless, in a large study involving thousands of substances, a computer program was developed that predicted LD_{50} values within a factor of 2.5 for 50 percent of the substances and within a factor of 6 for 80 percent. Considering the reproducibility of the test itself, this might be satisfactory for some purposes, and it certainly warrants further investigation. Furthermore, many of the larger deviations in this study, upon further examination, were found to involve reporting errors. This program relied on a multi-tiered classification scheme based on chemical structure (36).

SKIN AND EYE IRRITATION

The widely used Draize eye irritation test and, to a somewhat lesser extent, the skin irritation test have been criticized because of the amount of pain inflicted and because they are unsatisfactory models for human irritation (91,95). First, the rabbit eye has structural differences, such as a thinner cornea and differing tearing apparatus (103), and animal skin is much less sensitive and discriminating than human skin (56,63). Second, both of these tests are sensitive to too many variables, making reproducibility poor (83,118).

As with most tests, the number of animals used can sometimes be reduced. Several refinements have also been proposed. For example, screening tests based on pH or skin irritancy might also serve as alternatives to eye irritancy tests in limited circumstances, although preliminary studies indicate that this approach is frequently misleading (119). Other refinements involve local anesthetics (51,65, 110), applying smaller (43) or more dilute (120) doses, and testing whole eyes in vitro (20). The latter method has particular appeal when cow eyes are used because they are so readily available from slaughterhouses. In the case of smaller doses, a recent comparison with over 500 accidental human exposures showed that doses smaller than those now in use yielded results more predictive of the human response while causing less severe irritation (38).

Skin and eye irritation are similar in many respects. Thus, even though little work has been done to develop alternatives to skin irritation tests, the many approaches just summarized for eye irritation may eventually be applied to skin testing as well (91).

In Vitro Tests

Several in vitro alternatives have been examined, and it appears to some commentators that no single alternative will be adequate, but that a battery of in vitro tests might be a useful replacement (67). Several types of cell cultures have been used in developing an in vitro test for eye irritation. The cells used are rabbit and human corneal cells (72), mouse and hamster fibroblasts, human hepatoma cells, and mouse macrophages (96).

A variety of effects have been used as surrogates for eye irritation, such as the rate of uptake of uridine as an indication of cell functioning and recovery, visible changes in cell structure, decreases in the concentration of cell protein (96), and release of plasminogen activator from the injured cells (21). Some techniques appear promising, particularly in their ability to rank substances based on irritancy. Rapid progress is being made in the development of techniques, but none can be considered validated at this time (91).

To date, little work has been done on in vitro replacements for skin irritancy testing. However, the growth of skin in tissue culture is of interest for treating burn victims, and it is expected that culture techniques currently being developed for that purpose can be used in testing methods. In addition, it has also been suggested that suitable specimens can be obtained from cadavers and surgery and from judicious use of human volunteers (63).

Chick Embryo

One test system receiving considerable attention is the fertilized chicken egg. A part of the eggshell is removed and the test substance applied to the chorioallantoic membrane surrounding the developing embryo (see fig. 8-1). This test has the potential for assessing both eye and skin irritancy.

The chorioallantoic membrane of the chick embryo is a complete tissue, including arteries, capil-

Figure 8-1.—Chronological Sequence of Chick Embryo Chorioallantoic Membrane Assay

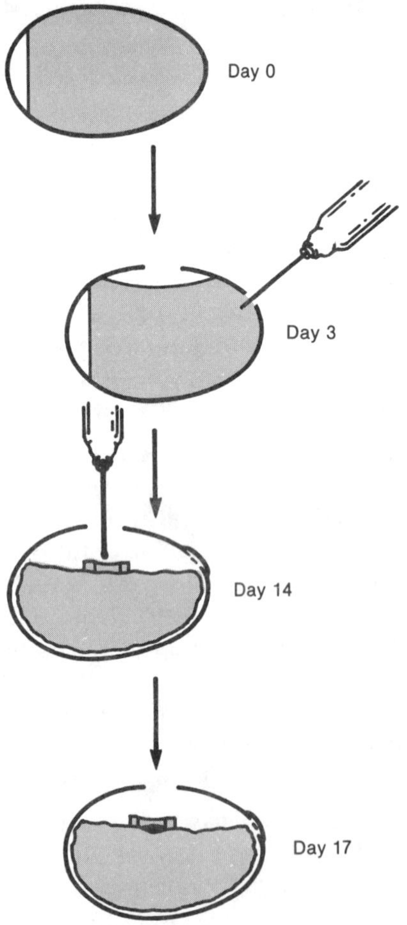

Day 0. Fertile eggs are incubated at 37° C. **Day 3.** The shell is penetrated in two places: A window is cut at the top, and 1.5 to 2 milliliters of albumin is removed with a needle and discarded. The chorioallantoic membrance forms on the floor of the air space, on top of the embryo. The window is taped. **Day 14.** A test sample is placed on the embryonic membrane and contained within a plastic ring. **Day 17.** The chorioallantoic membrane is evaluated for its response to the test substance, and the embryo is discarded.

SOURCE: J. Leighton, J. Nassauer, and R. Tchao, "The Chick Embryo in Toxicology: An Alternative to the Rabbit Eye," *Food Chem. Toxicol.* 23:293-298. Copyright 1985, Pergamon Press, Ltd.

laries, and veins, and is technically easy to study. An embryonic membrane tested after 14 days of incubation responds to injury with a complete inflammatory reaction, a process similar to that induced in the conjunctival tissue of the rabbit eye. The embryonic membrane can show a variety of signs of irritation and has capabilities for recovery (59,60).

Assessment of toxicity is made and the embryo is discarded on about day 17 of incubation. The criteria used for macroscopic rating of lesions on the chorioallantoic membrane are listed below (59):

- size,
- contours and surface,
- color,
- retraction of surrounding chorioallantoic membrane,
- spokewheel pattern of vessels,
- overall grade of severity, and
- necrosis (confirmed microscopically).

Although this is, strictly speaking, an in vivo test, the chorioallantoic membrane does not have nerve cells, and thus it is unlikely that the organism experiences any discomfort. In addition, fertile eggs are inexpensive and do not require elaborate animal room facilities.

REPEATED-DOSE TOXICITY TESTS

Repeated-dose toxicity testing involves the repeated application of a substance to a biological assay system and subsequent measurement of many different effects of the substance. In repeated-dose testing, the long-term effects of repeated, sublethal exposure to a substance are of interest, rather than acute, lethal effects. Cell cultures may be useful adjuncts for suspected tar-

Chick Embryo Chorioallantoic Membrane Assay

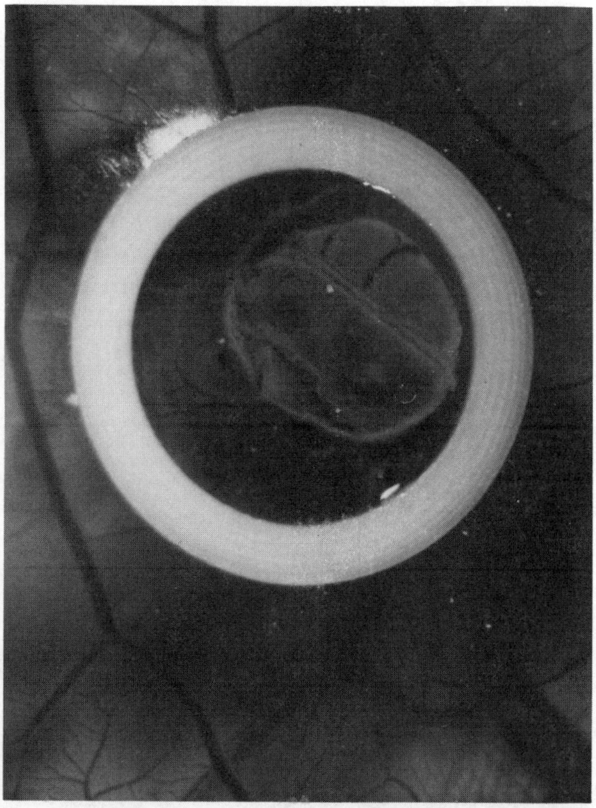

Photo credit: Joseph Leighton, Medical College of Pennsylvania

Typical reaction seen 3 days after certain concentrations of household products have been placed on the 14-day-old chorioallantoic membrane. The thin white plastic ring has an internal diameter of 10 millimeters. The area of injury within the ring is well defined with a distinct edge. All of the cells in the injured area are degenerating or dead. The severity of this positive lesion is quantified by measuring its diameter.

get organs or tissues, but they are not a replacement for whole-animal testing. The most promising alternatives in the near future involve modifications of animal use (for example, by combining tests), and the use of screening tests and computer simulation for improved experimental design. The screening tests with the greatest promise are for hepatotoxicity and neurotoxicity.

Hepatotoxicity

Several in vitro alternatives for hepatotoxicity have been developed, including perfused liver (108), liver cell suspensions (39), and liver cell cultures (39,44). Liver perfusions can only be maintained for a few hours, and with some difficulty. Cell cultures can retain the special functions of liver cells with specially prepared culture media (76,81). However, the cells are viable for only a limited period of time and do not replicate in a reproducible manner. Although these techniques have been used to study mechanisms of liver toxicity, only limited attention has been given to their use in screening or as alternatives (91).

Neurotoxicity

The development of alternatives for neurotoxicity is more difficult than for hepatotoxicity. The nervous system is the most complex organ in the body, both in terms of structure and its function. Because many neurotoxins affect only one kind of cell, a battery of in vitro tests would probably be required to replace whole-animal testing—if anything could. Substances can also affect various areas differently, partly because of distribution factors. For example, very few substances are able to enter the brain because of the "blood-brain barrier." Thus, pharmacokinetic studies will continue to be very important.

Some in vitro tests (41) and tests using invertebrates (8) seem useful, at least for screening. As yet, however, the primary use of in vitro techniques has been the elucidation of mechanisms of known toxic effects (31). Many toxic effects to neural tissue have been correlated with concentrations of specific chemicals in or around the cells, thus offering the means for developing in vitro tests (31).

MUTAGENICITY

Mutation, the change in the DNA sequence of genes, is a mechanism by which toxic effects may be initiated. If the DNA replicates, the mutation is passed from the mutated cell to its descendants. Mutation can lead to cell death or the gain or loss of certain functions. When it occurs in germ cells,

38-750 0 - 86 - 7

the gene pool is affected, even if the mutation is not expressed in the progeny. The mutations that occur in somatic cells that are of greatest concern are those that lead to cancer (18).

Recent advances in the techniques of cell biology have led to an increase in the types and sophistication of mutagenicity tests available. Mutations can be detected by analyzing DNA or its fragments or by observing changes in the size, shape, or number of the chromosomes (which contain DNA), as well as by observing changes in a whole organism (34). Mutation can also be detected by measuring the amount of DNA repair.

Micro-organism Tests

The most commonly used test for mutagenicity is the Ames test for "reverse mutation" in *Salmonella typhimurium* (3). Mutagenicity is detected by exposing an already mutated strain to potential mutagens. If the mutation is reversed, the bacteria regain their ability to produce the amino acid histidine and will proliferate in a histidine-deficient culture medium.

The Ames test, as well as most other mutagenicity tests involving micro-organisms, does not avoid animal use entirely. To determine whether the metabolic products of a substance might be mutagenic even if the substance itself is not, liver preparations from rats or other rodents are used to produce at least some of the likely metabolic products.

Micro-organism systems may fail to detect or may overpredict mutagenic changes that could occur in whole animals or humans. For example, the system provided for metabolism may not be capable of reproducing conditions in vivo, or in the case of screening for carcinogenicity, mutation may not be the initiating event. On the other hand, such systems may indicate mutagenicity when the DNA repair system of mammals would reverse the mutation.

Other bacterial tests have been developed using *S. typhimurium*, *Escherichia coli*, and *Bacillus subtilis*. These systems do not seem to offer any particular advantage over the Ames test, although thorough evaluation is hampered by lack of a comparable database of results (28). Tests have also been developed for molds (30), fungi (16), and yeasts (18,82).

In Vitro Tests

In vitro mutagenicity tests may be done with cultured mammalian cells that are exposed to toxic substances, although many mammalian in vitro tests also have an in vivo variant. Such tests typically measure acquired resistance or lost resistance to the effects of the toxic substance. Most commonly used are a mouse lymphoma cell line or hamster ovary cells, but almost any well-characterized cell can be used. Ovary cells are often used because, as germ cells, they have half the number of chromosomes to be evaluated (18).

A test known as the specific locus test can be done with Chinese hamster ovary cells. They are exposed to a test substance and their response to the normally lethal 8-azaguanine or 6-thioguanine in cell culture determined. The cell's ability to survive, requiring the ability to metabolize the 8-azaguanine or 6-thioguanine, is an indication of the occurrence of mutation as a result of exposure to the test substance. This test can also be done with mouse lymphoma cells exposed to 5-bromodeoxyuridine or trifluorothymidine (23).

The sister chromatid exchange test relies on the fact that certain substances will cause DNA breakage and reunion. This damage can be observed by staining the original chromosomes so that any segments exchanged during replication can be observed. Commonly used cells include human lymphocyte cells and rodent and human fibroblasts (37). Both the specific locus test and the sister chromatid exchange can also be performed as in vivo procedures (see ch. 7).

Although the cells are usually derived from animals, there is a considerable net savings in animal lives when in vitro mutagenicity tests are performed. For example, the rat mast cell assay can be used to screen severe irritants, and one rat can supply enough tissue to replace the use of 48 animals in in-vivo procedures (103).

Tests Using Insects

The most widely used insect for genetic studies is the fruit fly, *Drosophila melanogaster* (114,115). The fruit fly has well-characterized genetics and is similar to mammals in many key reactions. A variety of end points can be detected. The most common, and probably most sensitive, test is the sex-linked recessive lethal assay (18). Treated males are mated with untreated females, and the progeny are mated to each other. The number and characteristics of the male progeny are evaluated to determine if lethal mutations (that is, mutations that prevent viability) have occurred.

Other tests involving fruit flies also exist or are likely to be developed. End points that can be measured include the loss, gain, or breakage of chromosomes detected by examining germ cells. With the availability of mutant strains, the measurement of reverse mutations can be a valuable tool. Eye color is a popular method of following genetic effects in the fruit fly (18).

CARCINOGENICITY

Many assays meant to replace carcinogenicity testing are designed to detect the initiation of cancer rather than the formation of tumors. First, detecting initiation is faster and easier than detecting cancer. Second, although not all initiation leads to cancer, certain kinds are considered reliable surrogates for the disease.

A major problem with evaluating the predictiveness of alternatives to whole animals for carcinogenicity testing is that very few human carcinogens have been positively identified. Most substances treated as human carcinogens, although documented to be *known* animal carcinogens, must be viewed as *probable* or *suspected* human carcinogens. The development of alternatives is somewhat hampered by a lack of epidemiologic data on humans.

Various molecular and physicochemical properties of substances have been correlated to carcinogenicity. Some structure-activity models developed for families of chemicals have predicted the carcinogenic properties for 75 to 97 percent of them. The chemicals modeled include polycyclic aromatic hydrocarbons (123), nitrosamines (89,99, 121), and aromatic amines (124).

The Ames Test

Because mutation is often the first step in carcinogenesis, the Ames test has been suggested as a possible screen or replacement for carcinogenicity testing. It has been evaluated for this purpose, both alone and as one in a battery of tests. Alone, it is less predictive than whole-animal tests. In a battery, it has been shown to be about as predictive as animal testing for certain families of chemicals and substantially less predictive for others for the substances tested. Table 8-1 shows the predictiveness of mouse and rat bioassays and the Ames test for some known human carcinogens.

The Ames test has been performed thousands of times in over 2,000 laboratories throughout the world and has provided results on over 1,000 chemical substances since it was developed less than two decades ago. Portions of this large body of analytical data have been reviewed in over a dozen evaluation studies with the intent of determining the test's ability to predict carcinogenicity (6,19,66). These evaluations show that the percentage of human carcinogens that are also mutagens (mutagenic carcinogens) ranges from 50 to 93 percent and is most likely about 80 percent (48). About 20 percent of the human carcinogens were not mutagens (nonmutagenic carcinogens) in the Ames test, and it is believed that cancer associated with these carcinogens is initiated by a mechanism other than mutation.

A critical analysis of several studies (19) identified several sources of variation. These include methods of chemical selection, sample coding, use of a high proportion of chemicals known to work well or poorly with Ames testing, and differences in metabolic activation during the test procedure. The conclusion was that a reasonably careful application of the Ames technique to a nonbiased group of chemicals would be expected to yield a predictive accuracy of approximately 80 percent for mouse and rat carcinogens.

The Ames test tends to be positive for a large proportion (about 40 percent) of substances that have not been identified as carcinogens in rodent bioassays. It should be noted, however, that these

Table 8-1.—The Response of Known Human Carcinogens to Rodent Carcinogenicity and Bacterial Mutagenicity Assays

Chemical	Rat bioassay	Mouse bioassay	Ames test
4-Aminobiphenyl	+	+	+
Arsenic	–	–	–
Asbestos	+	+	–
Benzene	–	+	–
Benzidine	+	+	+
Bis(chloromethyl)ether	+	+	+
Chromium; some chromium compounds	+	–	+
Cyclophosphamide	+	+	+
Diethylstilbestrol	+	+	–
Melphalan	+	+	+
Mustard gas	n.d.	+	+
2-Naphthylamine	–	+	+
Soot, tars	–	+	+
Vinyl chloride	+	+	+

KEY: + = Positive results (carcinogenic to rodents or mutagenic to bacteria).
– = Negative results (not carcinogenic or not mutagenic).
n.d. = No data.

SOURCES: From H. Bartsch, L. Tomatis, and C. Malaveille, "Mutagenicity and Carcinogenicity of Environmental Chemicals," *Regul. Toxicol. Pharmacol.* 2:94-105, 1982; D. Brusick, "Evaluation of Chronic Rodent Bioassays and Ames Assay Tests as Accurate Models for Predicting Human Carcinogens," *Application of Biological Markets to Carcinogen Testing,* H. Milman and S. Sell (eds.) (New York: Plenum Press, 1983); B.D. Goldstein, C.A. Snyder, S. Laskin et al., "Myelogenous Leukemia in Rodents Inhaling Benzene," *Toxicol. Lett.* 13:169-173, 1982; and J.V. Soderman (ed.), *Handbook of Identified Carcinogens and Noncarcinogens, Vols. I and II* (Boca Raton, FL: CRC Press, 1982).

substances have not been shown to be noncarcinogenic, and many authorities maintain that the information is insufficient to make any statement about the proportion of noncarcinogens that are also nonmutagens in the Ames test (4,116).

Use of the Ames Test in a Battery of Tests

The predictive value of the Ames test, or other mutagenicity tests, can be improved by combining it with additional short-term assays to form a test battery. Although no U.S. regulatory agency has yet recommended a specific combination, most authorities recommend that an appropriate battery should include information from a minimum of three types of tests:

- gene mutation (Ames test, mouse lymphoma test);
- chromosomal mutation (in vivo Chinese hamster ovary cell cytogenetics); and
- DNA damage (sister chromatid exchange, unscheduled DNA repair).

At least one test should include a mammalian in vitro cell, tissue, or organ culture assay (4).

In a recent study, 18 Ames tests averaged 66 percent "accuracy" (number of chemicals correctly identified/number of chemicals tested). Comparative results from six batteries of short-term tests that included the Ames test increased the accuracy to 82 to 90 percent (58,111).

CURRENT TRENDS

As long as toxicological data continue to be required by regulators and by the courts to protect human health, animal testing will continue for the foreseeable future. Even major progress in the development and implementation of alternatives will not necessarily eliminate whole-animal tests. Furthermore, there are several impediments to development and implementation:

- A large number of scientists have been trained to solve health problems and to invent new products using animal models.

- Regulatory schemes, product liability law, and patent law also incorporate notions of animal models.
- A large body of animal testing information already exists that is useful in interpreting new testing data.
- There are substantial costs and delays associated with the development and adoption of alternatives. One study indicated that it takes about 20 years for an in vitro test to be developed, validated, adopted, and implemented (92).

At the same time, there are several factors facilitating the development and implementation of alternatives:

- Rapid progress is being made in techniques for culturing mammalian cells and organs, in instruments for detecting and quantifying cellular and molecular changes, and in the understanding of the cellular and molecular processes underlying toxicity. Improved understanding is leading to the ability to predict long-term effects and carcinogenicity from short-term biochemical and morphological changes.
- As such advances are made, the research laboratories that have developed the expertise are often willing to apply it to the development of new testing methods, and can do so efficiently (42).
- Organizations such as The Johns Hopkins Center for Alternatives to Animal Testing and the Rockefeller University laboratory have been set up to facilitate and coordinate research on alternatives (see ch. 12).
- Many organizations have been established to pressure those who conduct animal testing or use data based on it to adopt alternatives or conduct research that will lead to alternatives.

Strategies to speed the development and adoption of alternatives will depend on the needs and resources of the organization involved. The following recommendations encompass a variety of perspectives. They were promulgated by the Toxicity Committee of the Fund for the Replacement of Animals in Medical Experiments, which met from 1979 through 1982 (40). Some involve reassessment of testing needs and priorities; others involve technical strategies thought to be likely to lead to better methods, both in testing and in evaluating results:

- Provide a mechanism for reviewing the need for a given test.
- Investigate the consequences of not requiring or possessing testing data other than what already exists. Particular attention should be given to widely used tests such as the LD_{50} and skin and eye irritation tests with a view toward eliminating unnecessary requirements.
- Encourage flexible use of testing guidelines and frequent reappraisal of them in light of new knowledge.
- Strive for broader-based international harmonization and mutual recognition of data from other countries so that duplicative testing can be avoided.
- Encourage detailed publication of all testing results, particularly for costly or painful tests or those requiring many animals.
- Investigate the possibility of time limits on the confidentiality of test results.
- Make greater use of studies on absorption, distribution, biotransformation, and excretion in humans, as well as in test animals, to select the most relevant exposure conditions, to aid in extrapolation of results, and to improve the reliability of test results.
- Perform preliminary studies before undertaking long-term studies so that results can be as useful as possible.
- Make greater use of the structural and conformational computer models used in developing drugs for the prediction of toxicity.
- Standardize screening tests based on in vitro and nonanimal tests, both to promote efficient use of testing resources and to evaluate the predictiveness of these tests.
- Try to predict toxic reactions before testing, both as a means for improving prediction techniques and to avoid testing highly irritating substances, particularly in the eye, if possible.
- Conduct research on the mechanisms by which toxic effects occur to facilitate the development of new testing methods.
- Develop more accurate, reproducible instrumentation for measuring toxic effects, avoid-

ing subjective measurements and reducing measurement errors.

- Make greater use of depositories in standardizing cell lines or strains of micro-organisms used for testing.
- Study the relationship between physicochemical properties and pharmacokinetic properties, as well as between physicochemical and toxicologic properties.
- Develop techniques for detecting nonmutagenic carcinogens.
- Develop systematic methods for objectively evaluating new techniques.
- Conduct postmarketing surveillance for adverse effects, noting any discrepancies with test results from animals.
- Substitute very specific tests for the LD_{50} and other general toxicity tests, particularly for substances having specialized uses, such as drugs.
- Use skin irritation testing as a rough screening tool for eye irritation.
- Attempt to describe specific effects in eye irritation studies, rather than reporting only the magnitude of the response.
- Investigate specific effects such as neurotoxicity to the extent possible when conducting general toxicity tests.
- Search for cell lines that retain their special functions upon replication and develop techniques for culturing them.
- Evaluate the statistical precision needed in various circumstances with a view toward using the smallest number of animals likely to be adequate.
- Use statistics to maximize the utility of results. Techniques such as blocking, covariance analysis, and factorial design should be used routinely.
- Improve standards of care and diet to reduce background effects.
- Take care that those conducting tests are qualified to do so, including having been trained in humane handling of animals.
- Combine tests wherever possible and keep them as short as possible, compatible with the nature of the test.
- Place greater emphasis on "no observed effect levels" than on lethal doses when they have greater predictive value.
- Use more than one species only to answer specific questions, and not for general safety assessments.

SUMMARY AND CONCLUSIONS

There has been a small but significant shift away from whole-animal testing to in vitro and nonanimal techniques in recent years, partly as a result of advances in biological techniques and partly in response to political and economic pressures. Many new methods are being developed for commonly used tests. Most of these are not yet validated, but they already have potential uses for screening substances for the animal testing they may eventually replace.

There are several kinds of alternatives. The first entails the continued, but modified, use of animals—changes in experimental design or data analysis so that fewer animals are needed or changes in protocols to reduce pain or distress. Living tissues, organs, and cells derived from humans or animals can sometimes be used instead of whole animals. These systems require a larger investment of time and money to develop than do modifications of whole-animal techniques, but their advantages may also be greater. They are usually faster and often cheaper than the corresponding whole-animal test, and they have scientific advantages as well. However, they almost always are less predictive than whole-animal tests and often fail to provide reliable dose-response data, information that is critical in estimating potential toxicity to humans.

Data, both anecdotal and epidemiologic, on toxic effects in inadvertently exposed humans are sometimes useful. However, these data are often confounded by lifestyle and exposure to other toxic factors. Another drawback is that human exposure can be great if there are long delays between exposure and observable effects.

The LD_{50}, probably the most common and most criticized toxicity test, is well suited to the limited use for which it was first developed. The biggest obstacle to limiting or eliminating use of the LD_{50} is institutional: Many regulatory schemes rely on it for classifying substances. The most promising alternatives in the short term are testing sequences that require fewer animals. Cell culture techniques and computer modeling show some promise, but they have limited value at this time.

Another common and widely criticized test is the Draize eye irritation test. Several promising in vitro alternatives have been developed with cell cultures. Another technique uses the outer (chorioallantoic) membrane of a 14-day-old chicken embryo. This technique, although it uses a whole animal embryo, is thought to involve no pain because the membrane has no nerves. These alternatives may also apply to skin irritation.

Alternatives to carcinogenicity testing and repeated-dose toxicity testing are of special interest, in part because the potential savings in testing costs and time are quite large, and in part because these tests require large numbers of animals. The most promising replacements are batteries of tests involving cell cultures and living, nonanimal organisms. Mutagenicity testing uses many in vitro or nonanimal protocols. Mutagenicity is of particular interest because mutation can be the first event in other kinds of toxicity, including carcinogenicity, and because it can permanently affect the human gene pool. The most well known nonanimal mutagenicity assay is the Ames test. When it is combined with other tests, the Ames shows promise as an alternative to carcinogenicity testing, but it is not yet validated for this use.

In general, the development of alternatives is being facilitated by the rapid development of biological techniques, which are being applied to the search for alternatives in many different laboratories. Major contributions to the coordination of these developments in the United States are being made by Rockefeller University and The Johns Hopkins Center for Alternatives to Animal Testing.

The implementation of alternatives is hindered by various forms of institutional inertia, such as regulatory schemes (see ch. 7), product liability law (see ch. 7), and general resistance to change. Important impediments are the large body of existing information—derived from animals—that is relied on for the interpretation of new data and the lack of sufficient information to support the use of alternatives.

CHAPTER 8 REFERENCES

1. Adolphe M., Pointet, Y., Onot, W., et al., "Use of Fibroblast Cell Culture for the Study of Wound Healing Drugs," *Int. J. Cosmetic Sci.* 6:55-58, 1984.
2. Altman, P.L. (ed.), *Pathology of Laboratory Mice and Rats* (New York: Pergamon Press, 1985).
3. Ames, B.N., McCann, J., and Yamasaki, E., "Methods for Detecting Carcinogens and Mutagens With the *Salmonella*/Mammalian Microsome Mutagenicity Test," *Mutat. Res.* 31:347-364, 1975.
4. Auletta, A., Genetic Toxicologist, U.S. Environmental Protection Agency, Washington, DC, personal communication, 1984.
5. Banerjee, S.K., and Adal, T., "Ascorbic Acid in the Pars Intercerebralis Cells of Grasshopper: Its Concentrations During Induced Accumulation of Depletion of Neurosecretory Substances," *Anat. Anx.* 134:378-381, 1983.
6. Bartsch, L., Malaveille, C., Camus, A.M., et al., "Validation and Comparative Studies on 180 Chemicals with *S. typhimurium* Strains and V79 Chinese Hamster Cells in the Presence of Various Metabolizing Systems," *Mutat. Res.* 76:1-50, 1980.
7. Berky, J., and Sherrod, C. (eds.), *In Vitro Toxicity Testing* (Philadelphia, PA: Franklin Institute Press, 1977).
8. Best, J.B., Morita, M., Ragin, J., et al., "Acute Toxic Responses of the Freshwater Planarian *Dugesia dorotocephala* to Methylmercury," *Bull. Environ. Contam. Toxicol.* 27:49-54, 1981.
9. Blot, W.J., "Developing Clues to Environmental Cancer: A Stepwise Approach With the Use of Cancer Mortality Data," *Envir. Health Perspect.* 32:53-58 (1979).
10. Borsetti, A., Staff Scientist, U.S. Department of

Health and Human Services, Food and Drug Administration, Office of Science Coordination, Bethesda, MD, personal communication, Jan. 17, 1985.

11. Bournais-Vardiabasis, N., Teplitz, R.L., Chernoff, G.F., et al., "Detection of Teratogens in the *Drosophila* Embryonic Cell Culture Test: Assay of 100 Chemicals," *Teratology* 28:109-122, 1983.
12. Boyden, S., "The Chemotactic Effect of Mixtures of Antibody and Antigen on Polymorphonuclear Leucocytes," *J. Exp. Med.* 115:453-466, 1962.
13. British Pharmacopoeia Commission, Submission to the Advisory Committee to the Cruelty to Animals Act, 1876, London, 1977.
14. British Toxicology Society Working Party on Toxicity, "A New Approach to the Classification of Substances and Preparation on the Basis of Their Acute Toxicity," *Hum. Toxicol.* 3:85-92, 1984.
15. Brown, V.K., "Acute Toxicity," *Animals and Alternatives in Toxicity Testing,* M. Balls, R.J. Riddell, and A.N. Worden (eds.) (New York: Academic Press, 1983).
16. Brown, M.M., Wassom, J.S., Malling, H.V., et al., "Literature Survey of Bacterial, Fungal, and *Drosophila* Assay Systems Used in the Evaluation of Selected Chemical Compounds for Mutagenic Activity," *J. Natl. Cancer Inst.* 62:841-871, 1979.
17. Bruce, R.D., "An Up-and-down Procedure for Acute Toxicity Testing," *Fund. Appl. Toxicol.* 5:151-157, 1985.
18. Brusick, D.J., *Principles of Genetic Toxicology* (New York: Plenum Press, 1980).
19. Brusick, D.J., "Mutagenicity and Carcinogenicity Correlations Between Bacteria and Rodents," *Ann. N.Y. Acad. Sci.* 164:176, 1983.
20. Burton, A.B.G., York, M., and Lawrence, R.S., "The In Vitro Assessment of Severe Eye Irritants," *Food Cosmet. Toxicol.* 19:471-480, 1981.
21. Chan, K.Y., "An In Vitro Alternative To the Draize Test," *Alternatives to the Draize Eye Test,* A. Goldberg (ed.) (New York: Mary Ann Liebert, Inc., 1985).
22. *Chemical Week,* "Animals in Testing; How the CPI Is Handling a Hot Issue," 135(23):36, 1984.
23. Clive, D., Johnson, K.O., Spector, J.F.S., et al., "Validation and Characterization of the L5178Y/TK +/- Mouse Lymphoma Mutagen Assay System," *Mutat. Res.* 59:61-108, 1979.
24. Cloyd, G. Gilbert, Director, Product Development, Bone Metabolism Products, Norwich Eaton Pharmaceuticals, Inc., Norwich, NY, personal communication, 1985.
25. Cooper, J.F., Levin, J., and Wagner, H.N., "Quantitative Comparison of In Vitro and In Vivo Methods for the Detection of Endotoxic," *J. Lab. Clin. Med.* 78:138-148, 1971.
26. Creech, J.L., and Johnson, M.N., "Angiosarcoma of Liver in the Manufacture of Polyvinyl Chloride," *J. Occup. Med.* 16:150, 1975.
27. Dagani, R., "In-Vitro Methods May Offer Alternatives to Animal Testing," *Chem. Eng. News* 62 (46):25-28, 1984.
28. Dean, B.J., and Hodges, P., "Short-Term Tests for Genotoxicity," *Animals and Alternatives in Toxicity Testing,* M. Balls, R. J. Riddell, and A.N. Worden (eds.) (New York: Academic Press, 1983).
29. Deichmann, W.B., and Leblanc, T.J., "Determination of the Approximate Lethal Dose With Six Animals," *J. Ind. Hyg. Toxicol.* 25:415-417, 1943.
30. De Serres, F.J., and Malling, H.V., "Measurement of Recessive Lethal Damage Over the Entire Genome and Two Specific Loci of the ad-3 Region of *Neurospora crassa* With a Two Component Heterokaryon," *Chemical Mutagens, Principles and Methods for Their Detection, Vol. II,* A. Hollaender (ed.) (New York: Plenum Press, 1971).
31. Dewar, A.J., "Neurotoxicity," *Animals and Alternatives in Toxicity Testing,* M. Balls, R J. Riddell, and A.N. Worden (eds.) (New York: Academic Press, 1983).
32. Dezfulian, M., and Barlett, J.G., "Selective Isolation and Rapid Identification of *Clostridium botulinum;* Type A and Type B by Toxin Detection," *J. Clin. Microbiol.* 2:231-233, 1985.
33. Dixon, W.J., and Mood, A.M., "A Method of Obtaining and Analyzing Sensitivity Data," *J. Am. Stat. Assoc.* 43:109-126, 1948.
34. Doull, J., Klassen, C.D., and Amdur, M.O. (eds.) *Casserett and Doull's Toxicology: The Basic Science of Poisons* (New York: Macmillan Publishing Co., 2d ed., 1980).
35. Eakins, K.E., "Prostaglandins and the Eye," *Prostaglandins: Physiological, Pharmacological and Pathological Aspects,* S.M.M. Karim (ed.) (Baltimore, MD: University Park Press, 1976).
36. Enslein, K., Lander, T.R., Tomb, M.E., et al., *Benchmark Papers in Toxicology: Vol. 1, A Predictive Model for Estimating Rat Oral LD_{50} Values* (Princeton, NJ: Scientific Publishers, Inc., 1983).
37. Evans, H.J., and O'Riordan, M.L., "Human Peripheral Blood Lymphocytes for the Analysis of Chromosome Aberration in Mutagen Tests," *Handbook of Mutagenicity Test Procedures,* B.J. Kilbey, M. Legator, W. Nichols, et al. (eds.) (Amsterdam: Elsevier/North Holland, 1977).
38. Freeberg, F.E., Griffith, J.F., Bruce, R.D., et al., "Correlation of Animal Test Method With Human Experience for Household Products," *J. Toxicol.-Cut. Ocular Toxicol.* 1:53-64, 1984.
39. Fry, J.R., and Bridges, J.W., "The Metabolism of Xenobiotics in Cell Suspensions and Cell Cultures," *Progress in Drug Metabolism, Vol. 2,* J.W. Bridges

and L.F. Chasseand (eds.) (New York: John Wiley & Sons, 1977).

40. Fund for the Replacement of Animals in Medical Experiments, "Report of the FRAME Toxicity Committee," *Animals and Alternatives in Toxicity Testing,* M. Balls, R.J. Riddell, and A.N. Worden (eds.) (New York: Academic Press, 1983).
41. Goldberg, A.M., "Mechanisms of Neurotoxicity as Studied in Tissue Culture Systems," *Toxicology* 17:201-208, 1980.
42. Goldberg, A.M., Director, The Johns Hopkins Center for Alternatives to Animal Testing, Baltimore, MD, personal communication, 1985.
43. Griffith, J.F., Nixon, G.A., Bruce, R.D., et al., "Dose-Response Studies With Chemical Irritants in the Albino Rabbit Eye as a Basis for Selecting Optimum Testing Conditions for Predicting Hazard to the Human Eye," *Toxicol. Appl. Pharmacol.* 55:501-13, 1980.
44. Grisham, J.W., "Use of Hepatic Cell Cultures to Detect and Evaluate the Mechanisms of Action of Toxic Chemicals," *Int. Rev. Exp. Pathol.* 20:123-210, 1979.
45. Guy, R.H., and Fleming, R., "Transport Across a Phospholipid Barrier," *J. Colloid Interface Sci.* 83:130-137, 1981.
46. Hassid, A., and Levine, L., "Induction of Fatty Acid Cyclooxygenase Activity in Canine Kidney Cells (MDCK) by Benzo(a) Pyrene," *J. Biol. Chem.* 252: 6591-6593, 1977.
47. Healey, G.F., "Statistical Contributions to Experimental Design," *Animals and Alternatives in Toxicity Testing,* M. Balls, R.J. Riddell, and A.N. Worden (eds.) (New York: Academic Press, 1983).
48. Hertzfeld, H.R., and Myers, T.D., "Alternatives to Animal Use in Testing and Experimentation: Economic and Policy Considerations," contract report prepared for the Office of Technology Assessment, U.S. Congress, January 1985.
49. Hill, J., *Cautions Against the Immoderate Use of Snuff* (London: Baldwin and Jackson, 1761).
50. Huot, R., Fodart, J., Nardone, R., et al., "Differential Modulation of Human Chorionic Gonadotropin Secretion by Epidermal Growth Factor in Normal and Malignant Placental Cultures," *J. Clin. Endocrinol. Metab.* 53:1059-1063, 1981.
51. Johnson, A.W., "Use of Small Dosage and Corneal Anaesthetic for Eye Testing In Vivo," *Proceedings of the CTFA Ocular Safety Testing Workshop: In Vivo and In Vitro Approaches* (Washington, DC: Cosmetic, Toiletry, and Fragrance Association, 1980).
52. Johnson, H.J., Northup, S.J., Seagraves, P.A., et al., "Biocompatibility Test Procedures for Polymer Evaluation In Vitro: I. Comparative Test System Sensitivity," *J. Biomed. Mater. Res.* 17:571-586, 1983.
53. Johnson, H.J., Northup, S.J., Seagraves, P.A., et al., "Biocompatibility Test Procedures for Materials Evaluation In Vitro: II. Quantitative Methods of Toxicity Assessment," *J. Biomed. Mater. Res.* 19:489-508, 1985.
54. Kaufmann, J.J., Koski, W.S., Hariharan, P.C., et al., "Theoretical and Quantum Prediction of Toxic Effects," *Drug Metab. Rev.* 15:527-556, 1984.
55. King, L.A., and Moffatt, A.C., "Hypnotics and Sedatives: An Index of Fatal Toxicity," *Lancet* II:387-78, 1981.
56. Kligman, A.M., "Assessment of Mild Irritants," *Principles of Cosmetics for the Dermatologist,* P. Frost and S.N. Horwitz (eds.) (St Louis, MO: C.V. Mosby, 1982).
57. Knowles, B.B., Howe, C.C., and Aden, D.P., "Human Hepatocellular Carcinoma Cell Lines Secrete the Major Plasma Proteins and Hepatitis B Surface Antigen," *Science* 209:97-99, 1980.
58. Lave, L., Omenn, G., Hefferman, K., et al., "Model for Selecting Short Term Test of Carcinogenicity," *J. Am. Coll. Toxicol.* 2:125-130, 1983.
59. Leighton, J., Nassauer, J., and Tchao, R., "The Chick Embryo in Toxicology: An Alternative to the Rabbit Eye," *Food Chem. Toxicol.* 23:293-298, 1985.
60. Leighton, J., Nassauer, J., Tchao, R., et al., "Development of a Procedure Using the Chick Egg as an Alternative to the Draize Rabbit Test," *Product Safety Evaluation,* A.M. Goldberg (ed.) (New York: Mary Ann Liebert, Inc., 1983).
61. Lorke, D., "How Can We Save Animals in Toxicity Testing," *Progress Without Pain* (Lord Dowding Fund, National Anti-Vivisectionist Society, Ltd., London) 22: 1984.
62. MacMahon, B., and Pugh, T.F., *Epidemiology: Principles and Methods* (Boston, MA: Little, Brown & Co., 1970).
63. Marks, R., "Testing for Cutaneous Toxicity," *Animals and Alternatives in Toxicity Testing,* M. Balls, R.J. Riddell, and A.N. Worden (eds.) (New York: Academic Press, 1983).
64. Martin, Y.C., *Quantitative Drug Design: A Critical Introduction* (New York: Marcel Dekker, Inc., 1978).
65. Maurice, D., "Pain and Acute Toxicity Testing in the Eye," *Alternatives to the Draize Eye Test,* A. Goldberg (ed.) (New York: Mary Ann Liebert, Inc., 1985).
66. McCann, J., Choi, E., Yamasaki, E., et al., "Detection of Carcinogens as Mutagens in the *Salmonella*/ Microsome Tests: Assay of 300 Chemicals," *Proc. Natl. Acad. Sci.* USA 72:5135-5139, 1975.
67. McCulley, J.P., "Chairman's Summary," *Alterna-*

tives to the Draize Eye Test: Alternative Methodism Toxicology, Vol. 3, A. Goldberg (ed.) (New York: Mary Ann Liebert, Inc., 1985).

68. Miletich, D.J., Khan, A., Albrecht, R.F., et al., "Use of Heart Cell Cultures as a Tool for the Evaluation of Halothan Arrhythmia," *Toxicol. Appl. Pharmacol.* 70:181-187, 1983.
69. Molingengo, L., "The Curve Doses v. Survival Time in the Evaluation of Acute Toxicity," *J. Pharm. Pharmacol.* 31:343-344, 1979.
70. Morrison, J.K, Quinton, R.M., and Reinert, H., "The Purpose and Value of LD_{50} Determinations," *Modern Trends in Toxicology, Vol. I,* E. Boyland and R. Goulding (eds.) (London: Butterworths, 1968).
71. Muller, H., and Kley, H.P., "Retrospective Study of the Reliability of an Approximate LD_{50} Determined With a Small Number of Animals," *Arch. Toxicol.* 51:189-196, 1982.
72. Nardone, R.M., and Bradlaw, J., "Toxicity Testing With In Vitro Systems: 1. Ocular Tissue Culture," *J. Toxicol.-Cut. Ocular Toxicol.* 2:81-98, 1983.
73. Nardone, R.M., and Ouellette, L.A., "Scope of 'Alternatives': Overview of the State of the Art," contract report prepared for the Office of Technology Assessment, U.S. Congress, July 1984.
74. National Research Council, *Models for Biomedical Research: A New Perspective* (Washington, DC: National Academy Press, 1985).
75. Neal, R.A., President, Chemical Industry Institute of Toxicology, Research Triangle Park, NC, personal communication, June 1985.
76. Nelson, K.F., and Acosta, D., "Long-Term Maintenance and Induction of Cytochrome P-450 in Primary Cultures of Rat Hepatocytes," *Biochem. Pharmacol.* 31:2211-2214, 1982.
77. *New Scientist,* "Human Placenta Can Test Drug Safely," 1417:20, Aug. 16, 1984.
78. Northup, S.J., "Perspectives on Alternative Methods of Toxicological Testing," *J. Parenter. Sci. Technol.* 37:225-226, 1983.
79. Northup, S.J., "Mammalian Cell Culture Models," *Handbook of Biomaterials Evaluation,* A. Von Recum (ed.) (in press).
80. Organization for Economic Cooperation and Development, *Guidelines for Testing of Chemicals,* and addenda (Paris: 1981).
81. Paine, A.J., Hockin, L.J, and Allen, C.M., "Long Term Maintenance and Induction of Cytochrome P-450 in Rat Liver Cell Culture," *Biochem. Pharmacol.* 31:1175-1178, 1982.
82. Parry, J.M., Parry E.M., and Parrett, J.C., "Tumor Promoters Induce Mitotic Aneuploidy in Yeast," *Nature* 294:263-265, 1981.
83. Philips, L., Steinberg, M., Maibach, H.I., et al., "A Comparison of Rabbit and Human Skin Response to Certain Irritants," *Toxicol. Appl. Pharmacol.* 21:369-382, 1972.
84. Pomerat, C.M., and Leake, C.D., "Short Term Cultures for Drug Assays: General Considerations," *Ann. N.Y. Acad. Sci.* 58:1110-1128, 1954.
85. Pott, P., *Chirurgical Observations Relative to the Cataract, the Polypus of the Nose, the Cancer of the Scrotum, the Different Kinds of Ruptures, and the Mortification of the Toes and Feet* (London: Hawes, Clarke, and Collins, 1775).
86. Prasad, R., Shopsis, C., and Hochstadt, J., "Nutrient Transport in a Bovine Lens Epithelial Cell Line," *J. Cell Physiol.* 107:231-236, 1981.
87. Ramazzini, B., *Diseases of Workers,* 1700 (translation of the Latin text of 1713 by Wilmer Cage Wright) (Chicago: University of Chicago Press, 1940).
88. Rekker, R.F., "LD_{50} Values: Are They About to Become Predictable?" *TIPS* 383-384, October 1980.
89. Rose, S.L., and Jurs, P.C., "Computer Assisted Studies of Structure-Activity Relationships of N-nitroso Compounds Using Pattern Recognition," *J. Med. Chem.* 25:769-776, 1982.
90. Rowan, A.N., *Of Mice, Models, and Men: A Critical Evaluation of Animal Research* (Albany, NY: State University of New York Press, 1984).
91. Rowan, A.N., and Goldberg, A.M., "Perspectives on Alternative to Current Animal Testing Techniques in Preclinical Toxicology," *Ann. Rev. Pharmacol. Toxicol.* 25:225-247, 1985.
92. Sabourin, T.D., and Goss, L.B., *Study of Alternative Species for Biological Testing,* final report to the Energy Analysis and Environment Division of the Electric Power Research Institute, Battelle Laboratories, Columbus, OH, 1984.
93. Sabourin, T.D., Carlton, B.D., Faulk, R.T., et al. (Battelle Laboratories), "Animal Testing for Safety and Effectiveness," contract report prepared for the Office of Technology Assessment, U.S. Congress, 1985.
94. Schultz, E., and Fuchs, H., "A New Approach to Minimizing the Number of Animals Used in Acute Toxicity Testing and Optimizing the Information of Test Results," *Arch. Toxicol.* 51:197-220, 1982.
95. Sharpe, R., "Four Reasons Why a Rabbit Should Not Be Turned Into a Guinea Pig," *Progress Without Pain* (Lord Dowding Fund, National Anti-Vivisection Society, Ltd., London) 22: 1984.
96. Shopsis, C., Borenfreund, E., Walberg, J., et al., "In Vitro Cytotoxicity Assays as Potential Alternatives to the Draize Ocular Irritancy Test," *Alternative Methods in Toxicology: Alternative Approaches,* A.M. Goldberg (ed.) (New York: Mary Ann Leibert, Inc., 1984).
97. Simpson, J.M., Sowell, Z.L., Sarley, J.T., et al., "Ef-

fects of Implanted Medical Device Materials on Rat Peritoneal Macrophages," paper presented at 4th Annual Meeting of American College of Toxicologists, Washington, DC, Nov. 30-Dec. 2, 1983.

98. Simpson, J.M., Sowell, Z.L., Sarley, J.T., et al., "Cell Culture Methods for Detecting Immunotoxicity of Synthetic Polymers," paper presented at meeting of Society for Biomaterials, Washington, DC, Apr. 27-May 1, 1984.
99. Singer, G.M., Taylor, H.W., and Lijinsky, W., "Liposolubility as an Aspect of Nitrosamine Carcinogenicity-Quantitative Correlations and Qualitative Observations," *Chem. Biol. Interact.* 19:133-142, 1977.
100. Spira, H., "Coordinator's Report '83," Coalition to Abolish the LD_{50}, New York, June 1983.
101. Stark, D.M., and Shopsis, C., "Developing Alternative Assay Systems for Toxicity Testing," *Ann. N.Y. Acad. Sci.* 406:92-103, 1983.
102. Stark, D.M., Shopsis, C., Borenfreund, E., et al., "Alternative Approaches to the Draize Assay: Chemotaxis, Cytology, Differentiation, and Membrane Transport Studies," *Alternative Methods in Toxicology: Product Safety Evaluation,* A.M. Goldberg (ed.) (New York: Mary Ann Liebert, Inc., 1983).
103. Swanston, D.W., "Eye Irritancy Testing," *Animals and Alternatives in Toxicity Testing,* M. Balls, R. J. Riddell, and A.N. Worden (eds.) (New York: Academic Press, 1983).
104. Task Force of Past Presidents, "Animal Data in Hay and Evaluation," *Fund. Appl. Toxicol.* 2:101-107, 1982.
105. Tattersall, M.L., "Statistics and the LD_{50} Test," *Arch. Toxicol.* [suppl.] 5:267-270, 1982.
106. Thomas, D.J., "Liver Cells Used in Toxicity Tests," *The Johns Hopkins Center for Alternatives to Animal Testing,* 2(2):3, 1984.
107. Thompson, W.R., "Use of Moving Averages and Interpolation to Estimate Median-Effective Dose: I. Fundamental Formulas, Estimation of Error, and Relation to Other Methods," *Bacteriol. Rev.* 11:115-145, 1947.
108. Thurman, R.G., and Reinke, L.A., "The Isolated Perfused Liver: A Model to Define Biochemical Mechanisms of Chemical Toxicity," *Reviews in Biochemical Toxicology, Vol. 1,* E. Hodgson, J.R. Bend, and R.M. Philpot (eds.) (New York: Elsevier, 1979).
109. Tute, M.S., "Mathematical Modeling," *Animals and Alternatives in Toxicity Testing,* M. Balls, R.J. Riddell, and A.N. Worden (eds.) (New York: Academic Press, 1983).
110. Ulsamer, A.G., Wright, P.L., and Osterberg, R.E., "A Comparison of the Effects of Model Irritants on Anaesthetized and Nonanaesthetized Rabbits Eyes," *Toxicol. Appl. Pharmacol.* 41:191-192, 1977.
111. U.S. Congress, Congressional Research Service, *Cost Benefit Analysis in Federal Regulations: A Review and Analysis of Developments, 1978-1984,* Pub. No. 84-74E (Washington, DC: May 14, 1984).
112. U.S. Congress, Office of Technology Assessment, *Assessment of Technologies for Determining Cancer Risks From the Environment,* OTA-H-138 (Washington, DC: U.S. Government Printing Office, June 1981).
113. Vodra, W.W., "Paper NDAs and Real Problems," *Food Drug Cosmet. Law J.* 39:356-384, 1984.
114. Vogel, E., and Rama, C., "Mutagenesis Assays With *Drosophila,*" *Long-Term and Short-Term Screening Assays for Carcinogens: A Critical Appraisal* (Lyon, France: International Agency for Research on Cancer, 1980).
115. Vogel, E., and Sobels, F., "The Function of *Drosophila* in Genetic Toxicology Testing," *Chemical Mutagens: Principles and Methods for Their Detection, Vol. IV,* A. Hollander (ed.) (New York: Plenum Press, 1976).
116. Water, M., U.S. Environmental Protection Agency, Washington, DC, personal communication, 1984.
117. Weary, M., and Pearson, F., "Pyrogen Testing With Limulus Amebocyte Lysate," *Med. Device Diag. Ind.* 2(11):34-39, 1980.
118. Weil, C.S., and Scala, R.A., "Study of Intra- and Inter-laboratory Variability in the Results of Rabbit Eye and Skin Irritation Test," *Toxicol. Appl. Pharmacol.* 19:276-360, 1971.
119. Williams, S.F., "Prediction of Ocular Irritancy Potential From Dermal Irritation Test Results," *Food Chem. Toxicol.* 22:157-161, 1984.
120. Williams, S.J., Grapel, G.J., and Kennedy, G.L., "Evaluation of Ocular Irritancy Potential: Intralaboratory Variability and Effect of Dosage—Volume," *Toxicol. Lett.* 1:235-241, 1982.
121. Wishnok, J.S., Archer, M.C., Edelman, A.S., et al., "N-Nitrosamine Carcinogenicity—Quantitative Hansch-Taft Structure Activity Relationship," *Chem. Biol. Interact.* 20:43-54, 1978.
122. Wright, E.M., Marcell, K.L., and Woodson, J.F., "Animal Pain: Evaluation and Control," *Lab Anim.* 14(4):20-35, 1985.
123. Yuan, M. and Jurs, P.C., "Computer-Assisted Structure-Activity Studies of Chemical Carcinogens: A Polycyclic Aromatic Hydrocarbon Data Set," *Toxicol. Appl. Pharmacol.* 52:294-312, 1980.
124. Yuta, K., and Jurs, P.C., "Computer-Assisted Structure-Activity Studies of Chemical Carcinogens: Aromatic Amines," *J. Med. Chem.* 24:241, 1981.
125. Zbinden, G., *Progress in Toxicology* (Berlin: Springer-Verlag, 1973).
126. Zimmerman, F.K., "Mutagenicity Screening With Fungal Systems," *Ann. N.Y. Acad. Sci.* 407:186-196, 1983.

Chapter 9

Animal Use in Education and the Alternatives

Any experienced teacher of physiology knows that the "feeling" of a beating heart in the opened chest of a dog does more to reinforce the lessons about cardiac physiology than any words he can speak. This is not an argument for unlimited use of animals, but it is a recognition that biology is ultimately about living organisms and that learning about living organisms requires some experience with them.

Joel A. Michael
Rush-Presbyterian-St. Luke's Medical Center
March 4, 1985

Generations of surgeons and veterinary surgeons have been trained without practising on live animals and the Government intends future generations to do so as well.

Microsurgery will be the only *surgical skill which we at present contemplate permitting to be practised on living animals.*

Scientific Procedures on Living Animals, Command 9521
British Home Office
May 1985

CONTENTS

List of Tables

Figure

Chapter 9

Animal Use in Education and the Alternatives

Measured by the number of animals involved, the use of animals is far less significant in education than in research and testing. Yet few students emerge from the educational system without some contact with animals in the classroom—an interaction that may range from the observing and handling of small mammals in grade school to surgical training in medical school. In terms of fostering attitudes, education exerts a vital influence over the use of animals and the development and implementation of alternatives.

This chapter examines the patterns of animal use and the prospects for alternatives in primary, secondary, and college education and in the 127 accredited medical schools and the 27 accredited veterinary schools in the United States. Replacements, reductions, and refinements of animal use can today be found at all levels of education. Moreover, principles of humane treatment of animals are increasingly an integral part of curricula throughout the life sciences.

PATTERNS OF ANIMAL USE IN EDUCATION

Out of every 1,000 students entering the fifth grade, 285 will enter college and about 40 will obtain science degrees (21). Some of those 40 continue their education to become doctoral scientists and health professionals. As students journey from elementary school through high school and then perhaps on to college, universities, and other postgraduate programs, their educational exposure to animals takes many forms. The elements of the scientific method and scientific principles pervade every curriculum. In at least 21 States, some type of instruction in the value of animals and humane considerations is required. Acquaintance with animals instills a respect for and appreciation of life and conveys as well the fundamental principles of biology.

Three distinct educational goals dictate ways in which animals are used in the classroom:

- Development of positive attitudes toward animals. In the best instances, such development incorporates ethical and moral considerations into students' course of study.
- Introduction of the concept of "biological models," by which students learn to single out particular animal species as representative of biological phenomena. Such models vary in the degree to which they provide general information about a broader spectrum of life.
- Exercise of skills vital to intellectual, motor, or career development. Familiarity with living tissue, for example, enhances a student's surgical dexterity.

Alternatives to using animals in education therefore must satisfy these goals. In addition, the educational use of animals and alternatives can foster positive attitudes toward alternatives in research, testing, and education, which may in turn perpetuate the search for such options as these students themselves become scientists. The sum total of the educational use of animals and alternatives can be to reinforce as the guiding principle of the scientific method the judicious selection of the most appropriate system to generate the desired knowledge.

Primary and Secondary Education

Animals in the Classroom

Most students become initially acquainted with animals and their role in the biological sciences during primary and secondary education. In primary schools, animals are generally not subject to experimentation or invasive procedures of any sort. They are usually present in the classroom to teach students about care and to observe the social interactions of people and other animals.

Such interactions provide the vehicle for developing humane attitudes toward animals. In junior high and high school, students begin a more aggressive pursuit of science, which is reflected in the patterns of animal use. Dissections and investigational laboratory exercises are introduced into the curriculum. For most students, high school provides their last formal science education, in the form of biology class.

A recent study identified three stages in the development of students' attitudes about animals (6). The period from 2d to 5th grade (ages 6 to 10) was characterized by an increase in emotional concern about and affection for animals. The years between 5th and 8th grades (10 to 13 years of age) were marked by increased factual understanding and knowledge of animals. From 8th to 11th grade (ages 13 to 16), students exhibited broadening ethical concern about and ecological appreciation of animals.

Each phase of primary and secondary education appears to offer varying opportunities for education about animals. The 8th through 11th grades seem to be the most appropriate times for exercising meaningful influence on the development of attitudes toward animals (6).

Several national organizations and local school systems have issued specific policy statements on the use of animals; these suggest the practices both permitted and prohibited in the classroom at the secondary level (see table 9-1). All the policy documents generated by national groups share one distinct limitation: They have neither the power nor the mechanisms to enforce their provisions. They are merely guides and statements, not rules.

Science Fairs

Active involvement in the day-to-day aspects of science and the scientific method is not a usual component of primary and secondary science education. Science fairs provide an opportunity for some students to enhance their understanding of science by pursuing independent investigations and competing with their peers in various local,

Table 9-1.—Sample Policies Governing Animal Use in Primary and Secondary Schools

Group	Year last revised	Description of policy
Connecticut State Board of Education	1968	Policy urges that no vertebrate animal should be subjected to any procedure that interferes with its normal health or causes it pain or distress. No experiment should be carried out without the personal direction of an individual trained and experienced in approved techniques for such animals.
Alexandria (VA) City Public Schools	1969	No vertebrate animal used for secondary school teaching may be subjected to any experiment or procedure that interferes with its normal health or causes it pain or distress. Dissections are not banned; however, they are to be done only with commercially prepared specimens.
Canadian Council on Animal Care	1975	Guiding principles apply to animal use in the classroom, not to science fairs. No experimental procedures are permitted on vertebrates that subject them to pain or discomfort or that interfere with the organism's health.
National Association of Biology Teachers	1980	Guidelines for the use of live vertebrates at the pre-university level apply to classrooms as well as school-related activities. No experimental procedures should be attempted that would subject the animals to pain or distinct discomfort. No experimental studies should be done outside the school. No live vertebrates are permitted in science fair exhibits. Exemptions to these guidelines may be granted under limited conditions that include direct supervision by a qualified research scientist in the field, an appropriate facility designed for such projects, and the utmost regard for the humane care and treatment of the animals involved in the project.
National Science Teachers Association	1981	Code of practice applies to the use of vertebrates in schools or school-related activities. Experimental procedures conducted should include only those that do not involve pain or discomfort to the animal. Extracurricular protocols should be reviewed in advance of the start of the work by a qualified adult supervisor, and should preferably be conducted in a suitable area in the school. This code has been endorsed by the National Academy of Sciences and the American Veterinary Medical Association.

SOURCES: Connecticut State Board of Education, *State Board Policy on Animals in the School*, Feb. 7, 1968. Alexandria City Public Schools, Policy File 3107, Jan. 6, 1969. Canadian Council on Animal Care (Ottawa), *Guiding Principles Governing the Use of Animals in the Classroom at the Pre-University Levels*, May 1975. "National Association of Biology Teachers Guidelines for the Use of Live Animals at the Pre-University Level," *American Biology Teacher* 41:426, 1980. National Science Teachers Association, *Code of Practice on Animals in Schools*, Washington, DC, 1981.

State, and national competitions. The fairs stimulate an interest in science, and they reward active involvement. Many scientists have taken the first steps in their career paths by this route. The competitive nature of the fairs encourages budding scientists to stretch their skills to often sophisticated levels of investigation.

The National Science Teachers Association's *Code of Practice on Animals in Schools* (see table 9-1) applies to science fairs as well as animal use in the classroom and prohibits experimental procedures that would involve pain or discomfort to the animal (10). This code governs both projects conducted by students at schools that adhere to the policy, and science fairs that have adopted the standards. Several of the most prominent fairs have adopted other rules in addition.

The International Science and Engineering Fair (ISEF) is held annually with several hundred entrants in grades 9 through 12, drawn from many thousands of participants in local fairs. ISEF rules require that a Scientific Review Committee consider all research involving vertebrate animals prior to competition. Criteria include a completed research plan, evidence of a literature search, documentation of the type and amount of supervision, use of accepted techniques, demonstrated skill in such techniques, and compliance with any required certifications.

ISEF explicitly disallows procedures that would develop new surgical techniques or would refine existing ones, as well as research where the animal is not humanely killed (4). Surgical procedures may not be done at home. Sacrifices of animals and experiments involving anesthetics, drugs, thermal procedures, physical stress, pathogens, ionizing radiation, carcinogens, or surgical procedures must be done under the direct supervision of an experienced and qualified scientist or designated adult supervisor. Nutritional deficiency studies and studies of toxic effects may only proceed to the point where the symptoms appear. Steps must then be taken to correct the deficiency, or the animals are to be humanely killed. LD_{50} experiments (see chs. 7 and 8) are not permitted.

The Westinghouse Science Talent Search, an annual competition involving more than 15,000 participants, has since 1970 forbidden experimentation with live vertebrates with the exception of projects involving behavioral observations of animals in their natural habitat or of human subjects (17). In 1985, none of the 39 Westinghouse finalists carried out experiments on nonhuman vertebrate animals. One entrant studied gene expression in cultured mammalian cells. Living organisms used in the winning projects included leeches, butterflies, fruit flies, water fleas, and bacteria.

Finalist, 1985 Westinghouse Science Talent Search

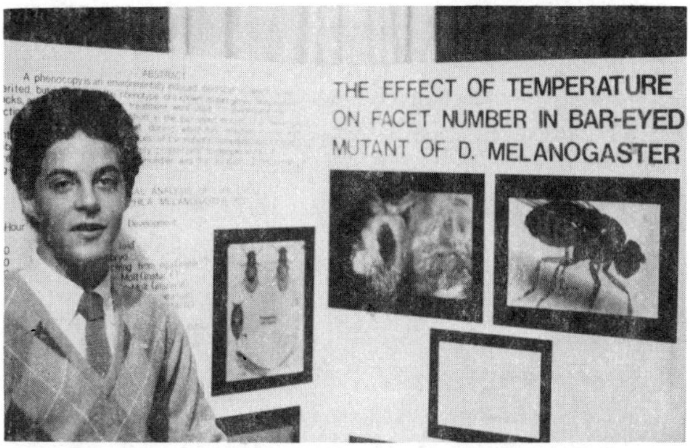

Photo credit: Gary B. Ellis

Louis C. Paul, age 18, Baldwin Senior High School, Baldwin, NY, with his research project, "Effect of Temperature on Facet Number in the Bar-Eyed Mutant of *Drosophila melanogaster.*"

In Canada, all animal experimentation for science fairs is subject to *Regulations for Animal Experimentation in Science Fairs,* the 1975 policy statement of the Youth Science Foundation of Ottawa, Ontario. Key provisions include:

- Vertebrate animals are not to be used except for observation of normal living patterns of: 1) wild animals in the free-living state or in zoos, aquaria, or gardens; or 2) pets, fish, or domestic animals.
- No living vertebrate animal shall be displayed in exhibits in science fairs.

Other rules include:

- Chick embryos may be used for observational studies only.
- If eggs are to be hatched, then humane considerations must be met in the disposal of the chicks.

- If humane requirements cannot be met, embryos must be destroyed by the 19th day of incubation.
- No eggs capable of hatching may be exhibited at science fairs.
- All experiments shall be carried out under the supervision of a competent science teacher.

Enforcement mechanisms for these restrictions specify that students sign a declaration of compliance, and that this compliance be certified by the science teacher supervising the project.

Animal Use at the Postsecondary Level

Animals are used in undergraduate education for both the acquisition of knowledge and the acquisition of particular skills. Procedures involving animals can, of course, serve both purposes. Graduate science education (and, in some instances, advanced undergraduate education) involves an additional component—the student's first genuine research experience. The distinction between teaching and research virtually disappears in graduate school because the student simultaneously learns the methods and actually conducts research. The guidelines that dictate practices of animal use in graduate education are those that govern animal use in research (see ch. 15). Effects of earlier exposure to humane concerns may manifest themselves in graduate education through the student's choice of avenues of research and selection of model systems for investigation.

Because attitudes about animals will almost certainly affect the ways in which students may use (or not use) animals in education and, later, professionally, it is noteworthy that U.S. colleges and universities offer about two dozen full-length courses on ethics and animals, according to a 1983 survey (see table 9-2). These courses cover the bioethical issues surrounding humans' responsibilities regarding laboratory, agricultural, and wildlife animals. The Scientists Center for Animal Welfare maintains information on college courses on ethics and animals and advocates the inclusion of such courses as a standard component of the education of all students entering careers in the biological sciences (18). At virtually all veterinary schools, lecture material on ethical considerations of working with animals is included in required courses as part of the veterinary curriculum.

Determining the number of animals used strictly for undergraduate and graduate education is difficult because laboratory education is often mixed with laboratory research. This is especially true for graduate education. The last survey of animal use that included questions regarding animals used for teaching purposes was done for fiscal year 1978 by the National Academy of Sciences/National Research Council's Institute of Laboratory Animal Resources (ILAR) under contract to the National Institutes of Health (23). Respondents that used animals for educational purposes included 69 medical schools, 10 veterinary schools, 42 additional health professional schools (e.g., dental, public health), 65 hospitals, and 149 colleges and univer-

BLOOM COUNTY by Berke Breathed

Reprinted with permission. © 1985 Washington Post Writers Group.

Table 9-2.—Courses on Ethics and Animals Offered at U.S. Colleges and Universities, 1983-84

Institution	Course name (department and course number)
Appalachian State University	People, Plants, and Animals (Philosophy 3560)
California State University	Animal Rights (Philosophy 1941; General Studies 4279)
Central Michigan State University	Religion and Social Issues (Religion 335)
Colorado State University	Attributes of Living Systems (Biology 102; Honors)
	Moral and Conceptual Issues in Veterinary Medicine (Veterinary Medicine 712)
Eastern Michigan State University	Introduction to Philosophy (Philosophy 100)
Elmira College	Mankind? We and Other Animals (Humanities 0530)
Indiana University-Purdue University	Ethics and Animals (Philosophy 493)
Michigan State University	Ethics and Animals (Philosophy 494)
	Perspective in Veterinary Medicine (Veterinary Medicine 517)
Moorhead State University	Animal Rights (Philosophy 215)
North Carolina State University	Philosophical Issues in Environmental Ethics (Philosophy 332)
Purdue University	Ethics and Animals (Philosophy 280)
Stanford University	Animal Rights: Issues and Politics (Stanford Workshop on Political and Social Issues Program 161)
State University of New York at Stony Brook	Human/Pet Bonds (Psychology 391)
University of Connecticut	Problems in Environmental Law: Issues in Animal Rights and Protection (Law 852)
University of Maryland	Philosophy and Environmental Ethics (Philosophy 0255)
University of Minnesota	Perspectives: Animal-Human Relationships and Community Health (Public Health 5-303)
Virginia Polytechnic Institute	Special Study, Ethics, and the Treatment of Animals (Philosophy 2980)
Wagner College	Bioethics (Biology 230)
Washington State University	Reverence for Life (Veterinary Anatomy, Physiology, and Pharmacology 499)

SOURCE: Scientists Center for Animal Welfare (Bethesda, MD), "College Course on Ethics and Animals," *Newsletter* 5(2):3-6, 1983.

sities. Some of the health professional schools were included in other categories (e.g., universities with affiliated professional schools) and thus accounted for a smaller number of such schools identified separately than expected.

For this assessment, animal use in medical education and veterinary education was examined in detail for the school year 1983-84. Comparisons with the 1978 ILAR survey are inappropriate because of different survey methodology.

Medical Education

Animals are used in many capacities in medical education. In the basic sciences, they are often used to illustrate the structure and function of the systems under study and the complex physiologic interactions within a single organism. They function as intermediaries during a medical student's transition from trainee to practicing physician, letting students cultivate their skills on other living creatures before they actually apply those same techniques to human patients. Techniques such as venipuncture, insertion of catheters, and other procedure-oriented exercises are those cited by medical educators as needing practice before patients are worked with. The need to practice invasive surgical procedures prior to human surgery is probably the most compelling use of animals by medical students.

It is generally held that doctors must learn the techniques of their profession. And most commentators acknowledge the need for students in the health professions to subject animals to some practice surgery, albeit closely regulated (17). The issue of animal use in medical education thus seems more a question of degree and manner of use rather than one of whether or not animals should be used at all.

Yet, practicing techniques on animals is not universally condoned. In the United Kingdom, live animals cannot be used by students practicing ordinary surgery solely to improve manual dexterity and technique. (This does not necessarily mean that medical and veterinary students do not improve their techniques by using live animals, but such activities must have some other purpose.) Physicians are trained by a process similar to apprenticeship, learning by observation, demonstration, and example. They assist an accomplished surgeon and expand their active role only as their abilities increase.

In 1985, the British Government relaxed its stricture in order to allow animal use in microsurgical training (22):

> Generations of surgeons and veterinary surgeons have been trained without practising on live animals and the Government intends future generations to do so as well. But the new development of microsurgery—which is surgery performed with miniature instruments under a microscope, for example, to repair blood vessels or nerves—presents special problems. The delicate techniques involved cannot be practised satisfactorily on dead subjects. Surgeons at present have to go abroad or practise on decerebrate animals which for this purpose is technically complicated and sometimes more wasteful of animals than using terminally anaesthetised ones. Microsurgery will be the *only* surgical skill which we at present contemplate permitting to be practised on living animals. The consent of the Secretary of State will be required in every case, and he will only give it to qualified surgeons working on approved microsurgical courses on rodents which are anaesthetised throughout the procedure and killed before the animal can recover consciousness.

In general, adequate training through staged exercises is regarded as a prerequisite for successful microsurgery (11).

To ascertain patterns of animal use in medical education during the school year 1983-84, the Association of American Medical Colleges (AAMC) surveyed 16 of the 127 accredited medical schools in the United States. The 16 schools surveyed were selected in an effort to achieve balance in three characteristics: ownership (10 public and 6 private); geographical region (4 each in the Northeast, Midwest, South, and West); and research expenditures (5 high, 5 medium, and 6 low) (2).

The AAMC distributed questionnaires to each department in the sample schools and followed up with telephone calls. Because differing curricula made analysis by department problematic, queries were oriented to each of the disciplines known to be present in undergraduate and graduate medical education. Anatomy, for example, is taught by the surgery department in some schools, but animal use in these exercises was still recorded in the discipline of anatomy (2).

Anatomy, biochemistry, microbiology, pathology, pharmacology, and physiology are part of the curriculum leading to the M.D. degree everywhere, and data for these disciplines were obtained from all 16 schools. The data for all other disciplines except family medicine and advanced trauma life support were obtained from at least 15 of the 16 schools surveyed. Family medicine is offered at only 10 of the 16 institutions (all responded). Advanced trauma life support, a course for house staff rather than medical students, is offered at only 7 of the 16 institutions (all responded) (2).

The use of animals was common in only a few disciplines (see table 9-3), although all 16 institutions used animals in some discipline. Animal use in medical education was most common in physiology (10 of 16 schools), surgery (10 of 16), and pharmacology (8 of 16). In other disciplines, no more than 7 of the 16 medical schools used animals for educational purposes. Advanced trauma life support involved animal use at all 7 schools where it was offered (2).

Table 9-3.—Instructional Use of Animals in 16 Selected U.S. Medical Schools, by Discipline, 1983-84

Discipline	Number of schools with discipline	Use animals	Do not use animals	No response
Advanced trauma life support	7	7	0	0
Anatomy	16	2	14	0
Anesthesiology	16	2	14	0
Biochemistry	16	3	13	0
Dermatology	16	0	15	1
Family medicine	10	0	10	0
Internal medicine	16	1	14	1
Microbiology	16	4	12	0
Neurology	16	0	16	0
Neurosurgery	16	5	11	0
Obstetrics and gynecology	16	1	14	1
Ophthalmology	16	3	13	0
Otolaryngology	16	2	14	0
Pathology	16	0	16	0
Pediatrics	16	3	12	1
Pharmacology	16	8	8	0
Physiology	16	10	6	0
Psychiatry	16	1	15	0
Radiology	16	0	16	0
Surgery	16	10	6	0
Surgery, orthopedic	16	4	12	0
Urology	16	1	15	0

SOURCE: Association of American Medical Colleges, *Use of Animals in Undergraduate and Graduate Medical Education* (Washington, DC: 1985).

Table 9-4 shows the numbers of animals used by the 16 medical schools. The principal species used by those surveyed were rats, dogs, and mice. Most animals (84 percent) were sacrificed either before or at the end of the demonstration or laboratory, but over half the cats and all the sheep were allowed to recover. Anesthesiology, psychiatry, and biochemistry were the disciplines most likely to subject animals to multiple recovery procedures. According to this survey, only slightly more than 10 percent of the animals used in surgery are allowed to recover at all (2).

The majority of animals used in the 16 schools surveyed were used in the teaching of surgery (51 percent) and physiology (16 percent). No other single discipline accounts for even 10 percent of all animals used. Most of the dogs (64 percent) were used in the teaching of surgery and physiology. The total of 7,274 animals can be placed in context by noting the number of students taking part in the laboratory exercises and demonstrations—approximately 7,900 medical students and 6,700 residents, for a total of approximately 14,600 students at both levels. Calculating roughly from this, approximately one animal is sacrificed each year to support the training of two students (2).

The purposes for which animals are used vary, even within a discipline. Several general surgery and surgical specialty departments offer their residents a course in microsurgery. Residents learn microvascular suture techniques that they will later apply in human surgery designed to restore circulation. Nearly all small-animal use (i.e., rats, hamsters, and rabbits) is for such microsurgery training. Some general surgery departments offer their residents training in major surgery (e.g., splenectomy) using dogs, cats, or pigs, with the goal of recovery of animals. Ophthalmology departments use rabbits to teach new residents the fundamentals of microsurgery of the eye (2).

Table 9-4.—Animals Used in Laboratory Exercises and Demonstrations in Medical Education in 16 Selected U.S. Medical Schools, 1983-84

	Kind of animal										
Discipline	Primate	Dog	Cat	Pig	Rabbit	Rat	Mouse	Guinea pig	Hamster	Other[a]	Total
Advanced trauma life support	—	39	13	10	—	—	—	—	—	—	62
Anatomy	—	—	—	—	—	75	—	—	—	—	75
Anesthesiology	—	6	1	—	—	—	—	—	—	—	7
Biochemistry	—	7	—	—	—	—	40	—	—	—	47
Dermatology	—	—	—	—	—	—	—	—	—	—	0
Family medicine	—	—	—	—	—	—	—	—	—	—	0
Internal medicine	—	115	—	—	—	—	—	—	—	—	115
Microbiology	—	—	—	—	2	—	12	9	3	—	26
Neurology	—	—	—	—	—	—	—	—	—	—	0
Neurosurgery	—	12	—	—	6	100	—	—	—	—	118
Obstetrics and gynecology	—	52	—	—	—	—	—	—	—	—	52
Ophthalmology	4	—	20	—	122	—	—	—	—	—	146
Otolaryngology	—	5	1	—	—	5	9	—	—	—	20
Pathology	—	—	—	—	—	—	—	—	—	—	0
Pediatrics	—	—	14	—	4	—	—	—	—	—	18
Pharmacology	—	44	50	—	—	264	300	—	—	—	658
Physiology	—	490	—	—	2	294	—	—	80	327	1,193
Psychiatry	—	—	—	—	—	—	—	—	—	4	4
Radiology	—	—	—	—	—	—	—	—	—	—	0
Surgery	10	612	151	54	113	1,689	930	27	130	—	3,716
Surgery, orthopedic	—	—	—	—	113	279	20	—	—	1	413
Urology	—	20	—	—	—	—	—	—	20	—	40
Miscellaneous/basic sciences	—	365	16	—	16	72	—	—	—	72	541
Other	—	4	13	—	—	—	6	—	—	—	23
Total	14	1,771	279	64	378	2,778	1,317	36	233	404	7,274

[a]Includes frogs, sheep, and pigeons.

SOURCE: Association of American Medical Colleges, *Use of Animals in Undergraduate and Graduate Medical Education* (Washington, DC: 1985).

Dogs and pigs are used to teach techniques for intubation (establishing an emergency airway) and the installation of intravenous/intra-arterial catheters. In the AAMC survey, one anesthesia department used dogs to teach insertion of Swan-Ganz catheters into the right chamber of the heart, a common procedure in cardiac intensive care units. Two otolaryngology departments used dogs to teach the musculature and innervation of the trachea and oropharynx to ear, nose, and throat residents. One obstetrics and gynecology department used dogs as models to teach exposure and isolation of the Fallopian tubes from the nearby ureters, and three pediatrics departments use young cats as models for instruction in intubation of premature newborn babies. All of the techniques taught in these graduate medical programs must be learned to achieve competence in the desired specialty. In those programs that do not use animals, the techniques are mastered through experience with human patients during surgery (2).

The AAMC survey found no relation between a medical school's level of research expenditures (high, medium, or low) and its use of animals in education. The medium-expenditure schools used the most animals in education, perhaps because in the more research-intensive schools there is a greater opportunity for students to observe animal surgery in the course of participation in faculty research and less need to include such experience in the curriculum. Most of the schools surveyed expressed regret that they were not able to use animals to a greater extent in student instruction, often citing cost as a factor limiting instruction with live animals (2).

National estimates of the numbers of animals used in medical education (see table 9-5) were calculated based on the assumptions that the 16 schools surveyed are typical of the 127 accredited schools in the United States. The mean number of animals of each species used in the sample schools was accepted as the best estimate of the mean for all schools, and an extrapolation was made to 127 schools (2).

Rats and dogs are the principal species used in medical education, accounting for about 70 percent of the estimated 36,700 animals used annually. These figures are very rough—the potential error inherent in the estimates ranges from 22 and 25 percent for rats and dogs to 100 percent for pigs and hamsters. The great uncertainty stems from variability among the 16 institutions in the sample. One school used 10 primates, for example, while another used 4, and 14 schools used none at all. Use of dogs and cats was more general; less uncertainty is associated with the national estimates of those species' use (2).

It is unlikely that any of the 127 medical schools in the United States train physicians without using any live animals. This is neither surprising nor alarming, particularly in light of the fact that the ultimate recipients of medical attention—humans—are not available for many of the types of educa-

Instruction in Intubation of Premature Newborn Babies, Using a Young Cat as a Model

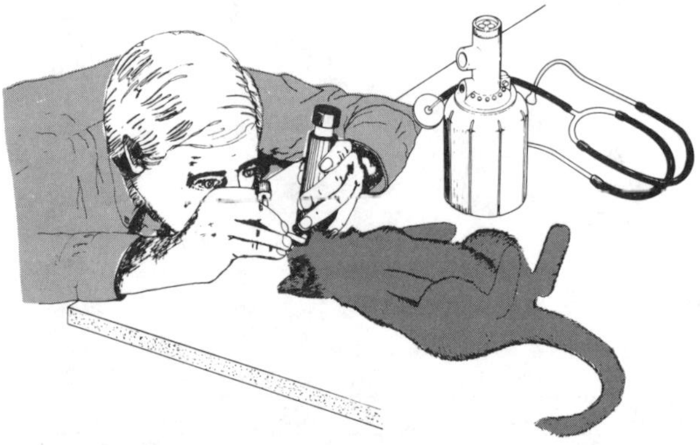

Redrawn by: Office of Technology Assessment.

Table 9-5.—Estimated Animal Use in Medical Education in the United States, 1983-84

Kind of animal	Number used[a]
Rat	14,000
Dog	12,000
Mouse	3,000
Rabbit	1,700
Cat	800
Hamster	800
Pig	200
Primate	130
Guinea pig	70
Other[b]	4,000
Total	36,700

[a]Estimate is based on an extrapolation of a survey of 16 selected medical schools evenly distributed by geographic region (Northeast, Midwest, South, or West), ownership (public or private), and research expenditures (low, medium, or high).
[b]Includes frogs, sheep, and pigeons.

SOURCE: Association of American Medical Colleges, *Use of Animals in Undergraduate and Graduate Medical Education* (Washington, DC: 1985).

tional exercises that medical students routinely must perform. It should be noted, however, that it is possible for a student to complete medical school without using animals.

Veterinary Education

> Being admitted to the profession of veterinary medicine, I solemnly swear to use my scientific knowledge and skills for the benefit of society through the protection of animal health, the relief of animal suffering, the conservation of livestock resources, the promotion of public health, and the advancement of medical knowledge.
>
> I will practice my profession conscientiously, with dignity, and in keeping with the principles of veterinary medical ethics.
>
> I accept as a lifelong obligation the continual improvements of my professional knowledge and competence.
>
> *The Veterinarian's Oath*
> American Veterinary Medical Association

Twenty-seven accredited veterinary schools in the United States educate and train veterinary scientists and veterinarians in the basic biomedical sciences and comparative animal health. An OTA survey of the 27 schools indicated that every veterinary school uses animals in its curriculum. As in medical education, the question of the use of animals in veterinary education is a matter of degree and practice.

Veterinary students—unlike medical students—train on models identical to their prospective patients. Animals are used in laboratory exercises and demonstrations, and students have the additional opportunity to interact with clinical cases owned by their schools as well as those brought in by clients. Privately owned pets, domestic livestock, and zoo animals all serve as resources for the clinical education of veterinary students.

Most animal use occurs in the third year of the curriculum, when surgical training takes place, using principally dogs and sheep. In earlier basic science courses, anatomy involves dissection of cadavers with live animals present in the lab for comparison, and physiology exercises involve the observation of live animals. The fourth year of veterinary studies is largely clinical apprenticeship.

With cooperation from the Association of American Veterinary Medical Colleges, OTA conducted a census of animal use in veterinary education in the 27 accredited veterinary schools in the United States for the school year 1983-84. The survey counted only those animals that began an exercise alive and either died or were subjected to euthanasia during the course of the laboratory session or demonstration. Cadavers or animals subjected to euthanasia prior to educational use were not counted, and clinical patients were not counted.

Of 16,655 animals used in 1983-84, half (8,020) were dogs. Mice, rats, and birds accounted for the bulk of the remaining animals (see table 9-6). No primates were killed during or after educational exercises in veterinary schools.

Laboratory-Animal Training

Technicians with specialized training in public health and animal care are needed at all levels by public health organizations, research institutions, pharmaceutical manufacturers, and universities. During the 1970s, several 2-year training programs were developed in response to an increasing need for personnel formally qualified to assist in pri-

Table 9-6.—Animals Used in Veterinary Education in the United States, 1983-84

Kind of animal	Number used[a]
Dog	8,020
Mouse	2,180
Rat	2,083
Bird	1,323
Reptile	433
Sheep	423
Cat	414
Horse	378
Rabbit	195
Goat	194
Pig	140
Guinea pig	112
Cow	111
Hamster	71
Other[b]	578
Total	16,655

[a]This census of all 27 U.S. veterinary schools does not include privately owned or pet animals used for clinical demonstrations, animals purchased as cadavers, or those subjected to euthanasia prior to the laboratory exercise. It includes only those animals that began the course alive and then either died or were subjected to euthanasia during the course of the laboratory session.
[b]Includes fish, frogs, and exotic species.

SOURCE: Office of Technology Assessment.

vate veterinary practices, biological laboratories, animal research, food inspection, and other areas requiring expertise in both science and animal care and use.

Graduates of these programs are generally referred to as animal technicians. The terminology may vary slightly among different schools or with individual State laws and regulations. Many employees of animal care and research and testing facilities have received training on the job, in secondary schools, or at less than the 2-year college level. These individuals are commonly referred to as animal attendants, animal caretakers, or animal health assistants. Two other types of animal-support personnel are laboratory-animal technicians (whose training has been oriented primarily toward laboratory animals) and animal technologists (who have had training in a 4-year baccalaureate degree program).

Most accredited animal technician programs cover 2 academic years of college-level study and lead to an Associate in Applied Science degree or its equivalent. The core curriculum usually includes animal husbandry, animal care and management, animal diseases and nursing, anesthetic monitoring and nursing, ethics and jurisprudence, veterinary anatomy and physiology, medical terminology, animal nutrition and feeding, necropsy techniques, radiography, veterinary urinalysis, veterinary parasitology, and animal microbiology and sanitation (1).

Many States require animal technicians to be registered or certified. The Laboratory Animal Technician Certification Board sponsored by the American Association of Laboratory Animal Science provides examinations and registry for technicians who are eligible and employed in laboratory-animal facilities.

In addition to increasing interest in laboratory-animal technician degree programs, a number of graduating veterinary students have begun to seek additional training and certification in laboratory-animal medicine. To date, about 700 full-time veterinarians are certified in this field nationwide (see ch. 15). As more laboratory-animal technicians are trained and as the number of veterinarians specializing in laboratory-animal medicine increases, the resulting base of skills and knowledge will likely improve animal care in the laboratory.

THE ALTERNATIVES

Finding alternatives to the use of animals in education is a complex challenge. Alternatives must satisfy the demands of science education, teaching both the scientific method and the fundamental skills and techniques necessary to carry out scientific investigation. Yet science education does more—as it trains aspiring students, it establishes a framework of values and molds attitudes that will long influence their work. Therefore, exposure to alternatives, particularly the concepts underlying animal use and alternative methods, strongly influences the paths investigators choose to follow in the future. Viewed from this perspective, the acceptance (or rejection) of a specific alternative method in education assumes an importance that is, in fact, secondary to the impact it may have on the development of a student's overall attitude toward animal use in research, testing, or education.

Implementing alternative technologies and methods in education does not necessarily mean banishing animals from the classroom or laboratory. As in research (see ch. 6) and testing (see ch. 8), certain techniques are available that allow for the continued, but modified, use of animals, the use of living systems, the use of nonliving systems, and the use of computers. In education, computer simulation stands as a particularly promising alternative.

Continued, But Modified, Use of Animals in Education

Demonstrations

In contrast to animal experimentation in research and testing, animal use in the educational laboratory is unlikely to result in novel findings.

In education, a traditional laboratory exercise with a well-known outcome is usually repeated by a new student or group of students. The process of self-discovery and training is generally of greater importance than the specific data being collected. Under these circumstances, live demonstrations can often provide experiences that combine the best of direct student participation in animal laboratories with a reduction in animal use. Such exercises, when carried out by practiced professional instructors, avoid clumsy errors that students may make at the expense of laboratory animals. They also provide a convenient intermediate in the constant tension between active student participation in the laboratory and the limitations imposed by large class sizes.

In a variation on the laboratory demonstration, students may work together in groups on a single animal, again using fewer animals than if each student worked alone on a single animal. Exercises based on animal cells, tissues, or organs may be coordinated such that the minimum number of animals required can be sacrificed. Or animals may be subjected to multiple procedures, although if these involve sequential survival surgeries the advantage of reducing the number of animals used stands in conflict with the undesirability of repeated insults imposed on a surviving animal.

Noninvasive Procedures

Observation can give rise to an appreciation of the diversity of the animal kingdom in general and important principles of physiology and behavior in particular. A sense of responsibility and an understanding of the life processes of animals are also conveyed when animals are maintained for observation in the laboratory. Areas for study in which animals can be used in a noninvasive manner include:

- simple Mendelian genetics (e.g., the inheritance of coat color in successive generations of small rodents);
- reproductive behavior (e.g., behavioral receptivity of a female during estrus);
- normal physiological processes of maturity, aging, and death (e.g., the relationship between aging and body weight);
- disease processes (e.g., the incidence of spontaneous tumor growth in a population);
- biological rhythms (e.g., nocturnal and diurnal feeding and drinking patterns); and
- social interactions (e.g., territoriality and dominance relationships among males).

Reduction in Pain

Reduction in pain and distress may be accomplished with the use of anesthetics, analgesics, and tranquilizers. In education, this is of primary importance in surgical training, when animals are anesthetized, operated on, and then subjected to euthanasia. Principles of pain and pain relief—common to research, testing, and education—are discussed in chapters 5, 6, and 8.

Substitution of Species

The substitution of nonmammalian for mammalian species, of cold-blooded vertebrates for warm-blooded ones, or of nonpet species for companion animals is occasionally possible in education. Swine have replaced dogs in one surgical teaching and research laboratory (20). The pigs were especially successful replacements in a basic operative surgery course offered as an elective to medical students. The principal advantages cited were closely shared anatomic and physiologic characteristics with humans, better health than dogs, and economic factors.

Use of Other Living Systems in Education

Invertebrates

The use of invertebrates as an alternative is already widespread in primary and secondary schools. Most laboratory manuals include common exercises that teach biological principles and introduce students to the scientific method of inquiry using organisms such as hydra, planaria (flatworms), annelids (earthworms), mollusks, and a variety of arthropods (e.g., insects and crustaceans). The use of invertebrates at the college and graduate levels may also increase as more is known about them. These deceptively simple systems are valuable resources for the laboratory investigation of sophisticated biological principles.

In Vitro Methods

Like the use of invertebrates, in vitro manipulation and maintenance of animal components such as cells, tissues, or organs (see chs. 6 and 8) can illustrate many biological principles. The incorporation of in vitro techniques into students' education and training also bears potential for shaping their later attitudes about the utility of in vitro methods. The stimulus provided by in vitro laboratory exercises can therefore ultimately alter the general course of research and testing.

One noteworthy endeavor in training researchers in in-vitro methods is the program of the Center for Advanced Training in Cell and Molecular Biology at Catholic University of America in Washington, DC. With funding from the American Fund for Alternatives to Animal Research, the American Anti-Vivisection Society, and the Albert Schweitzer Fellowship, the Center offers courses to students interested in the biomedical sciences and to professional researchers. In 1985, its third year of existence, the Center offered:

- Basic Cell and Tissue Culture,
- In Vitro Toxicology: Principles and Methods,
- Tissue Culture Technology in Neuroscience Research, and
- An Introduction to Tissue Culture and In Vitro Toxicology.

The first three courses were attended by technicians and Ph.D. and M.D. researchers. The last course was specifically designed for high school seniors and college freshmen (9). Activities of this nature are useful in that they enable professionals and, particularly, beginning students to become acquainted with and proficient in in-vitro methodologies and to comprehend the possibilities as well as the limitations of alternative methods.

The debate about whether or not the training of medical and veterinary students requires animals has spawned development of an alternative technique in microsurgery training. The most prominent use of microsurgery is for reconnecting arteries and veins, for example in restoring circulation to severed fingers. To reproduce vascular circulation for microsurgical training, a British plastic surgeon connected human placentas to a pump and an artificial blood supply, thereby simulating a heartbeat and typical blood pressures. Because the placenta contains blood vessels of widely ranging diameters, a single placenta can provide material for a substantial amount of practice (14).

At present, the human placenta cannot fully substitute for living animals. One of the problems is that the placenta contains an anti-blood-clotting agent or mechanism that is not understood and cannot be controlled. Clotting therefore does not occur in placental vessels. Since learning how to avoid clotting during repair is a critical aspect of training, and since students training on placental tissue cannot detect their errors that cause clotting, the existing system is not fully adequate in microsurgical training (14).

Use of Nonliving Systems in Education

Audiovisual presentations bring the abstract prose of lecture and text one step closer to the biological reality of living organisms. Films and videotapes can demonstrate principles and protocols performed with live animals, while sparing additional animals. They may also present experiments and situations that cannot be performed live in the average classroom setting. As replacements for animals, however, they lack the living dimension; most cannot behave interactively. Recently developed computerized videodisks offer an opportunity for student interaction with an audiovisual program.

When audiovisual aids are used in concert with animals, they may enhance the value of live animals used in the laboratory. Students may learn a technique from a taped demonstration, for example, and then build on that experience as they perform the actual laboratory exercise in vivo.

Medical education substitutes audiovisual techniques for animals in several cases. This has less to do with educational philosophy than with factors external to the particular laboratory exercise. Those factors include the costs of animals and the facilities required to perform quality experiments, large medical school classes, lack of faculty time, and competition within a tightly packed curriculum.

Animal cadavers (e.g., frogs, sharks, cats, and fetal pigs) are currently used at all levels of educa-

Use of the Human Placenta for Training in Microvascular Surgery

Human placenta perfused under dissecting microscope.

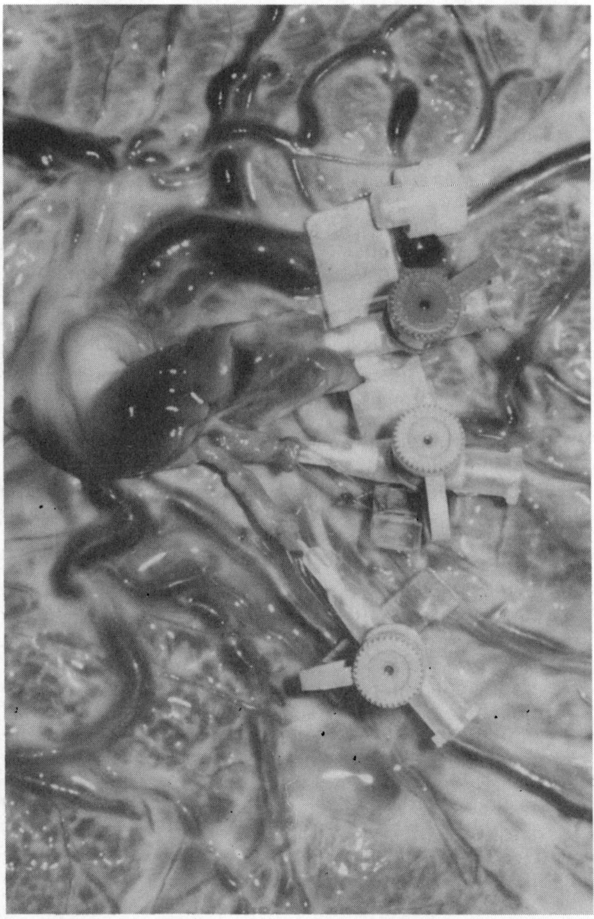

Photo credits: Paul LG. Townsend, Consultant Plastic Surgeon, Frenchay Hospital, Bristol

Sutures and valves implanted in vessels of human placenta.

tion as models for dissection. Commercially prepared specimens are often used in junior high and high school education; medical and veterinary schools are more likely to prepare their own specimens. In some situations, cadavers may provide adequate replacements where living animals were once used.

Computer Simulation in Education

Computer simulation offers a variety of alternatives for studying animal and human biology at all levels of education, and the field is evolving quickly as experience grows and computer technology advances. Although at this time popular expectations for computer simulation still outdistance actual performance, the options that simulations present to educators can be expected to increase. Educational computer simulations fall into two categories: computer models of biological events and interactive simulations of biological experiments.

Computer simulations of biological events—primarily mathematical models of physiological and cellular phenomena—present in quantitative form phenomena that might be difficult or impossible to study in animals or humans. By altering parameters within the programs and noting results, students learn principles of biology from an ersatz animal system, the computer program. For example, a dog's circulatory functions are converted to a series of mathematical equations, which are programmed into a computer. As students change individual values or groups of values, the program resolves the various equations and reports values that mimic the effects of altering those parameters of the circulatory system in a living dog. Figure 9-1 depicts a portion of such a simulation.

An array of computer models of physiological processes are used in undergraduate and graduate laboratory exercises. The range of physiological simulations includes simulations of blood chemistry, cardiovascular physiology, the digestive system, the musculoskeletal system, respiratory physiology, and renal physiology. Computer simulations currently used in physiology laboratory exercises include:

- HUMAN: a comprehensive physiological model (3),

Figure 9-1.—Computer Simulation of Cariovascular Dynamics for Use in Teaching Physiology

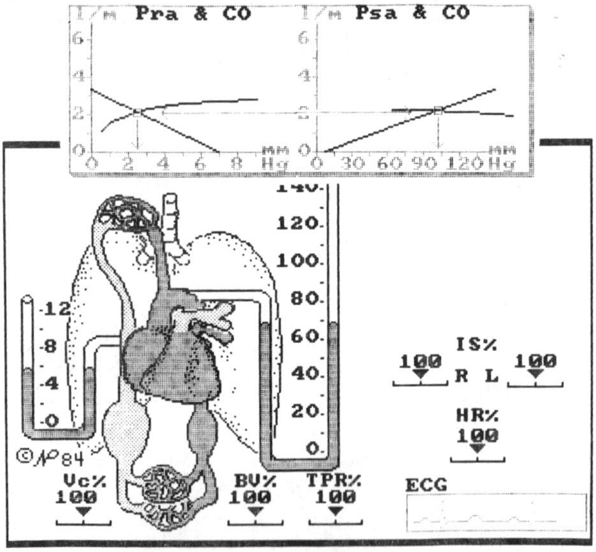

Overview of a computer simulation of the complete cardiovascular system, showing student-controlled variables such as heart rate (HR%), total active blood volume (BV%), and total peripheral resistance (TPR%).

SOURCE: N.S. Peterson and K.B. Campbell, "Teaching Cardiovascular Integrations With Computer Laboratories," *Physiologist* 28(3):159-169, 1985.

- pH regulation and carbon dioxide (24),
- pulsatile hemodynamics in the aorta (5),
- determinants of cardiac output (16),
- effects of medically important drugs on the circulatory system (25),
- simulation of the digestion of a meal (25),
- responses of organisms to exposure to high and low temperatures (25),
- influence of hormones on muscle cells (25), and
- renal excretory response to volume and osmolarity changes (12).

Computer simulation of a particularly sophisticated laboratory exercise—for example, one that is too difficult for beginning veterinary students to perform—can enable students to carry out laboratory exercises they otherwise would not have had (13).

Table 9-7 summarizes the advantages, disadvantages, and barriers to substituting computer models of biological systems for animals in education. Some characteristics apply to one type of computer application more than another. Viewed as a whole, the descriptors of computer simulations listed in table 9-7 illustrate the potential as well as the limi-

Table 9-7.—Advantages, Disadvantages, and Barriers to Using Computer Simulations in Education

Advantages:

Quality of teaching material:

- *Simplification.* Some biological events that are too complicated or not accessible to human study by vivisection or dissection are better approached through computer simulation.
- *Quantitative skills.* Physical mechanisms and mathematical variables that underlie biological events are emphasized.
- *Emphasis.* Student attention is shifted from techniques to concepts, supporting lecture and textbook material.
- *Reliability.* Strong consistency from experiment to experiment.
- *Response time.* Simulations yield immediate results.

Cost and efficiency:

- *Long-range cost reduction.* Following initial purchase of computer hardware, computer laboratory costs are often lower than relatively high animal laboratory costs.
- *Speed and coordination.* Increased teaching efficiency through expeditious testing, drills, and tutorials.
- *Laboratory availability.* Increased access for students to laboratories.

Disadvantages:

- *Biological complexity.* Computers cannot be programmed to simulate many integrative interactions between internal organs.
- *Missed experiences.* In the view of some teachers, students should have experience with living tissue.
- *Biological variability.* Computers do not accurately portray the large degree of uncertainty that arises from biological variability, whereas comparisons of animals do present this concept.
- *Publication of results.* Developers of computer simulations sometimes find publication of their work in the usual scientific journals difficult since some simulations require ponderous documentation; in cases where publications are intrinsic to tenure and other faculty decisions, computer modelers may be discriminated against.
- *Student attitudes.* In some cases, dubious student outlook on computer replacement of animals undermines teaching of concepts. In other cases, simulations may unintentionally train students (e.g., medical students) to ignore the behavior and appearance of patients and to place unwarranted importance on data from instruments.

Barriers:

- *Incompatibility.* Hardware components and software systems often are not interchangeable; this is especially true of graphic simulations.
- *Computer limitations.* Some complex digital computer programs are not fully realistic because they must approximate biological processes that are continuous and simultaneous by using a series of discrete steps. The only way to make such a computer approximation more realistic is to reduce the time the computer takes between steps. This may require more sophisticated hardware.
- *Tradition.* Widespread lack of training in mathematic modeling leads many talented people to write textbooks rather than computer models.
- *Proprietary considerations.* Many of those who are developing programs or catalogs of programs for commercial purposes will only disseminate useful information about computer simulations if they are paid, restricting applications.

SOURCE: Office of Technology Assessment.

tations of this alternative in a variety of teaching situations. Several of the disadvantages listed in table 9-7 underscore the small likelihood that computers can completely replace animals in the classroom. Those who are developing computer simulations are among the most vocal in maintaining that this technique is not the optimal method in every teaching situation; in some cases, they say, animals serve the lesson better (8,13,15,26).

In addition to providing models of biological experiments, computer programs serve in the classroom and laboratory as reusable training devices to teach specific skills, just as airline pilots train in flight simulators. These simulations are based on graphic presentation of the experiments and involve interaction between the program and trainee. An interactive videodisk program, for example, enables students to simulate dissections using photographic images stored on the disks, rather than animals. Production of such a videodisk can cost from $60,000 to $200,000 for a 30-minute program and involves thousands of still photographs, computer overlay, and touch screen interaction. The sales price of such a videodisk can range from $1,000 to $5,000.

The most sophisticated types of videodisk programs have not achieved widespread use, largely because of economic factors. Apart from steep initial production costs, the hardware supporting videodisk use is expensive.

Computer-linked mannequins and robots currently provide the most sophisticated simulations. Resusci-Dog, developed at the New York State College of Veterinary Medicine at Cornell University in Ithaca, NY, is a canine cardiopulmonary resuscitation training mannequin, the equivalent of the human dummies used in training paramedical technicians. Constructed of plastic, Resusci-Dog can simulate a femoral artery pulse, and pressure can be applied to its rib cage for cardiac massage or cardiopulmonary resuscitation. The first microprocessor-laden canine simulator cost $7,000; the second $700. Resusci-Dog has replaced about 100 dogs per year in veterinary classes at the New York school (19).

Despite the widespread enthusiasm for the potential of computer models and interactive simulations in the life sciences, three general problems confront computer-based education in the mid-1980s (7,8):

- The rapid advance of computer technology has resulted in many—frequently incompatible—machines in competition for the same market. This has limited the transportability of existing computer-based education materials. Users of different systems cannot eas-

Scenes From Interactive Videodisk Laboratory Exercise —Canine Hemorrhagic Shock

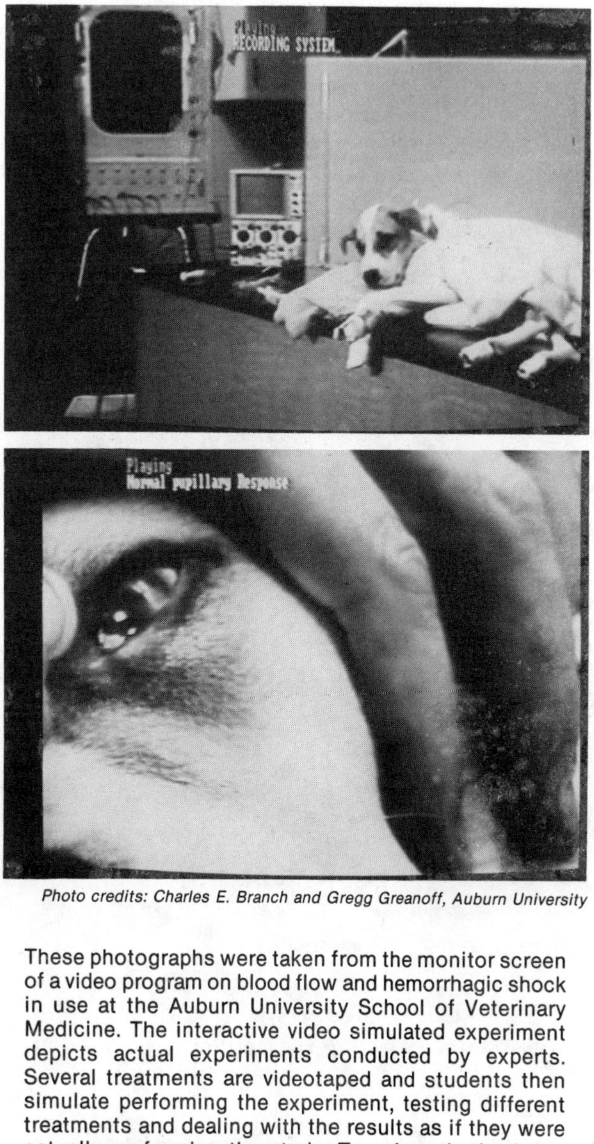

Photo credits: Charles E. Branch and Gregg Greanoff, Auburn University

These photographs were taken from the monitor screen of a video program on blood flow and hemorrhagic shock in use at the Auburn University School of Veterinary Medicine. The interactive video simulated experiment depicts actual experiments conducted by experts. Several treatments are videotaped and students then simulate performing the experiment, testing different treatments and dealing with the results as if they were actually performing the study. Top: Anesthetized dog in experimental setup. Bottom: Response of dog's pupil to light.

Canine Cardiopulmonary Resuscitation Simulator (Resusci-Dog) in Use

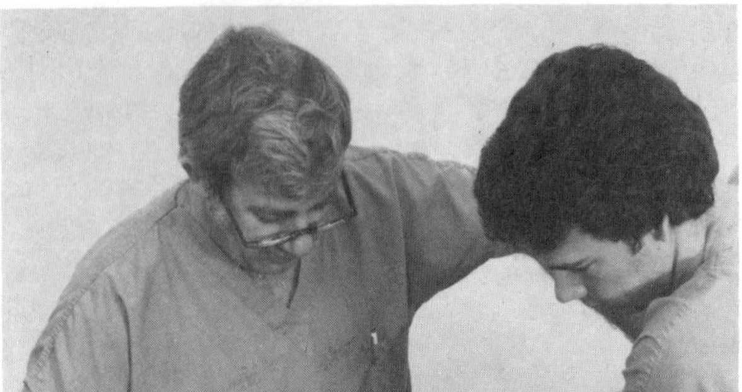

Photo credit: Charles R. Short, New York State College of Veterinary Medicine, Cornell University

ily share or exchange materials. As a result, there is a serious problem of duplication of effort, with individuals and institutions developing similar teaching programs. Although ideas are clearly portable, actual computer programs may not be, and the avenues for effective dissemination of programs remain limited.

- The resources available to support research and development in computer-based education are too limited. Few institutions have committed funds for such activity, and much current work is supported by departmental or individual resources. Many new computer-based education materials are developed by individuals on their own time out of personal interest. There is virtually no external funding available to support advances in this field.
- In the long run, the most serious problem may well be the lack of professional academic rewards for faculty members working in this area. Promotion, tenure, and salary increments are awarded predominantly for productivity in the research laboratory, not for efforts to develop innovative teaching techniques and materials. With essentially no external grant support for computer-based education activities and with few refereed high-quality journals in which to publish, two of the measures by which rewards are apportioned are not available to developers of novel educational software. This is a particular problem for junior faculty members, who often must devote their major efforts to climbing the academic ladder. Computer-based education seemingly fails to meet the perception of an academically valid and creditable enterprise.

SUMMARY AND CONCLUSIONS

In elementary school, student exposure to animals in the classroom generally takes the form of exercises in humane awareness. Later, involvement in science becomes more active and the role of the animal as a tool of science is explored. As students advance to and through college, animal use often becomes more invasive during instruction in laboratory techniques. At the highest levels, especially in professional and research training, students are expected to attain levels of skill that may be difficult to reach without the use of animals.

Taken together, the approximately 53,000 animals used in accredited medical and veterinary schools for education and training make up less than one-half of 1 percent of the estimated 17 million to 22 million animals used annually in the United States for research, testing, and education. (No data are available on the number of animals used in primary, secondary, and college education.) Yet the development of students' attitudes toward animals during the classroom years overshadows in importance the actual quantity of animal subjects used in education. Each phase of primary and secondary education appears to offer an opportunity for shaping students' attitudes toward animals. Grades 8 through 11 seem to be the most appropriate times for influencing the development of attitudes toward animals.

Alternatives applicable to different levels of schooling vary with the educational goals of each level. Whereas classroom demonstrations or noninvasive observation could be appropriate in primary and secondary education to teach the scientific method and aspects of biology, a nonliving system is inadequate to teach surgical technique and manual dexterity to medical and veterinary students. Computer models of biological phenomena and interactive simulations of biological experiments are especially promising alternatives to animal use, even in sophisticated laboratory physiology exercises. Interactive videodisk programs—although expensive and not currently widely available—offer particularly realistic training simulations.

CHAPTER 9 REFERENCES

1. American Veterinary Medical Association, *Your Career in Animal Technology* (Washington, DC: January 1981).
2. Association of American Medical Colleges, *Use of Animals in Undergraduate and Graduate Medical Education* (Washington, DC: 1985).
3. Coleman, T.G., and Randall, J.E., "HUMAN: A Comprehensive Physiological Model," *Physiologist* 26: 15-21, 1983.
4. International Science and Engineering Fair, *Rules of the 35th International Science and Engineering Fair* (Washington, DC: Science Service, Inc., 1984).
5. Katz, S., Hollingsworth, R.G., Blackburn, J.G., et al., "Computer Simulation in the Physiology Student Laboratory," *Physiologist* 21:41-44, 1978.
6. Kellert, S.R., "Attitudes Toward Animals: Age-Related Development Among Children," *J. Environ. Educ.* 16:29-39, 1985.
7. Michael, J.A., "Computer-Simulated Physiology Experiments: Where Are We Coming From and Where Might We Go?" *Physiologist* 27:434-436, 1984.
8. Michael, J.A., Associate Professor, Department of Physiology, Rush-Presbyterian-St. Luke's Medical Center, Chicago, IL, personal communication, Mar. 4, 1985.
9. Nardone, R.M., Director, Center for Advanced Training in Cell and Molecular Biology, Department of Biology, Catholic University of America, Washington, DC, personal communication, Sept. 4, 1985.
10. National Science Teachers Association, *Code of Practice on Animals in Schools* (Washington, DC: 1981).
11. Oelsner, G., Boeckx, W., Verhoeven, H., et al., "The Effect of Training in Microsurgery," *Am. J. Obstet. Gynecol.* 152:1054-1058, 1985.
12. Packer, J.S., and Packer, J.E., "A Teaching Aid for Physiologists—Simulation of Kidney Foundation," *The Physiology Teacher* 6:15, 1977.
13. Peterson, N.S., Professor, Department of Veterinary and Comparative Anatomy, Pharmacology, and Physiology, College of Veterinary Medicine, Washington State University, Pullman, WA, personal communication, Aug. 23, 1985.
14. *Progress Without Pain* (Lord Dowding Fund, National Anti-Vivisection Society, Ltd., London), "Development of a Dynamic Model Using the Human Placenta for Microvascular Research and Practice," 23:6-10, 1985.
15. Randall, J.E., Professor, Medical Sciences Program, Indiana University School of Medicine, Bloomington, IN, personal communication, Apr. 25, 1984.
16. Rothe, C.F., "A Computer Model of the Cardiovascular System for Effective Learning," *Physiologist* 22:29-33, 1979.
17. Rowan, A.N., *Of Mice, Models, & Men: A Critical Evaluation of Animal Research* (Albany, NY: State University of New York Press, 1984).
18. Scientists Center for Animal Welfare (Bethesda, MD), "College Courses on Ethics and Animals," *Newsletter* 5(2):3-6, 1983.
19. Short, C.E., Chief, Department of Anesthesiology, New York State College of Veterinary Medicine, Cornell University, Ithaca, NY, personal communication, March 1984.
20. Swindle, M.M., "Swine as Replacements for Dogs in the Surgical Teaching and Research Laboratory," *Lab. Anim. Sci.* 34:383-385, 1984.
21. Tarp, J., "Toward Scientific Literacy for All Our Students," *The Science Teacher* 45:38-39, 1978.
22. U.K. Home Office, *Scientific Procedures on Living Animals,* Command 9521 (London: Her Majesty's Stationery Office, 1985).
23. U.S. Department of Health and Human Services,

Public Health Service, National Institutes of Health, *National Survey of Laboratory Animal Facilities and Resources,* NIH Pub. No. 80-2091 (Bethesda, MD, 1980).

24. Veale, J.L., "Microcomputer Program for Teaching pH Regulation and CO_2 Transport," *Fed. Proc.* 43:1103, 1984.
25. Walker, J.R., "Computer Simulation of Animal Systems in the Medical School Laboratory," *Alternatives to Laboratory Animals* (U.K.) 11:47-54, 1983.
26. Walker, J.R., Assistant Director, Integrated Functional Laboratory, University of Texas Medical Branch at Galveston, TX, personal communication, Feb. 22, 1984.

Chapter 10

Information Resources and Computer Systems

One of the biggest barriers to using available information is that most people do not know how to use existing resources or what systems are available for use.

John S. Wassom
Oak Ridge National Laboratory
March 1985

The best computer programs evolve *into large creations. It is rarely possible to imagine a very large computer activity at the outset and build it as such.*

Charles S. Tidball
The George Washington University Medical Center
March 4, 1985

CONTENTS

List of Tables

List of Figures

Chapter 10

Information Resources and Computer Systems

Earlier chapters have described the quantity and variety of data generated by using animals in research, testing, and education. To assess fully the alternatives to animal use in these areas, therefore, it is important to consider how the data are shared once they are generated. Anything that increases information exchange reduces the need of other investigators to perform the same experiments. The pivotal role computers can play in that process has recently become an important topic for consideration and is examined in this chapter.

SOURCES OF RESEARCH AND TESTING DATA

Primary Literature

One of the most important ways to make data publicly available is through the "primary literature" in which they are published for the first time and in greatest detail. A significant form of this is the scientific journal, the most up-to-date and ubiquitous of the published sources available. Journal articles that are reviewed by knowledgable peers before they are accepted for publication are considered especially reliable. Most normally contain a description of the methodology of the experiment, the results obtained, the conclusions drawn by the author or authors, and references to and discussions of related published and unpublished information.

Other primary sources are published reports (e.g., of Government-sponsored research), proceedings of technical meetings, or similar collections of articles. As a rule, reports and proceedings are not as widely available as journal articles. They may or may not have been peer-reviewed.

Secondary Literature

Secondary sources contain information drawn solely from other published material. The most common forms are books, reviews, and reports. (A book that contains original material would not be considered a secondary source.) Handbooks are a useful secondary source for numerical data and for citations to the primary literature in which they were first published. Because secondary sources draw from primary sources, the information they report can be somewhat dated, as there is a timelag ranging from months to years between the publication of a primary source and that of any secondary sources that rely on it.

Many reviews and reports are prepared to meet the specific needs of various organizations. Government agencies, such as the Food and Drug Administration and the Environmental Protection Agency (EPA), prepare reports to support regulatory activities. Research institutions, such as the National Institutes of Health and the Chemical Industry Institute of Toxicology (CIIT), prepare reports to announce the results of a particular study. Other organizations, such as the Chemical Manufacturers Association and the World Health Organization, prepare reports to further their programs.

Unpublished Information

Unpublished information about recent, planned, and ongoing research and testing can be of even greater interest than older, published information. The timelag between submission or acceptance of data for publication and their actual publication is often a handicap to those waiting to learn of experimental results. Time lost while waiting to obtain another investigator's published research results can cost a laboratory its claim to priority in obtaining research results. In testing, proprietary interests create pressure to obtain information as quickly as possible.

One of the oldest sources of unpublished information is networking—that is, the use of personal contacts. Networking is affected by the economic factors discussed in chapter 11, such as the proprietary value of testing data and the incentives to make it public. Membership in scientific and professional societies and attendance at professional meetings facilitates this form of information exchange. Recent test results are often presented at meetings of professional societies, and valuable information about work in progress is exchanged by participants.

Unpublished data may not be written in report form, which makes it difficult to share the information. Although the data are stored in some kind of organized fashion, the way one person organizes information may not be useful to someone else. Thus, even if it is possible to determine that unpublished useful research or testing data do exist, it is often difficult to share them.

In addition to unpublished material, a separate category of information that is fairly inaccessible includes many Government reports, research institute reports, and obscure journals. This information falls into a grey area—"published" in a literal sense, but not in a practical one.

Information Centers

Because of the large volume of published and unpublished information that is generated, special services called "information centers" have been set up to collect, organize, and disseminate it. An information center, to be comprehensive, must have a fairly narrow scope. These centers are a good vehicle for sharing unpublished information, although they do not have the resources to seek it out.

The most well known information center with holdings of research and testing data is the International Agency for Research on Cancer, in Lyons, France. The United Nations maintains several collections of published and unpublished data on chemicals potentially of international interest, e.g., through the International Program on Chemical Safety and the International Registry for Potentially Toxic Chemicals in Geneva, Switzerland. These agencies have a much broader scope than a typical information center, although they carry out many of the same functions. The Oak Ridge National Laboratory in Oak Ridge, TN, has individual information centers for environmental carcinogens, teratogens, and mutagens. Statistics on the volume and rate of growth of publications in the areas for which Oak Ridge has holdings are given in table 10-1.

Table 10-1.—Growth and Publication Frequency of Literature Related to Genetic Toxicology, Carcinogenicity, and Teratogenicity

Subject	Papers published per year[a]	Increase in papers published per year[b]	Publication sources providing information[c]
Genetic toxicology	4,000-5,000	200-300	3,400
In vivo animal carcinogenicity studies	1,500-2,000	50-100	1,000
In vitro cell transformation studies	400-500	25-50	500
Teratogenicity	2,000-2,800	100-150	3,500

[a]Figures would be substantially greater if augmented with unpublished or inaccessible published material.
[b]Numbers shown are projected increases based on trends cataloged from the literature for the period 1979-84.
[c]Includes journals, books, symposium proceedings, government reports, and abstracts.

SOURCE: J.S. Wassom, Director, Environmental Mutagen, Carcinogen, and Teratogen Information Program, Oak Ridge National Laboratory, Oak Ridge, TN, personal communication, November 1985.

THE AVAILABILITY OF INFORMATION

One of the most important incentives to publish, both for people and for organizations, is to establish a professional reputation. Although "publish or perish" is an enduring part of academic tradition, in nonacademic research and testing sectors there is often little incentive to publish. As a rule, industry is more concerned with the protection of proprietary information and the conservation of financial resources than with publishing.

Federal organizations are likewise more interested in carrying out missions required by law than in the publication of research and testing data (unless that is their mission). As a result, many agencies' reports are never sent to the National Technical Information Service (NTIS) for distribution and cataloging, or too little time is spent indexing them in a fashion that facilitates easy retrieval of the information.

Journal Publication Policies

Because of the importance of journals as a source of testing data, their publication policies are crucial to the effective exchange of information. Some journal policies (e.g., the limitations on the length of an article and the amount of detail it contains) are related to high printing and distribution costs. Others, such as an unwillingness to publish results that have already been disclosed publicly, are a result of the stiff competition that exists among journals.

One of the most frustrating publication policies from the standpoint of avoiding duplicative research and testing is that most journals (and therefore secondary sources) rarely publish negative results. It is natural that people would be more interested in knowing, for example, which chemicals have been found to be hazardous than which chemicals have not. As a consequence, a certain number of experimental protocols are repeated because the negative results of earlier experiments were not published. This policy is not likely to change without dramatic alterations in the stance of journal publishers, the policies of professional societies, and, indeed, the tradition of scholarly publication in academia. One notable exception to this is the journal *Mutation Research,* which in 1977 made it a policy to also publish negative results.

Federal Laws Affecting Unpublished Data

One method available to the Federal Government for collecting testing data is to require them, either through registration requirements such as those under the Federal Insecticide, Fungicide, and Rodenticide Act (Public Law 92-516, as amended by Public Laws 94-140 and 95-396), or through reporting rules such as those promulgated under the Toxic Substances Control Act (TSCA) (Public Law 94-469). Section 8(d) of TSCA requires manufacturers and processors to submit citations or copies of health and safety studies they have sponsored, or about which they are aware, for specified chemicals. As of June 1984, EPA had received over 6,000 such submissions, about half of which were health-effects studies. For the specified chemicals, when regulatory notices were published in the Federal Register, about one-quarter of the citations were to data received under Section 8(d) (10).

Some unpublished data are given to Government agencies voluntarily, either through personal contacts or in response to publicity that the government is working on a particular problem. Much of the data concern adverse effects, but some concern negative results as well.

Unlike most countries, the United States has a policy of making information held by the Government as available as possible, consistent with protecting its proprietary value. Key laws in implementing this policy are the Administrative Procedures Act (Public Law 79-404, as amended by Public Law 89-554), which encompasses the Freedom of Information Act (Public Law 90-23, as amended by Public Laws 93-502, 94-409, and 95-454). This act makes all information held by the executive branch of the Federal Government available to anyone who asks for it, unless the information is specifically exempted or is protected under another law. The person requesting the information is frequently required to pay search and duplication costs, but the burden is on the Government to show why information should be withheld.

Under these laws, the public also has access to collections of published and unpublished nonproprietary data gathered to support administrative actions such as rulemaking. This "public docket" contains all reports, literature, memos, letters, and other information considered in taking the action.

Once information has been obtained by the Federal Government, it may be shared within and among Government agencies. Often such sharing is very informal, and with informality comes unpredictability and oversights. Various committees have been set up to facilitate intragovernmental networking, such as the Interagency Regulatory Liaison Group of the late 1970s, the Interagency Risk Management Council, and the Interagency Toxic Substances Data Committee. These efforts increase the amount of information available to solve particular problems. They also reduce duplicative information requests made of industry.

In 1980, an interagency Toxic Substances Strategy Committee examined the sharing of information, focusing principally on the data held by Federal agencies (20). The Committee noted there were then more than 200 independent data systems, mostly incompatible. Barriers to sharing information included diverse methods of identifying chemicals and differing reliability and review of the databases. The Committee noted that coordination of Federal agencies' chemical data systems could reduce duplication of information gathering, minimize delay, and, to some extent, decrease uncertainties in decisionmaking. The benefits of such coordination would likely extend beyond the Federal Government to State and local governments, industry, labor, public interest groups, academic institutions, international organizations, and foreign governments.

BARRIERS TO USING AVAILABLE INFORMATION

Data Quality and Comparability

Before data are to be used, the user must be confident of their quality. This judgment is based on a variety of facts and inferences. People will frequently take into account the professional reputation of the investigator or the investigator's industrial, academic, or professional affiliation or organization. If the person has no reputation, good or bad, many scientists will not rely on that investigator's data. This phenomenon is most acute with investigations carried out in foreign countries and published overseas (14). Further, many scientists will not (and perhaps should not) trust results that have not been peer-reviewed. Lastly, some organizations tend not to trust any data that they have not generated.

It is important to assess the quality of data. Thus, even though numerical databases are convenient because they contain data in summary form, often there is no way to determine from the information contained there how reliable the data are (unless they were peer-reviewed before being put into the system). This problem has been addressed by the National Bureau of Standards (NBS), the Chemical Manufacturers' Association, and others. A workshop held in 1982 (16) recommended that computerized databases (discussed at length later in this chapter) include the following "data quality indicators" that would allow the user to determine reliability for specific needs:

- the method(s) used to obtain the data,
- the extent to which the data have been evaluated,
- the source of the data, and
- some indication of the accuracy of the data.

An important part of evaluating data is comparing them with data obtained using similar methods—that is, validating the data. In deciding, for example, to rely on a particular test protocol, it is necessary to be confident not only that the test is a useful model of the effect of interest, but also that the results can be trusted, even though they are unexpected. For many investigators, validation involves repeating at least a portion of an experimental protocol in their own laboratories. They might also compare the results with those generated by other procedures with which they are more familiar.

International Barriers to Sharing Information

Animal research and testing is conducted in many countries (as described in ch.16). The importance of communicating scientific information among nations has been recognized in the United Nations, in the Organization for Economic Cooperation and Development (OECD), and in regional and bilateral forums. Although much has been done to facilitate this, many barriers must still be overcome.

International communications cost more and take longer than domestic communications. Moreover, there are fewer international personal acquaintances on whom to rely for information than there are on a national level. Communication problems are exacerbated by institutional differences. It is difficult for industry-to-industry communications to occur, for example, when one industry is privately owned and another is government-owned, because governments typically deal through diplomatic channels.

Political animosities hinder information exchange. Defense-related information is affected the most, but all information sharing must suffer in such a climate. Even political differences cause problems in sharing information. It is difficult for agencies within the U.S. Government to obtain information from governments that have close working relationships with their industries, such as Japan, particularly when any information received would be subject to Freedom of Information Act requests in the United States.

Language differences are a large problem, both in the use of written materials and in personal communications. Translation and interpreting are expensive, particularly in the United States, where the number of people who speak more than one language has been decreasing. English translation costs for the four principal languages of science (French, German, Russian, and Japanese) range from $40 to $88 per thousand words. An estimated $4 billion to $5 billion would be required to translate the current foreign-language holdings of the National Library of Medicine (NLM), for example, with an ongoing yearly translation cost of $150 million (9). Duplicative translations are avoided through the clearinghouse effort of the John Crerar Library in Chicago, IL. Translations donated by a variety of sources on a broad spectrum of topics are made available to others.

Common protocols can also facilitate the international exchange of, for example, testing data. OECD members decided in 1981 that health-effects data generated according to OECD test guidelines should be mutually acceptable in all member countries, regardless of where the testing was done (see app. A) (17). Although this decision has not been fully implemented, OECD test guidelines are readily available and are receiving considerable use.

RETRIEVING RESEARCH AND TESTING DATA

The ways data are obtained and the amount sought are functions of the resources available for searching, how the data are to be used, the likelihood that the information exists at all, and how reliable the information is likely to be. Many methods for finding information are available, and most of them overlap to some extent.

Abstracting and Citation Services

In research and testing, several hundred thousand scientific articles in thousands of journals are published each year in the primary literature (6). Abstracting and indexing services and bibliographic services play a vital role in making these accessible to those who need them. (An index based on references cited, or citations, permits the user to follow the literature into the future to locate pertinent articles. For example, a user with a 1981 article in hand who is seeking related, more recent publications can consult a citation index to identify 1985 publications that referenced the 1981 article.) Because animals are used for a variety of research purposes (see chs. 5 and 6), however, and because testing is interdisciplinary (see chs. 7 and 8), information may be indexed in the fields of chemistry, biology, pharmacology, medicine, and so on.

Abstracting and indexing services and bibliographic services have existed since the 17th century and have grown in number and size as published literature has expanded. The first major services for scientific information were published by professional societies (e.g., *Chemical Abstracts*). Some were sponsored by the Federal Government (e.g., *Air Pollution Abstracts* and *AGRICOLA*) or by commercial enterprises (e.g., *Current Contents* and *Environmental Abstracts*) (8). Some, such as the Chemical Information System, originated in Government and were later converted into commercial enterprises (12).

The largest abstracting and indexing service for biological and biomedical research is BIOSIS, the BioSciences Information Service. In 1985, its coverage extended to 440,000 items from over 9,000 sources worldwide. The file accumulated to date contains over 6 million items, the largest biological file in the English language. Items covered include abstracts and citations for journal articles and other serial publications, and citations to reports, reviews, and scientific meetings (6).

A typical abstract of a journal article and an illustration of how it is indexed by BIOSIS appear in figure 10-1. Information like this is contained in the semimonthly publication *Biological Abstracts*. Another publication, *Biological Abstracts/RRM,* contains bibliographic entries for research reports, reviews, meetings, and books (see fig. 10-2). BIOSIS also offers several computer-based services that provide citations tailored to the customer's information needs. All of these resources are regularly used by scientists. As the figures illustrate, however, it is often difficult to tell from a title, or even from an abstract, whether a particular article would satisfy a reader's needs.

Once a citation has been obtained, it is easy to acquire the full text of a research report. Most libraries have the necessary services available, or the inquirer can write to the author and ask for a reprint. In addition, some commercial vendors offer to supply by mail the full text of virtually any article (see fig. 10-3).

A recent comparison of databases for literature on 10 pesticides illustrates the problem of overlap (15). Eight databases had to be searched in order to get 90 percent of all data relevant to a particular regulatory decision. The share of citations produced by these databases that were not relevant ranged from 11 to 27 percent. Used together, the four most consistently relevant databases—TOXLINE, CAB Abstracts, BIOSIS, and *Chemical Abstracts*—produced 25 to 91 percent of all relevant citations, with an average of 69 percent.

These statistics illustrate the fragmentation that may accompany a literature search. Although the number of databases that need to be searched may be small for some fields, questions of an interdisciplinary nature require substantial resources for a complete literature search.

Retrieving Unpublished Information

Citation services are available for some unpublished data and testing in progress. Federal databases and publications include the *Bioassay Status Report* and *Tox-Tips* of the National Toxicology Program (NTP), the *EPA Chemical Activity Status Report,* the *Current Research Database* of the National Institute for Occupational Safety and Health, NTIS's *Federal Research in Progress,* and the *Smithsonian Science Information Exchange* (no longer active). There are also many small databases used to keep track of specialized data, such as information used in the implementation of a specific law.

Similar citation services to unpublished data or ongoing testing exist on an international level. The International Agency for Research on Cancer, which has substantial U.S. support, coordinates the sharing of information about current carcinogenicity testing in laboratories around the world and publishes an information bulletin, *Survey of Chemicals Being Tested for Carcinogenic Activity.* The International Program on Chemical Safety of the United Nations Environment Program (UNEP) is establishing a database for *Chemicals Currently Being Tested for Toxicological Effects.* This database is designed for long-term or otherwise expensive studies other than those on carcinogenicity. Participants in both programs include governments, industry, academia, and research institutes. In addition, Infoterra, a service of UNEP, publishes a directory through which experts in numerous subject areas can be located. Assistance is also provided by national representatives. The U.N.'s International Registry of Potentially Toxic Chemi-

Figure 10-1.—A Scientific Abstract and Corresponding Index Entry in BIOSIS

ABSTRACT FORMAT

TOXICOLOGY ← Major Heading

ENVIRONMENTAL AND INDUSTRIAL ← Subheading

Authors → CARSONS, JOANNE N and JOHN O. GOULDEN

Reference Number → 23330.

Author Address → (Arch Oceanogr. Inst., Phila., Pa. 19103, USA.)

Article Title → **The effects of chlorine pollution on growth and respiration rates of larval lobsters (*Homarus americanus*).**

Journal, Volume, (Issue), Pages, Year → BIOL RES 11(12): 1433-1438. 1985.

Abstract → The length, dry weight and standard respiration rate of larval lobsters (*H. americanus*) were measured following 20 days immersion in coastal waters surrounding a power plant. Significantly lower increases in dry weight ($P < .05$) and significant reductions in standard respiration rates ($P < .01$) were measured in exposed organisms when compared to control organisms. Water samples taken from the immersion site contained high concentrations of free Cl.

BIOSIS' INDEXING SYSTEM

Author Index (Personal or Corporate Names)

AUTHOR INDEX (Personal or Corporate Names)

NAME	REF. NO.	NAME	REF. NO.
CARSONS J N	23330◄	ELL A W	26787
CASEY N	29806	FINEMAN C	26884
DAVIES R	24001	GOULDEN J O	23330◄

Biosystematic Index (Broad Taxonomic Categories)

BIOSYSTEMATIC INDEX (Taxonomic Categories)

ARTHROPODA............. HIGHER TAXONOMIC CATEGORY

Crustacea..................
• **Malacostraca**............ } LOWER TAXONOMIC CATEGORIES

Environmental and Industrial Toxicology............. MAJOR CONCEPT

23330◄ 23572 25352............. REFERENCE NUMBERS

Generic Index (Genus-species Names)

GENERIC INDEX (Genus-species Names)

GENUS-SPECIES	MAJOR CONCEPT	REF. NO.
HOMARUS-AMERICANUS	TOXIC INDUS	23330◄
	WILDLIFE AQU	24063
MICROCERUS-BERONI	CRUSTAC SYST	19145*S

Subject Index (Specific Words)

SUBJECT INDEX (Specific Words)

ALPHABETIC POSITION

SUBJECT CONTEXT	▼KEYWORD	REF. NO.
GHT/ THE EFFECTS OF	CHLORINE POLLUTION ON GROWTH	23330◄
TOBACTER/ EFFECT OF	SUBSTITUTION ON THE	26575
LORINE POLLUTION ON	GROWTH AND RESPIRATION RATES	23330◄
GERMINATION RADICAL	BARRIER TEMPERATURE	27304

SOURCE: *The 1985 BIOSIS Information Catalog* (Philadelphia, PA: BioSciences Information Service, 1985).

Figure 10-2.—Sample Bibliographic Entries in *Biological Abstracts/RRM*

EXAMPLES OF BIBLIOGRAPHIC ENTRIES IN *BA/RRM:*

CONTENT SUMMARY FORMAT

TOXICOLOGY ← Major Heading

ENVIRONMENTAL AND INDUSTRIAL ← Subheading

Reference Number → 13003. BADASHKEYE, A.G., T.S. GALL, E.V. EFIMOVA, D. G. KNOORE, A. V. LEBEDEV and S. D. MYSINA. (Inst. Organic Chemistry; Siberian Div. USSR Acad. Sci., Novosibirsk, 630090, USSR.) ← Author Address

Biblio-graphic Detail: FEBS (FED EUR BIOCHEM SOC) LETT 155(2): 263-266. 1985. **Biological effects of chlorination on coastal waters.**/

HOMARUS AMERICANUS, LARVAE, JUVENILE MORTALITY, RESPIRATION DECLINE, POWER PLANT, POLLUTION ← Subject Terms

Subject Concepts → CON: Animal Ecology/Oceanography/ Air, Water, & Soil Pollution/ Comparative & Experimental Crustacea.

TAX: Malacostraca

BOOK SYNOPSIS FORMAT

Main Entry → 8720. OGLEVEY, O. C. and M. STIGGS (Ed.). (Lab. Biochem., Swiss Fed. Inst. Tech., Zurich, Switz.) Sprinter-Verlag; New York, N.Y. USA; Berlin, West Germany. Illus. Paper. ISBN 0-387-06842-1 ISBN 3-540-06842-1. x+175 p. 1984 (recd. 1985). **Membrane biochemistry: Bacterial membrane transport.**

Book Synopsis → This manual presents a series of 17 experiments on membrane transport and membrane bioenergetics in bacteria, covering a large spectrum of modern techniques in the field of membrane biochemistry. Tables, mathematical illustrations and diagrams complement the text. The work is intended for graduate and advanced undergraduate students, but should also be of value to researchers in the field.

Book Chapters →

8721. SPONSON, HAROLD. (Lab. Biochem., Swiss Fed. Inst. Technol., Zurich, Switz.) 164-170. **Characteristics of ionophores using artificial lipid membranes.**/ BLACK LIPID MEMBRANE, ANIONIC—CATIONIC PERMEABILITY, BIIONIC POTENTIAL, MEMBRANE CONDUCTANCE

8722. SCHLEUTER, HERMAN and PATRICK COLLETTI. (Lab. Biochem., Swiss Fed. Inst. Technol., Zurich, Switz.). 171-176. **Characterization of neural and charged ionophores using vesicular artificial lipid membranes (liposomes).**/ HYDROCARBON STRUCTURE, THERMODYNAMICS, MINERAL DIFFUSION

MEETING FORMAT

Main Entry → 4718. SLOAN, GARTH and I. WILLINGSBY (Ed.). (Dep. Physiol. Pharmacol., Vet. Sch., Toulouse, Fr.) ANN Rech VET 10 (2/3): 157-502. 1985 [In Fr.] **Communications on Rumen Physiology and Forage Degradation at the 5th International Symposium on Ruminant Physiology. Clermont-Ferrand, France. Sept. 3-7, 1985.** [ABSTRACTS ONLY]

Meeting Papers →

4719. CROFT, L. (Rowett Res. Inst., Bucksburn, Aberdeen, Scotl., U.K.) 157-159. [In Fr.] **Effects of cannulation on intestinal motility.**/ SHEEP, OCCLUSION, SURGERY, RADIOLOGY

4720. SCHWAB, R., E. SCHWAB, F. TANG and B. BEAUGEROUX. (Fac. Sci. Agron. Etat 5500 Grembloux, Belg.) 163-165. [In Fr.] **Rate of passage of digesta in sheep.**/ HAY, FECES, RADIOTRACER

SOURCE: *The 1985 BIOSIS Information Catalog* (Philadelphia, PA: BioSciences Information Service, 1985).

Figure 10-3.—Promotional Material From Commercial Supplier of Full Texts of Scientific Publications

THE Genuine Article™

Pick an article—any article from this issue of *CC*®! It can be in your hands *fast* when you order it from ISI®'s document delivery service, *The Genuine Article*.

The Genuine Article can supply you with original article tear sheets or quality photocopies of nearly all journal articles, editorials, letters, and other items you see in this issue of *Current Contents*® . . . To order, simply fill out the coupon below and mail it to ISI, together with your check or money order.

Price information: Any article of ten or fewer pages costs $7.50 (when order includes ISI Accession Number). This amount includes first class mail delivery to the U.S.A., Canada, and Mexico. Air mail to all other locations costs $8.50. For every additional ten pages or fraction of ten pages, there is an additional charge of $2 per article.

For complete information on our document delivery service, write ISI Customer Services at the address shown.

FAST, RELIABLE DOCUMENT DELIVERY

To receive your order from *The Genuine Article*™, fill in oval with ISI accession number adjacent to journal title in *CC*®.

Journal ____________

Vol. ______ No. ______

Date ______ 1st Page No. ______

Author ____________

☐ Check enclosed.

☐ ISI Stamps attached.

☐ Please send me information on volume discounts or deposit accounts.

Name Title ____________

Organization Dept. ____________

Address ____________

City ______ State / Province ______ Country ______

ZIP Postal Code ______ Telephone ______

Prices are subject to change. Payment must accompany order.

ISI® Institute for Scientific Information®

The Genuine Article, 3501 Market Street, Philadelphia, PA 19104 U.S.A.
Telephone: (215) 386-0100, ext. 1140, Cable: SCINFO, Telex: 84-5305
European Office: 132 High Street, Uxbridge, Middlesex UB8 1DP, U.K.
Telephone: 44-895-70016, Telex: 933693 UKISI

©1985 ISI
CC-3716

SOURCE: Institute for Scientific Information, Inc., Philadelphia, PA.

cals sometimes refers information requests among member countries through its national correspondents.

A recent U.S.-led project of the OECD, generally referred to as "Switchboard," has also addressed the problems of obtaining information from other countries. Unpublished information may be requested through the Switchboard system for use in risk assessments or to otherwise protect health and the environment. A pilot system is to be run in which two requests per participating country per month would be referred to some combination of government agencies, industry, academia, and research institutes that might have unpublished data relevant to the request. The mechanisms for referring requests on the national level and the enlistment of various organizations, either as requesters or responders, is the responsibility of Switchboard's national focal point. This project will begin on a small scale and will be monitored. If appropriate, it could be expanded (18).

COMPUTER SYSTEMS

Computers have two applications as an alternative to using animals in research, testing, and education. First, they can be used to model or simulate biological, chemical, and physical systems. In this way, a computer could be used as a direct replacement for some number of animals used in laboratories. This form of computer use is discussed in chapters 6, 8, and 9. Second, computers are used to disseminate information that has been generated from prior use of animals in research and testing, thus avoiding the needless repetition of a procedure by other scientists. It is this role of computers as information disseminators that is discussed in the rest of this chapter.

Advantages of Computers

Biological testing (see ch. 7) can be described as the repetitive use of a standard biological test situation, or protocol, employing different chemicals or different test parameters (e.g., species or biological end points). Because the protocols in testing are more stereotyped and less varied than those in research, biological testing is more amenable than research to the institution of a computerized data retrieval system. In fact, testing emerged in the 1970s as the first discipline in which such a system was developed.

If a comprehensive, computerized registry of biological research or testing data were established, certain benefits might accrue. These benefits are predicated on the inclusion in the computerized registry of both control and experimental data, and of both positive and negative results. (Data obtained from testing fall into two broad categories: those derived from untreated (control) subjects, and those from treated (experimental) subjects. Data obtained from treated subjects may either show an effect from the treatment ("positive results") or no effect ("negative results").) Furthermore, the advantages of such a registry depend on the acceptance by working scientists of the data contained in it—acceptance that seems possible only with the imprimatur of peer review of the data. The anticipated benefits of a computer-based registry of research or testing data include:

- **Decreased Use of Animals in Research or Testing.** In some instances, an investigator would locate the exact data desired, possibly from a previously unpublished source, thus avoiding unintentional duplication of animal research or testing. Baseline data could permit the selection of a dose, a route of administration, or a strain of animal without the need for new animal experiments to establish these factors. Efficiencies could also include the use of fewer doses on smaller numbers of animals. Conceivably, the number of animals required for control groups could be reduced, although many experimental protocols require the use of concomitant control subjects, rather than of data from a pool of control subjects, in order to achieve statistical significance.
- **A Check for Genetic Drift.** Certain experimental results can change over a span of many generations due to subtle, progressive changes in the underlying genetic constitution of the strain of animals ("genetic drift"). The regis-

try would provide baseline data within specified time frames of measurement, and make it easy to check for the possibility of genetic drift.

- **New Perspectives on Old Data.** By performing statistical comparisons across data sets and identifying relationships not already obvious, unforeseen relations could be established without animal experimentation.

The scientific community makes use of a number of computerized literature retrieval services to obtain bibliographic citations and abstracts to the published literature. Most abstracting and indexing services started as publications, but most are now available on-line as well. Others, such as *AGRICOLA,* are only available on-line.

Many handbooks and other numerical databases are also available on-line. Several numerical databases are sponsored by the Federal Government. The most comprehensive, the recently terminated Laboratory Animal Data Bank, is reviewed in detail in the next section. Two current systems, the Toxicology Data Bank and the Registry of Toxic Effects of Chemical Substances, are discussed in some detail here. Table 10-2 lists a number of databases available for searches of the research and testing literature. Table 10-3 lists some widely used databases of the NLM.

Toxicology Data Bank

The Toxicology Data Bank (TDB) was made public by NLM in 1978. It is designed to address some of the needs of the testing and regulatory communities for toxicity information. TDB is organized by individual chemicals or substances, now totaling more than 4,000. Its fixed format includes:

- data on the production and use of each chemical;
- a description of the physical properties of each chemical; and
- the results of pharmacological and biochemical experiments, and information on toxicological testing.

TDB is based on conventional published sources and does not include unpublished data. Thus, baseline data on control animals, which might be used in place of a control group, could not be included because so little has been published.

The most valuable feature of TDB is the fact that all the data it contains are peer-reviewed. As a consequence, its data summaries are acceptable to most users (5). (Another database containing only peer-reviewed data is the Environmental Protection Agency's Gene-Tox.)

Registry of Toxic Effects of Chemical Substances

The Registry of Toxic Effects of Chemical Substances (RTECS) has been published annually since 1971 by the National Institute for Occupational Safety and Health, under Section 20(a)(6) of the Occupational Safety and Health Act of 1970 (Public Law 91-596). RTECS is a compendium, extracted from the scientific literature, of known toxic and biological effects of chemical substances. RTECS does not evaluate the data it cites, leaving that responsibility to the reader. An example of the information contained in a typical substance entry in RTECS is given in figure 10-4.

By congressional mandate, those data that indicate a toxic effect of a chemical are to be included in RTECS; those that show no toxicity are to be excluded. Thus, RTECS does not include negative results. Moreover, a chemical might not be included in the registry for a variety of reasons, including the following:

- The test results could not be cited because the protocol of the study did not meet the RTECS selection criteria.
- The substance has not yet been tested or the results have not yet been published.
- The substance has been tested and the results published, but the information has not yet been entered into the RTECS file.

The exclusion of negative results from RTECS and its incompleteness for these other reasons may lead to the repetition of toxicity testing of essentially nontoxic substances.

The production of RTECS costs approximately $500,000 per year. The current quarterly update includes a total of 68,000 compounds, and it continues to grow steadily toward the estimated 100,000 unique substances for which toxicity data may be available. If RTECS were expanded to include all results of whole-animal toxicity testing, including

Table 10-2.—Examples of Databases Available[a] for Searches of Literature Involving Animal Research and Testing

Database	Description	First year covered
AGRICOLA	Worldwide journal and monograph literature on agriculture and related subjects; from the National Agricultural Library	1970
AQUACULTURE	Growth requirements, engineering, and economics of marine, brackish, and freshwater organisms; from National Oceanic and Atmospheric Administration	1970
AQUALINE	Abstracts from world literature on water, waste water, and aquatic environments; from Water Research Centre, Stevenage, U.K.	1974
ASFA (Aquatic Sciences and Fisheries Abstracts)	Life sciences of seas and inland waterways plus legal, political, and social implications of aquatic life; from UNESCO	1978
BIOSIS Previews	International coverage of life science research; from *Biological Abstracts*	1969
CA Search	International coverage of chemical sciences; from Chemical Abstract Service	1967
Comprehensive Dissertation Abstracts	Author, title, and subject guide to nearly all American dissertations since 1861 and many from foreign countries; abstracts added beginning in July 1981; from Xerox University Microfilms	1861
Conference Papers Index	Records of scientific and technical papers presented at major regional, national, and international meetings each year; from Data Courier, Inc.	1973
CRIS (Current Research Information System)	Research in agricultural sciences; from U.S. Department of Agriculture's State Research Service	1974
Enviroline	International coverage of biology, chemistry, economics, geology, law, management, planning, political science, and technology of environmental issues; from Environment Information Center, Inc.	1971
Environmental Bibliography	Atmospheric studies, energy, general human ecology, land resources, nutrition and health, and water resources; from Environmental Studies Institute	1973
Excerpta Medica	Worldwide citations and abstracts from 3,500 biomedical journals; from Excerpta Medica	1974
INSPEC	Coverage of literature in computers, electrotechnology, and physics; from the American Institute of Electrical Engineers	1969
IPA (International Pharmaceutical Abstracts)	Literature on drug development and use of drugs; from the American Society of Hospital Pharmacy	1970
IRL Life Sciences Collection	Worldwide coverage of life sciences including conferences; from Information Retrieval, Ltd.	1978
ISI/BIOMED	Index of 1,400 biomedical journals; from the Institute of Scientific Information	1979
ISI/COMPUMATH	Covers literature in computer science, mathematics, statistics, operations research, and related areas; from the Institute for Scientific Information	1976
ISI/ISTP&B	Computerized version of Scientific and Technical Proceedings and Books. Covers 3,000 proceedings and 1,500 books annually; from the Institute for Scientific Information	1978
LISA (Library Science Abstracts)	International coverage of library and information science literature; from Learned Information, Ltd.	1969
Microcomputer Index	Subject and abstract guide to 21 microcomputer journals; form Microcomputer Information Services	1981
NIMH	Mental health literature from 950 journals, symposia, government reports, and other sources; from the National Institute of Mental Health	1969
Oceanic Abstracts	International literature on geology, governmental and legal aspects of marine resources, marine biology, marine pollution, meteorology, and oceanography; from Data Courier, Inc.	1964
Pollution Abstracts	Literature on the sources and control of environmental pollution; from Data Courier, Inc.	1970
Population Bibliography	International coverage of population research: abortion, demography, family planning, fertility studies, and migration; from Carolina Population Center, University of North Carolina	1966
Psychological Abstracts	Worldwide coverage of literature in psychology and related social-behavioral literature; from the American Psychological Association	1967
SCISEARCH	International literature of sciences and technology; from the Institute for Scientific Information	1974

Table 10-2.—Examples of Databases Available[a] for Searches of Literature Involving Animal Research and Testing (Continued)

Database	Description	First year covered
SOCIAL SCISEARCH	Worldwide coverage of social and behavioral sciences literature; from the Institute for Scientific Information	1972
TELEGEN	Covers literature on biotechnology and genetic engineering in 7,000 sources including conference and symposia papers, government studies, periodicals, and the popular press; from Environment Information Center, Inc.	1973
Zoological Record	Covers zoological literature from 6,000 journals; from BioSciences Information Service and the Zoological Society of London	1978

[a]These databases are available by telephone connection to one or more of the following: Lockheed Information System DIALOG, System Development Corp.'s ORBIT, and Bibliographic Retrieval Service, Inc.

SOURCE: Adapted from R.V. Smith, *Graduate Research* (Philadelphia, PA: ISI Press, 1984).

Table 10-3.—Examples of On-Line Databases of the National Library of Medicine

Name	Description	Number of records (average length)	Type of record
MEDLINE	1966-present. Bibliographic citations and abstracts from primary biomedical literature	3,300,000 (1,250 char.)	Bibliographic
TOXLINE	1965-present. Abstracts from primary toxicological literature	1,400,000 (1,050 char.)	Bibliographic
CHEMLINE	Dictionary to chemicals contained in TOXLINE and other MEDLARS data bases	500,000 (275 char.)	Chemical compound
RTECS	Brief summaries of toxicity results from primary literature	68,000 (1,000 char.)	Chemical compound
TDB	Detailed chemical, pharmacological, and toxicological data and extracts from monographs and handbooks	4,000 (17,000 char.)	Chemical compound

SOURCE: Office of Technology Assessment.

negative results, its size would be increased by an estimated 10 to 15 percent (11). RTECS is available in hard copy (19), on microfiche, on magnetic tape, and on-line from both the MEDLINE service of NLM and the Chemical Information System, a joint resource of several Federal agencies that is managed by EPA.

On-Line Literature

The research community makes use of a number of computerized literature retrieval services to obtain bibliographic citations and abstracts from primary literature. Among these, for example, is NLM's MEDLINE database, a bibliographic file now exceeding 3,300,000 entries. In the private sector, BioSciences Information Services prepares hundreds of thousands of abstracts each year, providing access to essentially the entire published biological research literature. However, the research community is not presently served by a computerized database that includes comprehensive descriptions both of experimental protocols and of the resulting data.

Movement toward on-line delivery of the full text of scientific publications has begun in the private sector. For example, Mead Data Central (Dayton, OH) offers MEDIS, a medical literature database. In 1985, the MEDIS service included about 70 publications, with some stored journal articles going back to 1980. MEDIS includes the full text of the *Journal of the American Medical Association* (since 1982), *Archives of Internal Medicine,* and some textbooks and newsletters. In 1984, Bibliographic Retrieval Services (Latham, NY) joined with publisher W.B. Saunders Company to offer the full text of the *New England Journal of Medicine* and several other journals on-line. A serious limitation to any current full-text literature retrieval system is the inability to retrieve graphs, photographs, and other images (7).

Figure 10-4.—A Typical Substance Entry in the Registry of Toxic Effects of Chemical Substances (RTECS)

(A) AA1111111 (1) RTECSIUM (3) (4) (5)

(2) UPDT: 8209 CAS: 9999–99–9 MW: 357.88 MOLFM: C-Re-S-Te

(6) SYN: NIOSHRTECSIUM • RTECS (DOT) • RTECSIAM (French) • TSL (OBS.)

(7) *IRRITATION DATA AND REFERENCES:*

	skn-hmn 5%/1M nse MOD	(12) JAMAAP 135,1920,68
	skn-rbt 10 mg/24H open MLD	AMIHBC 10,61,54
	eye-rbt 20 mg	AMIHBC 10,61,54

(8) *MUTATION DATA AND REFERENCES:*

	mma-sat 50 ug/plate	PNASA6 72,5135,75
	cyt-hmn: leu 100 umol/L/8H	MUREAV4,53,67
	dlt-mus-orl 35 mg/kg	TXAPA9 23,288,72
	hma-mus/sat 400 ppm	GISAAA 42(1),32,77

(9) *REPRODUCTIVE EFFECTS DATA AND REFERENCES:*

1T03	orl-rat TDLo:270 mg/kg (5D male)	TJADAB 19,41A,79
3T25T46T52	ihl-rat TCLo:100 ppm (3D pre/4-7D preg)	NTIS** AD-900-000
2T35T75	mul-mus TDLo:900 mg/kg (1D male/6-15D preg/5D post)	TOXID9 1,125,81

(10) *TUMORIGENIC DATA AND REFERENCES:*

2V01M61	orl-rat TDLo:90 gm/kg/78W-I	29ZUA8 –,183,80
1V03	ihl-mus TCLo:400 ppm/8W-I	JTEHD6 – (Suppl.2),69,77
2V02K60	orl-rat TD :100 gm/kg/104W-I	BJCAAI 16,275,62

(11) *TOXICITY DATA AND REFERENCES:*

	ihl-hmn TCLo:500 mg/m3/7M	AIHAAP 23,95,62
2J13K18	orl-rat LD50:1500 mg/kg	MarJV# 26 Apr 76
•	scu-mus LDLo:1200 mg/kg	FCTXAV 17(3),357,79

(13) AQUATIC TOXICITY RATING: TLm96:100-10 ppm — WQCHM* 2,–,74

(14)

REVIEW: CARCINOGENIC DETERMINATION: ANIMAL POSITIVE	IARC** 20,151,80
REVIEW: TOXICOLOGY REVIEW	PLMJAP 6(1),160,75
REVIEW: TLV-TWA 10 ppm; STEL 25 ppm	DTLVS* 4,358,80
REVIEW: TLV-SUSPECTED CARCINOGEN	DTLVS* 4,358,80

(15) STANDARDS & REGULATIONS:

OSHA STANDARD-air:TWA 50 ppm	FEREAC 39,23540,74
DOT-ORM-A, LABEL: NONE	FEREAC 41,57018,76

(16) CRITERIA DOCUMENT: OCCUPATIONAL EXPOSURE TO RTECSIUM recm — NTIS**
std-air:CL 10 ppm/60M

(17) STATUS: SELECTED BY NTP FOR CARCINOGENESIS BIOASSAY AS OF SEPT 1982
STATUS: NTP SECOND ANNUAL REPORT ON CARCINOGENS, 1981
STATUS: NIOSH MANUAL OF ANALYTICAL METHODS, VOL 3 S255
STATUS: NIOSH CURRENT INTELLIGENCE BULLETIN 41, 1980
STATUS: REPORTED IN EPA TSCA INVENTORY, 1982
STATUS: EPA TSCA 8(a) PRELIMINARY ASSESSMENT INFORMATION FINAL RULE — FEREAC 47,26992,82

Key to Figure 10-4

A. RTECS accession number, a sequence number assigned to each substance in the Registry.
1. Substance name.
2. Date when substance entry was last revised.
3. American Chemical Society's Chemical Abstracts Service unique identification number for the substance.
4. Molecular weight of the substance.
5. Molecular or elemental formula of the substance.
6. Synonyms, common names, trade names, and other chemical names for the substance.
7. Skin and eye irritation data.
8. Mutation data.
9. Reproductive effects data.
10. Tumor-causing data.
11. Toxicity data.
12. Acronyms for the references from which the data and other citations were abstracted.
13. Aquatic toxicity rating.
14. Reviews of the substance.
15. Standards and regulations for the substance promulgated by a Federal agency.
16. A Criteria Document supporting a recommended standard has been published by NIOSH.
17. Status information about the substance from NIOSH, EPA, and the National Toxicology Program.

SOURCE: U.S. Department of Health and Human Services, National Institute for Occupational Safety and Health, *Registry of Toxic Effects of Chemical Substances*, R.L. Tatken and R.J. Lewis, Sr. (eds.) (Cincinnati, OH: DHHS (NIOSH) Pub. No. 83-107, 1983).

LABORATORY ANIMAL DATA BANK

The Laboratory Animal Data Bank (LADB) is a computerized set of records of baseline data of physiological, histological, and other biological properties of mammalian species (largely rodents) used in research and testing. The data contained in LADB were derived from both research and testing, and are relevant to both areas of animal use. Although LADB exists today only as an archival reference, and is no longer publicly available online, it is of great historical interest in a consideration of computer-based information resources.

In 1970-73, as the carcinogenesis bioassay program of the National Cancer Institute (NCI) was developed, NCI's Division of Cancer Cause and Prevention anticipated needing better access to baseline data for experimental animals. In 1973-74, NLM helped formulate the concepts leading to LADB. The major contributor of funding for LADB was NCI.

Data for LADB were derived from published and unpublished reports. Only control, or baseline, data from groups of animals were included. The data were collected and entered into LADB via a standard, eight-page form (reproduced in ref. 2) that surveyed 306 variables, including:

- name and manufacturer of the animals' feed,
- vaccinations given to the animals,
- organs or tissues routinely examined at autopsy,
- blood variables that were analyzed,
- detergent used in washing cages, and
- source of the animals.

The first page of that form is reproduced in figure 10-5.

Building Phase, 1975-80

Battelle Laboratories (Columbus, OH) was awarded an NLM contract in 1975, after a competitive procurement, and began detailed design activities in 1975-76. Methods for obtaining data were developed, and the data file was designed to permit interactive access, or time-sharing, by users. Sufficient data were entered to permit initial study by NLM staff in 1976, and in the following year 13 outside users were allowed to test the system.

In June 1976, NLM requested the Institute of Laboratory Animal Resources (ILAR) of the National Academy of Sciences to provide advice on scientific and technical aspects of LADB. A Committee on Laboratory Animal Data was formed by ILAR

Figure 10-5.—A Representative Page of the Eight-Page Data Input Form for the Laboratory Animal Data Bank

Animal Group Environment and Husbandry Conditions

FOR INTERNAL LADB USE ONLY
LADB Animal Group Number ______
Related Animal Group Numbers
______ ______ ______ ______
______ ______ ______ ______

NS = Not Specified NA = Not Applicable

01 Performing Laboratory (where animals were housed) [34]
02 City [35]
03 State [37]
04 Altitude feet [38]
05 Country United States ☐ Other [38]
06 Latitude deg North [39]
07 Latitude deg South [40]
08 Data Donor Organization (if different from performing lab) ☐
09 City ☐
10 State ☐
11 Country United States ☐ Other ☐
12 Animal Supplier or Breeder ☐
13 City ☐
14 State ☐
15 Country United States ☐ Other ☐
16 Testing Organization (if different from performing lab or data donor organization) ☐
17 City ☐
18 State ☐
19 Country United States ☐ Other ☐
20 Tests Performed by Testing Organization ☐
CBC ☐ Serum Chemistries ☐ Bone Marrows ☐
Histopathology ☐ Other
21 Common Animal Name ☐
Monkey ☐ Ape ☐ Cat ☐
Dog ☐ Rabbit ☐ Rat ☐
Mouse ☐ Minipig ☐ Hamster ☐
Other
22 Species Name [4]
23 Strain, Breed, or Stock Name [6]
24 Substrain Name (if not included in # 23) ☐

Rodents/Lagomorphs Now go to: Question 25 if Rodent or Lagomorph Question 30 if Carnivore

25 Type of Breeding [5]
Outbred ☐ now go to question (32)
Inbred ☐ now go to question (26)
Hybrid ☐ now go to question (27)
Congenic ☐ now go to question (28)
Mutant ☐ now go to question (29)

26 Type of Inbreeding ☐
BxS ☐ FxD ☐ MxS ☐
Gen (F #) ______ NS ☐
Now go to question 32

27 Hybrid Parentage
[8] Strain of Dam ______ Specify
[9] Strain of Sire ______ Specify
Now go to question 32

28 Congenic Parentage ☐
Background Strain (inbred partner) ______ Specify
Donor Strain ______ Specify
Now go to question 32

29 Mutant Parentage ☐
Strain on which carried ______ Specify
BxS ☐
Backcross ☐
Gen (F #) ______ Specify
(N #) ______ Specify
NS ☐ Now Go To Question 32

Carnivores

30 Mating System ☐
Outbred ☐
Inbred ☐
Linebred ☐

31 Type of Source ☐
Random Source, Unconditioned ☐
Random Source, Conditioned ☐
Kennel (Colony) Produced ☐
Now go to question 32

32 Microbial Status (check only one) [31]
Conventional ☐ } now go to question 35
Axenic (germ free) ☐ }
Gnotobiotic ☐ }
Defined Microbially Associated ☐ } now go to question 33
Barrier Maintained (SPF) ☐ }
Monitored ☐ now go to question 34

33 Designate Organisms ☐
Now go to question 35

34 Tests by Which Monitored ☐
Now go to question 35

35 Type of Control Animal [125]
Negative (untreated) ☐ - now go to question 42
Sham ☐ } now go to question 37 thru 41
Vehicle ☐ }
Pre-experiment * ☐ } now go to question 36
Quarantine ☐ }

36 Duration ☐
______ (days)
Now go to question 42

37 Designate Sham or Vehicle [126]
Distilled Water ☐ Tragacanth ☐
Saline Solution ☐ Agar ☐
Gelatin Capsule ☐ Corn Oil ☐
______ Other

38 Route and Site of Administration of Vehicle ☐

Route		Site
Oral (feed)	☐	N.A.
Oral (gavage)	☐	N.A.
Inhalation	☐	N.A.
Topical Application	☐	______ Specify
Parenteral Injection	☐	
I.M.	☐	______ Specify
I.V.	☐	______ Specify
Subcut	☐	______ Specify
I.P.	☐	N.A.
______ Other		______ Specify

39 Schedule of Vehicle Administration/Sham Procedure ☐
Continuous ☐ Other ______
Periodic: ______Times/Day for ______Days/Wk for ______Wks

40 Concentration of Vehicle (if applicable) (e.g., 0.85% Saline Solution, etc.) ☐

41 Amount of Vehicle Adminstered ☐
Constant Amount: ______ml (or) ______mg (or) ______ Other
Variable Amount (amount per unit body weight or body surface area):
______mg/kg ______mg/m²
______ml/kg ______ml/m²
Other ______

* Includes all animals postquarantine and under environmental conditions prior to treatment regimes

SOURCE: P.L. Altman and K.D. Fisher, *Review of Standards Related to the Laboratory Animal Data Bank—Interim Report* (Bethesda, MD: Federation of American Societies for Experimental Biology, 1980).

to advise NLM. It met in 1977 and 1978 to consider reports from the NLM and Battelle staff and to respond both to specific requests for guidance concerning LADB developmental aspects and to feedback from the 13 outside users. The NLM staff further requested ILAR to review the basic concept, purpose, scope, validation of data, and utility of LADB.

In 1978, ILAR prepared such a report and recommended that peer review of data for inclusion in LADB be performed, together with peer examination of the criteria for data acceptability (13). NLM contracted with the Life Sciences Research Office (LSRO) of the Federation of American Societies for Experimental Biology (FASEB) to organize an ad hoc LADB User Assessment Panel to review data descriptors and coverage of various disciplines by LADB.

In 1979, each member of the LSRO ad hoc panel had a computer terminal with unlimited access to the LADB database. The resulting hands-on experience provided the basis for an objective assessment of the data descriptors and the scope of coverage of LADB. The ad hoc panel's report, published in 1980 (2), made some 20 suggestions for improving LADB. The recommendations focused on increasing the data coverage, ensuring the quality of the data included, and facilitating statistical comparisons of data within LADB. The panel's principal recommendations were:

- put the individual animal data files on-line with the grouped animal data files;
- standardize diagnostic terms for pathology data, by using a system such as Systematized Nomenclature of Medicine;
- add new data elements to LADB for growth, development, reproduction, and teratology;
- provide capability for on-line statistical analysis for determining relationships between different data sets; and
- adopt new acceptance criteria for data submitted to LADB.

Public Accessibility, 1980-81

LADB first became available on-line to the public in April 1980, via the Battelle computer in Columbus, OH. Some 100 subscribing organizations logged 96 billable hours over the first 6 months of public availability. This usage was far lower than that of other databases operated by NLM, even in their beginning stages. The paucity of user hours, coupled with other financial considerations (see following section) led NLM to stop LADB file-building in January 1981. Slightly more than 1 million animal measurements were contained in LADB at this point, mainly obtained from 30,000 rats and mice. A small amount of data came from cats, dogs, hamsters, minipigs, monkeys, and tree shrews (2). Approximately 80 to 85 percent of the total was obtained from investigators holding contracts awarded by the National Cancer Institute, under its cancer treatment and bioassay programs. When the collection of data was halted, 44 organizations and 15 Federal contractors had contributed data, and 9 other sources had agreed to do so. The Federal commitment to LADB from 1975 through 1980 totaled slightly over $3 million.

Battelle continued to make the file available to the public, but usage did not increase sufficiently to make the project self-sustaining. In early 1982, just 2 years after becoming available on-line, LADB was taken off-line. The file was turned over to the National Technical Information Service for public distribution via licensing. One copy of LADB has been licensed by NTIS to date, to Pergamon International Information Corporation. In 1985, Pergamon, in a joint venture with FASEB, published hard-copy data books created from LADB records (1). There are no plans to add data to the existing file, or to make it publicly available on-line.

Reasons for the Failure of LADB

Financial Considerations

As mentioned, only 96 on-line hours were logged by about 100 LADB users over the first 6 months of public availability. This total was far too small to provide any useful base for self-sufficiency—one of the initial goals for the system. When the Federal Government was vigorously seeking ways to reduce its long-term financial commitments in late 1980, NCI dropped its major financial support in December, and other agencies of the Department of Health and Human Services declined to pick up the slack, under pressure from the Office of Management and Budget to reduce expenses. The LADB contract with Battelle was terminated in early 1981 for lack of funding.

User Friendliness and User's Needs

The interactive software used in LADB was designed in 1975. As such, it predated many major software developments that have emphasized "user friendliness." The users the system was aimed at—biologists—found it hard to retain procedural familiarity with infrequent use.

Another problem with the use of the LADB data, according to the FASEB ad hoc panel (2), was the inability to perform on-line statistical comparisons between different data sets. This limitation, which makes some desirable statistical comparisons difficult to perform, arose from inadequate design and would probably not be a problem with today's software.

User Community

LADB was publicly available for too short a time to permit many conclusions to be drawn about the users. By definition of the content, its users would be expected to be pharmacologists and toxicologists concerned with toxicity testing, particularly chronic toxicity testing. This community, numbering about 3,000 to 5,000 scientists, is far smaller than the community of basic biological scientists (about 200,000). The pool of prospective users of LADB, therefore, seems too small to sustain it.

Peer Review of LADB Design and Data

Although the Institute of Laboratory Animal Resources of the National Academy of Sciences evaluated LADB in 1978, it had not been involved in the original design considerations. Similarly, FASEB entered the review process in 1979—too late to have substantial impact on the design and most of the file-building process. The March 1980 FASEB review (2) pointed out several major design problems, including lack of on-line availability of the individual animal data files. The LADB records that are searchable on-line are composites from groups of animals. Failure to include data on individual animals prevents users from performing statistical comparisons between different data sets.

Lessons Learned From LADB

The acceptance of a biology data bank by the user community and its success in supplying useful research and testing data are actually determined well in advance of the collection or dissemination of data. The first step in assembling a computerized data registry should be the clear definition of its potential users and their specific needs. No adequate study of this nature was performed prior to the original design of LADB. The results of a preliminary feasibility study should identify the various users, their needs, and their desire (or lack thereof) to use and support the proposed database (3).

A 1981 FASEB report, "Guidelines for Development of Biology Data Banks" (4), emphasized three important steps in planning and developing a data bank of biological information. First, the stimulus for establishing a research and testing data bank may be the realization by a scientist, a government agency, or a private organization that the required information is not readily accessible from published, unpublished, or on-line resources. Nevertheless, the need for such an information resource must be determined independently. Most appropriately, this is done by an organization unrelated to the proposing institution. Determination of need involves answering the following questions:

- How many institutional, organizational, or individual users would find the database useful?
- How many would be willing to subscribe, and to what extent would cost be a factor in subscribing?
- How many institutions, organizations, or individual scientists could supply data? How many would?
- How are potential users distributed among disciplines?
- How much unpublished and presently inaccessible data could be made available to investigators by developing a data bank?

If the responses to these questions indicate a solid foundation of perceived need, then the establishment of the data bank is probably justified.

Second, the collection of descriptive data on those scientists interested in the proposed database and on their disciplinary specialties provides a basis for matching the scope of the database to the breadth of disciplinary interest. Specifically, the scope and design of the database depend on the range of purposes for collecting the research and testing data, the size of the prospective audience, and the needs of the users. It is essential to recognize that the needs of any user audience are dynamic and subject to change. A feasibility study should include an analysis of current trends in user application as a basis for inclusion of sufficient flexibility to permit later modification.

In identifying the potential user community, the following considerations are key:

- Can a model be developed to estimate with a high level of accuracy the number of potential users?
- Can a projection of the number of potential donors be made from a similar model?
- To what extent will the user community support assessment of operational charges to defray costs?
- What will it cost to collect, systematize, store, and retrieve the data for a computerized, online system?

Third, critical to the acceptance and success of a registry of research and testing data is peer review by experts, at all levels of database development. These levels include:

- system design;
- definition of data elements;
- establishment of standards for data acceptance;
- compilation and building of data files; and
- post-hoc evaluation of the system (i.e., feedback resulting from experience gained by actual use of the system).

The peer-review process assures that experienced researchers have judged the design, standards, and data to be used. The process enhances quality control, although it imposes the penalty of high costs and slow input of data.

EXPANDING THE LADB CONCEPT: A COMPUTERIZED REGISTRY OF RESEARCH AND TESTING DATA

The concept behind the LADB could be expanded in at least two important dimensions. First, the scope could be broadened beyond baseline results to include experimental results from research and testing. How great an increase in size would this be? For every measurement obtained from a group of control animals, measurements are obtained from an estimated one to nine groups of experimental animals. This makes a registry of control and experimental data from **2 to 10 times** the size of a registry of baseline data alone.

Second, the coverage could be enlarged beyond principally rodents to all vertebrate species. How great an increase would this entail? Several hundred vertebrate species could be involved. The number of species would increase by a factor of more than 100. Yet the bulk of the results would still be derived from rats and mice, since rats and mice account for 12 million to 15 million of the 17 million to 22 million animals used annually in the United States (see ch. 3). Increasing the scope from rats and mice to all vertebrates would therefore likely enlarge the size of the data registry by **a factor of 1.5** (17 million to 22 million animals divided by 12 million to 15 million rats and mice).

The creation and maintenance of a computerized registry of baseline and experimental results from all species of vertebrate animals would represent an enterprise **3 to 15 times more complex** than the unsuccessful Laboratory Animal Data Bank.

The factors that led in the 1970s to the assignment of the LADB project to the NLM remain valid today should a similar project be undertaken. NLM has related experience in handling substance-oriented databases (as detailed in table 10-3), such as the TDB and RTECS. NLM also operates much larger databases, such as TOXLINE and MEDLINE, that are bibliographic rather than substance-oriented.

Other entities that could be considered for operating a centralized registry of research and testing data include:

- **National Toxicology Program.** NTP never had as its mission the development of a data bank, and it is not presently equipped to do so. The scope of NTP's mission would have to be redefined if it were to undertake this responsibility.
- **National Bureau of Standards.** Although NBS specializes in physical, chemical, and engineering databases, it has never been involved in a biological database operation. NBS does not appear to be a viable candidate.
- **National Agricultural Library (NAL).** Unlike NLM, NAL has not developed any specialized computerized biological data registry systems. It does not appear to be a viable candidate for operating a centralized registry of research and testing data. The 1985 amendments to the Animal Welfare Act (see ch. 13) directed NAL—in cooperation with NLM—to provide information that could prevent unintended duplication of animal experimentation, and information on improved methods of animal experimentation.
- **Chemical Industry Institute of Toxicology.** Unless the chemical industry chose to increase funding to CIIT for this express purpose, it could not support this activity. Also, CIIT lacks personnel experienced in large-scale database development and operation.
- **Pharmaceutical Manufacturers' Association (PMA).** PMA is not independent of direction by its members (as is CIIT, for example). Further, PMA is not engaged in large database efforts, making it an unlikely candidate.
- **Federation of American Societies for Experimental Biology.** FASEB has published handbooks of biological data and is currently embarked on a venture to extract some data from LADB files. However, because of limited resources for data-base development and operation, FASEB's most appropriate role might be as the coordinator of peer-review groups.
- **Chemical Abstracts Service of the American Chemical Society,** and **BioSciences Information Services.** Each of these services annually prepares hundreds of thousands of abstracts that report biological research and testing results. These files are document-oriented and indexed systematically. However, the detail of the abstracts published does not begin to approximate the depth of information found even in LADB. Both services could conceivably undertake the development and operation of a computerized data registry, particularly with NLM supervision.

In summary, it appears that virtually no existing private or public entity, save the NLM, has the resources and expertise to design, develop, and maintain a computerized registry of research and testing data. If NLM were to undertake such a task, it would probably rely on contractors from the private and nonprofit sectors.

SUMMARY AND CONCLUSIONS

The sharing of information on research and testing is vital to scientific progress. There are a variety of ways in which such information can be shared.

Published materials, especially articles appearing in scientific journals, are an indispensable source of information on the results of completed research and testing. Unfortunately, a substantial body of information is not published, although some of it is publicly available.

Publication is a means of establishing a reputation in the scientific community. This is especially important to academics. For scientists in industry, however, the efforts required for publication compete with other demands on resources, as well as with the need to keep information with some proprietary value confidential.

Much data generated by the Government are published. Yet, when an agency's mission is regulatory, less attention is given to publication than to other concerns.

Because of the importance of journals, their publication policies have a great impact on the kinds of information available. The most troublesome policy is the tendency to publish only results that show an effect. Thus, protocols that yield negative results may be unintentionally duplicated in subsequent experiments.

Federal Government agencies have access to some of the unpublished information held by industry, through reporting rules promulgated under the Toxic Substances Control Act, for example, and through registration requirements of the Federal Insecticide, Fungicide, and Rodenticide Act. This information is used for a variety of regulatory activities and is frequently available to the public under the Freedom of Information Act. It may also be added to databases.

There are several barriers to using available information. One is that users who wish to base important decisions on data need to know how reliable the data are. In assessing reliability, scientists will consider not only the protocol used but also the professional reputation of the scientist, the journal in which the article is published, and where the research or testing was done. If the format of the data (e.g., a numerical database) does not allow the quality to be assessed, the data may have little value. The imprimatur of peer review is an additional factor when assessing data quality.

International barriers to sharing information include language, the delays and expense of communication, the lack of personal acquaintances who could facilitate networking, and political and institutional differences.

Hundreds of thousands of research and testing articles are published each year. Most of these articles and other resources are available through abstracting and indexing services and through bibliographic services. No service, unfortunately, is so comprehensive that it can be relied on as a sole source. However, when multiple sources are used, there can be a great deal of overlap. Another problem is that the summary information may be inadequate to judge whether the complete article should be obtained. Citation services also exist for unpublished data and ongoing experiments, some on an international level.

Computers are quite valuable in obtaining access to information. Many of the abstracting and indexing services and bibliographic services are available on computer. Recently, the full text of some scientific journals—except for graphs and images—has become available on-line. In principle, a computer-based registry of research and testing data could reduce the use of animals in research and testing. In practice, the best design of such a computerized database remains uncertain.

One attempt toward a modest, well-defined data registry, the Laboratory Animal Data Bank, failed. Any new effort to establish a comprehensive database that includes descriptions of experimental protocols, control and experimental results, and peer review will benefit from the lessons learned from LADB. The creation and maintenance of a computerized registry of baseline and experimental results from all species of vertebrate animals would be 3 to 15 times more complex than the defunct LADB.

The initial step towards assembling a computerized data registry is the clear definition of both its potential users and their specific needs. The acceptance of a new biological data bank by the user community and the registry's success in supplying useful research and testing data are closely linked to how well the data bank meets user needs. Thus, the probable success or failure of a new data bank can be predicted in advance of the collection or dissemination of the data.

CHAPTER 10 REFERENCES

1. Altman, P.L. (ed.), *Pathology of Laboratory Mice and Rats* (New York: Pergamon Press, 1985).
2. Altman, P.L., and Fisher, K.D., *Review of Data Standards Related to the Laboratory Animal Data Bank—Interim Report* (Bethesda, MD: Federation of American Societies for Experimental Biology, 1980).
3. Altman, P.L., and Fisher, K.D., *Assessment of the Laboratory Animal Data Bank in Meeting Needs of Users* (Bethesda, MD: Federation of American Societies for Experimental Biology, 1980).
4. Altman, P.L., and Fisher, K.D., *Guidelines for Development of Biology Data Banks* (Bethesda, MD: Federation of American Societies for Experimental Biology, 1981).
5. Altman, P.L., and Fisher, K.D., *A User Assessment of the Toxicology Data Bank* (Bethesda, MD: Feder-

ation of American Societies for Experimental Biology, 1982).
6. BIOSIS (BioSciences Information Service), "The 1985 BIOSIS Catalog," Philadelphia, PA, 1985.
7. Collen, M.F., and Flagle, C.D., "Full-Text Medical Literature Retrieval by Computer," *JAMA* 254:2768-2774, 1985.
8. Cooper, M., "Secondary Information Services in Science and Technology: A Wide-Angle View," *J. Am. Soc. Info. Sci.* 33:152, 1982.
9. Cummings, M.M., Consultant, Council on Library Resources, Inc., Washington, DC, personal communication, April 1985.
10. Davidson, J., "The Scope of Biological Testing Today," paper presented at the Annual Meeting of the Society for Information Science, Annual Meeting, Philadelphia, PA, October 1984.
11. Fang, J., Tracor Jitco, Inc., Rockville, MD, personal communication, June 1984.
12. Fox, J.L., "News and Comment," *Science* 226:816, 1984.
13. Institute of Laboratory Animal Resources, Committee on Laboratory Animal Data, *Review and Evaluation of the National Library of Medicine Laboratory Animal Data Bank* (Washington, DC: National Academy Press, 1979).
14. Loosjes, Th.P., *On Documentation of Scientific Literature* (London: Archon Books, 1967).
15. Meyer, D.E., Mehlman, D.W., Reeves, E.S., et al., "Comparison Study of Overlap Among 21 Scientific Databases in Searching Pesticide Information," *Online Review,* 7(1):33, 1983.
16. National Bureau of Standards, Workshop on Data Quality Indicators, Gaithersburg, MD, Feb. 10-12, 1982.
17. Organization for Economic Cooperation and Development, "Decision on the Mutual Acceptance of Data in the Assessment of Chemicals," [C(81)30 (Final)], addenda 1 to 4, adopted May 12, 1981.
18. Organization for Economic Cooperation and Development, "Improved Access to Unpublished Information," Report of the Expert Group (Paris: 1984).
19. U.S. Department of Health and Human Services, National Institute for Occupational Safety and Health, *Registry of Toxic Effects of Chemical Substances,* R.L. Tatken and R.J. Lewis, Sr. (eds.), DHHS (NIOSH) Pub. No. 83-107 (Cincinnati, OH: NIOSH, June 1983).
20. U.S. Executive Office of the President, Council on Environmental Quality, Toxic Substances Strategy Committee, *Toxic Chemicals and Public Protection* (Washington, DC: U.S. Government Printing Office, May 1980).

Chapter 11
Economic Considerations

It would not be reasonable to make decisions on alternatives to animal use without having some idea of the consequences to the health and welfare of the public.

Kennerly H. Digges
National Highway Traffic Safety Administration
U.S. Department of Transportation
March 20, 1985

CONTENTS

List of Tables

List of Figures

Chapter 11
Economic Considerations

Economic considerations play an important role in decisions on the use of animals in research, testing, and, to a lesser extent, education. It is demonstrable that many valuable techniques, pharmaceuticals, pesticides, and other products have been developed or tested using animals. Yet animal use is often very expensive and time-consuming. A new pesticide, for example, may require $5 million worth of testing with animals before it can be registered. Even higher animal costs may be incurred in developing a new drug. Large incentives thus exist to find alternatives that reduce the cost and time involved in animal research and testing while maintaining the ability to improve human health, assess and manage the risks of toxic substances, and acquire fundamental new biomedical knowledge. Considerable investments are required to develop and validate such alternatives before they can be implemented with confidence.

This chapter examines costs and benefits surrounding animal use and the development, validation, and implementation of alternatives in research and testing. Data are provided for biomedical research as it relates to human health and disease, but a precise determination of costs and economic benefits of animal use within biomedical research is elusive. Several aspects of using animals in toxicological testing are examined, including the development of pesticides, the economic incentives to develop and validate nonanimal tests, and the extent of liability a manufacturer might incur for insufficient product testing.

In education, it is hard to put a price tag on the use of animals. At the college and graduate levels, benefits of animal use include the training of biologists, psychologists, toxicologists, physicians, and veterinarians. Education involving animals contributes indirectly to research and testing by training those who eventually carry out this work. The benefits of using animals in primary and secondary education include increasing students' familiarity with animal behavior and care (see ch. 9).

HOW MUCH DOES ANIMAL USE COST?

In either research or testing, the principal cost associated with animal use is that of human labor. Animals must be fed, watered, and have their cages cleaned. They require attendant veterinary care and are housed in facilities needing labor-intensive sanitation. Such labor costs are the major component of both the expense of producing animals in breeding facilities and the cost of maintaining them in laboratory facilities prior to and during research and testing.

The total cost of animal use is the sum of the cost of acquisition of the animals and that of maintaining the animals prior to and during their use. Acquisition expenses vary widely among species. Mice, for example, cost on average about $2 apiece, hamsters about $5, and guinea pigs about $19. Dogs range in price from $5 for a pound animal to several hundred dollars for a purpose-bred animal. Primates can cost from $400 to more than $2,000. The actual cost for a particular species varies with the sex, strain, weight, age, quantity ordered, method of shipping, and distance shipped.

Maintenance costs also vary. Maintaining a mouse, for example, costs about 5 cents per day, a hamster about 11 cents per day, and a guinea pig about 40 cents per day. The actual cost varies among different laboratory facilities, depending, for example, on accounting practices and local labor costs. The total maintenance cost of an animal is directly related to its length of stay in the laboratory. It is important to note that maintenance expenses can quickly exceed and even dwarf acquisition costs. A 2-month-old hamster costing $5, for example, used in research until the age of 10 months costs $26 to maintain.

Figure 11-1 illustrates the relation between the number of animals used in research and testing

Figure 11-1.—Relation Between Number of Animals Used and Cost of Animal Use

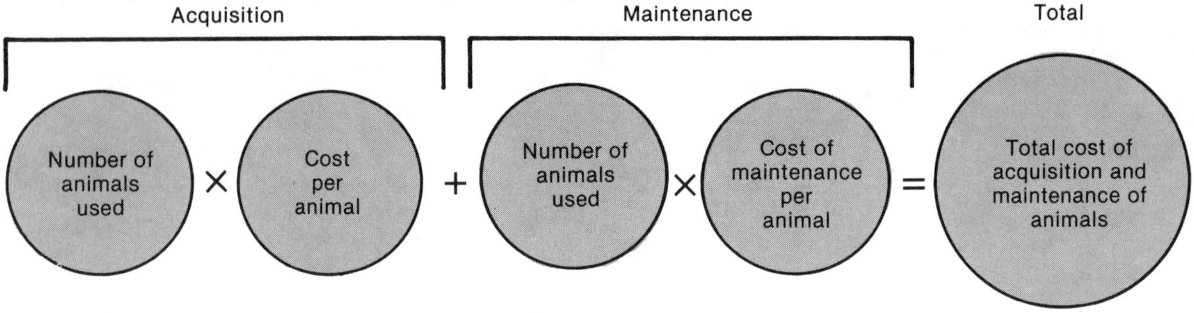

The total cost of animal acquisition and maintenance equals the sum of the acquisition cost and the maintenance cost. (The maintenance cost depends on the animal's length of stay in the animal facility.)

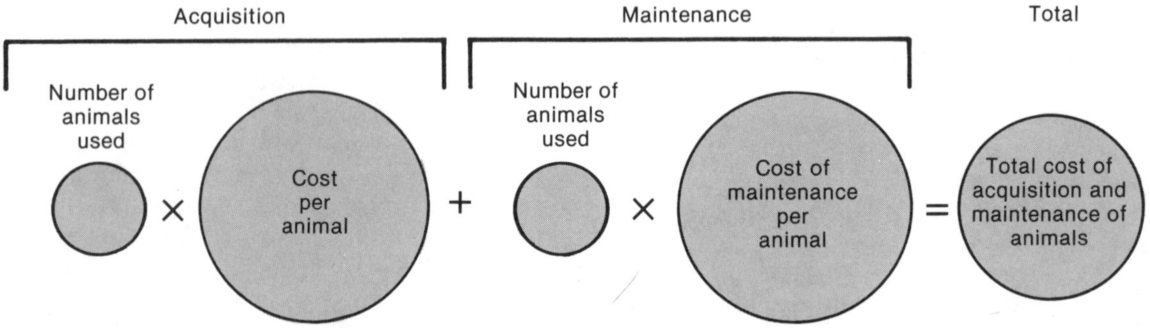

Using fewer animals will yield a decrease in the total cost of animal acquisition and maintenance, but the proportionate sav ings will be less than the decrease in the number of animals used. Both the price of each animal and the cost of maintenance per animal can be expected to increase to support the operating costs of breeding facilities and animal facilities.

SOURCE: Office of Technology Assessment.

and the total cost of animal use. Although the numbers and species of animals used (see ch. 3) and the price per animal can be estimated, it is currently impossible to estimate with any accuracy the laboratory lifetime—and hence the total maintenance costs—of animals used in the United States. Therefore no actual dollar figure can be affixed to the cost of animal acquisition and maintenance in research and testing. Beginning in 1986, the Public Health Service (PHS) will require reports on the average daily census of all species housed in PHS-funded facilities (see app. C). These data may permit an estimate of the total cost of animal use in a sizable portion of animal research—namely, that conducted in PHS-funded facilities.

The relationship shown in figure 11-1 emphasizes several aspects of the economics of animal use. If the number of animals used is reduced, the total cost of animal acquisition and maintenance will decline. But the proportional decrease in total cost will not match the proportional decrease in the number of animals used. Reducing animal use by 15 percent, for example, will not effect a cost savings of 15 percent; the savings will be somewhat less, for two reasons. First, if the number of animals used decreases, the cost of acquiring each animal can be expected to increase somewhat. (A temporary drop in price for some species that are in immediate oversupply may occur, but this would last only through the laboratory-useful lifespan of animals already on hand and ready for sale.) With reduced demand, vendors would have to raise prices to cover their overhead. Second, if the number of animals used decreases, the expense of maintaining each remaining animal in a laboratory facility can be expected to increase. Laboratory-animal facilities would have to spread the cost of operation over fewer animals. In both breeding and laboratory maintenance of animals, there are economies of scale such that breeding and maintenance of marginally fewer animals does not yield a corresponding decrease in costs.

COSTS AND BENEFITS IN RESEARCH

The many important economic contributions of research with animals are difficult to characterize. First, research does not lend itself to such analysis. Normally, one experiment will draw from many others and contribute to future research, making allocation of costs and benefits to a particular activity virtually impossible. Second, the outcome of each experiment is uncertain, and the experiences in one program would not necessarily apply to others. Third, the delay between research and commercialization is long, reaching a decade or more, with payoff taking even longer. Thus, it is not possible to evaluate with any reasonable confidence the costs and benefits of current or even recent animal and nonanimal research practices.

Biomedical Research

This section discusses biomedical research in general, which unavoidably averages many diverse research experiences. Biomedical research is of interest because it is a major user of animals, because it affects human health, and because it affects an important sector of the economy—the health care industry. As with most areas of research, many of the contributions are indirect and many are not easily quantified in economic terms (see ch. 5). Most benefits are realized in the health care industry, which in 1983 accounted for $355.4 billion (10.8 percent) of the gross national product (9). Drugs, which require both biomedical research and toxicological testing in their development, have annual sales of about $30 billion and contribute about 20,000 jobs to the economy (29).

The first medical discovery that was largely a result of research with animals was diphtheria antitoxin at the end of the 19th century. Its use reduced the likelihood of death for those contracting diphtheria from 40 to 10 percent (28). Animals eventually came to be used in all phases of biomedical research and in the development of medical products such as drugs and devices and of services such as surgery and diagnostic techniques.

Research with animals that leads to practical applications can last from a few days to many years. It may involve inexpensive equipment or hundreds of thousands of dollars' worth of instrumentation, may be performed by a laboratory technician with little supervision or by a team of highly educated scientists, and may be done with fruit flies or with primates. The costs will vary accordingly.

The benefits and rates of return on a given experiment vary widely. The rate of return for a given research program can only be determined reliably many years after commercialization. In the case of products with high research and testing costs and long lead times to commercialization, which applies to many of the products of biomedical research, the lag can be several decades.

A 1972 study on the rates of return for six large pharmaceutical companies for research they conducted in 1954 through 1961, when animals were widely used, estimated the pretax private rate of return to be 25 to 30 percent (2). The social rate of return—the benefits to the public, was estimated to be at least twice as high (20).

Another approach to gauging costs and benefits involves looking at expenditures from 1900 to 1975 and comparing them with the benefits of medical advances in preventing sickness and death in the work force over the same period (4). All data were adjusted to 1975 conditions. Analogous comparisons were made for 1930 to 1975.

Of course, this approach ignores both the costs of research before 1900 (or 1930) that contributed benefits after those years and any research conducted before 1975 for which the benefits had not fully accrued. The latter is more confounding because much more research was done in the last decade of the study than any other, so the benefits could not be fully counted. Undervalue also occurs because it is impossible to measure the value of not being ill. Yet, other assumptions in the study may overvalue the benefits by neglecting changes in nutrition, lifestyle, and working conditions.

Benefits exceeded costs in this study by factors ranging from 4 to 16, depending on the assumptions made in calculating benefits and whether the time period is from 1900 to 1975 or 1930 to 1975. Expressing the results in another way, the savings in health-related costs due to the increase in knowledge was estimated to be $115 billion to $407 billion (4,20).

Savings were also calculated for various disease categories. As can be seen in table 11-1, research costs in certain areas have exceeded benefits accruing over the same period (as indicated by a minus sign). Table 11-2 provides related information about levels of funding in selected years, showing how funding grew during the same period. The research budget for 1975 corresponded to almost 9 percent of the costs associated with neoplasms (data not shown in tables), whereas all other budget-to-cost ratios were below 1.4 percent (20).

Although economic and financial data such as these are useful in making policy judgments, most decisions about using animals are more complicated and take into account political and technical considerations, as well as economic ones. Monetary costs and benefits must be balanced with factors such as scientists' desire to be certain and society's desire to have animals treated in a humane fashion. Economic analysis focuses on only part of the equation, and cannot be the sole basis for decisions.

One example of the tension between financial and other criteria is exemplified by the question of whether pound animals should be used in laboratory studies. A recent survey indicates that about three times as many dogs and cats are obtained from pounds and dealers (who often purchase from pounds) as are purpose-bred for laboratory use (18). Scientists have argued that

Table 11-1.—Total Savings Attributable to Biomedical Research[a] (in billions)

Disease category	1900-75 simulation			1930-75 simulation		
Total[b]	**$299.37**	**to**	**$479.83**	**$145.65**	**to**	**$167.76**
Infective and parasitic diseases	118.35	to	174.16	63.15	to	69.23
Neoplasms	−2.66	to	−3.17	−1.17	to	−1.40
Endocrine, nutritional, and metabolic diseases	0.28	to	0.95	−1.57	to	−0.99
Diseases of the blood and blood-forming organs	0.76	to	1.27	5.22	to	5.45
Mental disorders	9.20	to	21.88	3.73	to	3.72
Diseases of the nervous system and sense organs	14.76	to	24.31	−3.32	to	−2.70
Diseases of the circulatory system	10.68	to	18.11	−6.42	to	−4.91
Diseases of the respiratory system	71.75	to	116.38	23.44	to	27.56
Diseases of the digestive system, oral cavity, salivary glands, and jaws	12.96	to	21.62	23.53	to	26.53
Diseases of the genitourinary system	23.58	to	37.28	9.27	to	10.96
Complications of pregnancy, childbirth, and postpartum	4.59	to	7.88	10.92	to	11.62
Diseases of the skin and subcutaneous tissue	0.93	to	1.76	2.98	to	3.04
Diseases of the musculoskeletal system and connective tissue	6.19	to	14.59	−11.04	to	−10.98
Congenital anomalies	7.56	to	10.08	−1.41	to	−1.11
Certain causes of perinatal morbidity and mortality	2.80	to	3.73	4.38	to	6.58
Symptoms and ill-defined conditions	14.46	to	19.80	−2.10	to	−1.67
Accidents, poisonings, and violence	4.08	to	9.39	26.05	to	26.86

[a]Minus signs indicate costs exceeded benefits.
[b]Totals may not add due to rounding.

SOURCES: **1900-75 simulation:** S.J. Mushkin, *Biomedical Research: Costs and Benefits* (Cambridge, MA: Ballinger Publishing Co., 1979); **1930-75 simulation:** A. Berk and L.C. Paringer, *Economic Costs of Illness, 1930-1975* (Washington, DC: Public Services Laboratory, Georgetown University, 1977).

Table 11-2.—Estimated Biomedical Research Outlays, Selected Years, 1900-75 (in millions)

Disease category	1900	1930	1963	1975
Total[a]	**$0.1570**	**$10.0180**	**$1,561.0**	**$4,640.0**
Infective and parasitic diseases	0.0476	1.0329	17.2	37.6
Neoplasms	0.0195	2.8291	847.6	2,464.8
Endocrine, nutritional, and metabolic diseases	0.0006	0.2775	33.2	109.0
Diseases of the blood and blood-forming organs	0.0003	0.0701	4.5	12.5
Mental disorders	0.0005	0.0461	4.1	22.7
Diseases of the nervous system and sense organs	0.0072	0.2164	14.2	41.3
Diseases of the circulatory system	0.0039	0.9136	252.4	876.0
Diseases of the respiratory system	0.0305	1.0609	96.5	261.7
Diseases of the digestive system, oral cavity, salivary glands, and jaws	0.0060	0.7273	62.3	175.4
Diseases of the genitourinary system	0.0129	0.9338	25.8	66.8
Complications of pregnancy, childbirth, and postpartum	0.0009	0.1142	1.2	0.9
Diseases of the skin and subcutaneous tissue	0.0002	0.0160	1.9	4.6
Diseases of the musculoskeletal system and connective tissue	0.0006	0.0240	3.3	12.1
Congenital anomalies	—	0.1092	18.4	32.0
Certain causes of perinatal morbidity and mortality	0.0085	0.4448	50.0	68.7
Symptoms and ill-defined conditions	0.0096	0.2725	19.4	74.2
Accidents, poisonings, and violence	0.0068	0.9377	109.0	379.6

[a]Totals may not add due to rounding.

SOURCE: Data from S.J. Mushkin, *Biomedical Research: Costs and Benefits* (Cambridge, MA: Ballinger Publishing Co., 1979).

pound animals are much cheaper than purpose-bred ones and that it would be wasteful to destroy them when they could be used. The difference in price between a purpose-bred and a pound dog ranges from $200 to $500 per animal. Estimates of the impact on research of a ban on using pound animals range from a tenfold increase in costs to effectively stopping research in Los Angeles County (25). Others have argued that pound animals are poorly suited to most laboratory work because they are often in poor health and their genetic background is usually uncertain (25).

It may seem ethically desirable to make use of animals that would be killed anyway, but an animal that had been a pet may find laboratory conditions more stressful than a purpose-bred animal would. Other nonpecuniary considerations are that people may hesitate to bring their animals to a pound if they oppose laboratory use of pound animals and that those using pound animals will see them as cheap, disposable experimental tools that need not be conserved (22).

Supporting Patent Claims

Data derived from animal research have proprietary value and are often used to support patent applications for drugs or devices for humans. Patents give the inventor an exclusive right to make and sell the patented invention, thus providing an incentive to invent, which in turn fuels a growing economy. Thus, animal use can have important economic consequences in addition to improvement in health.

To obtain a patent, an inventor must show that the invention is novel and useful and must disclose how to make it and use it. Data from studies with humans are normally obtained to support a patent on an invention to be used by humans, but data on animals can provide evidence of utility as well (12,15). And because they are normally obtained before research is done on humans, such data sometimes play a crucial role in determining the date of an invention, which could determine who gets the patent in the case of two competing inventors.

Utility can be demonstrated with animal studies, but only if the data would convince someone of ordinary skill in the art that the same effect would be observed in humans (14). The character and quantity of evidence needed to show utility depend, in part, on whether the results agree with established beliefs (13). Courts recognize that an animal may respond differently than a human would (16), and in demonstrating the utility of an invention it is not necessary to demonstrate safety (11,17).

In vitro experiments are sometimes sufficient to demonstrate utility for patent purposes. In one recent case (7), in vitro tests showed that the chemical to be patented, an imidazole derivative, inhibited thromboxane synthetase in blood platelets. The activity of thromboxane synthetase was thought to be related to hypertension, pulmonary vasoconstriction, and other cardiovascular diseases, and the demonstration of the chemical's ability to inhibit it was sufficient to show utility. Data showing therapeutic use were not required in showing that an invention had taken place. In another case, the fact that the inventor had given a detailed description of how the substance to be patented would behave was enough to support a showing of utility, thus fixing the date of invention (24).

Although the use of alternatives to support patents is interesting, it does not have much practical effect on the use of animals in developing medical products because safety and efficacy must be demonstrated to satisfy regulatory requirements (see ch. 7). These patent cases might have some application, however, in demonstrating the sufficiency of alternatives in other areas.

COSTS AND BENEFITS IN TESTING

There are several major economic benefits to using animals in toxicological testing. Drugs, food additives, pesticides, and many consumer products are tested for toxicity or other kinds of hazards before they can be marketed and begin to generate income for the manufacturer. This is often done to meet regulatory requirements, but the tests are also done to avoid marketing unsafe products. In addition, testing is done to confirm that a product does in fact confer a benefit.

Testing Pesticides for Toxicity

Over a billion pounds of pesticides are used in the United States annually, corresponding to over $4 billion in sales. About 130 firms produce the active ingredients in pesticides. Thirty of these produce common products in high volume; the others tend to produce specialty pesticides. Most of the pesticides are used in the agricultural sector. About 7 percent are purchased by consumers for home and garden use, while industrial and institutional use account for about 20 percent (31).

Because pesticides are designed to be biological poisons, they are among the most toxic substances commercially available. Most of the hazards result from chronic, low-level exposure. Exposure and the risk of it are widespread. About 2 million commercial farms in the United States use pesticides, some of which remain in or on the food and are eventually consumed. About 40,000 commercial applicators use pesticides to treat structures and facilities. The Environmental Protection Agency (EPA) estimates that 90 percent of all households regularly use or have used pesticides in the home, garden, or yard (31). The results of tests on animals are used by EPA to identify hazards and to develop acceptable exposure levels and safe handling and disposal practices (see ch. 7). Thus, animal testing plays an important role in the protection of virtually the entire U.S. population.

Acute poisonings have been estimated to cost over $15 million annually (1980 dollars), excluding the value of saving lives or avoiding suffering. The estimated cost of each death due to pesticide poisoning is $112,000, whereas the average cost of a nonfatal poisoning is $200 (23,31). The costs of cancer, the most important chronic effect, is over $34 billion in 1980 dollars, with each cancer costing $52,000 (31). One research goal is to find new pesticides that are less toxic and more effective than those now in use, a search that entails animal testing.

There are over 48,000 registered pesticide formulations, with an estimated 1,400 to 1,500 active ingredients (5). There are between 5 and 20 new registrations for active ingredients issued annually, each requiring a complete toxicological evaluation based on animal testing and other data. Another 1,500 to 2,000 new formulations or uses are also registered annually (5,31). These require little additional testing, as a rule, and often rely on data in EPA's files.

Testing costs vary with the product and its uses. Pesticides intended for food crops require much more testing than those for other uses. Some of the required testing depends on results obtained in screening tests. The cost of testing can range from $2 million to $5 million for a new active ingredient. This represents a small fraction of the total developmental expenses, which may approach $100 million (31). Testing costs are incurred primarily in the beginning of the developmental cycle (see fig. 11-2). As the figure illustrates, testing with animals—during testing for toxicity—is an integral part of the development of a new pesticide.

Testing and Product Liability

Toxicological testing of consumer products helps keep unsafe products off the market. It also may sometimes allow liability for injuries to be avoided. The cost of product liability litigation can be enormous, and companies are tending to drop risky products, as the current situation with vaccines illustrates.

Most States have "strict liability," in that a manufacturer is liable for whatever injuries its products cause. In most jurisdictions, there are exceptions, such as when the technology for determining that a product is unsafe does not exist. There are also exceptions when the product is known to be dangerous but also to confer a great benefit. Such is the case for rabies vaccine. A few jurisdictions merely require that a manufacturer not be negligent (see ch. 7.) Manufacturers are unlikely to adopt alternatives to animal tests until they believe such methods offer a level of assurance of product safety equal to that offered by animal testing.

Testing Costs of Animals and the Alternatives

An estimated 80 percent of the cost of testing, whether whole-animal or in vitro, is for labor (6). Testing costs vary widely with the assay used and somewhat with the facility. The cheapest, such as for eye or skin irritation, can be done for un-

Figure 11-2.—Development of a Typical Pesticide for Agriculture
(Note the integral role of animal toxicity testing in pesticide development, shown in boldface.)

Year	0 1 2 3 4 5 6 7 8
Research and development	△Synthesis △ Analytical methods development △ Preliminary tests for efficacy △Field trials, product development
Toxicity	**△ Acute and subacute tests, skin and eye sensitization ($25,000)** **△ Subchronic tests, fish and bird studies, teratogenicity ($500,000)** **△ Chronic effects, carcinogenicity, reproduction ($2-2.5 million)** **△ Metabolism and environmental studies ($2 million)**
Registration	△ Apply to EPA for experimental use permit △Submit application for registration to EPA
Marketing	△Market research △Develop marketing strategy △ Test market
Production	△Patent application △Process development △ Design small plant △ Start up small plant △ Final plant design △ Begin construction △ Start up plant
Commercialization	Full commercialization

SOURCE: Office of Technology Assessment, adapted from Haskell Laboratories, E.I. du Pont de Nemours & Company, Wilmington, DE, 1984.

38-750 O - 86 - 9

der $1,000. An LD_{50} test can be performed for less than $2,000. Subchronic toxicity tests can cost under $100,000, and those for long-term toxicity or carcinogenicity for two species can be done for less than $1 million, and perhaps for under $500,000 (10,31). As a rule, the cheaper tests require fewer animals, but more importantly they take far less time at each of three stages—planning, execution, and analysis. Another reason for large variations in testing costs is the species used, with maintenance costs approximating $0.05 per day for a mouse, $4 for a dog, and $11 for a chimpanzee. Most of the cost of maintaining animals is attributable to labor expenses.

Various short-term in vitro tests for mutagenicity have been developed over the past 15 years in an effort to replace the more costly and time-consuming carcinogenicity test (see ch. 8). The most popular mutagenicity test, and one of the first to be introduced, is the *Salmonella typhimurium*/microsome plate mutation assay (the Ames test), costing $1,000 to $2,000 (10). This assay has the most extensive database thus far (1). Used alone, it does not appear to be as predictive of human carcinogenicity as are animal tests.

If the Ames test, some yet-to-be-developed test, or a battery of tests proves to be more predictive of carcinogenicity than testing with animals, the savings could be enormous. A battery of tests that might indicate carcinogenicity has been suggested by the National Toxicology Program (30) and has shown some promise in preliminary evaluations (see ch. 8). Most testing laboratories could conduct this particular battery of tests for under $50,000, and costs would probably decline as the tests become more commonplace (10).

NATIONAL EXPENDITURES FOR RESEARCH AND TESTING

Research and testing in the United States are financed and conducted in a variety of ways. The sources of research funding are Government and industry. Some Government research funds support Government laboratories, but a larger share support research in academia. Industry research is done primarily at in-house industry laboratories, with some funds contracted to other laboratories and to academia.

Most testing is conducted by industry. The chemical industry is the sector most directly affected by regulatory policies concerning toxicological testing. In 1982, this industry (Standard Industrial Classification Code 28) had shipments worth over $170 billion and employed 866,000 people, which represented 8.7 percent of all industry shipments in the United States and 4.5 percent of the employees.

Drugs, soaps and toilet goods, and agricultural chemicals account for the greatest use of animals in testing, and constitute almost a third of their use by the chemical industry. The rest of the chemical industry, in order to satisfy transportation, disposal, and occupational health requirements, does simple tests such as the LD_{50} for substances for which the potential exposure is high (see ch. 7).

Corporate research and development (R&D) in the chemical industry is large and concentrated in the industrial chemicals and drug sectors. Expenditures by the industry totaled $7.6 billion in 1984 (8), a figure that includes in-house toxicological testing, research involving the use of animals, and many other activities. It has been estimated that the toxicological testing industry accounts for just under 10 percent of the R&D expenditures in the chemical industry (27), making testing an estimated $700 million expenditure in 1984. An unknown percentage is spent on research involving animals.

In the past 10 years, industry's R&D expenditures have grown at about 13 percent per year, following a slight decline in the early 1970s. R&D expenditures for drugs, as a percentage of sales, are twice as high as the industry average, and have grown at a slightly higher rate (8). Animal use could be growing at a similar rate, although survey estimates (see ch. 3) and other factors (see ch. 8) do not support this notion.

The Federal Government also plays a major role in animal research and testing, with almost $6 billion obligated for research in life sciences for 1985. University research in the life sciences, which is funded largely by Government and somewhat by industry, will cost an estimated $2.9 billion (8).

Projections of future expenditures depend on a number of factors, including the growth of the chemical industry and of R&D within it; the areas of R&D (e.g., new substances, new uses for old substances, new processes for making old substances); regulatory policies, both domestic and foreign; the growth of the overall economy; tax policy; and further developments in nonanimal tests.

International developments can have economic repercussions. For example, Swiss voters defeated in 1985 a referendum virtually banning all animal testing (see ch. 16). A number of companies have facilities in Switzerland, and such a change could have shifted testing to another country. Whether U.S. labs could compete for that business depends on the strength of the dollar.

Toxicological Testing Services

In 1984, the toxicity testing industry in the United States was estimated to be worth about $650 million per year (27). Sixty-five percent of the testing is done by corporations in-house. The remaining 35 percent (about $225 million annually) is conducted by commercial laboratories, universities, and other organizations. Although there are over 110 U.S. laboratories that sell testing services, most specialize in a small number of assays and are not "full service." Hazelton is the largest of the full-service labs, with domestic sales of $36 million in 1983. Except for Hazelton and several other large commercial labs, the industry is a dispersed one, with the many small commercial firms accounting for approximately two-thirds of the value of domestic sales (10).

The industry expanded its facilities in the 1970s in response to Federal regulatory changes and the passage of the Toxic Substances Control Act. Testing did not increase as much as expected, however, and in the early and mid-1980s the industry was operating at 60 to 70 percent capacity (27). This has led to fairly level prices over the past few years and, in some cases, price cutting to maintain market position. Because of this competition, current prices reflect the actual costs of testing. Testing laboratories often do not quote set prices for some testing procedures or for particular batteries of tests, preferring to negotiate on a case-by-case basis.

Government Toxicological Research and Testing

The U.S. Government programs with strong ties to toxicological testing are EPA, the National Center for Toxicological Research in the Food and Drug Administration, the Centers for Disease Control, and the National Institutes of Health (see table 11-3). Other programs are not identified with separate budget line items and are dispersed among various agencies and departments.

Table 11-3.—Selected Federal Expenditures Related to Toxicological Testing and Research, 1984-86 (in thousands)

	1984	1985[a]	1986[a]
Environmental Protection Agency:			
Program expenses	$327,145	$380,341	$376,074
Toxic substances	34,484	39,341	38,660
Pesticides	32,772	37,805	36,948
Research and development	144,903	195,449	212,061
Toxic substances	12,327	14,450	26,358
Pesticides	1,738	5,121	6,938
Interdisciplinary	18,522	22,423	14,876
Food and Drug Administration:			
National Center for Toxicological Research	21,132	21,575	22,284
Drug program	138,248	153,112	152,430
Food program	115,541	109,538	113,907
Devices and radiologic products	62,568	67,081	68,368
Centers for Disease Control:			
Occupational safety and health research	54,740	54,863	57,645
Research on chronic and environmental disease	25,953	28,568	23,726
National Institutes of Health:			
National Cancer Institute:			
Cause and prevention	276,075	301,655	285,844
Detection and diagnosis	63,182	70,524	66,839
Treatment	340,041	367,940	351,683
National Institute of Environmental and Health Sciences:			
Characterization of environmental hazards	19,152	21,136	21,601
Applied toxicological research and testing	57,781	57,303	56,737
Intramural research	48,643	55,051	52,536

[a]Estimates.

SOURCE: U.S. Executive Office of the President, Office of Management and Budget, *Budget of the United States Government, Fiscal Year 1986* (Washington, DC: U.S. Government Printing Office, 1985).

PROTECTING PROPRIETARY INTERESTS

In commercializing a particular product, animal use may be limited to toxicity testing, but many products rely on animals in the initial research phase as well. These research and testing results have proprietary value that is sometimes protected by secrecy, other times by obtaining a patent. The value of data that lead to a particular product may depend more on the size of the market and its profitability than on the cost of obtaining them, particularly when it takes a long time to generate the data.

Cooperative Research and Testing

Two major competing factors influence the sharing of research and testing costs— the desire to keep information that has proprietary value secret and the desire to share the very large expenses that may be involved in generating it. These business decisions are only slightly influenced by Government policies. Another factor is antitrust law, however, which is greatly affected by such policies.

In considering the role of antitrust law, it is important to recognize that the results of research and testing enable society to use resources efficiently. Antitrust laws help ensure that these efficiencies benefit consumers, by preventing manufacturers, for example, from colluding to maintain high prices. However, these statutes have sometimes been applied in a way that impedes technological development (3) by making it difficult for companies to pool resources for research so expensive that none would undertake it alone.

In recent years, antitrust policies have been changed or clarified so that resources can be pooled more easily (19). One component of this is the National Cooperative Research Act of 1984 (Public Law 98-462). The Sherman and Clayton antitrust acts still apply, but damages in private suits are reduced from three times the value of the unfair advantage to the actual value. This will certainly lower the risks involved in collaborating, and probably the likelihood of being sued as well.

Testing costs can be most equitably shared if potential participants can interact before testing begins rather than after it is completed, because a party who has already tested may have an unfair advantage (or disadvantage) in negotiating compensation. It is easiest to identify potential sponsors for a particular chemical when testing is required by a regulatory agency, because it is known that testing will take place and who is required to test. When industry forms testing consortia to share costs, it is most easily done through existing trade associations, such as the Chemical Manufacturers Association. Cooperative testing is also conducted by industry through the Chemical Industry Institute of Toxicology.

Many testing consortia have been put together to negotiate agreements in anticipation of required testing under Section 4 of the Toxic Substances Control Act. Such negotiations were ruled invalid in a recent case (21). Despite this ruling, testing consortia will continue to have appeal so long as testing is expensive and the results have little or no proprietary value other than in fulfillment of regulatory requirements.

Toxicity Testing Data

Many companies begin making other financial commitments to the commercialization of a product before testing is completed. Plant design and small-scale production may coincide with long-term toxicity testing. The practical costs of fulfilling lengthy testing requirements may greatly exceed the costs of testing. Thus, it is advantageous to be able to use any existing data generated by another laboratory in order to avoid the delays and uncertainties of testing. Conversely, this provides an incentive to prevent data from being made available to competitors.

The protection of pesticide testing data has been the subject of much litigation and several amendments to the Federal Insecticide, Fungicide, and Rodenticide Act (FIFRA). The most recent changes provide that data submitted after September 30, 1978, are protected from uncompensated use for 15 years. There are two kinds of protection. One requires that data be shared as long as compensation is offered. The terms of the compensation are subject to arbitration if the parties cannot agree. The other protection only applies to new pesticides (new active ingredients), not to new formulations of old ingredients. It gives exclusive use of the data to the data owner for 10 years unless the data owner explicitly agrees to sell the right to use the data.

The Supreme Court recently decided in *Ruckelshaus* v. *Monsanto* (26) that these provisions of FIFRA are constitutional. For data submitted before 1972 or after 1978, there is no expectation of a proprietary interest, thus nothing is taken; for data submitted between those years, the compensation and arbitration provision, in combination with the Tucker Act, provides adequate compensation. (See also the Environmental Protection Agency's regulations at 40 CFR 1984 ed. 152; 40 FR 30884.)

Congress has recognized the important business interest in keeping information from competitors, but it also supports the public's "right to know" and the Federal Government's need to know. An important barrier to the sharing of confidential business information among agencies is the differing standards and procedures for handling it. The ad hoc interagency Toxic Substances Strategy Committee, coordinated by the Council on Environmental Quality, thought it would be necessary to pass legislation permitting the sharing of confidential data between health and environmental agencies (32). Such legislation would establish a need-to-know standard, require uniform security procedures for the data to be shared, impose uniform penalties for disclosure, and provide for notification of the data submitted by the data holder at least 10 days prior to transfer.

SUMMARY AND CONCLUSIONS

The total dollar cost of animal acquisition and maintenance is directly related to the length of time animals stay in the laboratory. With no accurate source of data on various species' length of stay, it is impossible to calculate the total cost of animal use. Analysis of the factors involved in the costs of animal acquisition and maintenance indicates that a reduction in animal use will be accompanied by a reduction in cost—although the proportionate savings will be less than the proportionate decrease in the number of animals used.

Many of the issues involved with using animals in research and testing have economic implications, although they do not lend themselves well to rigorous quantitative economic analysis because many considerations are nonmonetary. A highly contested concern, for example, is the propriety of using unclaimed pound animals in laboratory studies.

An area of animal use that is of major economic importance is biomedical research, which contributes to health care through the development of drugs, medical devices, diagnostic techniques, and surgical procedures. Health care accounts for over 10 percent of the Nation's gross national product, or $355 billion in 1983. The results of research with animals might also reach the public through patented products. Although data on humans may also be required, and although nonanimal or in vitro methods are sometimes sufficient, many such patent applications use animals to show that the invention is useful.

Another use of animals with economic importance is toxicological testing, used to ensure that new products are sufficiently safe. One type of product for which such testing is of major consequence to public health is in the development of pesticides, which affect virtually all Americans through the production and contamination of food. The Environmental Protection Agency has estimated that 90 percent of all households use some pesticide product.

Whole-animal tests can be far more costly than in vitro and nonanimal alternatives, largely because they are labor-intensive. The incentives to find alternatives to the LD_{50} and Draize tests are primarily nonmonetary, however, as these tests can be performed for $1,000 to $2,000. This is in the price range of the cheaper, currently available in vitro and nonanimal replacements.

Most research and testing in the United States is financed by Government or industry. The chemical industry, including the production of drugs, has annual sales of over $170 billion and spends over $7 billion on research and development. An unknown fraction is spent on research involving animals and about $700 million is spent on toxicity testing.

The Federal Government sponsors much biomedical research and testing involving animals (see ch. 12). An unknown amount leads to the development or use of alternatives. The Government also has many programs related to testing, including the evaluation of testing data generated in other sectors. Agencies with significant budgets for such activities include the Environmental Protection Agency, the Food and Drug Administration, the Centers for Disease Control, and the National Institutes of Health.

The Federal Government also has a special role in the sharing of data derived from animal use, as the data have proprietary value. First, antitrust laws and policies affect industry's ability to share data and the costs of generating it. Such sharing is facilitated by the passage of the National Cooperative Research Act of 1984. It is also facilitated under the Federal Insecticide, Fungicide, and Rodenticide Act and the Toxic Substances Control Act.

CHAPTER 11 REFERENCES

1. Auletta, A., Genetic Toxicologist, U.S. Environmental Protection Agency, Washington, DC, personal communication, 1984.
2. Baily, M.N., "Research and Development Costs and Returns, the U.S. Pharmaceutical Industry," *J. Polit. Econ.* (Jan.-Feb.):70-85, 1972.
3. Baxter, W.F., "Antitrust Law and Technological Innovation," *Iss. Sci. Tech.* 1(2):80-91, 1985.
4. Berk, A., and Paringer, L.C., *Economic Costs of Illness, 1930-1975* (Washington, DC: Public Services Laboratory, Georgetown University, May 1977).
5. Bishop, F., Chief, Registration Support and Emergency Response Branch, Office of Pesticide Programs, U.S. Environmental Protection Agency, Washington, DC, personal communication, 1985.
6. Brusick, D.J., Director, Molecular Sciences Directorate, Litton Bionetics, Kensington, MD, personal communication, 1984.
7. *Cross* v. *Izuka*, 224 USPQ 745, 1985.
8. *Chem. Engin. News*, "Facts and Figures for Chemical R&D," 53(29):28, 1985.
9. Gibson, R.M., Levit, K.R., Lazenby, H., et al., "National Health Expenditures, 1983," *Health Care Finan. Rev.* 6(2):1-29, 1984.
10. Hertzfeld, H.R., and Myers, T.D., "Economic and Policy Considerations," contract report prepared for the Office of Technology Assessment, U.S. Congress, 1985.
11. *In re Anthony,* 56 CCPA 1443, 414 F.2d 1383, 162 USPQ 594 (1969).
12. *In re Bergel,* 48 CCPA 1102, 292 F.2d 955, 130 USPQ 206 (1961).
13. *In re Chilowsky,* 43 CCPA 775, 229 F.2d 457, 108 USPQ 321 (1956).
14. *In re Irons,* 52 CCPA 938, 340 F.2d 974, 144 USPQ 351 (1965).
15. *In re Jolles,* 628 F.2d 1322, 206 USPQ 885 (CCPA 1980).
16. *In re Krimmel,* 48 CCPA 1116, 292 F.2d 948, 130 USPQ 215 (1961).
17. *In re Watson,* 517 F.2d 465, 186 USPQ 11 ([Cust. and Pat. App.] 1975).
18. Institute of Laboratory Animal Resources, *National Survey of Laboratory Animal Facilities and Resources* (Washington, DC: National Academy of Sciences, 1980).
19. McGrath, J.P., Remarks at the 18th Annual New England Antitrust Conference, Boston, MA, Nov. 2, 1984.
20. Mushkin, S.J., *Biomedical Research: Costs and Benefits* (Cambridge, MA: Ballinger Publishing Co., 1979).
21. *Natural Resources Defense Council* v. *EPA,* 595 F.Supp. 1255 (S.D.N.Y., 1984).
22. Payton, N., Massachusetts Society for the Prevention of Cruelty to Animals, Testimony in Support of H1245, Boston, MA, February 1981.

23. Pimentel, D., Andow, D., Dyson-Hudson, R., et al., "Environmental and Social Costs of Pesticides: A Preliminary Assessment," *Oikos* 34:127-140, 1980.
24. *Rey-Bellet* v. *Englehardt,* 493 F.2d 1380, 181 USPQ 453 (1974).
25. Rowan, A.N., *Of Mice, Models, & Men: A Critical Evaluation of Animal Research* (Albany, NY: State University of New York Press, 1984).
26. *Ruckelshaus* v. *Monsanto,* 104 S.Ct. 2862 (1984).
27. *Stock Market Survey for Hazelton Labs* (New York, NY: Silverberg, Rosenthal, and Company, Apr. 9, 1984).
28. Turner, J., *Reckoning With the Beast: Animals, Pain and Humanity in the Victorian Mind* (Baltimore, MD: Johns Hopkins University Press, 1980).
29. U.S. Department of Commerce, *1982 Census of Manufactures, Drugs* (Washington, DC: U.S. Government Printing Office, 1985).
30. U.S. Department of Health and Human Services, Public Health Service, Food and Drug Admninistration, National Toxicology Program, Board of Scientific Counselors, *Draft Report—Ad Hoc Panel on Chemical Carcinogenesis Testing and Evaluation* (Bethesda, MD: Feb. 15, 1984).
31. U.S. Environmental Protection Agency, *Regulatory Impact Analysis: Data Requirements for Registering Pesticides Under the Federal Insecticide, Fungicide and Rodenticide Act,* EPA 540/9-82-013 (Washington, DC: 1982).
32. U.S. Executive Office of the President, Council on Environmental Quality, Toxic Substances Strategy Committee, *Toxic Chemicals and Public Protection* (Washington, DC: U.S. Government Printing Office, 1980).

Chapter 12

Public and Private Funding Toward the Development of Alternatives

The most authoritative source for information on alternatives to the use of live animals in research is the NIH itself.

Eleanor Seiling
United Action for Animals, Inc.
April 18, 1984

Cutting the NIH appropriation and eliminating this Federal agency will be an excellent place to start trimming waste from the Federal budget.

Helen Jones
International Society for Animal Rights, Inc.
July 1984

I become very suspicious when I see a grant for $5,664 or a grant for $22,000. What can a researcher accomplish with $22,000?

Sen. Alfonse M. D'Amato (R-NY)
Senate Hearing
October 2, 1984

CONTENTS

List of Tables

List of Figures

Chapter 12

Public and Private Funding Toward the Development of Alternatives

Attempts to find alternatives to using animals in research, testing, and education are so diverse that it is difficult to cite firm figures on funding levels. An investigation of public and private funding practices does make it clear, however, that no single policy covers such research and development (R&D). Much of the work that could lead to the replacement, reduction, or refinement of animal use is not even considered R&D of alternatives by the body that funds it.

Research is seldom targeted toward alternatives as ends in themselves. Few projects are initiated with this specific goal. Consequently, confining the inquiry to only those cases where development of an alternative method is the desired result, such as programs to find in vitro substitutes for the Draize eye irritancy test, drastically narrows the category of funding classified as supporting alternatives. In addition, it is especially difficult to examine funding policies related to reductions and refinements, because these considerations generally enter into the construction of any protocol.

This chapter covers targeted as well as incidental cases of research into alternatives—investigations directed toward the development of alternatives as well as those pursued for other reasons but that lead to or use alternatives. Also considered are research into laboratory-animal health and some types of pain research that may increase knowledge about the mechanisms of pain and improve methods of alleviating distress. Resources allocated to upgrading animal facilities are closely related, since inadequate facilities may skew experimental results, thereby requiring that more animals be used.

FUNDING TOWARD ALTERNATIVES IN RESEARCH

Developing replacements for the use of animals in research is far more likely to be incidental than targeted. Refinements and reductions may be incidental developments as well, but they are more likely to result from conscious efforts on the part of the investigator. Areas in which alternatives, especially replacements, are discovered will often be those in which animals are not used at all. This type of development is exemplified by basic research in cell biology that resulted in improved cell culture capabilities, and work in basic physics that led to noninvasive imaging techniques. Identifying funding in this area is particularly difficult: Few agencies view these projects as alternatives to animal use or label them as such, even though the methods may yield techniques and systems that could replace animals, reduce the numbers used, or refine the protocols. (Most testing-related research has been deliberately excluded from this category.)

In an attempt to obtain a rough indication of expenditures on alternatives, OTA examined the range of models in use, identifying the number of projects and amount of research money in each system area. Of course, not every nonanimal method evolves into an alternative to animal use. Yet research in specific techniques, such as biostatistics, may have broad or unanticipated applications across many areas of research and testing.

Public Funding

Two major granting agencies, the National Institutes of Health (NIH) and the National Science Foundation (NSF), account for most of the basic biomedical research sponsored by the Federal Government. Neither agency currently funds alternatives as a targeted goal. In few cases is the development of a replacement a major objective of the research that produces one. However, consideration of models of all types, and the selection of a research model appropriate to the problem under investigation, occurs with every grant. Other scientific and ethical considerations may lead to reductions and refinements within protocols during the grant review process (see ch. 15).

National Institutes of Health

In fiscal year 1985, national expenditures on health R&D exceeded $12.8 billion (24). Of this total, industry accounted for the largest portion (39 percent), followed by the National Institutes of Health (37 percent), other Federal research, and other funding groups (24). Of health R&D supported by the Federal Government, NIH has funded approximately 90 percent in recent years (13). About 60 percent of the research funded by NIH can be characterized as basic (25). NIH basic research has accounted in recent years for about 40 percent of all Federal basic research conducted (18).

Until recently, NIH had no concerted program under which it pursued the development of alternatives in research, as opposed to any such methods that may occur as byproducts during investigations. However, the new Biological Models and Materials Resources Section within the Division of Research Resources may assume this function.

This office was created in February 1985 and its function was mandated (Public Law 99-158) in November 1985 to address the need to explore and support the use of nonanimal models in biomedical research. Its missions include developing the use of cell systems, lower organisms, and nonbiological systems (mathematical and computer models) for biomedical research and actually providing biological materials that serve as critically important resources to the biomedical research community, such as those just mentioned (28).

The office intends to implement some of the recommendations offered in the recent report of the National Academy of Sciences' Committee on Models for Biomedical Research:

- As favorable systems are identified, the NIH should strive to make them readily available to the research community by providing support to supply organisms for research, maintaining stock centers for mutant strains and for cell lines, facilitating access to computer programs for biomedical modeling, maintaining databases like those for protein and DNA sequences, and providing long-term support for collections of cloned genes and useful vectors or collections of monoclonal antibodies.
- NIH should consider supporting proposals whose objective is the development of model systems for specific research areas. Indeed, funds might be targeted for the development of new model systems that appear to be particularly promising.
- NIH should encourage interest in nonmammalian systems through postdoctoral fellowships, symposia, and direct support of model development (12).

The office today tracks the use of model systems in research supported by NIH and serves as NIH's focal point for the exchange of information with individuals, organizations, and institutions concerning the use of model systems in biomedical research. In addition, the Biological Models and Materials Resources Section serves as the new home of four previously existing resources:

- **The American Type Culture Collection:** Support for this collection of cultured cells, $600,000 in fiscal year 1985, was recently transferred from the NIH Director's office.
- **The Massachusetts Institute of Technology Cell Culture Center:** This facility produces animal cells in large quantities tailored to specific investigator needs; 85 percent of its users are NIH grantees. Funding is in the process of being taken over from NSF in fiscal year 1985 (NIH contribution: $165,000) and will be complete in fiscal year 1986.
- ***Caenorhabditis elegans* Genetics Center:** This resource serves as a repository for nematodal mutants and a clearinghouse for the mapping of the *C. elegans* genome. It is supported jointly with the National Institute of Aging ($15,000 in fiscal year 1985).
- **National Diabetes Research Interchange:** This information resource is supported jointly with the National Institute of Arthritis, Dia-

betes, and Digestive and Kidney Diseases with funds ($25,000 in fiscal year 1985) provided through the General Clinical Research Centers Program (28).

An analysis of research systems within various projects and subprojects funded by NIH provides some idea of the patterns of subjects and models used overall for NIH; it may also indicate national patterns because NIH supports more than one-third of the health-related R&D in the United States (24). Use of both human subjects and mammals (expressed as the percentage of research projects using each) was essentially stable from 1977 through 1982 (see fig. 12-1). At the same time there was a slight increase (approximately 5 percent) in the percentage of research dollars being spent on mammalian systems and a corresponding decrease in the percentage of research dollars spent on research involving human subjects (see fig. 12-2). The data in these figures do not indicate, of course, the number of individual animals used; they only illustrate the relative percentages of projects funded and dollars spent among several types of research subjects.

NIH-supported research uses many models. Three widely used ones are in vitro cells and tissues, invertebrates, and mathematical and computer simulations, all commonly referred to in discussions about alternatives. In fiscal year 1981, 12 bureaus, institutes, or divisions (BIDs) of NIH supported 378 research projects that used human cells or tissues, for a total commitment of over $32 million (27). The projects included studies of cellular aging, in vitro studies of immune response and regulation of antibodies, the cellular basis of disease, and the mechanisms of DNA repair. A further 381 projects and subprojects used cells and tissues from sources other than humans in the course of their investigations. These accounted for nearly $34 million, directed toward research into models for diseases such as herpes, leprosy, and parasitic diseases; hormonal effects on the control and function of differentiated cells; differences between tumors and normal tissues; and other cellular and biochemical mechanisms. Invertebrates used in fiscal year 1981 included annelids, aplysia, cephalopods, crustaceans, *Drosophila,* echinoderms, gastropods, helminths, horseshoe crabs, mollusks, nematodes, platyhelminths, and protozoans, accounting for 608 subprojects and over $46 million.

Mathematical models were used by 8 BIDs, in 23 projects and subprojects for nearly $1.2 million, to analyze renal flow and neural networks, to model biological waves and kinetics, to model clinical trials, to predict fetal outcomes, and to support mathematical biology. Computer simulations

Figure 12-1.—Trends in NIH Research Subjects, 1977-82, as Percentage of Research Projects

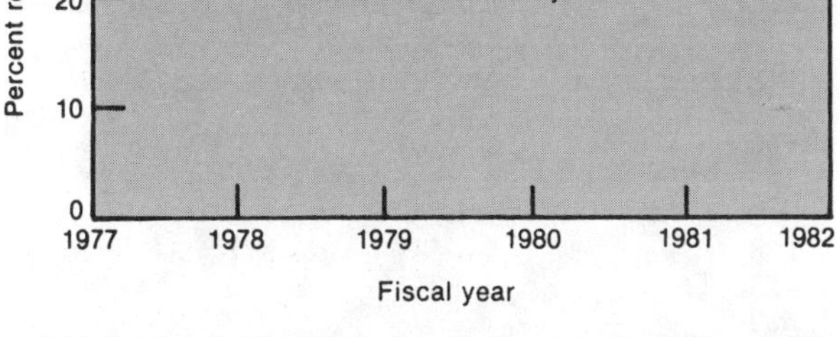

SOURCE: J.D. Willett, "Biological Systems Used as Research Models in NIH Programs," Animal Resources Program, Division of Research Resources, National Institutes of Health, Bethesda, MD, Sept. 24, 1984.

Figure 12-2.—Trends in NIH Research Subjects, 1977-82, as Percentage of Research Dollars

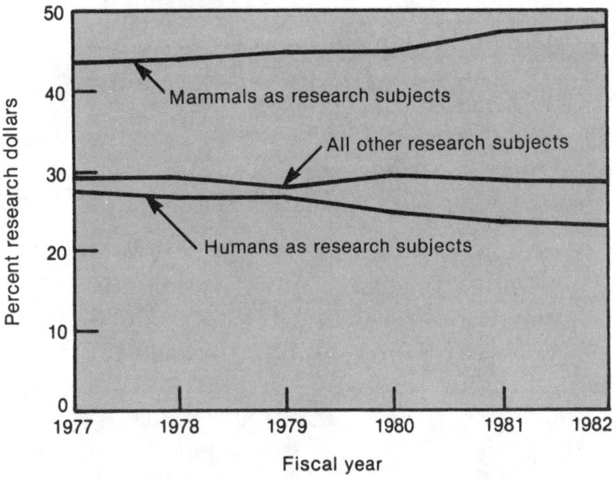

SOURCE: J.D. Willett, "Biological Systems Used as Research Models in NIH Programs," Animal Resources Program, Division of Research Resources, National Institutes of Health, Bethesda, MD, Sept. 24, 1984.

were supported by 10 BIDs to study a range of research questions including computer analyses of cellular differentiation and homeostatic control mechanisms, modeling of bladder cancer and structure-activity relationships in drugs, simulations of renal function, imaging reconstruction and display of biological surfaces, and the modeling of artificial intelligence. These 54 projects accounted for close to $6 million in awards.

Nonanimal models, including invertebrates and nonmammalian vertebrates in addition to those described above, account for approximately 26 percent of NIH's projects and an average of 29 percent of the funds in any given year. Mammalian systems account for slightly more than 43 percent of the projects and about 46 percent of the dollars spent. Many projects use several systems at once.

National Science Foundation

NSF considers project proposals for support in all fields of science. Among its programs are eight that have potential to support alternatives-related research:

- Behavioral and Neural Sciences,
- Biotic Systems and Resources,
- Information Science and Technology,
- Mathematical and Computer Sciences,
- Cellular Biosciences,
- Molecular Biosciences,
- Research Instrumentation and Equipment, and
- Science and Engineering Education (21).

The National Science Foundation normally does not support clinical research either with humans or animals, the development of animal models for specific diseases or conditions, or the development of drugs or other therapeutic procedures. For the most part, it supports only what can be classified as basic research.

The character of research projects and models used in investigations funded by NSF varies widely. Table 12-1 indicates the distribution of the approaches proposed in NSF research grants for fiscal year 1983. In the categories that include living organisms, only those projects involving actual experimentation manipulations have been included. Thus the data do not include studies on animals, plants, or micro-organisms that are observational or descriptive in nature; these might be ecologic studies, population dynamics, and studies of field behavior, for instance. However, field studies that included the actual capture of animals, involved invasive or noninvasive placement of electric tracking devices, or used physiological sampling were included.

In addition, NSF supports three additional awards that relate to the use of animals in research, although these projects do not directly use animals. The first is a grant to the Institute of Laboratory Animal Resources of the National Academy of Sciences for its activities in developing and making available to the biomedical community scientific and technical information on laboratory-animal science resources. The other two, related to research on ethical issues surrounding the use of animals, originate in the Ethics and Values in Science and Technology (EVIST) program in NSF's Directorate for Biological, Behavioral, and Social Sciences.

Table 12-1.—Approaches Used in National Science Foundation Research Grants, Fiscal Year 1983

Approach used	Number of awards	Range of award sizes (in thousands)	Total expenditure
Whole nonhuman primates	33	$9-$135	$ 1,875,956
Whole nonprimate vertebrates	552	2- 289	32,872,503
Culture of animal-derived components (cells, tissues, organs, or embryos)	166	6- 250	8,368,526
Mathematical modeling as an adjunct to animal use	22	9- 100	747,079
Mathematical modeling without animal use	9	25- 176	657,000
Invertebrates	298	5- 266	18,451,785
Micro-organisms	428	7- 250	21,440,070
Plants	398	9- 250	20,288,332
Total	1,906	$2-$289	$104,701,251

SOURCE: B.L. Umminger, Deputy Director, Division of Cellular Biosciences, National Science Foundation, Washington, DC, personal communication, 1984.

Although many of the projects listed in table 12-1 involve the culture of animal-derived components, invertebrate animals, micro-organisms, plants, or mathematical modeling, the intent of NSF-funded investigations usually is not the development of alternative methods to experimentation with live animals. Nevertheless, the outcome of some of these projects may lay the groundwork for the subsequent development of alternative techniques.

The Biological, Behavioral, and Social Sciences Directorate houses most of the work related to alternatives. NSF's total basic research budget is approximately $1.5 billion in fiscal year 1986, including approximately $260 million for this division. If past patterns continue, the bulk of these funds will not be spent on animal research but on a much broader group of projects.

Small Business Innovation Research

The Small Business Innovation Act (Public Law 97-219) requires agencies of the Public Health Service and certain other Federal agencies to reserve a specified portion of their R&D budgets for the Small Business Innovation Research (SBIR) program. The stated goals of this project are to "stimulate technological innovation, use small businesses to meet federal research and development needs, increase private sector commercialization of innovations derived from federal R&D, and to foster and encourage participation by minority and disadvantaged persons in technological innovation" (26). The NIH set-aside for the SBIR program totals $18.2 million. NSF retains a similar SBIR set-aside pool equal to 1.25 percent of its budget in fiscal year 1986.

Small businesses seeking to commercialize alternatives can take advantage of these funds for product research and development. The grants are generally in the range of $35,000 to $100,000, depending on how quickly commercialization is likely to follow the research. For fiscal year 1983, NIH's SBIR program funded many projects that might be related to alternatives, such as:

- phase I structure activity relationship estimation of skin and eye irritation,
- an interactive teaching system for medical students,
- CAT scanning for carcinogenesis bioassay in rodents,
- cell growth chambers for chemotherapeutic drug screening,
- continuous cell culture for monoclonal antibodies,
- a new method to detect immune complexes,
- synthetic peptides as animal vaccines,
- bacterial/laser bioassay to detect environmental pollutants,
- rapid methods to monitor genetic damage in humans, and
- development of mammalian cell culture aneuploidy assay.

Although not all of these will develop as replacements, reductions, or refinements of animal use, some may eventually produce commercially viable alternatives.

Private Funding

Private funding in research, especially basic research, is most difficult to evaluate and classify according to its applicability to alternatives. And because most basic biomedical and behavioral research is sponsored by the Federal Government, it is through public sector funding that alternatives in research are most likely to develop.

Private foundations and research institutes support biomedical research internally as well as extramurally. Although some of this research may pertain to alternatives, it is not often the case unless the mission of the institution is specifically related to animal welfare. Disease-oriented foundations conduct research on aspects of a particular system or affliction and support a variety of research approaches, animal as well as nonanimal. Though some of these initiatives may indeed qualify as alternatives, examining this research on a project-by-project basis is beyond the scope of this assessment.

In 1985, the Nation's first professorship in humane ethics and animal welfare was established at the University of Pennsylvania School of Veterinary Medicine with the an endowment of $1.25 million from Marie A. Moore. One goal of the endowed professorship will be to investigate alternatives to animal experimentation in medical research (15).

Several foundations have animal welfare as their primary mission or included as a principal goal. Since 1981, the Geraldine R. Dodge Foundation has disbursed over $450,000 in grants related to alternatives (7). The foundation awards grants in several categories, including that of animal welfare. Research grants include a 2-year contribution of $115,409 to the Baker Institute for Animal Health of Cornell University for the development of a cell hybridization laboratory to enhance diagnostic, therapeutic, and disease prevention capabilities. Dodge has also contributed $63,000 to the Center for Alternatives to Animal Testing (CAAT) at The Johns Hopkins University to help cover the costs of publishing the center's newsletter. Additionally, the Scientists' Center for Animal Welfare (Bethesda, MD) has received over $90,000 to date.

FUNDING TOWARD ALTERNATIVES IN TESTING

Funding of R&D on alternatives in testing is in many ways the support most easily identified, especially when the alternative is intended to replace a test that currently uses animals. This applied R&D draws on basic research from other areas, incorporates it into a testing methodology, and then validates the new test. Developing an alternative requires that the alternative system be shown to correlate with the effect that is of interest. Narrow efforts such as these contrast markedly with the broader goals of basic research, and the development of alternatives is correspondingly easier.

Public Funding

Public funding of research toward alternatives in testing stems from the Federal Government's role as regulator and guardian of safety. Federal agencies conduct toxicological and other tests on many substances and devices in order to establish effects as well as standards for safety (see ch. 7). The greatest impetus for Federal funding of replacements for animal tests would be a strong indication that an alternative could be found that would be superior to the comparable conventional assay with animals. This has not yet occurred in terms of technologies that would totally replace the use of animals, nor is it likely to in the near future, although promising areas like in vitro assays may someday replace some whole-animal tests. It is more likely that short-term in vitro tests, functioning primarily as screens, will reduce the number of substances run through the complete battery of tests with animals (see ch. 8).

Toxicological Testing

The National Toxicology Program (NTP) was chartered in 1978 as a cooperative effort by the Department of Health and Human Services (DHHS), involving four principal groups— the National Cancer Institute (NCI) and the National Institute of Environmental Health Sciences (NIEHS), both of which are part of NIH; the National Center for Toxicological Research (NCTR) of the Food and Drug Administration (FDA); and the National Institute for Occupational Safety and Health (NIOSH) of the Centers for Disease Control (CDC). Fiscal year 1985 funding for the NTP totaled $76.7 million, drawn from contributions by the DHHS member agencies that were negotiated after each agency received its congressional appropriation. NIEHS provides approximately 86 percent of the program's resources (8).

The stated goals of the NTP include the expansion of toxicological information obtained on chemicals nominated, selected, and tested; the expansion of the number of chemicals to be tested, within the constraints of funding; the development, validation, and coordination of tests and protocols to match regulatory needs; and the communication of program plans and results to the public (22,23). Figure 12-3 illustrates the relative priorities of these activities and their components with reference to spending in fiscal year 1985. Testing activities consume by far the largest share of resources. Within each of the three divisions, efforts are divided into four major areas: mutagenesis (cellular and genetic toxicology), carcinogenesis, toxicological characterization, and fertility and reproduction (reproductive and developmental toxicology).

According to the NTP's "Fiscal Year 1984 Annual Plan" (22), planning activities are directed toward reducing the number of chemicals that require chronic testing through the development, validation, and application of more efficient and more sensitive testing systems. It is in this area—establishing new batteries of tests and subsequently validating them—that the development of alternatives is most likely to occur.

NIEHS directs between $18 million and $20 million toward testing and research related to alternative test systems, especially short-term indicators of intoxication. Approximately 85 percent of this money is channeled through NTP in the form of grants for research and testing, R&D contracts for testing and development, and in-house research. These funds cover the actual testing in addition to methods validation and evaluation of alternatives. Test systems receiving the bulk of attention include bacteria, yeast, insects, and cultured cells from mammalian tissues including humans (10).

Figure 12-3.—Funding Levels of National Toxicology Program Activities, Fiscal Year 1985 (dollars in millions)

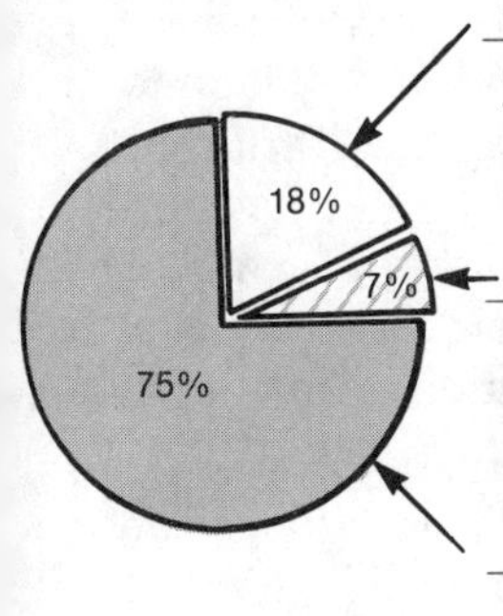

Methods development	$13.2
Carcinogenesis	2.0
Toxic characterization	4.2
Mutagenesis	5.5
Fertility and reproduction	1.5
Validation	$ 5.0
Carcinogenesis	0.6
Toxic characterization	1.5
Mutagenesis	0.9
Fertility and reproduction	2.0
Testing	$54.5
Carcinogenesis	28.4
Toxic characterization	17.0
Mutagenesis	6.9
Fertility and reproduction	2.2

SOURCE: L.G. Hart, Assistant to the Director, National Toxicology Program, Research Triangle Park, NC, personal communication, July 1985.

Beyond NCI, NIEHS, NCTR, and NIOSH (the four constituent agencies of NTP), DHHS support for research related to toxicology is also found within the Alcohol, Drug Abuse, and Mental Health Administration, CDC, FDA, and NIH. Substantial Federal support for toxicological research and testing is also provided by the Environmental Protection Agency (see ch. 11, table 11-3).

Food and Drug Administration

FDA conducts primarily mission-oriented, applied research. Its interest in alternatives derives from FDA requirements for product testing. Although intramural funds are not allocated on a project-by-project basis, the agency has tried to estimate expenditures on the basis of person-years involved in the work (4). Assuming a person-year is $40,000 (salary, overhead, and benefits), intramural research into alternatives to testing with animals was estimated at 35 person-years, an expenditure of roughly $1.2 million. Extramural work consists of one project, valued at $87,000, to develop an in vitro model as a primary screen to detect active agents against *Dirofilaria immitis* larvae (a heartworm found in the dog, wolf, and fox) and microfilariae (the prelarval stage of a parasitic roundworm). For the most part, these in vitro models have been developed elsewhere, and these projects involve the application to FDA-regulated products. Tables 12-2 and 12-3 list alternative tests currently under development and in use at the Food and Drug Administration.

Private Funding

Private sector motivation to develop alternatives in testing ranges from scientific concerns through economic and political ones. Investors in this sector account for perhaps the most diverse group of supporters of this type of research.

Trade and Industrial Groups

The development of alternatives in testing is supported by trade groups and industry for several reasons, mostly linked economically to the financial health of the company or industry. Commercial concerns find alternative methods generally take less time and labor and are therefore less expensive to perform than standard animal-based

Table 12-2.—Alternative Tests Under Development at the Food and Drug Administration

- Genetic probes for toxigenic strains of *Campylobacter jejuni*
- Genetic probes for invasive *Escherichia coli*
- In vitro invasiveness test based on siderophore avidity for iron
- Enzymatic and chemical in vitro evaluation of infant formula protein quality
- Development of an assay for genetic transposition in bacteria
- Cultures of rat embryos to detect agents that cause developmental toxicity and to determine the mechanism by which effects are produced
- Porcine kidney explant cultures for screening potentially nephrotoxic agents
- In vitro micromolecular biosynthesis as an index of potential tissue damage by chemical agents
- In vitro determination of effects of chemical agents of T- and B-lymphocyte function
- Improved procedures for use of unscheduled DNA synthesis for genotoxic effects
- In vitro use of renal cortex tissue to determine biochemical correlates for evaluating toxicity of natural toxicants
- In vitro assays to assess biological vaccine potency and safety (diphtheria antitoxin, rabies, polio vaccines)
- In vitro assays to assess drug potency (gonadotropin, lactogenic hormone, corticotropin, oxytocin, insulin)
- In vitro methods to determine percutaneous absorption of hydrophobic compounds
- In vitro immunoassay methods (RIA, ELISA) for assessment of immunotoxic effects of drugs and environmental pollutants
- Liquid and thin-layer chromatographic methods for ciguatera and paralytic shellfish toxins
- In vitro immunoassay methods (RIA, ELISA) for assessment of seafood toxins

SOURCE: A.P. Borsetti, Staff Scientist, Office of Science Coordination, Food and Drug Administration, U.S. Department of Health and Human Services, Rockville, MD, personal communication, 1985.

Table 12-3.—Alternative Tests in Use at the Food and Drug Administration

- Genetic probes for heat-labile and heat-stable enterotoxin of *Escherichia coli*
- Genetic probes for invasive strains of *Yersinia enterocolitica*
- Genetic probes for classical 01 cholera toxin
- Genetic probes for pathogenic organisms (01 and Non-01 *Vibrio cholerae, Vibrio parahemolyticus, Vibrio vulnificus)*
- In vitro tests for percutaneous absorption of cosmetic ingredients
- In vitro cell transformation assay
- Unscheduled DNA synthesis in primary rat hepatocytes
- *Salmonella* microsome assay for gene mutations
- *Limulus* amebocyte lysate test for pyrogenicity of drugs and biologics
- Sister-chromatid exchange for assessing mutagenic potential
- Use of primary myocytes and endothelial cells from neonatal rat heart ventricles for identification of potential cardiotoxic agents
- High-performance liquid chromatography as a screen for the vitamin D assay (used for products other than infant formula)
- Instrumental analysis assay for potency of three anticancer drugs for batch release (Dactinomycin, Doxorubicin hydrochloride, and Plicamycin)
- Instrumental analysis assays to determine the potency of biological vaccines
- Genetic probes for invasive *Shigella*
- In vitro assays for tumor-producing potential (HL 60 differentiation, V-79 metabolic cooperativity, and Epstein-Barr virus activation
- Assays for detection of mycotoxins (mass spectrometry, instrumental methods, brine shrimp assay)

SOURCE: A.P. Borsetti, Staff Scientist, Office of Science Coordination, Food and Drug Administration, U.S. Department of Health and Human Services, Rockville, MD, personal communication, 1985.

testing protocols. A desire for improved tests and responsiveness to public concern over animal use also drive the search for alternatives. As public relations tools, nonanimal methods have proved valuable in reassuring the public that these corporations share their concern about animal use and are exploring other systems, while being careful not to jeopardize public health and safety.

In 1980, Revlon Research Center, Inc., awarded a 3-year, $750,000 grant to Rockefeller University to establish the Rockefeller Laboratory for In Vitro Toxicology Assay. Revlon's investment was the first serious, publicly taken step by industry in the search for alternatives. The Revlon award has been extended into a fifth year and totals more than $1.25 million (5). The laboratory employs four scientific staff, working on projects including alternatives to the Draize eye irritancy test and other animal cell culture applications. Prior to the establishment of this facility, there were no laboratories committed to alternatives research.

The Johns Hopkins Center for Alternatives to Animal Testing has committed $2.1 million to the search for alternatives since 1981, funding 30 grants for research (19). The Center has both an information program (consisting of a regularly published newsletter, symposia, and a book series) and a research program (focused on in vitro acute and chronic toxicity testing and acute irritancy of the skin and eye). The center's enabling sponsor, the Cosmetic, Toiletry, and Fragrance Association (CTFA), is joined by other corporate donors, including the Bristol Myers Company, as well as by consumer and industrial groups and private individuals. CAAT solicits projects from scientists by

Solicitation for Proposals by The Johns Hopkins Center for Alternatives to Animal Testing

REQUEST FOR PROPOSALS

REQUEST FOR PROPOSALS

The Johns Hopkins Center for Alternatives to Animal Testing is soliciting proposals. These research proposals should provide the fundamental knowledge base to develop alternative methods to whole animals for the safety evaluation of commercial products.

The center is specifically interested in the use of human cells and tissues. Funds are available for studies of skin and eye irritation, inflammation, acute toxicity, and other organ specific toxicity. At the present time funds are unavailable for mutagenicity and carcinogenicity.

Grants will normally be funded up to a maximum of $20,000 per year including 15 percent overhead or actual costs, whichever is less. All grants will be on a yearly basis with continuation funding dependent upon an acceptable continuation of proposal.

Abstract deadline: 30 March 1985.
Application deadline: 30 May 1985.

Application instructions can be obtained by contacting: **Joan S. Poling, Secretary to the Director, Room 2306, School of Hygiene and Public Health.**

Taken from *Science* 227:212, 1985. Copyright 1985 by the American Association for the Advancement of Science.

circulating requests for proposals either for a broad, nonspecific area or for specific, investigator-initiated projects. In the first stage of a two-stage peer review, a group of scientific experts judges the proposal on the quality of the science proposed and its relevance to the mission of CAAT. Second, the advisory board votes on which projects to fund. The voting membership of the organization is academic, although nonvoting members do represent the sponsors, government, and animal welfare groups. Table 12-4 lists examples of some of the projects funded by The Johns Hopkins Center.

The Soap and Detergent Association is supporting work at the University of Illinois to develop alternatives to eye irritancy tests with a 3-year grant of $218,596. The program is designed to develop a mathematical model that would correlate the responses to a series of in vitro tests with the test material's potential to irritate the human eye (17). The Fund for Replacement of Animals in Medical Experiments (FRAME) reports that it is collaborating with both the Rockefeller and Illinois groups, providing chemicals for use in blind trials on alternative methods (3).

These various examples of private funding illustrate the variety of mechanisms to provide support for the development of alternatives. The first, the Rockefeller Laboratory, is a case in which a corporation endows a single laboratory facility and funds the work of scientists within that group. The research conducted in the lab is closely allied with the products manufactured by the sponsor and with the testing required by those products.

The second model, exemplified by The Johns Hopkins Center, is a central clearinghouse established to collect and disseminate funds in a wider variety of research areas. The source of the funds is also varied. The grants distributed within this structure are small (under $20,000) and not strictly comparable to the support accorded to the Rockefeller lab, but The Johns Hopkins Center funds many more grants.

The third example, the Soap and Detergent Association, shows a single project within a university funded by an industrial concern. In this case the association draws funds from its constituent members and then acts as their proxy in distributing them.

Table 12-4.—Selected Research Projects Supported by The Johns Hopkins Center for Alternatives to Animal Testing

Condition and organ/Project description
Irritation and inflammation:
Vagina: Tests for vaginal products
Eyes: Corneal cultures for tests
Corneal cultures—plasminogen activator as an indication of irritation
Skin: Human umbilical cord cells
Fibroblast damage by chemicals
Development of artificial skin
Phototoxic chemicals and skin
Architecture of skin in vitro
Biological change/toxic response
Cytotoxicity and acute toxicity:
Liver: Response to toxins in solution
Cells: In vitro production of metallothionein
In vitro production of peroxisomes
Effects of culture media on cells
Chemicals' effects on protein synthesis
Organ specific effects:
Heart, lung, kidney: Mechanistic data—acute and chronic organ toxicity
Other projects:
Nerves: Neurotoxicity/neuronal cell culture
Teratology: Fruit fly assays
Botulism: Evaluation of contamination of foods

SOURCE: A.M. Goldberg, Director, The Johns Hopkins Center for Alternatives to Animal Testing, Baltimore, MD, 1985.

Both the Animal Protection Institute and the Institute for the Study of Animal Problems have surveyed corporations that do animal research and testing (2,14). Many companies indicated that they were taking steps to promote alternatives. Support often took the form of membership in a trade association (e.g., CTFA) that sponsors research into alternatives. Others indicated that investigations were being undertaken within their own research programs. Responses and levels of commitment varied greatly among corporations.

Animal Welfare Groups

Groups such as the American Fund for Alternatives to Animal Research (AFAAR), the American Anti-Vivisection Society, the New England Anti-Vivisection Society, the Animal Welfare Foundation of Canada, the Lord Dowding Fund in Great Britain, the Millennium Guild, and the Muriel Lowrie Memorial Fund have supported research in the United States aimed at replacing animals in testing protocols. These grants range in size from a few thousand to several hundred thousand dollars.

AFAAR, for example, has provided some $130,000 in grants between 1977, when it was founded, and 1985 (1). Included among these are a grant of $25,905 to develop a test system to determine the nutritive value of protein in foodstuffs, using *Tetrahymena* (ciliate protozoans) in place of weanling mammals. This test enables food producers to provide correct diet supplements or therapeutic diets. In addition, a grant of $45,000 was awarded to develop a replacement for the Draize eye irritancy test using the chorioallantoic membrane of the chick embryo. Additional funding for this project has been supplied by other animal welfare groups (a total of $148,500 from the Lord Dowding Fund, the American Anti-Vivisection Society, the Muriel Lowrie Memorial Fund, and the Animal Welfare Foundation of Canada) and by the Colgate-Palmolive Company. In 1985, AFAAR joined three other animal welfare groups in awarding an additional $133,987 to develop procedures for toxicology testing using monolayer cell cultures in gradients of oxygen tension and temperature (1).

The Millennium Guild has offered $500,000 to encourage the development and implementation of testing methods that will replace or significantly reduce the use of animals (11). There is a breakthrough award of $250,000 for nonanimal replacements for the Draize eye, the Draize skin, or the LD_{50} tests for any scientist or team of scientists who develops a cost-effective test or battery of tests that can be validated and accepted by a U.S. regulatory agency. An equal sum is available to promote innovation and to reward the rapid reduction of widely used animal tests. These incentive awards have been granted in areas such as uses of liver culture, quantitative structure activity relationships, cell culture bioassays, and the use of protozoans as indicators of eye irritancy.

Foundations and Research Institutes

Foundations and research institutes often devote in-house and other private funds to research into alternate testing methodologies and systems. Battelle Columbus Laboratories (Columbus, OH), for example, is pursuing the development of many alternatives. Its efforts fall into two major divisions, mammalian and nonmammalian systems. The basic areas of system development include cell and organ culture, in vitro teratology, and neurotoxicity. A figure of $500,000 has been conservatively estimated as the investment in this area. The funding comes primarily from private sources and includes both internal and external funds. Some of the projects now under way are cell culture initiatives, including macrophage work, and teratology research using rat embryo and frog embryo cultures (16).

FUNDING TOWARD ALTERNATIVES IN EDUCATION

Funding of research toward alternatives in education, especially within the public sector, stems more from a renewed emphasis on science and math education and on computers than from substantial concerns with methods of animal use in education. Alternatives in education also often originate as research simulations, and then move back into the classroom. Exceptions to this are projects undertaken for the express purpose of developing replacements for animals in the classroom, or programs developed in order to cultivate attitudes conducive to the further development and implementation of alternatives (see ch. 9). Some of these other initiatives, such as those funded by groups interested in issues pertaining to animal use, have developed from concerns related to humane education.

The Health Professions Educational Assistance Amendments of 1985 (Public Law 99-129) authorized the Secretary of the Department of Health and Human Services to make grants to veterinary schools for work related to alternatives. These grants can support the development of curricula for:

- training in the care of animals used in research,
- the treatment of animals while being used in research, and
- the development of alternatives to the use of animals in research.

Since 1981 the Geraldine R. Dodge Foundation has given over $240,000 toward education-related alternatives programs including:

- $25,000 to the Biological Sciences Curriculum Study to support the development of materials at the high school level relating to animal welfare as a legitimate consideration in biology;
- more than $50,000 to the National Association for the Advancement of Humane Education to support the development of *People and Animals,* an interdisciplinary humane education guide for preschool through sixth-grade teachers;
- $50,000 to the American Society for the Prevention of Cruelty to Animals to broaden and strengthen its humane education component, particularly through four 15-minute humane education television programs for elementary-school children developed in cooperation with the New York City Board of Education; and
- $30,000 toward the development at Cornell University of Resusci-Dog, a canine cardio-pulmonary resuscitation mannequin (see ch. 9); this is the first of a series of simulators, including one that will demonstrate irregularities in heartbeat rhythm (7).

The American Fund for Alternatives to Animal Research supports a series of intensive training sessions on in vitro toxicology for students planning a biomedical career to promote the development of scientists who are well trained in the uses and limitations of replacement techniques. This $39,000 grant supports courses that cover the theory and practice of cell and tissue culture, in vitro mutagenesis, transformation, and cytotoxicity (20).

RELATED TYPES OF FUNDING

Three additional categories of funds may be considered in conjunction with efforts to develop alternatives. These types of projects are more likely to contribute to reductions and refinements than to replacements. Grants to improve animal facilities, research in animal health, and research into pain can have broad implications for research, testing, and education.

Animal-Facility Improvement Grants

Research support through grants to improve facilities for housing animals is not specifically designed to promote the development of alternatives, but it may assume that role nonetheless. The quality of animal care provided directly affects the health of experimental animals. Those maintained within a more controlled environment are less likely to exhibit variations stemming from exposure within that environment. And if they are kept under conditions better suited to their individual needs, they are less likely to exhibit symptoms of stress. These negative effects, all resulting from the intrusion of external stimuli, may skew the results of an experiment. Less reliable results may in turn demand that more animals be used for each protocol, perhaps a needless addition under better conditions.

To address this problem, the Division of Research Resources within NIH is offering grants for the development and improvement of animal facilities so that institutions can comply with the Animal Welfare Act and with DHHS policies on the care and treatment of animals. Eligibility is open to any nonprofit institutions engaged in research supported by NIH. Two programs currently exist. The first, an ongoing program, has funded from two to four proposals each year for the past several years.

Funds for alterations and renovations are limited to $100,000, although requests for funds for equipment may push the total above this amount.

The second program draws from a one-time pool of $5 million. Support for new construction is not available, and funding for alterations and renovations is limited to $500,000 for each award. Recipient institutions are required to match these funds dollar for dollar. As in the ongoing program, funds may be requested for equipment in addition to this amount. More than 100 applications have been received; of these, only 12 requested the maximum funds for renovations and alterations. Many, however, exceeded $700,000 in their total request. The applications averaged in the $300,000 to $400,000 range. Some 12 to 15 projects are likely to be funded, and grants will probably range from $65,000 to $750,000 (9).

It is important to note that at least two other sources of funding for improvement of animal facilities are available to NIH grantees. First, an institution's maintenance of facilities is an allowable indirect cost of research. Second, the National Cancer Institute is allowed to make awards for facilities renovation (6).

Groups other than NIH are also devoting resources to improvements in animal facilities. Industry laboratories, contract laboratories, and universities are mustering both internal and external funds to improve their facilities. For commercial groups, a longer term economic advantage is recognized in these efforts. Contract testing labs, in particular, have special incentives to maintain the highest laboratory standards in order to attract clients.

Research in Animal Health and Pain

Funding devoted to research in animal health can function in an analogous fashion to efforts to improve animal care facilities. It creates the scientific base on which improvements in facilities and practices may be based. The larger the knowledge base on animal research grows, the more exact and focused research using animals can become and, ultimately, the smaller the number of animals included in individual protocols.

Parallel with this, research into the mechanisms of pain and pain perception can contribute knowledge that allows researchers to alleviate pain in experimental protocols. This can include research on the detection of pain and distress, for example, that would allow an investigator to detect these phenomena with greater sensitivity. Advances in analgesics and anesthetics may produce less distortion in some protocols and allow animals a greater degree of comfort.

As an example, Humane Information Services, Inc., awarded $184,000 in research grants during 1984 to support eight agricultural research projects directed toward the alleviation of animal suffering. Included were studies on the behavioral effects of several types of housing for pigs and chickens, studies of electronic immobilization, and projects aimed at reducing the stress of weaning and pre-slaughter handling. Similar efforts could be undertaken in testing and research to maximize the information obtained from protocols while minimizing pain and suffering for the subjects.

SUMMARY AND CONCLUSIONS

Measuring the funding of alternatives is inexact at best. Funding of replacements is easiest to measure, while the data are poor for reductions and refinements. The easiest type of research to recognize and categorize as related to alternatives is targeted research. Such work is most often associated with technique development—for example, the effort to replace whole-animal testing assays with in vitro tests, as with the Draize eye irritancy test.

The development of alternatives, especially replacements, is likely to be the result of multidisciplinary efforts, executed over relatively long periods of time. The results of research can be transferred across the sciences—as has happened, for example, with the noninvasive imaging technologies developed by physicists that are now used in the biomedical sciences.

Three types of grants can augment the development of alternatives. Funding to improve animal facilities can result in healthier, less stressed animals and can free research from the confounding variables bred by a less well defined or inferior environment. Grants to investigate improvements in animal health in general can have the same effect. And research into the mechanisms governing pain may spare animals some measure of suffering when the techniques are incorporated into other protocols.

The development of alternatives in research is funded largely by incidental means through the support of basic biomedical research by the National Institutes of Health and the National Science Foundation plus a few targeted efforts that are supported privately. In a climate of finite research resources, research and development of alternatives to animal use take their place in the competition among research priorities. A noteworthy effort by NIH was the creation of the Biological Models and Materials Resources Section within the Division of Research Resources. With funding, this office may serve as a focal point for the exchange of both nonvertebrate biological materials and information about the use of model systems in biomedical research.

In testing, a solid organizational structure for R&D of alternatives is in place, best illustrated by the National Toxicology Program and the Food and Drug Administration in the public sector and by the Rockefeller Laboratory for In Vitro Toxicology Assay and The Johns Hopkins Center for Alternatives to Animal Testing in the private sector. Any strong indication that an alternative test method would be superior to a comparable conventional animal assay is likely to attract funding readily.

CHAPTER 12 REFERENCES

1. American Fund for Alternatives to Animal Research, "Presentation of Grant Awards by AFAAR at the Center for Advanced Training in Cell and Molecular Biology," Washington, DC, June 1985.
2. Animal Protection Institute, "The Product Testing Update: Who's Using Animals and Who's Not," response to "A Day That Counts" program, Sacramento, CA, January 1985.
3. Balls, M., Chairman of Trustees, Fund for the Replacement of Animals in Medical Experiments, Nottingham, UK, personal communication, Mar. 4, 1985.
4. Borsetti, A.P., Staff Scientist, Office of Science Coordination, Food and Drug Administration, U.S. Department of Health and Human Services, Rockville, MD, personal communication, 1985.
5. Brauer, E.W., Vice-President, Revlon Research Center, Inc., Edison, NJ, personal communication, January 1985.
6. *Fed. Proc.*, "NIH's McCarthy Discusses New Animal Policy" 44(10):10a-12a, 1985.
7. Geraldine R. Dodge Foundation, "Annual Reports," Morristown, NJ, 1981-85.
8. Hart, L.G., Assistant to the Director, National Toxicology Program, Research Triangle Park, NC, personal communication, July 1985.
9. Holman, J., Director, Laboratory Animal Sciences Program, Division of Research Resources, National Institutes of Health, Public Health Service, U.S. Department of Health and Human Services, personal communication, July 1985.
10. McKinney, P., Administrative Officer, Toxicology Research and Testing Program, National Institute of Environmental Health Sciences, Research Triangle Park, NC, personal communication, July 1985.
11. Millenium Guild, "Half Million Dollar Rewards to Get Rid of Lab Animal Suffering," press release, New York, Apr. 13, 1982.
12. National Research Council, *Models for Biomedical Research: A New Perspective* (Washington, DC: National Academy Press, 1985).
13. National Science Board, *Science Indicators 1982* (Washington, DC: National Science Foundation, 1983).
14. Nethery, L.B., and McArdle, J.E., *Animals in Product Development and Safety Testing: A Survey* (Washington, DC: The Institute for the Study of Animal Problems, Humane Society of the United States, 1985).
15. Resovsky, E.M., Director of Development, University of Pennsylvania School of Veterinary Medicine, Philadelphia, PA, personal communication, Oct. 1, 1985.
16. Sabourin, T.D., Battelle Columbus Laboratories, Columbus, OH, personal communication, February 1985.
17. Shadduck, J.A., "Alternative Testing Methods: A Proposal for the Development of Alternatives to Ocular Irritancy Tests," Grants and Contracts Office, University of Illinois at Champaign-Urbana, Nov. 24, 1982.
18. Shapley, W., "Special Analyses," *AAAS Report X: Re-*

search and Development, Fiscal Year 1986 (Washington, DC: American Association for the Advancement of Science, 1985).
19. *The Johns Hopkins Center for Alternatives to Animal Testing,* "New Grants Support Research to Simulate Human Exposure" 3(3):6, 1985.
20. Thurston, E., Director, American Fund for Alternatives to Animal Research, New York, personal communication, Apr. 25, 1985.
21. Umminger, B.L., Deputy Director, Division of Cellular Biosciences, National Science Foundation, Washington, DC, personal communication, February 1985.
22. U.S. Department of Health and Human Services (DHHS), National Toxicology Program, "National Toxicology Program: Fiscal Year 1984 Annual Plan," NTP-84-023 (Research Triangle Park, NC: DHHS, February 1984).
23. U.S. Department of Health and Human Services (DHHS), National Toxicology Program, "Review of Current DHHS, DOE, and EPA Research Related to Toxicology," NTP-84-024 (Research Triangle Park, NC: DHHS, February 1984).
24. U.S. Department of Health and Human Services (DHHS), Public Health Service, National Institutes of Health, *NIH Data Book* (Bethesda, MD: DHHS, 1985).
25. U.S. Department of Health and Human Services (DHHS), Public Health Service, National Institutes of Health, "NIH Federal Funds Data Submitted to NSF," Office of Program Planning and Evaluation (Bethesda, MD: DHHS, April 1985).
26. U.S. Department of Health and Human Services (DHHS), Public Health Service, *Omnibus Solicitation of the Public Health Service for the Small Business Innovation Research Grant Applications* PHS Pub. No. 86-1 (Bethesda, MD: DHHS, 1985).
27. Willett, J.D., "Biological Systems Used as Research Models in NIH Programs," Animal Resources Program, Division of Research Resources, National Institutes of Health, Public Health Service (Bethesda, MD: DHHS, Sept. 24, 1984).
28. Willett, J.D., Project Officer, Biological Models and Materials Resources Section, Animal Resources Program, Division of Research Resources, National Institutes of Health, Public Health Service, U.S. Department of Health and Human Services, Bethesda, MD, personal communication, July 1985.

Chapter 13

Federal Regulation of Animal Use

There is a debate as to what is the right of a mouse. Why are we wasting time in Washington with taking seriously this business?

James D. Watson
Cold Spring Harbor Laboratory
As quoted in *Science* 228:160, 1985

CONTENTS

List of Tables

Chapter 13

Federal Regulation of Animal Use

This chapter describes Federal law, as enacted and currently interpreted, that directly governs and regulates the acquisition and use of laboratory animals for research and testing. Federal laws and regulations governing the purchase, sale, handling, or transportation in commerce of animals for exhibition, domestic, or other purposes unrelated to research, testing, and education are not examined. Federal laws and regulations that have been interpreted to require testing with certain methodologies or protocols are considered in chapter 7, and appendix B describes regulations promulgated and guidelines issued by specific Federal agencies, pursuant to statutory authority, to regulate laboratory-animal use in required or sponsored research and testing.

FEDERAL LAWS AND REGULATIONS

Long before passage of the Laboratory Animal Welfare Act (Public Law 89-544) in 1966, Congress—following a trend against cruelty to animals that had manifested itself in some States throughout the 19th century—in 1873 passed the first Twenty-Eight Hour Law (Act of Mar. 3, 1873). Action was taken by the national legislature under its powers to regulate interstate commerce because of the toll exacted in animal flesh, literally, by inhumane conditions of rail transport for meat-producing livestock. The law barred confinement of livestock in rail cars for longer than 28 hours.

Continuing expressions of concern led to repeal of the original act and the passage in 1906 of the Twenty-Eight Hour Law still in effect today (45 U.S.C. 71-74). (In the intervening three decades, 22 States passed general anticruelty statutes (13).) Since enactment of the 1906 act preceded the rise of interstate motor traffic, its provisions regulating length of confinement and conditions of treatment during shipment do not apply to trucks (39). Similar concerns about needless suffering undergone by food-producing animals led Congress to pass the Humane Slaughter Act (Public Law 85-765) in 1958, permitting slaughter only by "humane" means.

After 1966, concerns about animals led to Federal protection of:

- **horses,** with the passage in 1970 of the Horse Protection Act (Public Law 91-929), against an unaesthetic physical practice on animals to produce a physical appearance aesthetically appealing to humans ("soring" the ankles to produce a high-stepping gait);
- **marine mammals** as a class (whales, porpoises, seals, and polar bears, for the most part), with the passage in 1972 of the Marine Mammal Protection Act (Public Law 92-522) against extinction or depletion from indiscriminate taking, including hunting, harassment, capture, and killing (permitted takings, including for subsistence and research purposes, must be accomplished humanely, with "the least degree of pain and suffering practicable to the animal"); and
- **endangered and threatened species,** with the passage in 1973 of the Endangered Species Act (Public Law 93-205), making it unlawful to buy, sell, or transport in interstate or foreign commerce any species found to be endangered and closely regulating commerce in any species threatened with extinction.

Thus, Congress has acted on several occasions over the past century to protect animals, both as individuals and as species (i.e., marine mammals and endangered species). The degree of commitment to protection of animals through proscription, regulation, and enforcement varied, with Congress exhibiting a tendency toward stricter controls beginning in the 1970s. Similarly, recent exercising of the constitutional authority of the Federal Government over interstate commerce seems to be based on interests broader than the welfare or treatment of individual animals—e.g., saving a species from extinction.

Congressional handling of humane treatment for experimental animals, discussed in this chapter, is an interesting mixture: It professes to protect the individual animal (e.g., the experimental subject), but it establishes classifications that favor some animals over others. It uses Federal authority over interstate commerce to regulate the procurement and housing of laboratory animals, but it does not use it to the same degree as for other animals in other circumstances. Though Congress has found less-than-humane treatment of laboratory animals to be worth exercising authority over interstate commerce in order to control, it has not judged the burden on commerce to be serious enough to preempt the regulatory field. By a cautious exercise of its power, Congress has acknowledged implicitly that there is some intrinsic public value in animal experimentation and that the uniqueness of the process of experimentation requires a deliberate approach, in order to achieve one policy objective without sacrificing the other.

The Laboratory Animal Welfare Act

The 1966 Act

Finding increasing evidence that dogs and cats owned as pets were being stolen by unscrupulous dealers, moved across State lines, and resold to research institutions to satisfy a demand for experimental subjects, Congress enacted the Laboratory Animal Welfare Act in 1966. The act sought to head off these abuses by requiring dealers and research facilities that handle, care for, treat, or transport certain animals "in commerce" to follow standards to be developed and issued by the U.S. Department of Agriculture (USDA). The purposes of the act were:

- to protect the owners of dogs and cats from theft of such pets;
- to prevent the use or sale of stolen dogs or cats for purposes of research or experimentation; and
- to establish humane standards for the treatment of dogs, cats, and certain other animals by animal dealers and medical research facilities.

"In commerce" meant interstate commerce between States, the District of Columbia, territories, and possessions; between points within a State, the District of Columbia, a territory, or a possession, but through an outside point; or within the District of Columbia, a territory, or possession. Thus, to be covered by the act a dealer or research facility would have to acquire, for a use covered by the act, a regulated animal that had moved, or at some point would move, "in commerce."

Although "animal" was defined to include nonhuman primates, guinea pigs, hamsters, and rabbits, recordkeeping requirements were restricted to dogs and cats. Humane treatment was required on the premises of animal dealers, in transit, and at research institutions. The act established a system for licensing dealers and registering research facilities, with monitoring by Federal regulators. The Secretary of Agriculture was vested with the power to promulgate and enforce standards for humane care, treatment, and housing of protected animals. The act provided for the suspension of the license of any dealer violating its provisions and, upon conviction, imprisonment of not more than 1 year and a fine of not more than $1,000. The law's reach extended to transportation of regulated animals by the supplier, but not by common carriers. The Secretary was authorized to cooperate with State and local officials to prevent theft of dogs and cats, apprehend pet thieves, and administer the provisions of the act. In addition, the Secretary was directed to establish rules for inspections of premises and of the required records of licensed dealers and registered research facilities, primarily to expedite the search for stolen pets.

As applied to research, the act's reach was short. Research facilities to be regulated were limited by definition to those that:

- used or intended to use dogs or cats in experiments, **and**
- either purchased them "in commerce" or received any Federal funds for research, tests, or experiments.

Covered facilities were required to register with the Secretary rather than be subject to more stringent licensure requirements. Research-animal suppliers were subject to the new law's requirements only if they bought, sold, or transported dogs or cats **and** if the dogs or cats supplied were used for research by the client institution. In other words, research facilities could continue to procure experimental animals from farms, municipal pounds and shelters, and "duly authorized agents of local governments," rather than having to acquire animals only from licensed dealers. Research facilities were defined to include "major research facilities and exclude the thousands of hospitals, clinics, and schools which use other animals for research and tests," though research or experimentation included use of animals as teaching aids in educational institutions associated with major research facilities.

A specific and unequivocal exemption from newly devised standards for humane treatment for actual research activities was included. USDA jurisdiction over research activities was confined to care and treatment of research animals in an institution's holding facilities. The drafters of the bill were careful to point out that the exemption of research procedures was not to be compromised. The conference report stated the legislation's intent was (38):

> . . . to provide protection for the researcher in this matter by exempting from regulation all animals during actual research or experimentation, as opposed to the pre- and post-research treatment. It is not the intention of the committee to interfere in any way with research or experimentation . . . [T]he Secretary is *not* authorized to prescribe standards for the handling, care, or treatment of animals during actual research or experimentation by a research facility. The important determination of when an animal is in actual research so as to be exempt from regulations under the bill is left to the research facility, but such determination must be made in good faith.

Regarding the power to require regular recordkeeping and to inspect premises to assure compliance, the committee intended:

> . . . that these inspectors will be employees of the U.S. Department of Agriculture . . . [and that] inspectors not be permitted to interfere with the carrying out of actual research or experimentation as determined by a research facility . . . [and] that inspection . . . be specifically limited to searches for lost and stolen pets by officers of the law (not owners themselves) and that legally constituted law enforcement authorities means agencies with general law enforcement authority and not those agencies whose law enforcement duties are limited to enforcing local animal regulations. It is *not* intended that this section be used by private citizens to harass or interfere in any way with the carrying out of research or experimentation. Such officers cannot inspect the animals when the animals are undergoing actual research or experimentation.

Unlike dealers, research facilities were subject only to civil penalties (a fine of up to $500 for each offense) for violation of the act.

In the Senate committee's report on its version of the bill leading to the act, comments from relevant executive agencies were included. The Departments of Commerce and the Treasury and the Federal Aviation Administration deferred to the views of USDA and the Department of Health, Education, and Welfare (DHEW). The Under Secretary of DHEW opposed licensure for research facilities and restrictions on procurement by them of experimental subjects from other than licensed sources. Noting that the agency charged with enforcing the new law would be USDA, the letter expressed support "for sound legislation to alleviate abuses which now exist in the transportation, purchase, sale, and handling of animals intended for use in research laboratories." The Secretary of Agriculture responded as follows (38):

> This Department conducts programs in research related to animal production and animal diseases. In addition, it is charged with the administration of programs for the control and eradication of infectious, contagious, and communicable diseases of livestock and poultry; for the prevention of the introduction and dissemination [in] the United States of such diseases; and for the prevention of the exportation of diseased livestock and poultry. It also administers laws regarding the humane slaughter and treatment of livestock.
>
> . . . There are many State laws covering [illicit traffic in family pets] and licensing requirements pertaining to dogs are common. Since the operating methods of people who steal family pets and the commercial aspects of the purchase and transfer of dogs and cats in commerce are not areas as to which this Department has expertise, we are unable to evaluate the effectiveness of existing State laws. In respect to animals, the functions of this Department relate basically to livestock and poultry. Accordingly, there is a question as to whether it would not be desirable that a law such as that in question be administered by a Fed-

eral agency more directly concerned and having greater expertise with respect to the subject than this Department.

USDA estimated that administration of the act would cost approximately $2 million per year. It was authorized to assess "reasonable" fees for licenses issued. Judging that the exact cost was undeterminable, because it was not known how many new dealers would be licensed, Congress included a general authorization for appropriations (38).

1970 Amendments

Continued allegations of poor treatment of animals by unregulated parties and expressions of concern for experimental animals besides dogs and cats prompted Congress to pass the Animal Welfare Act of 1970 (Public Law 91-579) to cover a broader class of animals, including those exhibited to the public and sold at auction, and to regulate anyone engaged in those activities.

The amendments broadened the 1966 act's coverage beyond dogs, cats, monkeys, guinea pigs, hamsters, and rabbits to protect all warm-blooded animals as the Secretary of Agriculture may determine are being used for research, testing, experimentation, exhibition, or as pets. Excluded specifically from the new definition were horses not used for research and other livestock, poultry, and farm animals used for food or fiber production (7 U.S.C. 2132(g)). The 1970 amendments define the word "animal" as:

> . . . any live or dead dog, cat, monkey (nonhuman primate animal), guinea pig, hamster, rabbit, or other such warm-blooded animal, as the Secretary may determine is being used, or is intended for use, for research, testing, experimentation, or exhibition purposes, or as a pet.

The act does not appear to give the Secretary the discretion to determine that a warm-blooded animal used for experimentation is not an "animal" for purposes of the act. The act gives the Secretary the authority to determine only whether or not a warm-blooded animal is being used or is intended for use for experimentation or another named purpose. If the warm-blooded animal is judged as being used in that way, it is an "animal" under the act's coverage (6).

In 1977, the Secretary promulgated regulations that specifically excluded rats, mice, birds, and horses and other farm animals from the definition of "animal" (9 CFR 1.1(n),(o)). The introductory comments published by the Secretary upon issuing the regulation did not discuss the basis for this exclusion (42 FR 31022) (6).

The Secretary's 1977 regulatory exclusion of rats and mice from coverage by the act appears to be inconsistent with the language of the 1970 amendments. The exclusion of rats and mice from the definition of "animal" appears to frustrate the policy Congress sought to implement in 1970 and consequently to be beyond the Secretary's statutory authority (6).

The Secretary's enforcement powers over the expanded classes of licensees and registrants were broadened by adding to the definitions of "commerce" and "affecting commerce." These expanded concepts made it plain that the act extended to trade, traffic, commerce, and transportation among States and, further, that Congress considered any activity leading to the inhumane care of animals used for purposes of research, experimentation, exhibition, or held for sale as pets as constituting a burden, obstruction, or a substantial effect on the free flow of commerce. Penalties exacted against persons convicted of interfering with, assaulting, or killing Federal inspectors were increased, and the Secretary's authority to obtain adequate information to sustain administration was augmented by broadening discovery procedures. A new provision was added, establishing a legal agency relationship between a covered entity and any person acting for or employed by that entity, essentially to ensure that the Secretary could hold licensees and registrants to account for the acts, omissions, and failures of their agents or employees.

The definition of research facility was amended to include those using covered live animals, not just live dogs and cats, but the Secretary was given the authority to exempt institutions not intending to use live dogs or cats, unless other animals would be used in "substantial numbers." Regulation of covered research facilities was increased to require annual reporting and to add civil penalties for any refusal to obey a valid cease and desist order from the Secretary.

The amendments announced a commitment to the humane ethic that animals should be accorded the basic creature comforts of adequate housing, ample food and water, reasonable handling, decent sanitation, sufficient ventilation, shelter from extremes of weather and temperature, and adequate veterinary care, including the appropriate use of pain killing drugs. Besides adding handling to the basic categories of care, treatment, and transportation of covered animals, the standard of "adequate veterinary care" was broadened to include the appropriate use of anesthetic, analgesic, or tranquilizing drugs, when the use of such drugs is considered proper in the opinion of the attending veterinarian at a research facility.

The prohibition on interference with research was qualified in 1970 with a proviso that every covered research facility must show, at least annually, that professionally acceptable standards of animal care, treatment, and use are being followed by each research facility during actual research or experimentation. However, the intent regarding the continued prohibition on interference in experimentation itself was clear (35):

> . . . it is the intention of the committee that the Secretary neither directly nor indirectly in any manner interfere with or harass research facilities during the conduct of actual research or experimentation. The important determination of when an animal is in actual research is left to the research facility itself.

Similarly, the House Committee on Agriculture's report on this bill stated that the inspection section applies only to agencies with general law enforcement authority and is not intended to "be used by private citizens or law enforcement officers to harass research facilities and in no event shall such officers inspect the animals when the animals are undergoing actual research or experimentation." In summarizing these provisions, the report said that "the research scientist still holds the key to the laboratory door. This committee and Congress, however, expect that the work that's done behind that laboratory door will be done with compassion and with care" (35).

The committee report included a letter from the USDA Under Secretary indicating the Department:

- was doing everything possible to carry out its assigned responsibilities under the act within the limitations of available resources of a fiscal year 1970 appropriation of $337,000;
- agreed with the objective of the legislation concerning the need for humane care and handling of laboratory animals during actual research and experimentation, but believed "that the Department of Health, Education, and Welfare is the appropriate agency to administer such an activity. We would expect to work with that Department to help assure consistency of standards and make other necessary arrangements to promote the objectives of both [laws]"; and
- suggested that regulating the humane care and handling of animals by exhibitors should be the responsibility of State and local agencies, rather than the Federal Government.

The committee's report, noting that license fee collections and appropriations in fiscal year 1971 were expected to total $376,600, projected that the responsibilities added by the 1970 amendments would increase related program costs by approximately $1.2 million annually. The report responded to research facilities' concerns that compliance with higher standards for adequate veterinary care would require substantial expenditures for new plants, equipment, and better trained personnel by urging "that adequate funds from Federal sources be made available for those research facilities which depend to a large extent on support derived from both State and Federal sources for laboratory facility improvements" (35).

1976 Amendments

Amendments to the Animal Welfare Act in 1976 (Public Law 94-279) enlarged its provisions to define more sharply and to simplify the regulation of animals treated inhumanely during transportation affecting interstate commerce and to combat ventures involving animal fighting. In brief, the amendments having an effect on experimentation:

- added a specific finding that activities or animals regulated by the act are in interstate and foreign commerce and do, in fact, burden or substantially affect the free flow of commerce, making regulation necessary to relieve those burdens;

- reordered the statement of policy to reflect Congress' desire to: "1) insure that animals intended for use in research facilities or for exhibition purposes or for use as pets are provided humane care and treatment; 2) to assure the humane treatment of animals during transportation in commerce; and 3) to protect the owners of animals from the theft of their animals by preventing the sale or use of animals which have been stolen"—in that order;
- simplified the definition of "commerce" by eliminating the definition of "affecting commerce," and substituting a definition of "State" (the conference committee resisted an attempt to narrow the definition of "commerce" by adopting a provision from the Senate-passed bill that would have done so with an amendment that retained the act's inclusion of commerce between intrastate points but through a place outside the State);
- extended required "dealer" licensure by redefining "dealer" to include persons who negotiate the purchase or sale of protected animals for profit;
- broadened the definition of animal to correct a then-existing interpretation that hunting, security, and breeder dogs did not fall within the act's protection;
- required carriers and intermediate handlers of animals, not otherwise required to be licensed, to register with the Secretary;
- extended the agency relationship, recordkeeping, and other existing regulatory requirements to carriers and intermediate handlers;
- increased the Secretary's options for enforcement and collections by revising the section on penalties and appeals and by increasing the daily civil penalty for violation of cease and desist orders from $500 to $1,000 for all classes of regulated parties;
- extended to Federal research facilities the existing requirement to demonstrate at least annually that professionally acceptable standards governing the care, treatment, and use of animals are being followed; and
- required the Secretary to consult and cooperate with other Federal departments, agencies, or instrumentalities concerned with the welfare of research animals, where transportation or handling in commerce occurs.

USDA estimated that the enlarged responsibilities for establishment and enforcement of humane transportation standards and certification practices and the oversight of compliance by carriers and intermediate handlers would increase its annual operating costs by $565,000 in fiscal year 1977 and $385,000 per year thereafter. (The decline in required outlays in future years was attributed to a reduced need for training and orientation.)

The Congressional Budget Office (CBO) estimated a total startup cost in fiscal year 1977 of $968,000—some $570,000 for transport standards and certification enforcement and $398,000 for investigation of animal fighting ventures. That estimate projected a gradual increase in each segment of new enforcement outlays for 5 years, with total costs for these new responsibilities rising to $1,304,000 by fiscal year 1981. CBO questioned USDA's estimates of declining costs, pointing out that USDA had factored in neither anticipated higher salary costs in the future nor the total anticipated cost of enforcing the new Federal ban on animal fighting. Neither agency projected any offsetting increase in miscellaneous receipts, since newly covered carriers and intermediate handlers would not be required to become licensed. Reflecting uncertainty about the total costs of the new effort to regulate animal transport, House and Senate conferees agreed to remove the House-passed funding ceiling of $600,000 per year, though the annual ceiling for enforcing animal-fighting prohibitions was fixed at $400,000 (36).

1985 Amendments

With the enactment of the Food Security Act of 1985 (Public Law 99-198), Congress amended the Animal Welfare Act for the third time. The amendments, effective December 1986, strengthen standards for laboratory-animal care, increase enforcement of the Animal Welfare Act, provide for the dissemination of information to reduce unintended duplication of animal experiments, and mandate training for personnel who handle animals. For the first time, the Department of Health and Human Services is brought into the enforcement of the Animal Welfare Act, as the Secretary of Agriculture is directed to "consult with the Secretary of Health and Human Services prior to the issuance of regulations" under the act.

The statute requires the Secretary of Agriculture to issue minimum standards for all aspects of the veterinary care of animals, including standards for the exercise of dogs and a physical environment adequate to promote the psychological well-being of primates. The Secretary shall require that no animal be used in more than one major operative experiment from which it is allowed to recover, except in cases of scientific necessity or by determination of the Secretary.

Each research facility covered by the Animal Welfare Act—including Federal facilities—is required to appoint an institutional animal committee that includes at least one doctor of veterinary medicine and one member not affiliated with the facility. The latter is intended "to provide representation for general community interests in the proper care and treatment of animals." Any member of the committee revealing confidential information is subject to a fine of up to $10,000 and three years' imprisonment. The committee must inspect all animal study areas at least twice a year. USDA shall inspect each facility at least once a year, and each facility is required to report at least annually to USDA that the provisions of the act are being followed. (Committees in Federal facilities will report not to USDA, but to the head of the Federal entity.)

This provision for institutional animal committees, taken in concert with similar provisions in the Health Research Extension Act of 1985 (Public Law 99-158) and the policy of the Public Health Service (see app. C), brings the overwhelming majority of experimental-animal users in the United States under the oversight of a structured, local review committee.

USDA is directed to establish an information service at the National Agricultural Library (NAL). The service, in cooperation with the National Library of Medicine, shall provide information that could prevent the unintended duplication of animal experimentation, reduce or replace animal use, minimize animal pain or distress, and aid in the training of personnel involved with animals.

The law requires research facilities to provide for scientists, animal technicians, and other personnel involved with animal care and treatment training on:

- the humane practice of animal maintenance and experimentation;
- methods that minimize or eliminate the use of animals or limit animal pain or distress;
- the utilization of the NAL information service; and
- the way to report deficiencies in animal care.

Current Provisions Governing Research

In addition to the provisions of the 1985 amendments, there are 14 key provisions[1] of the Animal Welfare Act, as amended, that affect research facilities:

- **Definition of "Research Facility."** The act defines "research facility" to cover any individual, institution, organization, or postsecondary school that uses or intends to use live animals in research, tests, or experiments **and** that purchases or transports live animals in commerce or receives Federal funds for research, tests, or experiments. Exemptions may be granted where dogs or cats are not used, except where the Secretary determines that substantial numbers of other types of warm-blooded animals are used and the principal purpose of the entity covered is biomedical research or testing [7 U.S.C.A. 2132(e)]. For these to be a violation under this provision, it must be established that Federal jurisdiction extends to the particular facility—either that some connection exists between animals acquired or used and interstate commerce, or that Federal funding support is received for the contemplated research. Research facilities that receive no Federal support for experimental work and that either purchase animals

[1]Pertinent provisions of the act are discussed in the order they appear in the U.S. Code, with cross-references where appropriate. All parenthetical references in this section are to current provisions of chapter 54 of Title 7 of the Code, which can be found in Title 7, "Agriculture," *U.S. Code Annotated*, §§ 2131-2152 (St. Paul, MN: West Publishing Co.), 1973 Edition (126-139) and 1984 Supplement (126-139).

38-750 O - 86 - 10

within their own State or maintain intramural breeding colonies are not "research facilities" under this definition.

- **Registration Requirement.** Research facilities not otherwise required to be licensed as a dealer or exhibitor are required to register with the Secretary [7 U.S.C.A. 2136]. Most U.S. research facilities covered by the act are thus required only to register, rather than to pay license fees and submit to more stringent compliance requirements and criminal penalties. A "dealer" is someone engaged in interstate trade of regulated animals for research, teaching, or exhibition, or for companion, hunting, breeding, or security purposes. "Exhibitors" include carnivals, circuses, and zoos touching commerce in some way, excluding "retail pet stores, organizations sponsoring and all persons participating in State and county fairs, livestock shows, rodeos, purebred dog and cat shows, and any other fairs or exhibitions intended to advance agricultural arts and sciences," as determined by the Secretary [7 U.S.C.A. 2132(h)].
- **Acquisition of Dogs and Cats.** Covered research facilities (including Federal agencies [7 U.S.C.A. 2138]) may not purchase dogs or cats from anyone other than a person holding a valid license, unless the seller is not required to be licensed by the act, or an operator of an auction sale [7 U.S.C.A. 2137], who may also need a license [7 U.S.C.A. 2142]. Only dealers and exhibitors who meet the act's definitions for those activities, and auction sellers who sell dogs or cats "affecting commerce," must be licensed.
- **Responsibility for Employees and Agents.** A principal-agent relationship between research facilities and their agents or employees concerning any "act, omission, or failure" is created by statute [7 U.S.C.A. 2139]. This provision creates a legal presumption that a covered research entity knows about, and is responsible for, transgressions of the act by its employees or authorized agents.
- **Recordkeeping for Animals.** Research facilities must make and retain records only with respect to the purchase, sale, transportation, identification, and previous ownership of live dogs and cats [7 U.S.C.A. 2140].
- **Animal Marking Requirements.** Generally, the act requires that all animals delivered for transportation, transported, purchased, or sold, in commerce by a dealer or exhibitor be marked or identified as required by the Secretary. Research facilities need only mark or identify live dogs and cats [7 U.S.C.A. 2141].
- **Compliance With Auction Sale Rules.** Research facilities involved in purchase, handling, or sale of animals in commerce at auction sales must comply with humane standards and recordkeeping requirements established by the Secretary to regulate those activities [7 U.S.C.A. 2142].
- **Standards of Care and Treatment.** The general grant of rulemaking authority to the Secretary for establishing minimum requirements for handling, housing, feeding, watering, sanitation, ventilation, shelter from extremes of weather and temperature, adequate veterinary care (including appropriate use of anesthetic, analgesic, or tranquilizing drugs, when such use would be proper in the opinion of the research facility's attending veterinarian), and separation of species when necessary may not be construed as authorizing the Secretary to promulgate rules, regulations, or orders with regard to design, outlines, guidelines, or performance of actual research or experimentation by a research facility as determined by such research facility. But the Secretary must require every facility to show annually that professionally acceptable standards governing animal care, treatment, and use, "including appropriate use of anesthetic, analgesic, and tranquilizing drugs, during experimentation are being followed by the research facility during actual research or experimentation" [7 U.S.C.A. 2143(a)].
- **Animal Certification Requirements.** Research facilities may not deliver for handling or transportation in commerce any dog, cat, or other designated animal without a certificate of inspection, executed by a licensed veterinarian not more than 10 days prior to delivery, for freedom from infectious diseases or physical abnormalities that would endanger the animal or other animals or endanger public health. The statute permits the Secretary by regulation to exempt from this require-

ment animals shipped to research facilities for purposes of research, testing, or experimentation requiring animals not eligible for such certification [7 U.S.C.A. 2143(b)].

- **Minimum Age for Transport.** Research facilities may receive dogs, cats, and other designated animals younger than the minimum age requirement for transportation in commerce established by the Secretary pursuant to the act [7 U.S.C.A. 2143(c)].
- **Federal Facilities.** Federal agencies with laboratory-animal facilities are required to comply with regulations for humane treatment in commerce as they apply to nongovernmental research facilities [7 U.S.C.A. 2144].
- **Inspections.** Research facilities are required to grant inspectors reasonable access to their places of business, facilities, animals, and records. Inspectors are empowered to confiscate or destroy in a humane manner any animal found to be suffering as a result of a failure to comply with the act, its regulations, or standards, if such animal is held by a research facility and is no longer required by such research facility to carry out the research, test, or experiment for which such animal has been utilized [7 U.S.C.A. 2146(a)]. Research facilities engaged in the purchase, handling, or sale of animals are also required to permit inspections by legally constituted law enforcement agencies in search of lost animals [7 U.S.C.A. 2147].
- **Penalties, Hearings, and Appeals.** For any violation of the act, its regulations, or standards, a research facility may be assessed a civil penalty up to $2,500 for each day of noncompliance. Knowing failure to obey a cease and desist order can result in an additional penalty of $1,500 for each day of noncompliance. Research facilities are not subject to criminal penalties for violations [7 U.S.C.A. 2149(b), (c),(d)].
- **Annual Report to Congress.** Each March, the Secretary of Agriculture is required to report to Congress the identification of all research facilities that are required or choose to be licensed, the nature of all investigations and inspections conducted and reports received, and the Secretary's suggestions for legislative changes to improve the administration of the act. The annual enforcement report cannot be released to non-Federal entities until it has been made public by a congressional committee [7 U.S.C.A. 2155].

Regulations

Congress intended that the broad statutory framework it had erected in the Animal Welfare Act be fleshed out to achieve the law's general objectives. USDA received common grants of discretionary power and ministerial duties, giving the Secretary both latitude to exercise judgment in enforcing the law and the obligation to execute a number of distinct duties.[2]

Responsibility for administration was delegated by the Secretary to the Administrator of the Animal and Plant Health Inspection Service (APHIS). Ministerial and enforcement duties are the province of the APHIS Deputy Administrator for Veterinary Services, and initial collection of records and supervision and assignment of inspectors are done by Veterinarians-in-Charge, based in APHIS's State offices in each of five geographic regions throughout the United States. Except for the Northeast region (served centrally by a Boston office), every State has an APHIS office, usually in the capital [7 CFR 371.2(a),(d); 9 CFR 1.1(a)-(j)]. Inspectors known as Veterinary Services Representatives perform investigative tasks in consultation with an attending veterinarian or with a three-member committee employed by a registered research facility (one of whom must be a licensed veterinarian), which is responsible for evaluating the type and amount of anesthetic, analgesic, and tranquilizing drugs used on animals during actual research, testing, or experimentation where appropriate to relieve all unnecessary pain and distress in the subject animals [9 CFR 1.1(ee)].

"Animal" includes "any live or dead dog, cat, monkey (nonhuman primate mammal), guinea pig, hamster, rabbit, or any other warm-blooded animal, which is domesticated or raised in captivity or which normally can be found in the wild state,

[2]Pertinent provisions are discussed in this section in the order in which they appear in the published regulations, with cross-references where appropriate. All parenthetical references are to Title 7, Part 371, and Title 9, Parts 1-4, of the U.S. *Code of Federal Regulations* (Washington, DC: General Services Administration, 1984).

and is being used, or is intended for use, for research, testing, experimentation or exhibition purposes, or as a pet" [9 CFR 1.1(n)]. By regulation, this definition excludes birds, rats, mice, and horses and other farm animals intended "for use as food or fiber, or livestock or . . . [for] improving animal nutrition, breeding, management, or production efficiency, or for improving the quality of food or fiber" [9 CFR 1.1(n),(o)]. The definition of "dog" is enlarged to include those used for hunting, security, or breeding purposes [9 CFR 1.1(l)-(n),(q)]. The farm-animal exemption and expanded dog definition reflect changes in the act made in 1970 and 1976. The only warm-blooded animals, other than those specified in the act, that the Secretary has chosen to designate are marine mammals.

A research facility not otherwise required to be licensed must register with APHIS by completing a standard registration form and filing it with the office in the State of its principal place of business. The registrant receives a copy of the form and "applicable standards" from APHIS and is required to acknowledge their receipt and agree to comply with the standards by signing a form [9 CFR 2.25-2.26].

Each "reporting facility" (each segment of a registered facility using experimental animals and for which an attending veterinarian has responsibility, including departments, agencies, and instrumentalities of the United States) must file an annual report, signed by a legally responsible official, showing that professionally acceptable standards governing the care, treatment, and use of animals, including appropriate use of anesthetic, analgesic, and tranquilizing drugs, during actual research, testing, or experimentation, were followed by the facility. The report, due by December 1 and covering the preceding Federal fiscal year (Oct. 1-Sept. 30), must include:

- the location of the facility where animals were used;
- common names and approximate numbers of animals on which research, experiments, or tests were conducted involving:
  (a) no pain, distress, or use of pain-relieving drugs;
  (b) accompanying pain or distress to the animals, for which appropriate anesthetic, analgesic, or tranquilizing drugs were used; and
  (c) pain or distress to the animals for which the use of appropriate anesthetic, analgesic, or tranquilizing drugs would adversely affect the procedures, results, or interpretation of the research, experiments, or tests and a brief statement explaining the reasons for the same (in all three cases, routine procedures—injections, tattooing, and blood sampling—need not be reported); and
- certification by the attending veterinarian or institutional committee that the type and amount of anesthetic, analgesic, and tranquilizing drugs used on animals during research, testing, or experimentation was appropriate to relive pain and distress for the subject animals (9 CFR 2.28).

Research facilities must observe certain requirements for maintaining identification of dogs and cats either received from or consigned for delivery into commerce. Live dogs and cats so consigned must bear either the original tag or tattoo, or a tag, tattoo, or collar supplied by the facility, that identifies each animal by description or number [9 CFR 2.50(e)].

Records on acquired dogs or cats must be kept and maintained to disclose the name and address of the person from whom the animal was acquired; the official tag number or tattoo; a description of each live dog or cat, including species, sex, date of birth or approximate age, color and distinctive markings, and breed or type; and the number assigned to the animal by the facility.

Facilities that transport, sell, or otherwise dispose of a live dog or cat must maintain on forms furnished by APHIS, in addition to the above information, the name and address of the person into whose custody the animal is delivered, the date of delivery, and the method and identification of mode of transportation.

Research facilities may not destroy or dispose of required records without the written consent of APHIS, and records must be held for longer where necessary to comply with any other Federal, State, or local law (9 CFR 2.100). Research facilities (like dealers, exhibitors, and auction operators) must open their records to APHIS requests for information and inspections related to the act's enforcement as well as their facilities, during ordinary business hours, and they must be willing to have the facility's name published in a periodic list of registered facilities (9 CFR 2.126-2.127). They must also open their premises to inspection by police or legally constituted law enforcement agencies with general law enforcement authority (other than agents whose sole authority is to enforce local animal regulations) for inspections for missing animals, where the authority provides a description of the animal and the owner's name and address and agrees to abide by institutional policies concerning spread of disease and animal escape, but such searches cannot be extended to animals undergoing actual research or experimentation, as determined by the facility (9 CFR 2.128).

An APHIS inspector can act to confiscate and destroy an animal found to be suffering as a result of a research facility's failure to comply with the act, its regulations, or its standards only:

- if the animal suffering through such failure is no longer required to carry out the research, test, or experiment for which it has been utilized;
- if the inspector has made a reasonable effort to notify the facility and request that the responsible condition be corrected or appropriate veterinary care be given, and the facility refuses to comply; **or**
- if the inspector is unable to locate or notify a representative of the facility, in which case a local law enforcement officer may be contacted to accompany the inspector to the premises to either provide veterinary care or confiscate and destroy the suffering animal.

Costs of care or destruction are to be borne by the violator facility. If the animal to be destroyed is an endangered species, the Deputy Administrator is required to consult with the Department of the Interior and the International Union for the Conservation of Nature and Natural Resources [9 CFR 2.129].

Research facilities are required to comply with detailed standards for humane care and treatment, except that nothing in the rules, regulations, or standards may affect or interfere with the design, outlines, guidelines, or performances of actual research or experimentation by a research facility as determined by such research facility (9 CFR 2.100(a)).

Part 3 of the regulations details specific standards for humane care and treatment according to category of defined animal—dogs and cats, guinea pigs and hamsters, rabbits, nonhuman primates, marine mammals, and warm-blooded animals other than the above species—under three headings:

- Facilities and Operating Standards (general, indoor, and outdoor facilities and primary enclosures);
- Animal Health and Husbandry Standards (feeding, watering, sanitation, employees, classification and separation, and veterinary care); and
- Transportation Standards (consignment to carriers and intermediate handlers, primary enclosures used for transport, primary conveyances [motor vehicle, rail, air, and marine], food and water requirements, care in transit, terminal facilities, and handling).

Although specific environmental requirements differ by category of defined animal, the pattern of each set of standards is quite similar. The primary difference with respect to research facilities pertains to the veterinary care standards for each animal, which contain the following common provisions: "Programs of disease control and prevention, euthanasia, and adequate veterinary care must be established and maintained under the supervision and assistance of a doctor of veterinary medicine." Specifically, research facilities must:

- include the appropriate use of anesthetic, analgesic, or tranquilizing drugs in their programs of veterinary care, when such use would be proper in the opinion of the attending veterinarian. The use of these three classes of drugs shall be in accordance with the currently accepted veterinary medical practice, as cited in appropriate professional journals or reference guides, which shall produce in the individual subject animal a high level of tranquilization, anesthesia, or analgesia consistent with the protocol or design of the experiment;

- provide guidelines and consultation to research personnel regarding type and amount of the three classes of drugs recommended as being appropriate for each species of animal, through the animal care committee or attending veterinarian; and
- assure that the use of the three classes of drugs effectively minimizes the pain and discomfort of the animals while under experimentation [9 CFR 3.10, 3.34, 3.59, 3.84, 3.110, 3.134].

Few petitions for changes in existing regulations have been made. No person or organization has used the formal rulemaking process to seek to add any classes of warm-blooded animals. In 1982, the Humane Society of the United States filed a petition for rulemaking and collateral relief that, among other things, sought definitions of the terms "pain," "distress," and "routine procedures" and a requirement that research facilities explain in adequate detail why pain-relieving drugs are withheld from animals used in experiments acknowledged to cause pain and distress (12).

In summary, USDA's approach has been literal and cautious with regard to research facilities. This position can be traced to two influences. First, both the act itself and its legislative history make clear Congress' desire to avoid any entanglement in the actual conduct of research. Second, both the legislative and executive commitments of funds and personnel for enforcement have never lived up to the expectations of those who believe the primary mission of the existing law to be the prevention or alleviation of experimental-animal suffering.

Enforcement

The responsibilities of APHIS in enforcing the Animal Welfare Act fall into three main categories:

- making, implementing, and enforcing policies and rules for national and international programs to protect the health of U.S. livestock and poultry resources, assuring quality and safety of veterinary biologics, and providing for the welfare and humane treatment of certain animals;
- cooperating and providing technical assistance to State and local governments regarding international quarantines and exotic animal disease programs; and
- providing professional development and training for APHIS personnel and training for foreign visitors in veterinary service programs.

Nineteen public laws outline APHIS's duties in the first area, including the Animal Welfare Act, the Horse Protection Act, and the Twenty-Eight Hour Law (49 FR 26674). By far, the most time- and resource-consuming APHIS objective is protecting domestic plants and livestock from diseases and pests. Of 841 pages in the *Code of Federal Regulations* on APHIS duties and programs, only 100 are devoted to animal welfare activities under the relevant acts (7 CFR 1984 ed. 371.2). Port-of-entry inspections by APHIS seek to prevent the introduction of insects, plant diseases, nematodes, and animal pests and diseases harmful to crops and crop products. Plant exports are controlled through a certification system administered by APHIS, and cooperative programs with States are conducted to eradicate domestically established plant pests.

The APHIS mission, then, is traditionally bound to certification, inspection, and cooperative assistance programs that govern agricultural activities, devoted almost exclusively to protecting plants and animals used to produce food and fiber.

The APHIS Assistant Deputy Administrator for Animal Health Programs, under the Deputy Administrator for Veterinary Services, is responsible for directing enforcement activities through four regional offices, located in Scotia, NY; Tampa, FL; Englewood, CO; and Fort Worth, TX (50 FR 31341). (Prior to 1985, five regional offices existed but this was changed in response to a review of APHIS activities by the General Accounting Office (GAO).) Licensing, registration, and inspection of all regulated entities—dealers, exhibitors, research facilities, carriers, intermediate handlers, and auction sales—are handled by a field force directed by Veterinarians-in-Charge in the APHIS offices in 45 State capitals. Field officials conducting animal welfare work include veterinary medical officers, compliance officers, and animal technicians. Six veterinarians trained in laboratory-animal husbandry procedures coordinate animal welfare activities among the four regions (43). APHIS has 286 Veterinary Medical Officers (inspectors), who spend approximately 6 percent of their time inspecting research facilities (25).

Table 13-1 summarizes funding and staff support dedicated to animal welfare activities, compared with the total APHIS budget and equivalent staff-years, for Federal fiscal years 1980-85. As a percentage of the total budget for APHIS activities, animal welfare has consistently constituted less than 2 percent.

Animal welfare appropriations have remained virtually constant since fiscal year 1982, despite gradual reductions in APHIS's overall budget. (Some of the decline in regular appropriations can be traced to increases in fees collected for a variety of activities, though program-specific reductions have occurred (4).) The total number of staff-years spent on APHIS activities (calculated from work-years available from authorized positions for which general appropriations are made) declined steadily from fiscal year 1980 through fiscal year 1985. That decline is reflected proportionately in animal welfare activities, but the percentage of staff-years devoted to those activities has remained constant and, as a percentage of the total staff time, is slightly higher than that of appropriated funds.

As of March 1985, a total of 1,286 research facilities had registered with APHIS as using covered animals, as having acquired them in commerce, or as receiving related Federal funding support. Sixty-four percent of the principal registered research facilities (RRFs) are located in just 10 populous States (California, New York, Pennsylvania, Ohio, Massachusetts, New Jersey, Texas, Illinois, Michigan, and Florida; see table 13-2); most facilities are close to urban centers. These numbers are for the principal registrants only, not the total number of research sites. A university campus system, for example, is only required to register once under the act, though it may have a number of sites where research or tests are performed. The location of licensees (dealers and exhibitors), other registrants (carriers and intermediate handlers), and violators of the act's animal-fighting prohibition may not, of course, exhibit a similar distribution. Given APHIS's traditional and overarching duties to protect food- and fiber-producing plants and animals as well as the Animal Welfare Act's exemption from coverage of most agricultural research, it seems that not even the major share of animal welfare enforcement resources could be targeted toward monitoring the care and treatment of experimental animals.

As the most widely used experimental subjects—mice and rats—have been excluded by USDA regulation from the act's coverage (9 CFR 1.1(n),(o)), current regulations probably do not affect a substantial percentage of animals used for experimental purposes. This can be tested in a crude way by comparing the 1984 Directory of Toxicology Laboratories, compiled by *Chemical Times and Trends (CT&T)*, with APHIS's 1984 List of Registered Research Facilities. Sixty-eight of 112 testing facilities, or 61 percent, listed in the *CT&T* directory also appear by name in the APHIS registration list; 39 percent are not registered. This implies no wrongdoing on the part of unregistered toxicity testing labs, since they may not fall under any of the definitional requirements for compliance with the act. The number of unregistered facilities is conservative, however; for purposes of comparison, it was assumed that all university-affiliated testing sites are covered by the parent institution's principal registration and that any nonuniversity lab whose name approximates that of another registrant is also covered. If rats and

Table 13-1.—Requests for Appropriations, Actual Appropriations, and Staff-Years, USDA Animal and Plant Health Inspection Service, Fiscal Years 1980-85

	1980	1981	1982	1983	1984	1985
Total appropriation, APHIS[a] (in thousands)	$249,098	$282,385	$281,967	$275,115	$263,238	$267,558
Executive request, Animal Welfare (in thousands)	$ 3,594	$ 4,355	$ 4,402	$ 1,509	$ 1,568	$ 3,655
Total appropriation, Animal Welfare[a] (in thousands)	$ 4,128	$ 4,291	$ 4,882	$ 4,886	$ 4,865	$ 4,865
Proportion (percent) of total appropriation	1.7	1.5	1.7	1.8	1.9	1.8
Total staff-years, APHIS[b]	5,286	5,099	5,069	4,637	4,416	4,440
Staff-years, Animal Welfare Act enforcement	150	137	137	120	119	120
Proportion (percent) of total	2.8	2.7	2.7	2.6	2.7	2.7

[a]All appropriations are actual (excluding pay supplementals).
[b]Staff-years are calculated from available work-years for authorized positions (appropriated funds only). All figures are actual, except for fiscal year 1985, which is projected.
SOURCE: Office of Technology Assessment.

Table 13-2.—Distribution of Research Facilities, by State, Registered With USDA/APHIS Under the Animal Welfare Act

State/jurisdiction	Number of registered research facilities	Percent of total	Rank out of 52
Alabama	12	0.9	24
Alaska	1	0.1	51
Arizona	9	0.7	34
Arkansas	3	0.2	46
California	175	13.6	1
Colorado	25	1.9	13
Connecticut	17	1.3	22
Delaware	8	0.6	36
District of Columbia	8	0.6	37
Florida	47	3.7	10
Georgia	12	0.9	25
Hawaii	4	0.3	41
Idaho	4	0.3	42
Illinois	63	4.9	8
Indiana	21	1.6	15
Iowa	11	0.9	27
Kansas	18	1.4	19
Kentucky	6	0.5	38
Louisiana	12	0.9	26
Maine	11	0.9	28
Maryland	33	2.6	11
Massachusetts	69	5.4	5
Michigan	49	3.8	9
Minnesota	19	1.5	16
Mississippi	3	0.2	47
Missouri	27	2.1	12
Montana	3	0.2	48
Nebraska	10	0.8	31
Nevada	1	0.1	52
New Hampshire	4	0.3	43
New Jersey	68	5.3	6
New Mexico	11	0.9	29
New York	120	9.3	2
North Carolina	19	1.5	17
North Dakota	3	0.2	49
Ohio	72	5.6	4
Oklahoma	13	1.0	23
Oregon	18	1.4	20
Pennsylvania	90	7.0	3
Puerto Rico	10	0.8	32
Rhode Island	9	0.7	35
South Carolina	5	0.4	39
South Dakota	2	0.2	50
Tennessee	11	0.9	30
Texas	67	5.2	7
Utah	10	0.8	33
Vermont	4	0.3	44
Virginia	23	1.8	14
Washington	18	1.4	21
West Virginia	5	0.4	40
Wisconsin	19	1.5	18
Wyoming	4	0.3	45
Total	1,286	100	

SOURCE: U.S. Department of Agriculture, Animal and Plant Health Inspection Service, *Animal Welfare: List of Registered Facilities*, Fiscal Year 1985.

mice used in testing and testing-related research merit the same coverage as other warm-blooded animals, and if inhumane treatment of such animals that are not part of interstate commerce is as much a burden on or affects commerce as much as the animals that are part of such commerce, this disparity assumes greater legislative and regulatory significance.

Table 13-3 summarizes annual registration and reporting activity as recorded by APHIS for fiscal years 1978-83. The total number of licensees and registrants covered by the act—all classes of regulated parties, from dealers through intermediate handlers—decreased slightly, and the total at the close of fiscal year 1983 remained smaller than in 1978. Increases in the number of RRFs over the preceding year occurred in 4 of the 6 years. The number of registered research facilities classified as "inactive" by APHIS (i.e., reporting no use of regulated animals for 2 consecutive years) has risen steadily but it remains below 7 percent of the total. As a class, RRFs rose from 15.8 percent of the total in fiscal 1978 to 19.3 percent in fiscal year 1983, due mainly to a simultaneous decrease in the number of licensed dealers.

APHIS indicated in its 1981 and 1982 Annual Enforcement Reports that the failure of qualified research facilities to register and report was a significant enforcement problem and stated that it "currently had no effective system for detecting research facilities that use laboratory animals without being registered." During 1981, one research facility was prosecuted for failure to register, resulting in registration and entry of a cease and desist order by an administrative law judge (41). Three cases were filed against registrants who had failed to report in 1981; in one case, a fine of $1,000 was assessed, the first time a research facility had been fined for failure to report (41,42).

A number of reports are late or not filed by actively registered research facilities either through inattention, ignorance of the law, lack of penalties with sufficient deterrent value, some incompatibility between the calendar or fiscal years of facilities and the established Federal fiscal year for reporting, the inability of APHIS to analyze and compile all reports to meet the congressionally

Table 13-3.—Licensing, Registration, and Reporting Activity of Registered Research Facilities Under the Animal Welfare Act, Fiscal Years 1978-83

	1978	1979	1980	1981	1982	1983
Total licensees/registrants	6,902	6,389	6,585	6,492	6,297	6,447
Licensed dealers	4,501	3,982	3,886	3,664	3,439	3,490
Exhibitors:						
Licensed	924	978	1,101	1,168	1,237	1,266
Registered	313	239	170	130	106	101
Intermediate handlers/carriers	66	139	274	312	339	346
Registered Research Facilities (RRFs):						
Active	1,057	1,051	1,092	1,169	1,113	1,166
Inactive[a]	35	—	62	49	63	78
New RRFs added	—	—	71	—	43	70
RRFs as proportion of total (percent)	16	17	18	19	19	19
Reports received from RRFs[b]	1,092	NA	1,061	1,111	968	1,127
Active	1,072	1,061	857	919	885	1,005
Negative[c]	—	169	138	143	73	73
Late or no report filed[d]	20	NA	66	49[e]	10	49

[a]Means no reported use of regulated animals for two consecutive years.
[b]Excludes reports from Federal facilities.
[c]Means no use of regulated animals during reporting year.
[d]Means no Annual Report received by December 1 of reporting year for inclusion in APHIS' Animal Welfare Enforcement Report to Congress for that year.
[e]Last reporting year for which late or no filings could be calculated from information given in Annual Animal Welfare Enforcement Report. Later figures supplied by APHIS.
NA = Not available.

SOURCE: Office of Technology Assessment.

established deadline for annual enforcement reports, or some combination of all these factors.

The method used by APHIS for monitoring compliance with the act's and its own standards is "regular, unannounced" inspections of licensee and registrant premises. For research facilities, the most important standard is that adequate veterinary care or, more particularly, "professionally acceptable standards" of relief of pain and distress are observed during and after experimentation, except where administration of anesthetics or pain relievers would interfere with the purpose of the experiment. Major inspections are characterized as:

- **recurring compliance inspections,** performed to "spot-check" active licensees and registrants for continued compliance with established standards;
- inspections to **investigate complaints** of noncompliance or substandard treatment;
- **status searches,** undertaken to determine whether a business (principally potential dealers) should be licensed; and
- inspections to investigate **apparent violations** that have come to the attention of inspectors (43).

Though a multi-sited facility may be required to register only as a single entity, obviously all sites where covered animals are held must be inspected on a regular basis if standards are to be enforced adequately. The precise number of sites of animal use in experimentation in the United States is unknown; it likely falls between 5,000 and 10,000.

In 1985, GAO completed a study for the Chairman of the Subcommittee on Agriculture, Rural Development and Related Agencies, Senate Committee on Appropriations, on USDA activities under the Animal Welfare Act. GAO focused on:

- the training and guidance given to USDA's inspectors;
- how USDA schedules its inspections of licensees and registrants and the frequency of those inspections; and
- the followup action USDA takes when inspectors find unsatisfactory conditions (32).

GAO reviewed animal welfare inspection activities at the APHIS area offices in California, Iowa, Kansas, Missouri, New York, and Texas. These offices accounted for 45 percent of the 19,473 recurring compliance inspections made in fiscal year 1982.

Regarding the training and guidance of inspectors, GAO found that 57 out of 73 inspectors had attended formal training courses. However, 43 of the 57 had received no training in recent years. The last training course for the 17 inspectors in Texas was given in 1979.

Although USDA personnel and planning documents state that four inspections a year per site is desirable, GAO found that the 3,379 sites in the six States were inspected, on the average, 1.7 times during fiscal year 1983. In California and New York, each site averaged 0.7 inspections per year. Between 6.4 percent (in Kansas) and 51.7 percent (in California) of the registered facilities in a given State were not inspected at all during fiscal year 1983.

When looking at followup action taken by USDA for unsatisfactory conditions, GAO reviewed inspection reports of 114 sites where major deficiencies were found. In general, GAO found that the APHIS offices complied with the Service's policy and met the timeframe goals for the various steps in the process. Only 17 of the 114 sites did not follow the prescribed procedure.

While conducting the review, GAO noted some additional matters affecting the APHIS Animal Welfare Program. First, there was no specified program or procedure to oversee the quality of inspections. Three of the six States surveyed did not have any program for monitoring inspection quality. Second, GAO found inconsistencies in the reporting of inspections. Finally, GAO found that funding of inspections for 1983 had been based on 1982 work levels rather than on estimates of current potential workloads and the severity of expected problems.

USDA is subject to the provisions of the Freedom of Information Act (FOIA) (Public Law 90-23), a Federal law that generally requires most Federal agencies to release to interested persons information in its possession, unless it is classified or meets one of the other exceptions established by Congress and interpreted by the courts. Congress, concerned about the potential for "harassment" of research facilities through the use and publication of their required inspection forms and reports, specified in the final sentence of Section 25 of the 1966 Animal Welfare Act that USDA could not release any such information (except to other agencies) "unless and until it [was] made public by an appropriate" congressional committee (Public Law 89-544).

Requests for information under FOIA have increased steadily since fiscal year 1979. Humane groups have usually made about half the petitions for information. In fiscal 1978, they accounted for 53 of 98 requests—54 percent (40). For fiscal years 1981-83, the proportions were 50, 53, and 52 percent (41,42,43). The highest numbers of documents released were in fiscal year 1981 and calendar year 1984, which coincided with renewed lobbying for amendments to strengthen the Animal Welfare Act or for new legislation increasing the Federal regulatory presence in research. No data are available on the proportion of requests for research facility records for prior years, but 1984 records show that 58 percent of total requests concerned research facilities, 62 percent of all documents released affected research, and 50 percent of all regulated parties affected were registered research facilities. The Animal Welfare Institute, a Washington, DC, organization interested in the act's application to research, entered most of the requests affecting such institutions (19). Documents most often requested are copies of inspection reports, reporting forms, records, and forms used to apply for licenses or registrations (43).

Litigation

No cases can be found where a Federal court has had to interpret the provisions of the Animal Welfare Act requiring humane care and treatment of research animals. Though some State courts have considered the act's provisions when interpreting the effect of other laws (see ch. 14), their decisions cannot affect the constitutionality of a Federal law's application under the Federal Constitution. In the only case where the U.S. Supreme Court considered any of the act's provisions, "exemplary" language in the 1970 amendments extending judicial enforcement powers to the Federal district courts was cited to sustain review jurisdiction asserted under another, similar provision in Federal law (14).

Three Federal appeals courts have had occasion to examine the language of the act, though none of the cases involved registered research facilities (11,21,27). One case is nevertheless germane because it is the only time the courts have had to examine the language and the intent of Congress in passing the act. In a 1976 decision denying a professional dog-and-pony-show owner's claim that he was not covered by the act, the U.S. Court of Appeals for the District of Columbia indicated the likelihood of a favorable judicial response to attacks on the act and of a liberal interpretation of the legislation. Quoting from the House report, the Court stated that (11):

> As the evolution of the Animal Welfare Act manifests, Congress has chosen a cautious approach to regulation in this area, increasing governmental intervention as the national interest seemed to warrant. . . . From the small beginning in 1966—confined to a few animals, and only when they were devoted to research purposes—the present legislation further, though still modestly, "implement[s] a statutory mandate that small helpless creatures deserve the care and protection of a strong and enlightened public." We perceive nothing in the Constitution outlawing this commendable "effort to demonstrate America's humanity to lesser creatures."

The U.S. Supreme Court refused to review the decision (11). Thus, the case's value rests in using it to support the notion that the highest court refused to disturb a lower court's decision upholding the reasonableness of Congress' effort to protect animals from inhumane treatment, including in research. The D.C. Federal appeals court has cited provisions of the act on three other occasions, once in support of judicial review of the delegated powers of the Secretary of Agriculture (29) and twice without comment (1,28).

At the district court level (the Federal system's usual courts of first resort, or "trial" courts), several cases have been brought in which the act's provisions have been raised (3,5,9,10), but no court has fully considered or decided any case invoking the act against a research facility.

A review of reported and unreported cases involving the Animal Welfare Act indicates that whatever case law has been developed bears little relation to the act's regulation of research activities. This can be traced to a single major factor. Congress—very deliberately, it appears, fearing harassment of research facilities—gave no party other than APHIS any statutory right to enforce the act or regulations promulgated pursuant to it. The degree of circumspection toward research evident in Congress' consideration of the act and its amendments must be seen as an obstacle to private enforcement of its standards through the courts, since at least one Federal court has held that humane groups have standing to sue on behalf of animals under another law enacted for humane objectives, the Marine Mammal Protection Act (2). Lack of standing—i.e., proof to a court that a claimant's stake in the accomplishment of the policy objectives of a statute is significant and the effect on the claimant's interests is real if those objectives are frustrated (see ch. 14)—makes it impossible to attain enforcement of laws from the bench.

The Health Research Extension Act of 1985

In 1985, Congress amended the Public Health Service Act (Public Law 78-184) by enacting the Health Research Extension Act of 1985 (Public Law 99-158), which contained provisions for the care and treatment of animals in research funded by the Public Health Service (PHS), including the National Institutes of Health (NIH). The act provided statutory authority for and recognition of certain elements of the PHS *Policy on Humane Care and Use of Laboratory Animals by Awardee Institutions* (see app. C).

The act also contained provisions for the development of alternative research methods. Thus, the concept of alternatives to animal use was explicitly described for the first time in Federal law in 1985. (The concept of alternatives first appeared in Federal law earlier in 1985, in fact. Public Law 99-129, The Health Professions Educational Assistance Amendments of 1985, also mentions the development of curriculum for veterinary students on alternatives to the use of animals. It is described in ch. 12.)

Care and Treatment of Animals in Research

The act requires that each entity receiving PHS support for research with animals establish a committee to monitor care and treatment of animals used in research. These committees shall consist of at least three members, of which one must be a veterinarian and one an individual having no association with the institution. The act thus specifies more modest requirements for the committees than does the PHS policy. The PHS policy requires a minimum of five committee members, and the veterinarian must have training or experience in laboratory-animal science or medicine.

The animal care committees are responsible for: 1) reviewing at least semiannually the care and treatment of animals in all animal study areas and facilities for compliance with NIH guidelines, 2) keeping appropriate records of such reviews, and 3) certifying to NIH that such reviews have been conducted. In requiring a minimum of two inspections per year, the law is more stringent than the PHS policy, which requires at least one per year.

The act requires applicants for NIH funds to file assurances with NIH indicating both that the applicant will meet the NIH guidelines for the care and treatment of animals and that the applicant's institution has an animal care committee. Applicants must also assure NIH of the availability of instruction at their institutions in the humane practices of animal care and in research methods that minimize the use of animals and limit animal distress. All applications for NIH funds must include a statement of the reasons for using animals in the research. If NIH determines that a research entity is not meeting the guidelines, and if no action is taken after notification of the noncompliance, the act provides that the NIH Director shall suspend or revoke funding.

Research on Alternatives

The act directs NIH to establish a plan for research into methods of biomedical and behavioral experimentation that do not require the use of animals, that reduce the number of animals used, or that produce less pain and distress than methods currently in use. NIH is further directed to develop plans for evaluating the validity and reliability of such methods, proceeding with development of methods found to be valid and reliable, and training scientists in the use of such methods. The law instructs NIH to disseminate information to investigators about alternative methods that are found to be valid and reliable, and to establish an internal coordinating committee (made up of the directors of each NIH institute) to assist in developing the NIH plan, which must be prepared by October 1, 1986. With the creation in 1985 of the Biological Models and Materials Resources Section (see ch. 12), NIH appears poised to respond to this legislative mandate.

Other Federal Laws and Regulations

Beyond the Federal laws and regulations that either directly require or have been interpreted to require the use of certain animals in testing or research and guidelines adopted pursuant to general statutory authority, several other Federal laws and regulations establish duties for research facilities concerning the acquisition and general care of animals used for experimentation.

Good Laboratory Practices

In the 1970s, concern at the Food and Drug Administration (FDA) about faulty toxicological data based on animals, generated both internally and externally (18), led to the promulgation of regulations requiring all regulated parties conducting nonclinical laboratory studies that test for safety or effectiveness to conduct, keep records about, and permit audits on all such tests in a specified manner. In 1978, FDA adopted Good Laboratory Practices (GLP) rules (43 FR 59986) and began a laboratory audit and inspection program. In 1984, FDA published a notice proposing some changes in these regulations primarily to streamline recordkeeping, data storage and retrieval, and reporting practice (49 FR 43530). Further action may occur in early 1986.

Drawing on the FDA experience and mindful of its responsibility to collect and analyze substantial amounts of testing data for approval of new chemicals and registration of pesticides, the Environmental Protection Agency (EPA) defined its own approach to GLPs (44 FR 27362). In 1978, EPA executed a Memorandum of Understanding to permit FDA to inspect toxicity testing labs and audit pesticide data submitted in support of registration applications (43 FR 14124). After much consideration—and the discovery by FDA of the submission of hundreds of fraudulent test results by one independent laboratory (22)—in 1983 EPA issued its own final GLP rules for its toxic substances control (48 FR 53922) and pesticides (48 FR 53946) programs.

The GLPs for FDA and EPA are similar. Both address all areas of laboratory operations, delineating requirements for the establishment of a Quality Assurance Unit to conduct periodic internal inspections and keep records for audit and reporting purposes; Standard Operating Procedures (SOPs) for all aspects of each study and for all phases of laboratory maintenance; a formal mechanism for evaluation and approval of study protocols and their amendments; and inclusion in reports of data in sufficient detail to support conclusions drawn from them. FDA performs four kinds of inspections in U.S. toxicology labs (8):

- **GLP compliance,** including examination of an ongoing study as well as a completed study (once every 2 years);
- **data audit** as needed, to verify that information submitted to the agency accurately reflects the raw data;
- **directed,** when prompted by questionable data, an informer's tip, etc.; and
- **followup,** to observe for correction of previously discovered deficiencies.

Inspections are conducted by investigators, who visit each facility and are given access to all parts of the premises where covered studies are performed and to all pertinent personnel and documentation. The Final Report and a more detailed Establishment Inspection Report are prepared after an audit is concluded; both can be obtained under FOIA. One (or more) of three sanctions can be imposed in cases of noncompliance: refusal to consider a study in support of an application; disqualification of the testing facility; or, in cases of alleged fraud, recommendation for criminal prosecution.

Provisions relating to care and housing of test animals are identical in both agencies' GLP rules. Both regulations provide that, where animals are housed, "facilities shall exist for the collection and disposal of all animal waste and refuse or for safe sanitary storage of waste before removal from the testing facility. Disposal facilities shall be so provided and operated as to minimize vermin infestation, odors, disease hazards, and environmental contamination." Finally, each GLP has a full section on animal care, specifying SOPs for housing, feeding, handling, and care, with additional standards on separation, disease control and treatment, identification, sanitation, feed and water inspection, bedding, and pest control (21 CFR 1984 ed. 58.43, 58.45, 58.49, 58.90; 40 CFR 1984 ed. 792.17, 792.43, 792.45, 792.90).

One chemical-industry representative summarized the benefits and problems of GLPs as follows:

- Benefits:
  1) promotion of good science through good documentation;
  2) credibility—"clean bill of health"; and
  3) self-assurance through knowledge—reducing chances of mistakes due to ignorance or use of shortcuts.
- Problems:
  1) duplication—possibility of six distinct audits in the animal care operation—FDA, EPA, USDA/APHIS, American Association for the Accreditation of Laboratory Animal Care (if accredited), State, and internal Quality Assurance Unit;
  2) adversarial climate—"guilty until proven innocent";
  3) confidentiality and accessibility—inadvertent disclosure of confidential business information or compromise of client confidentiality;
  4) time and cost—in larger facilities, single audits may occupy several hours per day for several weeks (7).

Noting that the GLP compliance record has been good, the commentator suggests that some duplication can be avoided by instituting a self-audit compliance program, using the *Guide for the Care and Use of Laboratory Animals* of the National Institutes of Health (47).

If consideration is given to broadening USDA's enforcement of the Animal Welfare Act to reach more testing facilities that may not now be covered—either by extending coverage to include rodents beyond only hamsters and guinea pigs or by increasing covered facilities' compliance duties—the problems of cost and duplication assume more significance. One indication of the cost of increasing an animal facility's compliance duties comes from a study commissioned by EPA to estimate the compliance costs for its new GLPs. That study concluded that additional costs to industrial laboratories would be $15 million ($80,000 per laboratory for 185 laboratories) (48 FR 53946).

Military Research and Training

In 1973, Congress prohibited the use of dogs for research and development of chemical or biological weapons (Public Law 93-365). At that time, Senate and House conferees stated that they did not support the use of dogs for research on chemical or biological agents whose only function was to destroy life. They believed it essential, however, that research to improve and save human and animal lives be continued, including establishing immunologic levels, occupational safety hazard levels, and other "vital medical research designed to improve and save lives."

Continued concern about this issue prompted a request for a GAO investigation of the U.S. Army's Edgewood Arsenal (Edgewood, NJ). The Comptroller General reported that the Army had complied with the restriction in fiscal year 1975 and, further, that compliance would continue. He responded to congressional concern about APHIS's lack of jurisdiction to inspect Federal facilities with the finding that, although dogs being used in toxic exposure research were treated well during experimental procedures, their housing facilities were deficient and needed physical improvements. He stated that legislation would be required to accomplish that purpose (33). Meanwhile, to implement the new restrictions, the Secretary of Defense issued three policy documents, in 1976 (44), 1982 (46), and 1984 (44), defining the types of investigations in which animals could be used.

In 1983, publicity about the use of dogs and pigs at the Uniformed Services University of Health Sciences (Bethesda, MD) to train military surgeons to treat wounds led to prohibitions on the expenditure of Department of Defense (DOD) funds in fiscal years 1984 and 1985 (Public Law 98-473) for the training of surgical personnel in treating weapon-produced wounds in dogs and cats (26). The Assistant Secretary of Defense for Health Affairs issued a memorandum in 1984 that explained the reach of the new limitation and superseded old policy directives (45):

> . . . effective October 1, 1983, dogs or cats will not be purchased or otherwise used for the purpose of training Department of Defense students or other personnel in surgical or other medical treatment of wounds produced by any type of weapon. In addition, the standards of such training with respect to the treatment of animals shall adhere to the Federal Animal Welfare Law and to those prevailing in the civilian medical community.

Current DOD policies and their effect on intramural and extramural defense research are examined in more detail in appendix B.

Animal welfare groups have expressed dissatisfaction about substitution of other animals for dogs and cats in ballistics training, and pressure on Congress to prohibit animals' use in this type of research is expected to continue (15).

Endangered Species, Public Health, and Import Legislation

Research facilities that plan to import, take, or otherwise use nonhuman primates or other animals protected by national or international laws and agreements must comply with provisions found in several laws. Besides prohibiting or controlling acquisition of some types of animals, these laws and agreements generally require, at a minimum, a permit or authorization from one or more Federal agencies. Relevant legislation includes:

- Section 7 of the Endangered Species Act of 1973, as amended (16 U.S.C. 1531 et seq.), and regulations administered by the Research Division of the Fish and Wildlife Service [50 CFR 10-24];
- Public Health Service Act regulations governing importation of nonhuman primates, both to control the spread of animal-borne disease (42 U.S.C. 264; 42 CFR 71) and for use in producing and testing viral vaccines (42 U.S.C. 262; 21 CFR 620 et seq.);
- the Airline Deregulation Act of 1978 and the Tariff Schedules of the Civil Aeronautics Board;
- Convention on International Trade in Endangered Species of Wild Fauna and Flora Treaty of 1973 (see app. E); and
- certificates of need for importing rhesus monkeys (a 1955 agreement between the United States and India, resulting in the Indian Rhesus Monkey Certification Program).

AGENCY GUIDELINES AND ACTIVITIES

Besides providing general assurances to USDA that intramural research activities involving warm-blooded animals meet the general requirements of the Animal Welfare Act, various Federal agencies have adopted general animal use guidelines or have taken steps to review relevant intramural and extramural policies. Most policies are confined to measures governing humane care and treatment of animals in testing and research—establishment of standards, review, and enforcement. Some policies mention the actual conduct of experimentation.

The Public Health Service Policy

Pursuant to a delegation of authority from the Secretary of the Department of Health and Human Services (DHHS), NIH is responsible for implementing the Public Health Service *Policy on Humane Care and Use of Laboratory Animals by Awardee Institutions* (PHS Manual, chs. 1 through 43). Each institution that receives Federal support from PHS for research involving live vertebrate animals is subject to the policy, including agencies of the PHS itself (NIH; FDA; the Alcohol, Drug Abuse, and Mental Health Administration; the Centers for Disease Control; and the Health Resources and Services Administration). Provisions of the PHS policy, revised in 1985, are discussed in detail in chapter 15 and the policy is reproduced in appendix C.

Interagency Activities

Governmentwide Standards

Representatives from 14 Federal entities[3] involved in animal use sit on the Interagency Research Animal Committee (IRAC) formed in recognition of the need for an interagency committee knowledgeable about the use, care, and welfare of research animals.

Staffed and sponsored by NIH, IRAC was established by the Assistant Secretary of Health in 1983 as an outgrowth of the Interagency Primate Steering Committee that had been established within NIH in 1974 to assure both short- and long-term supplies of primates critical to biomedical research, testing, and vaccine development programs (48).

Along with regular meetings to discuss current issues and needs, the Committee has undertaken two principal projects to date: serving in an advisory capacity to U.S. observers to the Council of Europe, which considered a draft convention on laboratory-animal use (see app. E), and writing the "Principles for the Utilization and Care of Vertebrate Animals Used in Testing, Research, and Training" (see box A). Developed and issued at the request of the Executive Office of Science and Technology Policy, the principles are intended to serve as a model for Federal agencies developing specific policies on the use of animals. The IRAC principles incorporate nine distinct injunctions on proper care and treatment of research animals, based primarily on similar principles promulgated by the Council for International Organizations of Medical Science (see app. E).

These statements on establishment, review, and enforcement of standards of humane care and treatment are part of the NIH *Guide for the Care and Use of Laboratory Animals* and are explicitly endorsed in the PHS *Policy on Humane Care and Use of Laboratory Animals by Awardee Institutions* (47).

Memorandum of Understanding

In 1983, APHIS, NIH, and FDA executed a Memorandum of Understanding and agreed to exchange information on animal welfare concerns and compliance with policies. Each has appointed liaison officers to serve on a standing committee to meet at least annually. Specifically, APHIS, NIH, and FDA have agreed to:

- share information contained in the registry/inventory/listing of establishments that fall under the purview of each;
- send to one another, each quarter, a listing of establishments that have been inspected

[3]USDA, Department of Defense, DHHS, Department of Energy, Department of State, Department of the Interior, EPA, the National Aeronautics and Space Administration, the National Science Foundation, and the Veterans' Administration. Components of the Public Health Service within DHHS that are represented on the committee include the Alcohol, Drug Abuse, and Mental Health Administration; the Centers for Disease Control; FDA; NIH; and the Office of International Health.

Box A.—U.S. Interagency Research Animal Committee "Principles for the Utilization and Care of Vertebrate Animals Used in Testing, Research, and Training"

The development of knowledge necessary for the improvement of the health and well-being of humans as well as other animals requires in vivo experimentation with a wide variety of animal species. When U.S. Government agencies develop requirements for testing, research, and training procedures involving the use of vertebrate animals, the following principles should be considered; and whenever these agencies actually perform or sponsor such procedures, the responsible institutional official shall ensure that these procedures are adhered to:

I. The transportation, care, and use of animals should be in accordance with the Animal Welfare Act and other applicable Federal laws, guidelines, and policies.

II. Procedures involving animals should be designed and performed with due consideration of their relevance to human or animal health, the advancement of knowledge, or the good of society.

III. The animals selected for a procedure should be of an appropriate species and quality and the minimum number required to obtain valid results. Methods such as mathematical model, computer simulation, and in vitro biological systems should be considered.

IV. Proper use of animals, including the avoidance or minimization of discomfort, distress, and pain when consistent with sound scientific practices is imperative. Unless the contrary is established, investigators should consider that procedures that cause pain or distress in human beings may cause pain and distress in other animals.

V. Procedures with animals that may cause more than momentary or slight pain or distress should be performed with appropriate sedation, analgesia, or anesthesia. Surgical or other painful procedures should not be performed on unanesthetized animals paralyzed by chemical agents.

VI. Animals that would otherwise suffer severe or chronic pain or distress that cannot be relieved should be painlessly killed at the end of the procedure or, if appropriate, during the procedure.

VII. The living conditions of animals should be appropriate for their species and contribute to their health and comfort. Normally the housing, feeding, and care of all animals used for biomedical purposes must be directed by a veterinarian or other scientist trained and experienced in the proper care, handling, and use of the species being maintained or studied. In any case, veterinary care shall be provided as indicated.

VIII. Investigators and other personnel shall be appropriately qualified and experienced for conducting procedures on living animals. Adequate arrangements shall be made for their in-service training, including the proper and humane care and use of laboratory animals.

IX. Where exceptions are required in relation to the provisions of these Principles, the decisions should not rest with the investigators directly concerned but should be made, with due regard to Principle II, by an appropriate review group such as an institutional animal research committee. Such exception should not be made solely for the purpose of teaching or demonstration.

SOURCE: 50 FR 20864.

or site-visited, to be used to avoid redundant evaluations;

- share information on significant adverse findings concerning animal care and welfare revealed by inspections or site visits and on followup actions taken;
- inform each other of evidence of serious noncompliance with required standards or policies for care and use of laboratory animals (including defective assurances of compliance with PHS policies) in establishments that fall under the authority of each agency;
- request from each other comments and advice on regulatory or policy proposals involving animal care and welfare under consideration; and
- provide to each other resource persons for scientific seminars, speeches, and workshops.

The agreement remains in effect indefinitely, may be modified by mutual consent, and may be terminated by any agency on 90-day advance written notice to the other two agencies (37).

Specific Agency Activities

Six departments and four agencies within the Federal Government do intramural research involving animals. At least 1.6 million animals were used by these branches for such research during fiscal year 1983 (see ch. 3). In addition, extramural research is conducted by many of these departments. Two departments, Commerce and Transportation, conduct almost all research extramurally and so have no specific policy regulating animal use other than the PHS policy (17,23). For a detailed discussion of the regulation of animal use within Federal departments and agencies, see appendix B.

CRITICISMS OF THE PRESENT SYSTEM OF FEDERAL REGULATION

The operation of the Animal Welfare Act, as applied to research, has been criticized since its passage. In addition to obvious shortcomings—lack of coverage for actual research practices and inadequate resources for enforcement—critics have questioned the presumption that researchers know best how to care for experimental animals (20,49) and the choice of APHIS as the primary enforcement agency (16,24). Complex recordkeeping requirements imposed on APHIS inspectors and other field enforcement staff have been decried; the process of noting, investigating, and evaluating violations for prosecution, and the attendant rights of suspected violators that can result in delay in disposition of cases, are viewed by some as too cumbersome and bureaucratic (20). Some question the expertise and the will of APHIS, pointing out its traditional reluctance to accept broader responsibilities under the act. Indeed, USDA remains opposed to its further extension (34,37). A 1982 review of the APHIS reporting system by the Humane Society of the United States concluded that the present system, as it is administered (24):

> . . . fails to achieve its primary statutory objective: it does not provide APHIS with information sufficient to demonstrate that researchers have used pain-relieving drugs "appropriately" and in accordance with "professionally acceptable standards." The chief reasons for this failing are: 1) regulations and guidelines do not define "pain" or "distress," 2) regulations and guidelines do not adequately define "routine procedures," and 3) regulations and guidelines do not require meaningful explanations for the withholding of pain-relieving drugs in procedures acknowledged to cause pain.
>
> The Reporting System, as presently administered, for the same reasons also fails to achieve a secondary—but nonetheless important—objective: it does not generate reliable and meaningful information to the public about the use of animals in research.

Humane groups have used the Freedom of Information Act with increasing frequency to obtain copies of inspection and annual reports in attempts to demonstrate their claims that the system does not work. Members of the research community opposed to the act's extension defend existing practices as adequate (16,34,37).

Could the Secretary of Agriculture require greater proof that "professionally acceptable" standards of care are being followed, require more detailed explanations of the use and withholding of anesthetics and pain relievers, and more effectively audit annual reports? The law permits such greater discretion. Several competing factors, however, are worth noting. First, consistent with Congress' enumerated powers to spend and to regulate interstate commerce, the objectives for the regulation of research are more limited than is often admitted by the critics. The remarks of congressional sponsors of the first bills, in the record of debates on the 1966 conference report, recognize that only a fraction of research animals would be covered (30) and that the new act was "nothing more than a very small first step toward the elimination of cruelty, mistreatment, and abuse of laboratory animals." The absolute power that remained with the experimenter to determine the nature of experimentation prompted the remark that "animals that are under research or experimentation for several years will have absolutely no protection under this law" (31). Subsequent amendments added more specific requirements but left the intra-research exemption undisturbed, retaining a post-hoc, audit-style enforcement system.

Second, creating an agency whose sole purpose is to regulate experimentation, or infusing more authority and funds into APHIS, are options that Congress has not chosen to exercise, even in the face of a lukewarm commitment to enforcement by existing executive agencies. Third, these choices have not been made because a consensus on the preferable mode and extent of control has never been apparent. Some regulation advocates, it appears, will settle for some degree of tinkering with the act; others will not rest until research on animals is done away with (27). Those differences have strong roots and are likely to persist.

There are important statutory and regulatory considerations regarding any attempt to modify existing law in order to effect replacements, reductions, or refinements of animal use. Statutory changes would reflect judgments on:

- whether the jurisdiction of enforcing agencies should be expanded to enforcement of adequate care, treatment, and use standards during actual conduct of experimentation;
- whether the scheme of regulation of experimentation should be scaled to a higher level of compliance responsibility, as is now the case for dealers and exhibitors;
- whether penalties for violations of research standards should be enacted that are commensurate with those assessed against other regulated parties;
- whether voluntary assurances or simple certifications of compliance are adequate;
- whether coverage of existing classes of animals is statutorily adequate to achieve even existing policy objectives; and
- whether proposed changes take into account the operation of other, overlapping laws that have different policy objectives.

Regulatory changes would involve judgments of:

- whether existing enforcement agencies are appropriate (and willing) to continue to fulfill current responsibilities and assume others;
- whether enforcement agencies should be given increased discretion in formulating and enforcing professionally acceptable standards of care, handling, treatment, and use of research animals;
- whether additional requirements for research regulation will be susceptible to consistent interpretation by inspection and enforcement agents in the field, in light of existing availability of training resources and aids for field inspectors; and
- whether efficient assignment of funds and enforcement resources on a state-to-state basis is likely to occur.

In addition, statutory or regulatory change would reflect a judgment of:

- whether funds authorized and appropriated will be adequate in relation to contemplated enforcement duties;
- whether regulated research institutions have sufficient financial resources and institutional and independent veterinary resources to effect meaningful compliance with a strengthened law, while avoiding any compromise of research or testing objectives; and
- whether strengthening existing laws will promote resolution of or enhance differences between the research and animal welfare communities.

Finally, the Animal Welfare Act is often criticized—inappropriately—for excluding mice and rats from its coverage. In fact, the act, as amended in 1970, covers all warm-blooded animals that the Secretary of Agriculture determines are being used or intended for use in research or for another named purpose. The Secretary does not appear to have the discretion to determine whether or not mice and rats are warm-blooded animals, only whether or not they are used in research. No amendment to the act is therefore necessary to bring mice and rats under its scope. The exclusion of mice and rats (and birds) from the definition of "animal" by USDA regulation in 1977 (9 CFR 1.1 (n),(o)) appears to frustrate the intent of Congress and to be beyond the Secretary of Agriculture's statutory authority (6).

SUMMARY AND CONCLUSIONS

The Animal Welfare Act and its amendments represent a cautious and deliberate attempt by Congress to improve care and treatment of research animals. Initially, the act was designed to regulate interstate traffic in dogs and cats used for research, with the goal of halting the use of stolen pets. This was accomplished by requiring Federal licenses for dealers, requiring research facilities to register, and instituting inspection and recordkeeping requirements for both. Enforcement responsibility was vested in the Animal and Plant Health Inspection Service of the U.S. Department of Agriculture, an agency not aligned with traditional, nonagricultural research interests. Three times the act was amended; twice the amendments extended interstate regulation to exhibition, transportation, and auction sales of covered animals (which, as enforced, now includes dogs, cats, rabbits, hamsters, guinea pigs, and nonhuman primates). The oversight of animal use by committees at every research facility was mandated in the most recent amendments.

A legislative reluctance to invade the actual conduct of research is clear. The Secretary of Agriculture is forbidden to enact any regulation that could be so construed. The closest the law comes is to require the Secretary to establish and enforce standards for care and treatment of experimental animals outside the laboratory door, and to require covered research facilities to certify that professionally acceptable standards of care, treatment, and use are being followed in the laboratory, including "appropriate" use of anesthetics and pain relievers, except when their use would interfere with experimental objectives. In addition, large classes of experimental animals—principally mice and rats—are not covered by the act as it is currently enforced by the Department of Agriculture, and the law's provisions remain weighted toward traffic in pet species. Since interstate regulation constitutionally requires some connection to interstate commerce, research institutions that use animals protected by the act but that receive no Federal funds and that maintain their own breeding colonies cannot be regulated. To date, there has been no significant judicial test of the provisions regulating research.

The Health Research Extension Act of 1985 amended the Public Health Service Act with provisions for the care and treatment of animals in PHS-funded research. The 1985 act also contained provisions for the development of alternatives to research methods using animals.

In addition to the Animal Welfare Act and the Health Research Extension Act of 1985, there is regulation of the use of laboratory animals at the Federal agency level. The Interagency Research Animal Committee was formed to provide a knowledgeable source about all vertebrate animal use in testing, research, and training within the Federal Government. It has developed the U.S. Government's "Principles for the Utilization and Care of Vertebrate Animals Used in Testing, Research, and Training" at the request of the Executive Office of Science and Technology Policy. The IRAC principles are endorsed by the Public Health Service, are part of the widely used NIH *Guide for the Care and Use of Laboratory Animals,* and are used by some Federal agencies in their own policies on animal use.

Six Federal departments and four Federal agencies conduct animal experimentation within Federal facilities (see app. B). Only the Departments of Commerce and Transportation, which use few animals, have no specific guidelines. The other entities all have some type of policy for such intramural research. In general, the more research conducted by an agency, the more extensive are its animal care guidelines. In addition, departments in which animal treatment has been targeted by animal welfare groups or spotlighted by the media tend to have more substantive guidelines.

CHAPTER 13 REFERENCES

1. *American Horse Protection Association* v. *U.S. Department of the Interior*, 551 F.2d 432, 434, n.17 (D.C. Cir. 1978).
2. *Animal Welfare Institute* v. *Kreps*, 561 F.2d 1002, 1007 (D.C. Cir. 1977).
3. Barnes, P., "Animal Advocates Are No Friends to Lawyer," *New Haven (CT) Register*, p. 17 (cols. 1-6), Aug. 17, 1984.
4. Becker, G., "The U.S. Department of Agriculture's FY 85 Budget," Issue Brief No. IB84043, Congressional Research Service, U.S. Congress, Washington, DC, Mar. 9, 1984.
5. *Californians for Responsible Research, Inc.* v. *Block, et al.*, (N.D.Calif., 1983).
6. Cohen, H., "Two Questions Concerning the Animal Welfare Act," Publication No. 85-927A, Congressional Research Service, U.S. Congress, Washington, DC, Aug. 7, 1985.
7. Conine, D., "Laboratory Audits: An Industry View," *Chem. Times Trends* 7(3):13-16, 1984.
8. Ford, D., and Mackler, B., "Good Laboratory Practices: A Perspective for Research Scientists," *BioTechniques* Jan./Feb. 1984:48-49.
9. *Friends of Animals, Inc.* v. *U.S. Surgical Corporation*, Civ. No. B81-643 (D.Conn., Feb. 17, 1982).
10. *Friends of Animals, Inc.* v. *U.S. Surgical Corporation*, Civ. No. B82-744, Plaintiff's Motion to Dismiss With Prejudice (D.Conn., Aug. 23, 1984).
11. *Haviland* v. *Butz*, 543 F.2d 169, 177 (D.C. Cir. 1976), cert. denied, 97 S.Ct. 95, 429 U.S. 832 (1976).
12. Holzer, H. (ed.), "Animal Welfare Act: Rulemaking Petition," *Anim. Rights Law Rep.* (Int. Soc. for Anim. Rights, Clarks Summit, PA) July 1982:14.
13. Leavitt, E., and Halverson, D., "The Evolution of Anti-Cruelty Laws in the United States," *Animals and Their Legal Rights*, E. Leavitt (ed.) (Washington, DC: Animal Welfare Institute, Third Ed., 1978).
14. *Marshall* v. *Barlow's, Inc.*, 436 U.S. 307, 98 S.Ct. 1816 (1978).
15. McArdle, J., Assistant Director, Institute for The Study of Animal Problems, Humane Society of the United States, Washington, DC, personal communication, Dec. 13, 1984.
16. Morrison, L., and Levey, G., "Animals and Research: Labs Already Take Steps to Protect the Animals' Health and Welfare," *L.A. Daily J.*, p. 4, June 29, 1983.
17. Mosed, R., Executive Director for Oceanic and Atmospheric Administration, National Oceanic and Atmospheric Administration, U.S. Department of Commerce, Rockville, MD, personal communication, September 1984.
18. Murray, C., "FDA-Proposed Lab Practice Regulations Scored," *Chem. Eng. News* 55(9):18, 1977.
19. Poore, S., Freedom of Information Act Coordinator, Veterinary Services Branch, Animal and Plant Health Inspection Service, U.S. Department of Agriculture, Washington, DC, personal communications, Jan. 11 and 18, 1985.
20. Rikleen, P., "The Animal Welfare Act: Still a Cruelty to Animals," *Boston Coll. Environ. Aff. Law Rev.* 7:129-142, 1978.
21. *Robinson* v. *United States*, 718 F.2d 336 (10th Cir. 1983).
22. Schneider, K., "Faking It: The Case Against Industrial Bio-Test Laboratories," *Amicus J.* 4(Spring):14-26, 1983.
23. Schultz, C., Chief, Sciences Branch, Technology Division, Office of Hazardous Materials Regulation, Materials Transportation Bureau, Research and Special Programs Administration, U.S. Department of Transportation, Washington, DC, personal communication, September 1984.
24. Solomon, M., and Lovenheim, P., "Reporting Requirements Under the Animal Welfare Act: Their Inadequacies and the Public's Right to Know," *J. Stud. Anim. Problems* 3:210-218, 1982.
25. Stewart, W., "Legal Standards for Humane Care: The Animal Welfare Act," *Lab Anim.* 13(6):33-41, 1984.
26. *Time*, "In the Doghouse: Protest Halts Animal Killings," 122:38, Aug. 8, 1983.
27. *Union County Jail Inmates* v. *DiBuono*, 718 F.2d 1247 (3rd. Cir. 1983).
28. *United States* v. *Fraley*, 538 F.2d 626 (D.C. Cir. 1974).
29. *United States* v. *Hill*, 694 F.2d 258, 264, n.19 (D.C.Cir. 1982).
30. U.S., *Congressional Record*, 112:19559, 19608, Statements of Reps. Rogers and Pepper (1966).
31. U.S., *Congressional Record*, 112:19785, Remarks of Sen. McIntyre (1966).
32. U.S. Congress, General Accounting Office, *Report to the Chairman, Subcommittee on Agriculture, Rural Development and Related Agencies, Committee on Appropriations, United States Senate: The Department of Agriculture's Animal Welfare Program*, GAO/RCED-85-8 (Gaithersburg, MD: May 16, 1985).
33. U.S. Congress, General Accounting Office, *Use of Dogs in Experiments at Edgewood Arsenal, Maryland: Department of the Army*, GAO Rep. No. PSAD-76-80 (Washington, DC: Mar.12, 1976).
34. U.S. Congress, House of Representatives, Committee on Agriculture, Subcommittee on Department Operations, Research, and Foreign Agriculture, *Im-*

proved Standards for Laboratory Animals, Hearing on H.R. 5725, hearings Sept. 19, 1984, Serial No. 98-086 (Washington, DC: U.S. Government Printing Office, 1984).

35. U.S. Congress, House of Representatives, Committee on Agriculture, *Report to Accompany H.R. 19846*, H. Rpt. 91-1651 (Dec. 2, 1970), reprinted in *U.S. Code Congressional and Administrative News*, 1970:5103-5113.
36. U.S. Congress, House of Representatives, Committee on Agriculture, *Report to Accompany H.R. 5808*, H. Rpt. 94-801 (Jan. 29, 1976), and Conference Committee, *Report to Accompany S. 1941*, Conf. Rpt. 94-976 (Mar. 29, 1976), reprinted in *U.S. Code Congressional and Administrative News*, 1976:758-797.
37. U.S. Congress, Senate, Committee on Agriculture, Nutrition, and Forestry, *Improved Standards for Laboratory Animals*, Hearing on S. 657, hearings July 20, 1983, Serial No. 98-470 (Washington, DC: U.S. Government Printing Office, 1983).
38. U.S. Congress, Senate, Committee on Commerce, *Report to Accompany H.R. 13881*, S. Rpt. 1281 (June 15, 1966) and Conference Committee, *Reports to Accompany H.R. 13881*, Conf. Rpt. 1848 (Aug. 11, 1966), reprinted in *U.S. Code Congressional and Administrative News*, 1966:2635-2658.
39. U.S. Department of Agriculture, Animal and Plant Health Inspection Service, "First Federal Law to Prevent Cruelty to Animals," *Animals and Their Legal Rights*, E. Leavitt (ed.) (Washington, DC: Animal Welfare Institute, Third Ed., 1978).
40. U.S. Department of Agriculture, Animal and Plant Health Inspection Service, *Animal Welfare Enforcement, FY 1978: Report of the Secretary of Agriculture to the President of the Senate and the Speaker of the House of Representatives* (Washington, DC: March 1979).
41. U.S. Department of Agriculture, Animal and Plant Health Inspection Service, *Animal Welfare Enforcement, FY 1981: Report of the Secretary of Agriculture to the President of the Senate and the Speaker of the House of Representatives* (Washington, DC: March 1982).
42. U.S. Department of Agriculture, Animal and Plant Health Inspection Service, *Animal Welfare Enforcement, FY 1982: Report of the Secretary of Agriculture to the President of the Senate and the Speaker of the House of Representatives* (Washington, DC: March 1983).
43. U.S. Department of Agriculture, Animal and Plant Health Inspection Service, *Animal Welfare Enforcement, FY 1983: Report of the Secretary of Agriculture to the President of the Senate and the Speaker of the House of Representatives* (Washington, DC: March 1984).
44. U.S. Department of Defense, "Clinical Investigation Program," DOD Directive 6000.4, Washington, DC, Apr. 16, 1976.
45. U.S. Department of Defense, Assistant Secretary of Defense for Health Affairs, "Memorandum to the Secretaries of the Uniformed Services, President of the Uniformed Services University of the Health Sciences, and Directors of Defense Agencies," Washington, DC, Jan. 4, 1984.
46. U.S. Department of Defense, "The Use of Animals in DoD Programs," DoD Instruction 3216.1, Washington, DC, Feb. 1, 1982.
47. U.S. Department of Health and Human Services, Public Health Service, National Institutes of Health, *Guide for the Care and Use of Laboratory Animals*, NIH Pub. No. 85-23 (Bethesda, MD: National Institutes of Health, 1985).
48. Wolfle, T., "The Interagency Research Committee [IRAC]," mimeo, National Institutes of Health, Bethesda, MD, 1984.
49. Zurvalec, L., "Use of Animals in Medical Research: The Need for Governmental Regulation," *Wayne Law Rev.* 24(5):1733-1774, 1978.

Chapter 14

State Regulation of Animal Use

It is time for states to stop having two sets of cruelty laws, one for the general public and a weaker one for the research community. Cruelty does not cease to exist by simply moving the activity within the four walls of a laboratory.

John E. McArdle
Humane Society of the United States
Physiologist 28(2):71, 1985

CONTENTS

List of Tables

Chapter 14
State Regulation of Animal Use

States have enacted a bewildering array of laws governing animals—their control, their ownership and disposition as human property, the responsibilities and liabilities of their owners, and the duty of care that is owed animals, including freedom from unnecessary and unjustified suffering. State laws in the last category are the most venerable; many predate any congressional action on the subject. These laws take several general forms, including the regulation of animal use in experimentation and the delegation of authority to local governments to regulate animal use and treatment (33). With Federal entry into the field, the potential for conflict and duplication arises.

This chapter summarizes State laws affecting the use of research animals and examines the potential for conflict or duplication with current Federal law. The analysis is restricted to laws with some bearing on the conduct of research and where some potential for conflict or duplication may exist. Examples of types of local laws or ordinances are cited to illustrate the contexts in which local law has affected research, but no attempt is made to describe such legislation independent of the operation of State law.

ANTICRUELTY LAWS

At common law, animals were entitled to no intrinsic right of protection, reflecting the prevailing belief that they were mere human instrumentalities. Two classes of animals existed, domestic and wild, with domestic animals considered the property of their owners and legally protected only as possessions. An owner could treat an animal in any manner, as long as no public nuisance was created. Abuse of an animal owned by another created liability in the abuser only for resulting damage to the economic value of the animal (2,4).

This means that any legal right or duty owed to animals by humans must have a statutory basis (33). Every U.S. jurisdiction has in place a statute prohibiting cruel treatment of some types of animals. These statutes generally apply criminal penalties (usually lower class misdemeanors) and civil sanctions for specified violations (74). Most of the original State anticruelty statutes were enacted prior to the turn of the century and have common, continental roots as offshoots of general societal concern for humane treatment. The first such statute, known as an "override, overdrive" law because it outlawed riding or driving farm animals beyond reasonable limits, was passed in the Massachusetts Bay Colony in 1641. It provided that "No man shall exercise any Tyranny or Cruelty towards any Brut Creatures which are usually kept for the use of man" (19).

The principal social goals promoted by the imposition of criminal or economic penalties for cruel or inhumane treatment of animals are threefold (3,33):

- protecting the *interests of society* and promoting morality by deterring conduct considered wanton or offensive, such as willful mistreatment of animals;
- protecting the *interests of animals* and preventing neglect by establishing enforceable minimum standards of care for animals; and
- protecting the *economic interests of animal owners* by shielding animals against treatment that invades or damages the owner's economic interest (including companionship and enjoyment).

Most anticruelty statutes serve the first two goals by prohibiting and punishing active cruelty to animals (beating, burning, castrating, shooting, pouring acid on hooves, or overworking) and, in some cases, passive cruelty occasioned by neglect, such as failure to provide basic necessities (food, water, shelter, or appropriate care) (36). Since most State anticruelty statutes combine elements of both active and passive cruelty, these concepts are discussed under this single rubric. Special duties of care, such as those imposed in some States on animal carriers, pet stores, and others, generally do not affect research facilities (39).

General Provisions

State anticruelty statutes often incorporate prohibitions on both active cruelty and failure to meet a generally described duty of care. Under these laws, several elements must be proved to sustain a conviction and penalty:

- The mistreated animal must come under the statute's coverage.
- The person charged with infliction or neglect must similarly be subject to the reach of the law, as must the conduct complained of.
- The act complained of must not be the subject of any exceptions to the statute.
- There must be no statutory defenses that can be sustained against the act complained of.
- The prescribed level of human knowledge or intent must be present if required by statute. Most States, however, do not require culpability to be proven (33).

Culpability depends on the presence of a specified state of mind at the time of the commission of the act. Except for statutes that create liability without culpability, conduct must generally fall into one of the following categories to result in the commission of an offense:

- **Intentional, Knowing, or Willful:** The individual must be conscious of his or her conduct, intend his or her voluntary actions or failure to act, and know or should know the actual consequences.
- **Recklessly Negligent:** This lesser level applies to an individual who is aware of and consciously disregards a substantial and unjustified risk to another interest (the animal's interest in avoiding cruel treatment).
- **Negligent:** This lowest level of culpability, also known as criminal negligence, applies to an individual who fails to perceive a substantial and unjustified risk incurred by his or her action or inaction. The standard applied in cases of criminal negligence is proof of a gross deviation from the standard of care observed by a reasonable person in similar circumstances.

Many statutes incorporate more than one level of culpability (33,36).

The other type of criminal statute, often combined with those that prohibit specified acts of cruelty, deals with nonfeasance or omissions. These laws establish a minimum duty of care toward an animal by making it a crime to fail to meet that duty in some specified way. Their objective is general care of covered animals, rather than protection from immediate harm. If no degree of culpability is required, defenses applicable under active statutes are not available. Nonetheless, if words like "willfully," "intentionally," or "knowingly" are used, then the appropriate degree of culpability must be proved. The most comprehensive "duty-of-care" statute is Virginia's Animal Welfare Act, which requires all companion-animal owners to provide adequate food, water, shelter, and space, as well as humane care and treatment and veterinary care necessary to prevent suffering. The maximum penalty upon conviction is a fine of $100 (117).

The variability of the basic elements of anticruelty statutes is demonstrated by a recent review by the Animal Welfare Institute of laws in the 50 States, the District of Columbia, Puerto Rico, Guam, the Virgin Islands, and the Canal Zone. The Institute found the following:

- **Definition of "Animal":** Twenty-nine anticruelty laws protect "any animal," including all living creatures except humans. Nineteen others provide no definition at all, and others apply the word to domestic animals, captive animals, or warm-blooded creatures.
- **Culpability:** Thirty-two jurisdictions have prohibitions on specified types of cruelty with no qualifying phrases—i.e., no requirement for proof of a particular state of mind on the part of the person charged. The other 23 have one or more of the qualifying phrases described above.
- **Food, Water, and Shelter:** Statutory prohibitions against failure to provide for basic animal survival vary in both definition and interpretation. Thirty-two jurisdictions have laws

requiring food and water, with no qualifying phrases. Twenty-three others qualify the duty of care to provide food and water with some requirement to prove at least a high degree of neglect; the word used most often as a qualifier here is "unnecessarily."

- **Other Living Conditions:** Requirements for adequate exercise or space, light, ventilation, and clean living conditions are found in some statutes. Eight jurisdictions require fresh air. Exercise or adequate space is required by 11. One requires sufficient light, and two laws mention clean living conditions.
- **Abandonment:** General anticruelty statutes in 42 jurisdictions prohibit the abandonment of animals. In several cases, abandonment is restricted to willful, cruel, or intentional abandonment, to abandoning animals to die, to abandoning disabled animals, or to abandoning domestic animals.
- **Humane Transport:** Thirty-eight jurisdictions incorporate provisions prohibiting cruel or inhumane transport of various classes of animals. Minnesota's statute is most specific, applying to "any live animal" and defining in detail requirements for humane transport. In most jurisdictions, however, laws governing humane transportation are much more general, often consisting of no more than a single section incorporating undefined or vaguely defined terms.
- **Poisoning:** Twenty-four jurisdictions prohibit or restrict the use of poison to inflict injury or death on an animal. Some statutes are modified with terms such as "needlessly," and others are found outside general anticruelty law, intended to apply primarily to livestock or other animals held and kept for specific purposes, usually related to their economic value in a given activity, such as racing or hunting (74).

Some statutes acknowledge the potential application of general anticruelty statutes to research facilities. Twenty-three jurisdictions specifically exclude experimental animals from the reach of criminal anticruelty statutes; 25 others make no mention of any possible relation (89) (see table 14-1). Interpretation of these statutes is discussed later in this chapter.

Table 14-1.—Laws on Research and Animal Cruelty, by Jurisdiction

State/jurisdiction	Research exemption	No mention in law	Other
Alabama		X	
Alaska	X		
Arizona		X	
Arkansas		X	
California	X		
Colorado		X	
Connecticut		X	
Delaware	X		
District of Columbia	X		
Florida	X		
Georgia	X		
Hawaii	X		
Idaho	X		
Illinois		X	
Indiana			([a])
Iowa		X	
Kansas	X		
Kentucky		X	
Louisiana	X		
Maine	X		
Maryland			([b])
Massachusetts		X	
Michigan		X	
Minnesota		X	
Mississippi		X	
Missouri	X		
Montana		X	
Nebraska		X	
Nevada	X		
New Hampshire		X	
New Jersey	X		
New Mexico		X	
New York	X		
North Carolina	X		
North Dakota		X	
Ohio		X	
Oklahoma		X	
Oregon		X	
Pennsylvania			([c])
Rhode Island		X	
South Carolina		X	
South Dakota	X		
Tennessee		X	
Texas	X		
Utah	X		
Vermont	X		
Virginia	X		
Washington	X		
West Virginia		X	
Wisconsin	X		
Wyoming		X	

[a]Exempts "veterinary practices."
[b]Expressly intends for animals used for "scientific or medical activity" to be protected from "intentional cruelty" but exempts "normal human activities to which the infliction of pain to an animal is purely incidental and unavoidable."
[c]Prohibits entry or search to enforce the law "where scientific research is being conducted by or under the supervision of graduates of reputable scientific schools or where biological products are being produced for the care or prevention of disease."

SOURCE: National Association for Biomedical Research, *State Laws Concerning the Use of Animals in Research* (Washington, DC: Foundation for Biomedical Research, 1985).

Most of the laws that do address the issue exempt "scientific experiments" or "investigations" entirely. In Alaska, one defense to prosecution is that the defendant's conduct "conformed to accepted veterinary practice [or] was part of scientific research governed by accepted standards" (1). Maine allows proof of "accepted veterinary practice or bona fide experimentation for scientific research" as an affirmative defense to a charge of cruelty as well, so long as the animal's destruction, if required, is not "unnecessarily cruel unless directly necessary to the veterinary purpose" (89). Florida's 59-year-old law states that cruelty "shall be held to include every act, omission, or neglect whereby unnecessary or unjustifiable pain or suffering is caused, except when done in the interest of medical science" (34). Georgia is more direct in establishing a connection between the exemption and the interest protected by it: "The killing or injuring of an animal for humane purposes or in the furtherance of medical or scientific research is justifiable" (53). Others contain specific provisos that the statutes not be construed to prohibit or interfere with scientific research, if done by qualified persons in a humane manner (18,30). The majority simply exempt "acceptable veterinary practices" and "bona fide experiments" or research "governed by accepted standards" (89).

Three other anticruelty statutes, all amended within the last 3 years, are equivocal. The Indiana Code was amended in 1983 to exempt "veterinary practices" from the general anticruelty statute (63). In Pennsylvania, neither an exemption nor a provision interpreting the statute as excluding scientific use is included in the law. The general grant of authority to police or humane society agents to enter premises for the purpose of seizing and destroying exploited animals prohibits entry or search "where scientific research work is being conducted by or under the supervision of graduates of reputable scientific schools or where biological products are being produced for the care or prevention of disease" (97).

The Maryland General Assembly, in a 1984 amendment, expressed its intention that "all animals . . . under private, local, state, or federally funded scientific or medical activity . . . be protected from intentional cruelty" but provided that no person is to be held liable for criminal prosecution due to "normal human activities to which the infliction of pain to an animal is purely incidental and unavoidable." Authorized enforcement officers otherwise permitted to take possession of animals to protect them from neglect or cruelty cannot do so without prior review and recommendation from the Division of Veterinary Medicine in the Department of Health and Mental Hygiene. Reports to the State's attorney for the county in which the facility is located must be made by the Division within 48 hours of receipt of a complaint (75).

Of greatest concern to those engaged in testing and research are older, general anticruelty statutes that prohibit cruelty to all animals without requiring proof of a culpable state of mind. Many of these statutes do not generally exempt scientific inquiry from the prohibitions, and those statutes that attempt to do so often fail to define "animal" or "science" or contain vague definitions of the terms. Virtually none of the statutes surveyed attempts to define what activities constitute scientific research, nor do they establish separate classifications for experimental animals.

Enforcement

Like Congress, State legislatures delegate enforcement to the executive branch of government, which is authorized to promulgate regulations and enforce them under authority of an enactment. The exercise of the police power to control and protect animals has been sustained in a variety of areas, including controlling migration of animals into a State, requiring registration and licensing of animals, controlling contagious and infectious diseases borne by animals, and compensating private parties for the destruction of animals in furtherance of anticruelty laws (33).

Because criminal penalties are imposed for violations of anticruelty statutes, primary enforcement responsibility generally rests with "duly constituted" law enforcement authorities—police and sheriff's departments. Most State legislatures, however, recognize the difficulty of ensuring enforcement of anticruelty statutes on the local level and have also delegated limited police powers to private, not-for-profit organizations, principally humane societies or societies for the prevention of cruelty to animals (74). These limited grants of authority are most frequently extended to seizure of animals found to be cruelly treated, neglected, or abandoned, in violation of an applicable State law. In some States, officers or agents of these groups possess specific powers for intervention, inspection, or the procurement of warrants or summonses or the ability to be deputized by local law enforcement officials for such purposes. In New York, for example, lawfully appointed agents of the American Society for the Prevention of Cruelty to Animals (ASPCA) have been judicially recognized as "peace officers" and are therefore authorized to issue summonses for violations of anticruelty laws. Another New York State case allowed the ASPCA to seize without a warrant and impound animals held in violation of cruelty statutes.

In States where no powers are specified or implied, societies formed for this purpose have developed investigative programs on which State or local law enforcement officers rely for preliminary investigative activities. There appears to be some movement away from statutory grants of authority to nongovernmental agencies for this purpose. Several States have repealed prior grants and others have left undisturbed laws with no mention of them. Beyond enforcement through specific grants of police power, many anticruelty groups initiate criminal investigations by filing complaints or resorting to civil actions against agencies or facilities to enjoin alleged cruelty to animals (33,36).

Constitutionality

Several State anticruelty statutes have been attacked on grounds that they are unconstitutionally vague, either because the statute allegedly fails to give a person of ordinary intelligence fair notice that a contemplated act is forbidden or because the statute as drafted encourages arbitrary arrests and convictions. In almost all instances, both active cruelty and duty-of-care provisions have survived constitutional challenges based on vagueness, even though their breadth and lack of definition and specificity makes them susceptible to such attacks (9,62).

Cruel Acts

An Arizona statute outlawing cockfighting was found to be unconstitutionally vague in its use of the terms "animal" and "needless suffering," and two convictions were overturned (104). Disparate results were reached in cases brought for convictions for the same activity in Kansas and Hawaii (86,105); the court was able to sustain the statute in the latter case because statutory definitions of "animals" and "cruelty" helped overcome problems of vagueness. These cases are instructive for another reason. When convictions have been thrown out, it is because courts have been unwilling to interpret general statutes to forbid cockfights in the absence of legislative action making these previously acceptable acts illegal.

Duty of Care

Courts have applied the same general principles of construction used in constitutional challenges to anticruelty statutes in upholding their components governing minimum husbandry or humane treatment standards. High courts in at least two States have sustained legislative establishment of broad standards of care, but judicial interpretations of the application of those standards varies. For example, a Texas court found, without explanation, that the duty-of-care statute "sufficiently informs an accused of the nature and cause of the accusation against him and that it is not unconstitutionally indefinite." Idaho's Supreme Court upheld the legislature's intent to establish broad standards of care, suggesting that "proper care" is that degree of care that a prudent person would use under similar circumstances. Virginia's statute attempts to define the terms "adequate feed" and "adequate water," but ultimately the standard adopted is a "reasonable level of nutrition," though it adds nothing to the law's specificity. Thus, the duty charged to anyone responsible for animal care is speculative, though the duty implicitly requires knowledge of the animal's requirements (33).

Review of the available case law indicates that courts are reluctant to accept constitutional attacks even against vague and undefined anticruelty statutes, preferring to limit themselves to measuring defendants' conduct against general statutory provisions on a case-by-case basis.

Judicial Interpretation of Applicability of Anticruelty Statutes to Research

Historically, those interested in protecting laboratory animals from cruelty have used general anticruelty statutes against research facilities or individual researchers, but (at least until 1981) to little effect. In 1914, for example, the Women's SPCA sued six faculty members at a Pennsylvania medical school for "wanton cruelty," but no conviction resulted (33).

Two recent cases give some indication how a modern State court might respond to a confrontation between anticruelty and research interests.

The *Taub* Decision

The most celebrated and controversial case in this area is *Maryland* v. *Taub*. Montgomery County police investigated conditions at a laboratory that was performing stroke research on nonhuman primates that was funded by the National Institutes of Health (NIH). The investigation resulted in seizure of the primate colony. In January 1982, the county's State's attorney filed 17 charges against the investigator, Edward Taub, charging him with violation of Maryland Code, Article 27, Section 59 (1957, 1976 Repl. Vol.), with respect to each of 17 primates. Following a trial in district court, the defendant was found guilty of failing to provide necessary veterinary care for 6 animals and acquitted of all other charges. On appeal to the circuit court, a jury hearing the case de novo found Taub guilty of one charge of failing to provide necessary veterinary care for 1 monkey, known as "Nero" (76).

Taub appealed to the Maryland Court of Appeals, asserting that the law was unconstitutional because the Federal Animal Welfare Act preempted State jurisdiction in the area of federally funded research, and attacking several of the trial court's evidentiary rulings. The Maryland high court reversed the circuit court's decision and remanded the case with instructions to dismiss the charges (32). Tracing the legislative history of the Maryland statute from 1890 to its last revision in 1976, the court concluded that the legislature had not intended the statute to apply to this type of research activity under a Federal program, basing its ruling on three points:

- The legislative intent was interpreted as exempting from punishment acts not involving "unnecessary" or "unjustifiable" pain, given exceptions for "customary and normal veterinary and agricultural husbandry practices" and the last sentence of Section 59, which states:

  > It is the intention of the General Assembly that all animals shall be protected from intentional cruelty, but that no person shall be liable for normal human activities to which the infliction of pain to an animal is purely incidental and unavoidable.

- The court imputed to the assembly "awareness" of the Federal Animal Welfare Act, which constituted a "comprehensive plan for the protection of animals used in research facilities, while at the same time recognizing and preserving the validity of use of animals in research."
- Taub's laboratory was subject to detailed regulations of the U.S. Department of Agriculture (USDA), which set forth specifications for humane handling, care, treatment, transportation, and veterinary care. With respect to the latter, the court noted that Federal law recognized and preserved the validity of animal research. The court also noted the application of NIH's grant requirements to the defendant's project (32).

The Maryland statute neither generally exempted scientific research from the reach of its anticruelty law nor regulated experimentation separately, as some others do. (In 1984, the Maryland General Assembly enacted a law that made the anticruelty statute's application to research activities less ambiguous.) The Maryland court's disposition of the case illustrates a judicial reluctance to find cruelty in an activity of some recognized social utility. Its value as a bellwether for other States is limited, however, for several reasons. First, although the case may be cited by other defendants as a helpful precedent, it is law only in Maryland. Second, the holding in this case may be limited to its particular facts. At the trial that resulted in conviction, a substantial amount of testimony was heard on the issue of adequate veterinary care in research involving intentional injury to the research subjects. The court's opinion did not fully address this issue. Third, the court relied heavily on its presumption that the General Assembly of Maryland had been aware of the Federal Animal Welfare Act when it last amended the statute, 8 years earlier. Many of the two dozen or so general anticruelty laws that contain no research exemption have not been amended since the 1966 passage of the Animal Welfare Act.

The Preemption Question

The *Taub* decision is also relevant to the question of research coverage by general anticruelty statutes because of what the case did not decide. On appeal, Taub asserted that his conviction was invalid for five main reasons, three of which addressed themselves to actions occurring in or taken by the trial court (sufficiency of evidence, permitting medical experts to define the term "veterinary care," and denial of a fair trial due to introduction of evidence of Nero's physical condition more than a month after he had been seized). But Taub also contended that the Maryland statute was unconstitutionally vague, because the definition of "animal" was excessively broad and because it was unclear as to what was "the most humane method reasonably available" and what were included or excluded from "normal human activities to which the infliction of pain to an animal is purely incidental and unavoidable." In addition, he claimed that his prosecution was barred by the Supremacy Clause of the Federal Constitution and that the reach of Maryland's general statute was therefore preempted by congressional passage of the Federal Animal Welfare Act (10).

Thus, the court was presented with two constitutional questions of considerable importance to the continued enforceability of general anticruelty statutes. First, do the old, nonspecific formulations of cruelty provide sufficient notice of what conduct is prohibited, under what circumstances, and how violation of the law can be avoided? Second, has Congress so occupied the field of research regulation that enforcement of a similar State law would violate the principle that the Federal Constitution and reasonable Federal laws enacted under it are the supreme law of the land? The Animal Legal Defense Fund (ALDF), formerly known as Attorneys for Animal Rights, Inc., a nonprofit professional legal group interested in better laws protecting animals, joined the State attorney general as a friend of the court in defending the appeal and briefing the constitutional issues raised by Taub's challenges (11,66).

Whether a State law is preempted by a Federal law is a matter of statutory interpretation by a State or Federal court. (Jurisdiction is concurrent where these questions arise, since both the State and the Federal Government have a stake in the outcome of the question.) Court decisions touching on this question over the years have established two general requirements for Federal preemption of a State statute. First, the Federal Government must have the *authority* to preempt the State's enactment. Second, Congress must have *intended* to preempt State law (115).

Preemptive authority is found where Congress legitimately exercises an enumerated power, such as the constitutional power to regulate interstate commerce (79,100,112,118). A Federal law may also be preemptive when, supported by application of the "Necessary and Proper Clause" (111), it gives effect to an enumerated power, even though the means used is not expressly enumerated in the Constitution (68). In either of those circumstances, if the law is found to have a rational basis for regulation and effectuation of an enumerated power, it is capable of preempting a State law (90). A Federal law does not have preemptive capability, however, if Congress uses its enumerated powers alone to go beyond its areas of enumerated concerns to achieve a result that a State could also achieve by the exercise of its reserved power.

Congress may exercise an enumerated power to achieve an end extraneous to the effectuation of that power. Thus, for example, Congress may exercise its spending power to encourage an extraneous goal such as humane treatment for research animals. As a general principle, however, if an enumerated power is used to affect an area not within the Federal "circle" of interests, it cannot compel the States to accept that exercise. In such cases, concurrent jurisdiction exists (16,68, 110). The ALDF brief relied on this principle in its assertion that, while Congress' power to appropriate funds for the general good may be used to require Federally funded research facilities to comply with Federal standards of animal care, this does not preempt similar State laws. Thus, the grantee of Federal funds may be bound to adhere to any conditions of the grant, but the State cannot be and is not so bound except to the extent that the State itself accepts Federal research funds. ALDF argued that denial of preemptive capability would promote valuable public policy by "preserving to the people of Maryland the right to determine what constitutes cruelty" (66).

Once a Federal law is shown to be constitutionally capable of preemption, it must be demonstrated against a generally applicable presumption in favor of State laws that Congress either explicitly or by inference intended for the Federal law to supersede conflicting State enactments (57,98). Determining legislative intent can sometimes be difficult, especially when Congress avails itself of more than one enumerated power, against which different constitutional standards must be applied (28). When the State law involves the exercise of its traditional police powers—to protect the welfare of its citizens—preemption will occur only when there is proof that such was the Federal law's clear purpose (35). If there is insufficient evidence that Congress intended to totally occupy the field regulated by the respective laws, there must be sufficient conflict between them for the State law to stand as "an obstacle to accomplishment and execution of the full purposes and objectives of Congress" (57).

Both the State and ALDF argued, first, that exercise of a traditional police power was involved and, second, that Section 2145(b) of the Animal Welfare Act made it sufficiently clear that Congress intended to establish a cooperative enforcement scheme rather than a conflicting one, so that no conflict or obstacle to attainment of Federal objectives was presented (11,66). (Section 2145(b) of the act authorizes USDA to cooperate with State and local governments carrying out "any State, local, or municipal legislation or ordinance on the same subject.") Taub, on the other hand, pressed the argument that the State law was in conflict with, and an obstacle to, the congressional objective of minimizing disruption of research (10). In any case, the court decided that the matter may be disposed of by the conclusion that the Maryland statute simply is inapplicable to Dr. Taub (32).

The decision was not at all surprising, given the publicity about the case over 2 years (8,73,88). Reaction was also predictable. One professional society's newsletter concluded that the Maryland court had "wisely recognized" the fact that the "ultimate goal [of biomedical research] is improvement of the human condition" and claimed that the decision provided an "important legal precedent that affirms the propriety of the use of animals in biomedical research" (31). One of the attorneys on the ALDF brief called the court's decision "opaque," observing that "one manifestation of the court's confused reasoning is that attorneys and commentators cannot agree on the grounds for the decision" (122). Writing in the *New England Journal of Medicine,* an attorney-professor who reviewed the decision and the resulting commentary reached this sober conclusion (27):

> It is now necessary for the Congress to consider whether or not it wishes to address this question and to remove the uncertainty in the law by making it clear that the Animal Welfare Act is intended to be a comprehensive, exclusive system of control over the use of animals in experimental facilities and activities in interstate and foreign commerce and under the National Institutes of Health research programs. Without such clarification, investigators and operators of facilities face the possibility of local criminal prosecution, seizure of animals, injunctions to close facilities, and cessation of animal investigations. It should be understood, however, that this Federal mandate, if accepted, means that the administrative system for monitoring, including on-site inspection, must be adequate to insure continued compliance with national standards for humane treatment. Otherwise, state-level organizations with a sincere and reasonable concern about the care of animals will be justified in demanding local enforcement and surveillance of biomedical research programs involving laboratory animals.

Winkler v. Colorado

Only one other State court case addresses the question of preemption by the Animal Welfare Act. In *Winkler* v. *Colorado*, that State's supreme court considered a preemptive challenge to Colorado regulations prohibiting the importation of pets for resale from States with less stringent licensing laws and regulations covering commercial pet dealers. The court found preemptive capability, holding that Congress used an enumerated power to effectuate an enumerated power: regulating interstate commerce. The challenge to the State law was not sustained, however; the court found that the act not only "clearly did not indicate preemptive intent, but rather, expressly endorsed state-federal cooperation" (119).

Criticisms

Despite the fact that it set the stage for future collisions between research and animal interests, the *Taub* case is not particularly valuable for resolving such conflicts, since the court avoided constitutional questions in reaching its decision. The decision suggests that when a court is confronted with a difficult case involving sharply contrasting but supportable interests and obscure legal principles whose potential impact on a decision far outweighs their understandability in application, it will go to extraordinary lengths to avoid that decision. It is a natural and conservative reaction for a judge to decline an invitation to make law that prejudices an existing enforcement system, however imperfect, when the legislature has shown no inclination to do so itself. The mixture of enumerated powers supporting the Animal Welfare Act, coupled with evidence that Congress did not intend to preempt the field of research regulation, are probably sufficient to avoid preemption. That result, however, cannot be predicted with any confidence.

Animal welfare advocates criticize general anticruelty laws as being ineffective in protecting animals from harm (19,29,124). The statutes' vagueness and the frequent requirement for some degree of culpability both exact high standards of proof and subject statutes to a greater risk of ineffectiveness. Other criticisms are that general anticruelty statutes fail to anticipate and prevent cruelty or neglect, instead taking effect only when a sustainable complaint is entered. Enforcement of these statutes is generally entrusted to local law enforcement agencies, which for a number of reasons typically assign them a comparatively low priority. State regulations and local procedures for investigating and building a criminal case against a violator are complex, involving complicated rules governing warrants and searches. Fines are low, as a rule, and criminal violations comparatively hard to prove. When convictions are obtained, fines assessed against violators are generally collected by the State, though humane societies or SPCAs with limited enforcement authority must spend their own funds to investigate and prove cases (33,36).

Recent Initiatives in Anticruelty Laws

Critics of current anticruelty statutes, who have pressed to extend the laws' reach to research activities, have not met with a great deal of success. They insist that two basic changes must be made if anticruelty laws are to be enforced meaningfully: First, animal welfare specialists must be trained and used; second, those trained specialists must be given increased enforcement authority (81). One situation hailed as a model is Massachusetts' creation of a private right-of-action and its delegation to the Massachusetts SPCA and, more recently, to the Animal Rescue League, of authority to act as agents of the Commissioner of Health in enforcing the State's anticruelty laws.

The private right-of-action allows citizens to bring civil suits to enjoin violations, reap statutory damages, and collect court costs and attorneys' fees if successful. Massachusetts SPCA officers are commissioned as special State police officers and given training by the police academy and the Massachusetts SPCA. They have arrest and prosecution authority for violations. Inspections are conducted when a problem becomes apparent. The officers can use selective enforcement procedures that focus on serious violations, which conserves time, money, and personnel while increasing the law's deterrent effect (77). Supporters of this model argue that efficient enforcement of the type contemplated by it would curtail animal abuse, including abuse occurring in laboratories. Skeptics point to the obvious increase in cost entailed by such qualification and training requirements, and they wonder if the research community would accept enforcement of anticruelty provisions by its chief antagonists (19).

38-750 0 - 86 - 11

Legislatures that have revised their anticruelty statutes within the last several years are mindful of the problems in applying and enforcing older laws. Virginia, for example, totally revised its Animal Welfare Act. Enforcement powers, duties, and training and skill requirements for "animal wardens" were increased, and local humane societies were granted limited warrant, search, and arrest powers (117). Florida, while not considering any animal welfare amendments per se, upgraded the maximum fine for active cruelty to animals from $1,000 to $5,000, and the fine for confinement without food, water, or exercise or for abandonment from $500 to $5,000 (58). The Michigan Humane Society has drafted a model anticruelty bill, as well as publishing a comprehensive guide to enforcement of the existing Michigan statute and supplements for use in Illinois and New York (69,70,71). (A model statute is a law proposed for State adoption by a group of experts, frequently a national conference of legal scholars, though advocacy groups are increasingly likely to offer model laws incorporating their positions. Although model statutes are intended to promote uniformity among the States, a State adopting such a law will often modify it to some extent to meet its own needs, or it may only adopt a portion of the model statute.) The Michigan guide and its supplements detail the process of investigating suspected cruel conduct and building a case against the suspected violator.

Another model anticruelty statute (26) includes provisions regulating research animals by dividing covered animals into three classes, with treatment depending on their classification. Class A animals are chimpanzees, gorillas, and dolphins. An experiment that causes a significant amount of pain to a Class A animal would be prohibited unless it is performed in a licensed research facility, it causes less suffering than any alternative experiment that would provide the same scientific information at a reasonable cost, and it is limited to gaining information about human or animal disease, injury, or mental disorder. In addition, weapons research on Class A animals would be banned unless the experiments dealt directly with counteracting the health effects of weapons. Furthermore, behavioral research with this group would be prohibited unless justified by health-related reasons.

Class B animals are all other mammals. The model statute prohibits scientific experiments that cause suffering to Class B animals unless the same restrictions that apply to Class A animals are met. Behavorial research is not prohibited, however.

Class C consists of any other vertebrate. Only two restrictions would apply to experiments causing pain to Class C creatures: The research facility would have to be licensed, and the experiment would have to produce less pain than any other reasonably priced experiment that would produce the same information.

This model statute provides both criminal penalties and civil damages for violations. The criminal provisions would be enforced by law enforcement officers and the others by any interested party (see discussion of private enforcement interests in the next section). Recordkeeping by facilities is required, and the records could be inspected at any time. Required entries include the number and types of animals used, the conditions under which animals were kept, and a description of the purpose and design of the experiment. Proponents contend that adoption of this statute would provide clear standards of research-animal care, resulting in less abuse. Critics cite the difficulty of classifying species so as to satisfy everyone and the inconsistency of arbitrarily excluding behavorial research for Class A animals (12,19).

RIGHT TO TAKE LEGAL ACTION ON AN ANIMAL'S BEHALF

Past Trends

There are two ways a State could allow legal action on an animal's behalf. First, an anticruelty statute could provide private citizens with a right to compel enforcement of the law. In nonanimal contexts, such a right is exercised by bringing against the enforcement agency a legal action seeking a court order directing the agency to enforce the law. Second, a legislature or court could confer upon private citizens "standing to sue" on an animal's behalf, such as by allowing citizens to act as legal guardians of an animal's welfare. The requirement of standing is satisfied either if it is conferred by statute or if a court holds that the plaintiff has a legally protectable and tangible interest at stake in the litigation.

One State trial court was called on in 1982 to decide whether the Animal Welfare Act or either or both of two Connecticut laws confer upon a private citizen a right to compel enforcement of the statutes against, and the right to seek damages from, a research entity on behalf of an animal. In *Friends of Animals, Inc.* v. *U.S. Surgical Corporation*, the plaintiffs filed a complaint alleging that the defendant's use of dogs in teaching its technical field representatives how to use surgical staplers violated both the Animal Welfare Act and the State's general anticruelty law. The Connecticut anticruelty law is a general misdemeanor statute with no qualifiers and contains no research exemption. (Similar attempts by this group to get a Federal hearing on these charges are described in ch. 13. For a complete chronology of the lawsuits between these parties and a more detailed examination of the attempted use of the act and the State's anticruelty laws against a research enterprise, see the case study at the end of this chapter.)

The group, claiming for its members "a personal stake and an intense interest in the prevention of cruelty to animals," asserted a private right of action against the company to enforce the laws and recover damages. The defendant moved to strike the complaint for failure to state a claim on which relief could be granted, a pleading that, under Connecticut rules of procedure, automatically tests the legal sufficiency of the complaint. The court struck the anticruelty counts, finding no legislative intent to create a private right of action and noting that the plaintiff introduced no legal authority in support of its contention that such a right existed.

To support the alleged right under the Animal Welfare Act, the plaintiff claimed the act was analogous to the Marine Mammal Protection Act (5). (A Federal court had previously interpreted the latter to support a private right to sue, as discussed in ch. 13.) The Connecticut court rejected this analogy. Citing a judicial-review provision in the latter statute that is not found in the Animal Welfare Act, the absence of any proof that the Congress intended to create a private right to enforce the Animal Welfare Act, and the absence of supporting case law, the judge struck the balance of the Friends of Animals complaint, leaving no issues for trial before the court (45).

Recent Initiatives to Create Legally Enforceable Rights for Animals

Support is growing in the animal welfare community for establishing independent and legally enforceable rights for animals, on the theory that effective enforcement of animal interests will never occur as long as they are balanced against, and almost always outweighed by, competing human or social considerations. This reflects a general historical progression toward treating animals as intrinsically valuable and away from treating them as mere chattels or personal property (7,29).

Interest in this concept is fed by the success of animal welfare groups in expanding the reach of statutes like the Marine Mammal Protection Act by winning the right to sue on behalf of protected animals, at least in a limited sense (5,120). Acceptance of other statutes with similar objectives, such as the Endangered Species Act, has led to a widening circle of protected and judicially enforceable interests for animals (22,29). Conferring standing to sue on animals would allow humans to sue on an animal's behalf (or on behalf of a class of animals) to protect the interests of the animal. Groups such as the Animal Welfare Institute have used their judicially conferred standing to sue the Federal Government and others under the Endangered Species Act, for example, on behalf of interests they believe are not being protected sufficiently (29).

Standing proposals have led naturally to other interest-protecting roles for those seeking to protect animals' rights. In particular, application of the familiar principles of guardianship is sought. Under guardianship principles, the legislative status of animals, especially companion species, would be changed from property to possessors of specified rights, while the definition of a guardian would be amended to include a person who "has elected to take responsibility for the care and well-being" of an animal. Thus, guardianship would commence on adoption or purchase. Legal guardians could be appointed by courts to assume duties as custodians and conservators of a laboratory animal's rights, including the right to sue. The relationship could be terminated by judicial removal for malfeasance or nonfeasance and would terminate on the animal's death or the guardian's incapacity. The guardian's ability to protect and enforce the animal's interests, by lawsuit if necessary, would afford animals better protection, it is argued (109).

As discussed, courts have thus far been unwilling to confer standing on human plaintiffs in the absence of a specific statutory grant. In the *U.S. Surgical* case, the Connecticut Superior Court found no sustainable private right to enforce either the Animal Welfare Act or the State's anticruelty statute. Even if courts were less conservative about granting standing, and even if the burden required for standing of showing actual injury were not as rigorous, the interest being affected still must be cognizable at law. Using the Endangered Species Act as an analogy, what would be required at a minimum is conferring the right to judicial review on "any person" affected by an action taken under the law containing the right of review. Thus, the likelihood of legislative, followed by judicial, acceptance of even some minimal version of animal standing is probably not imminent. Acceptance of novel interpretations of otherwise familiar concepts of guardianship to cover animals is likely to be even farther off.

As frustrated as animal advocates have been in their efforts to secure enforcement of laws protecting animals, they show no sign of abating. Several such cases, instituted or pending at the Federal level, are examined in chapter 13, and the case study at the end of this chapter discusses a series of cases, involving the same parties, that explores a variety of unsuccessful theories. Recently, Actors and Others for Animals and the Fund for Animals sued the Los Angeles County Board of Supervisors, alleging their failure to enforce the county's pound release ordinances, which require certification of humane treatment of animals by institutions seeking to purchase pound animals (108). Common-law theories, such as nuisance, have been used in these suits, and environmental statutes have been enlisted as well. In 1984, a California Superior Court dismissed a suit brought by a coalition of animal welfare groups, citing provisions of the California Environmental Quality Act, to include an evaluation of laboratory-animal use in an environmental impact report for a new, $46 million science building at the University of California at Berkeley (20).

REGULATION OF RESEARCH

Past Trends

Apart from regulating agricultural and other economically oriented uses of animals, some States regulate the use of animals for research purposes. Twenty-one jurisdictions regulate research specifically, either in the context of general registration, licensure or inspection laws, or independently:

- Four States allow or require regulation of research facilities: California (15,17), Michigan (84), Tennessee (107), and Virginia (117).
- Seven States and the District of Columbia require licensing or registration for a research facility to receive pound animals: D.C. (30), Illinois (61), Iowa (65), Minnesota (87), Ohio (95), Oklahoma (96), South Dakota (103), and Utah (116).
- Two States extend an exemption from their animal cruelty statutes only to research approved or licensed by the State: New Jersey (92) and New York (93).
- Two States require licenses to use dogs or cats in research: Connecticut (24) and Massachusetts (77).
- Five States exempt all research facilities or federally licensed facilities from State licensing programs: Colorado (23), Kansas (67), North Carolina (94), Pennsylvania (97), and Rhode Island (99).

Most State statutes deal with the procurement of animals for research. For example, the Michigan statute makes it unlawful to sell animals to an unlicensed research facility (84). Dogs used in research must be marked. Animals cannot be sold to research facilities at a public auction or by weight, and when an animal is purchased for research, a bill of sale signed by the seller must be retained. A facility failure to abide by those rules could result in revocation of its required license (85). Conditions in animal holding facilities are also common concerns in these laws. New York facilities must treat research animals kindly and humanely and must feed and house them properly (93). Animals held in California facilities must receive satisfactory food, shelter, and sanitation (15,17).

State legislatures have been as reluctant as Congress to go behind the laboratory door. California law provides that the Department of Health Services is required to promulgate rules for the control and humane use of animals in specified types of research (17). The New York statute specifies that:

> . . . commensurate with experimental needs and with the physiologic function under study, all tests, experiments, and investigations involving pain shall be performed under adequate anesthesia (93).

Under that statute, the Commissioner of Health has promulgated regulations applicable to research in the State university system to require ethical review of experimental procedures by the degree of pain and suffering caused the animal involved.

Some of the statutes extend their requirements only to the use of companion animals. Massachusetts requires a license prior to experimentation on dogs and cats (77), and Connecticut requires a license for research on dogs only (24). Institutions in Illinois, Iowa, or Oklahoma that plan to use live dogs or cats may apply for a license to obtain animals from a pound (61,65,96); in Ohio, to receive impounded dogs institutions must be certified by the Ohio Public Health Council as being engaged in teaching or research (95).

State research-regulation laws enacted since the passage of the Animal Welfare Act are mindful of the potential for duplication. California specifically exempts some laboratories from its licensure law, such as those regulated by the National Institutes of Health (17). Facilities in Kansas holding a current Federal registration under the Animal Welfare Act are exempt from State law (67), as are federally regulated facilities in North Carolina and Rhode Island (94,99). Facilities in Pennsylvania that have undergone a Federal inspection within the past year are exempt from regular inspections by Commonwealth animal wardens (97).

With the exception of Massachusetts and Kansas, inspection and enforcement authorities are State-level agencies. The California statute prohibits delegation of this authority to anyone other than an employee of the Department of Health Services (17). Conversely, Kansas law allows the Commissioner of Health to appoint county and city health commissioners as authorized representatives for inspection purposes (67). In Massachusetts, research institutions must apply to the Commissioner of Licenses for a license to "employ dogs or cats in scientific investigation, experiment or instruction or for the testing of drugs or medicines." The Commissioner must investigate the applicant prior to licensure to determine whether the public interest is served by granting a license and that the licensee "is a fit and proper institution to receive such license." Licenses are revocable, after notice and hearing, and must be renewed annually. Knowing violators are subject to a fine of up to $100 for each discovered violation of the statute. Local courts are authorized to enjoin violations "or to take such other actions as equity and justice require" in enforcing the licensing law. The Commissioner is given a general grant of rulemaking and inspection authority, and visitation and inspection powers may be delegated by regulation to the Massachusetts SPCA and the Animal Rescue League of Boston, "as agents of the commissioner" (77).

Recent Initiatives in Research Regulation

Proposals to enact or modify licensing statutes suggest such changes as increasing control over the research process; requiring stricter standards of treatment and care; increasing recordkeeping and inspection functions; streamlining investigation, complaint, and prosecution procedures; and providing additional enforcement resources. Other than these proposals, not many other initiatives have been put forward to prevent or reduce experimental-animal suffering. The model statute discussed above has not generated a great deal of interest (26). Bills routinely introduced in the legislatures of more populous States require percentage reductions in funds spent on animal research, require consideration and adoption of alternatives to animal use, or attack the legitimacy of animal usage in some other way. But none has yet been taken seriously. Nevertheless, House Bill 742 in Massachusetts would mandate a 5 percent annual reduction per institution in the number of animals used in that State's research laboratories.

POUND RELEASE LAWS

Past Trends

All States have statutes that provide for the seizure, holding, and humane destruction of unowned or unclaimed stray animals (74). These laws, which are most complex and aggressive in their application to dogs and cats, attempt to balance the need for protection of the public's health and safety from unmanaged animals against the rights and duties of private animal ownership, whether for aesthetic or commercial purposes. To serve the interests of public protection and welfare, most States provide for the release to research institutions of unowned or unclaimed animals, usually dogs and cats, under certain circumstances or when specified conditions are met, such as obtaining a license. Such statutes generally provide for a suitable holding period after collection or seizure, so that owners have an opportunity to claim their animals, and specify procedures to be followed by owners, holding facilities, and claiming institutions. Many municipalities also have laws either requiring or authorizing the release of "random-source" animals to research institutions. Definitions of what types of institutions qualify to claim random-source animals, and at what level of "scientific research," vary widely. As noted, there is little agreement on what legitimate scientific research is. Sometimes this is left to authorities responsible for regulating research, independent of general anticruelty laws, and some types of educational research activities are proscribed (33,36). These laws are summarized in table 14-2.

The authority of States to release unclaimed animals to appropriate research facilities has never been successfully challenged. In 1959, for example, the Supreme Judicial Court of Massachusetts declined to rule that such a scheme impaired any rights of petitioning humane societies or pet owners, or that it called for an unconstitutional expenditure of public funds or property (78). The force of the court's ruling was rendered moot by the recent passage in Massachusetts of a law, discussed below, prohibiting the release or importation of pound animals for research purposes.

Currently, nine States (Connecticut, Hawaii, Maine, Massachusetts, New Hampshire, New Jersey, Pennsylvania, Rhode Island, and Vermont) prohibit the release of dogs and cats from pounds for research purposes (89). The most far-reaching of these laws was passed by Massachusetts in 1983 and went into effect in October 1984. Besides repealing the State's old pound release statute and eliminating all pertinent references in general pound law, the new statute prohibits the release by "dog officers" or municipalities of any animal to any "business or institution licensed or registered as a research facility or animal dealer with the United States Department of Agriculture." A research "institution" is defined as (77):

> . . . any institution operated by the United States or by the Commonwealth or a political subdivision thereof, or any school or college of medicine, public health, dentistry, pharmacy, veterinary medicine or agriculture, medical diagnostic laboratory or biological laboratory, hospital or

Table 14-2.—Laws on Pound Animal Use, by Jurisdication

State/jurisdiction	Prohibit release	Require release	Allow release	No mention in law	Other
Alabama				X	
Alaska				X	
Arizona			X		
Arkansas				X	
California			X		
Colorado				X	
Connecticut	X				
Delaware				X	
District of Columbia		X			
Florida				X	
Georgia				X	
Hawaii	X				
Idaho				X	
Illinois					X
Indiana				X	
Iowa		X			
Kansas				X	
Kentucky				X	
Louisiana				X	
Maine	X				
Maryland					X
Massachusetts	X				
Michigan			X		
Minnesota		X			
Mississippi				X	
Missouri				X	
Montana				X	
Nebraska				X	
Nevada				X	
New Hampshire	X				
New Jersey	X				
New Mexico				X	
New York					X
North Carolina			X		
North Dakota				X	
Ohio			X		
Oklahoma		X			
Oregon				X	
Pennsylvania	X				
Rhode Island	X				
South Carolina				X	
South Dakota		X			
Tennessee			X		
Texas				X	
Utah		X			
Vermont	X				
Virginia					X
Washington				X	
West Virginia				X	
Wisconsin			X		
Wyoming				X	

SOURCE: National Association for Biomedical Research, *State Laws Concerning the Use of Animals in Research* (Washington, DC: Foundation for Biomedical Research, 1985).

other educational or scientific establishment within the Commonwealth above the rank of secondary school, which, in connection with any of its activities, investigates or gives instruction concerning the structure or functions of living organisms or the causes, prevention, control or cure of diseases or abnormal conditions of human beings or animals.

Effective October 1, 1986, Section 9 of the law will forbid the importation of similar animals into the Commonwealth for research purposes:

> . . . no person, institution, animal dealer or their authorized agents shall transport, or cause to be transported, any animal obtained from any municipal or public pound, public agency, or dog officer acting individually or in an official capacity into the Commonwealth for purposes of research, experimentation, testing, instruction or demonstration.

Under the provisions of Section 9, any institution obtaining animals before the deadline must have filed a report with the Department of Public Health "detailing its plans for discontinuation of the use of such animals."

The impact of recent laws forbidding the acquisition of unclaimed animals for research is uncertain. Research community representatives in Massachusetts have claimed that the new laws, when fully in effect, will add perhaps $6 million to the annual price of research conducted in the Commonwealth (80,82). The added cost to taxpayers of humanely destroying animals that remain unclaimed at pounds must also be considered, although it could be argued that taxpayers bear the cost of sacrificing animals in research as well, however indirectly (81). The effects of the new Massachusetts laws merit close observation.

Recent Initiatives in Pound Release Laws

The success of those who wish to repeal pound release laws or to prohibit the use of stray and abandoned companion animals in research by some other means has been spotty. Most of the laws permitting the use of pound animals in research were passed in the decade following World War II, when the need for inexpensive research models began to mount, and the vast majority of jurisdictions still permit it. As table 14-2 shows, 6 jurisdictions require release of impounded animals for research purposes, 7 permit it, 29 neither expressly require nor forbid release, and 9 prohibit the practice. Most delegate that authority to local animal control officers and authorities (89). Release repeals have succeeded in larger areas, which are perceived to have the resources for less-convenient means of disposition of unwanted animals. Smaller jurisdictions without those resources are faced with animal and disease control problems that are as persistent as ever. Thus, a senate committee in Florida reported a bill in 1984 that required more-humane methods of euthanasia for strays but rejected a proposal to prohibit city and county shelters from sending excess animals to the University of Florida for experimental purposes (114). Similarly, the Humane Society in Larimer County, CO, voted unanimously in May 1983 to sell animals to Colorado State University for veterinary research in order to raise funds.

Pound release laws, whether mandatory or permissive, have come under close scrutiny in the last 10 years at both the State and local level. A 25-year-old law in New York requiring the release of pound animals to State-run research institutions was repealed in 1979 (21). A bill defeated in the Wisconsin Senate by a vote of 2-97 would have amended the current law requiring pounds and shelters to release unclaimed dogs to State-accredited institutions, upon proper requisition, for research purposes (33,121).

A running legislative battle has been taking place in the California Assembly for several years. Two major bills dominated the legislative agenda in 1983 and 1984, but neither received approval. Senate Bill No. 883, defeated in 1984 in an assembly committee, would have repealed current requirements for pound signs warning owners and others that animals could be used in research and would have generally prohibited the release by local pounds and shelters of live dogs, cats, and other animals for the purpose of experimentation, testing, demonstration, or research (14). Assembly Bill No. 1735, left pending in the 1984 assembly session, would have modified the same law by permitting persons leaving strays to stipulate that the animal not be used for research purposes. Further, it would have extended the mandatory holding period for potential research animals and prohibited release of any pound animal to a research facility prior to a determination that the facility meets specified standards of humane animal care (13). (California law currently provides, in a regulation-of-research statute, that the Department of Health Services may not make any rule "compelling the delivery of animals for the purpose of research, demonstration, diagnosis, or experimentation," thus leaving the policy to the discretion of local jurisdictions (17).)

Substantial recent activity has occurred at the local level, as well. For 3 years, the City of Los Angeles has prohibited the release of cats or dogs for research (60). In 1984, commissioners in Jackson County, MI, refused to prohibit the release of pound animals to research institutions and educational facilities. Advocates of the measure subsequently failed in their drive to have the issue placed on a referendum ballot (102). In 1983, the Society for Humane Ethics and Principles petitioned the Board of Supervisors for Maricopa County, AZ, to adopt a policy prohibiting the sale of impounded animals to research facilities, following the State legislature's rejection of the society's proposal for a State law with identical restrictions (72,83). The board adopted the proposal and the policy has been sustained by an opinion issued by the State attorney general in 1984 (25).

In 1985, 11 influential animal welfare organizations joined in an effort to prevent all use of pound and shelter animals for scientific purposes. The new National Coalition to Protect Our Pets (Pro-Pets), which includes both humane societies and antivivisection groups, seeks legislation toward this end (64).

ANIMAL USE IN EDUCATION

Past Trends

Of all areas of State and local law dealing with the humane treatment of experimental animals, the realm of education is probably the most neglected. Statutes that refer to humane treatment in grammar and secondary schools usually contain very general terms, leaving the interpretation for instructional and curricular requirements to local school authorities.

Twenty-one States, in codes governing public instruction, list requirements for teaching students about the value of animals. These requirements vary widely and correspond to legislative perceptions of both the morality and utility of humane treatment. Some States, such as Pennsylvania and Wyoming, require a certain amount of time per week or other designated instruction period to be devoted to "kindness to" or "humane treatment of" animals. Others require such instruction, in more general terms, on designated days of the year—"bird, flower, and arbor day" in Tennessee, "arbor and bird day" in Wisconsin, "bird" day in Utah, and "conservation" day in New York. New York, however, also requires general-instruction programs in "moral and humane education" and "protection of wildlife and humane care of domestic animals," while Wisconsin mandates such programs regarding "kindness to and the habits, usefulness and importance of animals and birds, and the best methods of protecting, preserving and caring for all animal and bird life." California, besides requiring each teacher to "impress upon the minds of the pupils the principles of morality . . . including kindness toward domestic pets and the humane treatment of living creatures," requires public elementary and secondary schools to house and care for live animals in a "humane and safe" manner and prohibits killing or injuring, including anesthetizing, live vertebrates. Illinois and Massachusetts prohibit any "experiment upon any living animal for the purpose of demonstration in any study" in a public school. Further, dogs and cats may not be killed for vivisection, nor can any animal provided by or killed in the presence of a pupil be so used. Dissection of dead animals is limited to classrooms before students "engaged in the study to be illustrated thereby" (74).

Interest is increasing in laws restricting the use of at least some animals in experimentation below the undergraduate level. Recently introduced Kansas Senate Bill No. 529 forbids any school principal, administrator, or teacher from allowing any live vertebrate animal in a school or sponsored activity to be used as part of a scientific experiment or procedure in which the normal health of the animal is interfered with or in which fear, pain, suffering, or distress is caused. Covered experiments and procedures include, but are not limited to:

> . . . surgery, anesthetization, and the inducement by any means of painful, lethal, stressful, or pathological conditions through techniques that include but are not limited to:
> (a) administration of drugs;
> (b) exposure to pathogens, ionizing radiation, carcinogens, or to toxic, hazardous or polluting substances;
> (c) deprivation; and
> (d) electric shock or other distressing stimuli.

Dissection of dead animals would be permitted if confined to classrooms, and the bill requires that its provisions not be construed to prohibit "biological instruction involving the maintenance and study of living organisms or the vocational instruction in the practice of animal husbandry." Finally, the bill requires live animals in schools to be housed and cared for in a humane and safe manner, assigning personal responsibility to the teacher or other adult supervisor of a project or study. Violations would be punished as Class A misdemeanors.

A bill introduced in Florida seeks to set State policy regarding experimentation with live animals. The bill prohibits biological experiments on living subjects other than lower orders of life or anatomical specimens purchased from biological supply houses. Further, it permits only noninterventional observation of vertebrate animals (59). A similar bill was introduced in the New York Assembly in 1983 (58).

Only one case has tested the application of a State's general anticruelty statute to secondary school experimentation. For a science fair project, a New Jersey high school student intentionally inflicted two chickens with cancer and later killed them for dissection. The court first found that the State's general exemption for scientific research was unavailable to the student, since he was not a licensed institution. The plaintiff, the New Jersey SPCA, argued that experiments such as this one were needless and unnecessary. Adopting an expansive view of what constitutes scientific activity, the court found that the experiment did not violate the New Jersey anticruelty statute, for several reasons, including:

- the student had received proper supervision and normal protocols had been employed;
- there were general benefits to society in permitting such experimentation; and
- the chickens were given proper care during the term of the experiment, and it was unclear whether the chickens were in pain during the experiment (91).

Recent Initiatives in Education

Measures continue to be introduced that restrict the use of some types of animals for experimentation, teaching, or demonstration purposes and that prohibit painful or invasive procedures of any kind, as outlined above (56). An extreme example is Massachusetts House Bill No. 742, which would eliminate the use of animals for demonstration purposes at medical schools.

There appears to be growing interest among professional and humane-oriented organizations in establishing standards for animal use in teaching and promoting science to the young that also encourage humane attitudes. The Scientists' Center for Animal Welfare (Bethesda, MD), for example, has targeted science fairs (see ch. 9) as candidates for making students more sensitive to the needs of animals.

SUMMARY AND CONCLUSIONS

Unlike the Federal Animal Welfare Act, most State anticruelty statutes were enacted prior to the turn of the century, and they have been interpreted as protecting the interests of society, the animal owner, and the animal, in roughly that order. Most forbid both active cruelty (torture, "overriding") and failure to satisfy some specific (food, water, shelter) or nonspecific ("necessary sustenance") duty of care owed to animals. Many incorporate vague or undefined terms, require some proof of state of mind (culpability) to sustain a conviction, and are subject to a variety of defenses. Enforcement of most aspects of these statutes is usually delegated to local police and to humane societies. The members of humane societies are generally not trained to build criminal cases skillfully, they lack the enforcement tools to do so, and they are underfunded for the task.

The application of these statutes to the conduct of research is unclear, since many State anticruelty laws are general in nature and contain no specific exemption for research activity. The only case that offered the ideal forum for resolving conflicting research and animal protection interests at the Federal and State level—and for deciding whether Congress intended to occupy the field of laboratory-animal regulation or, rather, to establish a cooperative system of protection—was decided without addressing these issues. Another State court found no preemptive intent in Congress' passage of the Animal Welfare Act. It seems clear enough that the act is intended to complement, or at least operate concurrently, with State efforts at research regulation, but courts' reluctance to render broad decisions in cases on animals and the mixture of constitutional principles represented in the act make prediction of outcome difficult in any given case.

Twenty States and the District of Columbia regulate research to some extent. Like the Federal act, however, most address themselves to procurement and treatment of animals after experimentation, rather than to specific standards of care to be observed before and during research. These laws concern themselves primarily with dogs and cats, and some merely require or encourage licensing or some other type of certification to enable research facilities to obtain pound animals. Several States have passed regulatory laws that complement the Federal act, in the sense that they exempt facilities from compliance with certain responsibilities if they fulfill similar requirements under Federal law, regulations, or guidelines.

All States have laws providing for the control and disposition of stray and abandoned dogs and cats. Beginning in the late 1940s, States began adopting laws requiring or permitting research facilities to purchase strays from pounds and shelters. These laws have been the targets of repeal efforts.

All 50 States and the District of Columbia allow some form of pound animal use for research and training. To date, 9 States prohibit in-State procurement (although not importation from out-of-State) of pound animals for research and training. Of these, Massachusetts will in October 1986 prohibit the use of any animal obtained from a pound.

Twenty-one States have some provision in their codes requiring the teaching of "kindness" or "humanity" toward, or the "value" of, animals. A few place some restrictions on animal use in grammar and secondary schools.

Advocates of laboratory-animal protection criticize current State and local efforts to assure animals' humane treatment for several reasons, the main ones being that compliance schemes are overly complex and bureaucratic, that training and resources are inadequate, and that existing laws are not specific enough in their standards for care, treatment, and use. One model statute would regulate research use more closely by establishing classes of eligible research animals, based on comparative intelligence, with specific proofs to be met before animals in any class could be used in experiments.

Interest is growing in establishing direct, legally enforceable rights for animals. Some protection groups have endeavored to protect laboratory animals by seeking enforcement of anticruelty statutes or suing those they see damaging animals' interests. They have had virtually no success. Some have advocated conferring standing to sue on animals by applying the traditional concepts of guardianship to them.

Reviewing recent trends in each of these fields of law, it appears certain that animal welfare and humane groups will continue to press their case for reform on all fronts. Thus, it is likely that research and animal welfare interests will continue to collide in all three branches of Government at the State and local levels. Though some bills have been introduced that seek to reduce animal use in experimentation, promote other models, or eliminate the use of animals entirely, they have not been given serious consideration.

CASE STUDY: *FRIENDS OF ANIMALS, INC.* v. *U.S. SURGICAL CORPORATION*

> Every year, the United States Surgical Company used approximately 900 dogs to train sales representatives in the proper use of their [surgical] staple guns—a tool that is rapidly replacing conventional stitching of wounds or operation cuts. The representatives are chosen primarily for their sales ability and thus may have little or no medical knowledge. Before being sent out on the road, they must pass through a six-week training course. The company is now the focus for animal welfare protest in Connecticut. Their position has not been improved by allegations of animal abuse in a newspaper expose or the fact that one of the dealers who supplied them with dogs has been convicted of animal cruelty and of receiving stolen animals (101).

Thus was summarized a dispute between Friends of Animals, Inc., a major animal welfare organization, and U.S. Surgical Corporation, a large, private manufacturing interest using dogs to train its own personnel and customers in the use of its products. Behind local newspaper headlines on the case was a running legal battle involving several distinct lawsuits in Federal as well as State courts. Regardless of the positions or motives of the litigants, the cases in which they are parties provide an interesting view of the perceived roles that existing Federal and State animal welfare laws play when such disputes arise.

The Parties

Friends of Animals, Inc.

Friends of Animals, Inc. (FOA), is a not-for-profit, charitable organization incorporated under the laws of New York, with registered agents in a number of other States. FOA claims some 100,000 members nationwide, more than 5,000 of whom live in Connecticut, where these FOA complaints were filed. FOA is active in defense of all animals' right to humane treatment—politically, as well as legally. In the suits, FOA alleged that among its members are "individuals who are owners of dogs and . . . who have an intense interest in the proper administration and enforcement" of animal welfare laws (37).

U.S. Surgical Corporation

Headquartered in Norwalk, CT, U.S. Surgical Corporation is the leading producer of surgical stapling devices used for surgical tissue repair and wound closure. It has been in business for some 18 years and total sales in 1982 were $146 million. Its surgical products, marketed under the trade name AUTO-SUTURE, are sold in over 40 countries. U.S. Surgical has international subsidiaries in seven European countries and Australia, and the company employs about 1,900 people, two-thirds of whom work in Connecticut. Though it receives no Federal funding to support its product research or development, the company is subject to inspection and licensure by the Animal and Plant Health Inspection Service (APHIS) as a "research facility" under the Federal Animal Welfare Act, by the Drug Enforcement Administration under the Controlled Substances Act, and by the Departments of Health and Consumer Protection in Connecticut, which regulate the use and disposal of dogs in research (106,123). U.S. Surgical's president has expressed concern about the amendment of the Federal Animal Welfare Act that would require the company to appoint nonaffiliated persons to internal animal care review committees that have access to confidential business information (113).

The Controversy

U.S. Surgical's use of dogs purchased from local animal dealers to provide live-tissue training for its sales staff, also known as technical field representatives, in the use of surgical stapling equipment at the Norwalk teaching facility first came to the public's attention with the publication of a newspaper article in November 1981. That article contained a variety of allegations about the company's practices:

- "Sales personnel with no medical experience and surgeons destroyed at least 900 dogs at the Norwalk laboratory between October 1, 1980, and September 30, 1981. Additional hundreds of dogs are operated on each year for sales demonstration purposes by the company's traveling sales staff and at regional and national sales meetings."
- Anesthesia was "routinely administered to the dogs by persons with no medical training, including the sales staff."
- U.S. Surgical "failed to comply, for three consecutive years, with federal laws that [required it] to register with the U.S. Department of Agriculture."
- In at least one case, the personnel performing live-tissue training demonstrated the strength of the staple closure by lifting a dog by the clamp enclosing the abdominal fascia and by attempting to sunder the stapled cut.
- Some dogs appeared to be inadequately anesthetized, "jumping, jerking, writhing, and moaning" or showing other apparent signs of pain or distress during demonstrations, and others died prematurely, apparently from overdoses of barbiturates used for anesthesia.
- USDA officials quoted in the article were of the opinion that use of dogs for this purpose was a legal research activity although they "questioned the validity of sacrificing animals, especially in such large numbers, for this type of commercial purpose."
- One of the federally licensed dealers from whom the company had acquired dogs had

been "convicted in local court [in New Jersey] of receiving stolen dogs, animal cruelty, failing to keep proper records and failing to provide animals with adequate shelter from the cold" (54).

U.S. Surgical contended that its salespeople are given hands-on, live-tissue training in the use of its surgical stapling equipment, principally to "enable [them] to provide technical assistance in the operating room the first few times a surgeon uses the stapling instrumentation on a human patient." U.S. Surgical's technical field representatives also act as instructors, under the supervision of professors of surgery, in the laboratory portion of surgical-stapling seminars at postgraduate teaching hospitals. The company provides an "intense, five-week training program" for these purposes, consisting of instruction in "anatomy, physiology, surgical terminology, aseptic surgical techniques, surgical gowning, gloving, and scrubbing, and operating room protocol," in addition to supervised live-tissue training. Refresher courses on new surgical-stapling procedures are given to all sales staff at least once each year (106).

U.S. Surgical responded to major charges contained in the 1981 article as follows:

- In all, 974 dogs were acquired and used during the period mentioned, but only for "teaching regarding technical application and use of surgical instrumentation in well-accepted surgical procedures," and not for demonstration purposes. The company asserts that only foam wound and organ models are used for sales demonstration purposes.
- All anesthetic procedures are initiated and supervised by two "laboratory technicians trained in animal care and handling and who have been previously employed in animal laboratories responsible for both survival and nonsurvival animal research work."
- The company "complied in good faith" with Animal Welfare Act requirements. U.S. Surgical first applied for registration of its Stamford, CT, facility on June 4, 1976; it was first visited by USDA-APHIS inspectors in February 1979, and informed that it was not registered under the act. An inspection was conducted under "license-pending" status. The company reapplied for registration on February 20, 1979, and Registration No. 16-28 was issued on March 27, 1979.
- "The strength of the staples is tested to demonstrate their benefit when used in human clinical surgery; however, the methods described [lifting dogs by the staples and attempting to pull incisions apart by hand] are not employed."
- Although "the level of sedation may vary during the program," due to periodic administration of regulated doses to maintain unconsciousness without overdose, "the animal never regains consciousness or experiences discomfort." U.S. Surgical also stated that multiple teaching procedures are performed on single dogs in one session, "minimizing the need to use even more dogs and maximizing the teaching benefit provided by the animal."
- Expressing no specific opinion about the statements made by the quoted USDA-APHIS inspector as to the utility of using dogs for this purpose, U.S. Surgical noted that they had been contacted by a USDA veterinarian who would be writing to substantiate its need to use live animals.
- Dogs used in live-tissue training were acquired only from federally licensed dealers, their identification tags were checked and recorded, and their condition was evaluated prior to acceptance. If, as was stated in the article, the New Jersey dealer had had its Federal license revoked, then reinstated when violations had been corrected, the dealer "must be considered an acceptable source by the USDA" (123).

The Lawsuits

Friends of Animals filed its first lawsuit against U.S. Surgical in Federal court in Connecticut on December 29, 1981, a little less than 2 months after the newspaper article had appeared (37). Alleging that the defendant company, registered as a research facility as defined in the Federal Animal Welfare Act, had killed 974 dogs to demonstrate its surgical equipment, FOA contended that the demonstrations:

- were, "at times, performed without the proper administration of anesthesia";

- did not constitute "experimentation and/or research, as permitted by . . . the Animal Welfare Act"; and
- violated the Connecticut anticruelty statute.

The FOA complaint also contended that similar demonstrations performed from 1977 through 1979, when the company was not registered under the act, were not permitted experiments or research and violated the State anticruelty statute. FOA petitioned the court for a jury trial; unspecified compensatory damages; $5 million in punitive damages; interests, costs, and attorney's fees; and "other equitable relief." On February 8, 1982, U.S. Surgical filed a motion, under Rule 12 of the Federal Rules of Civil Procedure, to dismiss the suit because the plaintiff had failed to state a claim on which the court could base any warranted relief (38). Two days later, FOA filed a separate suit in the Superior Court of Connecticut, alleging the same facts, complaining of the same acts by the company, and requesting the same relief (41). On February 12, 1982, FOA filed a motion for voluntary dismissal without prejudice of the action filed in the Federal court, under Rule 41(a)(1)(i) of the Federal Rules of Civil Procedure, asserting that the Federal court lacked jurisdiction over the subject-matter of the suit (39). The court concurred and dismissed the suit without prejudice (40).

FOA amended the State court complaint on April 6, 1982, adding three additional counts to the original two (42). The third count alleged that the surgical-stapling demonstrations performed on anesthetized dogs from 1977 through 1981 violated Connecticut Statute 22a-15, which contains a general declaration of policy on environmental preservation. Counts Four and Five complained that the demonstrations constituted a nuisance and violated the provisions of the Animal Welfare Act. Thus, in addition to asserting that the company's complained-of activity violated Federal and State animal welfare laws, FOA contended that it amounted to a compensable common-law nuisance and also violated Connecticut's stated policies concerning protection of the public trust in natural resources.

U.S. Surgical countered with motions to strike the first two counts, on April 12, 1982, and the last three counts added by amendment, on May 19, 1982. In its memoranda in support of the motions, the company responded to the allegations as follows:

- The Connecticut anticruelty statute, being a criminal statute, created no private right of action to seek or compel enforcement of its provisions. According to U.S. Surgical, the law was not enacted to specially benefit a particular class and no evidence of legislative intent to create a private right of action could be found. The company claimed that such a right would be inconsistent with the statutory scheme of criminal and administrative enforcement erected by the legislature to protect both animals in general and dogs used in research.
- FOA lacked standing to sue, both on behalf of its members and on its own behalf, since the alleged injury was neither direct nor "distinct from a general interest shared with the public at large."
- Punitive damages could not be awarded to FOA since no allegation was made that the defendant's acts were committed to intentionally and wantonly violate FOA's rights or showed a reckless indifference to the rights of FOA.
- The Connecticut statute articulating the State's interest in natural resources as a "public trust" provided no basis for FOA's challenge to U.S. Surgical's use of dogs, for three reasons. First, it authorizes no private right of action. Second, the State's declared policy of protecting the public trust in natural resources does not apply to defendant's use of dogs. Third, the environmental statute does not supersede other State laws governing the use of dogs in research.
- FOA lacked standing to sue on grounds of nuisance, having suffered no direct and distinct injury of an interest in real property.
- The Federal Animal Welfare Act created no private right of action in favor of FOA, for the same reasons stated in U.S. Surgical's response to the first count (43,44).

FOA filed an opposition to U.S. Surgical's motion to strike on June 10, 1982, and the court heard oral arguments on the motion on November 3, 1982 (106).

The superior court entered a decision granting the company's motion to strike all five counts of FOA's complaint (45). With regard to the alleged violation of Connecticut's anticruelty law, the court construed the criminal-penalty law strictly and found no evidence of intent to create a private right to enforce its provisions. Although the Court did find legislative intent to create a private right to seek injunctive relief against pollution, under the Connecticut Environmental Protection Act, it rejected FOA's contention that dogs were covered by the statute.

The court also rejected FOA's charge that U.S. Surgical's destruction of dogs for surgical purposes constituted a common-law nuisance because FOA both "failed to set forth allegations that established a public nuisance" and based its claim for recovery "upon its peculiar and particular sensitivities and not upon its rights as a member of the general public." Additionally, the court rejected FOA's claim that the Federal Animal Welfare Act created a private right of enforcement similar to that created by the Marine Mammal Protection Act. Finally, the court agreed with U.S. Surgical that FOA could not collect punitive damages unless it pleaded and proved that the company had shown "a reckless indifference to the rights of others or an intentional and wanton violation of those rights" (45).

On December 21, 1982, before judgment had been entered on the motion to strike, FOA filed an amended complaint in Connecticut superior court, alleging again that U.S. Surgical's use of dogs for surgical demonstrations was reckless, wanton, sometimes without proper anesthetization, and constituted a public nuisance (46). FOA also claimed that the company's use of dogs violated a New Jersey anticruelty statute. The revised complaint added a new party to the proceedings: Pierre Quintana, a resident of Wilton, CT, who alleged that his springer spaniel, "George," was "stolen by agents or servants or employees of the U.S. Surgical Corporation and converted to said owner's use." FOA asked for a trial by jury and the same relief as earlier. U.S. Surgical, unaware that a substitute complaint had been filed, the following day filed a motion for early entry of judgment on the motion to strike (47,106).

While the action in State court continued, FOA refiled its case in Federal District Court on December 29, 1982, again asserting an interest on behalf of its members in "legally sufficient enforcement of the Animal Welfare Act" (48). Reiterating the allegations of the company's use of dogs in 1981, FOA renewed its contention that proper anesthetics were not used. It further alleged that U.S. Surgical had purchased live dogs from unlicensed dealers, in violation of the act, and that the company's surgery on live animals did not constitute experimentation and/or research as permitted by the act and was performed with "reckless indifference to the lives and well-being" of the animals.

Almost 4 months later, FOA moved for leave to amend the renewed complaint, and the motion was granted (49). In its amended complaint, filed on April 13, 1983, FOA charged that Rudolph Varana, a federally licensed animal dealer doing business as Varana Rabbit Farms, had committed "criminal acts"—i.e., received a stolen golden retriever, for which he was convicted under New Jersey Law—"as agent and servant for the U.S. Surgical Corporation . . . in direct violation of 7 U.S.C. 2131(3) which states that one of the purposes of the *Animal Welfare Act* is 'to protect the owners of animals from the theft of their animals by preventing the sale or use of animals which have been stolen'." FOA contended that the company knew or should have known of "its agent" Varana's "criminal acts" but continued to purchase dogs from him. As a result of Varana's "criminal acts" and U.S. Surgical's own negligence, FOA claimed that it had "been required to expend substantial amounts of money, [had] diverted substantial corporate resources, and [had] been forced to restructure [its] activities in order to investigate the criminal activities of said Rudolph Varana . . . and address the violations of the Animal Welfare Act and regulations enacted thereof [sic] by the U.S. Surgical Corporation." (FOA did not state that the golden retriever had been acquired and used by U.S. Surgical.)

Meanwhile, the company filed a request to revise the substituted complaint in the State court action, asserting that the second count of the substituted complaint reiterated allegations of public nuisance that had already been stricken by the Court (50). Failure by FOA to object to the request resulted in the request being granted on May 9, 1983, leaving intact the counts concerning the claimed violation of the New Jersey anticruelty statute and the alleged theft of Quintana's dog (106).

On December 9, 1983, FOA's lawyer moved to withdraw as counsel in the Federal case. The request was granted in March 1984. On August 23, 1984, FOA's new attorney filed a motion to dismiss the Federal complaint with prejudice, and moved to withdraw the State complaint and to set aside a judgment of dismissal entered in that case. Both motions were granted and the lawsuits were dismissed, not to be filed again (51,52,106). A newspaper story a week before the dismissal and withdrawal motions were filed by FOA reported that prior counsel had instituted suit against FOA for nonpayment of legal fees in the U.S. Surgical cases and others filed on FOA's behalf (6).

Discussion of the Case

Almost 3 years of legal sparring over an animal welfare controversy, conducted in both Federal and State courts, came to no substantive conclusion on the real issues in disagreement. There was no examination by a judge or a jury of the evidence to determine whether U.S. Surgical's use of anesthetized dogs to train its personnel in the use of surgical-stapling equipment on human patients was cruel or unjustified. FOA's attempts to invoke Federal and State animal use, anticruelty, animal theft, and even environmental statutes to "punish" or control behavior it deemed cruel or unjustified accomplished little more than the consumption of substantial amounts of time and judicial resources.

This result can be attributed to a number of factors, chief among which is a demonstrated reluctance on the part of judges to permit private enforcement of laws entrusted by legislation to administrative and law-enforcement agencies. Whether FOA decided to abandon its prosecution of U.S. Surgical as a result of disagreements with initial counsel or a realization of the unlikelihood of a victory on the merits is an open question. Statements attributed to FOA representatives in published press accounts could support both of those reasons (6,55).

Connecticut regulates the use of live companion animals (dogs) in research; its general anticruelty statutes make no mention as to whether its provisions also apply to the conduct of research. The same situation exists in 24 other States. If the complex and wholly inconclusive legal maneuvering in *Friends of Animals, Inc.* v. *U.S. Surgical Corporation* is indicative of what might occur in similar circumstances in other jurisdictions, it is unrealistic to expect a result that settles anything or satisfies any party with an ideological interest in the treatment of laboratory animals and the human benefits of animal research.

CHAPTER 14 REFERENCES

1. *Alaska Statutes,* Section 11.61.140(3)(b) (1982 Supp.).
2. *American Jurisprudence*, 2d. ed., vol. 4, sec. 27 (1982).
3. *American Law Reporter*, 2d. ed., vol. 82, sec. 794 (1984).
4. *American Law Reporter*, 2d. ed., vol. 56, sec. 1031 (1984).
5. *Animal Welfare Institute* v. *Kreps*, 561 F.2d 1002, 1007 (D.C. Cir. 1977).
6. Barnes, P., "Animal Advocates Are No Friends to Lawyer," *New Haven (CT) Register*, p. 17 (cols. 1-6), Aug. 17, 1984.
7. Bean, M., *Evolution of National Wildlife Law* (Washington, DC: Council on Environmental Quality, 1977).
8. *BioScience*, "Taub Animal Cruelty Trial Sparks Guideline Review," 32(1):15, 1982.
9. *Brackett* v. *State*, 142 Ga. App. 601, 236 S.E.2d 689 (1977).
10. Brief for Edward Taub, *Edward Taub* v. *Maryland*, 296 Md. 439, 463 A.2d 819 (1983).
11. Brief for State of Maryland, *Edward Taub* v. *Maryland*, 296 Md. 439, 463 A.2d 819 (1983).
12. Burr, S., "Toward Legal Rights for Animals," *Environ. Aff.* 4:205-219, 1975.

13. California, Assembly Bill No. 1735, Legislative Counsel's Digest, 1-10, Mar. 4, 1983.
14. California, Senate Bill No. 883, Legislative Counsel's Digest, Mar. 3, 1983.
15. *California Administrative Code*, Title 17, Sections 1150-1151 (1952).
16. *California Department of Human Resources Development* v. *Java*, 404 U.S. 121, 125 (1971).
17. *California Health and Safety Code*, Sections 1650-1673, 1676-1677 (West Cumulative Pocket Part 1984).
18. *California Penal Code*, Section 599c (West Pocket Part 1984).
19. Chambers, K., and Hines, C., "Recent Developments Concerning the Use of Animals in Medical Research," *J. Leg. Med.* 4(1):109-129, 1983.
20. *Chron. Higher Educ.*, "Cal. Judge Dismisses Animal-Rights Case," 27(18):6, 1984.
21. Coalition to Abolish Metcalf-Hatch, "Metcalf-Hatch Fact Sheet," New York, NY, 1978.
22. Coggins, G., "Wildlife and the Constitution: The Walls Come Tumbling Down," *Wash. Law Rev.* 55:295-358, 1980.
23. *Colorado Revised Statutes*, Sections 25-4-701 to 25-4-714, 25-4-1101 to 25-4-1109, and 35-42-114, (1973) as amended by Senate Bill No. 198, June 2, 1983.
24. *Connecticut General Statutes Annotated*, Sections 22-332a(b), 22-332b (West 1980 & Cumulative Annual Pocket Part 1984).
25. Corbin, C., Attorney General, State of Arizona, Letter to Hon. C. Walker, June 6, 1984.
26. Council of State Governments, *Model State Law to Supplement the Federal Laboratory Animal Welfare Act* (Washington, DC: Council of State Governments, 1970).
27. Curran, W., "Biomedical Laboratories and Criminal Liability for Cruelty to Animals," *N. Engl. J. Med.* 309:1564-1565, 1983.
28. *DeCanes* v. *Bica*, 424 U.S. 351, 360 n.8 (1976).
29. Dichter, A., "Legal Definitions of Cruelty and Animal Rights," *Boston Coll. Environ. Aff. Law Rev.* 7:147-164, 1978.
30. *District of Columbia Code*, Sections 22-812, 22-814 (1892 & Cumulative Annual Pocket Part 1984).
31. Edinger, H., "The Taub Case: A Final Report," *Neurosci. Newsletter* 15(5):6-8, 1984.
32. *Edward Taub* v. *Maryland*, 296 Md. 439, 463 A.2d 819 (Ct.App.Md. 1983).
33. Favre, D., and Loring, M., *Animal Law* (Westport, CT: Quorum Books, 1984).
34. *Florida Statutes Annotated*, Section 828.02 (1965 & Cumulative Annual Pocket Part 1984).
35. *Florida Lime and Avocado Growers, Inc.* v. *Paul*, 373 U.S. 132, 144 (1963).
36. Friend, C., "Animal Cruelty Laws: The Case of Reform," *U. Rich. Law Rev.* 8(2):201-231, 1974.
37. *Friends of Animals, Inc.* v. *U.S. Surgical Corporation*, No. B81-643, Plaintiff's Complaint (D. Conn. filed Dec. 29, 1981).
38. *Friends of Animals, Inc.* v. *U.S. Surgical Corporation*, No. B81-643, Defendant's Motion to Dismiss Complaint (D. Conn. filed Feb. 8, 1982).
39. *Friends of Animals, Inc.* v. *U.S. Surgical Corporation*, No. B81-643, Plaintiff's Motion for Voluntary Dismissal (D. Conn. filed Feb. 12, 1982).
40. *Friends of Animals, Inc.* v. *U.S. Surgical Corporation*, No. B81-643, Memorandum Order Dismissing Plaintiff's Complaint Without Prejudice (D. Conn. entered Feb. 17, 1982).
41. *Friends of Animals, Inc.* v. *U.S. Surgical Corporation*, CV 82-0202829S, Plaintiff's Complaint (Conn. Super. Ct. filed Feb. 10, 1982).
42. *Friends of Animals, Inc.* v. *U.S. Surgical Corporation*, CV 82-0202829S, Plaintiff's Motion to Amend Complaint (Conn. Super. Ct. filed Apr. 6, 1982).
43. *Friends of Animals, Inc.* v. *U.S. Surgical Corporation*, CV 82-0202829S, Defendant's Motion to Strike and Memorandum in Support of Motion to Strike (Conn. Super. Ct. filed Apr. 12, 1982).
44. *Friends of Animals, Inc.* v. *U.S. Surgical Corporation*, CV 82-0202829S, Defendant's Motion to Strike Amended Complaint and Memorandum in Support of Motion to Strike (Conn. Super. Ct. filed May 19, 1982).
45. *Friends of Animals, Inc.* v. *U.S. Surgical Corporation*, CV 82-0202829S, Memorandum of Decision on Motion to Strike No. 105 and Motion to Strike No. 107 (Conn. Super. Ct. entered Dec. 7, 1982 - Reynolds, J.).
46. *Friends of Animals, Inc.* v. *U.S. Surgical Corporation*, CV 82-0202829S, Plaintiff's Substituted Complaint (Conn. Super. Ct. filed Dec. 21, 1982).
47. *Friends of Animals, Inc.* v. *U.S. Surgical Corporation*, CV 82-0202829S, Defendant's Motion for Entry of Judgment on Motion to Strike (Conn. Super. Ct. filed Dec. 22, 1982).
48. *Friends of Animals, Inc.* v. *U.S. Surgical Corporation*, B82-744, Plaintiff's Complaint (D. Conn. filed Dec. 29, 1982).
49. *Friends of Animals, Inc.* v. *U.S. Surgical Corporation*, B82-744, Plaintiff's Motion for Leave to Amend Complaint (D. Conn. filed Apr. 21, 1983).
50. *Friends of Animals, Inc.* v. *U.S. Surgical Corporation*, CV 82-0202829S, Defendant's Request to Revise Substituted Complaint (Conn. Super. Ct. filed May 9, 1983).
51. *Friends of Animals, Inc.* v. *U.S. Surgical Corporation*, CV 82-0202829S, Plaintiff's Request to Withdraw Complaint and Motion to Set Aside

Judgement of Dismissal (Conn. Super. Ct. filed Aug. 23, 1983).
52. *Friends of Animals, Inc.* v. *U.S. Surgical Corporation,* No. B82-744, Plaintiff's Motion to Dismiss with Prejudice (D. Conn. filed Aug. 23, 1984).
53. *Georgia Code Annotated*, Section 16-12-4(b) (1972 & Cumulative Annual Pocket Part 1984).
54. Grunewald, C., "Firm Performing Surgery on Live Dogs," *The Hartford (CT) Sunday Advocate*, p. A1 (col. 1), Nov. 8, 1981.
55. Grunewald, C., "Suit Against U.S. Surgical Ended," *The Hartford (CT) Advocate*, pp. A1 (col. 1), A14, Sept. 8, 1984.
56. Harris, R., "UC Lab's Use of Monkeys Investigated," *San Francisco Examiner*, pp. B1, B8, Feb. 3, 1984.
57. *Hines* v. *Davidowitz*, 312 U.S. 52, 57 (1941).
58. Holzer, H. (ed.), *Anim. Rights Law Rep.* (Int. Soc. for Anim. Rights, Clarks Summit, PA), October 1983, pp. 10-11.
59. Holzer, H., (ed.) *Anim. Rights Law Rep.* (Int. Soc. for Anim. Rights, Clarks Summit, PA) April 1983, pp. 7, 9-10.
60. Holzer, H. (ed.), *Anim. Rights Law Rep.* (Int. Soc. for Anim. Rights, Clarks Summit, PA), July 1981, p. 8.
61. *Illinois Annotated Statutes*, Title 111-1/2, Section 129 (Smith-Hurd 1975 & Cumulative Annual Pocket Part 1984).
62. *In re William G.,* 52 Md. App. 131, 447 A.2d 493 (1982).
63. *Indiana Code Annotated*, Section 35-46-3-2(f) (Burns 1975 & Cumulative Pocket Supplement 1984).
64. *International Society for Animal Rights Report* (Int. Soc. for Anim. Rights, Clarks Summit, PA) April 1985, pp. 1-2.
65. *Iowa Code Annotated*, Sections 162.1-162.12 and 351A.1-351A.7 (West 1949 & Cumulative Annual Pocket Part 1984).
66. Joint Brief of Animal Legal Defense Fund and Animal Legal Defense Fund-Boston, Inc., as *Amici Curiae* for State of Maryland, *Edward Taub* v. *Maryland*, 296 Md. 439, 463 A.2d 819 (1983).
67. *Kansas Statutes Annotated*, Sections 21-4310 and 47-1709 to 47-1718 (1977 & Cumulative Pocket Part Supplement 1983).
68. *King* v. *Smith*, 392 U.S. 309, 316-318 (1968).
69. LaRene, S., *Michigan Humane Society Handbook of Animal Cruelty Law* (Detroit, MI: Michigan Humane Society, Rev. Ed. 1983).
70. LaRene, S., *Michigan Humane Society Handbook of Animal Cruelty Law: Illinois Supplement* (Detroit, MI: Michigan Humane Society, 1983).
71. LaRene, S., *Michigan Humane Society Handbook of Animal Cruelty Law: New York Supplement* (Detroit, MI: Michigan Humane Society, 1983).
72. *Lab Anim.*, "Pound Bill Fails," 13(4):13, 1984.
73. Lauter, D., "Dr. Taub's Animal House," *Nat. Law J.* 4:11, 1982.
74. Leavitt, E. (ed.), *Animals and Their Legal Rights* (Washington, DC: Animal Welfare Institute, Third Ed. 1978).
75. *Maryland Public Health Code Annotated* Art. 27, Sections 57, 59, 67, 67B, 70D (1976 & Cumulative Supplement 1984).
76. *Maryland* v. *Taub* (Dist. Ct. Md., Crim. No. 11848-81).
77. *Massachusetts General Laws Annotated*, Ch. 140, Sections 136A, 140, 151, 151A, 152, 153, and 174D, *as amended by* Acts of 1983, Ch. 631, sections 1-10.
78. *Massachusetts Society for the Prevention of Cruelty to Animals* v. *Commissioner of Public Health*, 339 Mass. 216, 158 N.E.2d 487 (1959).
79. *McCulloch* v. *Maryland*, 17 U.S. (4 Wheat.) 316, 405 (1819)(Marshall, C.J.).
80. McDonald, K., "Mass. Law May Cut Use of Dogs in Research," *Chron. Higher Educ.* 27(19):1, 1984.
81. Medlock, A., Executive Director, New England Anti-Vivisection Society, Boston, MA, personal communication, Jan. 13, 1984.
82. Melby, E., Dean, New York State College of Veterinary Medicine, Cornell University, Ithaca, NY, letter to A. Haffner, Mar. 14, 1980.
83. Messenger, P., Deputy Attorney, Maricopa County, AZ, personal communication, June 20, 1984.
84. *Michigan Compiled Laws Annotated*, Sections 12.580(21)-12.580(34), 14.15(2671)- 14.15(2686) (1948, 1975 & Cumulative Annual Pocket Part 1984).
85. *Michigan Compiled Laws Annotated*, Section 752.21 (1968, 1975 & Cumulative Annual Pocket Part 1984).
86. *Miller* v. *Clairborne,* 211 Kan. 264, 505 P.2d 732 (1973).
87. *Minnesota Statutes Annotated*, Sections 35.7, 346.35-346.44 (West 1972 & Cumulative Annual Pocket Part 1984).
88. Morrison, A., and Hand, P., "The Taub Case" (letter to the editor), *Science* 225:878, 1984.
89. National Association for Biomedical Research, *State Laws Concerning the Use of Animals in Research* (Washington, DC: Foundation for Biomedical Research, 1985).
90. *National League of Cities* v. *Usery*, 426 U.S. 833, 842 (1976).
91. *New Jersey Society for the Prevention of Cruelty*

to Animals v. *Board of Education of City of East Orange,* 91 N.J. Super. 81, 219 A.2d 200 (1966), aff'd. 227 A.2d 506 (1967).
92. *New Jersey Statutes Annotated,* Sections 4:22-15 to 4:22-26 (West 1973 & Cumulative Annual Pocket Part 1984).
93. *New York Laws,* Article 26, Section 353 (McKinney 1972, 1975 & Cumulative Annual Pocket Part 1984).
94. *North Carolina General Statutes,* Section 19A-37 (1969, 1975 & Cumulative Supplement 1981).
95. *Ohio Revised Code Annotated,* Sections 955.16-955.18 (Page 1958, 1964, 1968, 1969, 1975, 1979 & Supplement 1982).
96. *Oklahoma Statutes Annotated,* Title 4, Sections 391-399 (West 1958 & Cumulative Annual Pocket Part 1984).
97. *Pennsylvania Statutes Consolidated Annotated,* Sections 459-201 to 459-218 (Purdon 1971, 1973 & Cumulative Annual Pocket Part 1984).
98. *Ray* v. *Atlantic Richfield Company,* 435 U.S. 151, 156 (1978).
99. *Rhode Island General Laws,* Section 4-19-12 (1956 & Pocket Supplement 1984).
100. *Rice* v. *Santa Fe Elevator Corporation,* 331 U.S. 218 (1947).
101. Rowan, A.N., *Of Mice, Models, & Men: A Critical Evaluation of Animal Research* (Albany, NY: State University of New York Press, 1984).
102. Samuels, W., "Massachusetts Loses; Michigan Wins; Animal Welfare Bills Total 78," *Physiologist* 27:73, 1984.
103. *South Dakota Compiled Laws Annotated,* Sections 34-14-6 to 34-14-15 (1967 & Pocket Supplement 1984).
104. *State* v. *Stockton,* 85 Ariz. 153, 333 P.2d 735 (1958).
105. *State* v. *Kaneakua,* 61 Hawaii 136, 597 P.2d 590 (1979).
106. Taylor, D., Attorney for U.S. Surgical Corporation, Washington, DC, personal communication, Aug. 3, 1984.
107. *Tennessee Code Annotated,* Sections 44-17-109 to 44-17-116 (1975 & Cumulative Supplement 1984).
108. *The Fund for Animals,* "Fund Sues Los Angeles County," 16(4), 1983.
109. Tischler, J., "Rights for Nonhuman Animals: A Guardianship Model for Dogs and Cats," *San Diego Law Rev.* 14:484-506, 1977.
110. *Townsend* v. *Swank,* 404 U.S. 282, 292 (1971) (Burger, C.J., concurring).
111. U.S. Constitution, Article I, Section 8, clause 18.
112. U.S. Constitution, Article I, Section 10, clause 1.
113. U.S. Congress, Senate Committee on Agriculture, Nutrition, and Forestry, *Improved Standards for Laboratory Animals,* hearing on S. 657, July 20, 1983, Serial No. 98-470 (Washington, D.C.: U.S. Government Printing Office, 1984).
114. United Press International, "Group Protests Research on Animals," June 19, 1984.
115. *U. Colo. Law Rev.,* Note, "Federal Preemption: A New Method for Invalidating State Laws Designed to Protect Endangered Species," 47(2):261,265-268, 1976.
116. *Utah Code Annotated,* Sections 26-26-2, -3, (1981) and 76-9:301 (1981), 1984 Cumulative Pocket Supplement.
117. *Virginia Code,* Sections 18.2-403.1 to 18.2-403.3, and 29-213.36 to 29.213.100 (1975) as added by Chapter 492, Acts of 1984.
118. Wiggins, C., "Federalism Balancing and the Burger Court: California's Nuclear Law as a Preemption Case Study," *U.C. Davis Law Rev.* 13(1):1-87, 1979.
119. *Winkler* v. *Colorado Department of Health,* 193 Colo. 170, 564 P.2d 107 (1977).
120. Winters, M., "Cetacean Rights Under Human Laws," *San Diego Law Rev.* 21:911-940, 1984.
121. *Wisconsin Statutes Annotated,* Section 174.13 (West 1979 & Cumulative Annual Pocket Part 1984).
122. Wise, S., "Law-Medicine Notes: The Use of Animals in Research" (letter to the editor), *N. Engl. J. Med.* 311: 337, 1984.
123. Wolsch, R., Memorandum to D. Fisher, U.S. Surgical Corporation, Norwalk, CT, Nov. 9, 1981.
124. Zurvalec, L., "Use of Animals in Medical Research: The Need for Governmental Regulation," *Wayne Law Rev.* 24(5):1733-1751, 1978.

Chapter 15

Institutional and Self-Regulation of Animal Use

The public fears and distrusts science. Regulation—any regulation—may in the end make them fear it less. But scientists themselves have a duty, I believe, not just to argue their own case but to argue it in a manner acceptable to society as a whole. . . . [Fear] must be allayed if at all by scientists and doctors themselves, making their own case and making it intelligibly in public.

Baroness Mary Warnock
Girton College, Cambridge
Br. Med. J. 291: 187-190, 1985

What's happening in Washington is a red herring. The issue of the use of animals in research won't be resolved on Capitol Hill. The real action is right here on your front door step.

William M. Samuels
American Physiological Society
Address given at the University of South Florida Medical Center
March 21, 1984

CONTENTS

Table

List of Figures

Chapter 15

Institutional and Self-Regulation of Animal Use

The most important check on the proper treatment of animals is the conscience of the individual investigator (23). A person's view about animal welfare is influenced by many forces; some of the most formidable include exposure to professional peers, mentors, and formal course work on animal care or the ethics of animal experimentation.

Beyond individual conscience, the most visible means of self-regulation is institutional committee review of animal care and use. The use of animals is also overseen by the peer review of scientific colleagues and others outside of the research facility—an important part of the grants administration process.

In addition, most scientists are members of one or more professional associations, some of which have codes of ethics for research with animal subjects. These statements of principles can serve to inspire ethical behavior and alert researchers to ethical issues raised by their work. Codes can sometimes provide advice on specific cases and sanctions for violations (reviewed in ref. 21).

REVIEW OF ANIMAL CARE AND USE

All research supported by the Public Health Service (PHS), including that of the National Institutes of Health (NIH), is subject to the provisions of the PHS *Policy on Humane Care and Use of Laboratory Animals by Awardee Institutions* (revision effective Dec. 31, 1985) (44). Each institution so funded must submit an acceptable assurance to NIH's Office for Protection from Research Risks (OPRR) that commits the facility to active promotion of compliance with the policy and the NIH *Guide for the Care and Use of Laboratory Animals* (42).

The NIH peer-review system can be construed as external rather than self-regulation (46). Site visits to determine compliance can occur, and funding can be terminated for lack of compliance with contractual assurances, as happened in the *Taub* case (see ch. 14). In the broadest sense, however, NIH is fully dependent on grant recipients for effective policing of its provisions.

The enactment in 1985 of Public Law 99-158 (see ch. 13) provided statutory authority and recognition for some provisions of the PHS policy, requiring, for example, all entities conducting research with PHS funds to organize and operate institutional animal care and use committees. Also in 1985, amendments to the Animal Welfare Act (see ch. 13) extended the mandate for institutional committee oversight to research facilities covered by the Animal Welfare Act and to Federal research facilities.

NIH Assurance Review

To test the operation of written assurances of compliance with the PHS policy regarding humane care and treatment of experimental animals by investigators in the field, and perhaps in response to congressional and public pressure, the NIH Office of Extramural Research and Training in 1983 conducted site visits to 10 grantee facilities (43). These institutions were chosen from a stratified sample of the more than 800 awardees with general assurances on file at the NIH Office for Protection from Research Risks.

The 10 institutions were distributed among those receiving more than $10 million in annual support from NIH (3 institutions), between $5 million and $10 million (3 institutions), and less than $5 million (4 institutions). The sample was further defined by selecting institutions from each of those categories with valid written assurances on file but lacking accreditation by the American Association for Accreditation of Laboratory Animal Care (AAALAC). Awardee institutions were notified of the prospective visits by publication of the selection criteria and the site names (43), and the NIH chairperson notified the appropriate institutional representative(s) at least 1 month prior to the scheduled visit.

Site-visit team size depended on the size of the institution and the complexity of its physical facilities. At a minimum, teams consisted of a veterinarian, a biological scientist engaged in research using animals, and an NIH scientist/administrator. In addition, non-Federal consultants were included "with a view towards ensuring impartiality and enhancing expertise" (43). Between June and September 1983, the 10 site visits were conducted to receive information and impressions in order to answer the following questions:

- Is NIH's current assurance system adequate for promoting the proper care and use of animals involved in federally funded biomedical research?
- If it is adequate, how can it be further improved?
- If it is not adequate, what alternatives should be considered?

The NIH site visits were generally criticized within the animal welfare community on three grounds:

- 10 institutions may not represent a sizable enough sample to generate sufficiently representative data on which to base policy;
- the 1-month advance notification to the institutions to be visited may have skewed the findings; and
- too few smaller institutions were visited, since the majority of NIH-funded recipients fall into the unaccredited, less-than-$5-million category.

Despite these potential shortcomings, information generated by the 10 site visits led NIH to draw conclusions and make recommendations about the PHS policy regarding laboratory-animal welfare.

In early 1984, NIH reported on the site visits (43). Based on the finding of these visits, two general conclusions were reached:

- Reliance upon voluntary compliance with PHS policy and recommendations in the NIH *Guide* is a realistic approach to fostering proper care and use of laboratory animals in biomedical research. There is no reason to believe that regular NIH inspections are needed or would be more effective than the traditional assurance process.
- The present assurance system should be strengthened by modifying the 1979 PHS policy on animal welfare to promote more conscientious involvement by both NIH and its awardee institutions.

In addition, the report stated that "no incidents of animal abuse were observed" (43).

From the findings of the site-visit teams, a series of recommendations concerning the adequacy of the current policy and its enforcement were made. The site-visit report recommended that NIH:

- undertake a program for helping institutional officials, scientists, and responsible veterinarians "understand fully their responsibilities" for policy implementation;
- expand the policy to include "more specific information regarding responsibilities of the institution that receives funds for research involving the use of animals," including new and more specific assurances to be negotiated with institutions receiving funds "carefully and promptly";
- modify the policy to define more precisely institutional responsibilities, "particularly the role of the animal welfare committee," to which the appointment of a nonscientist and a person unaffiliated with the institution should be given serious consideration;
- conduct or sponsor a survey to assess whether the number of veterinarians trained in laboratory-animal science is sufficient to meet the needs of institutions conducting biomedical research involving animals; and
- conduct further assessments of the assurance process, including visiting more awardee institutions receiving total annual support of less than $5 million, since that category of institutions is the largest with assurance statements on file (43).

In response to the above recommendations and criticisms, five additional institutions receiving less than $5 million were visited in 1984. Using the same protocol as before, visits were made to a stratified sample of institutions without AAALAC accreditation during the months of July and August 1984. The site-visit teams consisted of a representative of the NIH Office of Extramural Research and Training, a scientist or administrator from OPRR, and two non-Federal consultants (a veterinarian experienced in laboratory-animal medicine and a biomedical scientist currently conducting research requiring laboratory animals) (44).

The conclusions following these additional visits are almost identical to the earlier ones. The teams noted that the small institutions were capable of both meeting the responsibilities of the 1979 PHS policy and assuming additional responsibilities in response to changes made in the 1985 PHS policy. The site visitors did find, however, that these institutions needed to improve the advisory and oversight roles of their institutional animal care and use committees (IACUCs) and upgrade their veterinary oversight (44).

Public Health Service Policy

In mid-1985, the Department of Health and Human Services (DHHS) released its new PHS *Policy on Humane Care and Use of Laboratory Animals by Awardee Institutions* (44) to replace the 1979 PHS *Extramural Animal Welfare Policy* (41). (For the full text of the new policy, see app. C.) This new policy is a result of the proposed PHS policy (43), the conclusions from the 15 site visits to animal care facilities by NIH, and 340 written and oral comments on the proposed policy. It took effect December 31, 1985, for all potential grantees of PHS wishing to use animals in experimentation.

This policy has many of the same features as the 1979 version. It applies to all PHS-supported activities involving animals in the United States. Animal is defined as "any live, vertebrate animal used or intended for use in research, research training, experimentation or biological testing or for related purposes." The Public Health Service includes the Alcohol, Drug Abuse, and Mental Health Administration; the Centers for Disease Control; the Food and Drug Administration; the Health Resources and Services Administration; and the National Institutes of Health. The policy relies on the NIH *Guide for the Care and Use of Laboratory Animals* for the standards for animal care and treatment. Finally, the PHS policy is based on a set of overall principles governing animal experimentation. The 1979 policy was based on 12 principles on the use of animals. The new policy implements and supplements the "Principles for the Utilization and Care of Vertebrate Animals Used in Testing, Research, and Training" (50 FR 20864) prepared by the U.S. Interagency Research Animal Committee (see ch. 13, box A). The principles contained in these two documents are very similar.

Two major requirements form the core of the PHS policy—the institutional animal welfare assurance to NIH and an institutional animal care and use committee. Each institution wishing to obtain PHS funding for a research project involving animals must have on file with NIH's Office for Protection from Research Risks a written assurance setting forth compliance with this policy. The assurance must describe in detail the institution's program for the care and use of animals in PHS-supported activities including:

- a list of every branch and major component of the institution;
- the lines of authority and responsibility for administering the program (each institution must identify an official who is ultimately responsible for the institution's animal program);
- the qualifications, authority, and responsibility of the veterinarian who will participate in the program;
- the membership list of the IACUC;
- the procedures that the IACUC will follow to implement this policy;
- the health-care practices for personnel who work with laboratory animals or their facilities; and
- the gross square footage of each animal facility (including satellite facilities), the species housed therein, and the average daily inventory, by species, of animals in each facility.

In addition, each assurance must categorize the evaluation of its program and facilities as either accredited by AAALAC or as evaluated by the institution itself. The second category requires that the IACUC assess its own program every year and maintain records on the nature and extent of the institution's adherence to the NIH *Guide* and the PHS policy. This report must also contain justifications for any departures from the policy. Deficiencies in an institution's program or facilities must be reported to NIH and the institution must adhere to an approved time frame for correction of the deficiencies.

The animal care and use committee required by the new PHS policy is specifically structured to consist of at least five members including:

> . . . one Doctor of Veterinary Medicine with training or experience in laboratory animal medicine, one practicing scientist experienced in research involving animals, one member whose primary concerns are in a nonscientific area, and one individual who is not affiliated with the institution in any way other than as a member of the IACUC.

New duties of this committee include reviewing the institution's program for animal care and use and inspecting the facilities (including satellites) at least annually. The policy also authorizes the IACUC to suspend any activity involving animals that is found to not be in compliance with the policy.

A new power of the IACUC is to "review and approve, require modifications in (to secure approval), or withhold approval of those sections of PHS applications or proposals related to the care and use of animals." The policy gives a detailed plan for the administrative structure to handle this task, along with certain specific animal care requirements that must be met by each proposal (e.g., minimization of discomfort of animals). Each application or proposal submitted to PHS must verify that the IACUC has approved those sections of the proposal related to the care and use of laboratory animals. It should be submitted along with the application but may be sent directly to the executive secretary of the initial review group within 60 days of the original submission. Figure 15-1 is the example NIH provides of an acceptable verification letter for a proposal. The letter must be signed either by the institutional official who signed the institution's Animal Welfare Assurance or by another individual authorized by the institution to provide verification of IACUC approval.

The PHS policy is implemented by the NIH's Office for Protection from Research Risks, which is responsible for approving, disapproving, or withdrawing approval of institutional assurances. It also has the power to evaluate allegations of noncompliance with the policy and to conduct site visits to selected institutions to check for proper implementation of the policy.

The new PHS policy differs from the 1979 version in the following ways:

- Institutions are required to designate clear lines of authority and responsibility for those involved in animal care and use in PHS-supported projects, including an institutional officer responsible for the entire program.
- The role and responsibilities of the IACUC have been upgraded. The requirements of specific types of committee members (e.g., a member unaffiliated with the institution or a member in a nonscientific area) are new, as is the policy that these committees review and approve those sections of research applications for PHS funding that relate to the care and use of animals before they are actually funded.
- If an institution is not AAALAC-accredited, stringent standards for self-assurances apply and more information about animal facilities must be made available to NIH.
- Following the policy is mandatory, as opposed to the earlier "commitment to comply."
- Recordkeeping requirements for institutions are explicitly addressed. Records of IACUC meeting deliberations, assurance forms, accrediting body determinations, and so forth must be maintained for 3 years and made accessible for inspection to PHS officials.
- OPRR has power to "evaluate allegations of noncompliance with the policy [and] . . . conduct site visits to selected institutions."

In general, the Public Health Service now has a much more structured animal welfare policy that specifically designates what individual institutions must do in order to achieve satisfactory compliance. The old policy had many of the same structures (e.g., institutional committees and assurances) but in a form that allowed different degrees of institutional animal care and treatment responsibility. The new policy defines a minimum standard animal care and use policy for an institution that wishes to obtain PHS funding. In 1979, OPRR released a sample assurance that was two pages long and only required a few specifics from the insti-

Figure 15-1.—Example of Acceptable Verification for Grant Submission to NIH

[Date]

Division of Research Grants
National Institutes of Health
5333 Westbard Avenue
Westwood Building, Room 240
Bethesda, Maryland 20205

Dear Sir:

The following application submitted to the Public Health Service was reviewed and approved by this institution's Animal Care and Use Committee on [insert date of approval]:

Title of application:

Name of principal investigator:

Name of institution:

This institution has an Animal Welfare Assurance on file with the Office for Protection from Research Risks. The Assurance number is [insert old assurance number until a new assurance number is assigned].

As a condition of approval, this institution's Animal Care and Use Committee required the following modifications to the above referenced application:

[This information is required when the modifications are not reflected in the original grant application or contract proposal.]

[Signature]
[Title]

SOURCE: Adapted from U.S. Department of Health and Human Services, Public Health Service, National Institutes of Health, "Laboratory Animal Welfare," *NIH Guide for Grants and Contracts* 14(8): June 25, 1985.

tution. The new sample assurance, released in 1985, is seven pages long, including two tables (one on membership of the IACUC and one summarizing the institution's individual animal facilities, their square footage, the species within, and the average daily inventory of species), and requires specific detailed data on the institution's animal welfare program.

REVIEW BY COMMITTEE

Recourse to committees to sort through a thicket of value questions occasioned by advances in biomedicine, and in particular biomedical research, is not unique to the area of research with animals. For example, there has been a recent explosion of interest in the formation of hospital ethics committees to develop policies and consult in individual cases. According to one newspaper account, "quietly and without fanfare, hundreds of American hospitals are organizing internal ethics committees that are coming to play crucial roles . . . involving life and death decisions for thousands of patients" (24).

Concern in this country about the objects of research—and the link between animal and human subjects—has been evident for decades. A recently published historical account describes nontherapeutic research into the cause of syphilis conducted at the beginning of the century and reviews the reaction to the use of orphans and hospital patients who had not given their consent. The result was a nearly 20-year campaign against "human vivisection" conducted by antivivisectionists who saw the use of human beings without their consent in nontherapeutic research as the logical outcome of a science built on animal suffering: "To whomsoever, in the cause of Science, the agony of a dying rabbit is of no consequence, it is likely that the old or worthless man which in the cause of learning may well be sacrificed" (22). A number of State and Federal legislative initiatives proposed 60 to 70 years ago regarding animal research were amended to regulate "human vivisection" as well.

Some egregious violations of human rights in the name of medical research occurred earlier in this century. The experiments conducted on prisoners of war during World War II that were revealed at Nuremberg are the most notorious and well-known examples; the trials resulted in a code of ethics to guide future research. Haunted by the specter of patently unethical and scientifically unsound research conducted by Nazi physicians, some commentators began to complain that it was not only in wartime that the rights of human subjects had been overlooked. In an influential series of articles by an American physician (12) and a British physiologist (28), hundreds of experiments published in major medical journals were reviewed, revealing many instances in which research subjects were abused or misinformed. In addition, there was concern that certain segments of the population—blacks, the poor, women, or the elderly —were bearing a disproportionate share of the burden of being research subjects.

In response to such revelations about the exploitation of vulnerable populations, a number of institutional review boards (IRBs) were set up in the mid-1960s under Federal regulations to oversee research with human subjects. Of all the committees formed to respond to value questions raised by medical practice and biomedical and behavioral research, IRBs have the most obvious parallels to animal care and use committees. Many of the questions raised now about committees on animals—whether they can both protect animal subjects and abet the scientific enterprise, whether they function to minimize pain and suffering in experiments, or are mere window dressings for public relations purposes—have been addressed in 15 years of experience with committees on human subjects. This experience includes not only the establishment of IRBs within institutions and oversight of the process through the general assurance process monitored by OPRR (31), but also frequent conferences, a spate of academic literature, and the publication of a journal devoted exclusively to the human-subjects review process, which includes case studies reviewing problematic protocols.

ANIMAL CARE AND USE COMMITTEES

Roles and Responsibilities

One commentator has summarized the potential functions for animal care and use committees as (26):

- to ensure compliance with local, State, and Federal laws and regulations on animal care and use;
- to inspect animal care facilities;
- to review protocols for animal welfare issues;
- to assess the qualifications of investigators;
- to oversee student use of animals;
- to advise on institutional needs, costs of animals, and animal procurement policies;
- to control allocation of animals within the institution;
- to act as a resource on animal welfare issues and to educate the university community and the community at large on animal welfare issues; and
- to serve as a community complaint forum.

Each IACUC may be mandated to perform all or some of the above responsibilities. Some committees oversee the care of all the research animals housed in an institution. This may include ensuring compliance with local, State, and Federal regulations; inspecting facilities; and advising on matters of care and feeding, design of facilities, and resource allocation. Some of the most difficult problems in this regard have been encountered in large institutions with farflung, decentralized facilities that may house only a few animals for use by individual researchers or small groups of students. Small, satellite facilities can present problems in ventilation, sanitation, care, and oversight during weekends and holidays (25). Some universities have countered this problem by centralizing a procurement system, so that the purchase of an animal by a researcher anywhere in the university triggers oversight mechanisms (32). At a minimum, the IACUC must comply with the PHS policy committee requirements.

According to NIH, approximately 26 percent of existing animal care and use committees review research protocols (25). Under the new PHS policy, all IACUCs will be required to approve all sections of each research protocol that involves animals. Some committees have established a system of expedited review where only protocols that raise questions regarding pain and suffering are considered by the full committee. More innocuous projects are reviewed perfunctorily by smaller subcommittees. Rating scales have been established for expedited reviews. One suggestion of such a scale has five categories, detailing a range of degree of harm inflicted on animals. This proposal, already in place in some form in a number of institutions, is designed to provide a calculus so that "ethical risks" can be weighed against "the benefit in terms of improvement of animal or human health or other societal good" (27). Other committees have a bifurcated review, with parallel processes for considering animal care and ethical issues (32).

In a broad sense, animal welfare concerns are by definition inextricably intertwined with scientific issues. The threshold question of the validity of an animal model approach and the possible availability of alternatives is followed closely by questions of the efficiency of animal use. Is the smallest number of animals of an appropriate species being used? Would a more sophisticated statistical methodology assure this is the case? Are genetic variables manipulated to the extent necessary? Will the data generated by the experiment be understood and of use to other scientists? Does the research answer an important question and has the researcher made sure it does not unintentionally duplicate already published work? Is the researcher qualified to undertake the project? These are among the questions that raise twin concerns of scientific and ethical appropriateness.

The dual nature of the scientific and care review issues were the focus of remarks by one committee proponent (20):

> Concern for the reduction or elimination of pain is inseparable from consideration of the potential scientific value or the benefits to humankind to be derived from the work . . . Decisions about, for example, the species and number of animals to be used, or the necessity for particular invasive procedures, simply cannot be made intelligently without reference to the scientific value of the work; or without an understanding of the scientific discipline represented in the proposal. Research of inferior quality should not be done on any species, regardless of how humanely it is done. Concern for humane treatment of animals is not only consistent with good science, but augments its quality by assuring us of well-maintained and nourished animals that are behaviorally comfortable.

Many people feel that the IACUC is not qualified to judge the science or "scientific merit" of an experiment. Yet, it may be impossible to discuss animal care and use issues without some discussion of the science involved. How does an IACUC draw the line between discussing and approving the animal care and use issues and the scientific merit, feasibility, and potential scientific gain of a particular experiment? Depending on the membership of a particular committee or the institution itself, science issues may or may not be addressed in the approval process. This may lead to an inconsistent system: A proposal that might be modified in one IACUC could be approved in a different committee depending on whether only animal care and use issues were addressed.

In addition to the above functions, animal care and use committees can also play an educational role. The process by which investigators justify their research can be an educational one and the committee can also be used to teach the research community as a whole. The availability of alternatives, ways to avoid unintentional duplication, and amelioration of pain are all subjects the committee can discuss. Some committees also monitor animal welfare legislation and advise institutional officials about pending State and Federal initiatives.

Financial and Procedural Issues

A number of questions about how committees operate involve "housekeeping" details that, as a practical matter, may be as important as substantive concerns. The operation of the committee in terms of recordkeeping and voting has important implications. Whether it operates on a consensus or majority vote may determine how much influence unaffiliated members have. In addition, some committees have provisions for investigators to appeal adverse findings; the rights of investigators in this regard, as well as the legal posture of the committee (and individual members), are still open to question. Other concerns include the committee's ability to monitor current research and to establish procedures ensuring that its advice is followed.

There is a paucity of data on operating costs for animal care and use committees for several reasons. Service on committees is part of the general responsibilities of salaried faculty or institutional officials. Additional overhead costs of office space, support staff, and recordkeeping are also often factored into general budgets. One cost estimate comes from Colorado State University, where the animal research committee costs about $24,000 per year to run, which was 0.43 percent of the university's biomedical research budget (35). In smaller institutions, requirements for more active committees would likely be a great administrative and financial burden, especially with a review process entailing prospective review of all protocols submitted for funding.

The parallel between the institutional review boards and IACUCs is the strongest when discussing procedural matters. The lessons learned by individual institutions in setting up, funding, finding administrative staff support, and structuring IRBs can help IACUCs avoid similar problems.

Membership

Much of the debate about the value of animal care and use committees has focused on who should be on them. One commentator, writing about the use of hospital ethics committees to advise on decisions about seriously ill newborns, maintained (10):

> . . . when it comes to matters of life and death, our society prefers procedure to substance. Instead of asking, "What is the right thing to do?" we ask, "Who should decide?" The attractiveness of such committees probably derives in large measure from their potential for transmuting a hard question (Who shall live?) into a more tractable one (Who shall sit on the committee?).

For animal care and use committees, however, the question may not be quite so tractable after all.

Practicing Research Scientists

Until the recent changes in the PHS policy, which now requires a diverse group of individuals on the IACUC, many institutional committees consisted primarily of practicing research scientists involved with animal research. Their contribution to an IACUC is important because of their knowledge on animal models, research protocols and procedures, and the use of animals in research. These members make sure that the views of the major users of animals are represented. At the same time, they have a conflict of interest with some of the goals of the IACUC since their jobs and livelihood are involved with research on animals. Ensuring their objectivity, therefore, is important.

Veterinarians

Having a veterinarian on the committee is essential since in many cases that person is responsible for the institution's animals. The PHS policy requires that each IACUC have one Doctor of Veterinary Medicine with training or experience in laboratory-animal science and medicine. The veterinarian must implement the institution's animal care and use program on a daily basis. The role of this person on an IACUC is to be the professional-level link between the committee and the daily operation of the institutional program.

Veterinarians for institutions doing animal research have come from all fields of veterinary medicine. In the late 1950s, veterinarians began to enter the specialty known as laboratory-animal medicine. To date, approximately 700 full-time veterinarians are certified in this field (out of a total of about 45,000 nationwide). The two organizations accrediting practitioners of laboratory-animal medicine are the American Society of Laboratory Animal Practitioners and the American College of Laboratory Animal Medicine. These veterinarians, along with any others with experience in laboratory-animal science and medicine, fulfill the PHS requirement on IACUC membership. For small institutions with only a few projects with animals, it can be difficult and costly to obtain a part-time laboratory-animal veterinarian as there are so few of them.

Unaffiliated Members

Most proposals for institutional animal review committees require that one or more persons not affiliated with the research entity (e.g., members of the local community) be included. This would be someone who is primarily responsible for representing community concerns regarding the welfare of animal subjects. This person can bring objectivity to the committee because there is no financial tie between the person and the institution and therefore no conflict of interest. The PHS policy requires one such unaffiliated member. (This person might also fill the nonscientific spot described below, but need not.) An unaffiliated member could well be a research scientist at a different institution.

The unaffiliated members who have generated the most controversy are representatives of the animal welfare and animal rights community. Scientists have feared that the involvement of such people might delay or derail research projects. There have also been concerns about confidentiality and unwarranted disclosure of research ideas in progress, a fear exacerbated in the commercial setting. On the other hand, not unlike individuals with strongly held views opposing capital punishment (who may be challenged during the jury selection process for a capital case), some animal welfare advocates have refused to cooperate with these committees at all.

This leads to another problem: How to certify the bona fides of such a committee member? Is membership in a local humane society sufficient or must it be a particular activist group? Some institutions may have difficulty finding members of the general community, let alone animal welfare advocates, who are willing to expend the considerable time necessary to participate in the process. Animal welfare proponents have complained that the fact they are generally not remunerated for such activities (whereas other committee members may be devoting salaried time to the committee) tends to greatly discourage their participation. (This has generally not been a problem in the human subjects area, however.) Paying unaffiliated members, which some schemes have proposed, would present a "Catch 22" situation: Payment would "affiliate" them with the institution and therefore disqualify them. Even with all these possible problems, many committees have been very successful at opening their deliberations to unaffiliated members.

Nonscientific Members

The presence of nonscientifically trained people on the IACUC has rankled some scientists; others have speculated that the need to translate research questions for nonspecialists "may well necessitate [the investigator's] use of a new vocabulary and new patterns of thought, especially if he is compelled to provide moral justifications for his use of animals" (34,37). Against the wishes of many scientists, the PHS policy requires that one member of the IACUC be from a nonscientific area.

Although nonscientific members are often spoken of as lay members, often they are simply professionals with different backgrounds. Lawyers, members of the clergy, and philosophers with training in bioethics have all been suggested as able to bring relevant outlooks to bear. On occasion, committees may also rely on specialists on an ad hoc basis to review particular projects. A professional statistician, for example, might be consulted in a determination of the appropriate number of animals to be used in a particular protocol.

Animal Care Staff

Many committees include an animal technician or a member of the technical staff who provide the daily service, health care, and personal care of the laboratory animals. Animal technicians, well trained in animal health care, animal maintenance, and facility design, can represent the view of the animal care facility on the committee. Animal care committees with technical staff find these members helpful with issues of protocol review (including whether the protocol can be done within the facility), space allocation, and management issues. On some committees, animal technicians act as full voting members of the IACUC; in others, they act as ad hoc advisory members without voting privileges.

Institutional Representatives

Representatives of the institutional administration are often members of animal care and use committees because of the insights they may have into the overall management of the institution, including the financial constraints under which it operates. Management personnel can often provide information on the physical plant that may bear on care and husbandry issues. For the committees to have clout, it is necessary to have a representative of the office of the president, dean, or provost.

Monitoring the Monitors

How can the successful functioning of animal care and use committees be determined? Some of the committee functions just described translate into fairly accessible benchmarks. The composition of the committees, the number of protocols reviewed, and the types of experiments given full review are all factors that can be examined. Yet even this relatively "hard" data can belie more elusive factors at work. For example, as in the area of human subjects review, often the process by which a committee approves a protocol is one of negotiation, during which an investigator may justify or change the number of animals, or species, or methods of experimental manipulation—a process that would not be reflected in a "yes" or "no" vote.

Since the review process itself is one that is difficult to study, site visits have been relied on to examine committee functioning. In addition to examining minutes of meetings, the composition of the committee, and number and types of protocols approved, site visits can afford the opportunity to interview scientists, committee members, and institutional officials and, perhaps, to sit in on a committee meeting.

THE AAALAC PROCESS

The American Association for Accreditation of Laboratory Animal Care is a voluntary organization that accredits institutions that conduct animal research. According to the group (2):

> . . . [the association] was organized in 1965 to conduct a voluntary program for the accreditation of laboratory animal care facilities and programs. The accreditation program is concerned with encouraging high standards for the care and use of laboratory animals including appropriate veterinary care, controlling variables that might adversely affect animal research, and protecting the health of animal research workers.

AAALAC is governed by a Board of Trustees composed of representatives of 27 professional organizations in education and research, including the American Association for Laboratory Animal Science, American Veterinary Medical Association, Pharmaceutical Manufacturers Association, and American Association for the Advancement of Science. A 16-member Council on Accreditation is appointed by the board to make recommendations. All the Council members have D.V.M. or Ph.D. degrees and are actively involved in laboratory-animal medicine or biomedical science. As of 1985, a total of 483 institutions had received AAALAC accreditation (see app. D) (3). Table 15-1 summarizes the types of facilities that have received accreditation.

To become AAALAC-accredited, a facility must pay a nonrefundable application fee prior to the

Table 15-1.—Distribution of AAALAC-Accredited Facilities by Category

Type of facility	Percent of total
Veterans' Administration medical centers	15
Commercial laboratories	14
Medical schools	13
Pharmaceutical manufacturers	9
Nonprofit research laboratories	9
Government laboratories	8
Hospitals	8
Universities (facilities serving an entire campus)	6
Combined facilities for health schools	4
Dental schools	4
Laboratory animal breeders	3
Colleges of pharmacy	3
Veterinary schools	1
Colleges of biological science	1
Colleges of arts	1
Universities (programs serving only a portion of a campus)	1
College of engineering	1
Total	100

SOURCE: American Association for Accreditation of Laboratory Animal Care, *AAALAC Activities Report*, vol. 13, New Lenox, IL, Apr. 1, 1985.

first site visit. Current application fees range from $1,050 to $1,650, depending on the size of the facility, and annual fees range from $600 to $900. AAALAC uses the NIH *Guide for the Care and Use of Laboratory Animals* as its primary standard for evaluating facilities and programs. In addition, the association recommends these sources about laboratory animal care:

- "Report of the AVMA Panel on Euthanasia" (19) and subsequent revisions.
- *NIH Guidelines for the Laboratory Use of Chemical Carcinogens* (45).
- *Biological Safety Manual for Research Involving Oncogenic Viruses* (40).
- *Classification of Etiologic Agents on the Basis of Hazard* (39) and subsequent revisions.
- Laboratory animal management and standards documents developed by committees of the Institute of Laboratory Animal Resources (3).

The accreditation procedure involves 11 steps. First, an application is requested from AAALAC. The completed application for accreditation is returned to AAALAC, which reviews it and determines whether the applicant is eligible to seek accreditation. After the application fee is paid, the Chairman of the AAALAC Council on Accreditation selects the site-visit team. Normally, this consists of one member of the council and one consultant. The institution is notified of the date and time of the visit and the names of the site visitors and is asked to have assembled materials ready. The site-visit team inspects the laboratory-animal care facility and evaluates all aspects of the animal care program with respect to AAALAC standards. Copies of the report are forwarded to two members of the council, who evaluate it for completeness and clarity. The final site visit report is then reviewed by the council during its next scheduled council meeting, and the accreditation status of the applicant is determined. The Board of Trustees confirms the action of the council. Finally, the applicant institution is provided with a letter summarizing the conclusions of the council (3).

After the initial site visit, an institution can be awarded full accreditation, provisional accreditation, or accreditation can be withheld. For accredited institutions, AAALAC reinspects facilities once every 3 years and can either decide to continue accreditation, provide a probationary accreditation while deficiencies are corrected, or revoke accreditation. Sixty-six percent (483 out of 731) of the institutions applying for accreditation since 1965 have received it.

Although AAALAC is a private, voluntary organization, its decisions carry great weight because the PHS recognizes AAALAC accreditation as a demonstration of institutional compliance with PHS policies. Moreover, the NIH *Guide for the Care and Use of Laboratory Animals* is the benchmark AAALAC uses in assessing the adequacy of laboratory facilities, sanitation, veterinary care, animal husbandry, and such basic but important details such as cage size. Approximately 25 percent of the close to 1,000 institutions with approved assurances on file with NIH are AAALAC-accredited.

POLICIES OF SCIENTIFIC AND PROFESSIONAL SOCIETIES

A number of scientific societies and professional organizations associated with science and research have generated policies on the standards of conduct expected of their members in the care or use of animals. Some of these are simple statements of support for research use and for humane care of research animals in accordance with Federal and State laws and the NIH *Guide.* For example, the American Association for Laboratory Animal Science (AALAS), an organization that emphasizes improved animal care and personnel training (13), has issued a four-paragraph statement of this nature (1). It states, in part: "The AALAS is committed to the principles of humane care and treatment of laboratory animals and endorses membership compliance with established scientific and legal standards."

The AALAS policy statement also contains some of the strong language that has only recently begun to appear in statements of scientific and professional organizations:

> Many of the factors that affect both animal and human life can only be studied in intact animal

> systems by systematically manipulating specific research variables. Given an incomplete knowledge of biological systems, it is inconceivable that animal experimentation can be replaced, in the foreseeable future, by mechanical models or other incomplete biological systems.

Several organizations have developed more comprehensive policies. These statements of principle have tended to evolve from early concern with solely humane animal care to a concentration on the humane care and use of animals.

Ethical standards and policies may be developed in a variety of ways. Some are prepared by committees or boards composed of members from different areas of research within a given discipline (e.g., American Psychological Association), from many countries (e.g., International Association for the Study of Pain), from several disciplines (e.g., Federation of American Societies for Experimental Biology), from the faculties and communities associated with a university (e.g., University of Southern California), or from within industry (e.g., Smith Kline & French Laboratories). Guidelines may also be issued by a professional society as part of the requirements for publication of research reports in a society's journal (e.g., Society for the Study of Reproduction).

The comprehensive statements of well-established organizations are examined here to provide insight into both the development and the promulgation of policies affecting large numbers of research investigators and their experimental subjects. The guidelines of the societies and associations reviewed by OTA share certain common elements, in that they all support or require:

- humane care and use of animals in accordance with relevant laws and the NIH guidelines;
- use of minimum numbers of animals of an appropriate species;
- limitations of the time and/or degree of allowable pain or discomfort during chronic experiments;
- use of proper types and amounts of analgesics or anesthesics or of euthanasia to prevent or terminate excessive pain during acute experiments; and
- assurance that all animal experiments are conducted by or under the supervision of qualified personnel.

Beyond these common elements, most policy statements contain principles tailored to the specific research interests of each organization's members. The *Animal Care Guidelines* of the Animal Behavior Society, for example, offer instruction on the observation of natural populations (9):

> Observation of free-living animals in their natural habitat may involve disruption, particularly if feeding, trapping, or marking is involved. While field studies may further scientific knowledge and advance awareness of human responsibility towards animal life, the investigator should always weigh any potential gain in knowledge against the adverse consequences of disruption for the animals used as subjects and also for other animals in the ecosystem.

American Psychological Association

The American Psychological Association (APA) was founded in 1892 to advance the understanding of basic behavioral principles and to contribute to the improvement of human health and welfare. Today, there are approximately 61,700 members of the APA in research, education, and clinical practice. Policies adopted in 1979, entitled *Principles for the Care and Use of Animals,* were designed to be posted in all facilities and included several additions to the common elements listed previously. They read, in part (5):

> All research conducted by members of the American Psychological Association or published in its journals must conform to these Principles.
>
> Investigators are strongly urged to consult with the Committee on Animal Research and Experimentation at any stage preparatory to or during a research project for advice about the appropriateness of research procedures or ethical issues related to experiments involving animals.
>
> Apparent violations of these Principles shall be reported immediately to the facility supervisor whose signature appears below.
>
> All persons in each laboratory, classroom, or applied facility shall indicate by signature and date . . . that they have read these Principles.

Although the issues of ethics and responsibility were briefly addressed in the 1979 *Principles,* the APA soon felt that a more complete statement was needed. The principles were extensively revised and issued in 1985 as the *Guidelines for Ethical Conduct in the Care and Use of Animals* (6).

The most comprehensive document of its type, the APA *Guidelines* is a detailed statement covering all aspects of animal care and use—personnel, facilities, acquisition of animals, care and housing, experimental design and procedures, field research, educational use of animals, and disposition and disposal of animals. The importance of the use of sound ethical judgment is reiterated throughout, and the new guidelines are to be signed by a supervisor and an administrative official and posted wherever animals are maintained or used.

The APA statement is distinguished by both the number and diversity of its requirements. In addition to supporting the principles previously mentioned, it states that "considerations limited to the time, convenience, or expense of a procedure do not justify violations of any of the principles." When violations are not resolved at the local level, they "should be referred to the APA Committee on Ethics, which is empowered to impose sanctions." The possible nature of such sanctions remains undefined.

The APA *Guidelines* state: "Psychologists should ensure that all individuals who use animals under their supervision receive explicit instruction in experimental methods and in the care, maintenance, and handling of the species being studied." All research should be justifiable, with "a reasonable expectation" that the research will:

- increase knowledge of the processes underlying the evolution, development, control, or biological significance of behavior;
- increase understanding of the species under study in the research; or
- provide results that benefit the health or welfare of humans or other animals.

These contributions "should be of sufficient potential significance as to outweigh any harm or distress to the animals used." Moreover, "when appropriate, animals intended for use in the laboratory should be bred for that purpose."

The APA stands virtually alone among scientific societies in offering guidance in the educational use of animals:

> When animals are used solely for educational rather than research purposes, the consideration of possible benefits accruing from their use vs. the cost in terms of animal distress should take into account the fact that some procedures which can be justified for research purposes cannot be justified for educational purposes.

The *Guidelines* further urge that alternatives to the use of animals be investigated and that alternatives to euthanasia, such as animal sharing and return of wild-trapped animals in the field, be considered. Following euthanasia, "no animal shall be discarded until its death is verified." Investigators are invited to seek assistance from the APA on relevant issues, and a list of references on the ethics of animal research is mentioned as available. The association supports the formation of institutional animal care and use committees (including representatives from the local community) to assist in the resolution of questions within individual institutions, but it recognizes that "laws and regulations notwithstanding, an animal's immediate protection depends upon the scientist's own conscience."

American Physiological Society

The minutes of the 1913 meeting of the Council of the American Physiological Society (APS) contain the first written statement by a U.S. scientific society in support of the prevention of cruelty to research animals. Although it did not receive much attention at that time, the statement later led to the development of the NIH *Guide* (33). The present APS policy statement, revised in 1980 as *Guiding Principles in the Care and Use of Animals* (30), is sent to each member to be signed and posted.

In addition to the principles they have in common with other societies, the APS *Guiding Principles* require that "animal experiments are to be undertaken only for the purpose of advancing knowledge" and that "consideration should be given to the appropriateness of experimental procedures."

"Only animals that are lawfully acquired shall be used," and, when muscle relaxants or paralytics are employed, "they should not be used alone for surgical restraint, [but] in conjunction with drugs known to produce adequate analgesia." In 1984, this provision concerning relaxants and paralytics became the object of a proposed revision, stating that they:

> . . . must only be used after administration of a general anesthetic, adequate to cause unconsciousness, so that when the muscle relaxant is given, the animal is already unconscious. The animal must then be kept unconscious until complete recovery from paralysis occurs. The only exception to this guideline would be in unusual cases where the use of an anesthetic would defeat the purpose of experiment and data cannot be obtained by any other humane procedure.

The revision was proposed in 1984 by the APS Animal Care and Experimentation Committee and is presently under consideration by APS members for comment on its impact on the design of their research.

Federation of American Societies for Experimental Biology

The Federation of American Societies for Experimental Biology (FASEB) is composed of six constituent societies (APS, the American Society of Biological Chemists, the American Society for Pharmacology and Experimental Therapeutics, the American Society of Pathologists, the American Institute of Nutritionists, and the American Association of Immunologists) and one affiliated society (the American Society for Cell Biology). As such, FASEB represents more than 28,000 research investigators and clinicians.

The organization adopted a policy on animal experimentation in 1913 that in 1984 it reaffirmed, while endorsing the APS *Guiding Principles* and issuing a policy statement on the appropriate use of animals for scientific experimentation and education (16). The latter document urges "appropriate safeguards to preclude inadvertent use of pet animals," supports the "wide application of accreditation procedures for animal experimental facilities," and resolves "that continuing collection of appropriate data on the conditions and number of animals used in scientific research and education is necessary for development of legislative or administrative remedies in the field."

International Association for the Study of Pain

The International Association for the Study of Pain publishes the journal *Pain,* which first appeared in 1975. In its first issue, the journal expressed its "one proper duty; to pursue knowledge for the alleviation of suffering in man and animals without any deviation in which we justify the passive observation or intentional production of suffering" (48). *Pain* refuses "to publish any reports where the animal was unable to indicate or arrest the onset of suffering" (48). In 1980, the association's Committee for Research and Ethical Issues published *Ethical Standards for Investigations of Experimental Pain in Animals* (15). These urge the acceptance of "a general attitude in which the animal is regarded not as an object for exploitation, but as a living individual" and offer a list of guidelines "concerned with the importance of the investigation, the severity and the duration of the pain." The statement speaks to the need for justification and review by colleagues, ethologists, and laypersons. In addition, it:

- states that "if possible, the investigator should try the pain stimulus on himself";
- urges careful assessment of the animal's "deviation from normal behavior" during the experiment;
- requires that by escape or avoidance, the animal "be able to control the effects of acute experimental pain" and be treated for chronic pain or "allowed to self-administer analgesic agents or procedures, as long as this will not interfere with the aim of the investigation"; and
- urges researchers to "choose a species which is as low as possible in the phylogenic order."

In 1983, the committee issued *Ethical Guidelines for Investigations of Experimental Pain in Conscious Animals* (50), containing two salient revisions from the 1980 document. First, when submitting a manuscript to *Pain,* authors are "required to show" that they have followed the ethical guidelines that are published in every issue. Second, "studies of pain in animals paralyzed with a neuromuscular blocking agent should not be performed without a general anesthetic or an appropriate surgical procedure that eliminates sensory awareness."

Society for Neuroscience

After more than 2 years of revision, review, and commentary by members of the Society for Neuroscience (17), an Ad Hoc Committee on Animals in Research published its *Guidelines for the Use of Animals in Neuroscience Research* in 1984 (14). In addition to the requirements in common with other societies, these *Guidelines* place particular emphasis on good experimental design and state that "advances in experimental methods, more efficient use of animals, within-subject designs, and modern statistical techniques all provide possible ways to minimize the numbers of animals used in research."

The *Guidelines* show particular concern about prolonged immobilization or restraint, suggesting that "reasonable periods of rest and readjustment should be included in the experimental schedule unless these would be absolutely inconsistent with valid scientific objectives." It is noteworthy that although the policy statement was formulated to deal with research using warm-blooded vertebrates, it includes a statement concerning invertebrates:

> As a general principle . . . ethical issues involved in the use of any species, whether vertebrate or invertebrate, are best considered in relation to the complexity of that species' nervous system and its apparent awareness of the environment, rather than physical appearance or evolutionary proximity to humans.

In this inclusion of invertebrates into its *Guidelines,* the Society for Neuroscience is unique among scientific organizations. This policy likely reflects an enhanced awareness in neurobiology of the degree of sophistication exhibited by some invertebrate nervous systems.

Society for the Study of Reproduction

The Society for the Study of Reproduction (SSR) publishes its *Guiding Principles for the Care and Use of Research Animals* in each issue of its journal, *Biology of Reproduction,* as part of the instructions to authors. Investigators are urged to give consideration to, among other things, "the use of in vitro models."

An investigator wishing to present data at the annual meeting of the SSR must first make a declaration regarding the use of animals in generating those data. The researcher is required to attest with his or her signature (see fig. 15-2) that the research described in the abstract is in strict accord with the guiding principles for experimental procedures endorsed by the society. Written affirmations of this nature are becoming increasingly common among scientific societies; the American Physiological Society, the Society for Neuroscience, and the International Association for the Study of Pain are among the groups with prerequisites of signed statements of humane treatment of experimental subjects for abstract presentations.

American College of Physicians

In a 1983 position paper entitled *Animal Research,* the American College of Physicians (ACP) stated that "scientists and animal welfare advocates share a belief that safeguards are necessary to ensure humane treatment of animals used in scientific research and testing" and that other issues needing to be addressed include "development of alternative testing methods" and "mechanisms to ensure that . . . treatment, care, and experimental methods limit animal pain and suffering."

ACP suggests that appropriate safeguards "may require the establishment of procedures not unlike human subjects protection review" and "recognizes the importance of standards that promote the conduct of quality research and ensure the humane care of healthy animals for research activities" (4).

Figure 15-2.— Declaration Required for the Presentation of Data at the Annual Meeting of the Society for the Study of Reproduction, July 1985

Abstract for

SOCIETY FOR THE STUDY OF REPRODUCTION

I have read and understand the Society's Guiding Principles for the Care and Humane Treatment of Research Animals and affirm that the research described in the above abstract is in strict accord with these principles.

Presenter's signature ______________________________

Telephone No. (Area Code) __________ No. ______________________

SOURCE: Society for the Study of Reproduction, Champaign, IL.

American Pharmaceutical Association

In 1981, the Policy Committee on Scientific Affairs of the American Pharmaceutical Association offered a number of recommendations on the use of animals in drug research (36). These included:

- provision for adequate regulation, controls, and enforcement directed toward the procurement, transportation, housing, care, and treatment of animals;
- encouragement of further development of alternative methods; and
- opposition of legislation penalizing properly controlled and conducted animal research and testing.

In what stands as one of the most strongly worded statements of support for the use of alternative methods from any scientific organization, the policy committee also observed that:

> . . . the use of animals for research, testing, control and production purposes is all inherently quite expensive when compared to other procedures, such as microbiological, chemical, instrumentation and tissue culture. Moreover, both the speed and accuracy of analytical tests and the yields of biological production are much superior when these alternate methods can be employed in place of animal procedures. As a result, there has been a continuing shift away from the use of animals and in favor of alternate procedures as the latter have been developed and have been demonstrated to be acceptable substitutes.

American Veterinary Medical Association

In 1982, the American Veterinary Medical Association (AVMA) approved the *AVMA Animal Welfare Guiding Principles* (7), which states that veterinarians must consider certain ethical, philosophical, and moral values relating to the welfare of animals. Among these considerations are the encouragement of humane care and proper stewardship, implementation of relevant laws and regulations, support of research to illuminate animal welfare issues, and identification of individuals qualified to speak to these issues as a continuing education resource. In 1983, an *AVMA Animal Welfare Positions* report recommended the voluntary establishment of standards of excellence for animal care and use (8). This report includes a number of recommendations on animal welfare issues outside of research use, such as ownership of exotic animals, declawing of domestic cats, and ear-trimming and tail-docking of dogs.

Association of American Veterinary Medical Colleges

In *A Policy on Standards and Procedures Related to the Use and Care of Animals in Veterinary Medical Education and Research,* the Association of

American Veterinary Medical Colleges recommended use of the NIH *Guide* and pursuit of AAALAC accreditation by all its member institutions (11). It also supports education in ethical considerations, use of alternatives where feasible, and continual monitoring of animal use and policies. It urges that "administrators . . . voluntarily establish standards of excellence for animal care and use programs rather than relying upon external enforcement agencies."

STATEMENTS OF INSTITUTIONAL POLICY

In addition to scientific and professional societies, several universities have formulated policies regarding animal use in research and education. Three such statements are reviewed here for purposes of illustration.

University of Southern California

In 1984, the University of Southern California published *Policies Governing the Use of Live Vertebrate Animals,* which contains a "Code of Ethics for the Use of Animals in Research and Teaching" adopted by the university's Animal Ethics Review Board. The code contains guidelines on avoidance of unnecessary pain or distress, searching for alternatives for all LD_{50} studies, prohibition of prolonged physical restraint or deprivation studies, the use of euthanasia and anesthesia, and consideration of alternatives to animal use. It further states that "this University shall expect each Investigator to consider alternatives to the use of animals in research or teaching before presenting a protocol for the use of live animals. The signed protocol should contain a statement to that effect." All protocols must be approved by the Animal Ethics Review Board. Principles governing the use of live animals for teaching are similar to those for research animals (47).

University of Wisconsin

The University of Wisconsin system began requiring in 1981 that all animals used for teaching and research on all of its campuses be used and cared for according to the NIH *Guide,* regardless of the species or source of funds used to conduct the teaching or research. The university at that time took a second extraordinary step and required the certification of all investigators, technicians, graduate students, or staff who supervise, use, or care for animals. On the main campus in Madison, for example, approximately 1,400 persons have been certified to date through instruction and examination (49).

Wisconsin Regional Primate Research Center

In 1982, the Director of the Wisconsin Regional Primate Research Center (WRPRC) published a *Policy Statement on Principles for the Ethical Uses of Animals at the Wisconsin Regional Primate Research Center* (18). This statement deals with the issues of respect for animals, care, choice of alternatives, use of animals in education, personnel training, appointment of animal rights advocates to oversight groups, and the use of good ethical judgment in evaluating the significance of proposed research. It is official WRPRC policy that "all animals under its control are recognized as creatures of great intrinsic value, remarkable complexity, and inherent dignity."

In a section of the *Policy* dealing with the unique value of nonhuman animals as models, researchers are charged to make the following choices when designing experiments:

- When the research question can be meaningfully pursued using nonanimal or in vitro models, the researcher must choose these alternatives.
- When animal experimentation is required, the researcher must seek the least traumatic techniques feasible, minimize the intensity and duration of any distress, and minimize the number of subjects.
- Nonhuman primates should be used only in projects for which they are the most suitable animal model.

All research at the WRPRC must have a "reasonable expectation that the experiment will contribute significantly to knowledge that may eventually lead to improvements in the health and welfare of humans or nonhuman animals" and the expected benefits must "clearly outweigh any pain and suffering experienced by the . . . animals." Consideration of time or expense alone may never justify violation of the principles. Sanctions for violation of the *Policy* include dismissal in accordance with due process and university regulations.

School of Veterinary Medicine, Purdue University

Purdue University's School of Veterinary Medicine drafted a *Policy Statement on the Utilization of Animals* in 1985 (38). The statement makes clear that the school "cannot fulfill its teaching, research, and service missions without the utilization of animals." Purdue's policy spells out the sources of animals for veterinary medical research and education:

> Animals must be legally acquired, and properly housed, fed, cleaned, and cared for to insure their comfort and well-being.
>
> The instructional programs require that preventive medicine, curative medicine, and surgery be practiced in a sequence involving, first, animals owned and maintained by the School and second, animals owned by the general populace who seek professional health services.

STATEMENTS OF CORPORATE POLICY

Industrial testing and research laboratories often have standard operating procedures in writing regarding animal care and use. One of the most comprehensive policy statements on animal welfare comes from the Research and Development Division of Smith Kline & French Laboratories of Philadelphia, PA. In its *Policies and Procedures for the Conservation and Humane Treatment of Experimental Animals,* Smith Kline & French adopted the following initiatives (29):

- Animal studies of a seemingly unwarranted nature, but that are required to meet regulations set by external agencies, will be reported to the Director of Laboratory Animal Science.
- Animal tests required by regulatory authorities in certain countries, but generally not by others, will be reported to the Director of Laboratory Animal Science.
- In vitro test methods developed to replace in vivo studies are to be documented so that other areas may consider potential applications.
- Mistreatment of animals is a serious violation of policy and may be grounds for dismissal.
- A series of Animal Welfare Achievement Awards will recognize and encourage a maximum effort toward conserving animals and developing in vitro techniques.

SUMMARY AND CONCLUSIONS

In mid-1985, the Public Health Service of the Department of Health and Human Services released a new policy on humane care and use of laboratory animals for all awardee institutions. The policy requires self-regulation of animal welfare by all institutions using animals in research and obtaining PHS funds. It is based on a PHS 1979 policy and on information obtained during 15 site visits by NIH to awardee institutions with general assurances on file with NIH. The new policy is more stringent and structured than the old one. It revolves around the institutional assurance to NIH and the institutional animal care and use committee. To obtain assured status with NIH, an institution must either be AAALAC-accredited or fulfill the steps outlined in the policy for self-assurance status.

In 1985, Congress gave the force of Federal law to some of the provisions of the PHS policy and, in separate action, mandated the establishment of institutional animal care and use committees at all research facilities covered by the Animal Welfare Act as well as at Federal facilities (see ch. 13). Taken together, the new PHS policy and Federal statutes bring the overwhelming majority of animal users in the United States under the oversight of institutional animal care and use committees.

Researchers who use animals, their institutional colleagues, their peers in science, laboratory-animal veterinarians, and local community members are today viewed as the appropriate arbiters of what constitutes acceptable care and use of animals. The PHS policy charges these individuals with membership on institutional animal care and use committees at each site where animals are involved in PHS-funded research. Each IACUC shall have broad oversight authority of the animal welfare program at the institution and approve all portions of research protocols involving animals for proper animal care and treatment.

The functions of animal care and use committees may include:

- ensuring compliance with local, State, and Federal laws and regulations on animal care and use;
- inspecting animal care facilities;
- reviewing protocols for animal welfare issues;
- assessing the qualifications of investigators;
- overseeing student use of animals;
- advising on institutional needs, costs of animals, and animal procurement policies;
- controlling allocation of animals within the institution;
- serving as a resource on animal welfare issues and as an educator of the university community and the community at large on animal welfare issues; and
- acting as a community complaint forum.

The concept of review by committee is not unique to the use of animals in experimentation. In fact, institutional review boards and human-subjects committees have overseen research using humans for a decade or more. Current thinking about animal care and use committees is modeled after experience with IRBs.

A voluntary private organization, the American Association for Accreditation of Laboratory Animal Care, functions as a respected agent of certification of an individual laboratory's standards of care. As of April 1985, a total of 483 institutions using animals had received AAALAC accreditation after passing an inspection based on the NIH *Guide for the Care and Use of Laboratory Animals.*

Several scientific and professional societies, universities, and corporations have promulgated statements of policy concerning their members' and employees' standards of conduct in the care and/or use of animals. An organization's policy statement usually reflects its characteristic interests. Some policies are brief enough to cover only one column of a page, while others (e.g., American Psychological Association) take many pages and go into great detail. These policies generally require:

- humane care and use of animals,
- use of a minimum number of animals,
- alleviation of pain and suffering, and
- supervision of animal use by qualified personnel.

At least eight of the organizations and institutions whose policies were reviewed by OTA support the concept of animal care and use committees. Twelve of the fifteen organizations reviewed specifically support or require consideration of the use of alternatives to animals in research, and three specify the maximum use of available statistical methodology.

Several statements of policy require signed statements attesting to humane animal care prior to the publication and/or presentation of papers. Only three policy statements, those of the American Psychological Association, the Wisconsin Regional Primate Research Center, and Smith Kline & French Laboratories, directly mention any sanctions against violators of their guidelines. As a rule, there are neither enforcement provisions accompanying the stated policies and principles of scientific and professional societies nor any apparent penalties for the violation of these policies. For these reasons, the practical significance of certain of these statements of principle is open to question.

CHAPTER 15 REFERENCES

1. *AALAS Bulletin,* "AALAS Policy Statement on Biomedical Research," 23(3):1, 1984.
2. American Association for Accreditation of Laboratory Animal Care, informational brochure, New Lenox, IL.
3. American Association for Accreditation of Laboratory Animal Care, *AAALAC Activities Report,* vol. 13 (New Lenox, IL: Apr. 1, 1985).
4. American College of Physicians, *Animal Research* (Philadelphia, PA: 1983).
5. American Psychological Association, *Principles for the Care and Use of Animals* (Washington, DC: 1979).
6. American Psychological Association, *Guidelines for Ethical Conduct in the Care and Use of Animals* (Washington, DC: 1985).
7. American Veterinary Medical Association, *AVMA Animal Welfare Guiding Principles* (Schaumburg, IL: 1983).
8. American Veterinary Medical Association, "AVMA Animal Welfare Positions," *J. Am. Vet. Med. Assoc.* 183(12):7, 1983.
9. *Animal Behavior Newsletter,* "ABS Animal Care Guidelines," May 1984.
10. Arras, J.D., "Toward an Ethic of Ambiguity," *Hastings Cent. Rep.* 14(2):29-33, 1984.
11. Association of American Veterinary Medical Colleges, *A Policy on Standards and Procedures Related to the Use and Care of Animals in Veterinary Medical Education and Research* (Washington, DC: 1975).
12. Beecher, H.K., *Research and the Individual* (Boston, MA: Little, Brown & Co., 1970).
13. Bennett, T., President, American Association for Laboratory Animal Science, Chicago, IL, personal communication, Dec. 17, 1984.
14. Burke, R.E., Edinger, H.M., Foreman, D.S., et al., "Guidelines for the Use of Animals in Neuroscience Research," *Neurosci. Newsletter* 15(5):3-4, 1984.
15. Covino, B.G., Dubner, R., Gybels, J., et al., "Ethical Standards for Investigations of Experimental Pain in Animals," *Pain* 9:141-143, 1980.
16. *Fed. Proc.,* "The Animal Issue: Some History," 43(11):8a-9a, 1984.
17. Fischbach, G.D., "An Open Letter From the President," *Neurosci. Newsletter* 15(5):3, 1984.
18. Goy R.W., "Policy Statement on Principles for the Ethical Uses of Animals at the Wisconsin Regional Primate Research Center," *Am. J. Primatol.* 3:345-347, 1982.
19. *J. Am. Vet. Med. Assoc.,* "Report of the AVMA Panel on Euthanasia," 173:59-72, 1978.
20. King, F.A., "The Concept of Pain and Its Reduction in Animal Research," paper presented at the 92d Annual Meeting of the American Psychological Association, Toronto, Aug. 25, 1984.
21. Ladd, J., "The Quest for a Code of Professional Ethics: An Intellectual and Moral Confusion," *Professional Ethics Activities in the Scientific and Engineering Societies,* R. Chalk, M.S. Frankel, and S.B. Chafer (eds.) (Washington, DC: American Association for the Advancement of Science, 1980).
22. Lederer, S.E., "The Right and Wrong of Making Experiments on Human Beings: Udo J. Wile and Syphilis," *Bull. Hist. Med.* 58:380-397, 1984.
23. Makarushka, J.L., "Learning To Be Ethical: Patterns of Socialization and Their Variable Consequences for the Ethical Standards of Bio-Medical Researchers," unpublished dissertation, Columbia University, 1971.
24. Malcolm, A.H., "Hospital Panels Consider Key Ethics Issues," *New York Times,* p. A1 (col. 3), Nov. 4, 1984.
25. McCarthy, C., Director, Office for Protection from Research Risks, National Institutes of Health, Public Health Service, U.S. Department of Health and Human Services, Washington, DC, personal communication, September 1984.
26. Orlans, F.B., "What Institutional Animal Research Committees Can Do to Improve Humane Care," paper presented at the 16th Annual Laboratory Animal Medicine Conference, University of Cincinnati, Apr. 26-27, 1984.
27. Orlans, F.B., "Classification of Animal Pain: Review of Protocols for Animal Welfare Concerns," paper presented at Animals and the Scientists: Institutional Responsibilities, The Johns Hopkins University, Baltimore, MD, May 21-22, 1984.
28. Pappworth, M.H., *Human Guinea Pigs: Experimentation on Man* (Boston, MA: Bascon Press, 1967).
29. Phelen, D., Director, Research and Development Technical Services, Smith Kline & French Laboratories, Philadelphia, PA, personal communication, Mar. 13, 1985.
30. *Physiologist,* "Guiding Principles in the Care and Use of Animals," 27(3):141, 1984.
31. President's Commission for the Study of Ethical Problems in Medicine and Biomedical and Behavioral Research, *The Official IRB Guidebook* (Washington, DC: U.S. Government Printing Office, 1983).
32. Ramsay, D., Academic Vice-Chancellor, University

of California, San Francisco, personal communication, September 1984.

33. Reynolds, O.E., Executive Secretary-Treasurer, American Physiological Association, Bethesda, MD, personal communication, Jan. 3, 1985.
34. Rollin, B.E., *Animal Rights and Human Morality* (Buffalo, NY: Prometheus Books, 1981).
35. Rollin, B.E., testimony before U.S. Congress, House of Representatives, Subcommittee on Health and Environment, Committee on Energy and Commerce, *Humane Care for Animals in Research,* hearing, Dec. 9, 1983, Serial No. 97-189 (Washington, DC: 1984).
36. Schwartz, M.A., Romankiewicz, J.A., Corr, M.M., et al., "Report of the Policy Committee on Scientific Affairs," American Pharmaceutical Association, House of Delegates, St. Louis, MO, Mar. 28-Apr. 1, 1981.
37. Stevens, C., "Mistreatment of Laboratory Animals Endangers Biomedical Research," *Nature* 311:295-297, 1984.
38. Stockton, J.J., Dean, School of Veterinary Medicine, Purdue University, West Lafayette, IN, personal communication, January 1985.
39. U.S. Department of Health, Education, and Welfare, Public Health Service, Centers for Disease Control, *Classification of Etiologic Agents on the Basis of Hazard,* 4th ed. (Atlanta, GA: 1974).
40. U.S. Department of Health, Education, and Welfare, Public Health Service, National Institutes of Health, *Biological Safety Manual for Research Involving Oncogenic Viruses,* NIH Pub. No. 76-1165 (Bethesda, MD: 1976).
41. U.S. Department of Health and Human Services, Public Health Service, "Extramural Animal Welfare Policy," *PHS Manual,* Chapters 1-43, and NIH Manual Issuances 4206 and 6000-3-4.58, Nov. 10, 1978.
42. U.S. Department of Health and Human Services, Public Health Service, National Institutes of Health, *Guide for the Care and Use of Laboratory Animals,* NIH Pub. No. 85-23 (Bethesda, MD: 1985).
43. U.S. Department of Health and Human Services, Public Health Service, National Institutes of Health, "Laboratory Animal Welfare," *NIH Guide for Grants and Contracts* 13(5): Apr. 5, 1984.
44. U.S. Department of Health and Human Services, Public Health Service, National Institutes of Health, "Laboratory Animal Welfare," *NIH Guide for Grants and Contracts* 14(8): June 25, 1985.
45. U.S. Department of Health and Human Services, Public Health Service, National Institutes of Health, *NIH Guidelines for the Laboratory Use of Chemical Carcinogens,* NIH Pub. No. 81-2385 (Bethesda, MD: 1981).
46. U.S. Department of Health and Human Services, Public Health Service, National Institutes of Health, *NIH Peer Review of Research Grant Applications* (Washington, DC: U.S. Government Printing Office, 1981).
47. University of Southern California, *Policies Governing the Use of Live Vertebrate Animals* (Los Angeles, CA: October 1984).
48. Wall, P.D., "Editorial," *Pain* 1:1-2, 1975.
49. Will, J.A., Director, Research Animal Resources Center, University of Wisconsin, Madison, WI, personal communication, Mar. 12, 1985.
50. Zimmermann, M., "Ethical Guidelines for Investigations of Experimental Pain in Conscious Animals," *Pain* 16:109-110, 1983.

Chapter 16

Regulation of Animal Use in Selected Foreign Countries

One of the tests of a civilized society is its treatment of animals.

Scientific Procedures on Living Animals, Command 9521
British Home Office
May 1985

We have come to the conclusion that the status of the dog in Western Society is such that it is desirable to minimize its use in the laboratory. Some 50 percent of Canadian households include a dog. These pets are regarded by most owners in an anthropomorphic way as being full members of the family. Clearly, such people are very receptive to emotional appeals to ban the use of animals—especially dogs like theirs—for research. Thus, it will probably be necessary to phase out the significant use of dogs if a major battle over the use of animals for research is to be avoided.

J.C. Russell and D.C. Secord
University of Alberta, Edmonton
Perspect. Biol. Med. 28:374-381, 1985

Possibly the most important feature of any legislation on behalf of laboratory animals is the acknowledgment that the ultimate responsibility for their welfare rests with society and not with the research community.

Anne Doncaster
Mississauga, Ontario
"Experiments on Animals—Review of the Scientific Literature," June 1982

CONTENTS

List of Tables

Chapter 16

Regulation of Animal Use in Selected Foreign Countries

The protections afforded animals vary greatly among countries, from almost complete disregard of animal welfare to the many cultural and legal protections provided in Western Europe and Canada. These protections are currently the subject of heated debate in many countries, particularly where animal protection is already significant. In 1985, for example, Switzerland's voters rejected a referendum that would have virtually banned the use of animals for experimental purposes. The use of the LD_{50} in safety testing continues to be given careful scrutiny by Government and scientific organizations in Switzerland (73,76, 77) and the United Kingdom (4,67,69).

Actions taken in other countries are relevant to U.S. policies for several reasons. First, steps taken by trading partners can lead to political and economic pressures to take similar actions. Second, decreased use of animals abroad, particularly by multinational corporations, can lead to an increased use in the United States. Finally, the experiences of other countries can serve as instructive models, both for policies and for their effects.

This chapter describes the laws of Australia, Canada, Denmark, the Federal Republic of Germany, Japan, the Netherlands, Norway, Sweden, Switzerland, and the United Kingdom. The most common provisions are prohibitions against painful experiments without anesthesia unless anesthesia would frustrate the purpose of the experiment; requirements for licensing or permitting of facilities, investigators, or experiments; limitations on animal use for education; and requirements for internal or external review of experiments by interdisciplinary committees. Two of the more unusual provisions are the protection of crustaceans (Norway) and of native nonvertebrates (the Netherlands).

The impact of these laws on the welfare of animals is affected by several factors other than the substantive requirements of the laws, including societal attitudes toward animals; training of scientists and technicians, both in techniques and in ethics; the composition and procedures of reviewing committees; and the vigor of animal welfare advocates. This chapter discusses the substantive and procedural aspects of these various laws and, where information was available, criticisms and comments on the effectiveness of the systems.

In addition to the array of national laws, there are international agreements—both in effect and proposed—that affect animal welfare. Among these, the Convention on International Trade in Endangered Species, bans on trade in primates, the Draft Convention of the Council of Europe, and the guidelines of the Council for International Organizations of Medical Sciences, are discussed in appendix E.

AUSTRALIA

In Australia, as in the United States, animal welfare is primarily a State concern. Each State has its own legislation and regulations for animal experimentation. At the Federal level, a select committee of the Australian Senate is in the early stages of an 18-month examination of animal welfare, and in 1985 the National Health and Medical Research Council revised its *Code of Practice* for experimental animals (41a).

Of the States, New South Wales has the most extensive laws. Its Prevention of Cruelty to Animals Act, passed in 1901 and amended many times, prohibits activities such as inflicting unnecessary pain; killing, mutilating, or poisoning; and failing to provided proper food, drink, shelter, or exercise. Experimentation is permitted only in the most humane manner available and pain must be alleviated. The most recent amendments, in 1979, primarily served to make the act more specific. Two levels of cruelty were defined and penalties specified—aggravated cruelty, resulting in death or severe injury or disease (fined at about $1,400 and/or 1 to 2 years imprisonment), and simple cruelty, resulting in pain or distress (fined at about $700 and/or 6 months) (2).

In addition to the act's prohibitions, it requires that those performing surgery have certain scientific credentials or a license. Recognizing that credentials alone do not prevent cruelty, the Minister for Local Government has the power to require those performing surgery as licensees to report the details of a procedure (1).

In 1985, the New South Wales Parliament passed legislation establishing an Animal Research Review Panel to oversee licensing of research institutions and animal suppliers. Each institution is required to establish its own review committee (56). These requirements make the laws of New South Wales quite similar in their comprehensiveness and approach to the laws existing in Western Europe.

CANADA

As in the United States and Australia, the Provinces have primary authority over animal use; national action is not taken unless there are interprovincial or national concerns. Although Canada has no national legislation pertaining specifically to protecting laboratory animals, it has a comprehensive voluntary national system.

Three Provinces have legislation affecting laboratory animal use: Two deal primarily with procurement of unclaimed pound animals (8,9,10), while Ontario has a more comprehensive Animals for Research Act, amended in 1979 (6) and accompanied by regulations (7). Many provisions of the Ontario law parallel the voluntary national program.

Although Canada is rather proud of its voluntary program, some Canadian animal protectionists are not satisfied. Vandalism and threats against an official have occurred at the University of British Columbia in Vancouver, the Clarke Institute of Psychiatry in Toronto has been firebombed, and protesters have campaigned against the use of pound animals at Dalhousie University (55).

Many years ago, scientists at the University of Alberta went further than their counterparts in other Provinces in protecting animal welfare. They employed a research veterinarian who upgraded their facilities to levels as high as animal hospitals and clinics, added various precautions against the use of stolen dogs, and established open communication with the press and the local community. Another policy, certainly welcomed by dog enthusiasts, has been the gradual replacement of the dog with the small Yucatan pig for many kinds of experiments. Some Alberta researchers feel that animal protectionists have not been active in Alberta because of these initiatives (55).

Canada's voluntary national program is run by the Canadian Council on Animal Care (CCAC). The first step toward the creation of the CCAC was taken in 1963, when the Canadian Medical Research Council requested the National Research Council (of Canada) to investigate the procurement of experimental animals, the facilities for their care, and control of experiments. This request followed on the heels of the inauguration of the Canadian Society for Animal Care (which became the Canadian Association for Laboratory Animal Science, an organization similar to the American Association for Laboratory Animal Science).

After completing its investigation, the National Research Council recommended that institutions voluntarily assess and control animal experimentation through:

- animal care committees that would monitor care and use of experimental animals and ensure compliance with uniform standards;
- Provincial advisory boards to deal with procurement matters; and
- a national, independent advisory body to establish guiding principles and oversee their application and to advise Provincial governments.

These recommendations led to the formation of the CCAC in 1968 as a committee of the Association of Universities and Colleges of Canada (AUCC). CCAC is independent of governmental and direct university control and is funded by the Medical Research Council and the National Research Council. Its 20 members are drawn from various sectors: 8 from national associations of higher education (including the AUCC), 5 from departments of the Federal Government, 4 from national agencies providing research grants, 2 from the Canadian Federation of Humane Societies, and 1 from the Pharmaceutical Manufacturers Association of Canada. The members of the CCAC also participate informally in curriculum committees for institutions that educate animal care attendants and technicians and, together with the Canadian Association for Laboratory Animal Science, certify laboratory animal personnel at five skill levels (28, 50,51,52).

The CCAC has two executive officers: the Executive Director, responsible for standards and overall operation; and the Director of the Assessment Program, responsible for compliance with the voluntary program. They organize the CCAC's activities around the *Guide to the Care and Use of Experimental Animals,* a two-volume publication much like the *Guide for the Care and Use of Laboratory Animals* issued by the U.S. National Institutes of Health (NIH). The CCAC's *Guide,* provided at no charge to every researcher using animals, details standards for the care and use of animals in experiments for government, university, and pharmaceutical research institutions.

The most important requirement of the *Guide* is that a local institutional Animal Care Committee (ACC) be set up. Volume I lists the following general requirements for a facility's committee:

- It must consist of senior scientific personnel experienced with laboratory animals. An experienced veterinarian or a biological scientist should be a member of the ACC or retained as a consultant.
- It must be kept informed of all activities involving animals.
- It must establish procedures to ensure that in any experiment likely to result in pain, the animal is anesthetized or given analgesics except when it would interfere with the experiment.
- It is responsible for all training and qualifications of personnel who care for animals.
- If its members believe required procedures are not being followed and unnecessary pain is being experienced, it has the power to stop the procedure and to destroy the animal humanely if necessary to alleviate distress (11).

In 1983, an addendum to Volume I, *The Use of Animals in Psychology,* provided additional guidelines to those engaged in psychological research (13). Volume II of the *Guide,* published in 1984, provides information on selection, acquisition, use, and care of 22 distinct classes of laboratory animals (14).

In addition to the *Guide,* CCAC has also published *Ethics of Animal Experimentation,* a set of principles for "all those utilizing vertebrates in the conduct of research, teaching, or testing." These stress the importance of:

- exhausting all alternative methods before animal use is considered;
- using the best methods on the smallest number of appropriate animals required to obtain valid information;
- having a reasonable expectation that the study will contribute significantly to knowledge that may eventually improve the health or welfare of humans or animals;
- avoiding unnecessary pain and duress, both in intensity and duration;
- humanely destroying animals when severe pain cannot be alleviated;
- seeking humane end points;
- withholding food or water on a short-term basis only;
- avoiding physical restraints; and
- using anesthetics or analgesics for surgery or traumatic procedures (burning, freezing, fracturing) (12).

CCAC publications that do not necessarily promote animal welfare, but that are useful to experimenters, include *Canadian Suppliers of Laboratory Animals* (a detailed list of suppliers, with species, producers, and locations) and annual editions of *Research Animals in Canada* (comprehensive information, by species, on laboratory-animal resources available to researchers) (15).

Compliance with the various guides and principles and the functioning of the local ACCs are overseen by assessment panels chosen by the CCAC. The typical panel consists of three scientists, one representative appointed by the Canadian Federation of Humane Societies, and the Director of Assessments, acting ex officio. Panelists are selected, to the extent possible, for the fields of research at the institution to be assessed.

Institutions, contacted in advance, complete a questionnaire describing the local ACC, the research facilities, the animals used, and the personnel. After the facility has been inspected (for as long as 4 days in large institutions), the panel discusses its general findings with the ACC and reports in confidence to the principal official of the institution. If the panel is dissatisfied, a followup visit may be scheduled. Major assessments occur approximately every 2 years; minor ones, or reassessments, occur less frequently (15,23).

Identified problems that are widespread are solved at the national level. For example, inappropriate use of certain animals as models, poor surgical or anesthesia techniques, dated equipment, and poor husbandry led the CCAC's ad hoc Education Committee to issue the *Syllabus of the Basic Principles of Laboratory Animal Science* in 1983 (16). Several Canadian universities have used the syllabus in short courses in basic laboratory-animal science, and one university proposed that such courses be mandatory for graduate students who may use animals during research (27).

Although there are no penalties in law or regulation for violating CCAC standards, an incentive for compliance has been provided by the Health Protection Branch of the Department of National Health and Welfare since 1975. It includes in its contracts with private sector institutions a requirement that the CCAC *Guide* be followed. All governmental departments with contracts involving animal experimentation have now adopted similar provisions, and a finding of noncompliance is grounds for terminating a contract (28,51).

Responding to increasing criticism from some quarters about CCAC's reliance on researchers to police themselves and to more frequent demands for Provincial legislation controlling research animal use, Canada's Minister of State for Science and Technology requested a review of CCAC's effectiveness in 1981. A special committee formed to conduct the review found that the CCAC has had considerable influence in eliminating those problems that led to its establishment and that it works effectively to produce further improvements. The site inspections involving the humane society and the facility upgrading were found to have resulted in Canadian animal care facilities now being among the best in the world (28).

JAPAN

The protections afforded animals in Japan are like those of Europe in their requirements for anesthetics and euthanasia, as well as in their concern, in particular, about dogs and cats. An interesting facet of the Japanese laws is that they combine the protection of animals with the responsibility of those possessing animals to protect other humans from them.

The principal law governing animal control and treatment in Japan (33) went into effect in 1974. Its purposes are to prevent cruelty to animals; to provide for appropriate treatment, taking natural habits into account; to engender a feeling of love for animals among people, thereby contributing to the development of respect for life and sentiments of friendship and peace; and to protect humans from any hazards to themselves or their property that could result from possession by others of domestic or laboratory animals. The law establishes a fine of up to $1,400 for violations of the law or of standards implementing it (32, 33,34).

The law protects all mammals and birds, but it is apparently intended to apply to other species as well. It establishes several responsibilities relevant to research:

- Those possessing animals are responsible for their maintenance, health, safety, and control.
- Where an animal is used for education, experimental research, manufacture of biotics, or other scientific purposes, the animal is to

suffer the minimum pain possible within the limits imposed by these purposes.

- If an animal will not recover from a scientific procedure, the person who used the animal must immediately dispose of the animal by a method that causes it the minimum pain possible.

These responsibilities do not apply to education and research in livestock husbandry or breeding or to experiments for the purpose of observing animal's roles in an ecosystem (37).

The Prime Minister has issued three standards in implementing this law: Standards for the Keeping and Custody of Dogs and Cats (1975); Standards Relating to the Keeping and Custody of Animals for Exhibition, etc. (1976); and Standards Concerning the Raising, Custody, etc. of Animals in Experimental Use (1980) (37). The first two establish general requirements for adequate food, water, shelter, exercise, care, safety, and disease control for animal owners, custodians, and exhibitors. As the title indicates, the first standard applies to dogs and cats; the most recent standard covers other mammals, birds, and reptiles. Enforcement guidance for local authorities was also provided in 1980 (37), and a licensing system was established for facilities conducting experiments (35).

The law establishes a decentralized system for general administration and enforcement. Local authorities at various levels—prefectures, cities, towns, villages, and wards—pass ordinances and establish custody and disposition programs. Prefectures, the largest units, can levy fees for custodial programs and can enlist the aid of animal protection societies. Such programs can also be granted subsidies by Cabinet Order (38).

An Animal Protection Council created by the Cabinet in 1974 (36) aids the Prime Minister at his request. Though the 15-member Council is advisory, the Prime Minister must consult with it before establishing, enlarging, or abolishing standards. The Council, together with the Government and the Japanese Science Council, recommended in 1980 that the Government establish guidelines for animal experimentation (39). The guidelines developed are quite like the NIH's *Guide for the Care and Use of Laboratory Animals*; they cover standards for housing, husbandry, veterinary care, handling during and after experimental procedures, anesthetics, euthanasia, and disposal (63).

In addition to these several publications on how to use animals, the Government has also published detailed information on licensed and regulated facilities, including statistics on experimental-animal use (75). According to this publication, mice accounted for 78 percent of total animal usage in 1980, while rats accounted for a little less than 17 percent. The total number of animals used has been declining from a peak in 1970 (13.6 million), though the use of hamsters, dogs, cats, and primates has increased (30).

WESTERN EUROPE

Throughout Western Europe, animals have legislative protections. The first such protections were anticruelty laws, many of which were passed in the late 19th century. Most anticruelty laws had only limited application to experiments, but in the last several decades, additional laws were passed to protect experimental animals, primarily from pain. This section describes the laws of seven of the more active countries. Table 16-1 compares the major provisions of these laws.

Denmark

The philosophy in Denmark, as in other Scandinavian countries, is that animal experiments are prohibited unless specifically allowed. This belief was first expressed by statute in 1953 (19). With amendments in 1977 (18), Denmark gave authority for all experiments involving animals to an Animal Experiment Board at the Ministry of Justice. This board has seven members who are doctors

Table 16-1.—National Laws for the Protection of Animals in Selected European Countries

Provisions	Denmark	Federal Republic of Germany	Netherlands	Norway	Sweden	Switzerland	United Kingdom
Species protected	Vertebrates	All animals	Vertebrates, native species	Vertebrates, crustaceans	Vertebrates	Vertebrates	Vertebrates
Distinctions among species	Should use lowest rank; dogs, cats, rabbits purpose-bred	Better to use invertebrates or cold-blooded vertebrates	Vertebrates better protected	Monkeys, dogs, cats better protected	Should use lowest rank; all purpose-bred	Should use lowest rank	Primates, dogs, cats, equidae preferred; no stray dogs
Alternatives must be used if available	Yes	Yes	Vertebrates	Yes	Alternatives promoted	Yes	Alternatives encouraged
Anesthetics, analgesics, or approval required for painful experiments	Except for minor or transient pain	If pain, suffering, or injury likely	If injury or pain likely	If pain is possible (unless Board approves)	Surgery on mammals unless committee approves	Slight pain or anxiety; if too painful, must forgo	Statute does not specify, but certificate may require
Educational uses	Higher education, technique	High school and above	University and vocational	Professional training	Allowed, but restricted	Not allowed	Some demonstration; not for practicing
Ban on animal use for more than one painful experiment	All dogs, cats, monkeys; most experiments	No multiple surgeries on vertebrates	Rarely reused because of pain requirements	Only one experiment allowed per animal	Rarely reused because of pain requirements	Only reused if pain was slight	If anesthetized or because of pain requirements
License/permit for dealers, facilities, and investigators	All facilities, head investigators	Dealers, facilities, investigators	Dealers (dogs and cats), facilities	Investigators or facilities licensed	Breeders, facilities	Breeders, facilities	Facilities registered, investigators licensed
Review of experiments	Most experiments need approval by national Board	Not needed; proposed that facility's animal welfare officer review	Head of institute reviews	Investigator or facility (licensee) review	Notification/application; tiered system	2 State committees review	Home Office and Advisory Committee
Administration	Centralized, government/nongovernment board; licensee is responsible	States enforce and administer (proposed that facilities have animal welfare officer)	Central enforcement and reporting; administration by institute	Central coordination, some functions delegated to licensees	Central coordination with oversight by facility head and committee	Central coordination, administered by States	Centralized, shared by Head Office, Advisory Committee, Royal Society
Animal welfare representation	3 nominees to national Board	Being considered	Not required, but facility reports are public	Not required	On all committees; being reconsidered	Members of national commission	Advisory Committee
Reporting	Annual report	In-house recordkeeping	Annual report	Annual report	Government recordkeeping	In-house recordkeeping	Annual report

SOURCE: Office of Technology Assessment.

or veterinarians. Members are nominated by various groups—two by the Medical, Agricultural, and Veterinarian Scientific Councils; one by the Public Health Authority; one by the Council for Industry; and three by associations for the protection of animals.

Because there are fewer than 300 experimenters, most of whom are clustered in a handful of facilities, the Board is able to oversee all experiments. A permit must be obtained from the Board for most experiments, and its decisions cannot be appealed. The only exceptions to the requirement for approval are nutrition studies that will cause conditions similar to what might occur naturally, and experiments that cause only transient and minor pain, as in the taking of blood samples or skin biopsies, but even these procedures are subject to the statute's other requirements. In a change from the earlier statute, Government institutes must obtain permits for experiments, although licensing of individual investigators in certain positions and of facilities is still automatic. Those having permission to conduct experiments may delegate this authority to others, but they remain responsible for the experiment.

There are two other important changes in statutory law. First, the use of animals in experiments is forbidden if alternative methods, such as cell, tissue, or organ cultures, could achieve the same results. Second, in the area of education, animals may only be used in universities and other institutions of higher learning, and then only to train people in experimental techniques. One troublesome provision, carried over from the 1953 act, is that animals of the lowest possible "rank" must be used. One can infer from the special protections given dogs, cats, and monkeys that these are the highest species, but the statute does not specify how rank is to be determined. A recent ordinance requires that as of January 1, 1986, all dogs, cats, and rabbits be purpose-bred. The Animal Experiment Board is also studying the need for the LD_{50} test, with decisions expected no earlier than mid-1986 (40).

The law requires the use of as few animals as possible and the prevention and alleviation of pain. Invasive (surgical) procedures and physically and chemically induced insults that might cause pain must be performed under anesthesia. The animal involved must be killed before recovery unless the experimenter can assume that pain will not endure or unless the procedures require that the animal be kept alive. If the latter, the animal must be given pain relievers and special care. If it survives in an abnormal state, any suffering that results must be relieved to the extent possible. The abnormal condition must be corrected as soon as possible, or the animal must be destroyed humanely. If dogs, cats, and monkeys are not killed at the conclusion of experiments, reasons must be given; the exact details of destruction and disposal must be included (40). This is similar in effect to those statutes requiring that an animal be used in no more than one painful experiment.

Licensees must keep records and file a detailed annual report on numbers and species of animals used; type of euthanasia performed on dogs, cats, horses, ungulates, and nonhuman primates; and purposes of experiments. Since 1979, the Board has required reporting that is unique. Research institutions must distinguish between the total numbers used in experiments (Category A), and those used as controls and sacrificed for harvesting organs or some other purpose only indirectly related to the performance of an experiment (Category B). Categories are further subdivided to reflect the risk of pain and suffering:

- procedures of short duration performed not under anesthetic (Category A-1);
- procedures of longer duration, when the animal is not sacrificed while still anesthetized (Category A-2);
- procedures performed under anesthetic, when the procedure is of short (Category A-3-a) or long (Category A-3-b) duration;
- procedures to produce or test substances performed without anesthetic and not included in the following two categories (Category A-4);
- procedures involving the induction of pathogens or infection (Category A-5); and
- procedures involving the injection of other matter (Category A-6).

There has been a steady growth in the number of licensees in Denmark, from 159 in 1970, to 276 in 1983, some of which is due to broadening scope of licensing requirements. Animal use has been fairly steady, but Category A uses have grown. Mice and rats accounted for 91 percent of all potentially painful experimental animal use in Denmark in 1983. Of those two species, 66 percent were used for toxicological testing. Nonhuman primates and companion animals (dogs and cats) were used in less than 0.25 percent of the total experiments. Most dogs and cats were used in longer term procedures under anesthetic, from which they recovered. In painful procedures, primates were used most often in long-term procedures under anesthetic, but 56 percent were used for purposes exempt from the law (40), that is, nutrition studies or experiments involving only minor or transient pain.

Federal Republic of Germany

West Germany's animal protection laws have been evolving since 1883, at which time anesthetics were required, if possible; experiments using animals could be done by trained persons only; the number of animals and amount of distress were to be minimized; and greater protection was afforded "higher" animals. Amendments in 1933 retained these requirements and added a licensing requirement for institutions using animals. In the 1972 Animal Protection Act, licenses were also required for individual scientists for each study (19).

The Parliament is considering new legislation that would create an ethics commission of scientists and animal protectionists that would review detailed applications for each project involving animals, require that each laboratory appoint an animal welfare officer, and require that the Government identify alternatives and promote their use. Finally, Parliament is also considering a special tax, probably 5 to 25 percent of costs, on animal experiments as a means of providing additional incentive to use alternatives (26,29).

Although the law is national, it is administered by the States (Länder). In enforcing the law, States can use sanctions ranging from stopping an experiment and seizing the animals or revoking a permit, to imposing penalties of about $3,800 and up to 2 years' imprisonment (24).

The basic goal of the law is that no one shall be permitted to cause pain, suffering, or injury to animals without acceptable reasons. Other provisions require that vertebrates not be used when invertebrates would suffice and that warm-blooded vertebrates not be used when cold-blooded ones would do. Further, experiments should be limited to the number absolutely necessary.

Those desiring a permit must be affiliated with a university or otherwise conducting research, and they must provide detailed information to the permitting authorities in the Länder documenting that:

- the desired results cannot be obtained by more humane methods;
- the experiment is necessary for the prevention, diagnosis, or cure of diseases in humans or other animals or serves scientific purposes;
- the director and deputy director of the experiment are reliable;
- the necessary equipment, facilities, supplies, and personnel are available; and
- proper care and medical treatment will be provided.

Permits may be restricted or revoked if requirements are not met by a specified time or if permit restrictions or regulations are not complied with. The permit contains the name of the director of the experiment and a deputy.

Unlike Denmark and other countries discussed in this chapter, educational uses are permitted at the high school level and a permit is not required. However, such activities must be reported to the authorities before they take place. Other experiments that do not require permits are those that fulfill governmental requirements and those used for diagnostic purposes.

Several restrictions pertain to pain. An animal should not endure pain, suffering, or harm if avoidable. Experiments on vertebrates may be performed only under anesthetic unless it is incompatible with the purpose of the research or the pain connected with the operation is less than the damage inflicted by anesthesia. A painful operation or treatment may be performed on an unanesthetized animal only once unless the purpose of the experiment cannot otherwise be achieved; the animal may be used for another experiment only if the second experiment does not involve pain, suffering, or harm. After an experiment, certain species must be presented immediately to a veterinarian, others to the experimenter, and killed painlessly if the animal can live only in great pain.

Animal experiments may be performed only by persons with the required professional knowledge in veterinary medicine, medicine, or biology. Surgery may only be performed by a certified veterinarian.

Detailed standards governing housing, care, and treatment of live vertebrates in experiments were published in 1977. The Federal Government has published a number of monographs and guidances for the use of the States and regulated facilities in interpreting the act in a variety of circumstances (25). In 1983, the German Veterinary Society issued *codex experiendi* providing advice and suggestions to investigators on the ethical use of experimental animals (26).

There are specific reporting requirements for regulated experiments. Each experiment for which permission was required must have a report on file that describes the purpose of the experiment, the number and types of animals used, and the nature and performance of the experiment. The reports must be signed both by experimenters and the director and retained for 3 years. Ownership histories must be kept for dogs and cats. Though no official national statistics are kept, the Ministry of Food, Agriculture, and Forestry estimates that approximately 7 million animals were used in experiments in West Germany in 1984 (71).

Netherlands

The Netherlands places a great deal of responsibility for animals' welfare on the head of the facility in which experiments are conducted. This oversight is coordinated by the Veterinary Chief Inspectorate of the Ministry of Public Health, who in 1984 began a major project in cooperation with five animal welfare organizations to identify potential alternatives to the use of animals in testing vaccines, serums, and other diagnostic methods. This report, and other initiatives, are expected to increase research on alternatives (53).

Like most other West European countries, the Netherlands has had a general statute that protects animals from cruelty since the late 19th century. It prohibits causing pain, suffering, or injury to an animal, or withholding proper care without reasonable cause. It provides criminal penalties for violations, but it has not been necessary to use them for animal experiments (21). A law governing trade in livestock confines trade in dogs and cats to licensed dealers, thus protecting pets (43), and an ordinance taking effect in 1986 requires that dogs, cats, and rabbits be purpose-bred (31). Finally, the Netherlands has a "protection of nature" law, which protects some invertebrate species—such as *Helix pomatia*, the Roman snail—and all native amphibians (42,44).

The Law for Experimental Animals, passed in 1976, established a comprehensive system for regulation of animal experimentation, including the filing of annual reports by all animal facilities with the Ministry of Public Health (45). The law is based on general guidelines issued by the International Committee for Laboratory Animals, and became the Council of Europe's model for the Draft Convention on protection of laboratory animals (see app. E).

The law requires justification for all animal experiments on vertebrates that are likely to be injurious or cause significant pain or other distress. Experiments must benefit human or animal health or food, or science, and must be approved by the head of the institute where they are to be done. Statistics on registered experiments compiled by the Dutch Government indicate that from 1978 to 1983 about 20 percent of the experiments were related to the production of serums, vaccines, and other biological products; about 30 percent were related to toxicological and pharmaceutical research; less than 10 percent were related to the diagnosis of pregnancy or disease; and about 30 percent were related to the solution of a scientific problem (and the vast majority of these were related to medical research). Less than 2 percent were for training and education. These statistics also indicate that about one-third of the experiments were done because of legal requirements, and less than 10 percent were toxicity tests.

As do many other countries, the Netherlands does not permit painful experiments on vertebrates when alternatives are available, and requires anesthetics for more than negligible pain except where their use would frustrate the purpose of the experiment. Where severe and prolonged pain will likely result from the procedure, the animal must be humanely killed without recovering from anesthesia (45). Statistics for 1978-83 indicate that some 20 to 30 percent of experiments do not require anesthetics (though the figure is steadily decreasing); that more than 10 percent of the animals are killed without treatment to obtain organs or blood; that about 10 percent of the operations end in euthanasia or slight pain; and that the greatest number of experiments producing significant pain are those involving pathogens, immunization, or toxic substances.

The Government entrusts most of the responsibility for administering the law to the head of the research enterprise to whom licenses are issued. The director of research need not be an expert, but he or she is responsible for appointing experts to ensure that:

- animal technicians involved in licensed experiments are qualified and accredited up to the level established by the Ministry;
- those engaged in animal experimentation cooperate in matters affecting the welfare of the subjects;
- research workers are qualified to perform assigned tasks; and
- the welfare of experimental animals is supervised by a qualified veterinary surgeon or equivalent professional.

From January 1986, licensed institutions are required to have an institutional ethics committee composed of persons of several disciplines, including ethics, who oversee all experiments (31).

Licensed institutions must keep records on experiments and care. They are further required to report research activities, including data on numbers of animals used by type and purpose. The information is available to the public.

The law also provides for establishment of a central veterinary inspectorate under the Ministry of Public Health, responsible for:

- registering research facilities, as of 1984 (22);
- periodically inspecting facilities conducting research;
- issuing regulations and guidelines governing laboratory animal housing; and
- regulating sources (breeders and suppliers) of laboratory animals.

In addition, the law also authorizes the appointment of an advisory committee of persons skilled in animal experimentation, laboratory-animal science, and animal welfare to advise the Ministry. This committee includes two representatives of animal welfare organizations. The committee participates in the drafting of regulations and other aspects of implementing the 1976 law.

The Ministry of Public Health is the central enforcement agency for the 1976 law. It has the power to issue detailed regulations on laboratory-animal treatment and presides over them using teams of veterinary inspectors who supervise and advise research institutions. The director of the research facility is also expected to enforce standards of care and treatment.

Regulations require that investigators and technicians complete training in laboratory-animal principles and techniques (22), including a 20-day course that emphasizes animal well-being and the social and ethical aspects of animal use (53). A 4-year program for training animal technicians is also available.

Data compiled from the 1983 annual reports indicate that there are 71 licensed institutes (containing 387 distinct research departments); 2,118 investigators working directly with animals; 2,541 persons involved in animal care management; and 4,683 students taking classes involving animal experiments.

Indications of the commitment to protecting animals are the use of experimental review committees in 17 percent of the departments surveyed and the fact that in 19 of 71 establishments, methods had been introduced to replace animals in experiments, reduce the use of animals, or refine procedures (54). Furthermore, there has been a steady decline in the use of experimental animals over the reporting years, from 1.6 million in 1978 to 1.3 million in 1983. Of these, mice account for about 56 percent and rats, about 26 percent.

Norway

Norway requires more of people in their behavior toward animals than most other countries. The Welfare of Animals Act, passed in 1974 and in effect since 1977, even goes as far as requiring people encountering a domestic animal or tame reindeer in pain to come to its assistance or to call the appropriate authority, and the act forbids the display of animals other than fish (46,47).

The act applies to vertebrates and crustaceans; it provides that animals shall be treated well and that due regard shall be given to their natural instincts and needs so that they are not in danger of being caused unnecessary suffering. Adequate care must be provided and many procedures can only be performed by a veterinarian or other highly qualified professional. Anesthetics must be used when there is reason to believe that a procedure may cause considerable suffering unless it would interfere with the purpose of the experiment, but such an experiment would require special permission from the National Experimental Animal Board. Experiments must be planned and carried out to avoid any unnecessary suffering, sometimes necessitating pilot studies. Destruction without delay is required where suffering after recovery will occur. Animals used in painful procedures without anesthetic may not be reused in further experiments.

The provisions of the act most applicable to research are its prohibitions on the use of live animals for educational purposes, except as a necessary part of professional training. It also requires permission to carry out biological tests on animals.

The purpose must be to diagnose animal or human disease, test a hypothesis, produce or control a product, or test medicines or other substances for effects. Such tests must not inflict greater suffering than is strictly necessary to achieve the purpose, and licensees are permitted to acquire and use local and general anesthetics for this purpose. Inspection authority is broad, and anyone "willfully or negligently" violating the act or authorized regulations is guilty of a misdemeanor, carrying penalties of a fine or imprisonment up to 6 months for the first offense, and up to a 1 year for subsequent offenses (47).

The Experimental Animal Board, first appointed under the statute by the Minister of Agriculture in 1976, has primary authority. Its five members issue and administer regulations on obtaining permission for experimentation on protected animals.

In 1985, the regulations were amended to provide that no experiment on a live animal can be carried out without the written consent of the institute's or organization's license holder. Copies of executed consent forms must be filed with the Board (20).

Sweden

Sweden's approach to experimental use of animals has much in common, both in substance and procedure, with that of the other countries of Western Europe surveyed here. For example, experiments involving pain or suffering receive greater scrutiny, anesthesia during painful experiments is generally required, and licenses are issued to facilities in which experiments are conducted. Its more unusual features are the close working relationships among scientists, technicians, and laypeople (most often animal welfare advocates) at all levels of review and the complex system of ethical review, which divides responsibilities among many organizations and committees.

The review procedures, which have evolved over many years, are being reevaluated by the Government. Matters being reconsidered include the extensive use of laypeople (who often disagree with other reviewers); the use of small subcommittees (which sometimes disagree with full committees); and the limited review given to experiments that cause little or no pain (which leaves their aim unexamined) (57). Sweden's active animal welfare representatives can be expected to vigorously oppose any changes that would decrease their input in the review process or that might reduce the protections provided to animals (17).

The first law pertaining to experimental use of animals, passed in 1944 (58), prohibited cruel treatment and governed care and transport of classes of animals. Painful experiments on animals were generally prohibited and experiments could be performed only in licensed institutions by persons with established qualifications for conducting such research (64). Furthermore, anesthetic was required where more than minor pain was produced, except where its use would frustrate the study's purpose (58).

Several ordinances and amendments were published between 1978 and 1982 (59,60,61). They added both substantive and procedural requirements. Experiments involving pain, suffering, or anxiety now have to be licensed by the National

Board of Agriculture (unless conducted by the Government). Vertebrates were ranked hierarchically, ranging from mammals to birds to reptiles to frogs to fish. The use of warm-blooded vertebrates in education at or below the secondary level became subject to approval, regardless of whether pain or suffering would occur. Animals used in laboratories now must be bred for that purpose, and dogs, cats, and rabbits must be marked and various records kept showing their origin. Most responsibility for the conduct of experiments is placed on individual licensees and heads of licensed institutions.

Several changes were also made in how experiments were to be reviewed. These changes were based on a voluntary system that began at the University of Uppsala. A Laboratory Animals Board, established by the National Medical Research Council in 1965, was called on in 1972 to help the Council review grant applications. Drawing from the considerable expertise of Karl-Johan Öbrink, a professor of physiology at the University of Uppsala's medical school, and of Lars Wass, a representative of the National Board of Universities, guidelines were developed for both the organization and operation of an ethics committee.

In response to the Board's request for a system through which the Council Administration could determine automatically whether a grant application involving the use of animals ought to be referred for ethical review, Öbrink and Wass proposed a scale of expected discomfort. Experiments causing little or no discomfort received little, if any, review, with other experiments receiving scrutiny in proportion to the pain they would cause. (This is not so different from other European systems—pain normally triggers review, and the reviewers would most likely take the degree of expected pain into account.) Other key provisions of the guidelines include:

- Members of the committee would be within easy reach of anyone planning animal work, even if the committee were large.
- The committee would be composed of animal technicians and laypeople, as well as researchers.
- The day-to-day work of the committee would be performed by ad hoc subcommittees, formed after submission of an investigator's proposal to a member of the parent committee.
- Experimentation could begin immediately upon approval of an experiment by the subcommittee.
- To protect an investigator's privacy, the committee and subcommittees would be voluntary only and would have no legal or administrative authority.
- Discussion between investigators and subcommittee members would promote increased awareness of research ethics.

The prototype committee consisted of 30 individuals, mostly investigators. Meetings were held frequently and applications were reviewed in full committee, with investigators present to discuss experiments and answer questions.

With the election of a new National Government in 1976, the Minister of Agriculture decided that the Uppsala system, with minor modifications, should be introduced throughout the country and incorporated into the National Board of Agriculture's regular system of experimental control. It was in place by 1979.

As the laws have become more comprehensive, their administration has become more complex. The National Board of Agriculture has the broadest range of responsibilities. In addition to its involvement with the ethical committees and the Board for Laboratory Animals, it oversees government laboratories that use animals, approves plans for new facilities for animals, conducts inspections, oversees breeding and transportation of animals, provides a variety of forms needed for review and recordkeeping, and keeps journals of experiments that have been approved (59,60).

The 1979 laws gave certain enforcement and administrative functions to the County Public Health Committee, with consultation and direction with the National Board of Agriculture. Operating somewhat independently of the National Board of Agriculture is the Swedish Laboratory Animals Board (referred to as CFN in Sweden). It has members nominated by Government (including the National Board of Agriculture), universities, the Swedish Medical Research Council, and the Swedish Natural Science Research Council. The Board, most recently the subject of a 1982 statute, is now charged with promoting cooperation between scientists, technicians, and animal welfare organizations; planning for long-term improvements in conditions for laboratory animals; promoting the development of alternatives, which it also funds; reviewing the work of ethical committees; and working toward the efficient use of animals by promoting cooperation among animal users (58).

The 1982 statute also required the establishment of six ethical committees, one in each university region. The requirements were based on the prototype committee developed in Uppsala. These committees, overseen by the National Board of Agriculture, advise and consult on individual experiments and report to their County's Public Health Committee. They have equal numbers of scientists, animal technicians, and laypeople.

The Central Veterinary Board of the National Board of Agriculture solicits nominees for review committees from each of six Regional Boards of Higher Education (that consist of university and political officials) and major animal welfare groups. Nominees are of three kinds: researchers, technicians, and laypeople. The animal welfare organizations nominate laypeople only. From the nominations submitted, the Board appoints six regional ethical committees, designating a chair and vice chair; six regional subcommittees for secret projects; and one special committee for military research. The special military-research group and the regional subcommittees for secret research were created to protect national defense interests and pharmaceutical trade secrets.

Although full committees meet at least twice annually, day-to-day application review is conducted by subcommittees, consisting of equal numbers of researchers, technicians, and laypeople. The technicians and laypeople are chosen from mandatory rotation lists, to avoid exclusion of any represented interest, and each subcommittee must have at least three members.

The applicant completes a one-page form, stating the objective of the research project; describing the experiment, with an emphasis on the use and disposition of the animals and the number of animals of different species that will be used; and describing what the investigator plans to do to alleviate and abbreviate suffering. When the subcommittee meets with the applicant, it may suggest improvements in the description of the procedure, modifications to the procedure itself, or a reduction in the number of animals used. If the subcommittee agrees to the applicant's proposal, it forwards a signed form to the central authority.

If an applicant or a subcommittee member disagrees with the decision of a subcommittee, the application is referred to the full committee, which can call a session to review appeals. All subcommittee decisions are discussed by the full committee at its regular meetings. A permit, valid for up to 3 years, is all that is needed to begin work. Rereview is required only if an investigator plans to conduct experiments more severe than those for which approval was granted.

Precise data on numbers of animals used for various kinds of procedures are not available. Reporting is only done in conjunction with the application process, although certain records must be submitted and others must be kept.

The time required to obtain a decision varies from region to region. Two contributing factors have been identified: difficulty in scheduling meetings, and some applicants' inability to use simple language, thus requiring extra time for clarification. To help remedy the lag problem, the 1982 ordinance required a subcommittee to reach a decision within 3 weeks of receipt of the application.

The 1982 ordinance also abolished the requirement that experiments be grouped into the traditional discomfort categories, thus eliminating needless discussion. Öbrink, the architect of the voluntary review mechanisms, has expressed worry over the system's potential, with increasing regulatory emphasis, to become bureaucratized to the point where it sacrifices the objectives of ethical review for the sake of control (5,48,49).

Switzerland

Switzerland has probably gone further to protect animals than any other country and recently came to the brink of going even further. In 1985, Swiss voters were presented with a constitutional amendment that read: "The vivisection of vertebrates as well as all cruel animal experimentation shall be forbidden in Switzerland." The proposal was rejected by a two-to-one margin. This law would have had a major impact on the three large pharmaceutical firms with facilities in Switzerland. Another, less restrictive referendum is being readied for Swiss voters, but may be 4 years away from a vote (74).

The Swiss antivivisection movement has become particularly active, if not violent in recent years. Research facilities have been broken into, scientists sued, and untrue or overstated stories publicized (for example, that vaccines had no part in fighting infectious diseases) (72).

Swiss scientists have not fought controls, and some have pointed out the benefits to good science—more attention is given to planning and scientists have greater incentives to keep abreast. Of course, there are also disadvantages to science—senior scientists must spend time answering simple questions and there can be delays of 4 to 6 weeks for licensing an experiment.

An indication of the importance of animal welfare to the Swiss is the fact that animal protection is addressed in the Constitution, which recognizes the necessity for and utility of humane treatment of animals. Controls on animal experimentation in Switzerland are found in the Federal Law of 1978 Regarding the Protection of Animals (as amended by the Ordinance of 1981 Regarding the Protection of Animals).

In response to antivivisectionist pressures, additional guidelines were developed in 1981 by the Swiss Academies of Medical Sciences and of Sciences. These have been adopted by government, industry, and academia. Under the guidelines, a permanent committee was set up to review animal experiments, and stringent requirements were set up for experiments involving severe pain—if the experiment cannot be modified to reduce pain, it must be forgone. Under the statute, any experiment that could cause pain to a protected animal or that would adversely affect its well-being must be licensed, whether conducted by government or by private institutions. Even where pain is not significant, licensing authorities must be satisfied that the expected benefits of the proposed experiment outweigh the adverse effects on experimental animals. Furthermore, animals that have suffered more than minor pain or anxiety may not be reused (62).

Licenses are issued to individual investigators for each experiment or series of related experiments. Licenses to perform experiments are issued by the cantons, or Swiss States. Special commissions must determine whether all legal requirements and qualifications are met before a license is issued. Thus, the commission must verify, in each instance, whether the proposed experiment:

- is essential in order to achieve the objective of the experiment, or whether alternative approaches are possible;
- is sound from a methodological point of view;
- can be performed with a lower order of species than the one proposed; and
- can be modified to reduce the number of animals to be used.

The conditions under which experimental animals are to be kept and used are specified in the law, setting standards for accommodations of differing species, by size and weight, and prescribing care. Animal caretakers must demonstrate their competency by passing a Federal examination. Records of licensed experiments must be kept for a minimum of 2 years after the experiment ends, and they must be available for inspection by local authorities (77).

Most licensed experiments in Switzerland are conducted by large pharmaceutical companies (74), with some work done by Government and universities. In addition, a few private institutes do testing and research. The experiments' purposes fall into four major categories: research and development (87 percent); production and quality assurance (12 percent); teaching (1 percent); and diagnostics (less than 1 percent).

According to the Swiss Government, the three pharmaceutical companies used 36 percent fewer animals in 1983 than in 1976; the decrease between 1981 and 1983 averaged 23 percent for all species, with the largest categorical decreases occurring in the use of mice (26 percent) and rabbits (25 percent). The authorities believe this indicates a general trend toward reduced animal use, since the firms involved account for about two-thirds of all experimental-animal use; one governmental representative has said the decline was hastened by the implementation of the 1981 ordinance (77).

United Kingdom

The United Kingdom has been a pioneer in the protection of experimental animals. The Cruelty to Animals Act, passed in 1876 (68), was the most protective statute of its kind for many decades. Although the act has not been amended, the protections afforded animals have continued to expand through administrative actions of the Home Office and by voluntary actions by institutions and individuals (69).

As in other parts of Western Europe, animal welfare advocates have been actively campaigning for more protective laws. Unlike many other countries, some of these groups have also made major scientific contributions to the development of alternatives. The most active of these scientifically, the Fund for the Replacement of Animals in Medical Experiments, was recently given over $200,000 by the Government to fund research on alternatives.

Contributing to the debate over how the act should be changed, the British Veterinary Association, the Committee for the Reform of Animal Experimentation, and the Fund for the Replacement of Animals in Medical Experiments made recommendations that became the basis for a 1983 White Paper by the Home Office. Several items in that paper provoked considerable debate, leading to the 1985 White Paper *Scientific Procedures on Living Animals* (70). This was presented by the Home Office to the Parliament in May 1985 and recommends substantial amendments to the 1876 Act, some of which would codify current practice. The 1876 act (as it is currently practiced) and the proposed legislation are summarized and compared in table 16-2.

Other acts that bear on these activities include the Dogs Act of 1906 and the Theft Act of 1968 (as amended by the Criminal Theft Act of 1977), which address the problem of stolen pets. Experiments regulated by the Cruelty to Animals Act are excluded specifically from the reaches of the Protection of Animals Act of 1911, the Protection of Animals (Scotland) Act of 1912, the Protection of Animals (Anaesthetics) Act of 1954 (65), and the Protection of Animals (Anaesthetics) Act of 1964 (66).

A basic philosophy of the act is that experiments should be permitted if they lead to new knowledge, but the use of animals to develop manual skills is not permitted. (Demonstrations—another educational use—are permitted, however, if the animal is anesthetized and does not recover.) In permitting the development of new knowledge, the authorities, as in many other countries, will not try to predict which experiments will result in useful knowledge or practical applications.

Control over experiments occurs in three ways: through the granting of licenses to experimenters, through the registration of facilities where experiments take place, and through the appointment of government inspectors. Although responsibility rests with the Home Office, assistance is provided by an Advisory Committee with representation by animal welfare organizations. In addition, many institutions have established their own informal review procedures (3).

The Secretary of State approves and registers every place for the performance of experiments or for the purpose of instruction, imposes conditions on licenses, and revokes licenses for cause. The Secretary may require reports, appoint inspectors, and require inspections. Most licenses are issued with one or more certificates. Certificates may be given for the period and series of experiments the persons signing the certificate may think expedient. There are six kinds of certificates, based on species use, pain, and the use of anesthetic.

A practical approach to the assessment of pain, suggested by a Royal Commission appointed in 1906, is that it would be unreasonable to impose greater restrictions on the infliction of pain for the advancement of knowledge than those imposed by public opinion in the pursuit of sport, in carrying out such operations as castration and spaying, or in the destruction of rabbits, rats, and other vermin (41).

The United Kingdom is able to compile detailed, accurate statistics on animal use through its reporting requirements as well as the through the issuance of licenses and certificates. Each licensee (except those who have no experiments to report for a given year) must submit an annual report for as many of each of the following reporting cate-

Table 16-2.—Comparison of the United Kingdom's Cruelty to Animals Act of 1876 and Proposed Amendments

Provision	Current law	Proposed amendments
Animals protected	All living vertebrates; additional protection for nonhuman primates, dogs, cats, and equidae	All living vertebrates, fetuses of mammals, embryonic or larval young of other species at specified stages, (would also add authority over breeding of animals with potentially disabling genetic defects; would allow the Home Secretary to protect invertebrates; would require justification of all species choices)
Permissable purposes	Advance new discovery of knowledge or lead to longer life, less suffering	Adopts permissible purposes of European Convention (Article 2) (see app. E), encompassing many procedures rather than experiments (e.g., production of serums, maintaining tumors or pathogens); Secretary must balance the severity (pain) against the purpose
Licensing system	Any person Home Secretary allows: difficult to alter issued license; restrictions must be specified	Personal license would only allow specified techniques and species; project license for each experiment, specifying purpose of work, species, number of animals, techniques; Secretary must answer to Parliament for balance of severity and purpose (Secretary must publish guidelines for the decision criteria)
Severity	No statutory limit on pain, but may be limited in certificates; pain may be severe or enduring, not both	An animal in severe pain or distress would have to be killed immediately and painlessly; severity would encompass pain, distress, suffering, morbidity, and mortality and would be tailored to each project license; would require licensees to minimize severity wherever possible; would broaden inspector's power to kill humanely
Assessors	No mechanism to assess integrity or competence for personal license	Senior licensee with personal knowledge of applicant and applicant's abilities would certify applicant's competence; Home Office would continue to issue license
Registering facilities	Most facilities for experiments are registered; most breeders and suppliers are not	All facilities would be registered; Secretary would have power to set standards for staffing, care, and accommodation; facilities would name person responsible for day-to-day care and outside veterinarian must be called for problems; breeders and suppliers would register
Fees	None	Registered facilities, based on number of procedures
Source of animals	Only stray dogs protected (Dog Act)	All animals purpose-bred in registered establishments (except for farm animals and animals taken from the wild); recordkeeping on source and disposal
Reuse of animals	Only anesthetized animals must be killed	Reuse would require Secretary's permission, and only if the animal has returned to normal
Killing of animals when procedure ends	Only if animal is in severe pain or was anesthetized	Not required to kill animals at the end of a procedure; if certified fit, surviving wild animals may be returned to the wild, farm animals to a farm, and certain domestic animals may be offered to private homes
Use of animals to attain manual skill	Not permitted unless decerebrated	Secretary would authorize for special, specific skills such as microsurgery on anesthetized animals
Use of alternatives	Encouraged but not required	License would not be issued until Secretary was convinced that alternatives were not suitable and that no further refinements or reductions could be made
Use for education and training	Only anesthetized animals that are killed before recovery for university lectures	Would be extended to allow other nonrecovery training for approved professional courses; would permit recovery if animal suffers only trivial pain or distress under exceptional circumstances, decerebration would become a licensed procedure and no longer permitted in schools
Advisory Committee	Not required, but has existed since 1912, with lay members since 1979	Would require Animal Procedures Committee, with lay members (including animal welfare advocates), doctors, veterinarians, and biologists; no more than half of the Committee would be licensees; would advise Secretary on procedures, standards, trends, licensing, and revisions of the law
Codes of practice	Voluntary codes are often used	Secretary would issue guidelines and codes of practice on animal husbandry and would give guidance on recognizing and alleviating stress and pain
Offenses and penalties	Experimenting without a license; 6 months and $3,000	Performing, aiding, or abetting performance of a procedure without authority; providing false information; disclosing information obtained in confidence; 2 years and an unlimited fine
Records	All licensees keep records of experiments	Same

SOURCE: Office of Technology Assessment.

gories as apply. (The number of distinct entry codes for each list subclassification is given in brackets.)

- anesthetic (none, for part of experiment, or entire experiment) [3];
- types of vertebrates (mammals—rodents, rabbits, primates, carnivores, ungulates, and others—birds, reptiles, amphibians, and fish) [16];
- neoplasia [4];
- infection and immunology [4];
- primary purpose (to study body function or structure, to develop or study the various products or chemicals, to develop transplant techniques) [15];
- toxicity tests [6];
- experiments in response to domestic or foreign legislation [14]; and
- use of particular painful techniques (such as eye irritation) [14].

These annual reports are compiled in detailed reports. Several tables from the 1984 report are included here. Table 16-3 shows the frequency with which various species are used in the United Kingdom, table 16-4 shows the primary purpose of the experiments, and table 16-5 shows the registered institutions performing experiments. These tables represent only highlights of the considerable data available.

Table 16-3.—Experiments by Species of Animal, 1977-84, United Kingdom

	Species of animal (thousands of experimental animals used)							
Year	Mouse	Rat	Guinea pig	Other rodent	Rabbit	Primate	Cat	Dog
1977	3,234.9	1,073.0	187.7	38.7	191.8	9.0	8.5	14.3
1978	3,168.5	1,062.6	193.4	39.4	199.2	7.2	7.9	13.7
1979	2,901.3	994.8	165.7	37.2	187.0	6.4	7.5	12.0
1980	2,780.7	957.9	166.6	36.4	181.5	5.2	6.8	11.5
1981	2,616.9	908.6	159.1	35.0	176.0	6.2	8.0	13.5
1982	2,442.7	932.3	154.7	36.8	165.0	5.7	7.3	13.1
1983	2,070.2	878.4	144.7	36.2	160.0	5.6	7.5	13.9
1984	1,903.8	888.0	141.7	36.5	156.0	6.0	6.4	14.4
	Other carnivore	Horse, donkey, or crossbred	Other ungulate	Other mammal	Bird	Reptile or amphibian	Fish	Total[a]
1977	2.2	0.5	31.9	3.0	344.3	7.2	157.5	5,385.6[b]
1978	2.7	0.6	36.0	2.6	314.3	6.6	140.6	5,195.4
1979	2.2	0.6	36.5	2.4	241.4	7.6	117.4	4,719.9
1980	1.3	0.5	33.4	2.6	211.6	7.8	175.5	4,579.5
1981	2.3	0.4	35.4	1.8	194.2	8.6	178.9	4,344.8
1982	1.9	0.5	33.6	2.7	251.8	7.8	165.8	4,221.8
1983	1.8	0.6	36.4	3.0	132.6	18.2	115.2	3,624.2
1984	1.7	0.6	33.1	2.7	155.0	8.1	143.2	3,497.3

[a]Columns do not add up to total due to rounding.
[b]Includes 81.3 thousand experimental animals that could not be classified.

SOURCE: U.K. Home Office, Secretary of State, *Statistics of Experiments on Living Animals: Great Britain, 1984* (London: Her Majesty's Stationery Office, 1985).

Table 16-4.—Primary Purpose of Experiments, 1977-84, United Kingdom
(thousands of experimental animals used)

Year	To study normal or abnormal body structure or function	To select, develop, or study the use, etc., of medical, dental, and veterinary products and appliances	To develop transplant techniques	To select, develop, or study the use, hazards, or safety of: Plant pesticides, including fungicides	Herbicides or substances modifying plant growth	Substances used in industry	Substances used in the household	Cosmetics and toiletries
1977	1,286.0	2,932.6	22.5	35.8	20.3	81.6	18.8	24.6
1978	1,164.8	2,925.7	16.2	50.4	18.8	88.0	14.9	28.2
1979	1,051.7	2,680.8	25.4	34.1	24.0	75.3	18.5	30.5
1980	909.3	2,680.1	14.7	40.1	17.5	80.4	13.8	31.3
1981	1,119.2	2,403.0	14.6	30.6	12.9	69.2	14.3	24.4
1982	997.0	2,373.0	15.2	33.0	15.1	66.2	13.9	18.9
1983	875.2	2,039.9	12.6	35.4	17.9	59.1	17.2	18.0
1984	824.8	1,915.7	15.0	46.7	18.1	64.5	12.9	17.5

Year	To select, develop, or study the use, hazards, or safety of: Food additives	Tobacco and its substitutes	Plants or animals and their toxins	General environmental pollutants	To demonstrate known facts	Other purposes	More than one purpose	Total[a]
1977	39.3	15.2	4.2	60.4	2.7	676.8	83.4	5,385.6[b]
1978	42.5	2.7	2.7	70.4	2.6	709.8	57.6	5,195.4
1979	27.7	4.6	3.3	33.6	1.8	600.5	108.1	4,719.9
1980	21.3	1.9	3.3	40.9	1.7	635.9	87.2	4,579.5
1981	20.2	2.3	2.7	45.8	1.9	519.4	64.3	4,344.8
1982	20.1	3.2	5.9	27.3	1.6	562.5	68.9	4,221.8
1983	14.1	2.7	4.8	34.4	1.6	444.9	46.4	3,624.2
1984	12.0	2.2	5.8	31.8	1.1	453.1	76.0	3,497.3

[a]Columns may not add up due to rounding.
[b]Includes 81.3 thousand experimental animals that could not be classified.

SOURCE: U.K. Home Office, Secretary of State, *Statistics of Experiments on Living Animals: Great Britain, 1984* (London: Her Majesty's Stationery Office, 1985).

Table 16-5.—Experiments by Type of Registered Facility, 1977-84, United Kingdom

Type of registered place[a]	1977	1978	1979	1980	1981	1982	1983	1984
	(thousands of experimental animals used)							
Public health laboratories[b]	37.8	41.8	120.6	106.7	117.0	106.4	78.4	63.7
Universities (including medical schools)	875.5	927.4	975.9	895.3	847.6	813.6	785.9	772.7
Polytechnics	32.9	46.7	38.4	37.7	34.9	29.5	36.9	29.8
Quasi-autonomous nongovernmental organizations	316.4	280.6	255.7	274.6	242.8	268.9	239.5	209.3
National health service hospitals (excluding medical schools)	180.5	157.4	147.7	159.4	154.3	144.2	132.2	134.4
Government departments[b]	323.9	273.5	163.7	169.8	174.0	154.0	101.9	103.2
Nonprofitmaking organizations	858.3	779.5	614.0	546.9	507.0	512.3	396.2	340.3
Commercial concerns	2,760.4	2,688.6	2,403.8	2,389.0	2,267.2	2,192.9	1,853.1	1,843.9
Total[c]	5,385.6[d]	5,195.4	4,719.9	4,579.5	4,344.8	4,221.8	3,624.2	3,497.3

[a]Recorded on the basis of the registered place that the licensees regard as their main place of work at the time the returns were issued. A licensee may have commenced experiments at more than one registered place during the year.
[b]The differences between 1978 and 1979 are partly because some establishments were reclassified from one type of registered place to another.
[c]Columns may not add up due to rounding.
[d]Includes 81.3 thousand experimental animals that could not be classified.

SOURCE: U.K. Home Office, Secretary of State, *Statistics of Experiments on Living Animals: Great Britain, 1984* (London: Her Majesty's Stationery Office, 1985).

SUMMARY AND CONCLUSIONS

Most of the countries examined for this assessment have laws far more protective of experimental animals than those in the United States. Despite these protections, animal welfare advocates have been applying considerable pressure for even stronger laws, and many countries, including Australia, Switzerland, West Germany, and the United Kingdom, are considering major changes.

Many of the laws have similar requirements. Almost all require anesthetics or analgesics for painful experiments unless these would frustrate the purpose of the experiment. Switzerland goes so far as to require that certain experiments be forgone because they are too painful. Some countries balance the importance of the experiment and the level of pain it would cause before giving approval.

Several countries require euthanasia after a painful experiment is finished; some require destruction of an animal even when it is no longer in pain, rather than allowing it to be reused. Euthanasia requirements sometimes apply only to certain animals, such as dogs, cats, and monkeys. These species are also preferred in other ways, such as requiring that lower animals be substituted for them wherever possible.

Many countries encourage the use of alternatives, and Denmark, West Germany, the Netherlands, Norway, and Sweden require that nonanimal alternatives be used if they are available. Sweden and the United Kingdom have provided funding for the development of alternatives, and West Germany is considering doing so. Many countries restrict educational uses of animals to professional or vocational training, and Switzerland prohibits even this.

All West European countries reviewed for this assessment require that facilities that use experimental animals be licensed. Some also license dealers, breeders, or experimenters. Many also require that individual experiments be approved, some by Government authorities, some by committees. Such committees, except in Sweden and the United Kingdom, do not require lay representatives, although Switzerland and Denmark have such representatives on national advisory boards. The use of ethics committees within the facilities that use animals is growing; their use is presently most well developed in Canada and Sweden.

The experiences of these selected countries can serve as useful models for various protections that are being considered in the United States. However, in trying to apply them, it is necessary to consider the size of a country, and perhaps more importantly, those cultural considerations that affect compliance with the laws.

CHAPTER 16 REFERENCES

1. Australia, Prevention of Cruelty to Animals Act Regulations, New South Wales Government Gazette, No. 68, May 24, 1929.
2. Australia, Prevention of Cruelty to Animals Act Regulations, New South Wales Government Gazette, No. 200, 1979.
3. Balls, M., Chairman of the Trustees, Fund for the Replacement of Animals in Medical Experiments, Nottingham, England, personal communication, March 1985.
4. Balls, M., Riddell, R.J., and Worden, A.N. (eds.), *Animals and Alternatives in Toxicity Testing* (New York: Academic Press, 1983).
5. Barany, E., "The Swedish System of Ethical Committees in the Laboratory Animals Field," *Conquest* 172:10-15, March 1983.
6. Canada, Animals for Research Act of 1970, Revised Statutes of Ontario, 1:103-117, 1980.
7. Canada, Animals for Research Act, Revised Regulations of Ontario, 1980, Regulations 16 and 18, 1:79-98, 1980.
8. Canada, Dog Control and Procurement Regulations for the Treatment of Animals, Alberta Regulation 33-72, November 1972.
9. Canada, the Universities Act of 1966, Province of Alberta, Section 50.

38-750 0 - 86 - 13

10. Canada, Urban Municipalities Act of 1970, Province of Saskatchewan, Section 177.
11. Canadian Council on Animal Care, *Animal Care Committees: Recommended Terms of Reference and Guidelines* (Ottawa, Ont., Canada: 1980).
12. Canadian Council on Animal Care, *Ethics of Animal Experimentation* (Ottawa, Ont., Canada: 1981).
13. Canadian Council on Animal Care, *Guide to the Care and Use of Experimental Animals,* Vol. I (Ottawa, Ont., Canada: 1980).
14. Canadian Council on Animal Care, *Guide to the Care and Use of Experimental Animals,* Vol. II (Ottawa, Ont., Canada: 1984).
15. Canadian Council on Animal Care, *Research Animals in Canada* (Ottawa, Ont., Canada: 1984).
16. Canadian Council on Animal Care, *Syllabus of the Basic Principles of Laboratory Animal Science* (Ottawa, Ont., Canada: 1984).
17. Carlsson, B., Nordic Society Against Painful Experiments on Animals, comments in discussion at Second CFN Symposium, *The Ethics of Animal Experimentation,* Stockholm, Sweden, Aug. 12-14, 1985.
18. Denmark, Statute No. 220 of May 18, 1977, on Animal Experiments, and Ordinance No. 106 of 1954, on the Maintenance and Submission of Records on the Use of Animals for Biological and Medical Research, in *Forsogsdyr og Dyreforsog,* Svendsen, P., and Hau, J., 1982.
19. Denmark, Statute No. 93, "On the Use of Animals for Biological and Medical Research," 1954.
20. Erichsen, S., National Institute of Public Health, Experimental Animal Board Member, Oslo, Norway, personal communication, January 1985.
21. Esling, R., "European Animal Experimentation Law," *Animals in Research: New Perspectives in Animal Experimentation,* D. Sperlinger (ed.) (New York: John Wiley & Sons, 1981).
22. Evers, T., Attache for Health and Environment Protection, Royal Netherlands Embassy, Washington, DC, personal communications, February and November 1984.
23. Farstad, M., Science and Agricultural Counsellor, Embassy of Sweden, Washington, DC, personal communication, October 1984.
24. Federal Republic of Germany, Animal Protection Act of July 24, 1972, Sartorius Band I, Verfassungsund Verwaltungsgesetze, 873, 1-12, Erganzungslieferung Marz (1982).
25. Federal Republic of Germany, Federal Ministry of Food, Agriculture, and Forestry, *List of Regulations Affecting the Conduct of Animal Experiments,* BML No. 321-3520-1/1 (Bonn: Oct. 17, 1984).
26. Federal Republic of Germany, Federal Ministry of Food, Agriculture, and Forestry, *Proposal to the Cabinet for Amendments to the Animal Protection Act of July 24, 1972* (Bonn: November 1984).
27. Flowers, F., *Educating the Scientist in Research Animal Care* (Ottawa, Ont., Canada: Canadian Council on Animal Care, 1984).
28. Flowers, F., "Research Animal Care in Canada: Its Control and Regulation," The Role of Animals in Biomedical Research, *Ann. N.Y. Acad. Sci.* 406: 144-149, 1983.
29. Gärtner, K., "100 Years of Regulations for Animal Welfare and for Animal Experimentation in Germany—Effects and Reasons," presented at Second CFN Symposium, *The Ethics of Animal Experimentation,* Stockholm, Sweden, Aug. 12-14, 1985.
30. Ikkaiat, S., Second Secretary, Embassy of Japan, Washington, DC, personal communication, December 1984.
31. Jansen, Veterinary Officer of Public Health, Veterinarie Hoofdinspectie, The Netherlands, personal communication, October 1985.
32. Japan, Prime Minister's Office, Deputy Chief Secretary for General Affairs, *Circular: On the Enforcement of the Law Concerning the Protection and Control of Animals,* Sokan, No. 60, Feb. 12, 1974.
33. Japan, Law Concerning the Protection and Control of Animals, Law No. 105, Oct. 1, 1973.
34. Japan, Enforcement Order, Law Concerning the Protection and Control of Animals, Cabinet Order No. 107, Apr. 7, 1975.
35. Japan, Prime Minister's Office, The Law and Related Standards for the Protection of Animals, Tokyo, Japan, 1982.
36. Japan, Order Concerning the Animal Protection Council, Cabinet Order No. 104, Apr. 11, 1974.
37. Japan, Prime Minister's Office, *Standards Concerning the Raising, Custody, etc. of Animals in Experimental Use,* Notification No. 6, Mar. 27, 1980.
38. Japan Experimental Animal Research Association, "Law Concerning the Protection and Control of Animals (Law No. 105), October 1, 1973," *Jikken Dobutsu* 31(3):221-231, 1982.
39. Japan Science Council, *On the Adoption of Guidelines for Animal Experimentation,* 80th General Meeting, Nov. 5, 1980.
40. Kjaersgaard, C., Chairman, The Permanent State Board for the Supervision of Use of Animals for Experiments, Copenhagen, Denmark, personal communication, January 1985.
41. Lane-Petter, W., et al., *The Welfare of Laboratory Animals: Legal, Scientific, and Humane Requirements* (Hertfordshire, England: Universities' Federation for Animal Welfare, 1977).
41a. National Health and Medical Research Council, *Code of Practice for the Care and Use of Animals for Experimental Purposes* (Canberra, Australia: Australian Government Publishing Service, 1985).
42. Netherlands, Decree of May 24, 1972, Staatsblad 311.

43. Netherlands, Law of Jan. 25, 1961, Staatsblad 19.
44. Netherlands, Law of Jan. 8, 1975, Staatsblad 48.
45. Netherlands, Law of Jan. 12, 1977, Staatsblad 67.
46. Norway, Regulation of Dec. 22, 1977, on Biological Experiments with Animals, 1977 Norsk Lovtidend, Avd. I, 1188-1192.
47. Norway, Statute No. 73 of Dec. 20, 1974, on Protection of Animals, Sections 20-22, Norges Lover, 1685-1981, at 2301-2306, 1982.
48. Öbrink, K., "Swedish Law of Laboratory Animals," *Scientists' Center for Laboratory Animal Welfare Newsletter* 4(1):1-3 and 4(2):5, 1982.
49. Öbrink, K., "Are Regulations to Protect Experimental Animals Adequate?" *Research Ethics,* K. Berg and K. Trany (eds.) (New York: Alan R. Liss, Inc., 1983).
50. Rowsell, H., Executive Director, Canadian Council on Animal Care, Ottawa, Ont., Canada, personal communications, April and November 1984 and March 1985.
51. Rowsell, H., *The Animal in Research: Perspective on Voluntary Control* (Ottawa, Ont., Canada: Canadian Council on Animal Care, 1984).
52. Rowsell, H., "The Voluntary Control Program of the Canadian Council on Animal Care," *J. Med. Primatol.* 9:5-8, 1980.
53. Rozemond, H., Veterinary Officer of Public Health, Veterinaire Hoofdinspectie, The Netherlands, personal communication, March 1985.
54. Rozemond, H., *Statistics of Animal Experimentation in the Netherlands: 1982* (Leischendam, The Netherlands: Veterinary Head Inspectorate, 1983).
55. Russell, J.C., and Secord, D.C., "Holy Dogs and the Laboratory: Some Canadian Experiences With Animal Research," *Perspect. Biol. Med.* 28:374-381, 1985.
56. Shewart, K., Minister for Local Government of New South Wales, Sydney, Australia, personal communication, Mar. 29, 1985.
57. Skogland, E., General Veterinary Division, National Board of Agriculture of Sweden, in discussion at Second CFN Symposium, *The Ethics of Animal Experimentation,* Stockholm, Sweden, Aug. 12-14, 1985.
58. Sweden, Ordinance No. 554 of 1982 on Amendment (and Republication) of the Ordinance on Use of Animals for Scientific Purposes, etc. (1979:286), 1982 Svensk Forfattningssamling, No. 554.
59. Sweden, Ordinance No. 29 of 1979, "The Ordinance of the National Board of Agriculture of Animal Breeding for Scientific Purpose, etc." (LSFS 1979:29).
60. Sweden, Ordinance No. 30 of 1979, "The Ordinance of the National Board of Agriculture of Keeping Journals etc. When Using Animals for Scientific Purpose" (LSFS: 1979:30).
61. Sweden, Statute No. 979 of 1978, "Statute on Alteration in the Animal Protection Act of 1944" (SFS 1978:979).
62. Switzerland, Federal Law of March 9, 1978, Regarding the Protection of Animals, RO 1981:562-571, as amended by the Ordinance of May 27, 1981, Regarding the Protection of Animals, RO 1981:572-598.
63. Tajima, Y., "History of the Development of Laboratory Animal Science in Japan," *Jikken Dobutsu* 33(1):1-23, 1984.
64. Trolle, I., *Animal Experiments* (Stockholm, Sweden: Robert Larson, 1971).
65. U.K., The Protection of Animals (Anaesthetics) Act 1954, 2 & 3 Elizabeth II, ch. 46, *Halsbury's Statutes of England,* 3d ed., vol. 2, 1966.
66. U.K., The Protection of Animals (Anaesthetics) Act 1964, ch. 39, *Halsbury's Statutes of England,* 3d ed., vol. 2, 1964.
67. U.K. Department of Health and Social Security, Committee on Toxicity of Chemicals in Food, Consumer Products and the Environment, *Guidelines for the Testing of Chemicals for Toxicity,* Report on Health and Social Subjects 27 (London: Her Majesty's Stationery Office, 1982).
68. U.K. Home Office, Veterinary Inspectorate, *Notes for Guidance in Completing Forms of Application Under the Cruelty to Animals Act, 1876* (London: 1971).
69. U.K. Home Office, Advisory Committee on the Administration of the Cruelty to Animals Act, 1876, *Report on the LD_{50} Test to the Secretary of State* (London, 1979).
70. U.K. Home Office, *Scientific Procedures on Living Animals* Command 9521 (London: Her Majesty's Stationery Office, 1985).
71. Voetz, D., Federal Ministry of Food, Agriculture, and Forestry, Federal Republic of Germany, Bonn, West Germany, personal communication, November 1984.
72. Weibel, E.R., "Man's Relation to Experimental Animals. Modern Times—The Present Situation in Switzerland," at the Second CFN Symposium, *The Ethics of Animal Experimentation,* Stockholm, Sweden, Aug. 12-14, 1985.
73. Weihe, W., "Problems of Alternatives to Animal Experiments," *Fortschritte der Medizin* 100:2162-2168, 1982.
74. Weihe, W., "Regulation of Animal Experimentation—The International Experience: Switzerland," presented at the Second CFN Symposium, *The Ethics of Animal Experimentation,* Stockholm, Sweden, Aug. 12-14, 1985.
75. Yokoyama, A., *Handbook on Experimental Animals* (Tokyo: Yokendo, 1983).

76. Zbinden, G., and Flury-Roversi, M., "Significance of the LD_{50} Test for the Toxicological Evaluation of Chemical Substances," *Arch. Toxicol.* 47:77-99, 1981.

77. Zobrist, S., Attache for Science and Technology, Embassy of Switzerland, Washington, DC, personal communications, October 1984 and December 1985.

Appendixes

Appendix A
Testing Guidelines

Testing Guidelines

Testing guidelines are developed for a variety of reasons: to allow results of various test substances or species to be easily compared, to encourage the use of certain protocols so that testing need not be repeated, and to facilitate the work of those who design and carry out tests. Many organizations have developed testing guidelines. Three such compilations have been selected for discussion.

FDA Guidelines Involving Whole Animal Testing

To the extent possible, the Food and Drug Administration (FDA) makes its animal testing guidelines consistent throughout the agency and consistent with those of other agencies and organizations. However, special uses of products require special testing, and guidance is available from agency staff to help manufacturers meet those requirements. In this table, tests that generally can be considered common or standard toxicological tests usually used throughout the agency are grouped together. Those that are more specific for evaluation of the safety of certain products are identified with the FDA Center responsible for regulating that product.

I. Agency-wide
- A. General Toxicity
  1. Acute oral—rodent, nonrodent
  2. Acute dermal—rodent, nonrodent
  3. Acute inhalation—rodent
  4. Subchronic oral—rodent, nonrodent
  5. Chronic oral—rodent, nonrodent
  6. Carcinogenicity—rodent
  7. Combined chronic/carcinogenicity—rodent
- B. Specific Effects
  1. Dermal sensitization—guinea pig
  2. Dermal irritation—rabbit
  3. Eye irritation—rabbit
  4. Teratogenicity—rodent, rabbit
  5. Reproduction—rodent
  6. Absorption, distribution, metabolism, elimination—rodent, nonrodent
  7. Neural-behavioral—rodent, rabbit

II. Center-oriented
- A. Human Drugs
  1. Subchronic inhalation—rodent, nonrodent
  2. Subchronic dermal—rodent, nonrodent
  3. Vaginal and rectal administration—rodent, nonrodent
  4. Immunotoxicity—rodent
- B. Food Additives/Color Additives
  1. Immunotoxicity—rodent
  2. Protein quality—rodent
  3. Vitamin D assay—rodent
- C. Biologics
  1. All biologics administered by injection
     - a. Safety—guinea pigs, mice
     - b. Pyrogenicity—rabbits
  2. Vaccines
     - a. Safety—mice, suckling mice, chimpanzees, monkeys, guinea pigs, rabbits
     - b. Potency—guinea pigs, mice, monkeys
     - c. Hypersensitivity—guinea pigs
     - d. Toxicity—mice
  3. Antitoxins
     - a. Potency—guinea pigs, mice
  4. Toxins
     - a. Potency—mice
  5. Toxoids
     - a. Potency—mice
  6. Immune globulins
     - a. Potency—guinea pigs
  7. Tuberculin
     - a. Safety—guinea pigs
     - b. Potency—mice
- D. Devices
  1. Corneal metabolism—rabbit
  2. Biomaterial implant—rabbit, primate, cat
  3. U.S.P. intracutaneous—rabbit
- E. Cosmetics
  1. Primary skin irritation and corrosivity—rabbit
  2. Phototoxicity—nude mouse, rabbit, guinea pig
- F. New Veterinary Drugs
  1. Safety, efficacy—target species
  2. Drug tolerance—target species
  3. Reproduction studies—target species
  4. Tissue irritation—target species
  5. Combination drug—target species
  6. Drug disposition—target species
  7. Route of administration—target species
  8. Intramammary infusion—dairy cows, goats

OECD Guidelines Involving Whole Animal Testing

The Organization for Economic Cooperation and Development (OECD) guidelines have wide acceptance in the United States and abroad because of the Mutual Acceptance of Data Decision (1). Under the terms of this decision, member countries of OECD must accept data generated in other countries if done so according to these guidelines. Animal tests contained in the guidelines are listed below.

1. Effects on Biotic Systems
   - 202 Daphnia, acute immobilization test and reproduction test
   - 203 Fish, acute toxicity test
   - 204 Fish, prolonged toxicity test: 14-day study
   - 205 Avian dietary toxicity test
   - 206 Avian reproduction test
2. Degradation and Accumulation
   - 305A Bioaccumulation: Sequential Static Fish Test
   - 305B Bioaccumulation: Semi-static Fish Test
   - 305C Bioaccumulation: Test for the Degree of Bioconcentration in Fish
   - 305D Bioaccumulation: Static Fish Test
   - 305E Bioaccumulation: Flow-through Fish Test
3. Health Effects

   Short-Term Toxicology
   - 401 Acute oral toxicity
   - 402 Acute dermal toxicity
   - 403 Acute inhalation toxicity
   - 404 Acute dermal irritation/corrosion
   - 405 Acute eye irritation/corrosion
   - 406 Skin sensitization
   - 407 Repeated dose oral toxicity—rodent: 14/28 day
   - 408 Subchronic oral toxicity—rodent: 90 day
   - 409 Subchronic oral toxicity—nonrodent: 90 day
   - 410 Repeated dose dermal toxicity: 14/28 day
   - 411 Subchronic dermal toxicity: 90 day
   - 412 Repeated dose inhalation toxicity: 14/28 day
   - 413 Subchronic inhalation toxicity: 90 day
   - 414 Teratogenicity
   - 415 One-generation reproduction toxicity study
   - 416 Two-generation reproduction toxicity study
   - 417 Toxicokinetics
   - 418 Acute delayed neurotoxicity of organophosphorous substances
   - 419 Subchronic delayed neurotoxicity of organophosphorous substances: 90 day

   Long-Term Toxicology
   - 451 Carcinogenicity studies
   - 452 Chronic toxicity studies
   - 453 Combined chronic toxicity/carcinogenicity studies

   Genetic Toxicology
   - 474 Genetic toxicity: micronucleus test
   - 475 In vivo mammalian bone marrow cytogenetic test—chromosomal analysis
   - 478 Rodent dominant lethal test

Pesticide Assessment Guidelines Involving Whole-Animal Testing

The Office of Pesticide Programs of the Environmental Protection Agency (EPA) has developed guidelines for testing required under the Federal Insecticide, Fungicide, and Rodenticide Act. These Pesticide Assessment Guidelines contain standards for conducting acceptable tests, guidelines for the evaluation and reporting of data, guidelines as to when additional testing might be required, and examples of acceptable protocols (2). Similar guidelines have been developed by EPA's Office of Toxic Substances (OTS) for testing required under the Toxic Substances Control Act (3).

Subdivision E: Hazard Evaluation: Wildlife and Aquatic Organisms

Series 70: General Information and Requirements

Series 71: Avian and Mammalian Testing
- 71-1 Avian single-dose oral LD_{50} test
- 71-2 Avian dietary LC_{50} test
- 71-3 Wild mammal toxicity test
- 71-4 Avian reproduction test
- 71-5 Simulated and actual field tests for mammals and birds

Series 72: Aquatic Organism Testing
- 72-1 Acute toxicity test for freshwater fish
- 72-2 Acute toxicity test for freshwater aquatic invertebrates
- 72-3 Acute toxicity test for estuarine and marine organisms
- 72-4 Fish early life-stage and aquatic invertebrate life-cycle studies
- 72-5 Life-cycle tests of fish
- 72-6 Aquatic organism accumulation tests
- 72-7 Simulated or actual field testing for aquatic organisms

Subdivision F: Hazard Evaluation: Humans and Domestic Animals

Series 80: Overview, Definition, and General Requirements

Series 81: Acute Toxicity and Irritation Studies
- 81-1 Acute oral toxicity study

81-2 Acute dermal toxicity study
81-3 Acute inhalation toxicity study
81-4 Primary eye irritation study
81-5 Primary dermal irritation study
81-6 Dermal sensitization study
81-7 Acute delayed neurotoxicity of organophosphorous substances

Series 82: Subchronic Testing
82-1 Subchronic oral toxicity (rodent and nonrodent): 90 day study
82-2 Repeated dose dermal toxicity: 21 day study
82-3 Subchronic dermal toxicity: 90 day study
82-4 Subchronic inhalation toxicity: 90 day study
82-5 Subchronic neurotoxicity: 90 day study

Series 83: Chronic and Long-Term Studies
83-1 Chronic toxicity studies
83-2 Oncogenicity studies
83-3 Teratogenicity study
83-4 Reproductive and fertility effects
83-5 Combined chronic toxicity/oncogenicity studies

Series 84: Mutagenicity
84-1 Purpose and general recommendations for mutagenicity testing
84-2 Mutagenicity tests (described in very general terms, with reference to the OTS guidelines)

Series 85: Special Studies
85-1 Metabolism study
85-2 Domestic animal safety testing

Subdivision G: Product Performance

Series 95: Efficacy of Invertebrate Control Agents
95-1 General considerations
95-8 Livestock, poultry, fur and wool-bearing animal treatments
95-9 Treatments to control pests of humans and pets

Series 96: Efficacy of Vertebrate Control Agents
96-1 General considerations
96-2 Fish control agents
96-3 Aquatic amphibian control agents
96-4 Terrestrial amphibian and reptilian control agents
96-5 Avian toxicants
96-6 Avian repellants
96-7 Avian frightening agents
96-8 Mole toxicants
96-9 Bat toxicants and repellants
96-10 Commensal rodenticides
96-11 Rodenticides in orchards
96-12 Rodenticides on farm and rangelands
96-13 Rodent fumigants
96-14 Rodent repellants on tree seeds
96-15 Rodent repellants on cables
96-16 Rodent reproductive inhibitors
96-17 Mammalian predacides
96-18 Domestic dog and cat repellants
96-19 Browsing animal repellants
96-30 Methods and protocols

Subdivision M: Biorational Pesticides

(This subdivision duplicates many of the provisions of other subdivisions, and is therefore not described in detail.)

Series 150: Overview, Definitions, and General Provisions

Series 152: Toxicology Guidelines
Subseries 152A: Toxicology Guidelines
Subseries 152B: Toxicology Guidelines for Microbial Pest Control Agents

Series 154: Nontarget Organism Hazard Guidelines
Subseries 154A: Nontarget Organism Hazard Guidelines for Biochemical Agents
Subseries 154B: Nontarget Organism Hazard Guidelines for Microbial Agents

Series 157: Experimental Use Permit Guidelines

Subdivision N: Environmental Fate

Series 165: Accumulation Studies
165-4 Laboratory Studies of Pesticide Accumulation in Fish
165-5 Field Accumulation Studies of Aquatic Nontarget Organisms

Appendix A References

1. Organization for Economic Cooperation and Development, *Guidelines for Testing of Chemicals*, and addenda (Paris: 1981).
2. U.S. Environmental Protection Agency, *Pesticide Assessment Guidelines* (Springfield, VA: National Technical Information Service, 1984).
3. U.S. Environmental Protection Agency, *Office of Toxic Substances Health and Environmental Effects Test Guidelines* (Washington, DC: update October 1984).

Appendix B

Regulation of Animal Use Within Federal Departments and Agencies

Six Federal departments and four Federal agencies conduct animal experimentation within Federal facilities, or "intramurally." Of those, only the Departments of Commerce and Transportation, which use few animals, have no specific guidelines. A seventh Federal department, the Department of Energy (DOE), conducts no intramural animal experimentation, but has a policy on animal experimentation for its extramural contracted work. The other entities all have some type of policy for intramural use of animals.

Effective December 1986, each Federal research facility will be required to establish an animal care and use committee with composition and function as described in the 1985 amendments to the Animal Welfare Act (see ch. 13). Each Federal committee will report to the head of the Federal entity conducting the animal experimentation.

Several generalizations can be drawn about the guidelines of the Federal entities conducting intramural animal experimentation. Most policies on proper animal care and treatment include:

- adherence to the Animal Welfare Act and to the *Guide for the Care and Use of Laboratory Animals* of the National Institutes of Health (NIH) (26) as well as the Public Health Service (PHS) *Policy on Humane Care and Use of Laboratory Animals by Awardee Institutions* (see app. C);
- an animal care and use committee with at least three members (the attending veterinarian and two scientists within the agency);
- an attending veterinarian responsible for maintaining the proper animal care standards;
- some prior review of protocols and animal species use, usually accomplished by an animal care and use committee;
- no real mechanism for enforcement of the policy, with the primary responsibility for maintaining the proper standards and adhering to agency guidelines lying with the individual investigator;
- a minimal number of site inspections and no real oversight mechanism; and
- a policy calling for using as few animals as possible and encouraging the use of alternative methods wherever feasible.

Some agency policies are noteworthy for additional provisions intended to promote high standards of animal care and use:

- NIH requires all animal research committees to include one member sensitive to bioethical issues and not employed in the same NIH bureau, institute, or division. This person must be a Federal Government employee and so may or may not be a layperson. These committees have explicit responsibilities and a detailed administrative structure in which to carry out duties.
- The Ames Research Center of the National Aeronautics and Space Administration (NASA) has demonstrated the successful participation of lay committee members in the consideration of animal welfare issues: 40 percent of the committee are laypeople, a format set up at NASA's instigation.
- Since 1971, the Veterans' Administration (VA) has required that all facilities using animals seek and obtain accreditation by the American Association for Accreditation of Laboratory Animal Care (AAALAC). The VA has a contract with AAALAC covering all its research facilities, thus prohibiting failure of accreditation of any constituent facility solely for financial reasons. The Department of Energy also requires the facilities of its extramural contractors to be AAALAC-accredited.
- The Department of Defense (DOD) has a policy and committee distinct from its general animal policy to ensure proper care and use of nonhuman primates.
- The policies at the Food and Drug Administration (FDA) and the Department of the Interior give a great deal of flexibility to the research centers to allow specific policies tailored to the needs and demands of each animal facility. Although this may have many advantages, it may make the maintenance and monitoring of a standard of care throughout the agency difficult.

Department of Agriculture

Regulation of animal use in research within the U.S. Department of Agriculture (USDA) involves adherence to the Animal Welfare Act and to the NIH *Guide* (26). Much of the animal research performed by USDA involves farm animals, which are largely excluded from these policies. The system of compliance involves periodic checking of intramural research facilities. For extramural research, no enforcement occurs; hence the system is largely voluntary and self-regulating (15).

Department of Defense

The general policy on animal use in all Department of Defense programs is contained in DOD Directive No.

3216.1, issued by the Deputy Secretary of Defense in 1982. This statement sets policy on the humane treatment and appropriate care of animals used in research and the responsibilities of different DOD personnel to carry out the directive. In general, it follows the Animal Welfare Act and the NIH *Guide,* along with attempting to incorporate alternatives to animal use in the form of replacement, reduction, and refinement. Other, special policies treat the general use of nonhuman primates and prohibit the use of dogs, cats, and nonhuman primates for developing nuclear weapons. The directive also requires that all proposals or designs for animal experiments undergo appropriate animal welfare review to confirm: "1) the need to perform the experiment or demonstration; 2) the adequacy of the design of the experiment or demonstration; and 3) compliance with established policy on the use of animals" (20).

Army Regulation 70-18 (a Joint Service regulation) implements the directive's policies uniformly for all DOD components. The authority for enforcing this regulation is conferred to the Secretary of the Army, who is required to develop and issue, in consultation with the other DOD components, regulations implementing the directive. Army Regulation 70-18 states that all DOD facilities using animals should seek AAALAC accreditation. Also, it sets up a long chain of responsibilities for establishing and policing animal welfare policies. The regulation states that the Under Secretary of Defense for Research and Engineering will: "1) issue policies and procedural guidance under DOD directive 3216.1, 2) allocate nonhuman primate resources, and 3) designate a veterinarian as the DOD representative to IRAC [Interagency Research Animal Committee]" (21). The Surgeon General of each DOD component involved in animal research must supervise animal use and implement this regulation in each component, establish a joint working group to identify and conserve nonhuman primate resources, and establish and provide representatives to a joint technical working group that periodically reviews the care and use of animals in DOD programs. Finally, the local commander of a facility must ensure that:

- all programs involving animals conform to the guidelines cited in Army Regulation 70-18;
- local animal care and use, procurement, and transportation policies and procedures comply with the regulation;
- animals used or intended to be used will experience no unnecessary pain, suffering, or stress, and their use will meet valid DOD requirements;
- alternatives to animal species will be used if they produce scientifically satisfactory results; and
- dogs, cats, or nonhuman primates are not used in research conducted to develop nuclear, biological, or chemical weapons (21).

Thus, the powers and responsibilities for carrying out DOD animal welfare policies are decentralized. DOD does not do any inspections of its facilities. The facilities are required to submit annual reports to USDA under the regulations implementing the Animal Welfare Act.

The Army regulation builds the institutional review structure around the local animal care committee. Local commanders must form a committee to oversee the care and use of animals in their facilities. The committee must have at least three members, including at least one person not involved in the proposed project and one veterinarian. The committee reviews: 1) all aspects of animal care to ensure that established policies, standards, and regulations are complied with; and 2) all research protocols and proposals for proper animal welfare policies and good animal experimentation standards. Sufficient information to do this animal care and treatment review must be presented with all research proposals. In addition, proposals that involve experimentation on nonhuman primates are reviewed separately by the proper DOD component office (21).

As with other departments in the Federal Government, DOD contracts with outside investigators for some of its research. The DOD extramural animal research policy requires that the same standards outlined in Army Regulation 70-18 be followed by contractors in order to receive DOD funds. Assurance is obtained by written statements from the recipient's animal care committee or other responsible official. An assurance is also required that the proposal or protocol has been reviewed and approved by the local animal care and use committee or by the attending veterinarian (21). Enforcement of these policies for extramural research is more difficult than the intramural policy, since investigators and administrators are not directly responsible to the military line of command.

In addition to DOD-wide policies issued by the Office of the Secretary, a recommendation is pending in the Army Medical Research and Development Command that an Advisory Committee on Animal Welfare be appointed, including non-DOD representatives, to meet periodically about concerns related to the use of animals for research and training purposes (7).

In 1983, the Air Force commissioned an outside review panel to study animal use in its Aerospace Medical Division. The panel looked at Brooks Air Force Base (San Antonio, TX) and Wright-Patterson Air Force Base (Dayton, OH), which together account for 95 percent of the service's animal use. The panel found the current policy in place to be satisfactory and was (17):

> . . . impressed with the thoroughness and genuine concern of all those involved to ensure that appropriate measures are taken to effect proper care and use of animals. Furthermore, there was a clear emphasis on selection of alternatives to animal use where feasible. Excellent progress was shown in the use of simulation models for a variety of radiation and toxicological studies.

The panel did note that the system of care and treatment policies was too informal and based on the current personnel; it was unconvinced the system would remain in place if staff were transferred. The Aerospace Medical Division of the Air Force drafted a Supplement to Army Regulation 70-18 to implement some of the review panel's recommendations. The most substantial change deals with the animal care and use committee membership (21):

> The local commander will appoint at least one lay person from the local community who has no direct Department of Defense connections to serve as a member of the Committee. This lay member should not be a veterinarian or research scientist who works with animals; however, a background in sciences would be helpful. The Committee may have permanent or ad hoc membership. Its specific purpose is to review all protocols, experimental designs, or lesson plans that involve the use of animals and assure compliance with [DOD policy].

The Air Force Supplement to Army Regulation 70-18 also requires that each organization using animals submit not just the Annual Report of Research Facility of USDA's Animal and Plant Health Inspection Service (APHIS), but also an Annual Animal Use Report, listing all species used, the inventory at the beginning of the year, additions and losses to the facility, the ending inventory, the utilization of the animals, the different experimental situations, and the projected use of animals for the next fiscal year (18).

Department of Energy

The Department of Energy has no intramural research facilities and so contracts for all its research. The division involved with animals is the Office of Health and Environmental Research (OHER); programs involving research with animals represented less than 15 percent of OHER's total research budget for fiscal year 1985 (5). Proposals for OHER-funded research are subjected to outside peer review for scientific merit. An OHER research committee from the Office's four divisions has final approval before funding a research proposal.

The OHER policy for animal use by its extramural contractors places the prime responsibility for the maintenance of animal facilities and for animal care on the contractor. OHER contract research facilities are bound by law to comply with the Animal Welfare Act and its regulatory policies, and OHER personnel maintain close liaison to assure such compliance. In addition, the IRAC principles are part of the OHER policy statement, along with the requirement to maintain AAALAC accreditation (5).

To enforce these policies, one OHER staff member has responsibility for monitoring animal research programs for compliance. This staff member must maintain contact with the research facilities to assure accreditation and to affirm, at least yearly, that it is being maintained. Site visits with at least one noncontract veterinarian who is an expert in laboratory-animal care may be conducted to evaluate the care and treatment of experimental animals (5,6).

Department of Health and Human Services

Food and Drug Administration

The Food and Drug Administration has recently played a major role in attempting to address animal welfare issues. In 1983, the agency took two steps in this direction by sponsoring an acute studies workshop and by establishing an Agency Steering Committee on Animal Welfare Issues.

The workshop helped clarify FDA's position on its need for toxicity data, especially from the LD_{50} test. The points emerging from the workshop were that:

- FDA had no regulations mandating use of the LD_{50} test;
- the requirement by Federal agencies for LD_{50} data from regulated parties was much less than perceived by the public;
- government and industry agreed that there are better determinants of acute toxicity than the LD_{50} test and that they supported developing valid alternatives to the use of animals for testing chemicals;
- U.S. Government agencies are cooperating with other countries through organizations like the Organization for Economic Cooperation and Development; and
- improvements in the way animals are used for toxicity testing can and should be made administratively rather than through legislation (1,22).

The steering committee, which in part grew out of the acute studies workshop, found several FDA references to the LD_{50} that could be misinterpreted as requirements to perform the test, and one involving three antitumor antibiotics where the requirement still existed (in contrast to the workshop findings). Its 1984 report states that, in all these instances (except for the antitumor antibiotics), regulations and guidelines are being rewritten to resolve any misunderstandings. They will then reflect the position of FDA that "the use of this test should be avoided except for those rare situations where no alternative exists." In the case of the antitumor antibiotics, FDA is considering eliminating the requirement (23).

Addressing five specific considerations, all part of its investigation of agency testing guidelines and practices to answer questions raised at the acute studies workshop, the steering committee concluded that:

- FDA practices and procedures are designed to obtain the maximum amount of data from the minimum number of animals;
- despite general references to the use of LD_{50} tests, FDA has no requirements for LD_{50} data obtained by using the classical, statistically precise test, except for batch release toxicity tests of three antitumor antibiotics;
- there are many alternative tests being studied and developed throughout FDA;
- practices and procedures for assuring humane care and treatment of animals are agency-wide; and
- FDA has a number of regular channels of communication to industry, consumers, and the private sector in general and efforts to improve communication channels will continue (23).

The steering committee recommended workshops on acute toxicity studies throughout the agency, on the use of in vitro alternatives by various centers, and on agency and PHS practices and procedures for the care and handling of animals. The recommendations also called for the establishment of an agency-wide animal welfare committee (23). FDA is now setting up two in-house workshops to address the first two topics (1). Furthermore, it has established a Research Animal Council to see that the recommendations of the report are carried out, to consider animal research issues at FDA in a broad context, and to serve as an oversight committee for individual FDA centers. FDA's Research Animal Council began meeting quarterly in 1984 and will report to the Commissioner; its membership includes one representative from each of the centers within FDA (3).

FDA's policies on humane animal care and treatment require compliance with the Animal Welfare Act as well as with other standards for humane care and use of animals. The steering committee report found that all centers have acceptable procedures, but that they varied in specific details. The centers conduct different amounts of research and testing; some have more formal procedures than others and stronger veterinary staff capabilities. Accreditation by AAALAC is sought on a voluntary basis, and two of FDA's animal facilities, the National Center for Toxicological Research (NCTR) and the Center for Drugs and Biologics of the Office of Biologics Research and Review, are fully accredited (23).

The policies and procedures in place at the National Center for Toxicological Research (Jefferson, AR) are a good example of FDA's system for addressing animal welfare issues, since NCTR is the primary animal research facility within FDA (24):

> The policy of NCTR management is to use laboratory animals under practical and reasonable conditions of humane treatment, in carefully planned experiments with in vitro methodologies balanced against minimally required test species numbers in in vivo bioassays, and via procedures set forth in national standards and guidelines.

The Director of NCTR has primary responsibility for assuring compliance with the policy but delegates some aspects of that control. The duties of the Senior Scientists in NCTR's Office of Research include technical overview of animal use, strain selection, genetic quality control, state-of-the-art reviews, and recommendations for adopting new concepts in animal care and control. The Director of the Division of Animal Husbandry is responsible for breeding-colony operations, animal production and laboratory-animal care in NCTR's various holding areas, and quarantine procedures (25). The animal care committee has adopted an "Animal Use Form for Experimental Protocols" and requires every investigator using animals to provide the committee with detailed information for evaluation (23). Finally, the Director has set up ad hoc committees of in-house personnel to evaluate specific areas of animal care, such as change in feed for the facility (1,24).

The FDA policy on extramural research requires adherence by awardee institutions to the PHS policy and procedures (23):

> This includes (1) having in place a program of animal care which meets federal and Department standards, (2) providing, through AAALAC accreditation or defined self-assessment procedures, assurance of institutional conformance, and (3) maintaining an animal research committee to provide oversight of the institution's animal program, facilities and associated activities.

National Institutes of Health

NIH has a specific animal care and use program for intramural research and for research within NIH-controlled space (25). The NIH policy requires individual investigators to adhere to the NIH *Guide.* In addition, each bureau, institute, or division (BID) is encouraged to pursue accreditation of its animal facilities by either AAALAC or any other NIH-approved accrediting body (at present AAALAC is the sole body) and to report its accreditation status each year to the Deputy Director, who ensures compliance with the policy by each BID.

The NIH policy delegates responsibility to five different authorities, including two types of committees. The first is the local BID Animal Research Committee (ARC). This committee must have at least five Federal Government employees; the BID Scientific Director is responsible for annual appointments of the chairperson and members and for carrying out the committee's recommendations. Included among the five ARC members must be the attending veterinarian on the BID staff, a tenured investigator representing laboratories and divisions that use animals, and "a person who is sensitive to bioethical issues, does not possess an advanced degree in one of the life sciences, and is an employee from outside that BID" (26).

The NIH policy gives the BID ARCs many specific responsibilities beyond the general duties of many such committees. As with other local animal care committees, each ARC is required to make recommendations on animal care matters to its Scientific Director and to review proposals and protocols for humane standards of animal care. It is also supposed to advise individuals on the BID's policies and oversee their implementation within the facility. The major specific duties of the ARC are:

- to hold quarterly meetings at which a majority of the ARC members are present;
- to maintain a file of all minutes, memorandums, waivers, and project review documents;
- to perform site visits of each facility within the BID at least annually to assess compliance, and to submit written reports on these inspections to the Scientific Director;
- to develop a plan for attaining accreditation of the animal facilities or for pursuing accreditation standards; and
- to prepare an annual report for the NIH Deputy Director for Intramural Research addressing problems and accomplishments related to attaining accreditation.

Individual investigators are responsible for submitting appropriate information needed for ARC review of a proposal, advising the ARC chairperson of any significant deviations from procedures described in the most recent project review, and ensuring that all personnel working directly with animals have been trained in the proper care and use of that species. Thus, the system puts much of the burden for proper animal care during an experiment on each investigator.

The second authority set up by the NIH intramural policy was the NIH Animal Research Committee (NIHARC). Committee members are appointed annually by the Deputy Director for Intramural Research and must include a veterinarian, the chairperson from each BID ARC, and a nonaffiliated member. NIHARC holds quarterly meetings, advises the Deputy Director on animal care and use at NIH, discusses issues referred from the BID ARCs, develops and coordinates training programs for NIH employees on animal care and use, and prepares NIH's Annual Report of Research Facility for USDA.

Department of the Interior

The Department of the Interior does more than 95 percent of its research in-house. All research and development facilities must comply with both the Animal Welfare Act and with the Department's *Research and Development Policy/Procedures Handbook* (27), which calls for an approved animal welfare plan. The National Wildlife Health Laboratory (NWHL) must provide assistance upon request in the development, implementation, and maintenance of each program. Due to the diversity of the research programs and the uniqueness of the species involved, each facility is allowed to develop an animal welfare plan peculiar to its own needs as long as it is approved by NWHL.

Each division plan must discuss:

- persons responsible for compliance;
- reporting and recordkeeping procedures for animals used;
- all components of the Animal Welfare Act and the Department animal health and husbandry standards that cannot be complied with, due either to the general design of anticipated studies or the unique natural requirements of the species involved;
- quarantine procedures for exotic species;
- personnel health monitoring and disease prevention programs;
- a schedule for periodic onsite evaluations by the NWHL Veterinary Medical Officer; and
- procedures for handling carcasses following unexpected mortalities (27).

The NWHL Veterinary Medical Officer oversees enforcement of these policies.

Consumer Product Safety Commission

The Consumer Product Safety Commission (CPSC), as part of its mission to enforce the labeling requirements of the Federal Hazardous Substances Act (FHSA) (see ch. 7), conducts its own oral acute toxicity studies to determine the toxic potential of regulated substances. If the demand for testing exceeds the capacity of the CPSC's Health Sciences Laboratory Division, the agency contracts with FDA's NCTR (13).

In addition to requiring its own personnel, contracting agencies, and regulated parties to observe the requirements of the Animal Welfare Act and the NIH *Guide* in performing required safety tests on animals, CPSC has published an Animal Testing Policy, "which is intended to reduce the number of animals tested to determine hazards associated with household products and to reduce any pain that might be associated with such testing" (49 FR 22522). The policy states that CPSC itself and manufacturers of substances covered by the FHSA "should wherever possible utilize existing alternatives to conducting animal testing [including] prior human experience, literature sources which record prior animal testing or limited human tests, and expert opinion."

Citing the provision in FHSA regulations that gives preference to studies based on humans over those with animals, the policy states that CPSC "resorts to animal testing only when the other information sources have been exhausted." It also states that:

- "limit" tests for acute toxicity studies, rather than the "classic" LD_{50}, are performed when necessary, requiring fewer animals;
- eye irritancy testing is not performed if the test substance is a known skin irritant; and
- agency-required Draize (eye irritation) tests are modified to eliminate the need for restraining test rabbits, allowing them full mobility and access to food and water (49 FR 22522).

Environmental Protection Agency

The guidelines and policies that the Environmental Protection Agency (EPA) follows governing humane treatment and appropriate veterinary care for laboratory animals involve AAALAC accreditation for its two major laboratories, adherence to the NIH *Guide*, and adherence to the Animal Welfare Act. In addition, EPA has an intra-agency committee that oversees animal research issues. There is no separate policy for extramural research; NIH *Guide* principles and requisites are enforced in such cases by a signed statement from the investigator that the proper animal care is being observed (16).

The EPA facility at Research Triangle Park, NC, has an animal care committee that oversees and carries out an institutional review of animal care and welfare issues. The committee is composed of representatives of the different research divisions within that facility along with the attending veterinarian. Its 8 to 10 members, who meet approximately once a month and keep records of their proceedings, are responsible for animal care issues only, and do not conduct scientific reviews of research proposals. Scientific review is done separately before proposals reach the committee. The overall responsibilities for the committee are to:

- oversee the functioning of the animal care facility,
- plan improvements for the facility and carry them out,
- set policy for humane treatment of animals,
- set policy for sharing facility resources,
- address any day-to-day animal care problems brought to its attention, and
- review proposals for appropriate animal use and care (2).

In addition, the committee can recommend experimental changes to improve animal care and treatment and has the authority to interrupt or terminate an experiment if it finds any instances of inhumane treatment or inappropriate care of the animals, a step that has been taken at least once since the committee was established (2).

The committee does not monitor experiments while in progress or handle the day-to-day activities of the animal care facility. These powers are delegated to the attending veterinarian (who is under contract with EPA to work at the facility 3 days a week) and a staff of approximately 20 (2).

National Aeronautics and Space Administration

The overall National Aeronautics and Space Administration policy on animal research is based on the Animal Welfare Act, the NIH *Guide,* and the IRAC principles. All NASA facilities, all users of NASA facilities, aircraft, or spacecraft, and all NASA contractors using animals are subject to this policy. The overriding philosophy of the policy is based on three principles:

- Animals will be used only to answer valid questions that improve the health, welfare, or general medical and scientific knowledge of humans.
- Experimental animals must not be subject to avoidable discomfort or distress.
- Experiments requiring the use of invasive procedures without benefit of anesthetic agents demand strong justification and attention to possible alternatives (12).

Although the NASA policy exists today as only a proposed NASA Management Instruction (NMI), it is already being implemented. For example, the NMI establishes an Animal Care and Use Committee (ACUC) in each facility with animals (12); the committee includes a research veterinarian, a biomedical scientist, a nonscientist, and a person not affiliated with NASA. It is responsible for overseeing the animal care facility, establishing specific guidelines, reviewing proposals, and making recommendations for approval or disapproval of funding (9). The committee must ask the following questions for each experiment (12):

- Will the minimum possible number of animals be used?
- Is the use of animals necessary in this experiment?
- Are provisions for care of these animals adequate?

Different compliance with these policies is needed for intramural versus extramural research. For NASA facilities, ACUC reports are required to be sent to the Director of the Life Sciences Division at NASA headquarters reviewing facility procedures. AAALAC accreditation is required for all NASA installations. Currently all facilities are moving toward AAALAC accreditation but have not yet obtained it (12). For extramural research, the institution must submit a written assurance that its animal care policies are equivalent to the NASA policy. (AAALAC accreditation is one way of showing compliance.) Noncompliance will result in termination of the research by the ACUC and possibly sanctions after review by the Director of the Life Sciences Division (19).

The Ames Research Center (Moffett Field, CA), NASA's primary center for nonhuman research, illustrates the implementation of NASA policy. The Ames Research Center has established the *Animal Users Guide* for Ames-sponsored laboratory experiments using animals. This guide sets up two entities to ensure that all legal requirements are met: The animal care facility is responsible for housing and maintaining the animals properly, and the animal care and use committee must monitor all animal care and experimentation progress at the center. In addition, the guide states (28):

> EVERY RESEARCH SCIENTIST AND ALL RESEARCH PERSONNEL, CONTRACTORS, AND GRANTEES ARE RESPONSIBLE FOR OBSERVING THE LEGAL REQUIREMENTS CONCERNING LABORATORY ANIMALS.

The Ames committee reports to the center's Director of Life Sciences and is responsible for:

- reviewing the use of animals in proposed and ongoing experiments;
- reviewing all animal experimentation performed by contractors or grantees;
- serving as an advisory committee on all questions of animal care and use, and as a forum for resolving differences that may occur; and
- reviewing animal-related inventions and devices (28).

At present, the Ames committee has 10 members—4 non-NASA, non-life-sciences laypersons; 1 veterinarian; 1 scientist-veterinarian; 1 engineer; 2 scientists; and 1 science manager. In addition, 2 veterinarians accredited in Laboratory Animal Medicine are advisors. The lay members include an attorney, a professor of religion (ethics), the chairman of the Department of Education at a local college, and the public relations director of the Santa Clara Valley Humane Society. This is one of the few such committees in the country with a 40 percent lay membership. According to the Acting Director of Life Sciences at Ames Research Center, "the out-of-house members have contributed materially to the [committee]." Two of the lay members head subcommittees that are reviewing and updating the *Animal Users Guide* and committee charter and developing an animal user's orientation program (14).

National Science Foundation

A summary of the animal care requirements of the National Science Foundation (NSF) is found in Section 713 of the *NSF Grant Policy Manual* (30) and included in the NSF document "Grant General Conditions," that is sent to each grantee when an award is made. Any grantee performing research on warm-blooded animals must comply with the Animal Welfare Act and its regulations and follow the NIH *Guide*. NSF has no formal inspection system to check on compliance with these policies, as that is judged to be the responsibility of USDA/APHIS (8). The result is a voluntary adherence system by NSF grantees.

Beginning in 1986, NSF imposed two new requirements on grant applicants and grantees who perform research on vertebrate animals:

- Each proposal must be reviewed by an institutional animal care and use committee.
- Each proposal must be accompanied by a statement from the grantee that assures the grantee's compliance with the PHS policy.

Grant proposals submitted to NSF thus face three separate reviews—one by the grantee's institutional committee, one by outside reviewers, and one by NSF staff. Although these are primarily scientific in nature, reviewers are asked to comment on animal welfare issues. If a proposal involves the use of animals, sufficient information must be provided to allow evaluation of the appropriateness of experimental protocols with respect to the choice of species, the number of animals to be used, and any necessary exposure of animals to discomfort, pain, or injury (29). With this information, the reviewers are asked to (29):

> . . . comment if you have any concerns regarding the violation of animal welfare laws or guidelines, the exposure of animals to unnecessary pain or mistreatment, or the use of excessive numbers of animals. If the species being used is not the one most appropriate, or if alternative or adjunct methods could be used to eliminate or reduce the need for animal experimentation, please comment.

Veterans' Administration

The Veterans' Administration is unique in its policies governing humane treatment and appropriate veterinary care for laboratory animals because it has required all its facilities using animals to seek and obtain AAALAC accreditation (see ch. 15). This policy was originated in 1971, and 81 out of 174 VA facilities (as of Apr. 1, 1985) had some level of AAALAC accreditation. Not all VA constituents apply for accreditation, since some do not engage in animal research. In fact, the VA has a contract with AAALAC covering all its research facilities that prohibits failure of accreditation of any constituent facility solely for financial reasons (10).

In addition to requiring adherence to the PHS policy, the VA has a lengthy research review process with a strong committee structure. At the local research facility, each research and development committee has a subcommittee for animal studies that oversees all such research. The membership varies, though it includes at least one member of the research and development committee, a Veterinary Medical Officer (VA employee), and two to four investigators who are involved in studies using animals. Thus, there are no laypersons or persons not affiliated with the research facility on the subcommittee. Except for the veterinarian, who serves indefinitely, members serve 3-year terms (31). The subcommittee has three primary functions:

- to approve the use or uses made of animal subjects in all research studies as they relate to animal welfare laws, regulations, and policies;
- to review all animal studies for need, adequacy, and availability of essential animal research facility support; for the appropriateness, quality, and availability of the animal models; for the humaneness and appropriateness of procedures and conditions surrounding animal subjects before and throughout the study; and
- to evaluate, at least annually, the animal research facility and recommend appropriate actions to correct deficiencies noted (11).

Proposals are reviewed again at a regional VA office by two committees, first for veterinary medical review (appropriate use and care of animals) and then for scientific merit (10). The animal welfare review is done by a Veterinary Medical Panel of specialists chosen for their experience, knowledge, and research in laboratory-animal science and medicine. This panel attempts "to assure that proposals include sound, acceptable animal medicine and husbandry practices in animal research facilities that are operated in conformance with all pertinent animal welfare laws, regulations, and policies" (11). Specifically, the panel conducts reviews:

- to ascertain the description of the animal model;
- to ascertain the biological and medical definition of the animal model;
- to ascertain the environmental and experimental-animal-related factors;
- to determine if there is evidence of adequate experience with the proposed technology of manipulations, monitoring, or measuring;
- to determine if use of intact animals is required or if animal parts could be obtained from or shared with other investigators who have scientifically compatible studies;
- to determine if painful procedures are involved and whether these can be avoided or if their control has been satisfactorily planned; and
- to relate the budget of the experiment to the animal costs and to the animal maintenance needs (11).

In 1984, the VA required that all research proposals have an appendix with a detailed discussion of animal protocols, the number of animals to be used, and why the specific choice of organism was made. This appendix is signed by three people from the local facility—the researcher, the animal committee chairperson, and the research and development chairperson—to guarantee that the procedures are carried out.

The enforcement of the VA's animal research policies rests with the committee structure and is overseen by the Chief Veterinary Medical Officer for the VA, whose duties include making sure all Federal and State animal research laws are observed and that the individual facilities have the funds to continue to remain AAALAC-accredited. In addition, the VA began in fiscal year 1984 strict enforcement of the completion of the Annual Reports of Animal Research Facilities for APHIS by every VA facility, whether the facility used animals in research the preceding year or not (10).

At the local VA facilities, the attending veterinarian has authority for veterinary medical matters. This person must monitor the housing, general treatment, and care of the experimental animals while the experiment is in progress as often as needed. If inhumane treatment or inappropriate care is found, the veterinarian and animal subcommittee do not have the authority to interrupt or terminate an experiment. The subcommittee would make a recommendation to the research and development committee and to the Associate Chief of Staff for Research and Development, who may make a decision or a recommendation to the Director (4). This means there is some enforcement of the proper animal care standards at each local VA facility on a day-to-day basis.

Appendix B References

1. Borsetti, A., Staff Scientist, Office of Science Coordination, Food and Drug Administration, U.S. Department of Health and Human Services, Rockville, MD, personal communications, October and November 1984 and March 1985.
2. Chernoff, N., U.S. Environmental Protection Agency, Research Triangle Park, NC, personal communication, 1984.

3. Crawford, L., Director, Bureau of Veterinary Medicine, Food and Drug Administration, U.S. Department of Health and Human Services, Rockville, MD, personal communication, November 1984.
4. Ditzler, J., Chief Medical Director, Department of Medicine and Surgery, Veterans' Administration, Washington, DC, personal communication, Jan. 17, 1985.
5. Edington, C., Associate Director, Office of Health and Environmental Research, Office of Energy Research, U.S. Department of Energy, Washington, DC, personal communication, Nov. 16, 1984.
6. Edington, C., Procedures for Selection of Animal Research Projects for Funding Through OHER/DOE (Washington, DC: Department of Energy, Jan. 24, 1985).
7. Kainz, R., Office of the Commander, U.S. Army Medical Research and Development Command, Ft. Detrick, MD, personal communication, September 1984.
8. Kingsbury, D., Assistant Director, National Science Foundation, Washington, DC, personal communication, Nov. 2, 1984.
9. Lewis, C.S., "NASA's Use of Animals in Research," prepared for the Life Sciences Division, National Aeronautics and Space Administration, Washington, DC, Sept. 28, 1983.
10. Middleton, C., Chief Veterinary Medical Officer, Veterans' Administration, Washington, DC, personal communication, Oct.3, 1984.
11. Moreland, A., "Animal Research Protocol Review Within the Veterans' Administration," mimeo, Gainesville, FL, 1984.
12. Nicogossian, A., Director, Life Sciences Division, National Aeronautics and Space Administration, Washington, DC, personal communication, Oct. 19, 1984.
13. Porter, W., Health Sciences Laboratory Division, Consumer Product Safety Commission, Washington, DC, personal communication, Nov. 19, 1984.
14. Sharp, J., Acting Director of Life Sciences, Ames Research Center, National Aeronautics and Space Administration, letter to A. Nicogossian, Director, Life Sciences Division, NASA, on Animal Care and Use Committee, Moffett Field, CA, Sept. 12, 1984.
15. Stewart, W., Senior Veterinarian, Animal and Plant Health Inspection Service, U.S. Department of Agriculture, Hyattsville, MD, personal communication, November 1984.
16. Ulvedal, F., Acting Director, Water and Toxic Substances Health Effects Research Division, U.S. Environmental Protection Agency, Washington, DC, personal communications, September and October 1984.
17. U.S. Department of Defense, Air Force, *Aerospace Medical Division Animal Use Review Panel Meetings* (Washington, DC: May 1984).
18. U.S. Department of Defense, Air Force, Aerospace Medical Division, "Animals in DOD Research and Training AMD Supplement 1" (draft), Brooks Air Force Base, TX, 1985.
19. U.S. Department of Defense, Assistant Secretary of Defense for Health Affairs, *Memorandum to the Secretaries of the Uniformed Services, President of the Uniformed Services University of the Health Sciences, and Directors of Defense Agencies* (Washington, DC: Jan. 4, 1984).
20. U.S. Department of Defense, *The Use of Animals in DOD Programs,* DOD Instruction 3216.1 (Washington, DC: Feb. 1, 1982).
21. U.S. Department of Defense, *The Use of Animals in DOD Programs,* Army Regulation 70-18 (Washington, DC: June 1, 1984).
22. U.S. Department of Health and Human Services, Food and Drug Administration, Office of Science Coordination, *Final Report of Acute Studies Workshop* (Washington, DC: Nov. 9, 1983).
23. U.S. Department of Health and Human Services, Food and Drug Administration, *Final Report to the Commissioner, FDA Agency Steering Committee on Animal Welfare Issues* (Rockville, MD: Aug. 15, 1984).
24. U.S. Department of Health and Human Services, Food and Drug Administration, National Center for Toxicological Research, *NCTR Quality Assurance Program* (Jefferson, AR: May 1983).
25. U.S. Department of Health and Human Services, Public Health Service, National Institutes of Health, *Animal Care and Use in the Intramural Program,* NIH Policy 3040-2 (Bethesda, MD: Dec. 30, 1983).
26. U.S. Department of Health and Human Services, Public Health Service, National Institutes of Health, *Guide for the Care and Use of Laboratory Animals,* NIH Pub. No. 85-23 (Bethesda, MD: National Institutes of Health, 1985).
27. U.S. Department of the Interior, *Research and Development Policy/Procedures Handbook* (Washington, DC: July 26, 1984).
28. U.S. National Aeronautics and Space Administration, Ames Research Center, *Animal Users Guide AHB 7180-1* (Moffett Field, CA: June 1982).
29. U.S. National Science Foundation, Office of the Assistant Director for Biological, Behavioral, and Social Sciences, *NSF AD/BBS Circular No. 13* (Washington, DC: June 15, 1982).
30. U.S. National Science Foundation, *NSF Grant Policy Manual, Section 713* (Washington, DC: Apr. 15, 1984).
31. U.S. Veterans' Administration, Department of Medicine and Surgery, *Research and Development in Medicine General* (Washington, DC: Apr. 27, 1982).

Appendix C

Public Health Service Policy on Humane Care and Use of Laboratory Animals by Awardee Institutions

The following is reprinted from U.S. Department of Health and Human Services, Public Health Service, National Institutes of Health, "Laboratory Animal Welfare," NIH Guide for Grants and Contracts *14(8), June 25, 1985.*

Introduction

It is the policy of the Public Health Service (PHS) to require institutions to establish and maintain proper measures to ensure the appropriate care and use of all animals involved in research, research training and biological testing activities (hereinafter referred to as activities) supported by the PHS. The PHS endorses the "U.S. Government Principles for the Utilization and Care of Vertebrate Animals Used in Testing, Research and Training" developed by the Interagency Research Animal Committee (IRAC). This policy is intended to implement and supplement those Principles.

Applicability

This policy is applicable to all PHS-approved activities involving animals, whether the activities are performed at an awardee institution or any other institution and conducted in the United States, the Commonwealth of Puerto Rico, or any territory or possession of the United States. Institutions in foreign countries receiving PHS support for activities involving animals shall comply with this policy, or provide evidence to the PHS that acceptable standards for humane care and use of the animals in PHS-supported activities will be met. No PHS support for an activity involving animals will be provided to an individual unless that individual is affiliated with or sponsored by an institution which can and does assume responsibility for compliance with this policy for PHS-supported activities, or unless the individual makes other arrangements with the PHS. This policy does not affect applicable state or local laws or regulations which impose more stringent standards for the care and use of laboratory animals. All institutions are required to comply, as applicable, with the Animal Welfare Act, and other Federal statutes and regulations relating to animals.

Definitions

A. Animal

Any live, vertebrate animal used or intended for use in research, research training, experimentation or biological testing or for related purposes.

B. Animal Facility

Any and all buildings, rooms, areas, enclosures, or vehicles, including satellite facilities, used for animal confinement, transport, maintenance, breeding or experiments inclusive of surgical manipulation. A satellite facility is any containment outside of a core facility or centrally designated or managed area in which animals are housed for more than 24 hours.

C. Animal Welfare Act

Public Law 89-544, 1966, as amended, (P.L. 91-579 and P.L. 94-279) 7 U.S.C. 2131 et seq. Implementing regulations are published in the Code of Federal Regulations (CFR), Title 9, Subchapter A, Parts 1, 2, 3 and 4, and are administered by the U.S. Department of Agriculture.

D. Animal Welfare Assurance or Assurance

The documentation from an awardee or a prospective awardee institution assuring institutional compliance with this policy.

E. Guide

Guide for the Care and Use of Laboratory Animals, DHEW, NIH Pub. No. 78-23, 1978 edition or succeeding revised editions.

F. Institution

Any public or private organization, business, or agency (including components of Federal, state and local governments).

G. Institutional Official

An individual who has the authority to sign the institution's Assurance, making a commitment on behalf of the institution that the requirements of this policy will be met.

H. Public Health Service

The Public Health Service includes the Alcohol, Drug Abuse, and Mental Health Administration, the Centers for Disease Control, the Food and Drug Administration, the Health Resources and Services Administration, and the National Institutes of Health.

I. Quorum
A majority of the members of the Institutional Animal Care and Use Committee.

Implementation by Awardee Institutions

A. Animal Welfare Assurance
No activity involving animals will be supported by the PHS until the institution conducting the activity has provided a written Assurance acceptable to the PHS, setting forth compliance with this policy for PHS-supported activities. Assurances shall be submitted to the Office for Protection from Research Risks (OPRR), Office of the Director, National Institutes of Health, 9000 Rockville Pike, Building 31, Room 4B09, Bethesda, Maryland 20205. The Assurance shall be typed on the institution's letterhead and signed by an institutional official. OPRR will provide the applicant institution with necessary instructions and an example of an acceptable Assurance. All Assurances submitted to the PHS in accordance with this policy will be evaluated by OPRR to determine the adequacy of the institution's proposed program for the care and use of animals in PHS-supported activities. On the basis of this evaluation OPRR may approve or disapprove the Assurance, or negotiate an approvable Assurance with the institution. Approval of an Assurance will be for a specified period of time (no longer than five years) after which time the institution must submit a new Assurance to OPRR. OPRR may limit the period during which any particular approved Assurance shall remain effective or otherwise condition, restrict, or withdraw approval. Without an applicable PHS approved Assurance no PHS-supported activity involving animals at the institution will be permitted to continue.

1. Institutional Program for Animal Care and Use
The Assurance shall fully describe the institution's program for the care and use of animals in PHS-supported activities. The PHS requires institutions to use the *Guide for the Care and Use of Laboratory Animals* (*Guide*) as a basis for developing and implementing an institutional program for activities involving animals. The program description must include the following:
a. a list of every branch and major component of the institution, as well as a list of every branch and major component of any other institution which is to be included under the Assurance;
b. the lines of authority and responsibility for administering the program and ensuring compliance with this policy;
c. the qualifications, authority and responsibility of the veterinarian(s) who will participate in the program;
d. the membership list of the Institutional Animal Care and Use Committee(s)[1] (IACUC) established in accordance with the requirements set forth in IV.A.3.;
e. the procedures which the IACUC will follow to fulfill the requirements set forth in IV.B.;
f. the health program for personnel who work in laboratory animal facilities or have frequent contact with animals;
g. the gross square footage of each animal facility (including satellite facilities), the species housed therein and the average daily inventory, by species, of animals in each facility; and
h. any other pertinent information requested by OPRR.

2. Institutional Status
Each institution must assure that its program and facilities are in one of the following categories:
- *Category 1*—Accredited by the American Association for the Accreditation of Laboratory Animal Care (AAALAC). All of the institution's programs and facilities (including satellite facilities) for activities involving animals have been evaluated and accredited by AAALAC, or other accrediting body recognized by PHS.[2]
- *Category 2*—Evaluated by the Institution. All of the institution's programs and facilities (including satellite facilities) for activities involving animals have been evaluated by the IACUC and will be reevaluated by the IACUC at least once each year. The IACUC shall use the *Guide for the Care and Use of Laboratory Animals* as a basis for evaluating the institution's program and facilities. A report of the IACUC evaluation shall be submitted to the institutional official and updated on an annual basis.[3] The initial report shall be submitted to

[1]The name Institutional Animal Care and Use Committee (IACUC) as used in this policy is intended as a generic term for a committee whose function is to ensure that the care and use of animals in PHS-supported activities is appropriate and humane in accordance with this policy. However, each institution may identify the committee by whatever name it chooses. Membership and responsibilities of the IACUC are set forth in IV.A.3. and IV.B.

[2]As of the issuance date of this policy the only accrediting body recognized by PHS is the American Association for Accreditation of Laboratory Animal Care (AAALAC).

[3]The IACUC may, at its discretion, determine the best means of conducting an evaluation of the institution's programs and facilities. The IACUC may invite ad hoc consultants to conduct or assist in conducting the evaluation. However, the IACUC remains responsible for the evaluation and report.

OPRR with the Assurance. Annual reports of the IACUC evaluation shall be maintained by the institution and made available to OPRR upon request. The report must contain a description of the nature and extent of the institution's adherence to the *Guide* and this policy.[4] The report must identify specifically any departures from provisions of the *Guide* and this policy, and state the reasons for each departure. If program or facility deficiencies are noted, the report must contain a reasonable and specific plan and schedule for correcting each deficiency. The report must distinguish significant deficiencies from minor deficiencies. A significant deficiency is one which, in the judgment of the IACUC and the institutional official, is or may be a threat to the health or safety of the animals. Failure of the IACUC to conduct an annual evaluation and submit the required report to the institutional official may result in PHS withdrawal of its approval of the Assurance.

3. Institutional Animal Care and Use Committee (IACUC)
   a. Each institution shall appoint an Institutional Animal Care and Use Committee (IACUC), qualified through the experience and expertise of its members to oversee the institution's animal program, facilities and procedures.
   b. The Assurance must include the names, position titles and credentials of the IACUC chairperson and the members. The committee shall consist of not less than five members, and shall include at least:
      (1) one Doctor of Veterinary Medicine, with training or experience in laboratory animal science and medicine, who has direct or delegated program responsibility for activities involving animals at the institution;
      (2) one practicing scientist experienced in research involving animals;
      (3) One member whose primary concerns are in a nonscientific area (for example, ethicist, lawyer, member of the clergy); and
      (4) one individual who is not affiliated with the institution in any way other than as a member of the IACUC, and is not a member of the immediate family of a person who is affiliated with the institution.
   c. An individual who meets the requirements of more than one of the categories detailed in IV.A.3.b.(1)-(4) may fulfill more than one requirement. However, no committee may consist of less than five members.

B. Functions of the Institutional Animal Care and Use Committee

As an agent of the institution the IACUC shall, with respect to PHS-supported activities:

1. review at least annually the institution's program for humane care and use of animals;
2. inspect at least annually all of the institution's animal facilities, including satellite facilities;
3. review concerns involving the care and use of animals at the institution;
4. make recommendations to the institutional official regarding any aspect of the institution's animal program, facilities or personnel training;
5. review and approve, require modifications in (to secure approval) or withhold approval of those sections of PHS applications or proposals related to the care and use of animals as specified in IV.C.;
6. review and approve, require modifications in (to secure approval), or withhold approval of proposed significant changes regarding the use of animals in ongoing activities; and
7. be authorized to suspend an activity involving animals in accord with specifications set forth in IV.C.5.

C. Review of PHS Applications and Proposals

1. In order to approve applications and proposals or proposed significant changes in ongoing activities, the IACUC shall conduct a review of those sections related to the care and use of animals and determine that the proposed activities are in accord with this policy. In making this determination, the IACUC shall confirm that the activity will be conducted in accord with the Animal Welfare Act insofar as it applies to the activity, and that the activity is consistent with the *Guide* unless acceptable justification for a departure is presented. Further, the IACUC shall determine that the activity conforms with the institution's Assurance and meets the following requirements:
   a. Procedures with animals will avoid or minimize discomfort, distress and pain to the animals, consistent with sound research design.
   b. Procedures that may cause more than momentary or slight pain or distress to the animals will be performed with appropriate sedation, analgesia, or anesthesia, unless the procedure is justified for scientific reasons in writing by the investigator.
   c. Animals that would otherwise experience severe or chronic pain or distress that cannot be relieved will be painlessly sacrificed at the

[4]If some of the institution's facilities are accredited by AAALAC or other accrediting body recognized by PHS, the report should identify those facilities and need not contain any further information about evaluation of those facilities.

end of the procedure or, if appropriate, during the procedure.

d. The living conditions of animals will be appropriate for their species and contribute to their health and comfort. The housing, feeding and nonmedical care of the animals will be directed by a veterinarian or other scientist trained and experienced in the proper care, handling and use of the species being maintained or studied.

e. Medical care for animals will be available and provided as necessary by a qualified veterinarian.

f. Personnel conducting procedures on the species being maintained or studied will be appropriately qualified and trained in those procedures.

g. Methods of euthanasia used will be consistent with the recommendations of the American Veterinary Medical Association (AVMA) Panel on Euthanasia,[5] unless a deviation is justified for scientific reasons in writing by the investigator.

2. Prior to the review, each IACUC member shall be provided with a list of applications and proposals to be reviewed. Those sections of applications and proposals that relate to the care and use of animals shall be available to all IACUC members, and any member of the IACUC may upon request obtain full committee review of those sections. If full committee review is not requested, at least one member of the IACUC, designated by the chairperson and qualified to conduct the review, shall review those sections and have the authority to approve, require modifications in (to secure approval) or request full committee review of those sections. If full committee review is requested, approval of those sections may be granted only after review at a convened meeting of a quorum of the IACUC and with the approval vote of a majority of the quorum present. No member may participate in the IACUC review or approval of an application or proposal in which the member has a conflicting interest (e.g., is personnaly involved in the project), except to provide information requested by the IACUC; nor may a member who has a conflicting interest contribute to the constitution of a quorum.

3. The IACUC may invite consultants to assist in the review of complex issues. Consultants may not approve or withhold approval of an application or proposal or vote with the IACUC.

4. The IACUC shall notify investigators and the institution in writing of its decision to approve or withhold approval of those sections of applications or proposals related to the care and use of animals, or of modifications required to secure IACUC approval. If the IACUC decides to withhold approval of an application or proposal, it shall include in its written notification a statement of the reasons for its decision and give the investigator an opportunity to respond in person or in writing.

5. The IACUC shall conduct continuing review of applications and proposals covered by this policy at appropriate intervals as determined by the IACUC, but not less than once every three years.

6. The IACUC may suspend an activity that it previously approved if it determines that the activity is not being conducted in accordance with applicable provisions of the Animal Welfare Act, the *Guide,* the institution's Assurance, or IV.C.1.a.-g. The IACUC may suspend an activity only after review of the matter at a convened meeting of a quorum of the IACUC and with the suspension vote of a majority of the quorum present.

7. If the IACUC suspends an activity involving animals, the institutional official in consultation with the IACUC shall review the reasons for suspension, take appropriate corrective action and report that action with a full explanation to OPRR.

8. Applications and proposals that have been approved by the IACUC may be subject to further appropriate review and approval by officials of the institution. However, those officials may not approve those sections of an application or proposal related to the care and use of animals if they have not been approved by the IACUC.

D. Information Required in Applications and Proposals Submitted to PHS

1. All Institutions

Applications and proposals submitted to PHS that involve the care and use of animals shall contain the following information:

a. identification of the species and approximate number of animals to be used;

b. rationale for involving animals, and for the appropriateness of the species and numbers to be used;

c. a complete description of the proposed use of the animals;

d. assurance that discomfort and injury to animals will be limited to that which is unavoid-

[5]Journal of the American Veterinary Medical Association (JAVMA), 1978, Vol. 173, No. 1, pp. 59-72, or succeeding revised editions.

able in the conduct of scientifically valuable research, and that analgesic, anesthetic, and tranquilizing drugs will be used where indicated and appropriate to minimize discomfort and pain to animals; and

e. a description of any euthanasia method to be used.

2. Institutions That Have an Approved Assurance

Applications or proposals covered by this policy from institutions which have an approved Assurance on file with OPRR shall include verification of approval by the IACUC of those sections related to the care and use of animals. With the authorization of PHS, such verification may be filed at a time not to exceed 60 days after submission of applications or proposals.[6]

If verification of IACUC approval is submitted subsequent to the submission of the application or proposal, the verification shall state the modifications, if any, required by the IACUC. The verification shall be signed by an individual authorized by the institution, but need not be signed by the institutional official who signed the Assurance.

3. Institutions That Do Not Have an Approved Assurance

Applications and proposals involving animals from institutions that do not have an approved Assurance on file with OPRR shall contain a declaration that the institution will establish an IACUC and submit an Assurance upon request by OPRR. After OPRR has requested the Assurance, the institution shall establish an IACUC as required by IV.A.3. and the IACUC shall review those sections of the application or proposal as required by IV.C. The institution shall then submit to OPRR the Assurance and verification of IACUC approval. The verification shall state the modifications, if any, required by the IACUC. The verification shall be signed by an individual authorized by the institution, but need not be signed by the institutional official who signed the Assurance.

E. Recordkeeping

1. The awardee institution shall maintain:
   a. an Assurance approved by the PHS;
   b. minutes of IACUC meetings, including records of attendance, activities of the committee, and committee deliberations;

[6]Until further notice, PHS hereby authorizes all institutions with approved Assurances to file verification of IACUC approval either along with the application or proposal or within 60 days of submission of the application or proposal. From time to time PHS will reevaluate this blanket authorization. Any decision to withdraw this authorization will take place only after ample opportunity is provided for comment by the public.

   c. records of applications, proposals and proposed significant changes in the care and use of animals and whether IACUC approval was given or withheld;
   d. records of any IACUC reports and recommendations as forwarded to the institutional official; and
   e. records of accrediting body determinations.
2. All records shall be maintained for at least three years; records that relate directly to applications, proposals, and proposed significant changes in ongoing activities reviewed and approved by the IACUC shall be maintained for the duration of the activity and for an additional three years after the completion of the activity. All records shall be accessible for inspection and copying by authorized OPRR or other PHS representatives at reasonable times and in a reasonable manner.

F. Reporting Requirements

1. On or before each anniversary of approval of its Assurance, the institution shall report in writing to OPRR:
   a. any change in the institution's program or facilities which would place the institution in a different category than specified in its Assurance (see IV.A.2.);
   b. any change in the description of the institution's program for animal care and use as required by IV.A.1.a.-h.;
   c. any changes in IACUC membership; and
   d. if the institution's program and facilities are in Category 2 (see IV.A.2.), verification that the IACUC has conducted an annual evaluation of the institution's program and facilities and submitted the evaluation to the institutional official.
2. Institutions that have no changes to report as specified in IV.F.1.a.-c. shall submit a letter to OPRR stating that there are no changes.
3. Institutions shall provide OPRR promptly with a full explanation of the circumstances and actions taken with respect to:
   a. any serious or continuing noncompliance with this policy;
   b. any serious deviation from the provisions of the *Guide;* or
   c. any suspension of an activity by the IACUC.

Implementation by PHS

A. Responsibilities of OPRR

OPRR is responsible for the general administration and coordination of this policy and will:

1. request and negotiate, approve or disapprove,

and, as necessary, withdraw approval of Assurances;

2. distribute to executive secretaries of initial review and technical evaluation groups, and to PHS awarding units, lists of institutions that have an approved Assurance;
3. advise awarding units and awardee institutions concerning the implementation of this policy;
4. evaluate allegations of noncompliance with this policy;
5. have the authority to review and approve or disapprove waivers to this policy (see V.D.); and
6. conduct site visits to selected institutions.

B. Responsibilities of PHS Awarding Units

PHS awarding units may not make an award for an activity involving animals unless the institution submitting the application or proposal is on the list of institutions that have an approved Assurance on file with OPRR, and the institution has provided verification of approval by the IACUC of those sections of the application or proposal related to the care and use of animals in PHS-supported activities. If an institution is not listed, the awarding unit will ask OPRR to negotiate an Assurance with the institution before an award is made. No award shall be made until the Assurance has been submitted by the institution, approved by OPRR, and the institution has provided verification of approval by the IACUC of those sections of the application or proposal related to the care and use of animals in PHS-supported activities.

C. Conduct of Special Reviews/Site Visits

Each awardee institution is subject to review at anytime by PHS staff and advisors, which may include a site visit, in order to assess the adequacy of the institution's compliance with this policy.

D. Waiver

Institutions may request a waiver of a provision or provisions of this policy by submitting a request to OPRR. No waiver will be granted unless sufficient justification is provided and the waiver is approved in writing by OPRR.

Appendix D

Laboratory-Animal Facilities Fully Accredited by the American Association for Accreditation of Laboratory Animal Care

As of April 1, 1985, there were 483 facilities listed as fully accredited by the American Association for Accreditation of Laboratory Animal Care (AAALAC) (New Lenox, IL). Institutions are categorized as universities, medical schools, combined facilities for health sciences, veterinary schools, dental schools, colleges of pharmacy, colleges of biological science, colleges of arts, colleges of engineering, Veterans' Administration medical centers, pharmaceutical manufacturers, government laboratories, commercial laboratories, hospitals, nonprofit research laboratories, or laboratory animal breeders. The following list of AAALAC-accredited facilities numbers 538, as some institutions are listed in more than one category. (Facilities receiving accreditation since April 1, 1985, are not listed.)

Universities (Programs serving an entire campus)

Alabama:
- University of Alabama, University
- University of Alabama at Birmingham and the Veterans' Administration Medical Center, Birmingham

Arkansas:
- University of Arkansas at Little Rock, Little Rock

California:
- University of California-Davis, Davis
- University of California-San Diego, San Diego
- University of California at Los Angeles, Los Angeles
- University of Southern California, Los Angeles

Georgia:
- Medical College of Georgia, Augusta

Illinois:
- University of Illinois at the Medical Center and the Veterans' Administration Medical Center, Chicago

Kansas:
- University of Kansas-Lawrence, Lawrence

Massachusetts:
- Massachusetts Institute of Technology, Cambridge

Michigan:
- University of Michigan, Ann Arbor, Dearborn, and Flint
- Wayne State University, Detroit

Missouri:
- University of Missouri-Kansas City, Kansas City

Montana:
- University of Montana, Missoula

Nebraska:
- University of Nebraska at Omaha, Omaha

New York:
- St. John's University, Jamaica
- State University of New York at Buffalo, Buffalo
- Rockefeller University, New York

North Carolina:
- Duke University, Durham

Oklahoma:
- Oral Roberts University, Tulsa

Rhode Island:
- Brown University, Providence

South Carolina:
- University of South Carolina, Columbia

Tennessee:
- Oak Ridge Associated Universities, Oak Ridge
- Vanderbilt University, Nashville

Utah:
- University of Utah, Salt Lake City

Virginia:
- Virginia Commonwealth University, Richmond
- University of Virginia, Charlottesville

Washington:
- University of Washington, Seattle

Universities (Programs serving only a portion of a campus)

California:
- Divisions of Animal Resources, University of California, Berkeley

Georgia:
- Yerkes Regional Primate Research Center, Emory University, Atlanta

Ohio:
- Laboratory Animal Center, The Ohio State University, Columbus

Medical Schools

Arizona:
- Arizona Medical Center, University of Arizona, Tucson

Arkansas:
- Medical Center, University of Arkansas, Little Rock

California:
- California College of Medicine, University of California, Irvine
- School of Medicine, University of California at Los Angeles, Los Angeles
- School of Medicine, University of California at San Diego, San Diego
- Charles R. Drew Postgraduate Medical School, Los Angeles
- School of Medicine, Loma Linda University, Loma Linda

Colorado:
- Medical School, University of Colorado, Denver

Connecticut:
- School of Medicine, University of Connecticut Health Center, Farmington
- School of Medicine, Yale University, New Haven

District of Columbia:
- School of Medicine, Georgetown University
- College of Medicine, Howard University

Florida:
- College of Medicine, University of Florida, Gainesville
- Medical Center, University of South Florida, Tampa

Illinois:
- Chicago College of Osteopathic Medicine, Chicago
- The Chicago Medical School/University of Health Services, North Chicago
- College of Medicine-Rockford, University of Illinois, Rockford
- Stritch School of Medicine, Loyola University, Maywood
- School of Medicine, Southern Illinois University, Springfield

Iowa:
- College of Osteopathic Medicine and Surgery, Des Moines

Kentucky:
- Medical Center, University of Kentucky, Lexington
- School of Medicine, University of Louisville, Louisville

Louisiana:
- School of Medicine, Tulane University, New Orleans
- Delta Regional Primate Research Center, Tulane University, Covington

Maryland:
- School of Medicine, University of Maryland at Baltimore, Baltimore
- School of Medicine, Uniformed Services University of the Health Sciences, Bethesda

Massachusetts:
- Medical School, Harvard University, Boston
- Medical Center, University of Massachusetts, Worcester
- School of Medicine, Tufts-New England Medical Center, Boston

Michigan:
- Medical Center, University of Michigan, Ann Arbor
- Medical School, Wayne State University, Detroit

Minnesota:
- School of Medicine, University of Minnesota-Duluth, Duluth
- Medical School, University of Minnesota, Minneapolis

Missouri:
- The University of Health Sciences, Kansas City
- Kirksville College of Osteopathic Medicine, Kirksville
- School of Medicine, University of Missouri, Columbia

Nebraska:
- College of Medicine, University of Nebraska, Omaha

New Hampshire:
- Dartmouth Medical School, Hanover

New Jersey:
- Medical School, College of Medicine and Dentistry of New Jersey, Newark

New Mexico:
- School of Medicine, University of New Mexico, Albuquerque

New York:
- Albany Medical College of Union University, Albany
- Albert Einstein College of Medicine, Bronx
- College of Physicians and Surgeons, Columbia University, New York
- Medical College, Cornell University, New York
- Mount Sinai Medical Center, New York
- Downstate Medical Center, State University of New York, Brooklyn

School of Medicine, University of Rochester, Rochester
North Carolina:
School of Medicine, University of North Carolina, Chapel Hill
Bowman Gray School of Medicine, Wake Forest College, Winston-Salem
Ohio:
Medical College of Ohio, Toledo
College of Medicine, University of Cincinnati, Cincinnati
College of Medicine, Northeastern Ohio Universities, Rootstown
Department of Animal Laboratories, Hospitals, and College of Medicine, The Ohio State University, Columbia
Oregon:
Oregon Health Sciences University, Portland
Pennsylvania:
School of Medicine, Hahnemann University, Philadelphia
Milton S. Hershey Medical Center, Pennsylvania State University, Hershey
Jefferson Medical College, Thomas Jefferson University, Philadelphia
School of Medicine, University of Pittsburgh, Pittsburgh
Puerto Rico:
Medical Sciences Campus, University of Puerto Rico, San Juan
South Carolina:
School of Medicine, University of South Carolina, Columbia
Tennessee:
Meharry Medical College, Nashville
Texas:
Texas College of Osteopathic Medicine, North Texas State University, Ft. Worth
Medical School, University of Texas at Houston, Houston
Utah:
College of Medicine, University of Utah, Salt Lake City
Vermont:
College of Medicine, University of Vermont, Burlington
Virginia:
Medical College of Virginia, Virginia Commonwealth University, Richmond
Medical Center, University of Virginia, Charlottesville
Eastern Virginia Medical School, Norfolk
Washington:
School of Medicine, University of Washington, Seattle
Wisconsin:
Medical College of Wisconsin, Milwaukee
Medical School, University of Wisconsin, Madison

Combined Facilities for Health Sciences

Connecticut:
University of Connecticut Health Center, Farmington
District of Columbia:
Georgetown University Medical Center
School of Medicine and Health Sciences, George Washington University
Florida:
University of Florida, J. Hillis Miller Health Center and the Veterans' Administration Medical Center, Gainesville
Illinois:
Life Sciences Vivarium, Southern Illinois University, Carbondale
Indiana:
Lobund Laboratory, University of Notre Dame, Notre Dame
Kansas:
University of Kansas-Lawrence, Lawrence
Louisiana:
Medical Center, Louisiana State University, New Orleans
Maryland:
Johns Hopkins Medical Institutions, Baltimore
Massachusetts:
Boston University School of Medicine and Graduate School of Dentistry, Boston
Harvard University Medical School, Dental School, School of Public Health, Animal Research Center, and the New England Regional Primate Research Center, Southboro
Tufts-New England Medical Center, Boston
Minnesota:
Health Sciences, University of Minnesota, Minneapolis
Missouri:
John M. Dalton Research Center, Graduate School, University of Missouri, Columbia
New Jersey:
College of Medicine and Dentistry of New Jersey, Newark
New York:
Health Sciences Center, State University of New York at Stony Brook, Stony Brook
School of Medicine and Dentistry, University of Rochester, Rochester
North Carolina:
School of Medicine and School of Dentistry, University of North Carolina, Chapel Hill

Oklahoma:
University of Oklahoma Health Sciences Center at Oklahoma City, Oklahoma City
Texas:
University of Texas Health Science Center, San Antonio
Virginia:
School of Basic Sciences, Virginia Commonwealth University, Richmond
West Virginia:
West Virginia University Medical Center, Morgantown
Wisconsin:
University of Wisconsin, Madison
Graduate School, University of Wisconsin, Madison

Veterinary Schools

California:
School of Veterinary Medicine, University of California-Davis, Davis
Florida:
College of Veterinary Medicine, University of Florida, Gainesville
Louisiana:
School of Veterinary Medicine, Louisiana State University, Baton Rouge
Massachusetts:
School of Veterinary Medicine, Tufts-New England Medical Center, Boston
New York:
New York State College of Veterinary Medicine, Cornell University, Ithaca
Tennessee:
College of Veterinary Medicine, University of Tennessee, Knoxville
Wisconsin:
School of Veterinary Medicine, University of Wisconsin, Madison

Dental Schools

California:
School of Dentistry, University of California at Los Angeles, Los Angeles
Connecticut:
Dental School, University of Connecticut Health Center, Farmington
District of Columbia:
School of Dentistry, Georgetown University
Florida:
College of Dentistry, University of Florida, Gainesville
Illinois:
Dental School, University of Illinois at the Medical Center, Chicago
School of Dentistry, Loyola University, Maywood
Indiana:
School of Dentistry, Indiana University, Indianapolis
Maryland:
School of Dentistry, University of Maryland, Baltimore
Massachusetts:
School of Dentistry, Harvard University, Boston
School of Dental Medicine, Tufts-New England Medical Center, Boston
Michigan:
School of Dentistry, University of Michigan, Ann Arbor
Minnesota:
School of Dentistry, University of Minnesota, Minneapolis
New Jersey:
School of Dentistry, Fairleigh Dickinson University, Hackensack
Dental School, College of Medicine and Dentistry of New Jersey, Newark
New York:
School of Dentistry, University of Rochester, Rochester
North Carolina:
School of Dentistry, University of North Carolina, Chapel Hill
Ohio:
College of Dentistry, The Ohio State University, Columbus
Oregon:
School of Dentistry, Oregon Health Sciences University, Portland
Washington:
School of Dentistry, University of Washington, Seattle

Colleges of Pharmacy

Florida:
College of Pharmacy, University of Florida, Gainesville
Indiana:
School of Pharmacy and Pharmaceutical Sciences, Purdue University, Lafayette
Kansas:
School of Pharmacy, University of Kansas-Lawrence, Lawrence

Massachusetts:
- Massachusetts College of Pharmacy and Allied Health Sciences, Boston

Michigan:
- College of Pharmacy, University of Michigan, Ann Arbor

Minnesota:
- College of Pharmacy, University of Minnesota, Minneapolis

Nebraska:
- School of Pharmacy, University of Nebraska, Omaha

New Mexico:
- College of Pharmacy, University of New Mexico, Albuquerque

Ohio:
- College of Pharmacy, The Ohio State University, Columbus

South Carolina:
- College of Pharmacy, University of South Carolina, Columbia

Virginia:
- School of Pharmacy, Virginia Commonwealth University, Richmond

Washington:
- School of Pharmacy, University of Washington, Seattle
- College of Pharmacy, Washington State University, Pullman

Wisconsin:
- School of Pharmacy, University of Wisconsin, Madison

Colleges of Biological Science

California:
- College of Biological Sciences and Scripps Oceanography, University of California-San Diego, San Diego
- Pomona College, Claremont

South Carolina:
- College of Humanities and Social Sciences, University of South Carolina, Columbia
- College of Science and Mathematics, University of South Carolina, Columbia

Utah:
- College of Science, University of Utah, Salt Lake City
- College of Social and Behavioral Science, University of Utah, Salt Lake City

Washington:
- College of Biological and Laboratory Animal Resource Center, Washington State University, Pullman

Colleges of Arts

Alabama:
- College of Arts and Sciences, University of Alabama, University

Tennessee:
- College of Liberal Arts, University of Tennessee, Knoxville

Virginia:
- School of Arts and Sciences, Virginia Commonwealth University, Richmond
- College of Arts and Science, University of Virginia, Charlottesville

Washington:
- College of Arts and Science, University of Washington, Seattle
- College of Arts, Washington State University, Pullman

College of Engineering

New York:
- Biomedical Engineering Laboratory, Rensselaer Polytechnic Institute, Troy

Veterans' Administration Medical Centers

Alabama:
- Birmingham

Arizona:
- Tucson
- Phoenix

Arkansas:
- Little Rock
- North Little Rock

California:
- Fresno
- Loma Linda
- Long Beach
- Martinez
- San Diego
- San Francisco
- Sepulveda
- West Los Angeles

Colorado:
- Denver

Connecticut:
- West Haven

Delaware:
- Wilmington

District of Columbia:
- Washington

Florida:
- Gainesville

Tampa
Miami
Lake City
Bay Pines

Georgia:
Decatur
Augusta

Illinois:
Chicago (2)
North Chicago
Hines

Indiana:
Indianapolis

Iowa:
Iowa City
Des Moines

Kentucky:
Lexington

Louisiana:
New Orleans
Shreveport

Maryland:
Perry Point
Baltimore

Massachusetts:
Bedford
Boston
Brockton
West Roxbury

Michigan:
Allen Park
Ann Arbor

Minnesota:
Minneapolis

Mississippi:
Jackson

Missouri:
Kansas City
Columbia
St. Louis

Nebraska:
Omaha

New Mexico:
Albuquerque

New Jersey:
East Orange

New York:
Albany
Brooklyn
Buffalo
Castle Point
New York
Northport
Syracuse

North Carolina:
Asheville
Durham

Ohio:
Cleveland
Cincinnati
Dayton

Oklahoma:
Oklahoma City

Oregon:
Portland

Pennsylvania:
Coatesville
Philadelphia

Puerto Rico:
San Juan

South Carolina:
Charleston

Tennessee:
Memphis
Nashville

Texas:
Dallas
Houston
San Antonio

Utah:
Salt Lake City

Virginia:
Richmond

Washington:
Seattle
Tacoma

West Virginia:
Huntington

Wisconsin:
Madison
Wood

Vermont:
White River Junction

Pharmaceutical Manufacturers

California:
Hyland Division, Travenol Laboratories, Glendale
Quidel, La Jolla

Connecticut:
Boehringer Ingelheim Ltd., Ridgefield
Miles Laboratories, Inc., West Haven
Medical Research Laboratory, Charles Pfizer & Co., Inc., Groton

Delaware:
Stuart Pharmaceuticals, Division of ICI Americas, Inc., Wilmington

Illinois:
- Abbott Laboratories, North Chicago
- American Critical Care, American Hospital Supply Corporation, McGaw Park
- Division of Biological Research, G.D. Searle & Co., Chicago
- Travenol Laboratories, Inc., Morton Grove

Indiana:
- Bristol-Myers Company, Evansville
- Eli Lilly and Company, Indianapolis and Greenfield
- Miles Laboratories, Inc., Elkhart

Michigan:
- The Upjohn Company, Kalamazoo
- Warner-Lambert/Parke-Davis, Ann Arbor and Detroit

Minnesota:
- Riker/3M, St. Paul

Missouri:
- Mallinckrodt, Inc., St. Louis
- Marion Laboratories, Inc., Kansas City

Mississippi:
- Travenol Laboratories, Inc., Cleveland

New Jersey:
- Berlex Laboratories, Inc., Cedar Knolls
- Biological Research Division, Bristol-Myers Products, Inc., Hillside
- Pharmaceuticals Division, Ciba-Geigy, Inc., Summit
- Hoechst-Roussel Pharmaceuticals, Inc., Somerville
- Ethicon Research Foundation, Somerville
- Hoffman-La Roche, Inc., Nutley
- Johnson & Johnson Baby Products Company, Skillman
- Johnson & Johnson Research Foundation, New Brunswick
- Merck Institute for Therapeutic Research, Merck Sharp & Dohme Research Laboratories, Rahway
- Merck Sharp & Dohme Research Laboratories, Branchburg Farm, Somerville
- Ortho Pharmaceutical Corporation, Raritan
- Sandoz Inc., East Hanover
- Biological Research Division, Schering Corp., Bloomfield
- Toxicology and Pathology Division, Schering Corp., Lafayette
- Squibb Institute for Medical Research, E.R. Squibb & Sons, Inc., Princeton and New Brunswick
- Wallace Laboratories, Carter Wallace, Inc., Cranbury

New York:
- American Cyanamid Company, Lederle Laboratories, Pearl River
- Bristol-Myers Company, Buffalo
- Norwich-Eaton Pharmaceuticals, Norwich
- Pennwalt Corporation, Rochester
- Revlon Health Care Group, Tuckahoe

North Carolina:
- Becton Dickinson and Company Research Center, Research Triangle Park and Durham
- Wellcome Research Laboratories, Burroughs-Wellcome, Co., Research Triangle Park

Ohio:
- Merrell Research Center, Merrell Dow Pharmaceuticals, Cincinnati

Pennsylvania:
- McNeil Pharmaceutical, Inc., Spring House
- Merck Institute for Therapeutic Research, Merck Sharp & Dohme Research Laboratories, West Point
- Veterinary Services and Veterinary Pathology, Merck Sharp & Dohme, West Point
- William H. Rorer, Inc., Fort Washington
- Research and Development Divison-Pharmaceuticals, Smith Kline & French Laboratories, Philadelphia
- Wyeth Laboratories, Radnor

Virginia:
- A.H. Robins Research Laboratories, A.H. Robins, Co., Richmond

France:
- Searle Recherche et Developpement, G.D. Searle and Company, Valbonne

Government Laboratories

Alabama:
- U.S Army Aeromedical Research Laboratory, Fort Rucker

Arizona:
- National Center for Toxicological Research, Jefferson

California:
- Health Protection Systems/Laboratory Services Program, California Department of Health, Berkeley
- Letterman Army Institute of Research, Animal Resources Division, Presidio of San Francisco, San Francisco

Colorado:
- Fitzsimons Army Medical Center, Aurora

Connecticut:
- Naval Submarine Medical Research Laboratory, Naval Submarine Medical Center, Groton

District of Columbia:
- Armed Forces Institute of Pathology, Washington

Florida:
- Naval Aerospace Medical Research Laboratory, Naval Aerospace Medical Institute, Pensacola
- John F. Kennedy Space Center, John F. Kennedy Space Center

Georgia:
- Centers for Disease Control, Atlanta

Hawaii:
- Tripler Army Medical Center, Honolulu

Illinois:
- Argonne National Laboratory, Argonne
- Naval Dental Research Institute, Great Lakes Naval Base, Great Lakes

Iowa:
- National Animal Disease Center, U.S. Department of Agriculture, Ames

Louisiana:
- Naval Biodynamics Laboratory, New Orleans

Maryland:
- Bureau of Biologics, Food and Drug Administration, Bethesda
- Frederick Cancer Research Facility, National Cancer Institute, Frederick
- Medical Laboratory Veterinary, Medicine Service, Department of Pathology, Ft.Meade
- Gerontology Research Center, National Institute on Aging, National Institutes of Health, Baltimore
- Veterinary Resources Branch, National Institutes of Health, Bethesda
- U.S. Army Environmental Hygiene Agency, Edgewood
- U.S. Army Medical Research Institute of Chemical Defense, Aberdeen Proving Ground
- U.S. Army Medical Research Institute of Infectious Diseases, Fort Detrick, Frederick

Massachusetts:
- Human Nutrition Research Center at Tufts University, Boston
- U.S. Army Research Institute of Environmental Medicine, Natick

Mississippi:
- USAF Medical Center Keesler, Keesler Air Force Base

Montana:
- National Institute of Allergy and Infectious Disease, National Institutes of Health, Hamilton

New Mexico:
- Los Alamos National Laboratory, University of California, Los Alamos

New York:
- Brookhaven National Laboratory, Upton
- Food and Drug Research Laboratories, Inc., Waverly

North Carolina:
- National Institute of Environmental Health Sciences, National Institutes of Health, Research Triangle Park
- United States Environmental Protection Agency, Research Triangle Park

Ohio:
- National Institute for Occupational Safety and Health, Cincinnati
- United States Environmental Protection Agency, Cincinnati
- USAF 6570th Aerospace Medical Research Laboratories, Wright-Patterson AFB

Oklahoma:
- Civil Aeromedical Institute, FAA Aeronautical Center, Oklahoma City

Oregon:
- Oregon Regional Primate Research Center, Beaverton

Pennsylvania:
- Naval Air Development Center, Warminster

Tennessee:
- Oak Ridge National Laboratory, Biology Division, Oak Ridge

Texas:
- William Beaumont Army Medical Center (U.S. Army), El Paso
- Brooke Army Medical Center, Department of Pathology and Laboratory Services, Fort Sam Houston
- Texas Research Institute of Mental Sciences, Houston
- USAF School of Aerospace Medicine, Brooks AFB

Washington:
- Madigan Army Medical Center, Tacoma

Commercial Laboratories

Arizona:
- Armour Research Center, Armour-Dial Company, Scottsdale

Arkansas:
- INTOX Laboratories, Inc., Little Rock

California:
- American Pharmaseal Laboratories, Irwindale
- Bio-Devices Laboratories, Inc., Orange
- Chevron Environmental Health Center, Richmond

- Edwards Laboratories, Santa Ana
- McGaw Laboratories, Irvine
- Science Applications, Inc., La Jolla
- North American Science Associates of California, Irvine
- Shell Development Company, Modesto
- Stauffer Chemical Company, Mountain View

Connecticut:
- United States Surgical Corporation, Norwalk
- Stauffer Chemical Company, Farmington

Delaware:
- Haskell Laboratory for Toxicology and Industrial Medicine, Newark

Florida:
- Life Sciences, Inc., St. Petersburg
- Sherwood Medical Laboratories, Inc., DeLand

Georgia:
- American McGaw, Milledgeville

Illinois:
- American Biogenics Corporation, Decatur
- Kendall Company Health Research Center, Barrington
- Quaker Oats Company, Barrington

Kansas:
- Mobay Chemical Corporation, Stilwell
- BAVET Division of Miles Laboratories, Inc., Shawnee Missions

Maryland:
- BioCon, Inc., Rockville
- Biotech Research Laboratories, Inc., Rockville
- Borriston Laboratories, Inc., Temple Hills
- Gillette Capital Corporation, Rockville
- Laboratory Animal Services, Inc., Rockville
- Litton Bionetics, Inc., Bethesda
- Microbiological Associates, Bethesda
- Tegeris Laboratories, Inc., Laurel

Massachusetts:
- Arthur D. Little, Inc., Cambridge
- Bioassay Systems Corporation, Woburn
- Biotek, Inc., Woburn
- EG & G Mason Research Institute, Inc., Worcester
- SISA Laboratories Inc., Cambridge

Michigan:
- Toxicology Research Laboratory, The Dow Chemical Company, Midland
- Dow Corning Corporation, Midland
- General Motors Research Laboratories, Warren
- International Research and Development Corporation, Mattawan
- Toxicity Research Laboratories, Ltd., Muskegon

Minnesota:
- Medtronic, Inc., Coon Rapids

Missouri:
- Environmental Health Laboratory, Monsanto Company, St. Louis

New Jersey:
- Bio/dynamics, Inc., East Millstone
- Colgate Palmolive Research Center, Piscataway
- Cyanamid Foundation for Agricultural Development, Princeton
- Exxon Biomedical Sciences, Inc., East Millstone
- FMC Corporation Toxicology Laboratory, Somerville
- FMC Corporation, Princeton
- Lever Brothers Company, Edgewater
- Mobil Oil Corporation, Princeton
- Revlon Research Center, Inc., Edison

New York:
- Eastman Kodak Company, Rochester

Ohio:
- Ben Venue Laboratories, Inc., Bedford
- Hill Top Research, Inc., Miamiville
- North American Science Associates, Inc., Northwood
- Procter and Gamble Company, Cincinnati
- Toilet Goods Division, Procter and Gamble Company, Cincinnati
- Springborn Institute for Bioresearch, Inc., Spencerville
- WIL Research Laboratories, Inc., Ashland

Pennsylvania:
- Biosearch, Inc. Philadelphia
- M.B. Research Laboratories, Inc., Spinnertown
- Pharmakon Research International, Inc., Waverly
- Rohm and Haas Company, Spring House

Texas:
- Alcon Laboratories, Fort Worth
- Health and Environmental Sciences, Dow Chemical, U.S.A., Lake Jackson
- STILLMEADOW, Inc., Houston

Virginia:
- Flow Laboratories, Inc., McLean
- Hazelton Laboratories America, Inc., Vienna
- Meloy Laboratories, Inc., Springfield

Washington:
- Genetics Systems Corp., Seattle
- Hollister-Stier, Division of Miles Laboratories, Inc., Spokane
- Oncogen, Seattle

Wisconsin:
- Hazelton Laboratories America, Inc., Madison

Canada:
- Bio-Research Laboratories, Ltd., Senneville, Quebec

38-750 O - 86 - 14

Hospitals

Arizona:
- Barrow Neurological Institute, St. Joseph's Hospital and Medical Center, Phoenix

California:
- Children's Hospital of San Francisco, San Francisco
- Sutter Hospitals Medical Research Foundation, Sutter Community Hospitals, Sacramento

Colorado:
- Denver General Hospital, Denver
- National Jewish Hospital, Denver

District of Columbia:
- Research Foundation of the Washington Hospital Center
- Research Foundation of Children's Hospital, Children's Hospital

Florida:
- Mount Sinai Medical Center, Miami Beach

Illinois:
- Evanston Hospital Association, Evanston
- Michael Reese Hospital and Medical Center, Chicago

Louisiana:
- Southern Baptist Hospital, New Orleans
- U.S. Public Health Service Hospital, Carville

Maryland:
- Maryland Psychiatric Research Center, Catonsville

Massachusetts:
- Beth Israel Hospital, Boston
- New England Deaconess Hospital, Boston
- St. Vincent Healthcare System, Inc., Worcester
- New England Medical Center Hospitals, Tufts-New England Medical Center, Boston

Michigan:
- Henry Ford Hospital, Detroit
- Sinai Hospital of Detroit, Detroit
- Wayne County General Hospital, Westland

Minnesota:
- Saint Paul-Ramsey Medical Center, St. Paul

New Jersey:
- Newark Beth Israel Medical Center, Newark

New York:
- Beth Israel Medical Center, New York
- Hospital for Special Surgery, New York
- Montefiore Hospital and Medical Center, Bronx
- Nassau Hospital, Mineola
- Nassau County Medical Center, East Meadow
- St. Luke's-Roosevelt Institute for Health Sciences, New York
- St. Vincent's Hospital and Medical Center of NY, New York

Ohio:
- Akron City Hospital, Akron
- Children's Hospital Research Foundation, Children's Hospital, Columbus
- Children's Hospital Research Foundation, Children's Hospital Medical Center, Cincinnati
- Cleveland Research Institute, Cleveland

Pennsylvania:
- Albert Einstein Medical Center, Northern Division, Philadelphia
- Graduate Hospital, Philadelphia
- Lehigh Valley Hospital Center, Allentown
- Skin and Cancer Hospital of Philadelphia, Philadelphia
- Joseph Stokes, Jr. Research Institute of the Children's Hospital of Philadelphia

Rhode Island:
- Miriam Hospital, Providence

Tennessee:
- St. Jude Children's Research Hospital, Memphis
- University of Tennessee Memorial Hospital and Research Center, Knoxville

Texas:
- Scott and White Memorial Hospital, Temple

Nonprofit Research Laboratories

California:
- Cedar-Sinai Medical Research Institute, Los Angeles
- Huntington Institute of Applied Medical Research, Pasadena
- Lawrence Berkeley Laboratory, Berkeley
- Palo Alto Medical Research Foundation, Palo Alto
- Research and Education Institute, Inc., Harbor-UCLA Medical Center, Torrance
- SRI International, Menlo Park
- Whittier Institute for Diabetes and Endocrinology, La Jolla

Connecticut:
- John B. Pierce Foundation Laboratory, New Haven

Florida:
- Miami Heart Institute, Miami Beach

Illinois:
- American Dental Association Research Institute, Chicago
- Life Sciences Division, IIT Research Institute, Chicago

Kansas:
- Menninger Foundation, Topeka

Louisiana:
- Division of Research, Alton Ochsner Medical Foundation, New Orleans
- USL New Iberia Research Center, New Iberia

Maine:
- Jackson Laboratory, Bar Harbor

Maryland:
- American Type Culture Collection, Rockville

Massachusetts:
- Worcester Foundation for Experimental Biology, Inc., Shrewsbury
- Center for Blood Research, Inc., Boston
- Dana-Farber Cancer Institute, Boston
- Forsyth Dental Center, Boston
- Eunice Kennedy Shriver Center for Mental Retardation, Waltham

Michigan:
- Michigan Cancer Foundation, Detroit

Missouri:
- Midwest Research Institute, Kansas City

Nebraska:
- Eppley Institute for Research in Cancer, Omaha

New Mexico:
- Lovelace Biomedical and Environmental Research Institute, Inc., Albuquerque

New Jersey:
- Institute for Medical Research, Camden

New York:
- American Health Foundation, Naylor Dana Institute for Disease Prevention, Valhalla
- Cold Spring Harbor Laboratory, Cold Spring Harbor
- Memorial Sloan-Kettering Cancer Center, New York
- New York Blood Center, New York
- Trudeau Institute, Inc., Saranac Lake

North Carolina:
- Chemical Industry Institute for Toxicology, Research Triangle Park
- Research Triangle Institute, Research Triangle Park

Ohio:
- Battelle Memorial Institute, Columbus
- Cleveland Clinic Foundation, Cleveland

Oklahoma:
- Oklahoma Medical Research Foundation, Oklahoma City

Pennsylvania:
- Bushy Run Research Center, Export
- Federated Medical Resources, Honey Brook
- Institute for Cancer Research, Philadelphia

Texas:
- Southwest Foundation for Research and Education, San Antonio
- Southwest Research Institute, San Antonio
- University of Texas Cancer Center, Houston
- Veterinary Resources Division, Science Park, The University of Texas Cancer Center, Bastrop

Utah:
- University of Utah Research Institute, Salt Lake City

Washington:
- Battelle, Pacific Northwest Laboratories, Richland
- Bob Hope International Heart Research Institute, Seattle
- Fred Hutchinson Cancer Research Center, Seattle
- Pacific Northwest Research Foundation, Seattle
- Virginia Mason Research Center, Seattle

Laboratory-Animal Breeders

Indiana:
- Engle Laboratory Animals, Inc., Farmersburg
- Harlan Sprague Dawley, Inc., Indianapolis
- Laboratory Supply Company, Indianapolis

Maryland:
- M.A. Bioproducts, Inc., Walkersville

Massachusetts:
- Charles River Breeding Laboratories, Inc., Wilmington

Michigan:
- Charles River-Portage, Portage

New Jersey:
- Camm Research Institute, Inc., Wayne
- Charles River Lakeview, Newfield
- H.A.R.E. Rabbits for Research, Marland Breeding Farms, Hewitt

New York:
- Carworth Division, The Charles River Breeding Laboratories Inc., Kingston
- Charles River Research Primates Corporation, Port Washington
- Taconic Farms, Inc., Germantown

Tennessee:
- Cumberland View Farms, Clinton

Virginia:
- Hazelton Research Primates, Reston
- Hazelton Research Animals, Inc., Vienna

Canada:
- Charles River Canada Incorporated, St. Constant, Quebec

Appendix E
International Agreements Governing Animal Use

Convention on International Trade in Endangered Species

In 1973, the Convention on International Trade in Endangered Species of Fauna and Flora (CITES) was signed by 61 nations. It has since been ratified by a total of 81 separate nations and has been enforced in the United States since 1977 (10,11).

In addition to protecting animals from extinction, the Convention specifies in seven different places that the Management Authority must be "satisfied that any living specimen will be so transported and cared for as to minimize the risk of injury, damage to health or cruel treatment." CITES is administered on an international basis by the International Union for the Conservation of Nature and Natural Resources headquartered in Gland, Switzerland. Endangered plants and animals are listed in three Appendixes to the Convention, according to level of endangerment. For purposes of monitoring, all primates have been included in Appendix II ("Threatened") except chimpanzees, which are classified as "Endangered." Under CITES provisions, the effect of the Appendix II classification has been to require export permits for all listed primates.

The U.S. agency responsible for administration of CITES provisions is the Research Division of the Fish and Wildlife Service, Department of the Interior, which has additional responsibilities regarding international trade in endangered or threatened species under Section 7 of the Endangered Species Act of 1973. (For a brief discussion of how this act affects experimentation in the United States, see ch. 13.) Current CITES Appendixes listings, by species of wildlife and family of plants, can be found in part 23 of title 50 of the *Code of Federal Regulations*; lists of endangered and threatened wildlife species and plant families affected by the Endangered Species Act are found in part 17.

The Convention's importance to research is twofold. First, it has limited trade in nonhuman primates and a few other species favored at one time or another in experiments (1). Second, continued review of the Convention by signatories has served as a forum for discussion of protection of laboratory animals. CITES signatories meet periodically in conferences, convened under CITES provisions, to discuss the required classification of species according to the terms of the Convention. Under regulations promulgated by the Fish and Wildlife Service (50 CFR 23.31-.39), members of the public must be given notice of the U.S. negotiating position at CITES conferences and an opportunity to provide information and comments on the proposed agenda, including at least one public meeting. Humane groups have used these meetings to raise the issue of humane treatment of laboratory-animal species in relation to the Convention's articles (12). Recently, for example, CITES delegates were petitioned to ratify proposed interpretations of the Convention to reach that very question. The petition was ruled outside the terms of the Convention (9).

Bans on Exporting Primates

From time to time, nations with indigenous populations of nonhuman primates that have been in demand for various types of traditional research have considered or implemented prohibitions on their export, either to protect dwindling populations or because of high mortality rates suffered in transit. India ordered such a ban in 1955, for the latter reason. Because rhesus monkeys were in demand for testing polio vaccines at the time, India agreed to reopen trade with the United States on condition that the Surgeon General sign a certificate of need for each order of monkeys, with assurances that they be used humanely and only for medical research and vaccine production. The ban was reimposed by the Indian Government when it was revealed that military experiments, specifically prohibited under the agreement, were being done with some of the monkeys. Other countries have considered similar bans or have imposed ceilings on exports. Bans were enacted in Malaysia and Bolivia in 1984, and a U.S. dealer was ousted from Bangladesh in 1979 for selling Rhesus monkeys for military research (5). Some commentators have been critical of U.S. estimates of need for nonhuman primates in research, finding them overstated, and have faulted the research community for attempts to circumvent export bans (13).

Draft Convention of the Council of Europe

The Council of Europe, headquartered in Strasbourg, France, and with 21 member countries, was organized in 1949 to work for greater European unity, to improve the conditions of life and develop humane values in Europe, and to uphold the principles of parliamentary democracy (6).

Historically, the Council has been concerned about the treatment of animals. It has drafted Conventions on the protection of animals in international transport (1968), on those kept for farming purposes (1976), on slaughter (1979), and on conservation of European wildlife and natural habitats (1979). In 1971, the Council adopted Recommendation 621, which contained three relevant proposals:

- Establish a documentation and information center on alternatives to animal use in testing and experimentation.
- Establish tissue banks for research.
- Establishment of an Ad Hoc Committee of Experts to study the problems rising out of the abuse of live animals for experimental industrial purposes. The Committee was given the task of drafting international legislation setting out the conditions under which, and the scientific grounds on which, experiments on live animals may be authorized (15).

The Ad Hoc Committee of Experts for the Protection of Animals began its work on the Draft Convention in 1978. In 1983, the committee presented a Draft Convention, guidelines for care and treatment, and a guidance note on data collection to the Council of Ministers plenary sessions and seven working party meetings under three successive chairmen. The committee was composed of experts from member countries. Observers from the United States and Europe, including representatives from several nongovernmental organizations (World Society for the Protection of Animals, Federation of Veterinarians of the European Economic Community, European Federation of Pharmaceutical Industries' Associations, and the International Council for Laboratory Animal Science) were admitted to the committee's meetings (2,14).

The form of the Draft Convention follows an earlier one on the treatment of farm animals. Its preamble, restating the general objective of European unity in the context of protection of experimental animals, balances the need of "man in his quest for knowledge, health and safety . . . to use animals where there is a reasonable expectation that the result will be to extend knowledge or be to the overall benefit of man or animal, just as he uses them for food, clothing and as beasts of burden" against the "moral obligation to respect all animals and to exercise due consideration for their capacity for suffering and memory." As stated in the preamble, the general objective of the Convention is "to limit wherever practicable the use of animals for experimental and other scientific purposes, in particular by seeking alternative methods to replace the use of animals" (2).

Prospects for final ratification of the Draft Convention remain unclear. Twice in 1983 the Council's assembly failed to achieve the required two-thirds vote on the committee's report to urge the Committee of Ministers to adopt it as soon as possible. Reported accounts stated that some delegates did not believe the Convention goes far enough in controlling animal experimentation. The assembly, however, rejected amendments that would have outlawed the use of experimental animals (8).

The Convention itself is divided into 10 parts, which are summarized below.

General Principles

Article 1 applies the Convention "to any animal being used or intended for use in any experimental or other scientific procedure where that procedure may cause pain, suffering, distress, or lasting harm. It does not apply to any nonexperimental agricultural or clinical veterinary practice." "Animal" means, "unless otherwise qualified . . . any live non-human vertebrate, including free-living larval and/or reproducing larval forms, but excluding other foetal or embryonic forms." "Procedure" is defined to include:

> . . . any experimental or other scientific use of an animal which may cause it pain, suffering, distress or lasting harm, including any course of action intended to, or liable to, result in the birth of an animal in any such condition, but excluding the least painful methods accepted in modern practice (i.e., "humane" methods) of killing or marking an animal; a procedure starts when the animal is first prepared for use and ends when no further observations are to be made for that procedure; the elimination of pain, suffering, distress or lasting harm by the successful use of anesthesia or analgesia or other methods does not place the use of an animal outside the scope of this definition.

Article 2 provides that a defined procedure can be performed on an animal for only one or more of the following purposes, subject to other restrictions contained in the Convention:

- the avoidance or prevention of disease, ill health or other abnormality, or their effects, in humans, vertebrate or invertebrate animals, or plants, including the production and the quality, efficacy, and safety testing of drugs, substances, or products;
- the diagnosis or treatment of disease, ill health or other abnormality, or their effects, in humans, vertebrate or invertebrate animals, or plants;
- the assessment, detection, regulation or modification of physiological conditions in humans, vertebrate and invertebrate animals, or plants;

38-750 O - 86 - 15

- the prolongation or saving of life of humans, vertebrate or invertebrate animals or plants;
- the protection of the environment;
- the production and quality control of foodstuffs;
- the breeding of vertebrate or invertebrate animals;
- scientific research;
- education and training; or
- forensic inquiries.

Article 3 requires all member nations "to take all necessary steps to give effect to [its] provisions . . . and to ensure an effective system of control and supervision" within 5 years of the Convention's approval for ratification.

Article 4 stipulates that ratification by a member country does not bar it from adopting stricter measures to control experimental animal use.

General Care and Accommodation

Article 5 requires any animal to be used in a procedure to be provided with "accommodation, an environment, at least a minimum freedom of movement, food, water, and care all appropriate to its health and well-being. Any restriction on the extent to which an animal can satisfy its physiological and ethological needs shall be limited as far as practicable." Environmental conditions must be checked daily and as needed to prevent avoidable suffering.

Conduct of Procedure

Article 6 requires that procedures not be performed where "another scientifically satisfactory method, not entailing the use of an animal, is reasonably and practicably available," and asks member nations to "encourage, if possible, scientific research into the development of methods which could provide the same information as that obtained in procedures."

Article 7 requires careful consideration of choice of species in procedures and that choices be explained, where required, to the responsible authority. Procedures should use the minimum number of animals, cause the least pain, suffering, distress, or lasting harm consistent with providing satisfactory results.

Article 8 requires all procedures to be performed under general or local anesthetic or by other methods designed to eliminate to the extent practicable pain, suffering, distress, or lasting harm unless the methods are judged to be more distressing than the procedure or are incompatible with the aim of the procedure.

Article 9 requires specific authorization of the authority where an animal may experience severe pain that is likely to endure. Authorization must be refused if the authority judges that the procedure is not of exceptional importance for meeting the essential needs of humans or animals, including the solution of scientific problems.

Article 10 declares that an animal under procedure remains subject to the provisions of article 5, except where those provisions are incompatible with the object of the procedure.

Article 11 provides for a decision at the end of procedures whether the animal shall be kept alive or killed by a humane method, subject to the condition that it shall not be kept alive if, even though it has been restored to normal health in all other respects, it is likely to remain in lasting pain or distress. Such decisions must be made by a veterinarian or a person responsible for the procedure. If an animal is not to be kept alive it should be killed by a humane method as soon as possible. Finally, the article provides that no animal be used in more than one painful procedure unless the second procedure is one in which the animal is subject throughout to general anesthesia, from which it is not allowed to recover, or the further procedure will involve minor interventions only.

Article 12 permits experimental animals to be set free as part of the procedure provided that the maximum practicable care has been taken to safeguard the animal's well-being. Procedures that involve setting the animal free are not permitted solely for educational or training purposes.

Authorization

Article 13 provides that procedures authorized by article 2 may be performed only by authorized persons or persons under their direct responsibility, or if the project is authorized by the legislation of a member country. Only persons deemed competent by the responsible authority may be so authorized.

Breeding or Supplying Establishments

The four articles contained in this part establish principles for breeders and suppliers of experimental animals, who would be required to:

- register and comply with article 5 (article 14);
- specify a competent person in charge with authority to administer or arrange for suitable care (article 15);
- keep detailed records on breeding, shipment, and transfer, to be maintained at least 3 years from the date of last entry (article 16); and
- mark humanely for identification dogs and cats and maintain complete records to promote their identification (article 17).

User Establishments

Under the provisions of the seven articles in this part, users (i.e., experimental facilities) would be required to:

- register with national authorities and comply with article 5 (article 18);
- provide equipment and facilities appropriate for species used and to ensure that the procedures are performed as effectively as practicable with the minimum number of animals and the minimum degree of pain, suffering, distress, or lasting harm (article 19);
- identify persons administratively responsible for care and equipment, provide sufficiently trained staff, and make adequate arrangements for veterinary advice and treatment (article 20);
- use only animals supplied by registered breeders or suppliers, subject to national exceptions (article 21);
- use only mice, rats, guinea pigs, golden hamsters, rabbits, dogs, cats, or quail originating in or acquired directly from registered breeding establishments, subject to national exemptions (member countries would add species to the list, particularly primates, as soon as there is a reasonable prospect of a sufficient supply of purpose-bred animals; straying domestic animals cannot be used and exemptions are not permitted) (article 22);
- conduct procedures outside their establishments only where authorized by the national authority (article 23); and
- keep records adequate to meet the requirements of article 27 and, in addition, to show the number and species of all animals acquired, from whom acquired, and date of arrival, and to make such records available for inspections by the responsible authority (article 24).

Education and Training

Article 25 specifies that professional and training procedures must be approved by responsible authorities before being used and must be carried out by or under the supervision of a qualified person. Procedures are not permitted at or below the secondary level except when it is specifically directed to preparing for a career involving treatment or care of animals and the procedures entail no severe or enduring pain or suffering. Only the minimum measures absolutely necessary for the purpose are permitted, and only if their objective cannot be achieved by audiovisual or any other suitable methods. Article 26 requires that persons who carry out, take part in, or take care of animals used for procedures, including supervisors, must have adequate education and training.

Statistical Information

Article 27 requires each agreeing nation to collect and make public, where lawful, statistical information on animals in experimentation, including:

- numbers and kinds of animals used;
- numbers of animals, by categories, used in procedures directly concerned with medicine and in teaching and learning;
- numbers of animals, by categories, used in procedures for the protection of humans and their environment; and
- numbers of animals, by categories, used in procedures required by legislation.

Article 28 specifies that, subject to its own secrecy laws, each nation must submit information annually in the form set out in Appendix B to the Secretary General of the Council, who is required to publish it. Each nation is invited to send the name and address of the corresponding authority, to be included in the Secretary General's compilation of statistics.

Recognition of International Procedures

Article 29 binds agreeing nations to share information on results of procedures and to provide mutual assistance in order to avoid unnecessary repetition of procedures for the purposes of satisfying national legislation on health and safety.

Final Provisions

Articles 30 through 36 specify the manner and conditions under which the Convention will become ratified and effective (i.e., 6 months after four member states express their consent to be bound and, for any ratifying or acceding state after that, 6 months after written ratification or accession), and reserve a member state's right to reservation, partial application, or denunciation (2).

Appendix A of the Draft Convention

Appendix A, *Guidelines on Accommodation and Care of Animals*, contains detailed specifications for physical facilities, holding-room environments and environmental control, and care. Though the specifications are comprehensive, article 5 does refer to them as "suggested" (3).

Appendix B of the Draft Convention

Appendix B consists of *Statistical Tables and Guidance Notes for Their Completion in Fulfillment of the Requirements in Articles 27 and 28 of the Draft European Convention for the Protection of Vertebrate Ani-*

mals Used for Experimental and Other Scientific Purposes. The appendix would require submission by agreeing nations of experimental-animal data, reported to the Secretary General for each calendar year under the general classifications established by the referenced articles. The method of data collection is left to each member nation (4).

Guidelines of the Council for International Organizations of Medical Sciences

Through the World Health Organization (WHO), headquartered in Geneva, Switzerland, more than 150 nations exchange information and share resources for laboratory-animal science training, technical information, consultative support, and other activities.

In 1985, in the culmination of a 3-year effort initiated in 1982, the Council for International Organizations of Medical Sciences (CIOMS), an international nongovernmental organization representative of many branches of medicine and cognate disciplines that was established under the auspices of WHO and UNESCO in 1949, issued *International Guiding Principles for Biomedical Research Involving Animals* (7).

Modeled after the Tokyo revision of the *Declaration of Helsinki* by the World Medical Association in 1975 and CIOMS's *Proposed International Guidelines for Biomedical Research Involving Human Subjects*, issued in 1982, the CIOMS *International Guiding Principles* are intended to provide a conceptual and ethical framework for whatever regulatory measure each country chooses to adopt with respect to animal use (7).

The *International Guiding Principles* enumerate 11 basic principles, as follows (7):

I. The advancement of biological knowledge and the development of improved means for the protection of the health and well-being both of man and of animals require recourse to experimentation on intact live animals of a wide variety of species.

II. Methods such as mathematical models, computer simulation and in vitro biological systems should be used wherever appropriate.

III. Animal experiments should be undertaken only after due consideration of their relevance for human or animal health and the advancement of biological knowledge.

IV. The animals selected for an experiment should be of an appropriate species and quality, and the minimum number required, to obtain scientifically valid results.

V. Investigators and other personnel should never fail to treat animals as sentient, and should regard their proper care and use and the avoidance or minimization of discomfort, distress, or pain as ethical imperatives.

VI. Investigators should assume that procedures that would cause pain in human beings cause pain in other vertebrate species although more needs to be known about the perception of pain in animals.

VII. Procedures with animals that may cause more than momentary or minimal pain or distress should be performed with appropriate sedation, analgesia, or anaesthesia in accordance with accepted veterinary practice. Surgical or other painful procedures should not be performed on unanesthetized animals paralysed by chemical agents.

VIII. Where waivers are required in relation to the provisions of article VII, the decisions should not rest solely with the investigators directly concerned but should be made, with due regard to the provisions of articles IV, V, and VI, by a suitably constituted review body. Such waivers should not be made solely for the purposes of teaching or demonstration.

IX. At the end of, or when appropriate during, an experiment, animals that would otherwise suffer severe or chronic pain, distress, discomfort, or disablement that cannot be relieved should be painlessly killed.

X. The best possible living conditions should be maintained for animals kept for biomedical purposes. Normally the care of animals should be under the supervision of veterinarians having experience in laboratory animal science. In any case, veterinary care should be available as required.

XI. It is the responsibility of the director of an institute or department using animals to ensure that investigators and personnel have appropriate qualifications or experience for conducting procedures on animals. Adequate opportunities shall be provided for in-service training, including the proper and humane concern for the animals under their care.

Additional special provisions accompany the basic principles. These deal with sources of supply of animal subjects; transport conditions; housing, including space allocation, hygienic standards, and protection against vermin; environmental conditions, including temperature, humidity, lighting, and social interaction; nutrition appropriate to the species; provision of veterinary care; and the keeping of records (7).

The CIOMS statement also urges that the development and use of alternatives be actively encouraged. Specifically mentioned are nonbiological methods—such as the study of structure-activity relationships or computer modeling—and biological methods, including the use of micro-organisms, in vitro preparations, and sometimes animal embryos (7).

Organization for Economic Cooperation and Development

The Organization for Economic Cooperation and Development (OECD) is a group of nations whose membership accounts for two-thirds of the world's chemical production, including the United States, Canada, Japan, and most of the countries of Western Europe. It also embraces six organizations that have a major role in international efforts to regulate chemicals (6).

In 1979-80, an international group of experts convened under the OECD's Special Program on the Control of Chemicals drafted and recommended for the Council's approval *OECD Principles of Good Laboratory Practice*. The Council approved the document in 1981 (OECD, *Guidelines for Testing of Chemicals*, C(81)30 (Final), Annex 2).

Though the main purpose for adopting the *Principles* was to promote international harmonization of chemical-testing practices and thereby help safeguard the integrity of test results required under health and environmental safety laws, the document is patterned very much after good laboratory practice regulations adopted in 1978 by the U.S. Food and Drug Administration (see ch. 13). Following the *Principles'* general command would certainly have an impact on use of test animals, but they do not contain the same detailed language on animal care, management, and housing that domestic regulations do, nor are any sanctions to be levied for failure to observe them.

Appendix E References

1. Caufield, C., "Animal Treaty is No Protection," *New Scientist* 1417:43, 1984.
2. Council of Europe, Ad Hoc Committee of Experts for the Protection of Animals, *Final Activity Report, Addendum I: Draft European Convention for the Protection of Vertebrate Animals Used for Experimental and Other Scientific Purposes and Draft Explanatory Report* (Strasbourg, France: May 18, 1983).
3. Council of Europe, Ad Hoc Committee of Experts for the Protection of Animals, *Final Activity Report, Addendum II: Draft European Convention for the Protection of Vertebrate Animals Used for Experimental and Other Scientific Purposes, Appendix A—Guidelines on Accommodation and Care of Animals* (Article 5 of the Draft Convention) (Strasbourg, France: May 18, 1983).
4. Council of Europe, Ad Hoc Committee of Experts for the Protection of Animals, *Final Activity Report, Addendum III: Draft European Convention for the Protection of Vertebrate Animals Used for Experimental and Other Scientific Purposes, Appendix B—Statistical Tables and Guidance Notes for Their Completion in Fulfillment of the Requirements in Articles 27 and 28 of the Draft Convention* (Strasbourg, France: May 18, 1983).
5. Gravitz, M., "Primates Get Top Priority," *The Animals' Agenda* 5(5):4-5, 1984.
6. Held, J., "Animals in Research: An International Overview," *Cal. Vet.* 1:93-95, 1983.
7. Howard-Jones, N., "A CIOMS Ethical Code for Animal Experimentation," *WHO Chronicle* 39:51-56, 1985.
8. Japan Science Council, *On the Adoption of Guidelines for Animal Experimentation,* 80th General Meeting, Nov. 5, 1980.
9. Lazarowitz, A., Management Authority, Division of Research, Fish and Wildlife Service, U.S. Department of the Interior, Washington, DC, personal communication, August 1984.
10. Leavitt, E. (ed.), *Animals and Their Legal Rights* (Washington, DC: Animal Welfare Institute, third ed., 1978), Appendix.
11. Nay, A., et al., *Animal Welfare Laws in Foreign Countries* (Washington, DC: Library of Congress, 1976).
12. *Humane Society News,* "Update: The Good With the Bad," 28:24, 1983.
13. Rowan, A.N., *Of Mice, Models, & Men: A Critical Evaluation of Animal Research* (Albany, NY: State University of New York Press, 1984).
14. Vallier, G., "European Concepts on the Use of Laboratory Animals in Relationship With Animal Welfare Problems," *Dev. Biol. Stand.* 45:189-195, 1980.
15. Weiderkehr, M., "The Council of Europe's Conventions," *Council of Europe Forum,* March 1982, p. 7.

Appendix F

List of Working Papers

For this assessment, OTA commissioned 10 reports on various topics concerning alternatives to animal use in research, testing, and education. The manuscripts of these contract reports are available in three volumes from the National Technical Information Service, 5285 Port Royal Road, Springfield, VA, 22161.

Volume I: Overview

"Survey and Estimates of Laboratory Animal Use in the United States," Kurt Enslein, Health Designs, Inc., Rochester, NY.

"Ethical Considerations," Arthur H. Flemming, Department of Philosophy, The University of Chicago, Chicago, IL.

"Scope of 'Alternatives': Overview of the State of the Art," Roland M. Nardone and Lucille Ouellette, Department of Biology, Catholic University, Washington, DC.

"Overview of Computer Use in Research, Testing, and Education," Paul N. Craig, Shadyside, MD.

Volume II: Research

"Alternatives to Animal Use in Biomedical Research," Eileen M. Cline, Springfield, VA.

"Alternatives to the Use of Animals in Behavioral Research," Gordon G. Gallup, Jr., Department of Psychology, State University of New York at Albany, Albany, NY.

"Alternatives to Animal Use in Veterinary Medicine," Bennie I. Osburn and faculty, School of Veterinary Medicine, University of California, Davis, CA.

Volume III: Testing and Economics

"Animal Testing for Safety and Effectiveness," Thomas D. Sabourin, Betsy D. Carlton, Robin T. Faulk, and L. Barry Goss, Environmental and Health Sciences Division, Battelle Columbus Laboratories, Columbus, OH.

"Animal Testing and Alternatives," Meyer, Faller, and Weisman, P.C., Washington, DC.

"Economic and Policy Considerations," Henry R. Hertzfeld and Thomas D. Myers, Washington, DC.

Appendix G

Acknowledgments

OTA would like to thank the members of the advisory panel who commented on drafts of this report, the contractors who provided material for this assessment, and the many individuals and organizations that supplied information for the study. In addition, OTA acknowledges the following individuals for their review of drafts of this report:

Robert F. Acker
National Foundation for Infectious Diseases

James Aftosmis
E.I. du Pont de Nemours and Co., Inc.

Donald G. Ahearn
Georgia State University

Gwynn C. Akin
Syntex Corporation

Robert L. Alkire
Society of Toxicologic Pathologists

Douglas L. Archer
Food and Drug Administration

John L. Bartholomew
U.S. Army

Michael Balls
Fund for the Replacement of Animals in Medical Experiments

Edward M. Barrows
Georgetown University

George W. Beran
Iowa State University

Richard N. Bergman
University of Southern California

Emmanuel M. Bernstein
Psychologists for the Ethical Treatment of Animals

Keith A. Booman
Soap and Detergent Association

Arnold P. Borsetti
Food and Drug Administration

Joseph F. Borzelleca
Medical College of Virginia

Richard C. Bostwick
Merck and Company, Inc.

Richard P. Bradbury
Food and Drug Administration

John E. Burris
National Research Council

Jack L. Carter
Biological Sciences Curriculum Study

Charles B. Cleveland
Pharmaceutical Manufacturers Association

Eileen M. Cline
Springfield, VA

Thomas G. Coleman
University of Mississippi School of Medicine

Frances K. Conley
Stanford University Medical School

Charles E. Cover
E.I. du Pont de Nemours and Co., Inc.

Geraldine V. Cox
Chemical Manufacturers Association

Paul N. Craig
Shady Side, MD

Arthur L. Craigmill
University of California, Davis

Lester M. Crawford
Food and Drug Administration

Lloyd E. Davis
The University of Illinois

Mary Dawson
University of Strathclyde

Charles DeLisi
National Cancer Institute

Kennerly H. Digges
National Highway Traffic Safety Administration

Rebecca Dresser
Baylor College of Medicine

Ronald Dubner
National Institute for Dental Research

Sarah Wells Duffy
U.S. House of Representatives

James L. Dwyer
Millipore Corporation

David M. Ferguson
ICI Americas, Inc.

Kenneth D. Fisher
Federation of American Societies for Experimental Biology

Michael Allen Fox
Queen's University

Gordon G. Gallup, Jr.
State University of New York at Albany

Roger W. Galvin
Animal Legal Defense Fund of Washington, DC

William I. Gay
National Institutes of Health

Michael A. Giannelli
The Fund for Animals, Inc.

Robert P. Giovacchini
The Gillette Company

Dawn G. Goodman
American College of Veterinary Pathology

L. Barry Goss
Battelle—Columbus Laboratories

Sidney Green
Food and Drug Administration

Lowell M. Greenbaum
Medical College of Georgia

Earl W. Grogan
National Research Council

Francis J. Haddy
Uniformed Services University for the Health Sciences

Richard E. W. Halliwell
University of Florida School of Medicine

Harlyn O. Halvorson
Brandeis University

Thomas E. Hamm
Stanford University Medical School

F. Gene Hampton
National Science Teachers Association

David G. Hattan
Food and Drug Administration

George A. Hedge
West Virginia University Medical Center

Lee A. Heilman
American Association for the Accreditation of Laboratory Animal Care

Joe R. Held
Pan American Zoonoses Center

John R. Herbold
Department of Defense

Henry R. Hertzfeld
Washington, DC

Karen M. Hiiemae
The University of Illinois at Chicago

Larry Horton
Stanford University

Peter J. Hyde
International League for Animal Rights

Robert Kainz
Walkersville, MD

Gerald S. Kanter
Albany Medical College

Donald Kennedy
Stanford University

Keith F. Killam, Jr.
University of California, Davis

Robert W. Krauss
Federation of American Societies for Experimental Biology

Sienna LaRene
Michigan Humane Society

C. Max Lang
The Pennsylvania State University

Thomas W. Langfitt
The University of Pennsylvania

Victor G. Laties
University of Rochester School of Medicine and Dentistry

Chung Lee
Northwestern University Medical School

Joel L. Mattsson
Dow Chemical U.S.A.

Charles R. McCarthy
National Institutes of Health

Basil E. McKenzie
Ortho Pharmaceutical Corporation

Donald E. McMillan
University of Arkansas for Medical Sciences

Donald R. Meyer
The Ohio State University

Joel A. Michael
Rush-Presbyterian-St. Luke's Medical Center

Robert J. Moolenaar
American Industrial Health Council

John A. Moore
Environmental Protection Agency

Ray E. Moseley
University of Arkansas for Medical Sciences

Thomas H. Moss
Case Western Reserve University

Laila A. Moustafa
World Health Organization

Arnauld E. Nicogossian
National Aeronautics and Space Administration

Sharon J. Northup
Travenol Laboratories, Inc.

Mike G. Norton
British Embassy

Karl Johan Öbrink
Uppsala Biomedicinska Centrum

F. Barbara Orlans
Scientists Center for Animal Welfare

Bennie I. Osburn
University of California, Davis

Robert E. Osterberg
Food and Drug Administration

Alex Pacheco
People for the Ethical Treatment of Animals

Douglas L. Park
Food and Drug Administration

Paul C. Rambaut
National Aeronautics and Space Administration

B. Randall, IV
Congressional Research Service

Walter C. Randall
Loyola University Medical Center

Tom Regan
North Carolina State University

Conrad B. Richter
National Institute of Environmental Health Sciences

Carol F. Rodgers
U.S. House of Representatives

Bernard E. Rollin
Colorado State University

Walter G. Rosen
National Research Council

Carl F. Rothe
Indiana University School of Medicine

Harry C. Rowsell
University of Ottawa

H. Rozemond
Staatstoezicht op de Volksgezondheid

Thomas D. Sabourin
Battelle—Columbus Laboratories

Jonathan D. Sackner
Philadelphia, PA

William M. Samuels
American Physiological Society

Robert A. Scala
Exxon Corporation

Trevor H. Scott
World Society for the Protection of Animals

Fred R. Shank
Food and Drug Administration

Kenneth J. Shapiro
Psychologists for the Ethical Treatment of Animals

John F. Sherman
Association of American Medical Colleges

Charles E. Short
New York State College of Veterinary Medicine

Lee R. Shull
University of California, Davis

Robert S. Shurtleff
Springfield, MA

Evan B. Siegel
The Proprietary Association

Sidney Siegel
National Library of Medicine

Richard C. Simmonds
Uniformed Services University of the Health Sciences

Peter Singer
Monash University

Cheryl L. Sisk
Michigan State University

Kendric C. Smith
Stanford University Medical School

Judy A. Spitzer
Louisiana State University Medical Center

Dennis M. Stark
The Rockefeller University

Donald G. Stein
Clark University

Marshall Steinberg
Society of Toxicology

Christine Stevens
Society for Animal Protective Legislation

Irving I. A. Tabachnick
Schering Corporation

Dennis J. Taylor
Rhodes and Taylor

J. W. Thiessen
Department of Energy

Robert Thomas
U.S. Department of Energy

Ethel Thurston
American Fund for Alternatives to Animal Research

Charles S. Tidball
George Washington University Medical Center

Richard J. Traystman
The Johns Hopkins Hospital

Bruce L. Umminger
National Science Foundation

James Vorosmarti, Jr.
Department of Defense

William J. Waddell
University of Louisville School of Medicine

James R. Walker
The University of Texas Medical Branch at Galveston

John S. Wassom
Oak Ridge National Laboratory

William L. West
Howard University College of Medicine

James A. Will
University of Wisconsin Research Animal Resources Center

James Willett
National Institutes of Health

Robert P. Williams
Baylor College of Medicine

Steven M. Wise
Attorneys for Animal Rights (Boston), Inc.

Earl H. Wood
Mayo Foundation and Mayo Medical School

Constantine J. Zervos
Food and Drug Administration

Appendix H

Glossary of Acronyms and Terms

Glossary of Acronyms

AAALAC —American Association for Accreditation of Laboratory Animal Care
AALAS —American Association for Laboratory Animal Science
AAMC —Association of American Medical Colleges
AAVMC —Association of American Veterinary Medical Colleges
ACC —Animal Care Committee (Canada)
ACP —American College of Physicians
ACUC —Animal Care and Use Committee
ADAMHA—Alcohol, Drug Abuse, and Mental Health Administration (PHS, DHHS)
AFAAR —American Fund for Alternatives to Animal Research
ALD —Approximate Lethal Dose
ALDF —Animal Legal Defense Fund
AMD —Aerospace Medical Division (U.S. Air Force)
APA —American Psychological Association
APHIS —Animal and Plant Health Inspection Service (USDA)
APS —American Physiological Society
ARC —Animal Research Committee
ASPCA —American Society for the Prevention of Cruelty to Animals
AUCC —Association of Universities and Colleges of Canada
AVMA —American Veterinary Medical Association
BID —bureau, institute, or division (NIH)
BIOSIS —Biosciences Information Service
CAAT —Center for Alternatives to Animal Testing (The Johns Hopkins University)
CALAS —Canadian Association for Laboratory Animal Science
CBO —Congressional Budget Office (U.S. Congress)
CCAC —Canadian Council on Animal Care
CDC —Centers for Disease Control (PHS, DHHS)
CERCLA —Comprehensive Environment Response, Compensation, and Liability Act
CFHS —Canadian Federation of Humane Societies
CFR —Code of Federal Regulations
CIIT —Chemical Industry Institute of Toxicology
CIOMS —Council of International Organizations of Medical Sciences
CITES —Convention on International Trade in Endangered Species
CPSC —U.S. Consumer Product Safety Commission
CTFA —Cosmetic, Toiletry, and Fragrance Association
CT&T —*Chemical Times and Trends*
DHEW —U.S. Department of Health, Education, and Welfare (see DHHS)
DHHS —U.S. Department of Health and Human Services
DOD —U.S. Department of Defense
DOE —U.S. Department of Energy
DOT —U.S. Department of Transportation
EPA —U.S. Environmental Protection Agency
EVIST —Ethics and Values in Science and Technology (NSF program)
FAA —U.S. Federal Aviation Administration
FASEB —Federation of American Societies for Experimental Biology
FDA —Food and Drug Administration (PHS, DHHS)
FIFRA —Federal Insecticide, Fungicide, and Rodenticide Act
FOA —Friends of Animals, Inc.
FOIA —Freedom of Information Act
FR —Federal Register
FRAME —Fund for Replacement of Animals in Medical Experiments
FTC —U.S. Federal Trade Commission
GAO —General Accounting Office (U.S. Congress)
GLP —Good Laboratory Practices
IACUC —Institutional Animal Care and Use Committee
ILAR —Institute for Laboratory Animal Resources (NRC)
IRAC —Interagency Research Animal Committee
IRB —Institutional Review Board
ISEF —International Science and Engineering Fair
LADB —Laboratory Animal Data Bank
LC_{50} —median lethal concentration
LD_{50} —median lethal dose
LSRO —Life Sciences Research Office (FASEB)
MRI —magnetic resonance imaging
NAL —National Agricultural Library

NAS —National Academy of Sciences
NASA —National Aeronautics and Space Administration
NBS —National Bureau of Standards (Department of Commerce)
NCI —National Cancer Institute (NIH)
NCTR —National Center for Toxicological Research (FDA)
NIDA —National Institute on Drug Abuse (ADAMHA)
NIEHS —National Institute of Environmental Health Sciences (NIH)
NIH —National Institutes of Health (PHS, DHHS)
NIHARC —National Institutes of Health Animal Research Committee
NIMH —National Institute of Mental Health (ADAMHA)
NIOSH —National Institute for Occupational Safety and Health (CDC)
NLM —National Library of Medicine (NIH)
NRC —National Research Council
NSF —National Science Foundation
NTIS —National Technical Information Service (Department of Commerce)
NTP —National Toxicology Program (NIEHS)
NWHL —National Wildlife Health Laboratory
OECD —Organization for Economic Cooperation and Development
OHER —Office of Health and Environmental Research (DOE)
ONR —Office of Naval Research (Navy)
OPRR —Office for Protection from Research Risks (NIH)
OSHA —Occupational Safety and Health Administration (U.S. Department of Labor)
OSTP —Office of Science and Technology Policy (Executive Office of the President)
OTA —Office of Technology Assessment (U.S. Congress)
OTS —Office of Toxic Substances (EPA)
PHS —U.S. Public Health Service (DHHS)
PMA —Pharmaceutical Manufacturers' Association
PRI —Primate Research Institute (University of New Mexico)
QSAR —quantitative structure-activity relationships
RCRA —Resource Conservation and Recovery Act
R&D —research and development
RRF —Registered Research Facility
RTECS —Registry of Toxic Effects of Chemical Substances (NIOSH)
SBIR —Small Business Innovation Research (program)
SPCA —Society for the Prevention of Cruelty to Animals
SSR —Society for the Study of Reproduction
TDB —Toxicology Data Bank (NLM)
TSCA —Toxic Substances Control Act
UNEP —United Nations Environment Program
UNESCO —United Nations Educational, Scientific, and Cultural Organization
USDA —U.S. Department of Agriculture
VA —U.S. Veterans' Administration
WHO —World Health Organization
WRPRC —Wisconsin Regional Primate Research Center

Glossary of Terms

Acute Toxicity Test: Tests that are used to detect the toxic effects of single or multiple exposures to a substance occurring within 24 hours. These are frequently the first tests performed to determine the toxic characteristics of a given substance. One of the most common acute toxicity tests is the LD_{50} test.

Alternatives to Animal Use: For purposes of this assessment, OTA has chosen to define "alternatives" as encompassing any subjects, protocols, or technologies that replace the use of laboratory animals altogether; reduce the number of animals required; or refine existing procedures or techniques so as to minimize the level of stress endured by the animal. These technologies involve the continued, but modified, use of animals; use of living systems; use of chemical and physical systems; and use of computers.

American Association for Accreditation of Laboratory Animal Care (AAALAC): A voluntary private organization that, by April 1985, provided accreditation for 483 institutions. AAALAC accreditation is based on the provisions of the NIH *Guide for the Care and Use of Laboratory Animals,* and is recognized by the PHS.

Ames Test: The most commonly used test for mutagenicity, it tests "reverse mutation" by exposing an already mutated strain of micro-organism to potential mutagens. If the mutation is reversed the micro-organisms regain their ability to produce the amino acid histidine and will proliferate in a histidine-deficient culture medium. However, when used alone the Ames test does not seem to be as predictive of human carcinogenicity as are animal tests.

Analgesic: An agent that relieves pain without causing loss of consciousness.

Anesthetic: An agent that causes loss of the sensation of pain, usually without loss of consciousness. Anesthetics may be classified as topical, local, or general.

Animal: For purposes of this assessment, animal is defined as any nonhuman member of five classes of vertebrates: mammals, birds, reptiles, amphibians, and fish. Within this group, two kinds of animals can be distinguished, warm-blooded animals (mammals and birds) and cold-blooded animals (reptiles, amphibians, and fish). Under this definition, invertebrates are not considered to be animals.

Animal Care and Use Committee (ACUC): An institutional committee that oversees housing and routine care of animals. The committee may also review research proposals. The committee's membership generally includes the institution's attending veterinarian, a representative of the institution's administration, users of research animals, and one or more nonscientist and lay members.

Animal and Plant Health Inspection Service (APHIS): A branch of USDA that, among other duties, is charged with the enforcement of the Animal Welfare Act. Enforcement of the act is directed through four regional offices and is carried out by 286 APHIS Veterinary Medical Officers (inspectors) who spend about 6 percent of their time inspecting over 1,200 research facilities (many of which have multiple sites).

Animal Use: The use of animals for research purposes. Three aspects of animal use are dealt with in this assessment: in behavioral and biomedical research; in testing products for toxicity; and in the education of students at all levels. This assessment does not cover animal use for food and fiber; animal use to obtain biological products; or animal use for sport, entertainment, or companionship.

Animal Welfare Act: This act, passed in 1966 and amended in 1970, 1976, and 1985, was originally an endeavor to stop traffic in stolen animals that were being shipped across State lines and sold to research laboratories. Amendments to the act have expanded its scope to include housing, feeding, transportation, and other aspects of animal care. However, the act bars regulation of the conduct of research and testing by USDA. Animals covered by the act, as currently enforced, are dogs, cats, hamsters, rabbits, guinea pigs, nonhuman primates, and marine mammals. The Animal Welfare Act is enforced by APHIS.

Animal Welfare Enforcement Report: Annual report submitted to Congress by APHIS, based on data collected from the Annual Report of Research Facility forms.

Animal Welfare Groups: There are a number of groups concerned with animal rights and animal welfare—e.g., the ASPCA, FOA, and AFAAR. These groups cover a broad spectrum of ethical concerns about animal use, they may question the objectives as well as the means of research, but they generally find common ground in the principle of humane treatment of animals.

Annual Report of Research Facility: This is required under the regulations stemming from the Animal Welfare Act. Research facilities must submit these annual reports, detailing animal use, to APHIS for evaluation. (Elementary and secondary schools are exempt, as are facilities using exempt species.) APHIS presents data collected from these reports to Congress in its annual *Animal Welfare Enforcement Report*.

Anticruelty Statutes: Laws passed by States that prohibit active cruelty, and in some cases passive cruelty (neglect), to animals. Some of these laws acknowledge the potential application of anticruelty statutes to research animals, but most of them exempt "scientific experiments" entirely. Twenty States and the District of Columbia regulate research to some extent. Twenty-one States have some provisions in their codes requiring the teaching of "kindness" to or the "value" of animals, and a few place restrictions on animal experimentation in secondary schools.

Behavioral Research: Research into the movements and sensations by which living things interact with their environment, with the purpose of better understanding human behavior. A further goal of behavioral research is the better understanding of animal species of economic or intrinsic interest to humans. Behavioral research differs from biomedical research in that it is difficult to study behavioral phenomena in isolation; therefore continued, but modified, use of animals holds most promise for this area of research.

Biological Model: A surrogate or substitute for a process or organ of interest to an investigator. Animals or alternatives can serve as biological models.

Biological Testing: The repetitive use of a standard biological test situation or protocol employing different chemicals or different test parameters. Such test protocols are more stereotyped than those used in research, and may be more amenable to the institution of a computerized data retrieval system.

Biomedical Research: A branch of research devoted to the understanding of life processes and the application of this knowledge to serve humans. A major user of animals, biomedical research affects human health and the health care industry. It is instrumental in the development of medical products such as drugs and medical devices, and in the development of services such as surgical and diagnostic techniques. Biomedical research covers a broad spectrum of disciplines, such as anatomy, biochemistry, biology, endocrinology, genetics, immunology, nutrition, oncology, and toxicology.

Carcinogen: An agent or process that significantly increases the incidence of abnormal, invasive, or uncontrolled cell growth in a population. Carcinogens fall into three classes: chemicals, viruses, and ionizing radiation. A variety of screening assays have been developed to detect chemical carcinogens, including the *Salmonella*-mediated mutagenesis assay (Ames test), the sister chromatid exchange assay, and traditional laboratory animal toxicity tests.

Cell Culture: Growth in the laboratory of cells isolated from multicellular organisms. Each culture is usually of one type. Cell culture may provide a promising alternative to animal experimentation, for example in the testing of mutagenicity, and may also become a useful adjunct in repeated-dose toxicity testing.

Center for Alternatives to Animal Testing (CAAT): Established by the Johns Hopkins University in 1981 to search for alternatives to animal use, CAAT puts out publications and supports intramural and extramural research. The Center is sponsored by the CTFA and corporate donors as well as consumer and industrial groups.

Chick Embryo Chorioallantoic Membrane Assay: A test used to determine the irritancy of a substance. A test sample is placed on the chorioallantoic membrane formed on top of a chick embryo. The membrane is then evaluated for response to the test substance and the embryo is discarded. This test may be a promising alternative to the Draize Test.

Chronic Toxicity Test: Repeated-dose toxicity test with exposure to a test substance lasting at least 1 year, or the lifetime of the test species.

Comprehensive Environment Response, Compensation, and Liability Act (CERCLA): Known as "Superfund," CERCLA authorizes the Federal Government to clean up or otherwise respond to the release of hazardous wastes or other pollutants that endanger public welfare.

Crossover Test: A useful laboratory or clinical method whereby an animal serves as its own control by first receiving a drug or a placebo and then receiving the reverse. This kind of test has potential applications in anesthesiology, endocrinology, radiology, and various other fields.

Computer Simulation: The use of specially devised computer programs to simulate cells, tissues, fluids, organs, and organ systems for research purposes; to develop mathematical models and algorithims for use in toxicity testing; and to simulate experiments traditionally done with animals, for educational purposes.

Data Sources: Can provide an alternative to animal testing by disseminating information generated from prior use of animals. The TDB and RTECS are two such sources, as was the LADB.

Descriptive Toxicology: A branch of toxicology dealing with phenomena above the molecular level. Descriptive toxicology relies heavily on the techniques of pathology, statistics, and pharmacology to demonstrate the relationship between cause and effect—e.g., that certain substances cause liver cancer in certain species within a certain time. It is most often used in regulatory schemes requiring testing.

Distress: Usually the product of pain, anxiety, or fear. However, distress can also occur in the absence of pain. For example, an animal struggling in a restraint device may be free from pain, but may be in distress. Distress can be eased with tranquilizers.

Draize Eye Irritancy Test: A test that involves placing a single dose of a test substance into one eye of four to six rabbits (the other eye remains untreated) and observing its irritating effects. A promising alternative to this test is the chick embryo chorioallantoic membrane assay.

Education: The aspect of education dealt with in this assessment is the use of animals and alternatives in the teaching of life sciences to secondary school students, university students, health professionals and preprofessionals, and research scientists.

Federal Environmental Acts: A number of these have been passed to protect human health and the environment from the adverse effects of toxic substances, and to regulate the release of such substances into the environment. Among these acts are FIFRA, TSCA, the Clean Air Act, the Clean Water Act, RCRA, CERCLA, and the Consumer Product Safety Act. Animal testing provides much of the data needed for the enforcement of these acts.

Federal Government Use of Animals for Research: Six Cabinet departments and four Federal agencies conduct intramural research and testing involving animals. They are: USDA, Department of Commerce, DHHS, DOD, Department of the Interior, DOT, CPSC, EPA, NASA, and the VA.

Federal Insecticide, Fungicide, and Rodenticide Act (FIFRA): Designed to protect the human environment from the adverse effects of pesticides and their use, FIFRA regulates various aspects of pesticide use by means of registration, labeling, and the setting of maximum residue levels. It also established procedures for safe application, storage, and disposal of pesticides.

Good Laboratory Practices (GLP): Rules adopted by FDA in 1978 requiring that all regulated parties conducting nonclinical laboratory studies keep records and permit audits of such studies. The GLP rules also contain specific provisions for animal housing, feeding, and care. In 1983, EPA issued similar GLP rules for its toxic substances and pesticides research programs.

Guidelines for Animal Care and Use: Various organizations outside the Federal Government have adopted their own guidelines—e.g., the APA's *Guidelines for Ethical Conduct in the Care and Use of Animals,* which is the most comprehensive and has been endorsed by FASEB; the APS's *Guiding Principles in the Care and Use of Animals*; and the AVMA's *Animal Welfare Guiding Principles*. For Federal guidelines, see Interagency Research Animal Committee, NIH *Guide for the Care and Use of Laboratory Animals,* and PHS *Policy*.

Hepatotoxicity: The quality of exerting a destructive or poisonous effect upon the liver.

Homology: The correspondence among organisms of structures and functions derived from a common evolutionary origin (e.g., a common gene structure).

Immunoscintigraphy: The use of external radioimaging techniques to locate tumors and to identify certain noncancerous diseases.

Institute for Laboratory Animal Resources (ILAR): A component of the National Research Council, ILAR performs periodic surveys on the use of laboratory animals.

Interagency Research Animal Committee (IRAC): This committee was formed by 14 Federal entities in recognition of a need for an interagency body knowledgeable about the welfare of research animals. IRAC meets regularly to discuss research needs and has written *Principles for the Utilization and Care of Vertebrate Animals Used in Testing, Research and Training*. These *Principles,* which incorporate nine injunctions on animal welfare, are intended to serve as a model for Federal agencies in developing policies on animal use.

Invertebrate: Any nonplant organism without a spinal column—e.g., worms, insects, and crustaceans. Invertebrates account for 90 percent of the Earth's nonplant species. For the purposes of this assessment, invertebrates are not considered to be animals.

In vitro: Literally, in glass; pertaining to a biological process or reaction taking place in an artificial environment, usually a laboratory. Human and animal cells, tissues, and organs can be cultured in vitro. In vitro testing may hold some promising alternatives to animal testing—e.g., in testing for eye irritation and mutagenicity.

In vivo: Literally, in the living; pertaining to a biological process or reaction taking place in a living cell or organism.

Laboratory Animal Data Bank (LADB): Founded by NCI and NLM in the late 1970s, the LADB was supposed to provide a computer-based registry of research and testing data. However, the data were limited and consequently LADB had few users. It was terminated in 1981 because of lack of funding. It exists today only as an archival reference.

LC_{50}: An acute toxicity test used to screen substances for their relative toxicity. LC_{50} is calculated to be the lethal concentration for half of the animals exposed to a test substance. Exposure may be by breathing vapor or immersion in liquid (e.g., fish in water).

LD_{50}: An acute toxicity test used to screen substances for their relative toxicity. LD_{50} is calculated to be the lethal dose for half of the animals exposed to a test substance. Exposure is often by ingestion.

Mechanistic Toxicology: An approach to testing that focuses on the chemical processes by which a toxic effect occurs. Mechanistic toxicology testing relies heavily on physiology, biochemistry, and analytical chemistry techniques to monitor these processes.

Micro-organism: A minute microscopic or submicroscopic living organism, such as bacteria, viruses, and protozoa.

Mutagen: An agent that induces chemical changes in genetic material. Chemicals, viruses, and ionizing radiation can be mutagenic. Most carcinogens are mutagens, therefore many screening tests to detect carcinogens are designed to detect the mutagenic potential of the compound. Some mutagens are not direct-acting, requiring metabolic activation in the body before they exert their mutagenic potential.

National Toxicology Program (NTP): NTP was chartered in 1978 as a cooperative effort by DHHS. Participants in NTP are NIH (through its agencies NCI and NIEHS), FDA (through NCTR), and CDC (through NIOSH). The stated goals of NTP include the expansion of toxicological information; expansion of numbers of chemicals to be tested; the validation, development, and coordination of tests to meet regulatory needs; and the communication of programs, plans, and results to the public.

Neurotoxicity: The quality of exerting a destructive or poisonous effect on nerve tissue.

NIH *Guide for the Care and Use of Laboratory Animals*: Revised in 1985, the *Guide* lays out detailed standards for animal care, maintenance, and housing. Its provisions apply to all research supported by NIH, and it is used by most animal research facilities, both within and outside the Federal Government. AAALAC and PHS also use it when assessing research facilities for accreditation.

Nonliving Systems: Inanimate chemical or physical systems used in testing.

Oncology: The study of tumors.

Organ Culture: The attempt to isolate and maintain animal or human organs in in-vitro culture. Long-term culture of whole organs is not generally feasible, but they can be sustained in cultures for short periods (hours or days).

Pain: Discomfort resulting from injury or disease. Pain can also be psychosomatic, the product of emotional stress. Pain can be induced by mechanical, thermal, electrical, or chemical stimuli, and it can be relieved by analgesics or anesthetics.

Pharmacokinetic Studies: A branch of toxicity testing that provides information about the mechanics of absorption.

PHS *Policy on Humane Care and Use of Laboratory Animals by Awardee Institutions*: Revised in 1985, the *Policy* applies to PHS-supported activities involving animals (including those of NIH). It relies on the NIH *Guide for the Care and Use of Laboratory Animals,* and uses institutional committees for the assessment of programs and maintenance of records.

Pound Release Laws: State laws that provide for the seizure, holding, and humane disposal of stray and unwanted animals. Most States permit the release of unowned animals to research institutions that have met specified conditions. These laws have been closely scrutinized in the past 10 years and nine States have passed laws prohibiting the release of stray animals to research institutions. The most far-reaching of these laws takes effect in Massachusetts in 1986. Also referred to as "pound seizure laws."

Protocol: The plan of a scientific experiment or treatment.

Reduction: Considered an alternative to animals when fewer animals are used in research and education through changed practices, sharing of animals, or better design of experimental protocols.

Refinement: An alternative to animal use by better use and modification of existing procedures so that animals are subject to less pain and distress. Examples of such refinements are the administration of anesthetics and tranquilizers, humane destruction, and the use of noninvasive imaging techniques.

Registry of Toxic Effects of Chemical Substances (RTECS): An annually published compendium, extracted from the literature, of known toxic and biological effect of chemical substances. RTECS is published by NIOSH under the provisions of the Occupational Safety and Health Act of 1970.

Repeated-Dose Toxicity Test: Repeated or prolonged exposure to measure the cumulative effects of exposure to a test substance. These tests involve chronic, subchronic, or short-term exposure to a test substance.

Replacement: An alternative to animal use, replacing methods using animals with those that do not. Examples include the use of a placenta instead of a whole animal for microsurgical training, the use of cell cultures instead of mice and rats, the use of nonliving systems, and the use of computer programs.

Research: The development of new knowledge and technologies, often with unpredictable but potentially significant results. Uncertainty, missteps, and serendipity are inherent in the research process. Research is distinguished from testing by the ways in which animals are used, and the identity of the investigators. There are more research procedures than there are tests, and researchers are more likely to develop their own procedures.

Research Facility: Under the Animal Welfare Act, any individual, institution, organization, or postsecondary school that uses or intends to use live animals in research, tests, or experiments. Facilities that receive no Federal support for experimental work and that either purchase animals only within their own State or that maintain their own breeding colonies are not considered research facilities under the act, however.

Resource Conservation and Recovery Act (RCRA): This act was passed to protect public health and the environment through the regulation of the management and handling of hazardous waste and through the control of solid waste disposal.

Resusci-Dog: A plastic mannequin linked to a computer. The Resusci-Dog can simulate an arterial pulse and pressure can be applied to its ribcage for cardiac massage or cardiopulmonary resuscitation.

Sequential Design Test: The comparison of treatment groups at set stages of experimentation. Further experimentation at higher doses is undertaken only if there is no significant difference between the two groups. This kind of test has potential application in anesthesiology, endocrinology, nutrition, and other fields.

Serial Sacrifice: The sequential killing of animals to examine the occurrence and progress of induced effects.

Short-Term Toxicity Test: Repeated-dose toxicity test that involves exposure to a test substance over a period of 2 to 4 weeks.

Speciesism: A term used by some animal rights activists, referring to the denial of animal rights as a moral breach analogous to racism or sexism.

State Environmental Acts: Legislation passed by States to regulate pesticides, air quality, water, and waste products. These laws are often the simple adoption or recodification of existing Federal laws.

Subchronic Toxicity Test: Repeated-dose toxicity test

of intermediate duration, with exposure to a test substance for 3 to 6 months.

Testing: Standardized procedures that have been demonstrated to predict certain health effects in humans and animals. Testing involves the frequent repetition of well-defined procedures with measurement of standardized biological endpoints. A given test may be used to test many different substances and may use many animals. Testing is used to establish the efficacy, safety, and toxicity of substances and procedures.

Tissue Culture: The maintenance in vitro of isolated pieces of a living organism. The various cell types are still arranged as they were in the original organism and their differential functions are intact.

Toxic Substances Control Act (TSCA): This act authorizes EPA to regulate substances that present an unreasonable risk of injury to health or to the environment. The act also requires the reporting or development of data to assess the risks posed by a given substance.

Toxicity Testing: The testing of substances for toxicity in order to establish conditions for their safe use. There are now more than 50,000 chemicals on the market and 500 to 1,000 new ones are introduced each year. The Federal agencies with the largest role in toxicity testing are FDA, EPA, CPSC, and OSHA.

Toxicology Data Bank (TDB): Made public by the NLM in 1978, the TDB provides toxicity information on more than 4,000 chemicals and substances. TDB information is based on conventional published sources.

Tranquilizer: An agent that quiets, calms, and reduces anxiety and tension, with some alteration of the level of consciousness.

T-test: An estimate of the difference between the mean values of one parameter of two treatments. This can be a powerful measure when the number of comparisons is small, but the potential for error increases as the number of parameters grows.

Veterinary Medicine: The maintenance and improvement of the health and well-being of animals, particularly the 30 to 40 different species of animals of economic, ecological, and environmental importance. Veterinary medicine is closely allied with veterinary research.

Veterinary Research: A branch of biomedical research devoted to the understanding of the life processes of animals and the application of this knowledge to serve animals as well as humans.

Index

Index